An Invitation to Spanish

¡ADELANTE!

DOS

José A. Blanco

VISTA
HIGHER LEARNING

Boston, Massachusetts

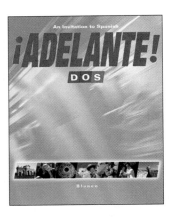

The ¡**ADELANTE!** cover gives you a glimpse into the many cultures of the Spanish-speaking world you will encounter in this program. Photos from left to right: **Puerta de Alcalá**, Madrid, Spain; **Flash cultura** correspondent Mari Carmen on location in Barcelona, Spain; Aztec pottery in Mexico; a Cuzqueña with a llama in Cuzco, Peru; papayas in a market in Costa Rica; Tango dancers in Buenos Aires, Argentina; the **El Morro** fortress in San Juan, Puerto Rico.

Publisher: José A. Blanco
Vice President and Editorial Director: Beth Kramer
Managing Editor: Sarah Kenney
Project Manager: Gabriela Ferland
Editors: Isabelle Alouane, Armando Brito
Director of Art and Design: Linda Jurras
Director of Production and Manufacturing: Lisa Perrier
Design Manager: Polo Barrera
Photo Researcher and Art Buyer: Rachel Distler
Production and Manufacturing Team: Oscar Diez, María Eugenia Castaño, Mauricio Henao, Nick Ventullo, Jeff Perron

President: Janet L. Dracksdorf
Sr. Vice President of Operations: Tom Delano
Vice President of Sales and Marketing: Scott Burns
Executive Marketing Manager: Benjamín Rivera

Student Text ISBN-13: 978-1-60007-611-4
ISBN-10: 1-60007-611-4

Instructor's Annotated Edition ISBN-13: 978-1-60007-612-1
ISBN-10: 1-60007-612-2

Library of Congress Control Number: 2007934476

1 2 3 4 5 6 7 8 9 R 12 11 10 09 08 07

LESSON PLANNING

Each lesson of ¡ADELANTE! has been designed with a consistent structure to allow for flexible use in the classroom. The following lesson plan for **Lección 4** of *¡ADELANTE!* **UNO** illustrates how **¡ADELANTE!** can be used in a three-semester program with five contact hours per week. It deals with order of presentation rather than specific instructional techniques and suggestions because those are provided in the annotations of the **¡ADELANTE!** IAE and because additional lesson plans are posted on the **¡ADELANTE!** Supersite (**adelante.vhlcentral.com**). You should feel free to depart from these suggestions and present the material in the order and manner that best suits your needs.

LECCIÓN 4
(10 days, including quiz given on tenth day)

GENERAL SUGGESTIONS
1. Assign the Workbook, Lab Manual, and Video Manual portions of the worktext on the first day of each lesson. Let students know they will be responsible for handing these in on the last day of the lesson, before the test.
2. Do not assign all of the **Práctica** and **Comunicación** activities until students have had an opportunity to complete **Recapitulación**. Based on their diagnostics, use the unassigned activities for areas in which students need additional practice.

Day 1

IN-CLASS
1. Warm up by chatting with the class using previously learned structures.
2. Present the Communicative Goals for **Lección 4**.
3. Present the **Contextos** vocabulary using the Overheads. Point out the **Variación léxica** information; ask heritage speakers for additional suggestions.
4. Present the **Vocabulario adicional** from the Supersite/IRCD. Encourage students to keep notes for new vocabulary words.
5. Have the class work through your choice of the **Práctica** activities, if needed.
6. Have students do your choice of the **Comunicación** activities.
7. Preview the **Fotonovela**.

ASSIGNMENT
1. Have students complete any remaining **Práctica** activities.
2. Have students complete the **Contextos** activities in the Workbook and Lab Manual. You may choose to assign all or some of them.

ADDITIONAL PRACTICE
1. Have students review expressions with **gustar** in **Estructura 2.1**.
2. Have students work through **Pronunciación** on the Supersite or in the Lab Manual.
3. Have students read the **Fotonovela** dialogue and **Expresiones útiles**, making a list of any **Contextos** vocabulary they find.
4. Have students complete the **Fotonovela** mouse icon activities on the Supersite.
5. Preview **En detalle** in the **Cultura** section and complete the first activity on the Supersite.

IN-CLASS

1. Warm up by chatting with the class using previously learned structures.
2. Present the **Fotonovela** by reviewing the **Expresiones útiles** as a class.
3. Watch the **Fotonovela** segment together, if time permits.
4. Have students work in pairs to complete your choice of the **¿Qué pasó?** activities.
5. Work through the **Pronunciación** section.
6. Present the **Cultura** section. Encourage students to add the **Así se dice** words to their vocabulary lists. Then complete the readings and your choice of activities in pairs.
7. If time permits, show the **Flash cultura** video, or assign it for homework.

ASSIGNMENT

1. Have students watch the **Lección 4 Fotonovela** video module on the Supersite and do the corresponding activities in the Video Manual.
2. Have students read **Estructura 4.1** and prepare **¡Inténtalo!** and your choice of the **Práctica** activities.
3. Have students complete the mouse icon activities for **Estructura 4.1** on the Supersite. Let students know that you will go over them the next day in class.

ADDITIONAL PRACTICE

1. Have students watch the **Flash cultura** video and complete the corresponding activities on the Supersite.
2. Have students complete the **Cultura** activities on the Textbook tab of the Supersite.

Day 3

IN-CLASS

Note: prior to teaching a new grammar point, review your students' work on the Supersite. Present aspects of the grammar that students did not understand.

1. For **Estructura 4.1**, go over the **¡Inténtalo!** activity. Work through your choice of **Práctica** activities, if needed.
2. Have students complete your choice of the **Comunicación** activities, as well as the **Síntesis** activity. For Activity 5, see the **Hojas de actividades** on the Supersite.
3. Use the Teaching Options in your IAE to activate the use of **ir**.
4. Preview **Estructura 4.2** by talking about students' habits.

ASSIGNMENT

1. Have students do the **Estructura 4.1** activities in the Workbook and Lab Manual. You may choose to assign all or some of them.
2. Have students read **Estructura 4.2** and prepare the **¡Inténtalo!** activity. Have them work through your choice of the **Práctica** grammar activities.
3. Have students complete the mouse icon activities for **Estructura 4.2** on the Supersite.

ADDITIONAL PRACTICE

1. See the Supersite for an Information Gap activity related to **Estructura 4.1**.
2. Have students work in pairs to find examples of the present tense of **ir** in the **Fotonovela,** or show the episode again and have them write examples that they hear.

IN-CLASS

1. Warm up by chatting with the class using previously learned structures.
2. Present **Estructura 4.2** and introduce the concept of "boot verbs." Have the class work through your choice of the **Práctica** and **Comunicación** activities.
3. Have students do the **Síntesis** activity in pairs. See the Information Gap Activities on the Supersite for materials.
4. Preview **Estructura 4.3** by talking about students' habits.

ASSIGNMENT

1. Have students do the **Estructura 4.2** activities in the Workbook and Lab Manual. You may choose to assign all or some of them.
2. Have students read **Estructura 4.3** and prepare the **¡Inténtalo!** activity. Have them work through your choice of the **Práctica** grammar activities.
3. Have students complete the mouse icon activities for **Estructura 4.3** on the Supersite.

ADDITIONAL PRACTICE

1. For slower-paced classes, review the present tense of regular -**ar** verbs in **Estructura 2.1**.

IN-CLASS

1. Warm up by chatting with the class using previously learned structures.
2. Present the **Estructura 4.3** concepts to the class, pointing out any similarities or differences with **Estructura 4.2**, including the idea of "boot verbs." Have the class work through your choice of the **Práctica** grammar activities, if needed.
3. Have students do the **Comunicación** activity and the **Síntesis** activity in pairs.
4. Preview **Estructura 4.4** by asking questions that elicit **yo** forms.

ASSIGNMENT

1. Have students do the **Estructura 4.3** activities in the Workbook and Lab Manual.
2. Have students read **Estructura 4.4** and prepare the **¡Inténtalo!** activity. Have them work through your choice of the **Práctica** grammar activities.
3. Have students complete the mouse icon activities for **Estructura 4.4** on the Supersite.

ADDITIONAL PRACTICE

1. Have students work individually or in pairs and look at news articles or magazines to find examples of stem-changing verbs like those in **Estructura 4.2** and **4.3**.

IN-CLASS

1. Warm up by chatting with the class using previously learned structures.
2. Present **Estructura 4.4**. Have the class work through the **Práctica** grammar activities.
3. Have students complete your choice of **Comunicación** activities and the **Síntesis** activity.

ASSIGNMENT

1. Have students do the **Estructura 4.4** activities in the Workbook and Lab Manual.
2. Have students complete the **Recapitulación** activities on the Supersite. Tell them to look at their diagnostics and come to class with questions about what topics they may need to review before the quiz.

ADDITIONAL PRACTICE

1. Review the differences between commonly confused verbs: **pedir/preguntar, escuchar/oír,** and **ver/mirar.** Find examples from authentic texts or the **Lectura** passages in the textbook.
2. Preview **Lectura** by having students read the **Estrategia** and skim the text.

Day 7

IN-CLASS

1. Warm up by chatting with the class using previously learned structures. Ask students to share what their diagnostics were from **Recapitulación** and review as necessary.
2. Present the **Lectura** in the ¡**Adelante!** section. Then go over the **Estrategia** section.
3. Have your students work on the **Lectura,** individually or in pairs. Have them begin with **Examinar el texto** and **Contestar** in order to familiarize themselves with the reading.
4. Go over the **Lectura** as a class. Ask a few comprehension questions about the reading selection, using grammatical structures and active vocabulary from the lesson.

ASSIGNMENT

1. Have students complete the **Después de leer** activities. Tell students to use complete sentences and let them know that you will go over them the next day in class.
2. Using the results of **Recapitulación** as a guide, assign any previously unassigned **Práctica** or Supersite activities for additional practice as homework.

ADDITIONAL PRACTICE

1. Have students complete the mouse icon activities for **Después de leer** on the Supersite.
2. Assign the additional reading and its activities on the Supersite.
3. Evaluate the results of the **Recapitulación** diagnostics and identify unassigned **Comunicación** activities for use in the following class.

Day 8

IN-CLASS

1. Warm up by chatting with the class using previously learned structures.
2. Go over the **Después de leer** activities from the **Lectura** section as a class. Spend a few minutes answering any remaining questions about the reading.
3. Present **Panorama** by using the Overheads. Ask questions about the map and encourage students who are familiar with Mexico to share what they know.
4. Have students complete the ¿**Qué aprendiste?** activity in pairs. Go over the answers as a class.
5. Show the **Panorama cultural** segment in class. Refer students to the Video Manual section of their worktext to familiarize themselves with unknown vocabulary.

ASSIGNMENT

1. Have students work through the **Panorama** and **Panorama cultural** activities in the Workbook and Video Manual sections of the worktext and on the Supersite.

ADDITIONAL PRACTICE

1. Have students prepare one of the items from **Conexión Internet** in **Panorama.**

Day 9

IN-CLASS

1. Warm up by chatting with the class using previously learned structures.
2. Complete the **Comunicación** activities identified based on the results of **Recapitulación**.
3. Preview the quiz by describing each section of the test and its point value.
4. Leave time for students to ask questions ahead of the next class' test.

ASSIGNMENT AND BEFORE TESTING

1. Remind students to consult the end-of-chapter vocabulary list when preparing for the test, or refer students to the Supersite or Lab MP3s for audio review of the lesson's active vocabulary.
2. Have students work through the practice quiz on the Supersite.
3. Have students complete the **Repaso** activities on the Supersite.

Day 10

IN-CLASS

1. Spend 5–10 minutes going over questions before the test.
2. Administer **Prueba A** or **Prueba C** for **Lección 4,** using the corresponding listening script. Reserve **Prueba B** and **Prueba D** for make-up exams.
3. Preview the **Lección 5** Communicative Goals and the **Lección 5 Contextos** section.

ASSIGNMENT

1. Have students read the **Lección 5 Contextos** section.
2. Have students prepare one or more of the **Práctica** activities for the next class session.
3. Have students complete the mouse icon activities for **Contextos** on the Supersite.

The lesson plan presented here is not prescriptive. You should feel free to present lesson materials as you see fit, tailoring them to your own teaching preferences and to your students' learning styles. You may, for example, want to allow extra time for concepts students find challenging. You may want to allot less time to topics they comprehend without difficulty or to group topics together when making assignments. Based on your students' needs, you may want to omit certain topics or activities altogether. If you have fewer than five contact hours per semester or are on a quarter system, you will find the ¡ADELANTE! program very flexible: simply pick and choose from its array of instructional resources and sequence them in the way that makes the most sense for your program.

Exciting ¡ADELANTE! Supersite,
powered by MAESTRO™

MAESTRO™ is an innovative and powerful learning management system specifically designed for the learning of foreign languages. Via the ¡ADELANTE! Supersite, MAESTRO™ delivers a wide array of electronic tools, including autograded activities, tracking and assessment of student progress, a gradebook and assignment options.

Instructor Resources available on the Supersite (<u>adelante.vhlcentral.com</u>)

▶ MAESTRO™ course management system, featuring roster, gradebook, and customizable assignment functionalities

▶ Instructor's Resource Manual*

▶ Testing Program*
  ▪ Ready-to-print PDF files
  ▪ Editable word processing files
  ▪ Answer Key
  ▪ Testing Program Audio MP3s

▶ Information Gap Activities*

▶ Workbook/Video Manual/Lab Manual Answer Key*

▶ **Contextos** and **Estructura** PowerPoints

▶ lesson plans

▶ complete access to the student site

  * Available as downloadable and printable PDFs

Your students' Supersite passcodes are free with the purchase of a new student text.

For information on the student resources available on the Supersite, see p. xxiv.

An Invitation to Spanish

¡ADELANTE!
DOS

José A. Blanco

VISTA
HIGHER LEARNING

Boston, Massachusetts

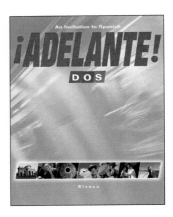

The **¡ADELANTE!** cover gives you a glimpse into the many cultures of the Spanish-speaking world you will encounter in this program. Photos from left to right: **Puerta de Alcalá,** Madrid, Spain; **Flash cultura** correspondent Mari Carmen on location in Barcelona, Spain; Aztec pottery in Mexico; a Cuzqueña with a llama in Cuzco, Peru; papayas in a market in Costa Rica; Tango dancers in Buenos Aires, Argentina; the **El Morro** fortress in San Juan, Puerto Rico.

Publisher: José A. Blanco
Vice President and Editorial Director: Beth Kramer
Managing Editor: Sarah Kenney
Project Manager: Gabriela Ferland
Editors: Isabelle Alouane, Armando Brito
Director of Art and Design: Linda Jurras
Director of Production and Manufacturing: Lisa Perrier
Design Manager: Polo Barrera
Photo Researcher and Art Buyer: Rachel Distler
Production and Manufacturing Team: Oscar Diez, María Eugenia Castaño, Mauricio Henao, Nick Ventullo, Jeff Perron

President: Janet L. Dracksdorf
Sr. Vice President of Operations: Tom Delano
Vice President of Sales and Marketing: Scott Burns
Executive Marketing Manager: Benjamín Rivera

Student Text ISBN-13: 978-1-60007-611-4
            ISBN-10: 1-60007-611-4

Instructor's Annotated Edition ISBN-13: 978-1-60007-612-1
            ISBN-10: 1-60007-612-2

Library of Congress Control Number: 2007934476

1 2 3 4 5 6 7 8 9 R 12 11 10 09 08 07

Welcome to ¡ADELANTE!

¡ADELANTE!—a unique new Spanish program—offers convenience, ease-of-use, and affordability to college students in introductory Spanish courses.

¡ADELANTE!'s three worktexts—**UNO**, **DOS**, **TRES**—are delivered in an easy-to-carry, spiral-bound format that includes all key components you need for learning and practicing Spanish. The workbook, lab, and video manual sections are conveniently placed after each lesson of the text. In addition, both **¡ADELANTE! DOS** and **TRES** begin with a review lesson that serves as a bridge between worktexts to help you review what you have learned.

¡ADELANTE! combines rich, authentic language with vibrant cultural presentations, clear and concise grammar and vocabulary sections, a carefully integrated dramatic video, and two cultural videos that will transport you all over the Spanish-speaking world. All three worktexts also offer access to the **¡ADELANTE!** Supersite, where you can view, learn, and practice much of the worktexts' dynamic content.

We know that **¡ADELANTE!** will make your journey through the Spanish language and Spanish-speaking world as rich and fulfilling as it can be!

table of contents

table of contents

	contexts	fotonovela

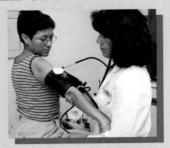

cultura	estructura	¡adelante!

New Worktext Format
delivers materials in a convenient, user-friendly package.

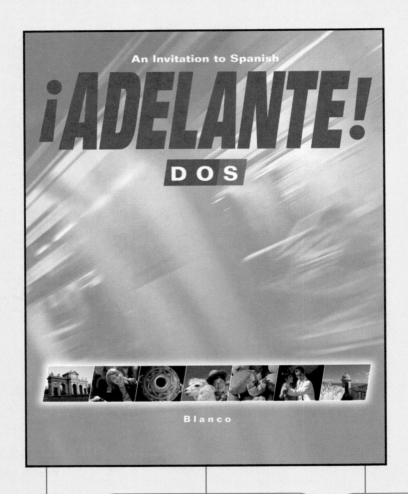

Spiral binding A unique binding allows easier handling of materials in class, at home, or wherever you may be.

Folders and notes For your convenience, folders and note papers are included.

Tab navigation Clearly marked tabs ensure that you always know exactly where you are in the worktext.

Perforation Perforated pages allow you to easily hand in assignments or travel with just what you need.

Built-in ancillaries The Workbook, Video Manual, and Lab Manual activities are included after each worktext lesson, eliminating the need to carry these components to and from class.

Lesson Openers
outline the content and features of each lesson.

Communicative Goals

You will learn how to:
- Talk about pastimes, weekend activities, and sports
- Make plans and invitations

Los pasatiempos 4

contextos

pages 168–171
- Pastimes
- Sports
- Places in the city

fotonovela

pages 172–175
Don Francisco informs the students that they have an hour of free time. Inés and Javier decide to take a walk through the city. Maite and Álex go to a park where they are involved in a minor accident. On their way back, Álex invites Maite to go running.

cultura

pages 176–177
- Soccer rivalries
- Anier García and Luciana Aymar

estructura

pages 178–193
- Present tense of **ir**
- Stem–changing verbs: e→ie; o→ue
- Stem–changing verbs: e→i
- Verbs with irregular **yo** forms
- **Recapitulación**

¡adelante!

pages 194–197
Lectura: Popular sports in Latin America
Panorama: México

Más práctica
Workbook pages 199–210
Video Manual pages 211–214
Lab Manual pages 215–220

Cross references help you navigate each lesson from the very start.

Communicative goals highlight the real-life tasks you will be able to carry out in Spanish by the end of each lesson.

¡ADELANTE!-at-a-glance

Contextos
presents vocabulary in meaningful contexts.

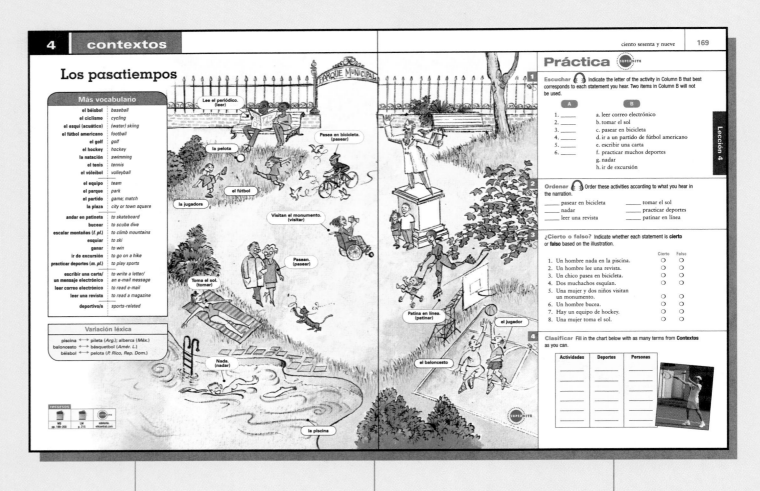

Más vocabulario boxes call out important theme-related vocabulary in easy-to-reference Spanish-English lists.

Illustrations High-frequency vocabulary is introduced through expansive, full-color illustrations.

Práctica This section always begins with two listening exercises and continues with activities that practice the new vocabulary in meaningful contexts.

Variación léxica presents alternate words and expressions used throughout the Spanish-speaking world.

Recursos These icons let you know which ancillaries you can use with every section. The Workbook, Video Manual, and Lab Manual activities are built right into your worktext, immediately following each lesson.

Comunicación activities allow you to use the vocabulary creatively in interactions with a partner, a small group, or the entire class.

Fotonovela
tells the story of four students traveling in Ecuador.

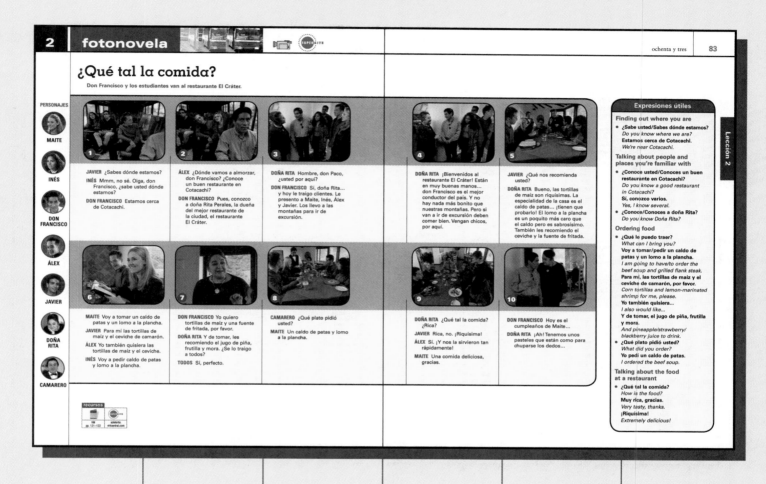

Personajes The photo-based conversations take place among a cast of recurring characters—four college students on vacation in Ecuador and the bus driver who accompanies them.

***Fotonovela* Video** The **Fotonovela** episode appears in the **Fotonovela** Video Program. To learn more about the video, turn to page xxii.

Conversations Taken from the **Fotonovela** Video, the conversations reinforce vocabulary from **Contextos**. They also preview structures from the upcoming **Estructura** section in context *and* in a comprehensible way.

Icons provide on-the-spot visual cues for various types of activities: pair, small group, listening-based, video-related, handout-based, information gap, and Supersite. For a legend explaining all icons used in the student text, see page xxv.

Expresiones útiles These expressions organize new, active structures by language function so you can focus on using them for real-life, practical purposes.

Pronunciación & Ortografía
present the rules of Spanish pronunciation and spelling.

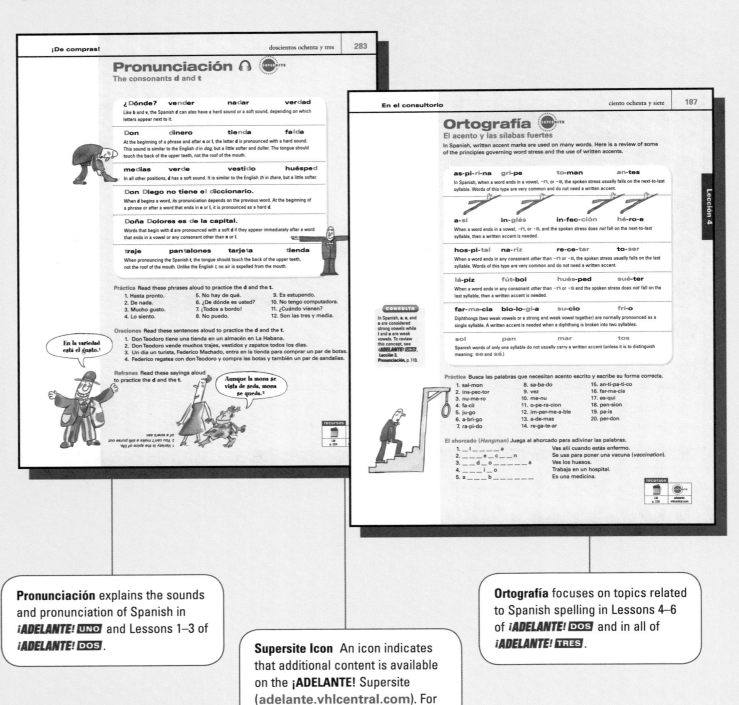

Pronunciación explains the sounds and pronunciation of Spanish in *¡ADELANTE!* UNO and Lessons 1–3 of *¡ADELANTE!* DOS.

Supersite Icon An icon indicates that additional content is available on the ¡ADELANTE! Supersite (adelante.vhlcentral.com). For more information on the Supersite, see page xxiv.

Ortografía focuses on topics related to Spanish spelling in Lessons 4–6 of *¡ADELANTE!* DOS and in all of *¡ADELANTE!* TRES.

Cultura

exposes you to different aspects of Hispanic culture tied to the lesson theme.

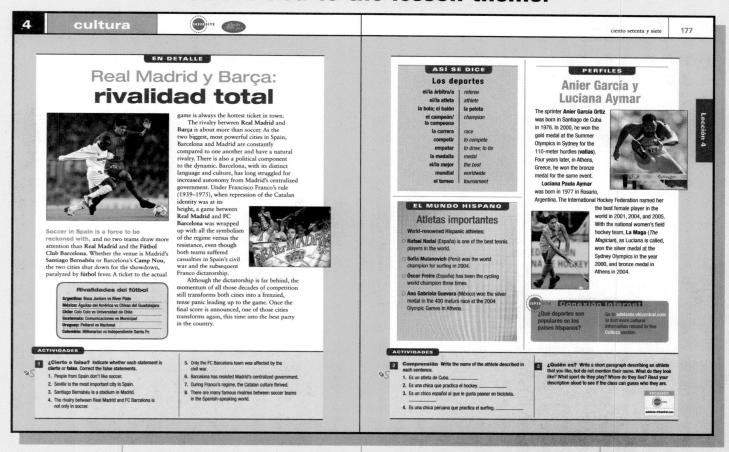

En detalle & Perfil(es) Two articles on the lesson theme focus on a specific place, custom, person, group, or tradition in the Spanish-speaking world. In Spanish, starting in *¡ADELANTE!* **DOS**, these features also provide reading practice.

Activities check your understanding of the material and lead you to further exploration. A mouse icon indicates that activities are available on the ¡ADELANTE! Supersite (adelante.vhlcentral.com).

Así se dice & El mundo hispano Lexical and comparative features expand cultural coverage to people, traditions, customs, trends, and vocabulary throughout the Spanish-speaking world.

Coverage While the **Panorama** section takes a regional approach to cultural coverage, **Cultura** is theme-driven, covering several Spanish-speaking regions in every lesson.

Video An icon lets you know that the exciting *Flash cultura* Video offers specially-shot content tied to the feature article. To learn more about the video, turn to page xxiii.

Conexión Internet An icon leads you to research a topic related to the lesson theme on the Supersite (adelante.vhlcentral.com).

Estructura
presents Spanish grammar in a graphic-intensive format.

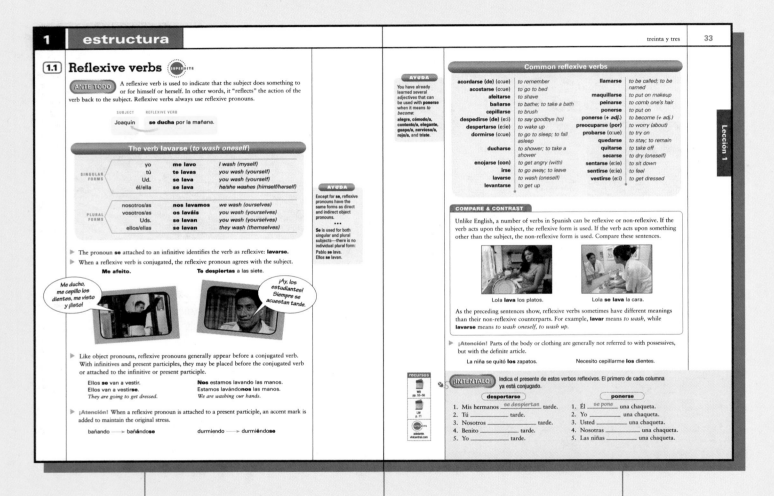

Ante todo This introduction eases you into the grammar with definitions of grammatical terms, reminders about what you already know of English grammar, and Spanish grammar you have learned in earlier lessons.

Compare & Contrast This feature focuses on aspects of grammar that native speakers of English may find difficult, clarifying similarities and differences between Spanish and English.

Diagrams To clarify concepts, grammar explanations are reinforced by diagrams that colorfully present sample words, phrases, and sentences.

Charts To help you learn, colorful, easy-to-use charts call out key grammatical structures and forms, as well as important related vocabulary.

Sidebars provide linguistic, cultural, or language-learning information and refer you to materials covered in other levels of ¡ADELANTE!

¡Inténtalo! offers an easy first step into each grammar point. A mouse icon indicates these activities are available with auto-grading at adelante.vhlcentral.com.

Estructura
provides directed and communicative practice.

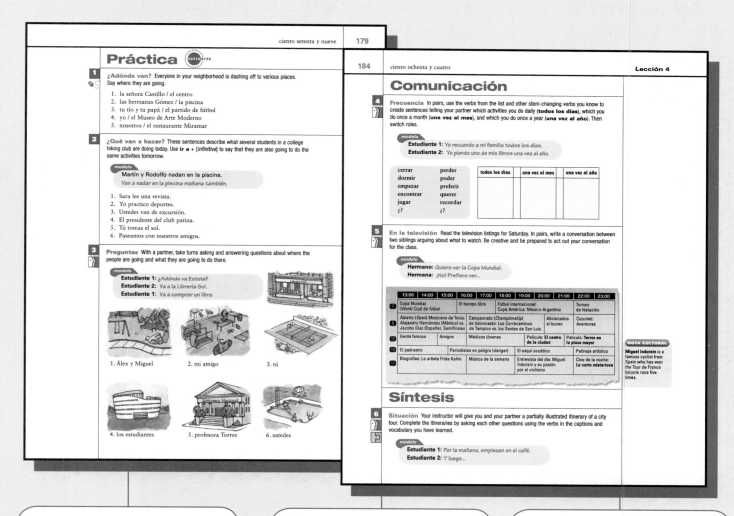

Práctica A wide range of guided, yet meaningful exercises weave current and previously learned vocabulary together with the current grammar point.

Comunicación Opportunities for creative expression use the lesson's grammar and vocabulary. These activities take place with a partner, in small groups, or with the whole class.

Síntesis activities integrate the current grammar point with previously learned points, providing built-in, consistent review and recycling as you progress through the text.

Supersite Icon An icon at the top of the page refers you to additional content on the ¡ADELANTE! Supersite (adelante.vhlcentral.com); mouse icons next to individual activities signal that these are available with auto-grading on the Supersite.

Information Gap Activities engage you and a partner in problem-solving and other situations based on handouts your instructor gives you. However, you and your partner each have only half of the information you need, so you must work together to accomplish the task at hand.

Sidebars The **Notas culturales** expand coverage of the cultures of Spanish-speaking peoples and countries, while **Ayuda** sidebars provide on-the-spot language support. **Consulta** refers you to other pages and levels of ¡ADELANTE! where appropriate.

¡ADELANTE!-at-a-glance

Estructura

Recapitulación reviews the grammar of each lesson and provides a short quiz, available with auto-grading on the Supersite.

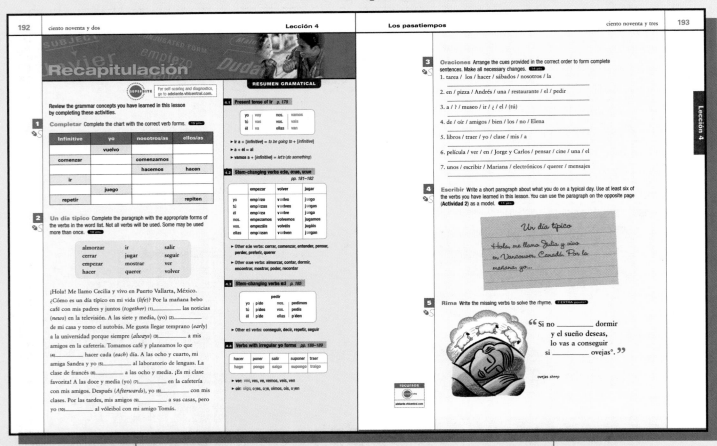

Resumen gramatical This review panel provides you with an easy-to-study summary of the basic concepts of the lesson's grammar, with page references to the full explanations.

Activities A series of activities, moving from directed to open-ended, systematically tests your mastery of the lesson's grammar. The section ends with a riddle or puzzle using the lesson's grammar.

Points Each activity is assigned a point value to help you track your progress. All **Recapitulación** sections add up to fifty points, with two extra-credit points for the last activity.

Supersite Icon An icon lets you know that **Recapitulación** can be completed online with automatic scoring and diagnostics to help you identify where you are strong or might need review.

¡Adelante!
Lectura develops reading skills in the context of the lesson theme.

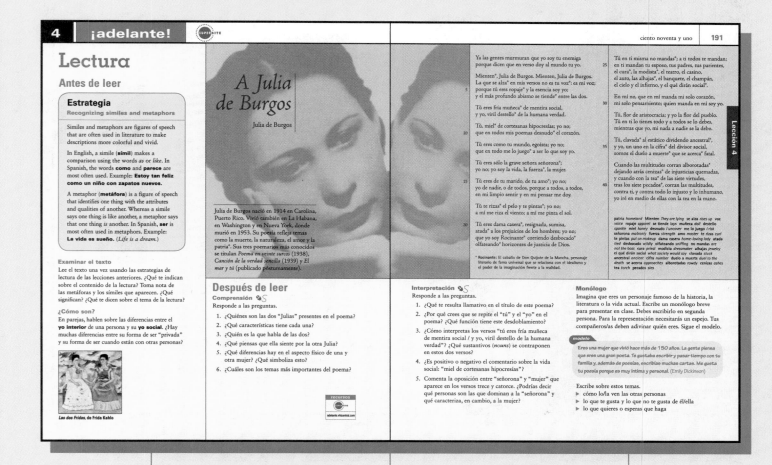

Antes de leer Valuable reading strategies and pre-reading activities strengthen your reading abilities in Spanish.

Readings Selections related to the lesson theme recycle vocabulary and grammar you have learned. The selections in *¡ADELANTE!* UNO and *¡ADELANTE!* DOS are cultural texts, while those in *¡ADELANTE!* TRES are literary pieces.

Después de leer Activities include post-reading exercises that review and check your comprehension of the reading and expansion activities.

Panorama
presents the nations of the Spanish-speaking world.

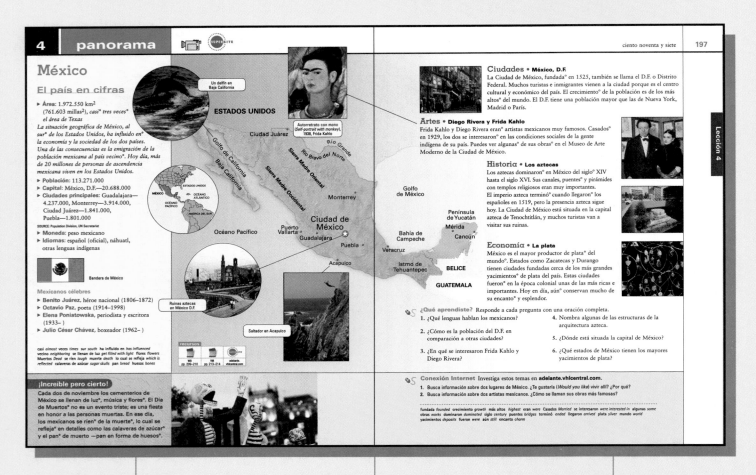

El país en cifras presents interesting key facts about the featured country.

Maps point out major cities, rivers, and geographical features and situate the country in the context of its immediate surroundings and the world.

Readings A series of brief paragraphs explores facets of the country's culture such as history, places, fine arts, literature, and aspects of everyday life.

¡Increíble pero cierto! highlights an intriguing fact about the country or its people.

Conexión Internet activities on the ¡ADELANTE! Supersite offer additional avenues of discovery.

***Panorama cultural* Video** The authentic footage of this video takes you to the featured Spanish-speaking country, letting you experience the sights and sounds of an aspect of its culture. To learn more about the video, turn to page xxiii.

Vocabulario
summarizes all the active vocabulary of the lesson.

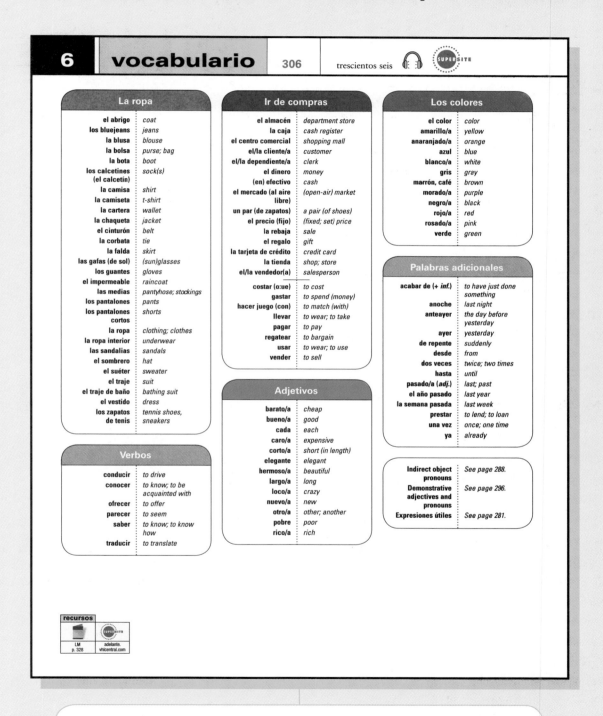

| 6 | vocabulario | 306 | trescientos seis |

La ropa

el abrigo	coat
los bluejeans	jeans
la blusa	blouse
la bolsa	purse; bag
la bota	boot
los calcetines (el calcetín)	sock(s)
la camisa	shirt
la camiseta	t-shirt
la cartera	wallet
la chaqueta	jacket
el cinturón	belt
la corbata	tie
la falda	skirt
las gafas (de sol)	(sun)glasses
los guantes	gloves
el impermeable	raincoat
las medias	pantyhose; stockings
los pantalones	pants
los pantalones cortos	shorts
la ropa	clothing; clothes
la ropa interior	underwear
las sandalias	sandals
el sombrero	hat
el suéter	sweater
el traje	suit
el traje de baño	bathing suit
el vestido	dress
los zapatos de tenis	tennis shoes, sneakers

Verbos

conducir	to drive
conocer	to know; to be acquainted with
ofrecer	to offer
parecer	to seem
saber	to know; to know how
traducir	to translate

Ir de compras

el almacén	department store
la caja	cash register
el centro comercial	shopping mall
el/la cliente/a	customer
el/la dependiente/a	clerk
el dinero	money
(en) efectivo	cash
el mercado (al aire libre)	(open-air) market
un par (de zapatos)	a pair (of shoes)
el precio (fijo)	(fixed; set) price
la rebaja	sale
el regalo	gift
la tarjeta de crédito	credit card
la tienda	shop; store
el/la vendedor(a)	salesperson
costar (o:ue)	to cost
gastar	to spend (money)
hacer juego (con)	to match (with)
llevar	to wear; to take
pagar	to pay
regatear	to bargain
usar	to wear; to use
vender	to sell

Adjetivos

barato/a	cheap
bueno/a	good
cada	each
caro/a	expensive
corto/a	short (in length)
elegante	elegant
hermoso/a	beautiful
largo/a	long
loco/a	crazy
nuevo/a	new
otro/a	other; another
pobre	poor
rico/a	rich

Los colores

el color	color
amarillo/a	yellow
anaranjado/a	orange
azul	blue
blanco/a	white
gris	gray
marrón, café	brown
morado/a	purple
negro/a	black
rojo/a	red
rosado/a	pink
verde	green

Palabras adicionales

acabar de (+ inf.)	to have just done something
anoche	last night
anteayer	the day before yesterday
ayer	yesterday
de repente	suddenly
desde	from
dos veces	twice; two times
hasta	until
pasado/a (adj.)	last; past
el año pasado	last year
la semana pasada	last week
prestar	to lend; to loan
una vez	once; one time
ya	already

Indirect object pronouns	See page 288.
Demonstrative adjectives and pronouns	See page 296.
Expresiones útiles	See page 281.

recursos

LM p. 328

adelante. vhlcentral.com

Recorded vocabulary The headset icon at the top of the page and the **Recursos** boxes at the bottom of the page highlight that the active lesson vocabulary is recorded for convenient study on the **¡ADELANTE!** Supersite (adelante.vhlcentral.com).

¡ADELANTE!-at-a-glance

Integrated Ancillaries
provide all the additional practice you need right in the worktext.

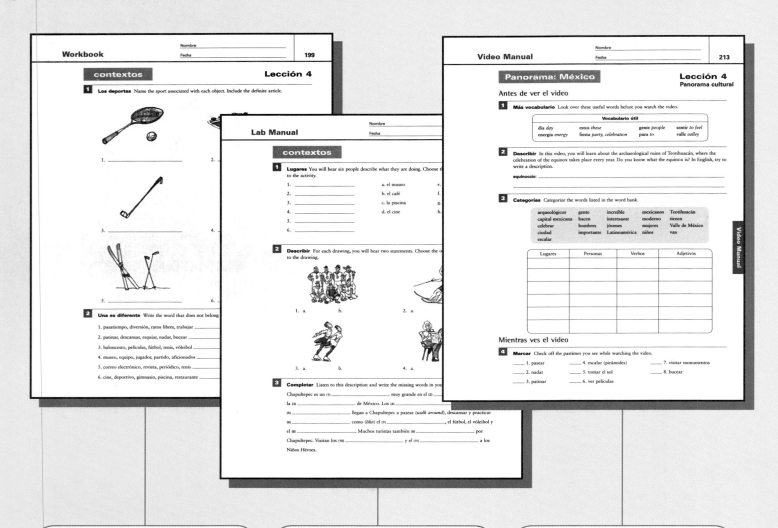

Workbook The Workbook section provides additional practice for the **Contextos, Estructura,** and **Panorama** sections.

Lab Manual The Lab Manual section further practices listening and speaking skills related to the **Contextos, Pronunciación,** and **Estructura** materials.

Video Manual The two Video Manual sections correspond to the **Fotonovela** and **Panorama cultural** video programs. These activities provide pre-, while-, and post-viewing practice.

Recursos Within each lesson, **recursos** boxes let you know which Workbook, Lab Manual, and Video Manual materials can be used. The boxes also lead you to additional material on the Supersite.

Audio and video All the audio and video material you need for these sections is available on the Supersite (**adelante.vhlcentral.com**).

¡ADELANTE! uno y tres
complete this three-volume program.

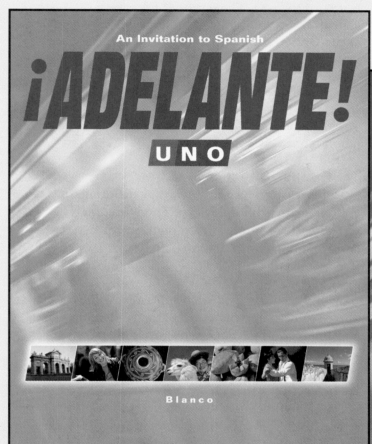

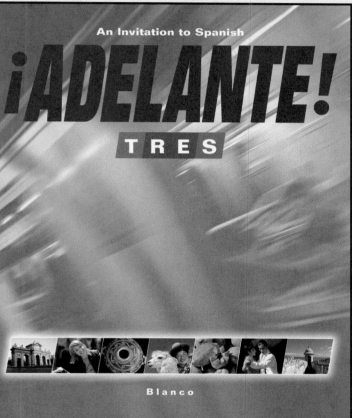

¡ADELANTE! **UNO** starts the program with the present tense and ends with an introduction to the preterite. These concepts will be reviewed and recycled throughout the next two volumes.

¡ADELANTE! **TRES** begins with a lesson that reviews what was covered in *¡ADELANTE!* **DOS**. You continue to expand your knowledge of the Spanish language by covering the subjunctive, the future, and the conditional tenses.

FOTONOVELA VIDEO PROGRAM

Fully integrated with your worktext, the **Fotonovela** Video contains eighteen episodes, one for each lesson of the text. The episodes present the adventures of four college students who are studying at the **Universidad de San Francisco** in Quito, Ecuador. They decide to spend their vacation break on a bus tour of the Ecuadorian countryside with the ultimate goal of hiking up a volcano. The video, shot in various locations in Ecuador, tells their story and the story of Don Francisco, the tour bus driver who accompanies them.

The **Fotonovela** section in each worktext lesson is an abbreviated version of the dramatic episode featured in the video. Therefore, each **Fotonovela** section can be done before you see the corresponding video episode, after it, or as a section that stands alone.

As you watch each video episode, you will first see a live segment in which the characters interact using vocabulary and grammar you are studying. As the video progresses, the live segments carefully combine new vocabulary and grammar with previously taught language. You will then see a **Resumen** section in which one of the main video characters recaps the live segment, emphasizing the grammar and vocabulary you are studying within the context of the episode's key events.

In addition, in most of the video episodes, there are brief pauses to allow the characters to reminisce about their home countries. These flashbacks—montages of real-life images shot in Spain, Mexico, Puerto Rico, and various parts of Ecuador—connect the theme of the video to everyday life in various parts of the Spanish-speaking world.

THE CAST
Here are the main characters you will meet when you watch the **Fotonovela** Video:

From Ecuador,
Inés Ayala Loor

From Spain,
María Teresa (Maite) Fuentes de Alba

From México,
Alejandro (Álex) Morales Paredes

From Puerto Rico,
Javier Gómez Lozano

And, also from Ecuador,
don Francisco Castillo Moreno

FLASH CULTURA VIDEO PROGRAM

The dynamic **Flash cultura** Video provides an entertaining supplement to the **Cultura** section of each lesson. Young people from all over the Spanish-speaking world share aspects of life in their countries: places, products, practices, and more. The similarities and differences among Spanish-speaking countries that come up through their experiences will challenge you to think about your own cultural practices and values.

The segments provide valuable cultural insights as well as linguistic input; the episodes will expose you to a wide variety of accents and vocabulary as they gradually move into Spanish.

PANORAMA CULTURAL VIDEO PROGRAM

The **Panorama cultural** Video is integrated with the **Panorama** section in each lesson of ¡ADELANTE! Each segment is 2–3 minutes long and consists of documentary footage from each of the countries featured. The images were specially chosen for interest level and visual appeal, while the all-Spanish narrations were carefully written to reflect the vocabulary and grammar covered in the worktexts.

As you watch the video segments, you will experience a diversity of images and topics: cities, monuments, traditions, festivals, archeological sites, geographical wonders, and more. You will be transported to each Spanish-speaking country, including the United States and Canada, thereby having the opportunity to expand your cultural perspectives with information directly related to the content of each level of ¡ADELANTE!

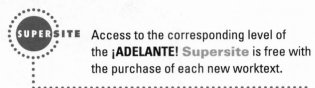

MAESTRO™ Supersite

The **¡ADELANTE!** Supersite, powered by **MAESTRO**™, provides a wealth of resources for both students and instructors.

SUPERSITE Access to the corresponding level of the **¡ADELANTE!** Supersite is free with the purchase of each new worktext.

Learning tools available to students:

▶ interactive practice activities with auto-grading and real-time feedback

- directed practice from the worktext, including audio activities
- additional practice for every strand of each lesson

▶ open-ended activities where students explore and search the Internet

- activities for the **Cultura** and **Panorama cultural** sections, including annotated interactive maps

▶ the complete **¡ADELANTE!** Video Program

- ***Fotonovela***: dramatic video episodes follow four students on their adventures through Ecuador

- ***Flash cultura***: shot on location in Latin America, the US, and Spain, this video in the form of a news program expands on the theme of each lesson in the book

- ***Panorama cultural***: one episode for every Spanish-speaking country highlights each country's culture

▶ MP3 files for the complete **¡ADELANTE!** Audio Program 🎧

- textbook audio files
- lab program audio files
- record-and-compare audio activities

▶ and more...

- auto-scored practice quizzes with feedback in every lesson
- flashcards with audio
- Flash-animated grammar tutorials (*Premium content*)

ICONS AND *RECURSOS* BOXES

Icons

Familiarize yourself with these icons that appear throughout ¡ADELANTE!

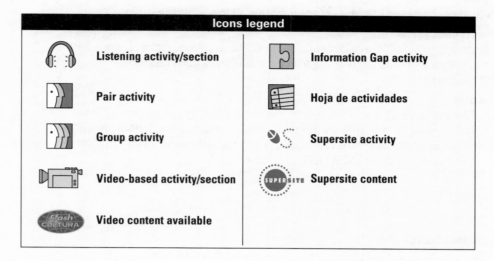

Icons legend	
Listening activity/section	Information Gap activity
Pair activity	Hoja de actividades
Group activity	Supersite activity
Video-based activity/section	Supersite content
Video content available	

- The Information Gap activities and those involving **Hojas de actividades** (*activity sheets*) require handouts that your instructor will give you.
- You will see the listening icon in each lesson's **Contextos**, **Pronunciación**, and **Vocabulario** sections.
- The video icons appear in the **Fotonovela**, **Cultura**, and **Panorama** sections of each lesson.
- Both Supersite icons and mouse icons appear in every strand of every lesson. Visit **adelante.vhlcentral.com**.

Recursos

Recursos boxes let you know exactly what supplementary materials you can use to reinforce and expand on every section of the lessons in your worktext. They even include page numbers when applicable. All print material is built right into your worktext, following the color pages of the lesson; all multimedia components are available on the Supersite. See the next page for a description of the ancillary program.

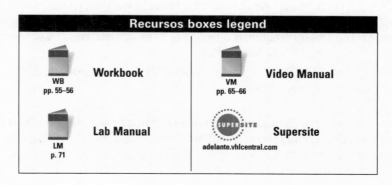

Recursos boxes legend	
Workbook WB pp. 55–56	Video Manual VM pp. 65–66
Lab Manual LM p. 71	Supersite adelante.vhlcentral.com

icons and ancillaries

STUDENT ANCILLARIES

▶ **Workbook/Video Manual/Lab Manual**
All of these materials are available right inside your worktext, at the end of each lesson.

▶ **Lab Audio Program**
The audio files to accompany the Lab Manual are available on the Supersite.

▶ **Textbook Audio Program MP3s**
The Textbook Audio Program MP3s, available on the Supersite, are the audio recordings for the listening-based activities and recordings of the active vocabulary in each lesson of the ¡ADELANTE! program.

▶ **Maestro™ Supersite**
Newly developed for ¡ADELANTE!, your passcode to the corresponding content on the Supersite (adelante.vhlcentral.com) is free with the purchase of each new worktext. Here you will find activities found in your worktext, available with auto-grading capability, additional activities for practice, all of the audio and video material for ¡ADELANTE!, and much more.

INSTRUCTOR ANCILLARIES

▶ **Instructor's Annotated Edition (IAE)**
The IAE contains a wealth of teaching information. Answers for discrete item activities are overprinted on the student pages for both the lesson itself and the Workbook, Lab Manual, and Video Manual tabs. Additionally, the principal lessons contain teaching suggestions, ideas for expansion, and more.

▶ **IRCD & DVD set**

   ▶ **Instructor's Resource CD (IRCD)**

      ▶ **Instructor's Resource Manual (IRM)**
      The IRM contains classroom handouts for the worktext, additional activities, answers to directed activities in the worktext, audioscripts and videoscripts, and transcripts and translations of the video programs.

      ▶ **PowerPoint Presentations**
      This feature provides the Overhead Transparencies as PowerPoint slides, including maps of all Spanish-speaking countries, the **Contextos** vocabulary drawings, and other selected drawings from the student text. Also included on PowerPoint are presentations of each grammar point in **Estructura**.

      ▶ **Workbook/ Video Manual/ Lab Manual Answer Key**
      Answers to the Workbook, Video Manual, and Lab Manual portions of each lesson are provided, should instructors wish to distribute them for self-correction.

      ▶ **Testing Program**
      The Testing Program contains four versions of tests for each worktext lesson, exams for each level of ¡ADELANTE!, listening scripts, test answer keys, and optional cultural, video, and reading test items. The Testing Program is provided in three formats: within a powerful Test Generator, in customizable RTF files, and as PDFs.

   ▶ One DVD for each level of ¡ADELANTE! provides the *Fotonovela*, *Flash cultura*, and *Panorama cultural* segments that correspond to each level.

▶ **Maestro™ Supersite**
In addition to access to the student site, the password-protected instructor site offers a robust course management system that allows instructors to assign and track student progress. The Supersite contains the full contents of the IRCD (with the exception of the Test Generator), and other resources, such as lesson plans and sample syllabi.

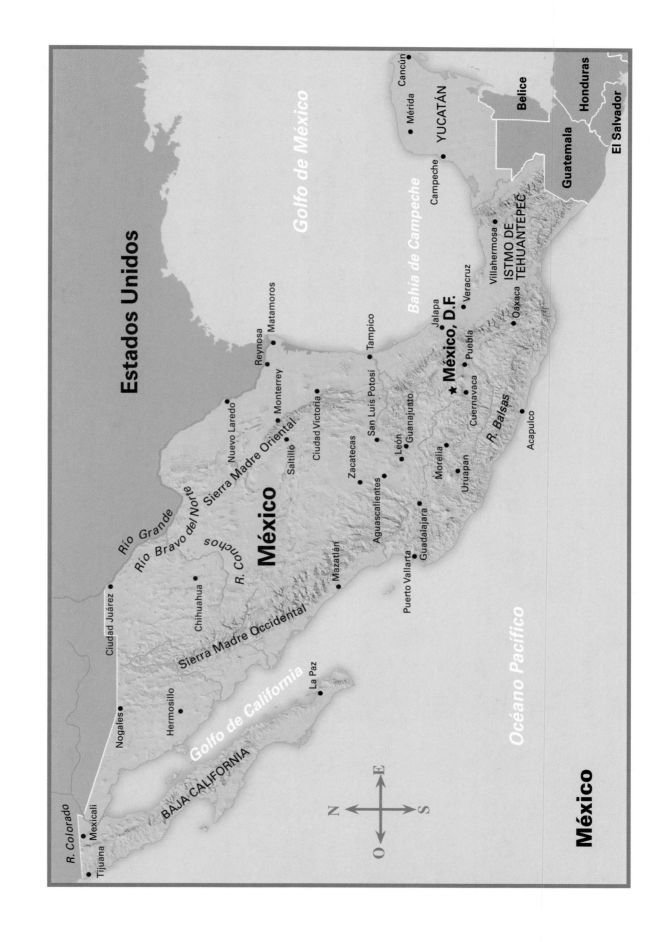

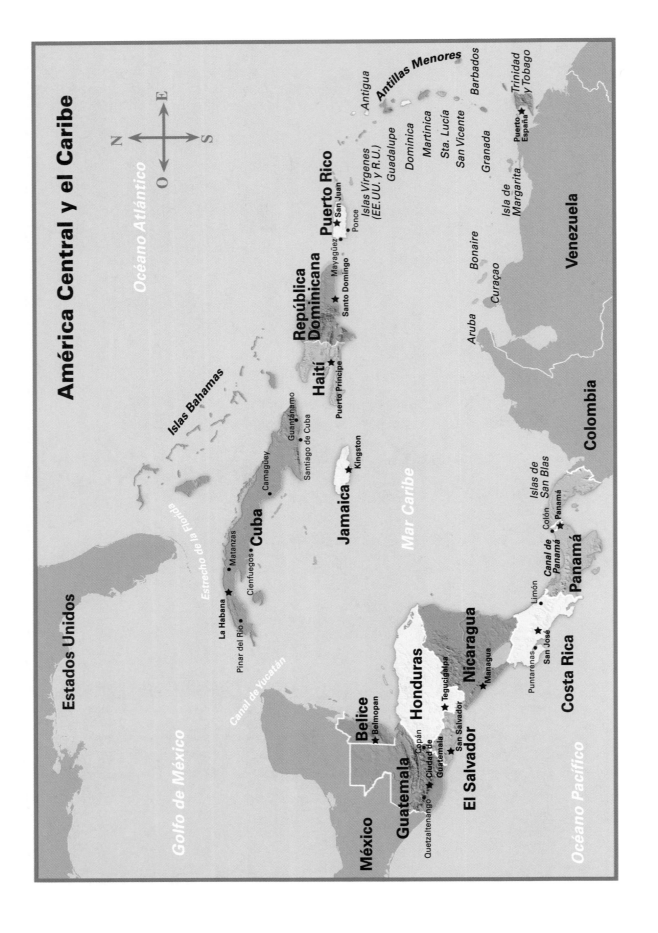

América Central y el Caribe

Estados Unidos

Golfo de México

Océano Atlántico

Océano Pacífico

México

Islas Bahamas

Estrecho de la Florida

Canal de Yucatán

Cuba
La Habana
Pinar del Río
Matanzas
Cienfuegos
Camagüey
Santiago de Cuba
Guantánamo

Belice
Belmopan

Guatemala
Ciudad de Guatemala
Quetzaltenango
Copán

El Salvador
San Salvador

Honduras
Tegucigalpa

Nicaragua
Managua

Costa Rica
San José
Puntarenas
Limón

Panamá
Canal de Panamá
Colón
Panamá
Islas de San Blas

Jamaica
Kingston

Mar Caribe

Haití
Puerto Príncipe

República Dominicana
Santo Domingo

Puerto Rico
San Juan
Mayagüez
Ponce

Islas Vírgenes
(EE.UU. y R.U.)

Antillas Menores
Antigua
Guadalupe
Dominica
Martinica
Sta. Lucía
San Vicente
Granada
Barbados

Aruba
Curaçao
Bonaire

Isla de Margarita

Trinidad y Tobago
Puerto España

Venezuela

Colombia

América del Sur

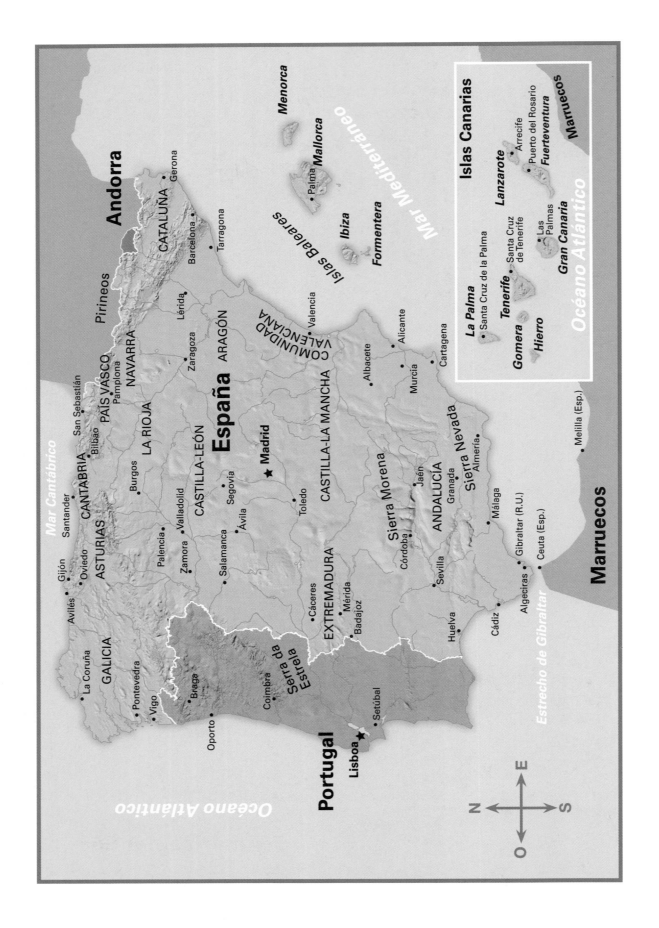

Lección de repaso

Communicative Goals

You will review how to:

- **Describe people and things**
- **Discuss pastimes and sports**
- **Talk about the seasons and the weather**
- **Tell what happened in the past**

Práctica SUPERSITE

1 **Identificar** Indica la palabra que no pertenece al grupo. **8 pts.**

1. lluvia • (tomar el sol) • botas • impermeable
2. traje de baño • bucear • playa • (abrigo)
3. (nadar) • nieve • esquiar • invierno
4. matemáticas • (mochila) • historia • computación
5. estudiar • tomar un examen • (viajar) • hacer la tarea
6. sandalias • camiseta • (guantes) • pantalones cortos
7. (semana) • ayer • mañana • hoy
8. tío • prima • abuelo • (dependienta)

2 **Listas** Completa cada lista con las palabras que faltan. **10 pts.**

DÍAS: lunes, (1) __martes__, miércoles, jueves, (2) __viernes__, sábado, (3) __domingo__

MESES: (4) __enero__, febrero, marzo, abril, (5) __mayo__, junio, julio, (6) __agosto__, septiembre, (7) __octubre__, noviembre, (8) __diciembre__

ESTACIONES: (9) __primavera__, verano, otoño, (10) __invierno__

3 **Oraciones** Completa cada oración con una palabra de la lista. **6 pts.**

biblioteca	periodismo
historia	pruebas
lápiz	psicología
lenguas extranjeras	reloj
matemáticas	ventana
mochila	vestido

1. Para ser reportero en la televisión, tienes que estudiar __periodismo__.

2. Si te gustan los números y las ecuaciones, puedes estudiar __matemáticas__.

3. Para comunicarte con personas de otros países y culturas, debes estudiar __lenguas extranjeras__.

4. El profesor les hace __pruebas__ a los estudiantes para comprobar (*check*) lo que aprendieron.

5. Cuando los estudiantes están aburridos, miran el __reloj__ esperando el final de la clase.

6. Para estudiar en un lugar tranquilo y tener acceso a muchos libros, puedes ir a la __biblioteca__.

For additional vocabulary, see p. 20.

This overview presents key vocabulary from *¡ADELANTE!* **UNO**. For further review, follow the cross-references.

El invierno

diciembre *December*
enero *January*
febrero *February*   **Nieva. (nevar)**

¿Qué tiempo hace? *What's the weather like?*
Hace frío. *It's cold.*

estudiar *to study*
patinar *to skate*
tomar el examen *to take an exam*
trabajar *to work*

el esquí *skiing*
el hockey *hockey*

esquiar

el abrigo *coat*
la bota *boot*
los guantes *gloves*

el año *year*
el día *day*
la semana *week*

lunes *Monday*
martes *Tuesday*
miércoles *Wednesday*
jueves *Thursday*
viernes *Friday*
sábado *Saturday*
domingo *Sunday*

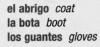

el mes

La primavera

marzo *March*
abril *April*
mayo *May*

Extra Practice In small groups, have students list as many related vocabulary words as they can remember. Call on several volunteers to share their lists with the class.

Hace mal tiempo. *The weather is bad.*

ir de excursión *to go on a hike*
pasear *to take a walk; to stroll*
pasear en bicicleta *to ride a bicycle*
practicar deportes *to play sports*

la contabilidad *accounting*
el periodismo *journalism*
la prueba *test; quiz*

Llueve. (llover)

la blusa *blouse*
la camisa *shirt*
el impermeable *raincoat*
el traje *suit*
el vestido *dress*

el reloj

El verano

junio *June*
julio *July*
agosto *August*

Hace buen tiempo. *The weather is good.*
Hace sol. *It's sunny.*

bucear *to scuba dive*
nadar *to swim*
tomar el sol *to sunbathe*
viajar *to travel*

el campo *countryside*
el mar *sea*

Hace (mucho) calor.

TPR To review additional vocabulary, play a word association game. Have students stand in a large circle, then throw a foam or paper ball to a student and call out a word. The student must quickly respond with a related word, then throw the ball to another student, who must come up with a new association for that word. (Ex: **jugar: deportes: el tenis: los zapatos de tenis: la ropa: lavar**) When a student is "stumped," he or she takes a seat. Call out another word and begin again. The last player standing is the winner.

la playa
el vóleibol *volleyball*

la camiseta *t-shirt*
las gafas de sol *sunglasses*
los pantalones cortos *shorts*
las sandalias *sandals*
el traje de baño *bathing suit*

El otoño

septiembre *September*
octubre *October*
noviembre *November*

Hace fresco. *It's cool.*

Hace viento.

comenzar las clases *to start clases*
escalar montañas *to climb mountains*
jugar (u:ue) al fútbol americano *to play football*

la biblioteca
la cafetería *cafeteria*
la computación *computer science*
las lenguas extranjeras *foreign languages*
las matemáticas *math*
la mochila *backpack*

montar a caballo

la chaqueta *jacket*
los bluejeans *jeans*
el suéter *sweater*

For a complete list of related vocabulary go to *¡ADELANTE!* UNO, pp. 34, 88, 144, 198, 254, and 306.

---

4 **Describir** Describe el tiempo que hace en cada escena y el tipo de actividad que hacen las personas. **12 pts.**

Some answers will vary. Sample answers:

> **modelo**
> Hace buen tiempo. Él está paseando en bicicleta.

1. Hace viento. Ella está paseando por la ciudad.

2. Hace fresco. Ellos están acampando.

3. Hace buen tiempo. Él está corriendo.

4. Está nublado. Él está montando a caballo.

5. Está lloviendo. Ella está paseando por el parque.

6. Hace calor. Ellos están jugando al vóleibol.

5 **Preparando un viaje** Escribe una conversación entre dos amigos que están haciendo las maletas para irse de viaje una semana. Uno va a esquiar en Argentina, donde es invierno, y el otro va a Florida, donde es verano. **14 pts.** Answers will vary.

- ¿Qué actividades pueden hacer?
- ¿Qué tiempo va a hacer?
- ¿Qué ropa tienen que llevar?
- ¿Qué medios de transporte van a usar?
- ¿Dónde se van a quedar?

Práctica

 SUPERSITE For self-scoring and diagnostics, go to adelante.vhlcentral.com.

1 **Género y número** Completa las tablas cambiando las palabras femeninas a masculinas, las singulares a plurales y viceversa. **14 pts.**

Masculino	Femenino
el pintor	la pintora
el cuñado	**la cuñada**
el huésped	**la huésped**
el turista	la turista
el dependiente	**la dependienta**
el pasajero	la pasajera
el inspector	**la inspectora**

Singular	Plural
una clase	unas clases
un autobús	unos autobuses
una excursión	**unas excursiones**
una comunidad	unas comunidades
un lápiz	**unos lápices**
una revista	**unas revistas**
un calcetín	unos calcetines

2 **Completar** Completa cada oración con el verbo **ser**. **6 pts.**

1. Maite ___es___ de España, ¿verdad?
2. ¿Quiénes ___son___ los huéspedes de la habitación 347?
3. Juan y yo ___somos___ vendedores en aquel centro comercial.
4. ¿De dónde ___eres___ tú?
5. ___Son___ las nueve de la mañana.
6. Yo ___soy___ puertorriqueño pero vivo en Costa Rica.

3 **El primer día de clases** Completa la conversación con las formas correctas del verbo **estar**. **5 pts.**

JULIO Hola, Martín. ¿Cómo (1) ___estás___ (tú)?

MARTÍN Bien. Oye, ¿sabes dónde (2) ___está___ el gimnasio? Mis compañeros del equipo de béisbol (3) ___están___ allí.

JULIO Pero, hombre, ¡yo también (4) ___estoy___ en el equipo! Vamos juntos al gimnasio, (nosotros) (5) ___estamos___ muy cerca.

MARTÍN ¡Pero qué tonto soy! No recordaba que tú también estás en el equipo. OK, vamos.

Resumen gramatical

This overview presents key grammatical concepts from *¡ADELANTE! UNO*. For further review, follow the cross-references.

R.1 Nouns and articles  *¡ADELANTE! UNO* L1 pp. 12–14

Gender of nouns

Nouns that refer to living things

	Masculine		Feminine
-o	el chico	-a	la chica
-or	el profesor	-ora	la profesora
-ista	el turista	-ista	la turista

Nouns that refer to non-living things

	Masculine		Feminine
-o	el libro	-a	la cosa
-ma	el programa	-ción	la lección
-s	el autobús	-dad	la nacionalidad

Plural of nouns

▶ ending in vowels + *-s*   **la chica → las chicas**

▶ ending in consonant + *-es* **el señor → los señores**

  (-z → -ces **un lápiz → unos lápices**)

Definite articles: el, la, los, las

Indefinite articles: un, una, unos, unas

R.2 Present of **ser** and **estar**  *¡ADELANTE! UNO* L1 pp. 19–21, L2 pp. 75–76

¿De dónde eres?

Yo soy de México.

ser			
yo	soy	nosotros/as	somos
tú	eres	vosotros/as	sois
Ud./él/ella	es	Uds./ellos/ellas	son

▶ Uses of **ser**: nationality, origin, profession or occupation, characteristics, generalizations, possession, what something is made of, time and date, time and place of events

estar

yo	estoy	nosotros/as	estamos
tú	estás	vosotros/as	estáis
Ud./él/ella	está	Uds./ellos/ellas	están

▶ **Uses of estar:** location, health, physical states and conditions, emotional states, weather expressions, ongoing actions

▶ **Ser** and **estar** can both be used with many of the same adjectives, but the meaning will change.

Juan **es** listo.	Juan **está** listo.
Juan is smart.	*Juan is ready.*

R.3 Adjectives   🔄 **¡ADELANTE! UNO**
L3 pp. 122–124, 127

> ¡Qué alto es tu papá! Y tu mamá, ¡qué bonita!

▶ Adjectives are words that describe nouns. In Spanish, adjectives agree with the nouns they modify in both gender and number.

Descriptive adjectives

Masculine		Feminine	
Singular	**Plural**	**Singular**	**Plural**
alt**o**	alt**os**	alt**a**	alt**as**
inteligente	inteligente**s**	inteligente	inteligente**s**
trabajad**or**	trabajad**ores**	trabajad**ora**	trabajad**oras**

▶ To refer to a mixed group, use the masculine plural form.

Juan y Ana son trabajad**ores**.

▶ Descriptive adjectives and adjectives of nationality follow the noun: **el chico rubio, la mujer española**

▶ Adjectives of quantity precede the noun: **muchos libros**

▶ Before a masculine noun, these adjectives are shortened.

bueno → **buen**	malo → **mal**	grande → **gran**

Possessive adjectives

Singular		Plural	
mi	nuestro/a	mis	nuestros/as
tu	vuestro/a	tus	vuestros/as
su	su	sus	sus

▶ Possessive adjectives are always placed before the nouns they modify: **nuestros amigos, mi madre**

---

4 **¿Ser o estar?** Completa el texto con **ser** o **estar**. `9 pts.`

🖱️ Me llamo Julio. Mis padres (1) __son__ de México, pero mi familia ahora (2) __está__ en Arizona. Mi padre (3) __es__ médico en el hospital; el hospital (4) __está__ cerca de nuestra casa. Nosotros tres (5) __somos__ altos y morenos. Yo (6) __soy__ estudiante de periodismo. Mis clases (7) __son__ buenas, pero a veces (yo) (8) __estoy__ demasiado ocupado con las tareas. Todos mis compañeros (9) __están__ nerviosos porque hoy empiezan los exámenes finales.

5 **Posesivos** Completa con el adjetivo posesivo correcto. `8 pts.`

🖱️ 1. Él es __mi__ (*my*) hermano.
2. __Tu__ (*Your*, fam.) familia es muy simpática.
3. __Nuestro__ (*Our*) sobrino es italiano.
4. ¿Ella es __su__ (*his*) profesora?
5. __Su__ (*Your*, form.) maleta es de color verde.
6. __Sus__ (*Her*) amigos son de Colombia.
7. Son __nuestras__ (*our*) compañeras de clase.
8. __Mis__ (*My*) padres están en el trabajo.

6 **Opuestos** Escribe oraciones completas con los elementos dados y los adjetivos opuestos a los que están subrayados. ¡Ojo! Recuerda conjugar los verbos. `8 pts.`

> **modelo**
> casa / de Silvia / ser / <u>grande</u> / pero / mi casa / ser / ¿?
> *La casa de Silvia es grande, pero mi casa es pequeña.*

1. habitación / de mi hermana / siempre / estar / <u>sucia</u> / pero / mi habitación / estar / ¿?
La habitación de mi hermana siempre está sucia, pero mi habitación está limpia/ordenada.

2. (yo) estar / <u>contento</u> / porque / (nosotros) estar / de vacaciones / pero / mis padres / estar / ¿? / porque / (ellos) tener / que trabajar
Estoy contento/a porque estamos de vacaciones, pero mis padres están tristes/enojados porque tienen que trabajar.

3. Tu primo / ser / <u>alto</u> y <u>moreno</u> / pero / tú / ser / ¿? y ¿?
Tu primo es alto y moreno, pero tú eres bajo/a y rubio/a.

4. Mi amigo Fernando / decir / que las matemáticas / ser / <u>difíciles</u> / pero / yo / creer / que / ser / ¿?
Mi amigo Fernando dice que las matemáticas son difíciles, pero yo creo que son fáciles.

Extra Practice Add a visual aspect to this grammar review. Bring in magazine pictures. Ask students to describe the people, places, and objects using **ser** and **estar**. Focus on verb forms, articles, and adjective agreement.

recursos

adelante.vhlcentral.com

Lección de repaso

Práctica y Comunicación

1 **Correo** Completa el mensaje de correo electrónico con la forma adecuada de **ser** o **estar**.

¡Hola Carlos!

¿Cómo estás? Yo (1) __estoy__ muy preocupada porque tenemos un examen mañana en la clase de español y el profesor (2) __es__ muy estricto. Mi amiga Ana (3) __está__ estudiando en la biblioteca y quiero ir a verla para que me ayude. Ella (4) __es__ una estudiante muy buena y sus notas (*grades*) (5) __son__ excelentes.

     Este fin de semana hay una excursión a las montañas. Mis amigos y yo (6) __estamos__ muy contentos porque el lugar que vamos a visitar (7) __es__ muy hermoso. Ana también quiere ir a la excursión, pero (ella) (8) __está__ enojada porque tiene que trabajar.

     Bueno, antes de ir a la biblioteca voy a dormir la siesta porque (9) __estoy__ muy cansada.

¡Hasta pronto!
Susana

1 To practice adjective agreement, have students circle all the adjectives in the e-mail, then replace them with different adjectives. Call on several volunteers to read their revised e-mails and have the class check for accuracy.

1 For expansion, have students write a similar e-mail to a friend, using at least six forms of **ser** and **estar**. Have them exchange their messages with a partner for peer editing.

2 **La vida de Marina** Completa cada oración con la forma correcta de los cuatro adjetivos.

1. Marina busca una compañera de cuarto __ordenada, honesta, alegre, amable__.
(ordenado, honesto, alegre, amable)
2. Se lleva bien con las personas __alegres, trabajadoras, interesantes, sensibles__
(alegre, trabajador, interesante, sensible)
3. Los padres de Marina son __simpáticos, inteligentes, altos, felices__.
(simpático, inteligente, alto, feliz)
4. A Marina le gusta la ropa __elegante, buena, bonita, barata__.
(elegante, bueno, bonito, barato)
5. Marina tiene un novio __trabajador, simpático, pelirrojo, listo__.
(trabajador, simpático, pelirrojo, listo)

Marina

2 For additional practice, have students add two more adjectives to each sentence.

3 **¿Es o no es?** Responde a cada pregunta usando el adjetivo opuesto.

modelo
¿Es alto tu tío? No, es bajo.

1. ¿Es viejo el agente de viajes? No, es joven.
2. ¿Son malas las amigas de Glenda? No, son buenas.
3. ¿Es antipática la vendedora? No, es simpática.
4. ¿Son guapos los primos de Omar? No, son feos.
5. ¿Son morenas las excursionistas? No, son rubias.
6. ¿Es feo el yerno de doña Ana? No, es guapo.

3 Give students these additional items: 7. ¿Es grande la biblioteca? (No, es pequeña.) 8. ¿Son difíciles tus clases? (No, son fáciles.) 9. ¿Son caros estos pantalones? (No, son baratos.) 10. ¿Es largo el vestido? (No, es corto.)

Extra Practice Briefly review adjectives that change in meaning when used with **ser** and **estar**. Ex: **listo, malo, aburrido, verde, vivo, seguro**

4 For expansion, bring in photos or magazine pictures that show several people performing a variety of activities. Have students use **ser** and **estar** to describe the scenes.

4

En el parque Mira la imagen y contesta las preguntas usando **ser** y **estar**. Puedes inventar las respuestas para algunas preguntas. Answers will vary.

1. ¿Quién es cada una de estas personas?

2. ¿Qué están haciendo?

3. ¿Cómo están?

4 Ask these additional questions about the drawing:
6. ¿Qué estación es?
7. ¿Qué tiempo hace?
8. ¿Quiénes están de vacaciones?

4. ¿Cómo son?

5. ¿Dónde están?

5 Encourage students to think about these categories: personality, physical characteristics, strengths and weaknesses, health, current feelings, and emotions.

5 Ask follow-up questions to practice gender and number agreement. Ex: **John es alto. ¿Y Paula? ¿Cómo es?** (Paula es baja.) **Carmen y Melissa son rubias. ¿Y Frank?** (Él es rubio también. / Los tres son rubios.)

5

Entrevista Escribe tantos (*as many*) adjetivos descriptivos como puedas (*as you can*) sobre ti mismo/a (*yourself*) en tres minutos. Luego, en parejas, usa **ser** o **estar** para preguntarle a tu compañero/a si él/ella tiene las mismas características. Finalmente, comparte con la clase lo que tienen en común. Answers will vary.

> **modelo**
> **(Yo):** *delgada, baja, morena, trabajadora, contenta, simpática*
> **(Preguntas):** *¿Tú eres trabajadora? ¿Estás contenta?*
> **(Oración):** *Somos morenas, estamos contentas y somos trabajadoras.*

6

Mi familia y mis amigos Escribe una breve descripción de tu familia, tus parientes y tus amigos. Usa tantos adjetivos posesivos como puedas para identificar a la(s) persona(s) que estás describiendo. Answers will vary.

¡AL RESCATE!

To review vocabulary related to family and friends, go to **¡ADELANTE!** **UNO**, **Lesson 3, Contextos,** pp. 112–113.

7

Una cita (*date*) Mañana vas a tener una cita con un(a) muchacho/a maravilloso/a. Quieres contarle a tu mejor amigo/a y pedirle consejos. Tu amigo/a es muy curioso/a y te va a hacer muchas preguntas. En parejas, representen la conversación. Éstos son algunos aspectos que pueden incluir. Answers will vary.

Tu amigo/a quiere saber:

- cómo te sientes (*you feel*) antes de la cita
- qué crees que va a pasar
- cómo es el lugar adonde van a ir
- cómo es la persona con quien vas a tener la cita

7 Circulate around the classroom, providing assistance as needed. If necessary, help students brainstorm useful verbs and briefly review present tense conjugations.

Tú quieres consejos sobre:

- qué ropa usar
- temas de los que pueden hablar
- adónde ir
- quién debe pagar la cuenta (*bill*)

EN DETALLE

Unas vacaciones de
voluntario

¿Qué hiciste durante las vacaciones de verano? Muchos estudiantes contestarían° esta pregunta con historias de cómo disfrutaron° de su tiempo libre. Pero hay otra actividad que ha recibido° atención recientemente: el trabajo voluntario durante las vacaciones.

En Latinoamérica, se le llama **aprendizaje-servicio°**, una combinación de educación formal y voluntariado°. En países como México, Argentina y Chile, los estudiantes reciben crédito académico mientras° usan su creatividad y su talento en beneficio de los demás°. Así se promueve° la participación activa de los estudiantes en la sociedad. Los

voluntarios también viven experiencias que no podrían° obtener en el salón de clases: en Buenos Aires, un grupo de alumnos° de los colegios más exclusivos ayuda con las tareas en centros comunitarios; en una escuela de Resistencia, en Argentina, los chicos de barrios marginales° les enseñan computación a los adultos desocupados° de su propia comunidad.

En 2001, la Secretaría de Educación de Argentina creó el Programa Nacional de Escuela y Comunidad para los proyectos de aprendizaje-servicio por todo el país. Y tú, ¿alguna vez has participado en servicio comunitario?

Otras vacaciones de voluntarios

En León, Nicaragua, 16 estudiantes costarricenses construyeron casas para familias nicaragüenses como parte del programa Hábitat para la Humanidad. Adrián, un voluntario, dijo: "Fue una experiencia increíble. Pude° divertirme y al mismo tiempo hacer algo útil° y beneficiar a otras personas durante mis vacaciones".

Los estudiantes de la escuela técnica de Junín de los Andes, Argentina, adaptaron molinos de viento° a las necesidades de las poblaciones mapuches°. Por este proyecto ganaron un premio° en la Feria Mundial de Ciencias de 1999.

contestarían *would answer* disfrutaron *they enjoyed* ha recibido *has received* aprendizaje-servicio *service learning* voluntariado *volunteerism* mientras *while* los demás *others* Así se promueve *Thus it promotes* no podrían *they could not* alumnos *students* barrios marginales *disadvantaged neighborhoods* desocupados *unemployed* Pude *I was able to* útil *useful* molinos de viento *windmills* mapuches *indigenous people of Central and Southern Chile and Southern Argentina* premio *prize*

ACTIVIDADES

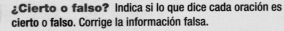

1 **¿Cierto o falso?** Indica si lo que dice cada oración es cierto o falso. Corrige la información falsa.

1. El aprendizaje-servicio es ir a cursos de verano. Falso. Es una combinación de educación formal y voluntariado.
2. En este programa, los jóvenes voluntarios aprenden cosas que no se aprenden en el salón de clases. Cierto.
3. Los estudiantes de Resistencia, Argentina, les enseñan computación a los chicos de los colegios más exclusivos. Falso. Les enseñan computación a los adultos desocupados de su propia comunidad.

4. En 2001, la Secretaría de Educación de Argentina creó un programa nacional de aprendizaje-servicio. Cierto.
5. De su experiencia como voluntario en Nicaragua, el joven Adrián dijo: "Fue una experiencia horrible". Falso. Adrián dijo: "Fue una experiencia increíble".
6. Los estudiantes de una escuela técnica adaptaron molinos de viento a las necesidades de las poblaciones indígenas de su país. Cierto.

ASÍ SE DICE

el buceo	*diving*
la carrera de autos	*car race*
el ciclismo	*cycling*
la lucha libre	*freestyle wrestling*
la ola	*[ocean] wave*
los países hispanohablantes	**los países donde se habla español**
surfear, hacer surf	*to surf*
el/la surfista, el/la surfero/a, el/la surfo/a, el/la tablista	*surfer*

EL MUNDO HISPANO

Deportes importantes

No cabe duda° que el fútbol es el deporte más popular en Latinoamérica. Sin embargo°, también se practican otros deportes en el mundo hispano.

Deporte	Lugar(es)
el béisbol	Puerto Rico, República Dominicana, Cuba, México, Venezuela
el ciclismo	Colombia, España y otras regiones montañosas
el rugby	Argentina, Chile
el baloncesto (básquetbol)	España, Puerto Rico, Colombia, Centroamérica
el jai-alai	Originado en el País Vasco (España), también es popular en México y los EE.UU.
la equitación (montar a caballo)	México, Argentina, España
el surf	las Islas Canarias (España), México, Chile, Perú, Colombia

No cabe duda *there is no doubt* Sin embargo *nevertheless*

PERFIL

Surfistas hispanos

Se dice que para hacer surf hay que "sentir" la ola°, pararse° en la tabla° y "agarrarla°". La frase "agarrar la ola" tiene un significado que sólo entienden realmente los que practican el surf. Originado en Hawai, es popular en muchas partes del mundo. Sólo necesitas una tabla y una costa marina. Dos de los surfistas hispanos más reconocidos son **Gabriel Villarán** y **Ornella Pellizari**.

Ornella Pellizari

Gabriel Villarán es probablemente el surfista hispanoamericano más famoso del mundo. Nació en 1984 en Lima, Perú, donde su madre, su padre y su hermano eran° surfistas. Villarán fue campeón° latinoamericano dos veces y en enero de 2006 ganó el primer lugar en los Juegos Panamericanos de Surf.

A los once años, la argentina Ornella Pellizari se compró una tabla con el dinero que había ahorrado°. A los dieciocho años, ganó el Campeonato Latinoamericano de Surf Profesional femenino. Dice Pellizari: "Una vez que empecé a surfear, no salí más del agua".

ola *wave* pararse *to stand* te paras *you stand* la tabla *surfboard* agarrarla *to grab it* eran *were* el campeón *champion* había ahorrado *she had saved*

SUPERSITE **Conexión Internet**

¿Quiénes son otros atletas hispanos famosos?

Go to **adelante.vhlcentral.com** to find more cultural information related to this **Cultura** section.

ACTIVIDADES

2 **Comprensión** Completa las oraciones.
1. El deporte del surf se originó en ___Hawai___.
2. Gabriel Villarán nació en ___Lima, Perú___.
3. Los países donde se habla español son conocidos como países ___hispanohablantes___
4. A los dieciocho años, Pellizari ganó el Campeonato Latinoamericano de Surf Profesional para ___mujeres___.
5. El deporte del ___jai-alai___ tiene su origen en el País Vasco.

3 **¿Qué vamos a hacer?** Your class has the opportunity to go on a week's vacation. Working in a small group, decide whether **el aprendizaje-servicio** or **los deportes** best suits the group's talents and interests. Plan activities you can agree on, including where you might go. Present your vacation plans to the class. Answers will vary.

recursos

adelante.vhlcentral.com

Práctica

For self-scoring and diagnostics, go to adelante.vhlcentral.com.

1 **Verbos** Completa la tabla con las formas de los verbos. **10 pts.**

Infinitive	yo	nosotros/as	ellos/as
comprar	compro	compramos	**compran**
poder	**puedo**	podemos	pueden
comenzar	comienzo	**comenzamos**	comienzan
hacer	hago	**hacemos**	**hacen**
oír	oigo	oímos	oyen
jugar	**juego**	jugamos	juegan
repetir	repito	repetimos	**repiten**
estudiar	estudio	**estudiamos**	estudian

2 **Ir** Completa el párrafo con las formas de **ir**. **8 pts.**

El sábado yo (1) ___voy___ al Museo de Bellas Artes porque mi artista favorito (2) ___va___ a presentar una exposición. Mis amigos no (3) ___van___ al museo conmigo porque todos (4) ___van___ a jugar al fútbol, pero yo voy a (5) ___ir___ porque yo (6) ___voy___ a ser artista. ¿(7) ___Vas___ (tú) al museo también? ¿Por qué no (8) ___vamos___ juntos?

3 **Conversación** Completa la conversación con las formas de los verbos. Puedes usar algunos verbos más de una vez. **7 pts.**

empezar	poder
jugar	querer
pensar	recordar
perder	volver

PABLO Óscar, voy al centro ahora. Necesito hacer varias diligencias (*errands*).

ÓSCAR ¿A qué hora (1) ___vuelves___? El partido de fútbol (2) ___empieza___ a las dos.

PABLO Regreso a la una. (3) ___Quiero/Pienso___ ver el partido. ¡Va a estar muy reñido (*hard-fought*)!

ÓSCAR ¿(4) ___Recuerdas___ (tú) que nuestro equipo ganó los tres partidos anteriores (*previous*)? Es muy bueno. ¡Estoy seguro de que vamos a ganar!

PABLO No, yo (5) ___pienso___ que vamos a (6) ___perder___. Los jugadores de Guadalajara son salvajes (*wild*) cuando (7) ___juegan___.

Resumen gramatical

This overview presents key grammatical concepts from ¡ADELANTE! **UNO** . For further review, follow the cross-references.

R.4 Present of regular verbs  *¡ADELANTE!* **UNO**
L2 pp. 66–68, L3 pp. 130–131

▶ To create the present-tense forms of most regular verbs, drop the infinitive endings (-ar, -er, -ir) and add the endings that correspond to the different subject pronouns.

	hablar	comer	escribir
yo	**habl**o	**com**o	**escrib**o
tú	**habl**as	**com**es	**escrib**es
él	**habl**a	**com**e	**escrib**e
nos.	**habl**amos	**com**emos	**escrib**imos
vos.	**habl**áis	**com**éis	**escrib**ís
ellas	**habl**an	**com**en	**escrib**en

R.5 Present of **tener** and **venir**  *¡ADELANTE!* **UNO**
L3 pp. 134–135

Tengo cuatro hermanas y un hermano mayor.

tener		venir	
tengo	**ten**emos	**veng**o	**ven**imos
tienes	**ten**éis	**vien**es	**ven**ís
tiene	**tien**en	**vien**e	**vien**en

▶ **Tener** is used in many common phrases.

tener años *to be... years old*
tener calor *to be hot*
tener frío *to be cold*
tener ganas de [+ *inf.*] *to feel like doing something*
tener hambre *to be hungry*
tener prisa *to be in a hurry*
tener que [+ *inf.*] *to have to do something*
tener razón *to be right*
tener sed *to be thirsty*

R.6 Present of **ir** 🔄 **¡ADELANTE! UNO**
L4 p. 178

ir			
yo	voy	**nos.**	vamos
tú	vas	**vos.**	vais
él	va	**ellas**	van

▶ **Ir** has many everyday uses, including expressing future plans:

ir a + [infinitivo] = *to be going to* + [*infinitive*]

vamos a + [infinitivo] = *let's do something*

R.7 Present of irregular verbs 🔄 **¡ADELANTE! UNO**
L4 p. 181–182, 185, 188–189

*Álex y Maite
vuelven al autobús.*

e:ie, o:ue, u:ue stem-changing verbs

	empezar	volver	jugar
yo	empiezo	vuelvo	juego
tú	empiezas	vuelves	juegas
él	empieza	vuelve	juega
nos.	empezamos	volvemos	jugamos
vos.	empezáis	volvéis	jugáis
ellas	empiezan	vuelven	juegan

▶ Other e:ie verbs: **comenzar, entender, pensar, querer**
▶ Other o:ue verbs: **almorzar, dormir, encontrar, mostrar**

e:i stem-changing verbs

pedir			
yo	pido	**nos.**	pedimos
tú	pides	**vos.**	pedís
él	pide	**ellas**	piden

▶ Other e:i verbs: **conseguir, decir, repetir, seguir**

Verbs with irregular yo forms

hacer	poner	salir	suponer	traer
hago	pongo	salgo	supongo	traigo

▶ **ver:** veo, ves, ve,
vemos, veis, ven

▶ **oír:** oigo, oyes, oye,
oímos, oís, oyen

> 🔄 For a complete list of verb conjugations, go to Apéndice D, pp. 353–362, at the end of your worktext.

4 **Oraciones** Escribe oraciones completas con estos elementos. **¡Ojo!** Recuerda conjugar los verbos. **10 pts.**

1. tú / tener / unos amigos / muy interesante
Tú tienes unos amigos muy interesantes.

2. yo / venir / en autobús / de / el centro comercial
Yo vengo en autobús del centro comercial.

3. ellos / no / tener / mucho / dinero / hoy
Ellos no tienen mucho dinero hoy.

4. yo / ir / a / el cine / todos / el sábado
Yo voy al cine todos los sábados.

5. los estudiantes / de español / ir / a / leer / una revista
Los estudiantes de español van a leer una revista.

5 **Tener** Describe qué hacen las personas. Usa expresiones con **tener** y sigue el modelo. **15 pts.**

Él **tiene (mucha) prisa.**

1. Ella tiene (mucho) calor.

2. Ella tiene veintiún años.

3. Ellos tienen (mucha) hambre.

4. Ellos tienen (mucho) frío.

5. Él tiene (mucha) sed.

TPR Make sets of cards with infinitives of verbs that are easy to act out (include regular and stem-changing verbs, as well as **tener** expressions). Divide the class into groups of five. Have students take turns drawing a card and acting out the verb for the group. Once someone has guessed the verb, the group members must take turns providing the conjugated forms.

recursos

SUPERSITE

adelante.vhlcentral.com

Práctica y Comunicación

1 Completar
Completa las oraciones con las formas apropiadas de los verbos de la lista. *Some answers may vary.*

aprender	correr	jugar	pedir	salir	vivir
bailar	hablar	oír	recibir	ver	volver

1. Rosa ___baila___ un tango en el teatro.
2. Mis amigos ___hablan___ francés muy bien.
3. Yo no ___salgo___ de casa cuando hace demasiado calor.
4. Mi hermano y yo ___aprendemos___ a nadar en la piscina.
5. Nosotros ___vivimos___ en la residencia estudiantil.
6. ¿Tú ___recibes___ regalos en el día de tu cumpleaños?
7. Los estudiantes ___corren___ a casa por la tarde.
8. Yo ___veo___ una película.
9. Usted nunca ___pide___ ayuda, ¿verdad?
10. Mis hermanos ___juegan___ al fútbol después de las clases.
11. Ustedes siempre ___oyen___ ese programa de radio.
12. ¿Mañana ___vuelven___ tus padres de Roma?

1 For additional practice, call out different subject pronouns for each item and have volunteers restate the sentence.

2 Contestar
Trabaja con un(a) compañero/a para formar preguntas completas. Luego, túrnense para hacerse las preguntas que crearon. *Answers will vary.*

modelo
> pedir / en la cafetería
> **Estudiante 1:** ¿Qué pides en la cafetería?
> **Estudiante 2:** En la cafetería, yo pido pizza.

1. horas / dormir cada noche
2. preferir / hacer la tarea de matemáticas
3. ir / cuando salir con amigos/as
4. empezar / tus clases los miércoles
5. tipo de música / preferir
6. pensar / ir a / ser / esta clase

2 For expansion, ask pairs to write one question for each of the interrogative words listed in ¡Al rescate! Then have them exchange their questions with another pair and take turns asking and answering the questions.

¡AL RESCATE!
Here are some interrogative words.
¿A qué hora? *At what time?*
¿Adónde? *Where to?*
¿Cómo? *How?*
¿Cuál(es)? *Which?; Which one(s)?*
¿Cuándo? *When?*
¿Cuántos/as? *How many?*
¿Dónde? *Where?*
¿Qué? *What?*

To review more about forming questions in Spanish, go to *¡ADELANTE!* UNO, Estructura 2.2, pp. 71–72.

3 Combinar
En parejas, túrnense para combinar elementos de las dos columnas y crear oraciones completas. *Answers will vary.*

A	B
yo	hacer la tarea todas las tardes
mis compañeros/as de clase	dormir hasta las doce del día
mi mejor amigo/a	ir al cine todos los viernes
tú	conseguir gangas en Internet
mi familia	pedir favores
mis amigos/as y yo	almorzar en casa los domingos

4

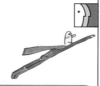

Frecuencia Indica qué actividades haces **todos los días**, cuáles haces **una vez al mes**, cuáles haces **una vez al año** y cuáles estás haciendo **ahora mismo** (*right now*). Escribe por lo menos (*at least*) dos oraciones para cada categoría. Intercambia tus oraciones con las de un(a) compañero/a.
Answers will vary.

> **modelo**
>
> **Estudiante 1:** *Yo juego al baloncesto todos los días.*
> **Estudiante 2:** *Yo pierdo mis llaves una vez al año.*

decir	jugar
dormir	leer
encontrar	pedir
hablar	perder
hacer	trabajar
¿?	¿?

4 Before beginning this activity, briefly review the present progressive, including **-ir** stem-changing verbs. Ex: **diciendo, durmiendo, sintiendo.**

¡AL RESCATE!

The present progressive indicates what someone is doing *right now*. It consists of the present tense of **estar** and the present participle of another verb.

Estamos hablando.

To review the present progressive, go to **¡ADELANTE! UNO**, Estructura 5.2, pp. 236–237.

5

Encuesta Circula por la clase preguntándoles a tus compañeros si hacen estas actividades con frecuencia (*frequently*). Trata de encontrar personas que respondan **sí** o **no** a cada pregunta y escribe sus nombres en la columna correcta. Prepárate para compartir tus conclusiones con la clase.
Answers will vary.

> **modelo**
>
> **Tú:** *¿Escribes tarjetas postales con frecuencia?*
> **Ana:** *Sí, las escribo con frecuencia.*
> **Luis:** *No, no las escribo con frecuencia.*

Actividades	Sí	No
1. escribir tarjetas postales	Ana	Luis
2. jugar al béisbol		
3. ver películas de horror		
4. pensar en el futuro		
5. decir mentiras		
6. oír música en español		

5 Call on several students to share their results and ask follow-up questions.
Ex: ¿_____, cuándo escribes tarjetas postales? ¿_____, qué otros deportes juegas con frecuencia?

5 To practice **ir a** + [*infinitive*], have the students repeat the activity, this time asking classmates which activities they plan to do today. Ex: **¿Vas a leer correo electrónico hoy?**

¡AL RESCATE!

Use direct object pronouns to keep your writing concise and clear by avoiding repeating nouns already mentioned.

El domingo voy a visitar a mi abuela. **La voy a ver a las nueve para desayunar.**

To read more about direct object nouns and pronouns go to **¡ADELANTE! UNO**, Estructura 5.4, pp. 244–245.

6

Escribir Escribe lo que haces en un día típico y tus planes para el fin de semana. Answers will vary.

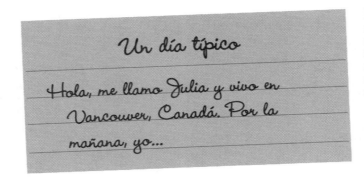

Un día típico

Hola, me llamo Julia y vivo en Vancouver, Canadá. Por la mañana, yo...

6 Remind students that direct object pronouns can be placed before an infinitive construction (Ex: **te voy a llamar**) or attached to the infinitive. (Ex: **voy a llamarte**).

¡Los primeros días del viaje!

Los viajeros se presentan y vemos lo que pasó en los seis primeros episodios.

PERSONAJES

 INÉS

 JAVIER

 ÁLEX

 MAITE

 DON FRANCISCO

INÉS Hola, me llamo Inés y soy de Ecuador, de Portoviejo. Este semestre tomo cinco clases: geografía, inglés, historia, sociología y arte. Mi familia es grande, están mis papás, mis abuelos, cuatro hermanas, un hermano y muchos tíos y primos. A mí me gusta pasear por los lugares que visito y conocer su historia.

JAVIER ¿Qué tal? Yo soy Javier y vengo de Puerto Rico. Mi familia es pequeña, yo no tengo hermanos. Este semestre estoy tomando tres clases: historia, arte y computación, pero no me gustan nada las computadoras. La clase de arte es mi favorita porque me gusta mucho dibujar.

ÁLEX Buenos días. Mi nombre es Álex y vengo de la Ciudad de México. A mí me gustan mucho las computadoras, creo que son muy interesantes. Siempre estoy en contacto con mi familia y mis amigos a través de Internet. También soy aficionado a los deportes, me gusta el fútbol y nadar.

Cuatro estudiantes de la Universidad San Francisco de Quito van a ir de excursión a las montañas. Son dos chicas y dos chicos. El primer lugar que visitan es la Mitad del Mundo, que marca la división entre los hemisferios norte y sur.

Durante el viaje, los chicos hablan de sus materias favoritas. A Álex le gusta mucho la computación, pero Javier prefiere el arte y encuentra inspiración para hacer un dibujo en el autobús. Ellos también hablan de sus familias.

Los estudiantes tienen una hora libre. Inés y Javier deciden salir a explorar la ciudad. Maite y Álex prefieren ir al parque. Mientras ella escribe unas postales, él juega al fútbol con un joven. Álex y Maite hablan sobre lo que les gusta hacer.

ACTIVIDADES

1 **¿Se te olvidó?** Indica si lo que dice cada oración sobre los primeros seis episodios es **cierto** o **falso**. Corrige la información falsa.

1. Javier es de Mayagüez, Puerto Rico.
   Falso. Javier es de San Juan, Puerto Rico.
2. Maite y Álex salen de las cabañas a explorar la ciudad.
   Falso. Inés y Javier salen a explorar la ciudad.
3. Javier piensa que los mercados al aire libre son interesantes.
   Cierto.

4. Inés quiere comprarle unos zapatos a su hermana Graciela.
   Falso. Inés quiere comprarle una bolsa./Inés le quiere comprar una bolsa.
5. La reservación en las cabañas está a nombre de Ecuatur.
   Cierto.
6. Cuando está en Madrid, Maite va a pasear al Parque del Retiro.
   Cierto.
7. Álex hace un dibujo de Maite.
   Falso. Javier hace un dibujo de Maite.
8. Maite escribe sobre el viaje en su diario.
   Cierto.

1 In pairs, have students come up with six additional true-false statements based on the previous episodes. Then have them exchange papers with another pair and complete the activity.

Lección de repaso

MAITE ¿Cómo estás? Yo me llamo María Teresa Fuentes de Alba, pero mis amigos me dicen Maite. Soy de Madrid, España y me gusta mucho escribir. Cuando termine la universidad quiero trabajar como periodista. También me gustan los deportes y salgo a correr todos los días.

DON FRANCISCO Buenas, soy don Francisco, el conductor del autobús donde viajan los estudiantes. Los llevo a una excursión por las hermosas montañas de mi país, Ecuador. Yo conozco muchos lugares interesantes y siempre comparto lo que sé con los viajeros. A mí me gusta mucho leer el periódico y tomar café.

Los viajeros llegan al hotel. Inés y Javier van a visitar un mercado al aire libre. Inés quiere comprarle un regalo a su hermana. Javier mira unos suéteres que le gustan y compra uno de color gris.

Ahora vamos a seguir con el viaje de los estudiantes por Ecuador. ¿Qué nuevas personas van a conocer? ¿Qué lugares interesantes van a visitar? ¿Qué otras aventuras les esperan?

¿Cuánto recuerdas?

Contesta el cuestionario para ver cuánto recuerdas sobre los primeros seis episodios de **Fotonovela**.

1. Al comenzar el viaje, _____ despide a los estudiantes.
   a. la profesora de geografía
   b. la Sra. Ramos de Ecuatur ✓
   c. una señora que va pasando

2. Maite piensa que el paisaje es como _____.
   a. un documental del canal Discovery
   b. las fotos de los libros de geografía ✓
   c. una película que vio el año pasado

3. Hay muchas chicas en la clase de _____ que toma Inés.
   a. sociología ✓
   b. historia
   c. inglés

4. Parece que a Javier le gusta _____.
   a. Maite
   b. la Sra. Ramos
   c. Inés ✓

5. El sobrino de Inés _____ pero es muy _____. ¡Qué raro!
   a. come mucho; delgado ✓
   b. juega al fútbol; malo
   c. tiene muchos amigos; antipático

6. _____ golpea (hits) a Maite cuando está en el parque.
   a. Un bumerán (boomerang)
   b. Una pelota ✓
   c. El viento

7. A don Francisco no le gusta _____.
   a. leer el periódico
   b. viajar por su país
   c. practicar deportes ✓

ACTIVIDADES

2 **Relacionar** Indica qué elemento de la segunda columna está relacionado con cada personaje.

1. __c__ Javier   a. café
2. __e__ Maite   b. computadoras
3. __a__ don Francisco   c. arte
4. __f__ Inés   d. aeropuerto
5. __b__ Álex   e. diario
       f. grabadora

3 **Predicciones** En grupos pequeños, escriban qué piensan que va a pasar en los próximos episodios con cada uno de los personajes. Después, compartan sus ideas con la clase.
Answers will vary.

 3 Before writing their predictions, have students read and discuss the questions in the caption for video still 10.

recursos

SUPERSITE
adelante.vhlcentral.com

Práctica

For self-scoring and diagnostics, go to adelante.vhlcentral.com.

1 **Verbos** Completa la tabla con las formas correctas de los verbos. `10 pts.`

Infinitive	yo	él/ella/usted	ellos/as
buscar	busqué	buscó	**buscaron**
cerrar	**cerré**	cerró	cerraron
comer	comí	comió	**comieron**
jugar	jugué	**jugó**	jugaron
leer	**leí**	leyó	leyeron
pagar	pagué	pagó	**pagaron**
salir	salí	**salió**	salieron
volver	volví	volvió	**volvieron**

2 **El sábado** Completa el mensaje con el pretérito de los verbos. `8 pts.`

De: cecilia@webmail.es
Para: julián@todomail.com
Asunto: El sábado
Fecha: 24 de noviembre

¡Hola, Julián!

¿Cómo estás? Yo estoy muy bien. El sábado mi amiga Matilde me (1) ___invitó___ (invitar) a ir con ella al cine. La película (2) ___empezó___ (empezar) a las siete y media, pero nosotras (3) ___llegamos___ (llegar) un poco tarde. Sólo perdimos los primeros diez minutos.

Yo (4) ___pensé___ (pensar) que la película fue (*was*) un poco larga, pero de todas maneras (5) ___me divertí___ (yo, divertirse). Se llama *Un día en el centro comercial*, te la recomiendo. Después de salir del cine, (6) ___tomamos___ (nosotras, tomar) un taxi a Mama Pizza con más amigos. Las pizzas (7) ___resultaron___ (resultar) (*turned out*) deliciosas. Yo pedí la de salami, ¡qué ricura!

Y tú, ¿cómo (8) ___pasaste___ (pasar) la noche del sábado? María Luisa me dijo que te vio (*saw you*) en la fiesta de Antonio y que estabas (*you were*) muy bien acompañado. ¿Nos vemos el miércoles por la tarde y me cuentas los detalles?

Un abrazo,
Cecilia

Resumen gramatical

This overview presents key grammatical concepts from *¡ADELANTE!* **UNO**. For further review, follow the cross-references.

R.8 Preterite of regular verbs *¡ADELANTE!* **UNO** L6 p. 292

Compré esta bolsa.

► To form the preterite of most regular verbs, attach the appropriate ending to the infinitive stem.

comprar	vender	escribir
compré	vendí	escribí
compraste	vendiste	escribiste
compró	vendió	escribió
compramos	vendimos	escribimos
comprasteis	vendisteis	escribisteis
compraron	vendieron	escribieron

► **-Ar** and **-er** verbs that have a stem change in the present tense are regular in the preterite. They do *not* have a stem change.

Infinitive	Present	Preterite
cerrar (e:ie)	La tienda cierra a las seis.	La tienda cerró a las seis.
volver (o:ue)	Carlitos vuelve tarde.	Carlitos volvió tarde.
jugar (u:ue)	Él juega al fútbol.	Él jugó al fútbol.

► **¡Atención!** **-Ir** verbs that have a stem change in the present tense also have a stem change in the preterite.

	dormir	conseguir
yo	dormí	conseguí
tú	dormiste	conseguiste
él	durmió	consiguió
nos.	dormimos	conseguimos
vos.	dormisteis	conseguisteis
ellas	durmieron	consiguieron

R.9 | Some irregular preterites 🔄 *¡ADELANTE!*  UNO
L6 p. 293

► There are many verbs with irregularities in the preterite. Here are some of them. You will learn more in **Lecciones 1, 2,** and **3**.

► Verbs that end in **-car**, **-gar**, and **-zar** have a spelling change in the first person singular (**yo** form).

buscar	>	busc-	>	qu-	>	yo bus**qu**é
llegar		lleg-		gu-		yo lle**gu**é
empezar		empez-		c-		yo empe**c**é

Llegué a Otavalo con mucho sueño.

► Except for the **yo** form, all other forms of **-car**, **-gar**, and **-zar** verbs are regular in the preterite.

► Three other verbs—**creer**, **leer**, and **oír**—have spelling changes in the preterite.

creer	>	cre-	>	cre**í**, cre**í**ste, cre**y**ó, cre**í**mos, cre**í**steis, cre**y**eron
leer		le-		le**í**, le**í**ste, le**y**ó, le**í**mos, le**í**steis, le**y**eron
oír		o-		o**í**, o**í**ste, o**y**ó, o**í**mos, o**í**steis, o**y**eron

¿Cuántos libros leíste el verano pasado?

► **Ver** is regular in the preterite, but none of its forms has an accent.

    ver → vi, viste, vio, vimos, visteis, vieron

   —¿A quiénes **vieron** en su viaje a Costa Rica?

   —**Vimos** a nuestra prima Mariana y a nuestros amigos Leonardo y Teresa.

---

3 **Preguntas** Completa la conversación con el pretérito de los verbos de la lista. **7 pts.**

atacar	olvidar
correr	robar
leer	sufrir (*to suffer, to undergo*)
ocurrir	

SANDRA ¿Cuándo (1) ___corriste___ en el parque por última vez?

MARCOS Corrí en el parque el domingo por la mañana. ¿Por qué?

SANDRA ¿(2) ___Leíste___ las noticias (*news*) de ayer?

MARCOS No, (3) ___olvidé___ comprar el periódico ¿Qué (4) ___ocurrió___?

SANDRA Unos ladrones (*thieves*) (5) ___atacaron___ a un corredor.

MARCOS ¿En serio?

SANDRA Sí, y le (6) ___robaron___ el reproductor de MP3.

MARCOS ¿Y resultó herido (*harmed*)?

SANDRA No, sólo (7) ___sufrió___ rasguños (*scratches*).

MARCOS ¡Qué fuerte! Mejor vamos a correr juntos. Es más seguro.

4 **Oraciones** Escribe oraciones completas con estos elementos, conjugando los verbos en el pretérito. **10 pts.**

1. tú / esperar / quince minutos / en / la puerta de / el cine
Tú esperaste quince minutos en la puerta del cine.

2. nosotros / tomar / café / ayer / por la noche
Nosotros tomamos café ayer por la noche.

3. los jugadores / no / perder / la esperanza / de ganar / el partido
Los jugadores no perdieron la esperanza de ganar el partido.

4. yo / llegar / tarde / a / la cita / de anoche
Yo llegué tarde a la cita de anoche.

5. ustedes / leer / el anuncio (*ad*) / con / mucha atención
Ustedes leyeron el anuncio con mucha atención.

5 **La semana pasada** Escribe un mensaje electrónico de al menos cinco oraciones donde les cuentas a tus padres lo que hiciste durante la semana. Usa al menos cinco verbos diferentes en el pretérito. **15 pts.**
Answers will vary.

modelo

¡Hola, papá y mamá! ¿Cómo están? Esta semana por fin *compré* el libro de Esmeralda Santiago que me *recomendaron*...

Extra Practice Briefly review the use of **acabar de** + [*infinitive*] to say that something has just occurred. Ex: **Acabo de llegar.**

recursos

adelante.vhlcentral.com

Práctica y Comunicación

Completar y contestar Completa las preguntas con las formas apropiadas de los verbos de la lista y luego hazle las preguntas a un(a) compañero/a. Some answers may vary.

acompañar	estudiar	llamar	oír	perder	ver
aprender	leer	llegar	pasar	recibir	volver

¿Cuándo fue (*was*) la última vez que...
1. (tú) ____viste____ un espectáculo de baile?
2. tus padres te ____llamaron____ por teléfono?
3. (tú) ____perdiste____ las llaves de tu casa?
4. tu mejor amigo/a te ____acompañó____ a ir de compras?
5. nosotros ____estudiamos____ juntos para un examen?
6. (tú) ____recibiste____ una mala nota?
7. tus amigos ____volvieron____ a casa más temprano que tú?
8. (tú) ____leíste____ una novela?
9. tu familia y tú ____pasaron____ el fin de semana juntos?
10. el/la profesor(a) ____llegó____ tarde a clase?

2 Contestar Trabaja con un(a) compañero/a para formar preguntas completas. Luego, túrnense para hacerse las preguntas que crearon. Answers will vary.

> **modelo**
> desayunar / esta mañana
> **Estudiante 1:** *¿Qué desayunaste esta mañana?*
> **Estudiante 2:** Esta mañana desayuné cereales.

1. comprar / la ropa que llevas hoy
2. llegar / a clase hoy
3. salir a divertirte / el fin de semana pasado
4. jugar / tu último partido
5. sentirse triste / por última vez
6. pasar / tus últimas vacaciones

3 Completar y combinar En parejas, túrnense para completar las frases con el pretérito de los verbos. Luego inventen un complemento para crear oraciones lógicas. Answers will vary.

> **modelo**
> cuando el/la profesor(a) / entrar / en la clase
> *Cuando la profesora entró en la clase, todos los estudiantes aplaudieron (clapped).*

1. cuando yo / cumplir / dieciocho años
2. el/la estudiante / abrir / el libro
3. yo / sentirse / decepcionado/a (*disappointed*)
4. cuando / mis padres / visitarme / por última vez
5. cuando nosotros / salir / de casa
6. mis hermanos/as / regalarme / un perrito

1 Write these verbs on the board and ask students to come up with additional questions using the preterite: **bailar, hablar, jugar, pedir, salir.**

Pairs For additional practice with the preterite of **-ir** stem-changing verbs, list these verbs on the board: **dormir, conseguir, morir, pedir, preferir, repetir, seguir, servir.** Have students work in pairs to write sentences with the **Ud./él/ella** and **Uds./ellos/ellas** preterite forms.

2 To practice additional preterite forms, divide the class into groups of three. Have each student take turns asking questions to the other two students, using the **ustedes** form. Call on group members to compare each other's responses. Encourage a variety of **yo, nosotros, él/ella,** and **ellos/as** forms. Ex: **Sara y yo llegamos a clase a las nueve. / Yo me sentí triste el lunes, pero Carlos se sintió triste esta mañana. / Anita y Will compraron en Gap la ropa que llevan.**

3 To simplify, have students write down all the conjugated phrases before creating complete sentences.

4

En el parque En parejas, túrnense para describir lo que hicieron (*did*) estas personas en el parque el sábado pasado.

4 To help students get started, help them brainstorm a list of infinitive verbs that could be used to describe the activities in each drawing. Review previously learned vocabulary as needed.

1. Ella tomó el sol.

2. Ellos leyeron (el periódico).

3. Él nadó en la piscina.

4. Ellos pasearon.

5. Ellos jugaron a la pelota/al fútbol.

6. Ella patinó (en línea).

5

Encuesta Circula por la clase preguntando a tus compañeros si hicieron estas actividades la semana pasada. Trata de encontrar personas que respondan **sí** o **no** a cada pregunta y escribe sus nombres en la columna correcta. Prepárate para compartir tus conclusiones con la clase. Answers will vary.

5 Have students add two more items to the list before they begin the activity.

modelo

Tú: ¿Hablaste por teléfono con tus padres la semana pasada?
Pepe: Sí, hablé por teléfono con mis padres el sábado.
Victoria: No, no hablé por teléfono con mis padres la semana pasada.

Game Divide the class into two teams. Call on a team member. Give an infinitive and a subject, and have the team member supply the correct preterite form. Award one point for each correct answer. Award a bonus point for correctly writing the verb on the board. The team with the most points wins.

Actividades	Sí	No
1. hablar por teléfono con sus padres	Pepe	Victoria
2. leer las noticias por Internet		
3. comer en un restaurante elegante		
4. ver deportes en la televisión		
5. practicar español		
6. reunirse con los amigos en el parque		

6 Have students exchange their paragraphs with a partner for peer editing.

6

Escribir Escribe una entrada en tu diario contando lo que hiciste (*you did*) durante el verano pasado. Usa por lo menos (*at least*) seis verbos de las páginas 16 y 17. Answers will vary.

La clase y la universidad

el/la compañero/a de clase	classmate
el/la compañero/a de cuarto	roommate
el/la estudiante	student
el/la profesor(a)	teacher
el borrador	eraser
el escritorio	desk
el libro	book
el mapa	map
la mesa	table
la mochila	backpack
el papel	paper
la papelera	wastebasket
la pizarra	blackboard
la pluma	pen
la puerta	door
el reloj	clock; watch
la silla	seat
la tiza	chalk
la ventana	window
la biblioteca	library
la cafetería	cafeteria
la casa	house; home
el estadio	stadium
el laboratorio	laboratory
la librería	bookstore
la residencia estudiantil	dormitory
la universidad	university; college
la clase	class
el curso, la materia	course
la especialización	major
el examen	test; exam
el horario	schedule
la prueba	test; quiz
el semestre	semester
la tarea	homework
el trimestre	trimester; quarter

Lugares

el café	café
el centro	downtown
el cine	movie theater
el gimnasio	gymnasium
la iglesia	church
el lugar	place
el museo	museum
el parque	park
la piscina	swimming pool
la plaza	city or town square
el restaurante	restaurant

Las materias

la administración de empresas	business administration
el arte	art
la biología	biology
las ciencias	sciences
la computación	computer science
la contabilidad	accounting
la economía	economics
el español	Spanish
la física	physics
la geografía	geography
la historia	history
las humanidades	humanities
el inglés	English
las lenguas extranjeras	foreign languages
la literatura	literature
las matemáticas	mathematics
la música	music
el periodismo	journalism
la psicología	psychology
la química	chemistry
la sociología	sociology

Preposiciones

al lado de	next to; beside
a la derecha de	to the right of
a la izquierda de	to the left of
en	in; on
cerca de	near
con	with
debajo de	below; under
delante de	in front of
detrás de	behind
encima de	on top of
entre	between; among
lejos de	far from
sin	without
sobre	on; over

For a complete list of related vocabulary go to *¡ADELANTE!* UNO, pp. 34, 88, 144, 198, 254, and 306.

Pasatiempos

andar en patineta	to skateboard
bucear	to scuba dive
escalar montañas (f. pl.)	to climb mountains
escribir una carta	to write a letter
escribir un mensaje electrónico	to write an e-mail message
esquiar	to ski
ganar	to win
ir de excursión	to go on a hike
leer correo electrónico	to read e-mail
leer un periódico	to read a newspaper
leer una revista	to read a magazine
nadar	to swim
pasear	to take a walk; to stroll
pasear en bicicleta	to ride a bicycle
patinar (en línea)	to (in-line) skate
practicar deportes (m. pl.)	to play sports
tomar el sol	to sunbathe
ver películas (f. pl.)	to see movies
visitar monumentos (m. pl.)	to visit monuments
la diversión	fun activity; entertainment; recreation
el fin de semana	weekend
el pasatiempo	pastime; hobby
los ratos libres	spare (free) time
el videojuego	video game

Deportes

el baloncesto	basketball
el béisbol	baseball
el ciclismo	cycling
el equipo	team
el esquí (acuático)	(water) skiing
el fútbol	soccer
el fútbol americano	football
el golf	golf
el hockey	hockey
el/la jugador(a)	player
la natación	swimming
el partido	game; match
la pelota	ball
el tenis	tennis
el vóleibol	volleyball

La rutina diaria

1

La rutina diaria

Más vocabulario

el baño, el cuarto de baño	bathroom
el inodoro	toilet
el jabón	soap
el despertador	alarm clock
el maquillaje	makeup
la rutina diaria	daily routine
bañarse	to bathe; to take a bath
cepillarse el pelo	to brush one's hair
dormirse (o:ue)	to go to sleep; to fall asleep
lavarse la cara	to wash one's face
levantarse	to get up
maquillarse	to put on makeup
antes (de)	before
después	afterwards; then
después (de)	after
durante	during
entonces	then
luego	then
más tarde	later
por la mañana	in the morning
por la noche	at night
por la tarde	in the afternoon; in the evening
por último	finally

Variación léxica

afeitarse ⟷	rasurarse *(Méx., Amér. C.)*
ducha ⟷	regadera *(Col., Méx., Venez.)*
ducharse ⟷	bañarse *(Amér. L.)*
pantuflas ⟷	chancletas *(Méx., Col.);* zapatillas *(Esp.)*

Supersite/IRCD: Lesson Plans, MP3 Audio Files and Listening Scripts, Overheads, *Vocabulario adicional*

recursos

WB pp. 53–54

LM p. 69

adelante. vhlcentral.com

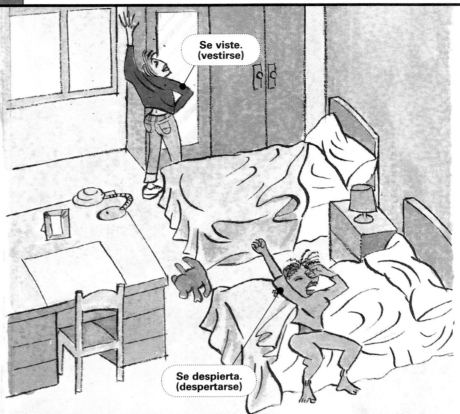

En la habitación por la mañana

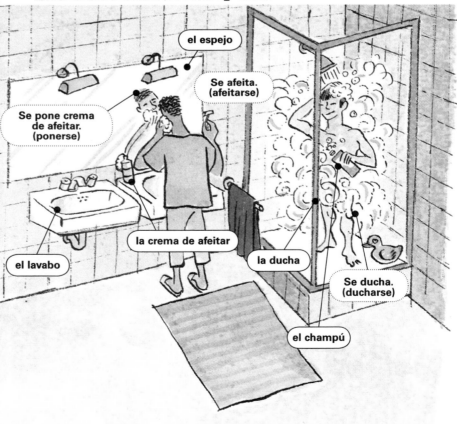

Por la mañana

Se peina.
(peinarse)

Se acuesta.
(acostarse)

En la habitación por la noche

Se lava las manos.
(lavarse las manos)

Se cepilla los dientes.
(cepillarse los dientes)

la toalla

la pasta de dientes

las pantuflas

Por la noche

Práctica

1 **2** Supersite/IRCD: MP3 Audio Files, Scripts

Escuchar 🎧 Escucha las oraciones e indica si cada oración es **cierta** o **falsa**, según el dibujo.

1 **2** To prepare students for the listening activities, have volunteers provide the third-person forms of each verb in **Contextos**. Additional reflexive verb forms will be presented in **Estructura 1.1**.

1. ___falsa___
2. ___cierta___
3. ___falsa___
4. ___cierta___
5. ___falsa___
6. ___falsa___
7. ___falsa___
8. ___cierta___
9. ___falsa___
10. ___cierta___

Ordenar 🎧 Escucha la rutina diaria de Marta. Después ordena los verbos según lo que escuchaste.

_5_ a. almorzar
_2_ b. ducharse
_4_ c. peinarse
_7_ d. ver la televisión
_3_ e. desayunar
_8_ f. dormirse
_1_ g. despertarse
_6_ h. estudiar en la biblioteca

Seleccionar Selecciona la palabra que no está relacionada con cada grupo.

1. lavabo • toalla • despertador • jabón ____despertador____
2. manos • antes de • después de • por último ____manos____
3. acostarse • jabón • despertarse • dormirse ____jabón____
4. espejo • lavabo • despertador • entonces ____entonces____
5. dormirse • toalla • vestirse • levantarse ____toalla____
6. pelo • cara • manos • inodoro ____inodoro____
7. espejo • champú • jabón • pasta de dientes ____espejo____
8. maquillarse • vestirse • peinarse • dientes ____dientes____
9. baño • dormirse • despertador • acostarse ____baño____
10. ducharse • luego • bañarse • lavarse ____luego____

Identificar Con un(a) compañero/a, identifica las cosas que cada persona necesita. Sigue el modelo. Some answers will vary.

> **modelo**
>
> Jorge / lavarse la cara
> **Estudiante 1:** ¿Qué necesita Jorge para lavarse la cara?
> **Estudiante 2:** Necesita jabón y una toalla.

1. Mariana / maquillarse maquillaje y un espejo
2. Gerardo / despertarse un despertador
3. Celia / bañarse jabón y una toalla
4. Gabriel / ducharse una ducha, una toalla y jabón
5. Roberto / afeitarse crema de afeitar
6. Sonia / lavarse el pelo champú y una toalla
7. Vanesa / lavarse las manos jabón y una toalla
8. Manuel / vestirse su ropa/una camiseta/unos pantalones/etc.
9. Simón / acostarse una cama
10. Daniela / cepillarse los dientes pasta de dientes

Heritage Speakers Ask heritage speakers to look at the illustration and provide additional lexical variations.
Ex: **cepillarse los dientes/lavarse la boca; la toalla/el paño; la habitación/la alcoba.**

Lección 1

5 **La rutina de Andrés** Ordena esta rutina de una manera lógica.

a. Se afeita después de cepillarse los dientes. __4__

b. Se acuesta a las once y media de la noche. __9__

c. Por último, se duerme. __10__

d. Después de afeitarse, sale para las clases. __5__

e. Asiste a todas sus clases y vuelve a su casa. __6__

f. Andrés se despierta a las seis y media de la mañana. __1__

g. Después de volver a casa, come un poco. Luego estudia en su habitación. __7__

h. Se viste y entonces se cepilla los dientes. __3__

i. Se cepilla los dientes antes de acostarse. __8__

j. Se ducha antes de vestirse. __2__

5 To simplify, have students read all items and identify the expressions of time before putting the sentences in order.

6 **La rutina diaria** Con un(a) compañero/a, mira los dibujos y describe lo que hacen Ángel y Lupe. Some answers may vary.

1.

Ángel se afeita y mira la televisión.

2.

Lupe se maquilla y escucha la radio.

3.

Ángel se ducha y canta.

4.

Lupe se baña y lee.

5.

Ángel se lava la cara con jabón.

6.

Lupe se lava el pelo con champú en la ducha.

7.

Ángel se cepilla el pelo.

8.

Lupe se cepilla los dientes.

Extra Practice Name daily routine activities and have students list all the words that they associate with each activity, such as things, places, and parts of the body. Ex: **lavarse las manos: el jabón, el cuarto de baño, el agua, la toalla.** How many associations can the class make for each activity?

5 Ask students if **Andrés's** schedule represents that of a "typical" student. Ask: **Un estudiante típico, ¿se despierta normalmente a las seis y media de la mañana? ¿A qué hora se despiertan ustedes?**

6 Ask brief comprehension questions about the actions in the drawings. Ex: **¿Quién se maquilla? (Lupe) ¿Quién se cepilla el pelo? (Ángel)**

6 If students ask, point out that in drawing number 7, **Ángel se mira en el espejo.** Reflexive pronouns and verbs will be formally presented in **Estructura 1.1.** For now it is enough just to explain that *he is looking at himself,* hence the use of the pronoun **se.**

6 For item 7, point out that **el pelo** is used only with the verb **cepillarse,** never with **peinarse.**

Small Groups In groups of three or four, students think of a famous person or character and describe his or her daily routine. In their descriptions, students may use names of friends or family of the famous person or character. Have groups read their descriptions aloud for the rest of the class to guess.

NATIONAL communication STANDARDS

Lección 1

Comunicación

7

La farmacia Lee el anuncio y responde a las preguntas con un(a) compañero/a. Answers will vary.

LA FARMACIA NUEVO SOL tiene todo lo que necesitas para la vida diaria.

Esta semana tenemos grandes rebajas.

Por poco dinero puedes comprar lo que necesitas para el cuarto de baño ideal.

Para los hombres ofrecemos... Buenas cremas de afeitar de Guapo y Máximo

Para las mujeres ofrecemos... Nuevos maquillajes de Marisol y jabones de baño Ilusiones y Belleza

Y para todos tenemos los mejores jabones, pastas de dientes y cepillos de dientes.

¡Visita **LA FARMACIA NUEVO SOL**! Te ofrecemos los mejores precios. Tenemos una tienda cerca de tu casa.

1. ¿Qué tipo de tienda es? Es una farmacia.
2. ¿Qué productos ofrecen para las mujeres? maquillajes, jabones de baño
3. ¿Qué productos ofrecen para los hombres? cremas de afeitar
4. Haz (*Make*) una lista de los verbos que asocias con los productos del anuncio.
5. ¿Dónde compras tus productos de higiene? Answers will vary.
6. ¿Tienes una tienda favorita? ¿Cuál es? Answers will vary.

Suggested answers: afeitarse, maquillarse, cepillarse los dientes

8

Rutinas diarias Trabajen en parejas para describir la rutina diaria de dos o tres de estas personas. Pueden usar palabras de la lista. Answers will vary.

antes (de)	entonces	primero
después (de)	luego	tarde
durante el día	por último	temprano

- un(a) profesor(a) de la universidad
- un(a) turista
- un hombre o una mujer de negocios (*businessman/woman*)
- un vigilante (*night watchman*)
- un(a) jubilado/a (*retired person*)
- el presidente de los Estados Unidos
- un niño de cuatro años
▶ • Daniel Espinosa

¡Jamás me levanto temprano!

communication cultures NATIONAL STANDARDS

Álex y Javier hablan de sus rutinas diarias.

1

JAVIER Hola, Álex. ¿Qué estás haciendo?

ÁLEX Nada… sólo estoy leyendo mi correo electrónico. ¿Adónde fueron?

2

JAVIER Inés y yo fuimos a un mercado. Fue muy divertido. Mira, compré este suéter. Me encanta. No fue barato pero es chévere, ¿no?

ÁLEX Sí, es ideal para las montañas.

3

JAVIER ¡Qué interesantes son los mercados al aire libre! Me gustaría volver pero ya es tarde. Oye, Álex, sabes que mañana tenemos que levantarnos temprano.

ÁLEX Ningún problema.

6

JAVIER ¡Increíble! ¡Álex, el superhombre!

ÁLEX Oye, Javier, ¿por qué no puedes levantarte temprano?

JAVIER Es que por la noche no quiero dormir, sino dibujar y escuchar música. Por eso es difícil despertarme por la mañana.

7

JAVIER El autobús no sale hasta las ocho y media. ¿Vas a levantarte mañana a las seis también?

ÁLEX No, pero tengo que levantarme a las siete menos cuarto porque voy a correr.

8

JAVIER Ah, ya… ¿Puedes despertarme después de correr?

ÁLEX Éste es el plan para mañana. Me levanto a las siete menos cuarto y corro por treinta minutos. Vuelvo, me ducho, me visto y a las siete y media te despierto. ¿De acuerdo?

JAVIER ¡Absolutamente ninguna objeción!

Video Synopsis **Javier** returns from the market and shows **Álex** the sweater he bought. Since they have to get up early the next day, **Álex** agrees to wake up **Javier** after his morning run. **Don Francisco** comes by to remind them that the bus will leave at 8:30 a.m.

Preview In groups of three, have students use the captions to role-play the episode. Ask whether their own routines are more similar to those of **Álex** or **Javier**.

Lección 1

Expresiones útiles Draw attention to preterite forms of **ser** and **ir** in the captions for video stills 1 and 2. Ask volunteers to use context to determine which verb is used in each example. Point out first- and second-person reflexive verb forms and call on students to provide the infinitive form of each verb. Explain that **siempre, nunca,** and **jamás** are examples of indefinite and negative words. Tell students they will learn more about these concepts in **Estructura**.

JAVIER ¿Seguro? Pues yo jamás me levanto temprano. Nunca oigo el despertador cuando estoy en casa y mi mamá se enoja mucho.

ÁLEX Tranquilo, Javier. Yo tengo una solución.

ÁLEX Cuando estoy en casa en la Ciudad de México, siempre me despierto a las seis en punto. Me ducho en cinco minutos y luego me cepillo los dientes. Después me afeito, me visto y ¡listo! ¡Me voy!

DON FRANCISCO Hola, chicos. Mañana salimos temprano, a las ocho y media... ni un minuto antes ni un minuto después.

ÁLEX No se preocupe, don Francisco. Todo está bajo control.

DON FRANCISCO Bueno, pues, hasta mañana.

DON FRANCISCO ¡Ay, los estudiantes! Siempre se acuestan tarde. ¡Qué vida!

Expresiones útiles

Telling where you went

- **¿Adónde fuiste/fue usted?**
  Where did you go?
  Fui a un mercado.
  I went to a market.
- **¿Adónde fueron ustedes?**
  Where did you go?
  Fuimos a un mercado. Fue divertido.
  We went to a market. It was fun.

Talking about morning routines

- **(Jamás) me levanto temprano/tarde.**
  I (never) get up early/late.
- **Nunca oigo el despertador.**
  I never hear the alarm clock.
- **Es difícil/fácil despertarme.**
  It's hard/easy to wake up.
- **Cuando estoy en casa, siempre me despierto a las seis en punto.**
  When I'm home, I always wake up at six on the dot.
- **Me ducho y luego me cepillo los dientes.**
  I take a shower and then I brush my teeth.
- **Después me afeito y me visto.**
  Afterwards, I shave and get dressed.

Reassuring someone

- **No hay problema.**
  No problem.
- **No te/se preocupes/preocupe.**
  Don't worry. (fam.)/ (form.)
- **Tranquilo.**
  Don't worry.; Be cool.

Additional vocabulary

- **sino**
  but (rather)
- **Me encanta este suéter.**
  I love this sweater.
- **Me fascinó la película.**
  I liked the movie a lot.

Teaching Tips
- Play the video segment and have students jot down notes on what they see and hear. Then have them work in groups of three to prepare a brief plot summary. Play the segment again and then ask groups to refine their summaries. Discuss the plot as a class.
- For expansion, ask students to write a short description of **don Francisco's** daily routine, then compare their ideas with a partner.

TPR Ask students to write **Javier** and **Álex** on separate pieces of paper. Read several statements aloud and have students hold up the corresponding name. Ex: **No me gusta levantarme temprano. (Javier); Mañana me ducho después de correr. (Álex)**

¿Qué pasó? (SUPERSITE)

1 **¿Cierto o falso?** Indica si lo que dicen estas oraciones es **cierto** o **falso.** Corrige las oraciones falsas.

1. Álex está mirando la televisión.
   Falso. Álex está leyendo su correo electrónico.
2. El suéter que Javier acaba de comprar es caro pero es muy bonito.
   Cierto.
3. Javier cree que el mercado es aburrido y no quiere volver.
   Falso. Javier piensa que el mercado es muy interesante.
4. El autobús va a salir mañana a las siete y media en punto.
   Falso. El autobús sale mañana a las ocho y media en punto. ◄
5. A Javier le gusta mucho dibujar y escuchar música por la noche.
   Cierto.

¡LENGUA VIVA!

Remember that **en punto** means *on the dot.* If the group were instead leaving at *around seven thirty,* you would say **a eso de las siete y media.**

2 **Identificar** Identifica quién puede decir estas oraciones. Puedes usar cada nombre más de una vez.

1. ¡Ay, los estudiantes nunca se acuestan temprano!
   __don Francisco__

2. ¿El despertador? ¡Jamás lo oigo por la mañana!
   __Javier__

3. Es fácil despertarme temprano. Y sólo necesito
   cinco minutos para ducharme. __Álex__

4. Mañana vamos a salir a las ocho y media.
   __Javier, don Francisco__

5. Acabo de ir a un mercado fabuloso. __Javier__

6. No se preocupe. Tenemos todo bajo control
   para mañana. __Álex__

DON FRANCISCO

JAVIER

ÁLEX

1 Give students these additional items: **6. Javier siempre se despierta temprano.** (Falso) **7. Don Francisco cree que los estudiantes siempre se acuestan temprano.** (Falso) **8. Álex va a despertar a Javier después de ducharse.** (Cierto)

2 Give students these additional items: **7. Quiero volver al mercado, pero no hay tiempo.** (Javier) **8. Cuando estoy en casa, siempre me despierto muy temprano.** (Álex)

3 **Ordenar** Ordena correctamente los planes que tiene Álex.

- __5__ a. Me visto.
- __2__ b. Corro por media hora.
- __6__ c. Despierto a Javier a las siete y media.
- __3__ d. Vuelvo a la habitación.
- __1__ e. Me levanto a las siete menos cuarto.
- __4__ f. Me ducho.

3 Ask pairs to imagine another character's plans for the following day and list them using the **yo** form of the verbs, as in the activity. Then have pairs share their lists with the class.

4 **Mi rutina** En parejas, hablen de sus rutinas de la mañana y de la noche. Indiquen a qué horas hacen las actividades más importantes. Answers will vary. ◄

> **modelo**
>
> **Estudiante 1:** ¿Prefieres levantarte temprano o tarde?
> **Estudiante 2:** Prefiero levantarme tarde… muy tarde.
>
> **Estudiante 1:** ¿A qué hora te levantas durante la semana?
> **Estudiante 2:** A las once. ¿Y tú?

4 Possible conversation:
E1: ¿Prefieres levantarte tarde o temprano?
E2: Prefiero levantarme tarde… muy tarde.
E1: ¿A qué hora te levantas durante la semana?
E2: A las once. ¿Y tú?

E1: Siempre me levanto muy temprano… a las cinco y media.
E2: Y, ¿a qué hora te acuestas?
E1: Siempre me acuesto temprano, a las diez o a las once. ¿Y tú?
E2: Yo prefiero acostarme a las doce.

CONSULTA

To review telling time in Spanish, see **¡ADELANTE! UNO**, **Estructura 1.4,** pp. 24–25.

4 Encourage students to use as many reflexive infinitives from **Contextos** as they can.

Supersite/IRCD: MP3 Audio Files, Listening Scripts

Lección 1

Pronunciación
The consonant r

ropa	rutina	rico	Ramón

In Spanish, **r** has a strong trilled sound at the beginning of a word. No English words have a trill, but English speakers often produce a trill when they imitate the sound of a motor.

gustar	durante	primero	crema

In any other position, **r** has a weak sound similar to the English *tt* in *better* or the English *dd* in *ladder*. In contrast to English, the tongue touches the roof of the mouth behind the teeth.

pizarra	corro	marrón	aburrido

The letter combination **rr,** which only appears between vowels, always has a strong trilled sound.

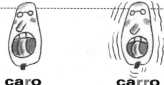

caro	carro	pero	perro

Between vowels, the difference between the strong trilled **rr** and the weak **r** is very important, as a mispronunciation could lead to confusion between two different words.

Práctica Lee las palabras en voz alta, prestando (*paying*) atención a la pronunciación de la **r** y la **rr**.

1. Perú
2. Rosa
3. borrador
4. madre
5. comprar
6. favor
7. rubio
8. reloj
9. Arequipa
10. tarde
11. cerrar
12. despertador

Oraciones Lee las oraciones en voz alta, prestando atención a la pronunciación de la **r** y la **rr**.

1. Ramón Robles Ruiz es programador. Su esposa Rosaura es artista.
2. A Rosaura Robles le encanta regatear en el mercado.
3. Ramón nunca regatea… le aburre regatear.
4. Rosaura siempre compra cosas baratas.
5. Ramón no es rico pero prefiere comprar cosas muy caras.
6. ¡El martes Ramón compró un carro nuevo!

Refranes Lee en voz alta los refranes, prestando atención a la **r** y a la **rr**.

Perro que ladra no muerde.[1]

No se ganó Zamora en una hora.[2]

1 A dog's bark is worse than its bite.
2 Rome wasn't built in a day.

recursos

LM p. 70

adelante. vhlcentral.com

EN DETALLE

La siesta

¿Sientes cansancio° después de comer? ¿Te cuesta° volver al trabajo° o a clase después del almuerzo? Estas sensaciones son normales. A muchas personas les gusta relajarse° después de almorzar. Este momento de descanso es **la siesta**. La siesta es popular en los países hispanos y viene de una antigua costumbre° del área del Mediterráneo. La palabra *siesta* viene del latín; es una forma corta de decir "sexta hora". La sexta hora del día es después del mediodía, el momento de más calor. Debido al° calor y al cansancio, los habitantes de España, Italia, Grecia e incluso Portugal, tienen la costumbre de dormir la siesta desde hace° más de° dos mil años. Los españoles y los portugueses llevaron la costumbre a los países americanos.

La siesta es muy importante en la cultura hispana. Muchas oficinas° y tiendas cierran dos o tres horas después del mediodía. Los empleados van a su casa, almuerzan, duermen la siesta y regresan al trabajo entre las 2:30 y las 4:30 de la tarde. Esto ocurre especialmente en Suramérica, México y España.

Los estudios científicos explican que una siesta corta después de almorzar ayuda° a trabajar más y mejor° durante la tarde. Pero, ¡cuidado! Esta siesta debe durar° sólo entre veinte y cuarenta minutos. Si dormimos más, entramos en la fase de sueño profundo y es difícil despertarse.

Hoy día, algunas empresas° de los Estados Unidos, Canadá, Japón, Inglaterra y Alemania tienen salas° especiales en las que los empleados pueden dormir la siesta.

¿Dónde duermen la siesta?

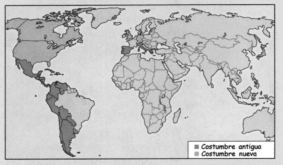

Costumbre antigua
Costumbre nueva

En los lugares donde la siesta es una costumbre antigua, las personas la duermen en su casa. En los países donde la siesta es una costumbre nueva, la gente duerme en sus lugares de trabajo o en centros de siesta.

Sientes cansancio *Do you feel tired* Te cuesta *Is it hard for you* trabajo *work* relajarse *to relax* antigua costumbre *old custom* Debido al *Because (of)* desde hace *for* más de *more than* oficinas *offices* ayuda *helps* mejor *better* durar *last* algunas empresas *some businesses* salas *rooms*

ACTIVIDADES

1 **¿Cierto o falso?** Indica si lo que dicen las oraciones es **cierto** o **falso**. Corrige la información falsa.

1. La costumbre de la siesta empezó en Asia. Falso. La costumbre de la siesta empezó en el área del Mediterráneo.
2. La palabra *siesta* está relacionada con la sexta hora del día. Cierto.
3. Los españoles y los portugueses llevaron la costumbre de la siesta a Latinoamérica. Cierto.
4. La siesta ayuda a trabajar más y mejor durante la tarde. Cierto.
5. Los horarios de trabajo de los países hispanos son los mismos que los de los Estados Unidos. Falso. En muchos países hispanos las oficinas y las tiendas cierran dos o tres horas después del mediodía.
6. Una siesta larga siempre es mejor que una siesta corta. Falso. La siesta sólo debe durar entre veinte y cuarenta minutos.
7. En los Estados Unidos, los empleados de algunas empresas pueden dormir la siesta en el trabajo. Cierto.
8. Es fácil despertar de un sueño profundo. Falso. Es difícil despertar de un sueño profundo.

ASÍ SE DICE

El cuidado personal

el aseo; el excusado; el servicio; el váter (Esp.)	el baño
el cortaúñas	*nail clippers*
el desodorante	*deodorant*
el enjuague bucal	*mouthwash*
el hilo dental/la seda dental	*dental floss*
la máquina de afeitar/ de rasurar (Méx.)	*electric razor*

EL MUNDO HISPANO

Costumbres especiales

○ **México y El Salvador** Los vendedores pasan por las calles gritando° su mercancía°: tanques de gas y flores° en México; pan y tortillas en El Salvador.

○ **Costa Rica** Para encontrar las direcciones° los costarricenses usan referencias a anécdotas, lugares o características geográficas. Por ejemplo: *200 metros norte de la Iglesia Católica, frente al° Supermercado Mi Mega.*

○ **Argentina** En El Tigre, una ciudad en una isla del Río° de la Plata, la gente usa barcos particulares°, colectivos° y barcos-taxi para ir de un lugar a otro. Todas las mañanas, un barco colectivo recoge° a los niños y los lleva a la escuela.

gritando *shouting* mercancía *merchandise* flores *flowers* direcciones *addresses* frente al *opposite* río *river* particulares *private* colectivos *collective* recoge *picks up*

PERFIL

Ir de tapas

En España, **las tapas** son pequeños platos°. **Ir de tapas** es una costumbre que consiste en comer estos platillos en bares, cafés y restaurantes. Dos tapas muy populares son la tortilla de patatas° y los calamares°. La historia de las tapas empezó cuando los dueños° de las tabernas tuvieron° la idea de servir el vaso de vino° tapado° con una rodaja° de pan°. La comida era° la "tapa"° del vaso; de ahí viene el nombre. Con la tapa, los insectos no podían° entrar en el vaso. Más tarde los dueños de las tabernas pusieron° la

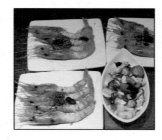

tapa al lado del vaso. Luego, empezaron a servir también pequeñas porciones de platos tradicionales.

Para muchos españoles, ir de tapas con los amigos después del trabajo es una rutina diaria.

platos *dishes* tortilla de patatas *potato omelet* calamares *squid* dueños *owners* tuvieron *had* vaso de vino *glass of wine* tapado *covered* rodaja *slice* pan *bread* era *was* tapa *lid* no podían *couldn't* pusieron *put*

Conexión Internet

¿Qué costumbres son populares en los países hispanos?

Go to adelante.vhlcentral.com to find more cultural information related to this **Cultura** section.

ACTIVIDADES

2 Comprensión Completa las oraciones.

1. Uso <u>el hilo dental/la seda dental</u> para limpiar (*to clean*) entre los dientes.

2. En <u>El Salvador</u> las personas compran pan y tortillas a los vendedores que pasan por la calle.

3. Muchos españoles <u>van de tapas</u> después del trabajo.

4. En Costa Rica usan anécdotas y lugares para dar <u>direcciones</u>

3 ¿Qué costumbres tienes? Escribe cuatro oraciones sobre una costumbre que compartes con tus amigos o con tu familia (por ejemplo: ir al cine, ir a eventos deportivos, leer, comer juntos, etc.). Explica qué haces, cuándo lo haces y con quién. Answers will vary.

3 To simplify, write time expressions on the board that students can use in their descriptions (Ex: **siempre, todos los años, cada mes**).

recursos

adelante.vhlcentral.com

Lección 1

1.1 Reflexive verbs

ANTE TODO   A reflexive verb is used to indicate that the subject does something to or for himself or herself. In other words, it "reflects" the action of the verb back to the subject. Reflexive verbs always use reflexive pronouns.

SUBJECT	REFLEXIVE VERB
Joaquín	**se ducha** por la mañana.

The verb **lavarse** (*to wash oneself*)

SINGULAR FORMS	yo	**me lavo**	*I wash (myself)*
	tú	**te lavas**	*you wash (yourself)*
	Ud.	**se lava**	*you wash (yourself)*
	él/ella	**se lava**	*he/she washes (himself/herself)*
PLURAL FORMS	nosotros/as	**nos lavamos**	*we wash (ourselves)*
	vosotros/as	**os laváis**	*you wash (yourselves)*
	Uds.	**se lavan**	*you wash (yourselves)*
	ellos/ellas	**se lavan**	*they wash (themselves)*

▶ The pronoun **se** attached to an infinitive identifies the verb as reflexive: **lavarse.**

▶ When a reflexive verb is conjugated, the reflexive pronoun agrees with the subject.

Me afeito.   **Te despiertas** a las siete.

Me ducho, me cepillo los dientes, me visto y ¡listo!

¡Ay, los estudiantes! Siempre se acuestan tarde.

▶ Like object pronouns, reflexive pronouns generally appear before a conjugated verb. With infinitives and present participles, they may be placed before the conjugated verb or attached to the infinitive or present participle.

Ellos **se** van a vestir.	**Nos** estamos lavando las manos.
Ellos van a vestir**se**.	Estamos lavándo**nos** las manos.
They are going to get dressed.	*We are washing our hands.*

▶ **¡Atención!** When a reflexive pronoun is attached to a present participle, an accent mark is added to maintain the original stress.

bañando ⟶ bañ**á**ndo**se**   durmiendo ⟶ durmi**é**ndo**se**

Extra Practice To provide oral practice with reflexive verbs, create sentences that follow the pattern of the sentences in the examples. Say the sentence, have students repeat it, then say a different subject, varying the gender and number. Have students then say the sentence with the new subject, changing pronouns and verbs as necessary.

Lección 1

Common reflexive verbs

acordarse (de) (o:ue)	to remember	**llamarse**	to be called; to be named
acostarse (o:ue)	to go to bed		
afeitarse	to shave	**maquillarse**	to put on makeup
bañarse	to bathe; to take a bath	**peinarse**	to comb one's hair
cepillarse	to brush	**ponerse**	to put on
despedirse (de) (e:i)	to say goodbye (to)	**ponerse (+ adj.)**	to become (+ adj.)
despertarse (e:ie)	to wake up	**preocuparse (por)**	to worry (about)
dormirse (o:ue)	to go to sleep; to fall asleep	**probarse** (o:ue)	to try on
		quedarse	to stay; to remain
ducharse	to shower; to take a shower	**quitarse**	to take off
		secarse	to dry (oneself)
enojarse (con)	to get angry (with)	**sentarse** (e:ie)	to sit down
irse	to go away; to leave	**sentirse** (e:ie)	to feel
lavarse	to wash (oneself)	**vestirse** (e:i)	to get dressed
levantarse	to get up		

COMPARE & CONTRAST

Unlike English, a number of verbs in Spanish can be reflexive or non-reflexive. If the verb acts upon the subject, the reflexive form is used. If the verb acts upon something other than the subject, the non-reflexive form is used. Compare these sentences.

Lola **lava** los platos.

Lola **se lava** la cara.

As the preceding sentences show, reflexive verbs sometimes have different meanings than their non-reflexive counterparts. For example, **lavar** means *to wash,* while **lavarse** means *to wash oneself, to wash up.*

▶ **¡Atención!** Parts of the body or clothing are generally not referred to with possessives, but with the definite article.

La niña se quitó **los** zapatos.   Necesito cepillarme **los** dientes.

recursos
WB pp. 55–56
LM p. 71
SUPERSITE adelante. vhlcentral.com

¡INTÉNTALO! Indica el presente de estos verbos reflexivos. El primero de cada columna ya está conjugado.

despertarse
1. Mis hermanos *se despiertan* tarde.
2. Tú *te despiertas* tarde.
3. Nosotros *nos despertamos* tarde.
4. Benito *se despierta* tarde.
5. Yo *me despierto* tarde.

ponerse
1. Él *se pone* una chaqueta.
2. Yo *me pongo* una chaqueta.
3. Usted *se pone* una chaqueta.
4. Nosotras *nos ponemos* una chaqueta.
5. Las niñas *se ponen* una chaqueta.

TPR Model gestures for a few of the reflexive verbs. Ex: **acordarse** (tap side of head), **acostarse** (lay head on folded hands). Have students stand. Begin by practicing as a class using only the **nosotros** form, saying expressions at random (Ex: **Nos lavamos la cara.**). Then vary the verb forms and point to the student who should perform the appropriate gesture. Keep a brisk pace. Vary by pointing to more than one student (Ex: **Ustedes se peinan.**).

Práctica   SUPERSITE

1   Nuestra rutina

Nuestra rutina La familia de Blanca sigue la misma rutina todos los días. Según Blanca, ¿qué hacen ellos?

> **1** To practice the formal register, describe situations and have students tell you what you are going to do. Ex: **Hace frío y nieva, pero necesito salir. (Usted va a ponerse el abrigo.)**

> **modelo**
>
> mamá / despertarse a las 5:00
> Mamá se despierta a las cinco.

1. Roberto y yo / levantarse a las 7:00   Roberto y yo nos levantamos a las siete.
2. papá / ducharse primero y / luego afeitarse   Papá se ducha primero y luego se afeita.
3. yo / lavarse la cara y / vestirse antes de tomar café   Yo me lavo la cara y me visto antes de tomar café.
4. mamá / peinarse y / luego maquillarse   Mamá se peina y luego se maquilla.
5. todos (nosotros) / sentarse a la mesa para comer   Todos nos sentamos a la mesa para comer.
6. Roberto / cepillarse los dientes después de comer   Roberto se cepilla los dientes después de comer.
7. yo / ponerse el abrigo antes de salir   Yo me pongo el abrigo antes de salir.
8. nosotros / despedirse de mamá   Nosotros nos despedimos de mamá.

2   La fiesta elegante

La fiesta elegante Selecciona el verbo apropiado y completa las oraciones con la forma correcta.

1. Tú ___lavas___ (lavar / lavarse) el auto antes de ir a la fiesta.
2. Nosotros no _nos acordamos_ (acordar / acordarse) de comprar regalos.
3. Para llegar a tiempo, Raúl y Marta ___acuestan___ (acostar / acostarse) a los niños antes de irse.
4. Yo ___me siento___ (sentir / sentirse) bien hoy.
5. Mis amigos siempre ___se visten___ (vestir / vestirse) con ropa muy cara.
6. ¿___Se prueban___ (Probar / Probarse) ustedes la ropa antes de comprarla?
7. Usted ___se preocupa___ (preocupar / preocuparse) mucho por sus amigos, ¿no?
8. En general, ___me afeito___ (afeitar / afeitarse) yo mismo, pero hoy el barbero (*barber*) me ___afeita___ (afeitar / afeitarse).

> **2** For expansion, ask students to write five sentence pairs contrasting reflexive and non-reflexive forms. Ex: **Me despierto a las siete. Despierto a mi compañero de cuarto a las ocho.**

> **3** Repeat the activity as a pattern drill, supplying different subjects for each drawing. Ex: **Número uno, yo. (Me quito los zapatos.) Número cinco, nosotras. (Nosotras nos maquillamos.)**

3   Describir

Describir Mira los dibujos y describe lo que estas personas hacen.   Some answers may vary.

1. el joven   El joven se quita los zapatos.

2. Carmen   Carmen se duerme.

3. Juan   Juan se pone la camiseta.

4. ellos   Ellos se despiden.

5. Estrella   Estrella se maquilla.

6. Toni   Toni se enoja con el perro.

Extra Practice Repeat the activity using the present progressive. Ask students to provide both possible sentences.
Ex: **1. El joven se está quitando los zapatos./El joven está quitándose los zapatos.**

Comunicación

4 **Preguntas personales** En parejas, túrnense para hacerse estas preguntas.   Answers will vary.

1. ¿A qué hora te levantas durante la semana?
2. ¿A qué hora te levantas los fines de semana?
3. ¿Prefieres levantarte tarde o temprano? ¿Por qué?
4. ¿Te enojas frecuentemente con tus amigos?
5. ¿Te preocupas fácilmente? ¿Qué te preocupa?
6. ¿Qué te pone contento/a?
7. ¿Qué haces cuando te sientes triste?
8. ¿Y cuando te sientes alegre?
9. ¿Te acuestas tarde o temprano durante la semana?
10. ¿A qué hora te acuestas los fines de semana?

4 Ask volunteers to call out some of their answers. The class should add information by speculating on the reason behind each answer. Ex: **Hablas por teléfono con tus amigos cuando te sientes triste porque ellos te comprenden muy bien.** Have the volunteer confirm or refute the speculation.

5 Ask each group to present their best **charada** to the class.

5 **Charadas** En grupos, jueguen a las charadas. Cada persona debe pensar en dos frases con verbos reflexivos. La primera persona que adivina la charada dramatiza la siguiente. Answers will vary.

6 Before assigning groups, go over some of the things men and women do to get ready to go out. Ex: **Las mujeres se maquillan. Los hombres se afeitan.** Then ask students to indicate their opinion on the question and divide the class into groups accordingly.

6 **Debate** En grupos, discutan este tema: ¿Quiénes necesitan más tiempo para arreglarse (*to get ready*) antes de salir, los hombres o las mujeres? Hagan una lista de las razones (*reasons*) que tienen para defender sus ideas e informen a la clase. Answers will vary.

Síntesis   **Supersite/IRCD:** Information Gap Activities

7 **La familia ocupada** Tú y tu compañero/a asisten a un programa de verano en Lima, Perú. Viven con la familia Ramos. Tu profesor(a) te va a dar la rutina incompleta que la familia sigue en las mañanas. Trabaja con tu compañero/a para completarla.   Answers will vary.

> **modelo**
>
> **Estudiante 1:** ¿Qué hace el señor Ramos a las seis y cuarto?
> **Estudiante 2:** El señor Ramos se levanta.

7 Ask groups of four to imagine they all live in the same house and have them put together a message board to reflect their different schedules.

Extra Practice Add an auditory aspect to this grammar practice. Prepare descriptions of five celebrities or fictional characters, using reflexives. Write their names randomly on the board. Then read the descriptions aloud and have students match each one to a name. Ex: **Se preocupa por todo. Siempre se viste de pantalones cortos negros y una camiseta amarilla. Tiene un amigo que nunca se baña y se llama Linus. (Charlie Brown)**

Lección 1

1.2 Indefinite and negative words

ANTE TODO Indefinite words refer to people and things that are not specific, for example, *someone* or *something*. Negative words deny the existence of people and things or contradict statements, for instance, *no one* or *nothing*. Spanish indefinite words have corresponding negative words, which are opposite in meaning.

Indefinite and negative words

Indefinite words		Negative words	
algo	*something; anything*	**nada**	*nothing; not anything*
alguien	*someone; somebody; anyone*	**nadie**	*no one; nobody; not anyone*
alguno/a(s), algún	*some; any*	**ninguno/a, ningún**	*no; none; not any*
o... o	*either... or*	**ni... ni**	*neither... nor*
siempre	*always*	**nunca, jamás**	*never, not ever*
también	*also; too*	**tampoco**	*neither; not either*

▶ There are two ways to form negative sentences in Spanish. You can place the negative word before the verb, or you can place **no** before the verb and the negative word after.

Nadie se levanta temprano.
No one gets up early.

No se levanta nadie temprano.
No one gets up early.

Ellos **nunca gritan**.
They never shout.

Ellos **no gritan nunca**.
They never shout.

Yo siempre me despierto a las seis en punto. ¿Y tú?

Pues yo jamás me levanto temprano. Nunca oigo el despertador.

▶ Because they refer to people, **alguien** and **nadie** are often used with the personal **a**. The personal **a** is also used before **alguno/a, algunos/as,** and **ninguno/a** when these words refer to people and they are the direct object of the verb.

—Perdón, señor, ¿busca usted **a alguien**?
—No, gracias, señorita, no busco **a nadie**.

—Tomás, ¿buscas **a alguno** de tus hermanos?
—No, mamá, no busco **a ninguno**.

▶ **¡Atención!** Before a masculine, singular noun, **alguno** and **ninguno** are shortened to **algún** and **ningún**.

—¿Tienen ustedes **algún** amigo peruano?

—No, no tenemos **ningún** amigo peruano.

Teaching Tips
• Present negative words by complaining dramatically in a whining tone. Ex: **Nadie me llama por teléfono. Jamás recibo un correo electrónico de ningún estudiante. Ni mi esposo ni mis hijos se acuerdan de mi cumpleaños.** Then smile radiantly and state the opposite. Ex: **Alguien me llama por teléfono.**
• Add a visual aspect to this grammar presentation. Use magazine pictures to compare and contrast indefinite and negative words. Ex: **La señora tiene algo en las manos. ¿El señor tiene algo también? No, el señor no tiene nada.**

AYUDA

Alguno/a, algunos/as are not always used in the same way English uses *some* or *any*. Often, **algún** is used where *a* would be used in English.

¿Tienes algún libro que hable de los incas?
*Do you have **a** book that talks about the Incas?*

Note that **ninguno/a** is rarely used in the plural.

—**¿Visitaste algunos museos?**
—**No, no visité ninguno.**

Lección 1

recursos

WB
pp. 57–58

LM
p. 72

SUPERSITE
adelante.
vhlcentral.com

COMPARE & CONTRAST

In English, it is incorrect to use more than one negative word in a sentence. In Spanish, however, sentences frequently contain two or more negative words. Compare these Spanish and English sentences.

Nunca le escribo a **nadie**.
I never write to anyone.

No me preocupo por **nada nunca**.
I do not ever worry about anything.

As the preceding sentences show, once an English sentence contains one negative word (for example, *not* or *never*), no other negative word may be used. Instead, indefinite (or affirmative) words are used. In Spanish, however, once a sentence is negative, no other affirmative (that is, indefinite) word may be used. Instead, all indefinite ideas must be expressed in the negative.

▶ Although in Spanish **pero** and **sino** both mean *but*, they are not interchangeable. **Sino** is used when the first part of a sentence is negative and the second part contradicts it. In this context, **sino** means *but rather* or *on the contrary*. In all other cases, **pero** is used to mean *but*.

Los estudiantes no se acuestan temprano **sino** tarde.
The students don't go to bed early, but rather late.

Las toallas son caras, **pero** bonitas.
The towels are expensive, but beautiful.

María no habla francés **sino** español.
María doesn't speak French, but rather Spanish.

José es inteligente, **pero** no saca buenas notas.
José is intelligent but doesn't get good grades.

¡INTÉNTALO! Cambia las oraciones para que sean negativas. La primera se da como ejemplo.

1. Siempre se viste bien.
   <u>Nunca</u> se viste bien.
   <u>No</u> se viste bien <u>nunca</u>.
2. Alguien se ducha.
   <u>Nadie</u> se ducha.
   <u>No</u> se ducha <u>nadie</u>.
3. Ellas van también.
   Ellas <u>tampoco</u> van.
   Ellas <u>no</u> van <u>tampoco</u>.
4. Alguien se pone nervioso.
   <u>Nadie</u> se pone nervioso.
   <u>No</u> se pone nervioso <u>nadie</u>.
5. Tú siempre te lavas las manos.
   Tú <u>nunca / jamás</u> te lavas las manos.
   Tú <u>no</u> te lavas las manos <u>nunca / jamás</u>.
6. Voy a traer algo.
   <u>No</u> voy a traer <u>nada</u>.
7. Juan se afeita también.
   Juan <u>tampoco</u> se afeita.
   Juan <u>no</u> se afeita <u>tampoco</u>.
8. Mis amigos viven en una residencia o en casa.
   Mis amigos <u>no</u> viven <u>ni</u> en una residencia <u>ni</u> en casa.
9. La profesora hace algo en su escritorio.
   La profesora <u>no</u> hace <u>nada</u> en su escritorio.
10. Tú y yo vamos al mercado.
    <u>Ni</u> tú <u>ni</u> yo vamos al mercado.
11. Tienen un espejo en su casa.
    <u>No</u> tienen <u>ningún</u> espejo en su casa.
12. Algunos niños se ponen el abrigo.
    <u>Ningún</u> niño se pone el abrigo.

Práctica

1

¿Pero o sino? Forma oraciones sobre estas personas usando **pero** o **sino**.

> **modelo**
>
> muchos estudiantes viven en residencias estudiantiles / muchos de
> ellos quieren vivir fuera del *(off)* campus
> *Muchos estudiantes viven en residencias estudiantiles, pero muchos*
> *de ellos quieren vivir fuera del campus.*

1. Marcos nunca se despierta temprano / siempre llega puntual a clase
   Marcos nunca se despierta temprano, pero siempre llega puntual a clase.
2. Lisa y Katarina no se acuestan temprano / muy tarde
   Lisa y Katarina no se acuestan temprano sino muy tarde.
3. Alfonso es inteligente / algunas veces es antipático
   Alfonso es inteligente, pero algunas veces es antipático.
4. los directores de la residencia no son ecuatorianos / peruanos
   Los directores de la residencia no son ecuatorianos sino peruanos.
5. no nos acordamos de comprar champú / compramos jabón
   No nos acordamos de comprar champú, pero compramos jabón.
6. Emilia no es estudiante / profesora
   Emilia no es estudiante sino profesora.
7. no quiero levantarme / tengo que ir a clase
   No quiero levantarme, pero tengo que ir a clase.
8. Miguel no se afeita por la mañana / por la noche
   Miguel no se afeita por la mañana sino por la noche.

2

Completar Completa esta conversación. Usa expresiones negativas en tus respuestas. Luego,
dramatiza la conversación con un(a) compañero/a.   Answers will vary.

AURELIO   Ana María, ¿encontraste algún regalo para Eliana?
ANA MARÍA (1)_____ No, no encontré ningún regalo/nada para Eliana. _____

AURELIO   ¿Viste a alguna amiga en el centro comercial?
ANA MARÍA (2)_____ No, no vi a ninguna amiga/ninguna/nadie en el centro comercial. _____

AURELIO   ¿Me llamó alguien?
ANA MARÍA (3)_____ No, nadie te llamó./No, no te llamó nadie. _____

AURELIO   ¿Quieres ir al teatro o al cine esta noche?
ANA MARÍA (4)_____ No, no quiero ir ni al teatro ni al cine. _____

AURELIO   ¿No quieres salir a comer?
ANA MARÍA (5)_____ No, no quiero salir a comer (tampoco). _____

AURELIO   ¿Hay algo interesante en la televisión esta noche?
ANA MARÍA (6)_____ No, no hay nada interesante en la televisión. _____

AURELIO   ¿Tienes algún problema?
ANA MARÍA (7)_____ No, no tengo ningún problema/ninguno. _____

2 For follow-up, ask students to summarize the conversation. Ex: **Ana María no encontró ningún regalo para Eliana. Tampoco
vio a ninguna amiga en el centro comercial.**

Lección 1

Comunicación

3 Give students these additional items: **5. Mis padres no son ____ sino ____. 6. Mi compañero/a de cuarto es ____ pero ____.**

3 **Opiniones** Completa estas oraciones de una manera lógica. Luego, compara tus respuestas con las de un(a) compañero/a. Answers will vary.

1. Mi habitación es _____ pero _____ .
2. Por la noche me gusta _____ pero _____ .
3. Un(a) profesor(a) ideal no es _____ sino _____ .
4. Mis amigos son _____ pero _____ .

3 Use personal examples to preview the activity. Ex: **Mi hijo es inteligente, pero no le gusta estudiar. Mi esposa no es norteamericana, sino española.**

4 **En el campus** En parejas, háganse preguntas para ver qué hay en su universidad: residencias bonitas, departamento de ingeniería, cines, librerías baratas, estudiantes guapos, equipo de fútbol, playa, clases fáciles, museo, profesores estrictos. Sigan el modelo. Answers will vary.

> **modelo**
>
> **Estudiante 1:** ¿Hay algunas residencias bonitas?
> **Estudiante 2:** Sí, hay una/algunas. Está(n) detrás del estadio.
>
> **Estudiante 1:** ¿Hay algún museo?
> **Estudiante 2:** No, no hay ninguno.

4 Have pairs of students create two additional sentences about your school.

5 **Quejas (Complaints)** En parejas, hagan una lista de cinco quejas comunes que tienen los estudiantes. Usen expresiones negativas. Answers will vary.

> **modelo**
>
> Nadie me entiende.

Ahora hagan una lista de cinco quejas que los padres tienen de sus hijos.

> **modelo**
>
> Nunca limpian sus habitaciones.

5 Divide the class into all-male and all-female groups. Then have each group make two different lists: **Quejas que tienen los hombres de las mujeres** and **Quejas que tienen las mujeres de los hombres.** After five minutes, compare and contrast the answers and perceptions.

6 **Anuncios** En parejas, lean el anuncio y contesten las preguntas. Some answers will vary.

1. ¿Es el anuncio positivo o negativo? ¿Por qué? Answers will vary.
2. ¿Qué palabras indefinidas hay? algún, siempre, algo
3. Escriban el texto del anuncio cambiando todo por expresiones negativas. ¿No buscas ningún producto especial? ¡Nunca hay nada para nadie en las tiendas García!
4. Ahora preparen su propio (own) anuncio usando expresiones afirmativas y negativas.

¿Buscas algún producto especial?

¡Siempre hay algo para todos en las tiendas García!

Síntesis

7 Have students write five sentences using information obtained through the survey. Ex: **Nadie va a la biblioteca durante el fin de semana, pero muchos vamos durante la semana.**

7 **Encuesta** Tu profesor(a) te va a dar una hoja de actividades para hacer una encuesta. Circula por la clase y pídeles a tus compañeros/as que comparen las actividades que hacen durante la semana con las que hacen durante los fines de semana. Escribe las respuestas. Answers will vary.

Supersite/IRCD: *Hojas de actividades*

Extra Practice Have students complete this cloze activity using **pero, sino,** and **tampoco: Yo me levanto temprano y hago mi tarea, ____ mi compañera de apartamento prefiere hacerla por la noche y acostarse muy tarde. (pero) Ella no tiene exámenes este semestre ____ proyectos. (sino) Yo no tengo exámenes ____ . (tampoco) Sólo tengo mucha, mucha tarea.**

1.3 **Preterite of ser and ir** 〔SUPERSITE〕

ANTE TODO　In ¡*ADELANTE!* ʊɴᴏ, **Lección 6,** you learned how to form the preterite tense of regular **-ar, -er,** and **-ir** verbs. The following chart contains the preterite forms of **ser** (*to be*) and **ir** (*to go*). Since these forms are irregular, you will need to memorize them.

NATIONAL STANDARDS / comparisons

Teaching Tips
• Use pairs of sentences to contrast the preterite of ser and ir. Ex: **Ayer fue domingo. No fui al supermercado ayer.**

		ser (*to be*)	**ir** (*to go*)
SINGULAR FORMS	yo	**fui**	**fui**
	tú	**fuiste**	**fuiste**
	Ud./él/ella	**fue**	**fue**
PLURAL FORMS	nosotros/as	**fuimos**	**fuimos**
	vosotros/as	**fuisteis**	**fuisteis**
	Uds./ellos/ellas	**fueron**	**fueron**

Preterite of ser and ir

AYUDA

Note that, whereas regular **-er** and **-ir** verbs have accent marks in the **yo** and **Ud./él/ella** forms of the preterite, **ser** and **ir** do not.

► Since the preterite forms of **ser** and **ir** are identical, context clarifies which of the two verbs is being used.

Él **fue** a comprar champú y jabón.　　¿Cómo **fue** la película anoche?
He went to buy shampoo and soap.　　*How was the movie last night?*

• Ask questions to further clarify how context determines meaning. Ex: **¿Quiénes fueron al partido de fútbol el sábado? ¿Fue divertido el partido?**

¿Adónde fueron ustedes?

Inés y yo fuimos a un mercado. Fue muy divertido.

Video Replay the *Fotonovela* segment and have students listen for preterite forms of **ser** and **ir**. Stop the video with each example to illustrate how context makes the meaning of the verb clear.

¡INTÉNTALO!　Completa las oraciones usando el pretérito de **ser** e **ir**. La primera oración de cada columna se da como ejemplo.

ir	**ser**
1. Los viajeros __fueron__ a Perú.	1. Usted __fue__ muy amable.
2. Patricia __fue__ a Cuzco.	2. Yo __fui__ muy cordial.
3. Tú __fuiste__ a Iquitos.	3. Ellos __fueron__ simpáticos.
4. Gregorio y yo __fuimos__ a Lima.	4. Nosotros __fuimos__ muy tontos.
5. Yo __fui__ a Trujillo.	5. Ella __fue__ antipática.
6. Ustedes __fueron__ a Arequipa.	6. Tú __fuiste__ muy generoso.
7. Mi padre __fue__ a Lima.	7. Ustedes __fueron__ cordiales.
8. Nosotras __fuimos__ a Cuzco.	8. La gente __fue__ amable.
9. Él __fue__ a Machu Picchu.	9. Tomás y yo __fuimos__ muy felices.
10. Usted __fue__ a Nazca.	10. Los profesores __fueron__ buenos.

recursos

WB p. 59

LM p. 73

〔SUPERSITE〕
adelante.
vhlcentral.com

Extra Practice To reverse the activity, have students close their books. Read several completed sentences at random and have students state whether the verb is **ser** or **ir**.

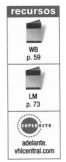

Lección 1

Práctica

1

Completar Completa estas conversaciones con la forma correcta del pretérito de **ser** o **ir**. Indica el infinitivo de cada forma verbal.

Conversación 1

RAÚL ¿Adónde (1)___fueron___ ustedes de vacaciones? ___ir___

PILAR (2)___Fuimos___ al Perú. ___ir___

RAÚL ¿Cómo (3)___fue___ el viaje? ___ser___

▶ **PILAR** ¡(4)___Fue___ estupendo! Machu Picchu y El Callao son increíbles. ___ser___

RAÚL ¿(5)___Fue___ caro el viaje? ___ser___

PILAR No, el precio (6)___fue___ muy bajo. Sólo costó tres mil dólares. ___ser___

Conversación 2

ISABEL Tina y Vicente (7)___fueron___ novios, ¿no? ___ser___

LUCÍA Sí, pero ahora no. Anoche Tina (8)___fue___ a comer con Gregorio y la semana pasada ellos (9)___fueron___ al partido de fútbol. ___ir___ ___ir___

ISABEL ¿Ah sí? Javier y yo (10)___fuimos___ al partido y no los vimos. ___ir___

2 Ask a volunteer to say one of his or her sentences aloud. Point to another student, and call out an interrogative word in order to cue a question. Ex: **E1: No fui a un restaurante anoche.** Say: **¿Adónde?** **E2: ¿Adónde fuiste? E1: Fui al cine.**

2

Descripciones Forma oraciones con estos elementos. Usa el pretérito. *Answers will vary.*

A	**B**	**C**	**D**
yo	(no) ir	a un restaurante	ayer
tú	(no) ser	en autobús	anoche
mi compañero/a		estudiante	anteayer
nosotros		muy simpático/a	la semana pasada
mis amigos		a la playa	el año pasado
ustedes		dependiente/a en una tienda	

Comunicación

3 Have pairs team up to form groups of four. Each student should report three things about his or her partner to the group.

TPR Read aloud a series of sentences using **ser** and **ir** in the preterite. Have students raise their right hand if the verb is **ser**, and their left hand for **ir**. Ex: **Yo fui camarero a los dieciocho años.** (right hand)

3

Preguntas En parejas, túrnense para hacerse estas preguntas. *Answers will vary.*

1. ¿Adónde fuiste de vacaciones el año pasado? ¿Con quién fuiste?
2. ¿Cómo fueron tus vacaciones?
3. ¿Fuiste de compras la semana pasada? ¿Adónde? ¿Qué compraste?
4. ¿Fuiste al cine la semana pasada? ¿Qué película viste? ¿Cómo fue?
5. ¿Fuiste a la cafetería hoy? ¿A qué hora?
6. ¿Adónde fuiste durante el fin de semana? ¿Por qué?
7. ¿Quién fue tu profesor(a) favorito/a el semestre pasado? ¿Por qué?

4

El viaje En parejas, escriban un diálogo de un(a) viajero/a hablando con el/la agente de viajes sobre un viaje que tomó recientemente. Usen el pretérito de **ser** e **ir**. *Answers will vary.*

> **modelo**
>
> **Agente:** ¿Cómo fue el viaje?
> **Viajero:** El viaje fue maravilloso/horrible…

Small Groups Have small groups of students prepare and perform a TV interview with astronauts who have just returned from a long stay on Mars. Review previous vocabulary as needed. Students should include three uses each of **ser** and **ir** in the preterite.

1.4 # Verbs like **gustar**

ANTE TODO In *¡ADELANTE!* **UNO**, **Lección 2**, you learned how to express preferences with **gustar**. You will now learn more about the verb **gustar** and other similar verbs. Observe these examples.

Me gusta ese champú.

> **ENGLISH EQUIVALENT**
> *I like that shampoo.*
> **LITERAL MEANING**
> *That shampoo is pleasing to me.*

¿Te gustaron las clases?

> **ENGLISH EQUIVALENT**
> *Did you like the classes?*
> **LITERAL MEANING**
> *Were the classes pleasing to you?*

▶ As the examples show, constructions with **gustar** do not have a direct equivalent in English. The literal meaning of this construction is *to be pleasing to (someone)*, and it requires the use of an indirect object pronoun.

INDIRECT OBJECT PRONOUN	SUBJECT		SUBJECT		DIRECT OBJECT
Me	**gusta** ese champú.		*I*	*like*	*that shampoo.*

▶ In the diagram above, observe how in the Spanish sentence the object being liked **(ese champú)** is really the subject of the sentence. The person who likes the object, in turn, is an indirect object because it answers the question: *To whom is the shampoo pleasing?*

¿No te gustan las computadoras?

Me gustan mucho los parques.

▶ Other verbs in Spanish are used in the same way as **gustar**. Here is a list of the most common ones.

Verbs like **gustar**

aburrir	to bore	**importar**	to be important to; to matter
encantar	to like very much; to love (inanimate objects)	**interesar**	to be interesting to; to interest
faltar	to lack; to need	**molestar**	to bother; to annoy
fascinar	to fascinate; to like very much	**quedar**	to be left over; to fit (clothing)

Heritage Speakers Ask heritage speakers to add to the list of verbs like **gustar**. Ex: **doler, preocupar, sorprender**. Have them use each verb in a sentence about themselves, then ask volunteers to report on their statements.

▶ The forms most commonly used with **gustar** and similar verbs are the third person (singular and plural). When the object or person being liked is singular, the singular form (**gusta/molesta**, etc.) is used. When two or more objects or persons are being liked, the plural form (**gustan/molestan**, etc.) is used. Observe the following diagram:

| SINGULAR | me, te, le | | encanta / interesó | ▶ | la película / el concierto |
| PLURAL | nos, os, les | | importan / fascinaron | ▶ | las vacaciones / los museos de Lima |

▶ To express what someone likes or does not like to do, use an appropriate verb followed by an infinitive. The singular form is used even if there is more than one infinitive.

Nos molesta comer a las nueve.
It bothers us to eat at nine o'clock.

Les encanta cantar y **bailar** en las fiestas.
They love to sing and dance at parties.

▶ As you learned in *¡ADELANTE!* **UNO**, **Lección 2**, the construction **a** + [*pronoun*] (**a mí, a ti, a usted, a él,** etc.) is used to clarify or to emphasize who is pleased, bored, etc. The construction **a** + [*noun*] can also be used before the indirect object pronoun to clarify or to emphasize who is pleased.

A los turistas les gustó mucho Machu Picchu.
The tourists liked Machu Picchu a lot.

A ti te gusta cenar en casa, pero **a mí** me aburre.
You like to eat dinner at home, but I get bored.

▶ **¡Atención! Mí** (*me*) has an accent mark to distinguish it from the possessive adjective **mi** (*my*).

¡INTÉNTALO!   Indica el pronombre del objeto indirecto y la forma del tiempo presente adecuados en cada oración. La primera oración de cada columna se da como ejemplo.

fascinar

1. A él ___le fascina___ viajar.
2. A mí ___me fascina___ bailar.
3. A nosotras ___nos fascina___ cantar.
4. A ustedes ___les fascina___ leer.
5. A ti ___te fascina___ correr.
6. A Pedro ___le fascina___ gritar.
7. A mis padres ___les fascina___ caminar.
8. A usted ___le fascina___ jugar al tenis.
9. A mi esposo y a mí ___nos fascina___ dormir.
10. A Alberto ___le fascina___ dibujar.
11. A todos ___nos/les fascina___ opinar.
12. A Pili ___le fascina___ ir de compras.

aburrir

1. A ellos ___les aburren___ los deportes.
2. A ti ___te aburren___ las películas.
3. A usted ___le aburren___ los viajes.
4. A mí ___me aburren___ las revistas.
5. A Jorge y a Luis ___les aburren___ los perros.
6. A nosotros ___nos aburren___ las vacaciones.
7. A ustedes ___les aburren___ las fiestas.
8. A Marcela ___le aburren___ los libros.
9. A mis amigos ___les aburren___ los museos.
10. A ella ___le aburre___ el ciclismo.
11. A Omar ___le aburre___ el Internet.
12. A ti y a mí ___nos aburre___ el baile.

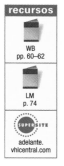
Lección 1

Práctica

1 Have students use the verbs in the activity to write a paragraph describing their own musical tastes.

1 **Completar** Completa las oraciones con todos los elementos necesarios.

1. _____A_____ Adela __le encanta__ (encantar) la música de Enrique Iglesias.
2. A ____mí____ me __interesa__ (interesar) la música de otros países.
3. A mis amigos __les encantan__ (encantar) las canciones (*songs*) de Maná.
4. A Juan y ____a____ Rafael no les __molesta__ (molestar) la música alta (*loud*).
5. _____A_____ nosotros __nos fascinan__ (fascinar) los grupos de pop latino.
6. ____Al____ señor Ruiz __le interesa__ (interesar) más la música clásica.
7. A ____mí____ me __aburre__ (aburrir) la música clásica.
8. ¿A ____ti____ te __falta__ (faltar) dinero para el concierto de Carlos Santana?
9. Sí. Sólo __me quedan__ (quedar) cinco dólares.
10. ¿Cuánto dinero te __queda__ (quedar) a ____ti____?

1 To simplify, have students underline the subject in each sentence before filling in the blanks

NOTA CULTURAL

Hoy día, la música latina es popular en los EE.UU. gracias a artistas como **Shakira**, de nacionalidad colombiana, y **Enrique Iglesias**, español. Otros artistas, como **Carlos Santana** y **Gloria Estefan**, difundieron (*spread*) la música latina en los años 60, 70, 80 y 90.

2 **Describir** Mira los dibujos y describe lo que está pasando. Usa los verbos de la lista.
Some answers will vary.

aburrir	faltar	molestar
encantar	interesar	quedar

1. a Ramón   A Ramón le molesta despertarse temprano.

2. a nosotros   A nosotros nos encanta esquiar.

3. a ti   A ti no te queda bien este vestido.
A ti te queda mal/grande este vestido.

LIBROS DE ARTE MODERNO

4. a Sara   A Sara le interesan los libros de arte moderno.

2 Repeat the activity using the preterite. Invite students to provide additional details. Ex: **1. A Ramón le molestó el despertador ayer. 2. A nosotros nos encantó esquiar en Vail.**

TPR Have students stand and form a circle. Begin by tossing a foam or paper ball to a student, who should state a complaint using a verb like **gustar** (Ex: **Me falta dinero para comprar los libros**) and then toss the ball to another student. The next student should offer advice (Ex: **Debes pedirle dinero a tus padres**) and throw the ball to another person, who will air another complaint. Repeat the activity with positive statements (**Me fascinan las películas cómicas**) and advice (**Debes ver las películas de Will Ferrell**).

3 **Gustos** Forma oraciones con los elementos de las tres columnas. Answers will vary.

> **modelo**
> A ti te interesan las ruinas de Machu Picchu.

A	B	C
yo	aburrir	despertarse temprano
tú	encantar	mirarse en el espejo
mi mejor amigo/a	faltar	la música rock
mis amigos y yo	fascinar	las pantuflas rosadas
Bart y Homero Simpson	interesar	la pasta de dientes con menta (*mint*)
Shakira	molestar	las ruinas de Machu Picchu
Antonio Banderas		los zapatos caros

3 Ask students to create two additional sentences using verbs from column B. Have students read their sentences aloud. After everyone has had a turn, ask the class how many similar or identical sentences they heard and what they were.

Lección 1

Comunicación

4

Preguntas En parejas, túrnense para hacer y contestar estas preguntas. Answers will vary.

4 Take a class survey of the answers and write the results on the board. Ask volunteers to use verbs like **gustar** to summarize them.

1. ¿Te gusta levantarte temprano o tarde? ¿Por qué? ¿Y a tu compañero/a de cuarto?
2. ¿Te gusta acostarte temprano o tarde? ¿Y a tu compañero/a de cuarto?
3. ¿Te gusta dormir la siesta?
4. ¿Te encanta acampar o prefieres quedarte en un hotel cuando estás de vacaciones?
5. ¿Qué te gusta hacer en el verano?
6. ¿Qué te fascina de esta universidad? ¿Qué te molesta?
7. ¿Te interesan más las ciencias o las humanidades? ¿Por qué?
8. ¿Qué cosas te molestan?

5

Completar Completa estas frases de una manera lógica. Answers will vary.

1. A mi novio/a le fascina(n)…
2. A mi mejor (*best*) amigo/a no le interesa(n)…
3. A mis padres les importa(n)…
4. A nosotros nos molesta(n)…
5. A mis hermanos les aburre(n)…
6. A mi compañero/a de cuarto le aburre(n)…
7. A los turistas les interesa(n)…
8. A los jugadores profesionales les encanta(n)…
9. A nuestro/a profesor(a) le molesta(n)…
10. A mí me importa(n)…

5 For items that start with **A mi(s)…** , have pairs compare their answers and then report to the class: first answers in common, then answers that differed. Ex: **A mis padres les importan los estudios, pero a los padres de _____ les importa más el dinero.**

6 Have pairs compare their matches by circulating around the classroom until they have all compared their answers with one another.

Supersite/IRCD: Information Gap Activities

6

La residencia Tú y tu compañero/a de clase son los directores de una residencia estudiantil en Perú. Su profesor(a) les va a dar a cada uno/a de ustedes las descripciones de cinco estudiantes. Con la información tienen que escoger quiénes van a ser compañeros de cuarto. Después, completen la lista. Answers will vary.

Síntesis

7

Situación Trabajen en parejas para representar los papeles de un(a) cliente/a y un(a) dependiente/a en una tienda de ropa. Usen las instrucciones como guía. Answers will vary.

Pairs Have pairs prepare short TV commercials in which they use the target verbs presented in **Estructura 1.4** to sell a particular product.

Extra Practice Add a visual aspect to this grammar practice. Bring in magazine pictures of people enjoying or not enjoying what they are doing. Have them create sentences with verbs like gustar. Ex: **A los chicos no les interesa estudiar biología.**

Dependiente/a	**Cliente/a**
Saluda al/a la cliente/a y pregúntale en qué le puedes servir.	→ Saluda al/a la dependiente/a y dile (*tell him/her*) qué quieres comprar y qué colores prefieres.
Pregúntale si le interesan los estilos modernos y empieza a mostrarle la ropa.	→ Explícale que los estilos modernos te interesan. Escoge las cosas que te interesan.
Habla de los gustos del/de la cliente/a.	→ Habla de la ropa (me queda(n) bien/mal, me encanta(n)…).
Da opiniones favorables al/a la cliente/a (las botas te quedan fantásticas…).	→ Decide cuáles son las cosas que te gustan y qué vas a comprar.

7 To simplify, have students prepare for their roles by brainstorming a list of words and phrases. Remind students to use the formal register in this conversation.

Recapitulación

SUPERSITE For self-scoring and diagnostics, go to **adelante.vhlcentral.com.**

Completa estas actividades para repasar los conceptos de gramática que aprendiste en esta lección.

RESUMEN GRAMATICAL

1 Completar Completa la tabla con la forma correcta de los verbos. **6 pts.**

yo	tú	nosotros	ellas
me levanto	te levantas	nos levantamos	se levantan
me afeito	**te afeitas**	nos afeitamos	se afeitan
me visto	te vistes	**nos vestimos**	se visten
me seco	te secas	nos secamos	**se secan**

1.1 Reflexive verbs   pp. 32–33

lavarse	
me lavo	nos lavamos
te lavas	os laváis
se lava	se lavan

2 Hoy y ayer Cambia los verbos del presente al pretérito. **5 pts.**

1. Vamos de compras hoy. ___Fuimos___ de compras hoy.
2. Por último, voy a poner el despertador. Por último, ___fui___ a poner el despertador.
3. Lalo es el primero en levantarse. Lalo ___fue___ el primero en levantarse.
4. ¿Vas a tu habitación? ¿___Fuiste___ a tu habitación?
5. Ustedes son profesores. Ustedes ___fueron___ profesores.

1.2 Indefinite and negative words   pp. 36–37

Indefinite words	Negative words
algo	nada
alguien	nadie
alguno/a(s), algún	ninguno/a, ningún
o... o	ni... ni
siempre	nunca, jamás
también	tampoco

3 Reflexivos Completa cada conversación con la forma correcta del presente del verbo reflexivo. **11 pts.**

TOMÁS Yo siempre (1) ___me baño___ (bañarse) antes de (2) ___acostarme___ (acostarse). Esto me relaja porque no (3) ___me duermo___ (dormirse) fácilmente. Y así puedo (4) ___levantarme___ (levantarse) más tarde. Y tú, ¿cuándo (5) ___te duchas___ (ducharse)?

LETI Pues por la mañana, para poder (6) ___despertarme___ (despertarse).

DAVID ¿Cómo (7) ___se siente___ (sentirse) Pepa hoy?

MARÍA Todavía está enojada.

DAVID ¿De verdad? Ella nunca (8) ___se enoja___ (enojarse) con nadie.

BETO ¿(Nosotros) (9) ___Nos vamos___ (Irse) de esta tienda? Estoy cansado.

SARA Pero antes vamos a (10) ___probarnos___ (probarse) estos sombreros. Si quieres, después (nosotros) (11) ___nos sentamos___ (sentarse) un rato.

1.3 Preterite of ser and ir   p. 40

► The preterite of ser and ir are identical. Context will determine the meaning.

ser and ir	
fui	fuimos
fuiste	fuisteis
fue	fueron

1.4 Verbs like gustar   pp.42–43

aburrir	importar
encantar	interesar
faltar	molestar
fascinar	quedar

SINGULAR	me, te, le		encanta interesó	la película el concierto
PLURAL	nos, os, les		importan fascinaron	las vacaciones los museos

► Use the construction a + [noun/pronoun] to clarify the person in question.

    A mí me encanta ver películas, ¿y a ti?

3 Remind students of the different positions for reflexive pronouns and the need for an infinitive after a phrase like **antes de** or a conjugated verb, such as **puedo**.

4 Have students create four additional sentences using the remaining indefinite and negative words from the word bank.

Game Play a game of **Diez Preguntas.** Ask a volunteer to think of a person in the class. Other students get one chance each to ask a question using indefinite and negative words. Ex: **¿Es alguien que siempre llega temprano a clase?**

4 **Conversaciones** Completa cada conversación de manera lógica con palabras de la lista. No tienes que usar todas las palabras. **8 pts.**

algo	nada	ningún	siempre
alguien	nadie	nunca	también
algún	ni... ni	o... o	tampoco

1. —¿Tienes __algún__ plan para esta noche?

   —No, prefiero quedarme en casa. Hoy no quiero ver a __nadie__.

   —Yo __también__ me quedo. Estoy muy cansado.

2. —¿Puedo entrar? ¿Hay __alguien__ en el cuarto de baño?

   —Sí. Ahora mismo salgo.

3. —¿Puedes prestarme __algo__ para peinarme? No encuentro __ni__ mi cepillo __ni__ mi peine.

   —Lo siento, yo __tampoco__ encuentro los míos (*mine*).

4. —¿Me prestas tu maquillaje?

   —Lo siento, no tengo. __Nunca__ me maquillo.

5 Remind students to use the personal **a** in their answers.

5 Give students these sentences as items 5–8:
5. yo / faltar / dinero (A mí me falta dinero.) 6. Pedro y yo / fascinar / cantar y bailar (A Pedro y a mí nos fascina cantar y bailar.)
7. usted / quedar / muy bien / esas gafas de sol (A usted le quedan muy bien esas gafas de sol.)
8. ¿ / ustedes / interesar / conocer / otros países / ? (¿A ustedes les interesa conocer otros países?)

5 **Oraciones** Forma oraciones completas con los elementos dados (*given*). Usa el presente de los verbos. **8 pts.**

1. David y Juan / molestar / levantarse temprano A David y a Juan les molesta levantarse temprano.
2. Lucía / encantar / las películas de terror A Lucía le encantan las películas de terror.
3. todos (nosotros) / importar / la educación A todos nos importa la educación.
4. tú / aburrir / ver / la televisión A ti te aburre ver la televisión.

6 **Rutinas** Escribe seis oraciones describiendo las rutinas de dos personas que conoces. **12 pts.**
Answers will vary.

> **modelo**
>
> Mi tía se despierta temprano, pero mi primo...

7 **Adivinanza** Completa la adivinanza con las palabras que faltan y adivina la respuesta. **¡2 puntos EXTRA!**

66 **Cuanto más°** __te seca__ (*it dries you*), **más se moja°.** 99
¿Qué es? __La toalla__

Cuanto más *The more* **se moja** *it gets wet*

recursos
SUPERSITE
adelante.vhlcentral.com

7 To challenge students, have them work in small groups to create a riddle using grammar and/or vocabulary from this lesson. Have groups share their riddles with the class.

Lectura

Antes de leer

Estrategia

Predicting content from the title

Prediction is an invaluable strategy in reading for comprehension. For example, we can usually predict the content of a newspaper article from its headline. We often decide whether to read the article based on its headline. Predicting content from the title will help you increase your reading comprehension in Spanish.

Examinar el texto

Lee el título de la lectura y haz tres predicciones sobre el contenido. Escribe tus predicciones en una hoja de papel.

Compartir

Comparte tus ideas con un(a) compañero/a de clase.

Cognados

Haz una lista de seis cognados que encuentres en la lectura. Answers will vary.

1. _____
2. _____
3. _____
4. _____
5. _____
6. _____

¿Qué te dicen los cognados sobre el tema de la lectura?

Teaching Tip Display or make up several cognate-rich headlines from Spanish newspapers and ask students to predict the content of each article. Ex: **Científicos anuncian que Plutón ya no es planeta. Decenas de miles recuerdan la explosión atómica en Hiroshima.**

¡Qué día!

Anterior ▼   ⬇ Siguiente ▼   ⬆ Responder   Responder a todos   Ree◄

Fecha: Lunes, 10 de mayo
De: Guillermo Zamora
Asunto: ¡Qué día!
Para: Lupe; Marcos; Sandra; Jorge

Hola, chicos:

La semana pasada me di cuenta° de que necesito organizar mejor° mi rutina... pero especialmente necesito prepararme mejor para los exámenes. Me falta mucha disciplina, me molesta no tener control de mi tiempo y nunca deseo repetir los eventos de la semana pasada.

El miércoles pasé todo el día y toda la noche estudiando para el examen de biología del jueves por la mañana. Me aburre la biología y no empecé a estudiar hasta el día antes del examen. El jueves a las 8, después de no dormir en toda la noche, fui exhausto al examen. Fue difícil, pero afortunadamente° me acordé de todo el material. Esa noche me acosté temprano y dormí mucho.

Me desperté a las 7, y fue extraño° ver a mi compañero de cuarto, Andrés, preparándose para ir a dormir. Como° siempre se enferma° y nunca

Extra Practice Ask students to skim the selection for verbs like **gustar**, then use **le** and **les** to rewrite the sentences in third person. Ex: **A Guillermo le aburre la biología.**

hablamos mucho, no le comenté nada. Fui al baño a cepillarme los dientes para ir a clase. ¿Y Andrés? Él se acostó. "Debe estar enfermo°, ¡otra vez!", pensé.

Mi clase es a las 8, y fue necesario hacer las cosas rápido. Todo empezó a ir mal... eso pasa siempre cuando uno tiene prisa. Cuando busqué mis cosas para el baño, no las encontré. Entonces me duché sin jabón, me cepillé los dientes sin cepillo de dientes y me peiné con las manos. Tampoco encontré ropa limpia, y usé la sucia. Rápido, tomé mis libros. ¿Y Andrés? Roncando°... ¡a las 7:50!

Cuando salí corriendo para la clase, la prisa no me permitió ver el campus desierto. Cuando llegué a la clase, no vi a nadie. No vi al profesor ni a los estudiantes. Por último miré mi reloj, y vi la hora. Las 8 en punto... ¡de la noche!

¡Dormí 24 horas!

Guillermo

me di cuenta *I realized* **mejor** *better* **afortunadamente** *fortunately* **extraño** *strange* **Como** *Since* **se enferma** *he gets sick* **enfermo** *sick* **Roncando** *Snoring*

Después de leer

Seleccionar

Selecciona la respuesta correcta.

1. ¿Quién es el/la narrador(a)? c
   a. Andrés
   b. una profesora
   c. Guillermo
2. ¿Qué le molesta al narrador? b
   a. Le molestan los exámenes de biología.
   b. Le molesta no tener control de su tiempo.
   c. Le molesta mucho organizar su rutina.
3. ¿Por qué está exhausto? c
   a. Porque fue a una fiesta la noche anterior.
   b. Porque no le gusta la biología.
   c. Porque pasó la noche anterior estudiando.
4. ¿Por qué no hay nadie en clase? a
   a. Porque es de noche.
   b. Porque todos están de vacaciones.
   c. Porque el profesor canceló la clase.
5. ¿Cómo es la relación de Guillermo y Andrés? b
   a. Son buenos amigos.
   b. No hablan mucho.
   c. Tienen una buena relación.

Ordenar

Ordena los sucesos de la narración. Utiliza los números del 1 al 9.

a. Toma el examen de biología. __2__
b. No encuentra sus cosas para el baño. __5__
c. Andrés se duerme. __7__
d. Pasa todo el día y toda la noche estudiando para un examen. __1__
e. Se ducha sin jabón. __6__
f. Se acuesta temprano. __3__
g. Vuelve a su cuarto a las 8 de la noche. __9__
h. Se despierta a las 7 y su compañero de cuarto se prepara para dormir. __4__
i. Va a clase y no hay nadie. __8__

Contestar

Contesta estas preguntas. Answers will vary.

1. ¿Cómo es tu rutina diaria? ¿Muy organizada?
2. ¿Cuándo empiezas a estudiar para los exámenes?
3. ¿Tienes compañero/a de cuarto? ¿Son amigos/as?
4. Para comunicarte con tus amigos/as, ¿prefieres el teléfono o el correo electrónico? ¿Por qué?

Perú

NATIONAL connections cultures STANDARDS

El país en cifras

▶ **Área:** 1.285.220 km² (496.224 millas²),
un poco menos que el área de Alaska

▶ **Población:** 30.063.000

▶ **Capital:** Lima—7.590.000

▶ **Ciudades principales:** Arequipa—915.000,
Trujillo, Chiclayo, Callao, Iquitos

SOURCE: Population Division, UN Secretariat

*Iquitos es un puerto muy importante en el río
Amazonas. Desde Iquitos se envían° muchos
productos a otros lugares, incluyendo goma°,
nueces°, madera°, arroz°, café y
tabaco. Iquitos es también un
destino popular para los ecoturistas
que visitan la selva°.*

▶ **Moneda:** nuevo sol

▶ **Idiomas:** español (oficial),
quechua (oficial), aimará

Bandera del Perú

Peruanos célebres

▶ **Clorinda Matto de Turner,** escritora (1854–1901)

▶ **César Vallejo,** poeta (1892–1938)

▶ **Javier Pérez de Cuéllar,** diplomático (1920–)

▶ **Mario Vargas Llosa,** escritor (1936–)

Mario Vargas Llosa

se envían *are shipped* **goma** *rubber* **nueces** *nuts* **madera** *timber*
arroz *rice* **selva** *jungle* **Hace más de...** *More than... ago* **grabó**
engraved **tamaño** *size*

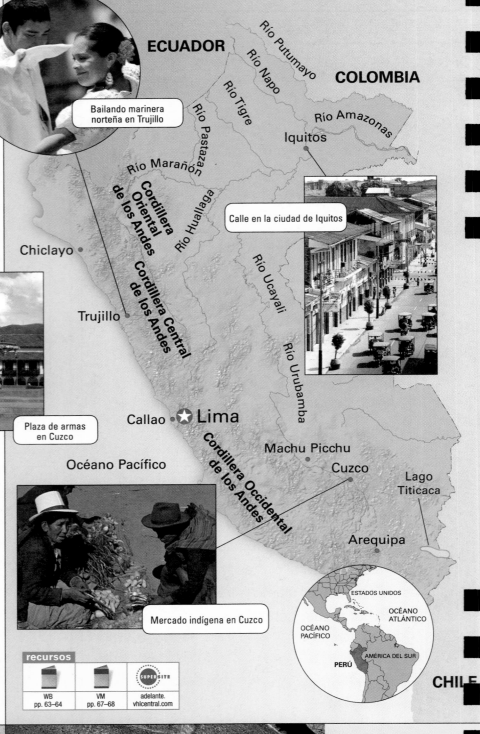

ECUADOR

COLOMBIA

Río Putumayo
Río Napo
Río Tigre
Río Pastaza
Río Amazonas

Iquitos

Río Marañón

Cordillera Oriental de los Andes

Río Huallaga

Cordillera Central de los Andes

Chiclayo

Río Ucayali

Río Urubamba

Bailando marinera
norteña en Trujillo

Calle en la ciudad de Iquitos

Trujillo

Plaza de armas
en Cuzco

Callao • ☆ Lima

Machu Picchu

Océano Pacífico

Cuzco

Lago Titicaca

Mercado indígena en Cuzco

Cordillera Occidental de los Andes

Arequipa

CHILE

ESTADOS UNIDOS
OCÉANO ATLÁNTICO
OCÉANO PACÍFICO
AMÉRICA DEL SUR
PERÚ

recursos

WB
pp. 63–64

VM
pp. 67–68

SUPERSITE
adelante.
vhlcentral.com

¡Increíble pero cierto!

Hace más de° dos mil años la civilización
nazca de Perú grabó° más de 2.000 kilómetros
de líneas en el desierto. Los dibujos sólo son
descifrables desde el aire. Uno de ellos es un
cóndor del tamaño° de un estadio. Las Líneas de
Nazca son uno de los grandes misterios de
la humanidad.

Lugares • Lima

Lima es una ciudad moderna y antigua° a la vez°. La Iglesia de San Francisco es notable por la influencia de la arquitectura barroca colonial. También son fascinantes las exhibiciones sobre los incas en el Museo Oro del Perú y en el Museo Nacional de Antropología y Arqueología. Barranco, el barrio° bohemio de la ciudad, es famoso por su ambiente cultural y sus bares y restaurantes.

BRASIL

Historia • Machu Picchu

A 80 kilómetros al noroeste de Cuzco está Machu Picchu, una ciudad antigua del imperio inca. Está a una altitud de 2.350 metros (7.710 pies), entre dos cimas° de los Andes. Cuando los españoles llegaron al Perú, nunca encontraron Machu Picchu. En 1911, el arqueólogo norteamericano Hiram Bingham la descubrió. Todavía no se sabe ni cómo se construyó° una ciudad a esa altura, ni por qué los incas la abandonaron. Sin embargo°, esta ciudad situada en desniveles° naturales es el ejemplo más conocido de la arquitectura inca.

Artes • La música andina

Machu Picchu aún no existía° cuando se originó la música cautivadora° de las antiguas culturas indígenas de los Andes. La influencia española y la música africana contribuyeron a la creación de los ritmos actuales de la música andina. Dos tipos de flauta°, la quena y la antara, producen esta música tan particular. En las décadas de los sesenta y los setenta se popularizó un movimiento para preservar la música andina, y hasta° Simon y Garfunkel la incorporaron en su repertorio con la canción *El cóndor pasa*.

Economía • Llamas y alpacas

El Perú se conoce por sus llamas, alpacas, guanacos y vicuñas, todos ellos animales mamíferos° parientes del camello. Estos animales todavía tienen una enorme importancia en la economía del país. Dan lana para hacer ropa, mantas°, bolsas y artículos para turistas. La llama se usa también para la carga y el transporte.

BOLIVIA

 ¿Qué aprendiste? Responde a cada pregunta con una oración completa.

1. ¿Qué productos envía Iquitos a otros lugares? Iquitos envía goma, nueces, madera, arroz, café y tabaco.
2. ¿Cuáles son las lenguas oficiales del Perú? Las lenguas oficiales del Perú son el español y el quechua.
3. ¿Por qué es notable la Iglesia de San Francisco en Lima? Es notable por la influencia de la arquitectura barroca colonial.
4. ¿Qué información sobre Machu Picchu no se sabe todavía? No se sabe ni cómo se construyó ni por qué la abandonaron.
5. ¿Qué son la quena y la antara? Son dos tipos de flauta.
6. ¿Qué hacen los peruanos con la lana de sus llamas y alpacas? Hacen ropa, mantas, bolsas y artículos para turistas.

 Conexión Internet Investiga estos temas en **adelante.vhlcentral.com**.

1. Investiga la cultura incaica. ¿Cuáles son algunos de los aspectos interesantes de su cultura?
2. Busca información sobre dos artistas, escritores o músicos peruanos y presenta un breve informe a tu clase.

....

antigua *old* a la vez *at the same time* barrio *neighborhood* cimas *summits* se construyó *was built* Sin embargo *However* desniveles *uneven pieces of land* aún no existía *didn't exist yet* cautivadora *captivating* flauta *flute* hasta *even* mamíferos *mammalian* mantas *blankets*

Supersite/DVD: You may want to wrap up this section by playing the *Panorama cultural* video footage for this lesson.

Variación léxica Point out familiar words that have entered both Spanish and English from the Quechua language. Ex: **el cóndor, la llama, el puma, la vicuña**

Los verbos reflexivos

acordarse (de) (o:ue)	to remember
acostarse (o:ue)	to go to bed
afeitarse	to shave
bañarse	to bathe; to take a bath
cepillarse el pelo	to brush one's hair
cepillarse los dientes	to brush one's teeth
despedirse (de) (e:i)	to say goodbye (to)
despertarse (e:ie)	to wake up
dormirse (o:ue)	to go to sleep; to fall asleep
ducharse	to shower; to take a shower
enojarse (con)	to get angry (with)
irse	to go away; to leave
lavarse la cara	to wash one's face
lavarse las manos	to wash one's hands
levantarse	to get up
llamarse	to be called; to be named
maquillarse	to put on makeup
peinarse	to comb one's hair
ponerse	to put on
ponerse (+ *adj.*)	to become (+ adj.)
preocuparse (por)	to worry (about)
probarse (o:ue)	to try on
quedarse	to stay; to remain
quitarse	to take off
secarse	to dry oneself
sentarse (e:ie)	to sit down
sentirse (e:ie)	to feel
vestirse (e:i)	to get dressed

Palabras de secuencia

antes (de)	before
después	afterwards; then
después (de)	after
durante	during
entonces	then
luego	then
más tarde	later (on)
por último	finally

Palabras afirmativas y negativas

algo	something; anything
alguien	someone; somebody; anyone
alguno/a(s), algún	some; any
jamás	never; not ever
nada	nothing; not anything
nadie	no one; nobody; not anyone
ni... ni	neither... nor
ninguno/a, ningún	no; none; not any
nunca	never; not ever
o... o	either... or
siempre	always
también	also; too
tampoco	neither; not either

En el baño

el baño, el cuarto de baño	bathroom
el champú	shampoo
la crema de afeitar	shaving cream
la ducha	shower
el espejo	mirror
el inodoro	toilet
el jabón	soap
el lavabo	sink
el maquillaje	makeup
la pasta de dientes	toothpaste
la toalla	towel

Verbos similares a gustar

aburrir	to bore
encantar	to like very much; to love (inanimate objects)
faltar	to lack; to need
fascinar	to fascinate; to like very much
importar	to be important to; to matter
interesar	to be interesting to; to interest
molestar	to bother; to annoy
quedar	to be left over; to fit (clothing)

Palabras adicionales

el despertador	alarm clock
las pantuflas	slippers
la rutina diaria	daily routine
por la mañana	in the morning
por la noche	at night
por la tarde	in the afternoon; in the evening

Expresiones útiles	See page 27.

Supersite/IRCD: MP3 Audio Files, Testing Program, *Vocabulario adicional*

contextos

1 **Las rutinas** Complete each sentence with a word from **Contextos**.

1. Susana se lava el pelo con _____champú_____.

2. La ducha y el lavabo están en el _____baño/cuarto de baño_____.

3. Manuel se lava las manos con _____jabón_____.

4. Después de lavarse las manos, usa la _____toalla_____.

5. Luis tiene un _____despertador_____ para levantarse temprano.

6. Elena usa el _____espejo_____ para maquillarse.

2 **¿En el baño o en la habitación?** Write **en el baño** or **en la habitación** to indicate where each activity takes place.

1. bañarse _____en el baño_____

2. levantarse _____en la habitación_____

3. ducharse _____en el baño_____

4. lavarse la cara _____en el baño_____

5. acostarse _____en la habitación_____

6. afeitarse _____en el baño_____

7. cepillarse los dientes _____en el baño_____

8. dormirse _____en la habitación_____

3 **Ángel y Lupe** Look at the drawings, and choose the appropriate phrase to describe what Ángel or Lupe are doing. Use complete sentences.

| afeitarse por la mañana | cepillarse los dientes después de comer |
| bañarse por la tarde | ducharse antes de salir |

1. Lupe se cepilla los dientes después de comer.

2. Ángel se afeita por la mañana.

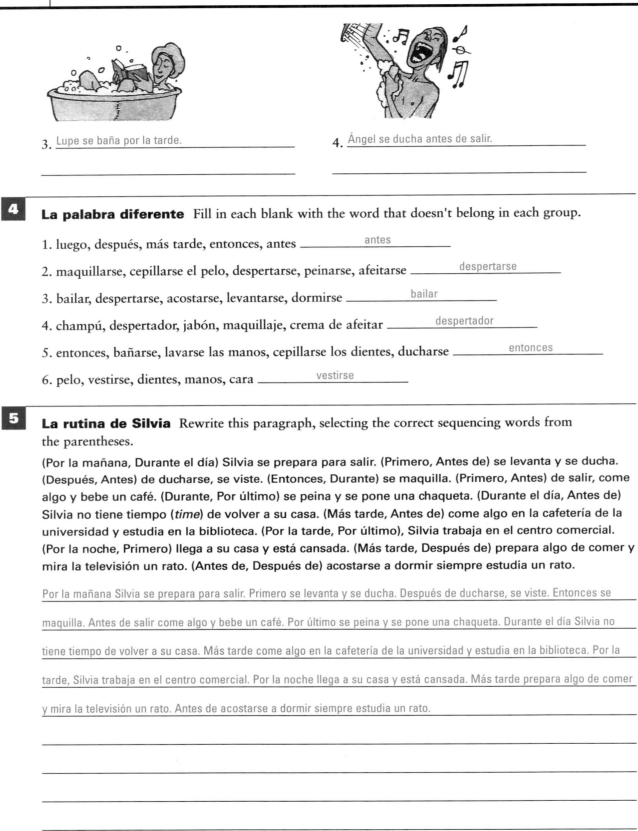

3. Lupe se baña por la tarde. _____

4. Ángel se ducha antes de salir. _____

_____

_____

4 **La palabra diferente** Fill in each blank with the word that doesn't belong in each group.

1. luego, después, más tarde, entonces, antes _____ antes _____

2. maquillarse, cepillarse el pelo, despertarse, peinarse, afeitarse _____ despertarse _____

3. bailar, despertarse, acostarse, levantarse, dormirse _____ bailar _____

4. champú, despertador, jabón, maquillaje, crema de afeitar _____ despertador _____

5. entonces, bañarse, lavarse las manos, cepillarse los dientes, ducharse _____ entonces _____

6. pelo, vestirse, dientes, manos, cara _____ vestirse _____

5 **La rutina de Silvia** Rewrite this paragraph, selecting the correct sequencing words from the parentheses.

(Por la mañana, Durante el día) Silvia se prepara para salir. (Primero, Antes de) se levanta y se ducha. (Después, Antes) de ducharse, se viste. (Entonces, Durante) se maquilla. (Primero, Antes) de salir, come algo y bebe un café. (Durante, Por último) se peina y se pone una chaqueta. (Durante el día, Antes de) Silvia no tiene tiempo (*time*) de volver a su casa. (Más tarde, Antes de) come algo en la cafetería de la universidad y estudia en la biblioteca. (Por la tarde, Por último), Silvia trabaja en el centro comercial. (Por la noche, Primero) llega a su casa y está cansada. (Más tarde, Después de) prepara algo de comer y mira la televisión un rato. (Antes de, Después de) acostarse a dormir siempre estudia un rato.

Por la mañana Silvia se prepara para salir. Primero se levanta y se ducha. Después de ducharse, se viste. Entonces se

maquilla. Antes de salir come algo y bebe un café. Por último se peina y se pone una chaqueta. Durante el día Silvia no

tiene tiempo de volver a su casa. Más tarde come algo en la cafetería de la universidad y estudia en la biblioteca. Por la

tarde, Silvia trabaja en el centro comercial. Por la noche llega a su casa y está cansada. Más tarde prepara algo de comer

y mira la televisión un rato. Antes de acostarse a dormir siempre estudia un rato.

_____

_____

_____

_____

estructura

1.1 Reflexive verbs

1 **Completar** Complete each sentence with the correct present tense forms of the verb in parentheses.

1. Marcos y Gustavo _____ se enojan _____ (enojarse) con Javier.

2. Mariela _____ se despide _____ (despedirse) de su amiga en la estación del tren.

3. (yo) _____ Me acuesto _____ (acostarse) temprano porque tengo clase por la mañana.

4. Los jugadores _____ se secan _____ (secarse) con toallas nuevas.

5. (tú) _____ Te preocupas _____ (preocuparse) por tu novio porque siempre pierde las cosas.

6. Usted _____ se lava _____ (lavarse) la cara con un jabón especial.

7. Mi mamá _____ se pone _____ (ponerse) muy contenta cuando llego temprano a casa.

2 **Lo hiciste** Answer the questions positively, using complete sentences.

1. ¿Te cepillaste los dientes después de comer?

Sí, me cepillé los dientes después de comer.

2. ¿Se maquilla Julia antes de salir a bailar?

Sí, Julia se maquilla antes de salir a bailar.

3. ¿Se duchan ustedes antes de nadar en la piscina?

Sí, nos duchamos antes de nadar en la piscina.

4. ¿Se ponen sombreros los turistas cuando van a la playa?

Sí, los turistas se ponen sombreros cuando van a la playa.

5. ¿Nos ponemos las pantuflas cuando llegamos a casa?

Sí, se ponen/nos ponemos las pantuflas cuando llegan/llegamos a casa.

3 **Terminar** Complete each sentence with the correct reflexive verbs. You may use some verbs more than once.

| acordarse | cepillarse | enojarse | maquillarse |
| acostarse | dormirse | levantarse | quedarse |

1. Mamá, no _____ te enojes _____ porque no tenemos que _____ levantarnos _____ temprano.

2. La profesora _____ se enoja _____ con nosotros cuando no _____ nos acordamos _____ de los verbos.

3. Mi hermano _____ se cepilla _____ los dientes cuando _____ se levanta _____.

4. Mis amigas y yo _____ nos quedamos _____ estudiando en la biblioteca por la noche y por la mañana _____ nos levantamos _____ muy cansadas.

5. Muchas noches _____ me duermo _____ delante del televisor, porque no quiero _____ acostarme _____.

4 **Escoger** Choose the correct verb from the parentheses, then fill in the blank with its correct form.

(lavar/lavarse)

1. Josefina ___se lava___ las manos en el lavabo.

   Josefina ___lava___ la ropa en casa de su madre.

(peinar/peinarse)

2. (yo) ___Peino___ a mi hermana todas las mañanas.

   (yo) ___Me peino___ en el baño, delante del espejo.

(poner/ponerse)

3. (nosotros) ___Nos ponemos___ nerviosos antes de un examen.

   (nosotros) ___Ponemos___ la toalla al lado de la ducha.

(levantar/levantarse)

4. Los estudiantes ___se levantan___ muy temprano.

   Los estudiantes ___levantan___ la mano y hacen preguntas.

5 **El incidente** Complete the paragraph with reflexive verbs from the word bank. Use each verb only once.

acordarse	irse	maquillarse	quedarse
afeitarse	lavarse	ponerse	secarse
despertarse	levantarse	preocuparse	sentarse
enojarse	llamarse	probarse	vestirse

Luis (1) ___se levanta/se despierta___ todos los días a las seis de la mañana. Luego entra en la

ducha y (2) ___se lava___ el pelo con champú. Cuando sale de la ducha, usa la crema de

afeitar para (3) ___afeitarse___ delante del espejo. Come algo con su familia y él y sus

hermanos (4) ___se quedan___ hablando un rato.

Cuando sale tarde, Luis (5) ___se preocupa___ porque no quiere llegar tarde a la clase de

español. Los estudiantes (6) ___se ponen___ nerviosos porque a veces (*sometimes*) tienen

pruebas sorpresa en la clase.

Ayer por la mañana, Luis (7) ___se enojó___ con su hermana Marina porque ella

(8) ___se levantó/se despertó___ tarde y pasó mucho tiempo en el cuarto de baño con la puerta cerrada.

—¿Cuándo sales, Marina? — le preguntó Luis.

—¡Tengo que (9) ___maquillarme___ porque voy a salir con mi novio y quiero estar bonita!

—dijo Marina.

—¡Tengo que (10) ___irme___ ya, Marina! ¿Cuándo terminas?

—Ahora salgo, Luis. Tengo que (11) ___vestirme___. Me voy a poner mi vestido favorito.

—Tienes que (12) ___acordarte___ de que viven muchas personas en esta casa, Marina.

1.2 Indefinite and negative words

1 **Alguno o ninguno** Complete the sentences with indefinite and negative words from the word bank.

alguien	algunas	ninguna
alguna	ningún	tampoco

1. No tengo ganas de ir a _____ ningún _____ lugar hoy.

2. ¿Tienes _____ algunas _____ ideas para la economía?

3. ¿Viene _____ alguien _____ a la fiesta de mañana?

4. No voy a _____ ningún _____ estadio nunca.

5. ¿Te gusta _____ alguna _____ de estas corbatas?

6. Jorge, tú no eres el único. Yo _____ tampoco _____ puedo ir de vacaciones.

2 **Estoy de mal humor** Your classmate Jaime is in a terrible mood. Complete his complaints with negative words.

1. No me gustan estas gafas. _____ No _____ quiero comprar _____ ninguna _____ de ellas.

2. Estoy muy cansado. _____ No _____ quiero ir a _____ ningún _____ restaurante.

3. No tengo hambre. _____ No _____ quiero comer _____ nada _____.

4. A mí no me gusta la playa. _____ No _____ quiero ir a la playa _____ nunca _____.

5. Soy muy tímido. _____ No _____ hablo con _____ nadie _____ nunca _____.

6. No me gusta el color rojo, _____ ni _____ el color rosado _____ tampoco _____.

3 **¡Amalia!** Your friend Amalia is chronically mistaken. Change her statements as necessary to correct her; each statement should be negative.

> **modelo**
>
> Buscaste algunos vestidos en la tienda.
> **No busqué ningún vestido en la tienda.**

1. Las dependientas venden algunas blusas.

   Las dependientas no venden ninguna blusa/ninguna.

2. Alguien va de compras al centro comercial.

   Nadie va de compras al centro comercial.

3. Siempre me cepillo los dientes antes de salir.

   Nunca te cepillas los dientes antes de salir.

4. Te voy a traer algún programa de la computadora.

   No me vas a traer ningún programa de la computadora/ninguno.

5. Mi hermano prepara algo de comer.

   Tu hermano no prepara nada de comer.

6. Quiero tomar algo en el café de la librería.

   No quieres tomar nada en el café de la librería.

4 **No, no es cierto** Now your friend Amalia realizes that she's usually wrong and is asking you for the correct information. Answer her questions negatively.

> **modelo**
> ¿Comes siempre en casa?
> No, nunca como en casa./No, no como en casa nunca.

1. ¿Tienes alguna falda?

   No, no tengo ninguna falda./no tengo ninguna.

2. ¿Sales siempre los fines de semana?

   No, nunca salgo los fines de semana./no salgo nunca los fines de semana.

3. ¿Quieres comer algo ahora?

   No, no quiero comer nada.

4. ¿Le prestaste algunos discos de jazz a César?

   No, no le presté ningún disco de jazz (a César)./no le presté ninguno (a César).

5. ¿Podemos ir a la playa o nadar en la piscina?

   No, no podemos ni ir a la playa ni nadar en la piscina.

6. ¿Encontraste algún cinturón barato en la tienda?

   No, no encontré ningún cinturón barato en la tienda./no encontré ninguno.

7. ¿Buscaron ustedes a alguien en la playa?

   No, no buscamos a nadie en la playa.

8. ¿Te gusta alguno de estos trajes?

   No, no me gusta ninguno de estos trajes./no me gusta ninguno.

5 **Lo opuesto** Rodrigo's good reading habits have changed since this description was written. Rewrite the paragraph, changing the positive words to negative ones.

Rodrigo siempre está leyendo algún libro. También lee el periódico. Siempre lee algo. Alguien le pregunta si leyó alguna novela de Mario Vargas Llosa. Leyó algunos libros de Vargas Llosa el año pasado. También leyó algunas novelas de Gabriel García Márquez. Siempre quiere leer o libros de misterio o novelas fantásticas.

Rodrigo nunca está leyendo ningún libro. Tampoco lee el periódico. Nunca lee nada. Nadie le pregunta si leyó una novela

de Mario Vargas Llosa. No leyó ningún libro de Vargas Llosa el año pasado. Tampoco leyó ninguna novela de Gabriel

García Márquez. Nunca quiere leer ni libros de misterio ni novelas fantásticas.

1.3 Preterite of **ser** and **ir**

1 **¿Ser o ir?** Complete the sentences with the preterite of **ser** or **ir**. Then write the infinitive form of the verb you used.

1. Ayer María y Javier _____fueron_____ a la playa con sus amigos. ____ir____

2. La película del sábado por la tarde _____fue_____ muy bonita. ____ser____

3. El fin de semana pasado (nosotros) _____fuimos_____ al centro comercial. ____ir____

4. La abuela y la tía de Maricarmen _____fueron_____ doctoras. ____ser____

5. (nosotros) _____Fuimos_____ muy simpáticos con la familia de Claribel. ____ser____

6. Manuel _____fue_____ a la universidad en septiembre. ____ir____

7. Los vendedores _____fueron_____ al almacén muy temprano. ____ir____

8. Lima _____fue_____ la primera parada (stop) de nuestro viaje. ____ser____

9. (yo) _____Fui_____ a buscarte a la cafetería, pero no te encontré. ____ir____

10. Mi compañera de cuarto _____fue_____ a la tienda a comprar champú. ____ir____

2 **Viaje a Perú** Complete the paragraph with the preterite of **ser** and **ir**. Then fill in the chart with infinitive form of the verbs you used.

El mes pasado mi amiga Clara y yo (1) _____fuimos_____ de vacaciones a Perú. El vuelo (flight) (2) _____fue_____ un miércoles por la mañana, y (3) _____fue_____ cómodo. Primero Clara y yo (4) _____fuimos_____ a Lima, y (5) _____fuimos_____ a comer a un restaurante de comida peruana. La comida (6) _____fue_____ muy buena. Luego (7) _____fuimos_____ al hotel y nos (8) _____fuimos_____ a dormir. El jueves (9) _____fue_____ un día nublado. Nos (10) _____fuimos_____ a Cuzco, y el viaje en autobús (11) _____fue_____ largo. Yo (12) _____fui_____ la primera en despertarme y ver la ciudad de Cuzco. Aquella mañana, el paisaje (13) _____fue_____ impresionante. Luego Clara y yo (14) _____fuimos_____ de excursión a Machu Picchu. El cuarto día nos levantamos muy temprano y (15) _____fuimos_____ a la ciudad inca. El amanecer sobre Machu Picchu (16) _____fue_____ hermoso. La excursión (17) _____fue_____ una experiencia inolvidable (unforgettable). ¿(18) _____Fuiste_____ tú a Perú el año pasado?

1. ir	7. ir	13. ser
2. ser	8. ir	14. ir
3. ser	9. ser	15. ir
4. ir	10. ir	16. ser
5. ir	11. ser	17. ser
6. ser	12. ser	18. ir

1.4 Verbs like **gustar**

1 **La fotonovela** Rewrite each sentence, choosing the correct form of the verb in parentheses.

1. Maite, te (quedan, queda) bien las faldas y los vestidos.

   Maite, te quedan bien las faldas y los vestidos.

2. A Inés y a Álex no les (molesta, molestan) la lluvia.

   A Inés y a Álex no les molesta la lluvia.

3. A los chicos no les (importa, importan) ir de compras.

   A los chicos no les importa ir de compras.

4. A don Francisco y a Álex les (aburre, aburren) probarse ropa en las tiendas.

   A don Francisco y Álex les aburre probarse ropa en las tiendas.

5. A Maite le (fascina, fascinan) las tiendas y los almacenes.

   A Maite le fascinan las tiendas y los almacenes.

6. A Javier le (falta, faltan) dos años para terminar la carrera (*degree*).

   A Javier le faltan dos años para terminar la carrera.

7. A los chicos les (encanta, encantan) pescar y nadar en el mar.

   A los chicos les encanta pescar y nadar en el mar.

8. A Inés le (interesan, interesa) la geografía.

   A Inés le interesa la geografía.

2 **Nos gusta el fútbol** Complete the paragraph with the correct forms of the verbs in parentheses.

A mi familia le (1) _____ fascina _____ (fascinar) el fútbol. A mis hermanas les

(2) _____ encantan _____ (encantar) los jugadores porque son muy guapos. También les

(3) _____ gusta _____ (gustar) la emoción (*excitement*) de los partidos. A mi papá le

(4) _____ interesan _____ (interesar) mucho los partidos y cuando puede los sigue por Internet.

A mi mamá le (5) _____ molesta _____ (molestar) nuestra afición porque no hacemos las tareas

de la casa cuando hay un partido. A ella generalmente le (6) _____ aburren _____ (aburrir) los

partidos. Pero cuando le (7) _____ falta _____ (faltar) un gol al equipo argentino para ganar,

le (8) _____ encantan _____ (encantar) los minutos finales del partido.

3 **El viaje** You and your friend are packing and planning your upcoming vacation to the Caribbean. Rewrite her sentences, substituting the subject with the one in parentheses.

1. Te quedan bien los vestidos largos. (la blusa cara)

   Te queda bien la blusa cara.

2. Les molesta la música estadounidense. (las canciones populares)

   Les molestan las canciones populares.

3. ¿No te interesa aprender a bailar salsa? (nadar)

   ¿No te interesa nadar/aprender a nadar?

4. Les encantan las tiendas. (el centro comercial)

   Les encanta el centro comercial.

5. Nos falta practicar el español. (unas semanas de clase)

   Nos faltan unas semanas de clase.

6. No les importa esperar un rato. (buscar unos libros nuestros)

   No les importa buscar unos libros nuestros.

4 **¿Qué piensan?** Complete the sentences with the correct pronouns and forms of the verbs in parentheses.

1. A mí _____me encantan_____ (encantar) las películas de misterio.

2. A Gregorio _____le molestan_____ (molestar) mucho la nieve y el frío.

3. A ustedes _____les falta_____ (faltar) un libro de esa colección.

4. ¿_____Te quedan_____ (quedar) bien los sombreros a ti?

5. A ella no _____le importan_____ (importar) las apariencias (*appearances*).

6. Los deportes por televisión a mí _____me aburren_____ (aburrir) mucho.

5 **Mi rutina diaria** Answer these questions about your daily routine, using verbs like gustar in complete sentences. Answers will vary.

1. ¿Te molesta levantarte temprano durante la semana?

   _____

2. ¿Qué te interesa hacer por las mañanas?

   _____

3. ¿Te importa despertarte temprano los fines de semana?

   _____

4. ¿Qué te encanta hacer los domingos?

   _____

Síntesis

Interview a friend or relative about an interesting vacation he or she took. Then gather the answers into a report. Answer the following questions:

- What did he or she like or love about the vacation? What interested him or her?
- Where did he or she stay, what were the accommodations like, and what was his or her daily routine like during the trip?
- Where did he or she go, what were the tours like, what were the tour guides like, and what were his or her travelling companions like?
- What bothered or angered him or her? What bored him or her during the vacation?

Be sure to address both the negative and positive aspects of the vacation. Answers will vary.

_____

_____

_____

_____

_____

_____

_____

_____

_____

_____

_____

_____

_____

_____

_____

_____

_____

_____

_____

_____

_____

_____

_____

_____

panorama

Perú

1   **Datos de Perú**   Complete the sentences with the correct words.

1. _____Lima_____ es la capital de Perú y _____Arequipa_____ es la segunda ciudad.

2. _____Iquitos_____ es un puerto muy importante del río Amazonas.

3. El barrio bohemio de la ciudad de Lima se llama _____Barranco_____.

4. Hiram Bingham descubrió las ruinas de _____Machu Picchu_____ en los Andes.

5. Las llamas, alpacas, guanacos y vicuñas son parientes del _____camello_____.

6. Las Líneas de _____Nazca_____ son uno de los grandes misterios de la humanidad.

2   **Perú**   Fill in the blanks with the names and places described. Then use the word in the vertical box to answer the final question.

1. barrio bohemio de Lima
2. animales que se usan para carga y transporte
3. en Perú se habla este idioma
4. capital de Perú
5. montañas de Perú
6. dirección de Machu Picchu desde Cuzco

7. puerto del río Amazonas
8. animales que dan lana
9. esta civilización peruana dibujó líneas
10. profesión de César Vallejo

¿Por dónde se llega caminando a Machu Picchu?

Se llega por el _____Se llega por el Camino Inca._____.

1.B	a	r	r	a	n	**c**	o
2.l	l	a	m	**a**	s		
3.a	i	m	a	**r**	á		
4.L	i	m	**a**				
5.A	n	d	**e**	s			
6.n	o	r	**o**	e	s	t	e

7.I	q	u	**i**	t	o	s
8.g	u	a	**n**	a	c	o	s
9.n	a	z	**c**	a		
10.p	o	e	**t**	a		

3   **Ciudades peruanas**   Fill in the blanks with the names of the appropriate cities in Peru.

1. ciudad al sureste de Cuzco _____Arequipa_____

2. se envían productos por el Amazonas _____Iquitos_____

3. Museo del Oro de Perú _____Lima_____

4. está a 80 km de Machu Picchu _____Cuzco_____

5. ciudad antigua del imperio inca _____Machu Picchu_____

4 **¿Cierto o falso?** Indicate whether each statement is **cierto** or **falso**. Correct the false statements.

1. Machu Picchu es un destino popular para los ecoturistas que visitan la selva.

   Falso. Iquitos es un destino popular para los ecoturistas que visitan la selva.

2. Mario Vargas Llosa es un novelista peruano famoso.

   Cierto.

3. La Iglesia de San Francisco es notable por la influencia de la arquitectura árabe.

   Falso. La Iglesia de San Francisco es notable por la influencia de la arquitectura barroca colonial.

4. Las ruinas de Machu Picchu están en la cordillera de los Andes.

   Cierto.

5. Las llamas se usan para la carga y el transporte en Perú.

   Cierto.

6. La civilización inca hizo dibujos que sólo son descifrables desde el aire.

   Falso. La civilización nazca hizo dibujos que sólo son descifrables desde el aire.

5 **El mapa de Perú** Label the map of Peru.

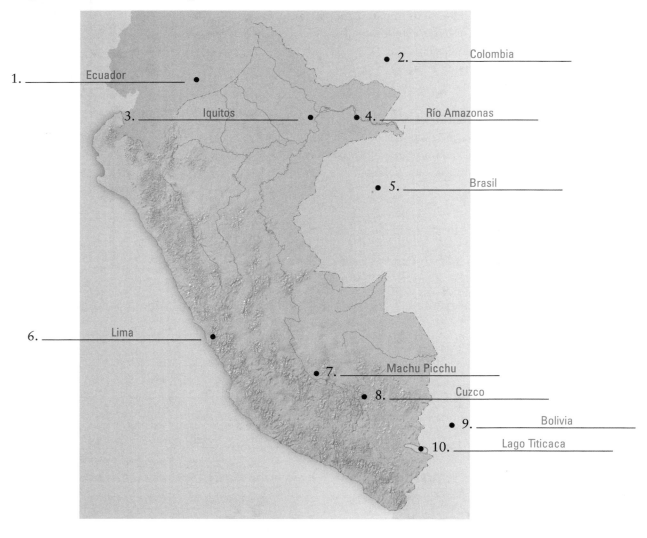

1. _____ Ecuador

2. _____ Colombia

3. _____ Iquitos

4. _____ Río Amazonas

5. _____ Brasil

6. _____ Lima

7. _____ Machu Picchu

8. _____ Cuzco

9. _____ Bolivia

10. _____ Lago Titicaca

¡Jamás me levanto temprano!

Lección 1
Fotonovela

Antes de ver el video

1 **La rutina diaria** In this video module, Javier and Álex chat about their morning routines. What kinds of things do you think they will mention? Answers will vary.

_____
_____
_____
_____
_____
_____
_____
_____

Mientras ves el video

2 **¿Álex o Javier?** Watch the **¡Jamás me levanto temprano!** segment of this video module and put a check mark in the appropriate column to indicate whether each activity is part of the daily routine of Álex or Javier.

Actividad	Álex	Javier
1. levantarse tarde		x
2. dibujar por la noche		x
3. despertarse a las seis	x	
4. correr por la mañana	x	
5. escuchar música por la noche		x

3 **Ordenar** Watch Álex's flashback about his daily routine and indicate in what order he does the following things.

__3__ a. ducharse   __1__ d. despertarse a las seis

__6__ b. vestirse   __5__ e. afeitarse

__2__ c. levantarse temprano   __4__ f. cepillarse los dientes

4 **Resumen** Watch the **Resumen** segment of this video module and fill in the missing words in these sentences.

1. **JAVIER** Álex no sólo es mi _____ amigo _____ sino mi despertador.

2. **ÁLEX** Me gusta _____ levantarme _____ temprano.

3. **ÁLEX** Vuelvo, me ducho, _____ me visto _____ y a las siete y media te _____ despierto _____.

4. **JAVIER** Hoy _____ fui _____ a un mercado al aire libre con Inés.

5. **ÁLEX** _____ Me _____ levanto a las siete menos cuarto y _____ corro _____ por treinta minutos.

Después de ver el video

5 **Preguntas** In Spanish, answer these questions about the video module.

1. ¿Qué está haciendo Álex cuando vuelve Javier del mercado?
   Álex está leyendo su correo electrónico cuando vuelve Javier del mercado.

2. ¿Le gusta a Álex el suéter que compró Javier?
   Sí. Álex piensa que es ideal para las montañas.

3. ¿Por qué Javier no puede despertarse por la mañana?
   Javier no puede despertarse por la mañana porque no duerme por la noche.

4. ¿A qué hora va a levantarse Álex mañana?
   Álex va a levantarse a las siete menos cuarto.

5. ¿A qué hora sale el autobús mañana?
   El autobús sale a las ocho y media.

6. ¿Dónde está la crema de afeitar?
   La crema de afeitar está en el baño.

6 **Preguntas personales** Answer these questions in Spanish. Answers will vary.

1. ¿A qué hora te levantas durante la semana? ¿Y los fines de semana?
   _____
   _____

2. ¿Prefieres acostarte tarde o temprano? ¿Por qué?
   _____
   _____

3. ¿Te gusta más bañarte o ducharte? ¿Por qué?
   _____
   _____

4. ¿Cuántas veces por día (*How many times a day*) te cepillas los dientes?
   _____
   _____

5. ¿Te lavas el pelo todos los días (*every day*)? ¿Por qué?
   _____

7 **Tus vacaciones** In Spanish, describe your morning routine when you are on vacation. Answers will vary.

_____
_____
_____
_____
_____

Panorama: Perú

Antes de ver el video

1 **Más vocabulario** Look over these useful words and expressions before you watch the video.

Vocabulario útil		
canoa *canoe*	**exuberante naturaleza**	**ruta** *route, path*
dunas *sand dunes*	*lush countryside*	**tabla** *board*

2 **Preferencias** In this video you are going to learn about unusual sports. In preparation for watching the video, answer these questions about your interest in sports. Answers will vary.

1. ¿Qué deportes practicas?

_____

2. ¿Dónde los practicas?

_____

3. ¿Qué deportes te gusta ver en televisión?

_____

Mientras ves el video

3 **Fotos** Describe the video stills. Write at least three sentences in Spanish for each still. Answers will vary.

_____
_____
_____
_____
_____
_____

_____
_____
_____
_____
_____

Después de ver el video

4 **¿Cierto o falso?** Indicate whether each statement is **cierto** or **falso**. Correct the false statements.

1. Pachamac es el destino favorito para los que pasean en bicicletas de montaña.

   Cierto.

2. El *sandboard* es un deporte antiguo de Perú.

   Falso. El sandboard es un deporte nuevo de Perú.

3. El *sandboard* se practica en Ocucaje porque en este lugar hay muchos parques.

   Falso. El sandboard se practica en Ocucaje porque allí hay grandes dunas.

4. El Camino Inca termina en Machu Picchu.

   Cierto.

5. El Camino Inca se puede completar en dos horas.

   Falso. El camino Inca se puede completar en tres o cuatro días.

6. La pesca en pequeñas canoas es un deporte tradicional.

   Cierto.

5 **Completar** Complete the sentences with words from the word bank.

aventura	kilómetros	pesca
excursión	llamas	restaurante
exuberante	parque	tradicional

1. En Perú se practican muchos deportes de _____aventura_____.

2. Pachamac está a 31 _____kilómetros_____ de Lima.

3. La naturaleza en Santa Cruz es muy _____exuberante_____.

4. En Perú, uno de los deportes más antiguos es la _____pesca_____ en pequeñas canoas.

5. Caminar con _____llamas_____ es uno de los deportes tradicionales en Perú.

6. Santa Cruz es un sitio ideal para ir de _____excursión_____.

6 **Escribir** Imagine that you just completed the **Camino Inca** in the company of a nice llama. Write a short letter to a friend in Spanish telling him or her about the things you did and saw. Answers will vary.

_____

_____

_____

_____

_____

contextos

1 **Describir** For each drawing, you will hear two statements. Choose the one that corresponds to the drawing.

1. a.   (b.)   2. a.   (b.)

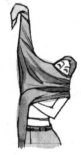

3. (a.)   b.   4. (a.)   b.

2 **Preguntas** Clara is going to baby-sit your nephew. Answer her questions about your nephew's daily routine using the cues in your lab manual. Repeat the correct response after the speaker.

> **modelo**
> *You hear:* ¿A qué hora va a la escuela?
> *You see:* 8:30 A.M.
> *You say:* Va a la escuela a las *ocho* y *media de la mañana.*

1. 7:00 A.M.
2. se lava la cara
3. por la noche

4. champú para niños
5. 9:00 P.M.
6. después de comer

3 **Entrevista** Listen to this interview. Then read the statements in your lab manual and decide whether they are **cierto** or **falso**.

	Cierto	Falso
1. Sergio Santos es jugador de fútbol.	○	☑
2. Sergio se levanta a las 5:00 A.M.	○	☑
3. Sergio se ducha por la mañana y por la noche.	☑	○
4. Sergio se acuesta a las 11:00 P.M.	☑	○

pronunciación

The consonant r

In Spanish, **r** has a strong trilled sound at the beginning of a word. No English words have a trill, but English speakers often produce a trill when they imitate the sound of a motor.

ropa	**r**utina	**r**ico	**R**amón

In any other position, **r** has a weak sound similar to the English *tt* in *better* or the English *dd* in *ladder*. In contrast to English, the tongue touches the roof of the mouth behind the teeth.

gusta**r**	du**r**ante	p**r**imero	c**r**ema

The letter combination **rr**, which only appears between vowels, always has a strong trilled sound.

piza**rr**a	co**rr**o	ma**rr**ón	abu**rr**ido

Between vowels, the difference between the strong trilled **rr** and the weak **r** is very important, as a mispronunciation could lead to confusion between two different words.

ca**r**o	ca**rr**o	pe**r**o	pe**rr**o

1 **Práctica** Repeat each word after the speaker, to practice the **r** and the **rr**.

1. Perú
2. Rosa
3. borrador
4. madre
5. comprar
6. favor
7. rubio
8. reloj
9. Arequipa
10. tarde
11. cerrar
12. despertador

2 **Oraciones** When you hear the number, read the corresponding sentence aloud, focusing on the **r** and **rr** sounds. Then listen to the speaker and repeat the sentence.

1. Ramón Robles Ruiz es programador. Su esposa Rosaura es artista.
2. A Rosaura Robles le encanta regatear en el mercado.
3. Ramón nunca regatea… le aburre regatear.
4. Rosaura siempre compra cosas baratas.
5. Ramón no es rico pero prefiere comprar cosas muy caras.
6. ¡El martes Ramón compró un carro nuevo!

3 **Refranes** Repeat each saying after the speaker to practice the **r** and the **rr**.

1. Perro que ladra no muerde.
2. No se ganó Zamora en una hora.

4 **Dictado** You will hear seven sentences. Each will be said twice. Listen carefully and write what you hear.

1. Ramiro y Roberta Torres son peruanos.
2. Ramiro es pelirrojo, gordo y muy trabajador.
3. Hoy él quiere jugar al golf y descansar, pero Roberta prefiere ir de compras.
4. Hay grandes rebajas y ella necesita un regalo para Ramiro.
5. ¿Debe comprarle una cartera marrón o un suéter rojo?
6. Por la tarde, Ramiro abre su regalo.
7. Es ropa interior.

estructura

1.1 Reflexive verbs

1 **Describir** For each drawing, you will hear two statements. Choose the one that corresponds to the drawing.

1. (a.)   b.   2. a.   (b.)

3. (a.)   b.   4. a.   (b.)

2 **Preguntas** Answer each question you hear in the affirmative. Repeat the correct response after the speaker. (*7 items*)

> **modelo**
>
> ¿Se levantó temprano Rosa?
> Sí, Rosa se levantó temprano.

3 **¡Esto fue el colmo! (*The last straw!*)** Listen as Julia describes what happened in her dorm yesterday. Then choose the correct ending for each statement in your lab manual.

1. Julia se ducha en cinco minutos porque...
   a. siempre se levanta tarde.   (b.) las chicas de su piso comparten un cuarto de baño.
2. Ayer la chica nueva...
   (a.) se quedó dos horas en el baño.   b. se preocupó por Julia.
3. Cuando salió, la chica nueva...
   a. se enojó mucho.   (b.) se sintió (*felt*) avergonzada.

1.2 Indefinite and negative words

1 **¿Lógico o ilógico?** You will hear some questions and the responses. Decide if they are **lógico** or **ilógico**.

	Lógico	Ilógico			Lógico	Ilógico
1.	○	⦿	5.		⦿	○
2.	⦿	○	6.		○	⦿
3.	⦿	○	7.		⦿	○
4.	○	⦿	8.		⦿	○

2 **¿Pero o sino?** You will hear some sentences with a beep in place of a word. Decide if **pero** or **sino** should complete each sentence and circle it.

> **modelo**
> *You hear:* Ellos no viven en Lima (*beep*) en Arequipa.
> *You circle:* sino because the sentence is Ellos no viven en
> Lima sino en Arequipa.

1.	pero (sino)	5.	(pero) sino
2.	(pero) sino	6.	pero (sino)
3.	pero (sino)	7.	(pero) sino
4.	pero (sino)	8.	(pero) sino

3 **Transformar** Change each sentence you hear to say the opposite is true. Repeat the correct answer after the speaker. (*6 items*)

> **modelo**
> Nadie se ducha ahora.
> Alguien se ducha ahora.

4 **Preguntas** Answer each question you hear in the negative. Repeat the correct response after the speaker. (*6 items*)

> **modelo**
> ¿Qué estás haciendo?
> No estoy haciendo nada.

5 **Entre amigos** Listen to this conversation between Felipe and Mercedes. Then decide whether the statements in your lab manual are **cierto** or **falso**.

		Cierto	Falso
1.	No hay nadie en la residencia.	⦿	○
2.	Mercedes quiere ir al Centro Estudiantil.	⦿	○
3.	Felipe tiene un amigo peruano.	○	⦿
4.	Mercedes no visitó ni Machu Picchu ni Cuzco.	⦿	○
5.	Felipe nunca visitó el Perú.	⦿	○

1.3 Preterite of **ser** and **ir**

1 **Escoger** Listen to each sentence and indicate whether the verb is a form of **ser** or **ir**.

1. ser (ir)
2. (ser) ir
3. ser (ir)
4. ser (ir)

5. ser (ir)
6. (ser) ir
7. (ser) ir
8. ser (ir)

2 **Cambiar** Change each sentence from the present to the preterite. Repeat the correct answer after the speaker. (*8 items*)

> **modelo**
> Ustedes van en avión.
> **Ustedes fueron en avión.**

3 **Preguntas** Answer each question you hear using the cue in your lab manual. Repeat the correct response after the speaker.

> **modelo**
> *You hear:* ¿Quién fue tu profesor de química?
> *You see:* el señor Ortega
> *You say:* El señor Ortega fue mi profesor de química.

1. al mercado al aire libre
2. muy buenas
3. no

4. fabulosa
5. al parque
6. difícil

4 **¿Qué hicieron (*did they do*) anoche?** Listen to this telephone conversation and answer the questions in your lab manual.

1. ¿Adónde fue Carlos anoche?

   Carlos fue al estadio.

2. ¿Cómo fue el partido? ¿Por qué?

   El partido fue estupendo porque su equipo favorito ganó.

3. ¿Adónde fueron Katarina y Esteban anoche?

   Katarina y Esteban fueron al cine.

4. Y Esteban, ¿qué hizo (*did he do*) allí?

   Esteban se durmió durante la película.

1.4 Verbs like **gustar**

1 **Escoger** Listen to each question and choose the most logical response.

1. (a.) Sí, me gusta.   b. Sí, te gusta.
2. (a.) No, no le interesa.   b. No, no le interesan.
3. (a.) Sí, les molestan mucho.   b. No, no les molesta mucho.
4. (a.) No, no nos importa.   b. No, no les importa.
5. a. Sí, le falta.   (b.) Sí, me falta.
6. a. Sí, les fascina.   (b.) No, no les fascinan.

2 **Cambiar** Form a new sentence using the cue you hear. Repeat the correct answer after the speaker. (*6 items*)

modelo

A ellos les interesan las ciencias. (a Ricardo)
A Ricardo le interesan las ciencias.

3 **Preguntas** Answer each question you hear using the cue in your lab manual. Repeat the correct response after the speaker.

modelo

You hear: ¿Qué te encanta hacer?
You see: patinar en línea
You say: Me encanta patinar en línea.

1. la familia y los amigos   4. $2,00   7. no / nada
2. sí   5. el baloncesto y el béisbol   8. sí
3. las computadoras   6. no

4 **Preferencias** Listen to this conversation. Then fill in the chart with Eduardo's preferences and answer the question in your lab manual.

Le gusta	No le gusta
nadar (la natación)	el tenis
ir de excursión al campo	el sol
el cine	ir de compras

¿Qué van a hacer los chicos esta tarde? Los chicos van a quedarse/se van a quedar en casa esta tarde.

vocabulario

You will now hear the vocabulary found in your worktext on the last page of this lesson. Listen and repeat each Spanish word or phrase after the speaker.

Additional Vocabulary

Additional Vocabulary

Notes

Notes

La comida

2

Communicative Goals

You will learn how to:
- **Order food in a restaurant**
- **Talk about and describe food**

La comida

Más vocabulario

el/la camarero/a	waiter/waitress
la comida	food; meal
el/la dueño/a	owner; landlord
los entremeses	hors d'oeuvres; appetizers
el menú	menu
el plato (principal)	(main) dish
la sección de (no) fumar	(non) smoking section
el agua (mineral)	(mineral) water
la bebida	drink
la cerveza	beer
la leche	milk
el refresco	soft drink
el ajo	garlic
las arvejas	peas
los cereales	cereal; grain
los frijoles	beans
el melocotón	peach
el pollo (asado)	(roast) chicken
el queso	cheese
el sándwich	sandwich
el yogur	yogurt
el aceite	oil
la margarina	margarine
la mayonesa	mayonnaise
el vinagre	vinegar
delicioso/a	delicious
sabroso/a	tasty; delicious
saber	to taste; to know
saber a	to taste like

Variación léxica

camarones	⟷	gambas (*Esp.*)
camarero	⟷	mesero (*Amér. L.*), mesonero (*Ven.*), mozo (*Arg., Chile, Urug., Perú*)
refresco	⟷	gaseosa (*Amér. C., Amér. S.*)

Las frutas — la pera, la banana, las uvas, la naranja, el limón

Las verduras — la lechuga, la cebolla, el maíz, el champiñón, la zanahoria, el tomate

Supersite/IRCD: Lesson Plans, MP3 Audio Files and Listening Scripts, Overheads, *Vocabulario adicional*

recursos

WB pp. 109–110	LM p. 125	adelante. vhlcentral.com

Heritage Speakers Ask heritage speakers to share regional variations in food-related vocabulary. Ex: **el guisante, el banano, el cambur, el hongo, la habichuela, la patata.**

1 2 Supersite/IRCD: MP3 Audio Files, Scripts

Práctica

Lección 2

1

Escuchar Indica si las oraciones que vas a escuchar son **ciertas** o **falsas**, según el dibujo. Después, corrige las falsas.

1. Cierta.
2. Falsa. El hombre compra una naranja.
3. Cierta.
4. Falsa. El pollo es una carne y la zanahoria es una verdura.
5. Cierta.
6. Falsa. El hombre y la mujer no compran vinagre.
7. Falsa. La naranja es una fruta.
8. Falsa. La chuleta de cerdo es una carne.
9. Falsa. El limón es una fruta y el jamón es una carne.
10. Cierta.

2

Seleccionar Paulino y Pilar van a cenar a un restaurante. Escucha la conversación y selecciona la respuesta que mejor completa cada oración.

1. Paulino le pide el ___menú___ (menú / plato) al camarero.
2. El plato del día es (atún / salmón) ___atún___.
3. Pilar ordena ___agua mineral___ (leche / agua mineral) para beber.
4. Paulino quiere un refresco de ___naranja___ (naranja / limón).
5. Paulino hoy prefiere ___la chuleta___ (el salmón / la chuleta).
6. Dicen que la carne en ese restaurante es muy ___sabrosa___ (sabrosa / mal).
7. Pilar come salmón con ___zanahorias___ (zanahorias / champiñones).

3

Identificar Identifica la palabra que no está relacionada con cada grupo.

1. champiñón • cebolla • banana • zanahoria banana
2. camarones • ajo • atún • salmón ajo
3. aceite • leche • refresco • agua mineral aceite
4. jamón • chuleta de cerdo • vinagre • carne de res vinagre
5. cerveza • lechuga • arvejas • frijoles cerveza
6. carne • pescado • mariscos • camarero camarero
7. pollo • naranja • limón • melocotón pollo
8. maíz • queso • tomate • champiñón queso

4

Completar Completa las oraciones con las palabras más lógicas.

1. ¡Me gusta mucho este plato! Sabe __b__.
   a. feo b. delicioso c. antipático
2. Camarero, ¿puedo ver el __c__, por favor?
   a. aceite b. maíz c. menú
3. Carlos y yo bebemos siempre agua __b__.
   a. cómoda b. mineral c. principal
4. El plato del día es __a__.
   a. el pollo asado b. la mayonesa c. el ajo
5. Margarita es vegetariana. Ella come __a__.
   a. frijoles b. chuletas c. jamón
6. Mi hermana le da __c__ a su niña.
   a. ajo b. vinagre c. yogur

SUPERSITE

Game Play a modified version of **20 Preguntas**. Ask a volunteer to think of a food item from the vocabulary list or illustration. Other students get one chance each to ask a yes-no question until someone guesses the item.

el desayuno

Teaching Tips
• Ask students to name their favorite foods for each of the three meals. Introduce additional items as necessary (Ex: **la pizza, los espaguetis**).

el jugo (de fruta)
el café
el pan (tostado)
el azúcar
la mantequilla
la salchicha
el huevo

el almuerzo

• Point out that in Spanish-speaking countries, lunch (also called **la comida**) is usually the main meal of the day. **La cena** is typically much lighter than **el almuerzo**.

el té helado
la manzana
la hamburguesa
el pan
las papas/patatas fritas

• At this point you may want to present *Vocabulario adicional: Más vocabulario relacionado con la comida* (Supersite/IRCD).

Más vocabulario

escoger	*to choose*
merendar (e:ie)	*to snack*
probar (o:ue)	*to taste; to try*
recomendar (e:ie)	*to recommend*
servir (e:i)	*to serve*
el té	*tea*
el vino blanco	*white wine*

la cena

• For expansion, discuss favorite desserts (**postres**) and snacks (**meriendas**). Introduce new terms as needed (Ex: **el helado, el pastel, las galletas**).

la sal
el vino tinto
la pimienta
la sopa
la ensalada
el arroz
los espárragos
el bistec

SUPERSITE

Extra Practice Add an auditory aspect to this vocabulary presentation. Prepare descriptions of five to seven different meals, with a mix of breakfasts, lunches, and dinners. As you read each description aloud, have students write down what you say as a dictation and then guess the meal it describes.

5 Get students to talk about what they eat. Ex: **¿Comen ustedes carne sólo una vez a la semana o menos? ¿Qué comidas comen ustedes dos o más veces al día?**

5 Ask students if they know which food groups and food products comprise the food pyramid used in this country. If you can get a copy of one, bring it to class and have student compare similarities and differences between the dietary requirements.

Extra Practice Have students draw food pyramids based not on what they should eat, but on what they actually do eat as part of their diet. Encourage them to include drawings or magazine cutouts to enhance the visual presentation. Then have students present their pyramids to the class.

5

Completar Trabaja con un(a) compañero/a de clase para relacionar cada producto con el grupo alimenticio (*food group*) correcto.

modelo

____La carne____ es del grupo uno.

el aceite	las bananas	los cereales	la leche
el arroz	el café	los espárragos	el pescado
el azúcar	la carne	los frijoles	el vino

1. ____La leche____ y el queso son del grupo cuatro.
2. ____Los frijoles____ son del grupo ocho.
3. ____El pescado____ y el pollo son del grupo tres.
4. ____El aceite____ es del grupo cinco.
5. ____El azúcar____ es del grupo dos.
6. Las manzanas y ____las bananas____ son del grupo siete.
7. ____El café____ es del grupo seis.
8. ____Los cereales____ son del grupo diez.
9. ____Los espárragos____ y los tomates son del grupo nueve.
10. El pan y ____el arroz____ son del grupo diez.

5 Ask follow-up questions about the food pyramid. Ex: **¿Qué se debe comer todos los días? ¿Cuáles son los productos que aparecen en el grupo cuatro? ¿Y en el grupo siete?**

Lección 2

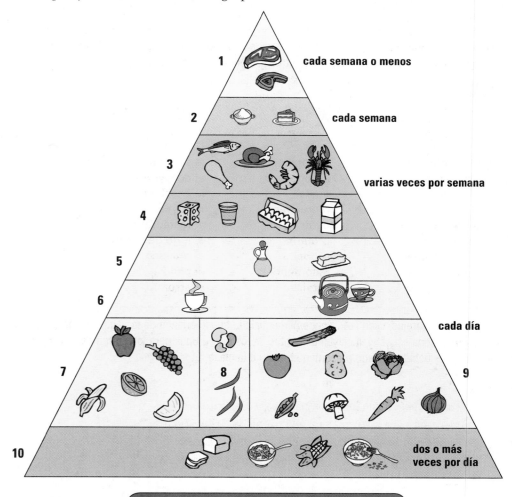

1 cada semana o menos

2 cada semana

3 varias veces por semana

4

5

6 cada día

7 8 9

10 dos o más veces por día

La Pirámide Alimenticia Latinoamericana

6 ¿Cierto o falso? Consulta la Pirámide Alimenticia Latinoamericana de la página 79 e indica si las oraciones son **ciertas** o **falsas**. Si la oración es falsa, escribe las comidas que sí están en el grupo indicado.

> **modelo**
> El queso está en el grupo diez.
> Falsa. En ese grupo están el maíz, el pan, los cereales y el arroz.

1. La manzana, la banana, el limón y las arvejas están en el grupo siete.
   Falsa. En ese grupo están la manzana, las uvas, la banana, la naranja y el limón.
2. En el grupo cuatro están los huevos, la leche y el aceite.
   Falsa. En ese grupo están los huevos, la leche, el queso y el yogur.
3. El azúcar está en el grupo dos.
   Cierta.
4. En el grupo diez están el pan, el arroz y el maíz.
   Cierta.
5. El pollo está en el grupo uno.
   Falsa. En ese grupo están el bistec y la chuleta de cerdo.
6. En el grupo nueve están la lechuga, el tomate, las arvejas, la naranja, la papa, los espárragos y la cebolla. Falsa. En ese grupo están la lechuga, el tomate, las arvejas, la zanahoria, la papa, los espárragos, la cebolla y el champiñón.
7. El café y el té están en el mismo grupo.
   Cierta.
8. En el grupo cinco está el arroz.
   Falsa. En ese grupo están el aceite y la mantequilla.
9. El pescado, el yogur y el bistec están en el grupo tres.
   Falsa. En ese grupo están el pescado, el pollo, el pavo, los camarones y la langosta.

7 Combinar Combina palabras de cada columna, en cualquier (*any*) orden, para formar diez oraciones lógicas sobre las comidas. Añade otras palabras si es necesario. Answers will vary.

> **modelo**
> La camarera nos sirve la ensalada.

A	B	C
el/la camarero/a	almorzar	la sección de no fumar
el/la dueño/a	escoger	el desayuno
mi familia	gustar	la ensalada
mi novio/a	merendar	las uvas
mis amigos y yo	pedir	el restaurante
mis padres	preferir	el jugo de naranja
mi hermano/a	probar	el refresco
el/la médico/a	recomendar	el plato
yo	servir	el arroz

8 Un menú En parejas, usen la Pirámide Alimenticia Latinoamericana de la página 79 para crear un menú para una cena especial. Incluyan alimentos de los diez grupos para los entremeses, los platos principales y las bebidas. Luego presenten el menú a la clase. Answers will vary.

> **modelo**
> La cena especial que vamos a preparar es deliciosa. Primero, hay dos entremeses: una ensalada César y una sopa de langosta. El plato principal es salmón con una salsa de ajo y espárragos. También vamos a servir arroz...

Extra Practice To review and practice the preterite along with food vocabulary, have students write a paragraph in which they describe what they ate up to this point today. Students should also indicate whether this meal or collection of meals represents a typical day for them. If not, they should explain why.

---

6 In pairs, have students create three additional true-false statements for their partners to answer.

7 To simplify, ask individual students what people in the activity logically do. Point out that there are many possible answers to your questions. Ex: **¿Qué hace la camarera en el restaurante? ¿Qué hace el dueño?**

8 Emphasize that students must include at least one item from each group in the **pirámide alimenticia.**

NOTA CULTURAL

El arroz es un alimento básico en el Caribe, Centroamérica y México, entre otros países. Aparece frecuentemente como acompañamiento del plato principal y muchas veces se sirve con frijoles. Un plato muy popular en varios países es el **arroz con pollo** (*chicken and rice casserole*).

Small Groups In groups of three, students role-play a situation in a restaurant. Two students play the customers and the other plays the **camarero/a**. Write these sentences on the board as suggested phrases: **¿Están listos para pedir?, ¿Qué nos recomienda usted?, ¿Me trae ____, por favor?, ¿Y para empezar?, A sus órdenes. La especialidad de la casa.**

Comunicación

9

9 Ask the same questions of individual students. Ask other students to restate what their classmates answered.

Small Groups In groups of two to four, ask students to prepare brief skits related to food. The skits may involve being in a market, in a restaurant, in a café, inviting people over for dinner, and so forth. Allow groups time to rehearse before performing their skits for the class, who will vote for the most creative one.

Conversación En grupos, contesten estas preguntas. Answers will vary.

1. ¿Meriendas mucho durante el día? ¿Qué comes? ¿A qué hora?
2. ¿Qué comidas te gustan más para la cena?
3. ¿A qué hora, dónde y con quién almuerzas?
4. ¿Cuáles son las comidas más (*most*) típicas de tu almuerzo?
5. ¿Desayunas? ¿Qué comes y bebes por la mañana?
6. ¿Qué comida deseas probar?
7. ¿Comes cada día comidas de los diferentes grupos de la pirámide alimenticia? ¿Cuáles son las comidas y bebidas más frecuentes en tu dieta?
8. ¿Qué comida recomiendas a tus amigos? ¿Por qué?
9. ¿Eres vegetariano/a? ¿Crees que ser vegetariano/a es una buena idea? ¿Por qué?
10. ¿Te gusta cocinar (*to cook*)? ¿Qué comidas preparas para tus amigos? ¿Para tu familia?

10

Describir Con dos compañeros/as de clase, describe las dos fotos, contestando estas preguntas.

Answers will vary.

▶ ¿Quiénes están en las fotos?

▶ ¿Dónde están?

▶ ¿Qué hora es?

▶ ¿Qué comen y qué beben?

10 For expansion, repeat the activity with additional photos of people in eating situations.

11

Supersite/IRCD: Information Gap Activities

11 Have groups create another type of word puzzle, such as a word-find, to share with the class. It should contain additional food- and meal-related vocabulary.

Crucigrama (*Crossword puzzle*) Tu profesor(a) les va a dar a ti y a tu compañero/a un crucigrama incompleto. Tú tienes las palabras que necesita tu compañero/a y él/ella tiene las palabras que tú necesitas. Tienen que darse pistas (*clues*) para completarlo. No pueden decir la palabra necesaria; deben utilizar definiciones, ejemplos y frases. Answers will vary.

> **modelo**
> **6 vertical:** *Es un condimento que normalmente viene con la sal.*
> **12 horizontal:** *Es una fruta amarilla.*

Game Play a game of continuous narration. One student begins with **Voy a preparar** (*name of dish*) **y voy al mercado. Necesito comprar...** and names one food item. Each student repeats the entire narration, adding an additional food item. Repeat the prompt with a new dish as necessary.

¿Qué tal la comida?

communication · cultures · NATIONAL STANDARDS

Don Francisco y los estudiantes van al restaurante El Cráter.

PERSONAJES

MAITE

INÉS

DON FRANCISCO

ÁLEX

JAVIER

DOÑA RITA

CAMARERO

JAVIER ¿Sabes dónde estamos?

INÉS Mmm, no sé. Oiga, don Francisco, ¿sabe usted dónde estamos?

DON FRANCISCO Estamos cerca de Cotacachi.

ÁLEX ¿Dónde vamos a almorzar, don Francisco? ¿Conoce un buen restaurante en Cotacachi?

DON FRANCISCO Pues, conozco a doña Rita Perales, la dueña del mejor restaurante de la ciudad, el restaurante El Cráter.

DOÑA RITA Hombre, don Paco, ¿usted por aquí?

DON FRANCISCO Sí, doña Rita... y hoy le traigo clientes. Le presento a Maite, Inés, Álex y Javier. Los llevo a las montañas para ir de excursión.

MAITE Voy a tomar un caldo de patas y un lomo a la plancha.

JAVIER Para mí las tortillas de maíz y el ceviche de camarón.

ÁLEX Yo también quisiera las tortillas de maíz y el ceviche.

INÉS Voy a pedir caldo de patas y lomo a la plancha.

DON FRANCISCO Yo quiero tortillas de maíz y una fuente de fritada, por favor.

DOÑA RITA Y de tomar, les recomiendo el jugo de piña, frutilla y mora. ¿Se lo traigo a todos?

TODOS Sí, perfecto.

CAMARERO ¿Qué plato pidió usted?

MAITE Un caldo de patas y lomo a la plancha.

recursos

VM pp. 121–122

adelante. vhlcentral.com

Video Synopsis **Don Francisco** takes the travelers to the **restaurante El Cráter** for lunch. The owner of the restaurant, **Doña Rita**, welcomes the group and makes recommendations about what to order. After the food is served, **Don Francisco** and **Doña Rita** plan a birthday surprise for **Maite**.

Preview Have the class predict the content of the episode based on the title and the video stills.

Expresiones útiles Draw attention to the verb **pidió** and explain that **pedir** has a stem change in the preterite. Have the class read the captions for video stills 5 and 9. Point out that **más** + [*adjective*] + **que** is used to make comparisons, and that **nos la** is an example of an indirect object pronoun and a direct object pronoun used together. Tell students that they will learn more about these concepts in **Estructura**.

Lección 2

DOÑA RITA ¡Bienvenidos al restaurante El Cráter! Están en muy buenas manos... don Francisco es el mejor conductor del país. Y no hay nada más bonito que nuestras montañas. Pero si van a ir de excursión deben comer bien. Vengan chicos, por aquí.

JAVIER ¿Qué nos recomienda usted?

DOÑA RITA Bueno, las tortillas de maíz son riquísimas. La especialidad de la casa es el caldo de patas... ¡tienen que probarlo! El lomo a la plancha es un poquito más caro que el caldo pero es sabrosísimo. También les recomiendo el ceviche y la fuente de fritada.

DOÑA RITA ¿Qué tal la comida? ¿Rica?

JAVIER Rica, no. ¡Riquísima!

ÁLEX Sí. ¡Y nos la sirvieron tan rápidamente!

MAITE Una comida deliciosa, gracias.

DON FRANCISCO Hoy es el cumpleaños de Maite...

DOÑA RITA ¡Ah! Tenemos unos pasteles que están como para chuparse los dedos...

Expresiones útiles

Finding out where you are

- **¿Sabe usted/Sabes dónde estamos?**
  Do you know where we are?
  Estamos cerca de Cotacachi.
  We're near Cotacachi.

Talking about people and places you're familiar with

- **¿Conoce usted/Conoces un buen restaurante en Cotacachi?**
  Do you know a good restaurant in Cotacachi?
  Sí, conozco varios.
  Yes, I know several.
- **¿Conoce/Conoces a doña Rita?**
  Do you know Doña Rita?

Ordering food

- **¿Qué le puedo traer?**
  What can I bring you?
  Voy a tomar/pedir un caldo de patas y un lomo a la plancha.
  I am going to have/to order the beef soup and grilled flank steak.
  Para mí, las tortillas de maíz y el ceviche de camarón, por favor.
  Corn tortillas and lemon-marinated shrimp for me, please.
  Yo también quisiera...
  I also would like...
  Y de tomar, el jugo de piña, frutilla y mora.
  And pineapple/strawberry/ blackberry juice to drink.
- **¿Qué plato pidió usted?**
  What did you order?
  Yo pedí un caldo de patas.
  I ordered the beef soup.

Talking about the food at a restaurant

- **¿Qué tal la comida?**
  How is the food?
  Muy rica, gracias.
  Very tasty, thanks.
  ¡Riquísima!
  Extremely delicious!

Teaching Tips
- Photocopy the ***Fotonovela*** Videoscript (Supersite/IRCD) and white out words related to food, meals, and other key vocabulary in order to create a master for a cloze activity. Distribute the photocopies and have students fill in the target words as they watch the episode.
- Play the first half of the episode and pause to write students' observations on the board. Ask them to use the information they already know to guess what happens in the rest of the segment. Go over their predictions after viewing the rest of the episode.

¿Qué pasó?

1

Escoger Escoge la respuesta que completa mejor cada oración.

1. Don Francisco lleva a los estudiantes a __c__ al restaurante de una amiga.
   a. cenar   b. desayunar   c. almorzar
2. Doña Rita es __b__.
   a. la hermana de don Francisco   b. la dueña del restaurante
   c. una camarera que trabaja en El Cráter
3. Doña Rita les recomienda a los viajeros __a__.
   a. el caldo de patas y el lomo a la plancha
   b. el bistec, las verduras frescas y el vino tinto   c. unos pasteles (*cakes*)
4. Inés va a pedir __c__.
   a. las tortillas de maíz y una fuente de fritada (*mixed grill*)
   b. el ceviche de camarón y el caldo de patas
   c. el caldo de patas y el lomo a la plancha

2

Identificar Indica quién puede decir estas oraciones.

1. No me gusta esperar en los restaurantes.
   ¡Qué bueno que nos sirvieron rápidamente! Álex
2. Les recomiendo la especialidad de la casa. doña Rita
3. ¡Maite y yo pedimos los mismos platos! Inés
4. Disculpe, señora... ¿qué platos recomienda usted? Javier
5. Yo conozco a una señora que tiene un restaurante
   excelente. Les va a gustar mucho. don Francisco
6. Hoy es mi cumpleaños (*birthday*). Maite

ÁLEX

INÉS   **DOÑA RITA**

DON FRANCISCO

MAITE   **JAVIER**

3

Preguntas Contesta estas preguntas sobre la **Fotonovela**.

1. ¿Dónde comieron don Francisco y los estudiantes?
   Comieron en el restaurante de doña Rita/El Cráter.
2. ¿Cuál es la especialidad de El Cráter?
   La especialidad de la casa es el caldo de patas.
3. ¿Qué pidió Javier? ¿Y Álex? ¿Qué tomaron todos? Javier pidió tortillas de maíz y el
   ceviche. Álex también pidió las tortillas de maíz y el ceviche. Todos tomaron jugo.
4. ¿Cómo son los pasteles en El Cráter?
   Los pasteles en El Cráter son sabrosísimos.

4

En el restaurante Answers will vary.

1. Prepara con un(a) compañero/a una conversación en la que le preguntas si conoce algún buen ◄
   restaurante en tu comunidad. Tu compañero/a responde que él/ella sí conoce un restaurante que
   sirve una comida deliciosa. Lo/La invitas a cenar y tu compañero/a acepta. Determinan la hora
   para verse en el restaurante y se despiden.

2. Trabaja con un(a) compañero/a para representar los papeles de un(a) cliente/a y un(a) camarero/a
   en un restaurante. El/La camarero/a te pregunta qué te puede servir y tú preguntas cuál es
   la especialidad de la casa. El/La camarero/a te dice cuál es la especialidad y te recomienda
   algunos platos del menú. Tú pides entremeses, un plato principal y escoges una bebida. El/La
   camarero/a te sirve la comida y tú le das las gracias.

Large Groups Have students work in groups of five or six to prepare a skit in which a family goes to a restaurant, is seated by a waitperson, examines the menu, and orders dinner. Each family member should ask a few questions about the menu and then order an entree and a drink. Have one or two groups perform the skit in front of the class.

2 For expansion, give students additional items. Ex: **¿Les gustó la comida? (doña Rita)**

4 Possible conversation (1):
E1: Oye, María, ¿conoces un buen restaurante en esta ciudad?
E2: Sí... el restaurante El Pescador sirve comida riquísima.
E1: ¿Por qué no vamos a El Pescador esta noche?
E2: ¿A qué hora?
E1: ¿A las ocho?
E2: Perfecto.
E1: Está bien. Nos vemos a las ocho.
E2: Adiós.
Possible conversation (2):
E1: ¿Qué le puedo traer?
E2: Bueno, ¿cuáles son las especialidades de la casa?
E1: La especialidad de la casa es el lomo a la plancha. También, le recomiendo el caldo de patas.
E2: Mmm... voy a pedir los camarones y el lomo a la plancha. De tomar, voy a pedir el jugo de piña.
E1: Gracias, señor.

CONSULTA

To review indefinite words like **algún,** see **Estructura 1.2,** p. 36.

Pronunciación

ll, ñ, c, and z

 SUPERSITE Supersite/IRCD: MP3 Audio Files, Listening Scripts

Teaching Tips
• As you model the pronunciation of these sounds with the class, write additional words on the board and have students repeat.
• You may wish to bring in additional audio samples to compare and contrast the pronunciation of **c** and **z** in Spain and Latin America.

Video Play the video segment again and pause to have students repeat and write down words with **ll, ñ, c, and z**. Go over as a class to check spelling.

Pairs Have the class work in pairs to practice the pronunciation of the sentences in **Actividad 2** on p. 84. Encourage students to help their partner if he or she has trouble pronouncing a particular word.

Game Divide students into teams of four. With books closed, give them two minutes to write down as many words as they can with **ll**. Then have students in each group take turns reading the words aloud. Groups earn a point for each word that is spelled and pronounced correctly. Repeat with **ñ, c, and z**.

pollo	**llave**	**ella**	**cebolla**

Most Spanish speakers pronounce the letter **ll** like the *y* in *yes*.

mañana	**señor**	**baño**	**niña**

The letter **ñ** is pronounced much like the *ny* in *canyon*.

café	**colombiano**	**cuando**	**rico**

Before **a**, **o**, or **u**, the Spanish **c** is pronounced like the *c* in *car*.

cereales	**delicioso**	**conducir**	**conocer**

Before **e** or **i**, the Spanish **c** is pronounced like the *s* in *sit*. (In parts of Spain, **c** before **e** or **i** is pronounced like the *th* in *think*.)

zeta	**zanahoria**	**almuerzo**	**cerveza**

The Spanish **z** is pronounced like the *s* in *sit*. (In parts of Spain, **z** is pronounced like the *th* in *think*.)

Práctica Lee las palabras en voz alta.

1. mantequilla	5. español	9. quince
2. cuñada	6. cepillo	10. compañera
3. aceite	7. zapato	11. almorzar
4. manzana	8. azúcar	12. calle

Heritage Speakers Call on heritage speakers to model pronunciation for the class. Ask them to list several additional words on the board for practice. You may wish to point out regional variations in the pronunciation of **ll**.

Oraciones Lee las oraciones en voz alta.

1. Mi compañero de cuarto se llama Toño Núñez. Su familia es de la ciudad de Guatemala y de Quetzaltenango.
2. Dice que la comida de su mamá es deliciosa, especialmente su pollo al champiñón y sus tortillas de maíz.
3. Creo que Toño tiene razón porque hoy cené en su casa y quiero volver mañana para cenar allí otra vez.

Refranes Lee los refranes en voz alta.

Las apariencias engañan.[1]

Panza llena, corazón contento.[2]

[1] Looks can be deceiving.
[2] A full belly makes a happy heart.

recursos

LM p. 126

SUPERSITE adelante. vhlcentral.com

Lección 2

EN DETALLE

Frutas y verduras de las Américas

Imagínate una pizza sin salsa° de tomate o una hamburguesa sin papas fritas. Ahora piensa que quieres ver una película, pero las palomitas de maíz° y el chocolate no existen. ¡Qué mundo° tan insípido°! Muchas de las comidas más populares del mundo tienen ingredientes esenciales que son originarios de las Américas. Estas frutas y verduras no fueron introducidas en Europa sino hasta° el siglo° XVI.

El tomate, por ejemplo, era° usado como planta ornamental cuando llegó por primera vez a Europa porque pensaron que era venenoso°. El maíz, por su parte, era ya la base de la comida de muchos países latinoamericanos muchos siglos antes de la llegada de los españoles.

La papa fue un alimento° básico para los incas. Incluso consiguieron deshidratarlas para almacenarlas° durante mucho tiempo. El cacao (planta con la que se hace el chocolate) fue muy importante para los aztecas y los mayas. Ellos usaron sus semillas° como moneda° y como ingrediente de diversas salsas. También las molían° para preparar una bebida, mezclándolas° con agua ¡y con chile!

El aguacate°, la guayaba°, la papaya, la piña y el maracuyá (o fruta de la pasión) son sólo algunos ejemplos de frutas originarias de las Américas que son hoy día conocidas en todo el mundo.

Mole

¿En qué alimentos encontramos estas frutas y verduras?

Tomate: pizza, ketchup, salsa de tomate, sopa de tomate

Maíz: palomitas de maíz, tamales, tortillas, arepas (Colombia y Venezuela), pan

Papa: papas fritas, frituras de papa°, puré de papas°, sopa de papas, tortilla de patatas (España)

Cacao: salsa mole (México), chocolatinas°, cereales, helados°, tartas°

Aguacate: guacamole (México), cóctel de camarones, sopa de aguacate, nachos, enchiladas hondureñas

salsa *sauce* palomitas de maíz *popcorn* mundo *world* insípido *flavorless* hasta *until* siglo *century* era *was* venenoso *poisonous* alimento *food* almacenarlas *to store them* semillas *seeds* moneda *currency* las molían *they used to grind them* mezclándolas *mixing them* aguacate *avocado* guayaba *guava* frituras de papa *chips* puré de papas *mashed potatoes* chocolatinas *chocolate bars* helados *ice cream* tartas *cakes*

ACTIVIDADES

1 **¿Cierto o falso?** Indica si lo que dicen estas oraciones es **cierto** o **falso**. Corrige la información falsa.

1. El tomate se introdujo a Europa como planta ornamental. Cierto.

2. Los aztecas y los mayas usaron las papas como moneda. Falso. Los aztecas y los mayas usaron las semillas de cacao como moneda.

3. Los incas sólo consiguieron almacenar las papas por poco tiempo. Falso. Los incas pudieron almacenar las papas por mucho tiempo.

4. En México se hace una salsa con chocolate. Cierto.

5. El aguacate, la guayaba, la papaya, la piña y el maracuyá son originarios de las Américas. Cierto.

6. Las arepas se hacen con cacao. Falso. Las arepas se hacen con maíz.

7. El aguacate es un ingrediente del cóctel de camarones. Cierto.

8. En España hacen una tortilla con papas. Cierto.

Lección 2

ASÍ SE DICE

La comida

el banano (Col.), el cambur (Ven.), el guineo (Nic.), el plátano (Amér. L., Esp.)	la banana
el choclo (Amér. S.), el elote (Méx.), el jojoto (Ven.), la mazorca (Esp.)	*corncob*
las caraotas (Ven.), los porotos (Amér. S.), las habichuelas	los frijoles
el durazno	el melocotón
el jitomate (Méx.)	el tomate

EL MUNDO HISPANO

Algunos platos típicos

○ **Ceviche peruano:** Es un plato de pescado crudo° que se marina° en jugo de limón, con sal, pimienta, cebolla y ají°. Se sirve con lechuga, maíz, camote° y papa amarilla.

○ **Gazpacho andaluz:** Es una sopa fría típica del sur de España. Se hace con verduras crudas y molidas°: tomate, ají, pepino° y ajo. También lleva pan, sal, aceite y vinagre.

○ **Sancocho colombiano:** Es una sopa de pollo o de carne con plátano, maíz, zanahoria, yuca, papas, cebolla y ajo. Se sirve con arroz blanco.

crudo *raw* se marina *gets marinated* ají *pepper* camote *sweet potato* molidas *mashed* pepino *cucumber*

PERFIL

Ferrán Adrià: arte en la cocina°

¿Qué haces si un amigo te invita a comer croquetas líquidas o paella de Kellogg's? ¿Piensas que es una broma°? ¡Cuidado! Puedes estar perdiendo la oportunidad de cenar en el restaurante más innovador de España: **El Bulli**.

Ferrán Adrià, el dueño de El Bulli, está entre los mejores° chefs del mundo. Su éxito° se basa en su creatividad. Adrià modifica combinaciones de ingredientes y juega con contrastes de gustos y sensaciones:

Aire de zanahorias

frío-caliente, crudo-cocido°, dulce°-salado°... Sus platos son sorprendentes° y divertidos: cócteles en forma de espuma°, salsas servidas en tubos y sorbetes salados.

Adrià también creó **Fast Good** (un restaurante de comida rápida de calidad), escribe libros de cocina y participa en programas de televisión.

cocina *kitchen* broma *joke* mejores *best* éxito *success* cocido *cooked* dulce *sweet* salado *savory* sorprendentes *surprising* espuma *foam*

Conexión Internet

¿Qué platos comen los hispanos en los Estados Unidos?	Go to adelante.vhlcentral.com to find more cultural information related to this **Cultura** section.

ACTIVIDADES

2 **Comprensión** Empareja cada palabra con su definición.

1. fruta amarilla d
2. sopa típica de Colombia c
3. ingrediente del ceviche e
4. restaurante español b

a. gazpacho
b. El Bulli
c. sancocho
d. guineo
e. pescado

3 **¿Qué plato especial hay en tu región?** Escribe cuatro oraciones sobre un plato típico de tu región. Explica los ingredientes que contiene y cómo se sirve. Answers will vary.

3 For expansion, ask students to create a **menú del día** in which they suggest complementary dishes (appetizers, drinks, or dessert).

2.1 Preterite of stem-changing verbs

Teaching Tips
- Review present-tense forms of -ir stem-changing verbs like **pedir** and **dormir**. Also review formation of the preterite of regular -ir verbs using **escribir** and **recibir**.
- Ask students questions using stem-changing -ir verbs in the preterite. Ex: ¿**Cuántas horas dormiste anoche?** Then have other students summarize the answers. Ex: _____ **durmió seis horas, pero _____ durmió ocho. _____ y _____ durmieron cinco horas.**
- Point out that **morir** means to die and offer sample sentences using stem-changing preterite forms of the verb. Ex: **No tengo bisabuelos. Ya murieron.**
- Other -ir verbs that change their stem vowel in the preterite are **conseguir, despedirse, divertirse, pedir, preferir, repetir, seguir, sentir, sugerir,** and **vestirse.**

ANTE TODO As you learned in *¡ADELANTE!* **UNO**, **Lección 6**, **-ar** and **-er** stem-changing verbs have no stem change in the preterite. **-Ir** stem-changing verbs, however, do have a stem change. Study the following chart and observe where the stem changes occur.

Preterite of -ir stem-changing verbs		
	servir *(to serve)*	**dormir** *(to sleep)*
SINGULAR FORMS yo	serví	dormí
tú	serviste	dormiste
Ud./él/ella	s**i**rvió	d**u**rmió
PLURAL FORMS nosotros/as	servimos	dormimos
vosotros/as	servisteis	dormisteis
Uds./ellos/ellas	s**i**rvieron	d**u**rmieron

▶ Stem-changing **-ir** verbs, in the preterite only, have a stem change in the third-person singular and plural forms. The stem change consists of either **e** to **i** or **o** to **u**.

(e → i) pedir: p**i**dió, p**i**dieron   (o → u) morir *(to die)*: m**u**rió, m**u**rieron

Perdón, ¿quiénes pidieron las tortillas de maíz?

¿Y qué plato pidió usted?

¡INTÉNTALO! Cambia cada infinitivo al pretérito.

1. Yo _____serví_____. (servir, dormir, pedir, preferir, repetir, seguir)
   dormí, pedí, preferí, repetí, seguí

2. Usted _____. (morir, conseguir, pedir, sentirse, despedirse, vestirse)
   murió, consiguió, pidió, se sintió, se despidió, se vistió

3. Tú _____. (conseguir, servir, morir, pedir, dormir, repetir)
   conseguiste, serviste, moriste, pediste, dormiste, repetiste

4. Ellas _____. (repetir, dormir, seguir, preferir, morir, servir)
   repitieron, durmieron, siguieron, prefirieron, murieron, sirvieron

5. Nosotros _____. (seguir, preferir, servir, vestirse, despedirse, dormirse)
   seguimos, preferimos, servimos, nos vestimos, nos despedimos, nos dormimos

6. Ustedes _____. (sentirse, vestirse, conseguir, pedir, despedirse, dormirse)
   se sintieron, se vistieron, consiguieron, pidieron, se despidieron, se durmieron

7. Él _____. (dormir, morir, preferir, repetir, seguir, pedir)
   durmió, murió, prefirió, repitió, siguió, pidió

recursos
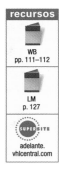
WB
pp. 111–112

LM
p. 127

adelante.
vhlcentral.com

Extra Practice Have students write five original sentences using stem-changing preterite forms. Encourage them to include lesson vocabulary.

Práctica

1

Completar Completa estas oraciones para describir lo que pasó anoche en el restaurante El Famoso.

▶ 1. Paula y Humberto Suárez llegaron al restaurante El Famoso a las ocho y ____siguieron____ (seguir) al camarero a una mesa en la sección de no fumar.
2. El señor Suárez ____pidió____ (pedir) una chuleta de cerdo.
3. La señora Suárez ____prefirió____ (preferir) probar los camarones.
4. De tomar, los dos ____pidieron____ (pedir) vino tinto.
5. El camarero ____repitió____ (repetir) el pedido (*the order*) para confirmarlo.
6. La comida tardó mucho (*took a long time*) en llegar y los señores Suárez ____se durmieron____ (dormirse) esperando la comida.
7. A las nueve y media el camarero les ____sirvió____ (servir) la comida.
8. Después de comer la chuleta, el señor Suárez ____se sintió____ (sentirse) muy mal.
9. Pobre señor Suárez... ¿por qué no ____pidió____ (pedir) los camarones?

2

El camarero loco En el restaurante La Hermosa trabaja un camarero muy distraído que siempre comete muchos errores. Indica lo que los clientes pidieron y lo que el camarero les sirvió.

modelo
Armando / papas fritas
Armando pidió papas fritas, pero el camarero le sirvió maíz.

1. nosotros / jugo de naranja Nosotros pedimos jugo de naranja, pero el camarero nos sirvió papas.

2. Beatriz / queso Beatriz pidió queso, pero el camarero le sirvió uvas.

3. tú / arroz Tú pediste arroz, pero el camarero te sirvió arvejas/sopa.

4. Elena y Alejandro / atún Elena y Alejandro pidieron atún, pero el camarero les sirvió camarones (mariscos).

5. usted / agua mineral Usted pidió agua mineral, pero el camarero le sirvió vino tinto.

6. yo / hamburguesa Yo pedí una hamburguesa, pero el camarero me sirvió zanahorias.

Comunicación

3

El almuerzo Trabajen en parejas. Túrnense para completar las oraciones de César de una manera lógica. Answers will vary.

> **modelo**
>
> Mi compañero de cuarto se despertó temprano, pero yo...
> Mi compañero de cuarto se despertó temprano, pero yo me
> desperté tarde.

1. Yo llegué al restaurante a tiempo, pero mis amigos...
2. Beatriz pidió la ensalada de frutas, pero yo...
3. Yolanda les recomendó el bistec, pero Eva y Paco...
4. Nosotros preferimos las papas fritas, pero Yolanda...
5. El camarero sirvió la carne, pero yo...
6. Beatriz y yo pedimos café, pero Yolanda y Paco...
7. Eva se sintió enferma, pero Paco y yo...
8. Nosotros repetimos el postre (*dessert*), pero Eva...
9. Ellos salieron tarde, pero yo...
10. Yo me dormí temprano, pero mi compañero de cuarto...

3 To check preterite verb forms, ask volunteers to write their sentences on the board. Have the class correct errors as needed.

¡LENGUA VIVA!

In Spanish, the verb **repetir** is used to express *to have a second helping* (*of something*).

Cuando mi mamá prepara sopa de champiñones, yo siempre repito.
When my mom makes mushroom soup, I always have a second helping.

4

Entrevista Trabajen en parejas y túrnense para entrevistar a su compañero/a. Answers will vary.

1. ¿Te acostaste tarde o temprano anoche? ¿A qué hora te dormiste? ¿Dormiste bien?
2. ¿A qué hora te despertaste esta mañana? Y ¿a qué hora te levantaste?
3. ¿A qué hora vas a acostarte esta noche?
4. ¿Qué almorzaste ayer? ¿Quién te sirvió el almuerzo?
5. ¿Qué cenaste ayer?
6. ¿Cenaste en un restaurante recientemente? ¿Con quién?
7. ¿Qué pediste en el restaurante? ¿Qué pidieron los demás?
8. ¿Se durmió alguien en alguna de tus clases la semana pasada? ¿En qué clase?

4 To practice the formal register, have students ask you the same questions.

Síntesis

5

Describir En grupos, estudien la foto y las preguntas. Luego, describan la cena romántica de Eduardo y Rosa. Answers will vary.

▶ ¿Adónde salieron a cenar?

▶ ¿Qué pidieron?

▶ ¿Les sirvieron la comida rápidamente?

▶ ¿Les gustó la comida?

▶ ¿Cuánto costó?

▶ ¿Van a volver a este restaurante en el futuro?

▶ ¿Recomiendas el restaurante?

CONSULTA

To review words commonly associated with the preterite, such as **anoche**, see *¡ADELANTE!* **UNO**, **Estructura 6.3**, p. 293.

5 Have groups present their description to the class in the form of a narration. Remind them to use transition words, such as **primero, después, luego,** and **también**.

Pairs For expansion, have students describe their most memorable experience in a restaurant (Ex: a first date, a celebration, a wonderful or terrible meal).

Lección 2

2.2 Double object pronouns

ANTE TODO In *¡ADELANTE! UNO*, **Lecciones 5** and **6**, you learned that direct and indirect object pronouns replace nouns and that they often refer to nouns that have already been referenced. You will now learn how to use direct and indirect object pronouns together. Observe the following diagram.

Indirect Object Pronouns			Direct Object Pronouns	
me	nos		lo	los
te	os	**+**	la	las
le (se)	les (se)			

▶ When direct and indirect object pronouns are used together, the indirect object pronoun always precedes the direct object pronoun.

I.O. D.O.		DOUBLE OBJECT PRONOUNS
El camarero **me** muestra **el menú**.	⟶	El camarero **me lo** muestra.
The waiter shows me the menu.		*The waiter shows it to me.*
Nos sirven **los platos**.	⟶	**Nos los** sirven.
They serve us the dishes.		*They serve them to us.*
Maribel **te** pidió **una hamburguesa**.	⟶	Maribel **te la** pidió.
Maribel ordered a hamburger for you.		*Maribel ordered it for you.*

Y de tomar, les recomiendo el jugo de piña... ¿Se lo traigo a todos?

Sí, perfecto.

▶ In Spanish, two pronouns that begin with the letter **l** cannot be used together. Therefore, the indirect object pronouns **le** and **les** always change to **se** when they are used with **lo, los, la,** and **las.**

I.O. D.O.		DOUBLE OBJECT PRONOUNS
Le escribí **la carta**.	⟶	**Se la** escribí.
I wrote him the letter.		*I wrote it to him.*
Les sirvió **los sándwiches**.	⟶	**Se los** sirvió.
He served them the sandwiches.		*He served them to them.*

Extra Practice Write six sentences on the board for students to restate using double object pronouns.
Ex: **Doña Rita les sirvió la cena a los viajeros. (Doña Rita se la sirvió.)**

Teaching Tips
• Briefly review direct and indirect object pronouns. Give sentences and have students convert objects into object pronouns. Ex: **Sara escribió la carta. (Sara la escribió.) Mis padres escribieron una carta. (yo) (Mis padres me escribieron una carta.**

• Model additional examples for students, asking them to make the conversion with **se**. Ex: **Le pedí papas fritas. (Se las pedí.) Les servimos café. (Se lo servimos.)**

Pairs In pairs, ask students to write five sentences that contain both direct and indirect objects (not pronouns). Have them exchange papers with another pair, who will restate the sentences using double object pronouns.

Video Show the *Fotonovela* again to give students more input containing double object pronouns. Stop the video where appropriate to discuss how double object pronouns were used and to ask comprehension questions.

Teaching Tips
• Ask questions to elicit
third-person double
object pronouns.
Ex: **¿Le recomiendas el
restaurante Acapulco
a _____? (Sí, se lo
recomiendo.) ¿Le traes
sándwiches a tus
compañeros? (No, no se
los traigo.)**

• Practice pronoun placement
with infinitives and present
participles by giving
sentences that show
one method of pronoun
placement and asking
students to restate them
another way. Ex: **Se lo
voy a mandar. (Voy a
mandárselo.)**

▶ Because **se** has multiple meanings, Spanish speakers often clarify to whom the pronoun refers by adding **a usted, a él, a ella, a ustedes, a ellos,** or **a ellas.**

¿El sombrero? Carlos **se** lo vendió **a ella.**
The hat? Carlos sold it to her.

¿Las verduras? Ellos **se** las compran **a usted.**
The vegetables? They buy them for you.

▶ Double object pronouns are placed before a conjugated verb. With infinitives and present participles, they may be placed before the conjugated verb or attached to the end of the infinitive or present participle.

DOUBLE OBJECT PRONOUNS
Te lo voy a mostrar.

DOUBLE OBJECT PRONOUNS
Voy a mostrár**telo.**

DOUBLE OBJECT PRONOUNS
Nos las están sirviendo.

DOUBLE OBJECT PRONOUNS
Están sirviéndo**noslas.**

¿Qué tal la comida, rica?

Sí. ¡Y nos la sirvieron tan rápidamente!

▶ As you can see above, when double object pronouns are attached to an infinitive or a present participle, an accent mark is added to maintain the original stress.

Game Play **Concentración.**
Write sentences that use
double object pronouns on
each of eight cards. Ex: **Óscar
se las muestra.** On another
eight cards, draw or paste a
picture that matches each
sentence. Ex: A photo of a
boy showing photos to his
grandparents. Place the cards
face-down in four rows of
four. In pairs, students select
two cards. If the two cards
match, the pair keeps them.
If they do not match, students
replace them in their original
position. The pair with the
most cards at the end wins.

¡INTÉNTALO! Escribe el pronombre de objeto directo o indirecto que falta en cada oración.

Extra Practice Have students create five
dehydrated sentences for their partner to
complete. They should include the following
elements: subject / action / direct object /
indirect object (name or pronoun). Ex: **Carlos /
escribe / carta / Marta** Their partners should
"hydrate" the sentences using double object
pronouns. Ex: **Carlos se la escribe (a Marta).**

(Objeto directo)

1. ¿La ensalada? El camarero nos ___la___ sirvió.
2. ¿El salmón? La dueña me ___lo___ recomienda.
3. ¿La comida? Voy a preparárte___la___.
4. ¿Las bebidas? Estamos pidiéndose___las___.
5. ¿Los refrescos? Te ___los___ puedo traer ahora.
6. ¿Los platos de arroz? Van a servírnos___los___ después.

(Objeto indirecto)

1. ¿Puedes traerme tu plato? No, no ___te___ lo puedo traer.
2. ¿Quieres mostrarle la carta? Sí, voy a mostrár___se___la ahora.
3. ¿Les serviste la carne? No, no ___se___ la serví.
4. ¿Vas a leerle el menú? No, no ___se___ lo voy a leer.
5. ¿Me recomiendas la langosta? Sí, ___te___ la recomiendo.
6. ¿Cuándo vas a prepararnos la cena? ___Se___ la voy a preparar en una hora.

recursos

WB
pp. 113–114

LM
p. 128

SUPERSITE
adelante.
vhlcentral.com

Práctica

1

Responder Imagínate que trabajas de camarero/a en un restaurante. Responde a las órdenes de estos clientes usando pronombres.

> **modelo**
>
> Sra. Gómez: Una ensalada, por favor.
>
> *Sí, señora. Enseguida (Right away) se la traigo.*

1. Sres. López: La mantequilla, por favor. Sí, señores. Enseguida se la traigo.
2. Srta. Rivas: Los camarones, por favor. Sí, señorita. Enseguida se los traigo.
3. Sra. Lugones: El pollo asado, por favor. Sí, señora. Enseguida se lo traigo.
4. Tus compañeros/as de cuarto: Café, por favor. Sí, chicos. Enseguida se lo traigo.
5. Tu profesor(a) de español: Papas fritas, por favor. Sí, profesor(a). Enseguida se las traigo.
6. Dra. González: La chuleta de cerdo, por favor. Sí, doctora. Enseguida se la traigo.
7. Tu padre: Los champiñones, por favor. Sí, papá. Enseguida te los traigo.
8. Dr. Torres: La cuenta (*check*), por favor. Sí, doctor. Enseguida se la traigo.

2

¿Quién? La señora Cevallos está planeando una cena. Se pregunta cómo va a resolver ciertas situaciones. En parejas, túrnense para decir lo que ella está pensando. Cambien los sustantivos subrayados por pronombres de objeto directo y hagan los otros cambios necesarios.

> **modelo**
>
> ¡No tengo carne! ¿Quién va a traerme <u>la carne</u> del supermercado? (mi esposo)
>
> *Mi esposo va a traérmela./Mi esposo me la va a traer.*

1. ¡Las invitaciones! ¿Quién les manda <u>las invitaciones</u> a los invitados (*guests*)? (mi hija) Mi hija se las manda.
2. No tengo tiempo de ir a la bodega. ¿Quién me puede comprar <u>el vino</u>? (mi hijo) Mi hijo puede comprármelo./Mi hijo me lo puede comprar.
3. ¡Ay! No tengo suficientes platos (*plates*). ¿Quién puede prestarme <u>los platos</u> que necesito? (mi mamá) Mi mamá puede prestármelos./Mi mamá me los puede prestar.
4. Nos falta mantequilla. ¿Quién nos trae <u>la mantequilla</u>? (mi cuñada) Mi cuñada nos la trae.
5. ¡Los entremeses! ¿Quién está preparándonos <u>los entremeses</u>? (Silvia y Renata) Silvia y Renata están preparándonoslos./Silvia y Renata nos los están preparando.
6. No hay suficientes sillas. ¿Quién nos trae <u>las sillas</u> que faltan? (Héctor y Lorena) Héctor y Lorena nos las traen.
7. No tengo tiempo de pedirle el aceite a Mónica. ¿Quién puede pedirle <u>el aceite</u>? (mi hijo) Mi hijo puede pedírselo./Mi hijo se lo puede pedir.
8. ¿Quién va a servirles la cena a los invitados? (mis hijos) Mis hijos van a servírsela./Mis hijos se la van a servir.
9. Quiero poner buena música de fondo (*background*). ¿Quién me va a recomendar <u>la música</u>? (mi esposo) Mi esposo va a recomendármela./Mi esposo me la va a recomendar.
10. ¡Los postres! ¿Quién va a preparar los postres para los invitados? (Sra. Villalba) La señora Villalba va a preparárselos./La señora Villalba se los va a preparar.

Comunicación

3 **Contestar** Trabajen en parejas. Túrnense para hacer preguntas y para responderlas usando las palabras interrogativas **¿Quién?** o **¿Cuándo?** Sigan el modelo. Answers will vary.

> **modelo**
> nos enseña español
> **Estudiante 1:** ¿Quién nos enseña español?
> **Estudiante 2:** La profesora Camacho nos lo enseña.

3 To simplify, begin by having students read through each item. Guide them in choosing **¿Quién?** or **¿Cuándo?** for each one.

3 Continue the **modelo** exchange by asking: **¿Cuándo nos lo enseña?** (Nos lo enseña los lunes, miércoles, jueves y viernes.)

1. te puede explicar (*explain*) la tarea cuando no la entiendes
2. les vende el almuerzo a los estudiantes
3. vas a comprarme boletos (*tickets*) para un concierto
4. te escribe mensajes electrónicos
5. nos prepara los entremeses
6. me vas a prestar tu computadora
7. te compró esa bebida
8. nos va a recomendar el menú de la cafetería
9. le enseñó español al/a la profesor(a)
10. me vas a mostrar tu casa o apartamento

4 **Preguntas** Hazle estas preguntas a un(a) compañero/a. Answers will vary.

> **modelo**
> **Estudiante 1:** ¿Les prestas tu casa a tus amigos? ¿Por qué?
> **Estudiante 2:** No, no se la presto a mis amigos porque no son muy responsables.

1. ¿Me prestas tu auto? ¿Ya le prestaste tu auto a otro/a amigo/a?
2. ¿Quién te presta dinero cuando lo necesitas?
3. ¿Les prestas dinero a tus amigos? ¿Por qué?
4. ¿Nos compras el almuerzo a mí y a los otros compañeros de clase?
5. ¿Les mandas correo electrónico a tus amigos? ¿Y a tu familia?
6. ¿Les das regalos a tus amigos? ¿Cuándo?
7. ¿Quién te va a preparar la cena esta noche?
8. ¿Quién te va a preparar el desayuno mañana?

Síntesis

5 **Regalos de Navidad (*Christmas gifts*)** Tu profesor(a) te va a dar a ti y a un(a) compañero/a una parte de la lista de los regalos de Navidad que Berta pidió y los regalos que sus parientes le compraron. Conversen para completar sus listas. Answers will vary.

> **modelo**
> **Estudiante 1:** ¿Qué le pidió Berta a su mamá?
> **Estudiante 2:** Le pidió una computadora. ¿Se la compró?
> **Estudiante 1:** Sí, se la compró.

Supersite/IRCD: Information Gap Activities

Game Divide the class into two groups. Give each member of the first group a strip of paper with a question on it. Ex: **¿Te compró ese suéter tu novia?** Give each member of the second group the answer to one of the questions. Ex: **Sí, ella me lo compró.** Students must find their partners. Take care not to create sentences that can have more than one match. With a different partner, ask pairs to make a list of the gifts they each received for their last birthday or other occasion. Then have them point to each item on their list and, using double object pronouns, tell their partner who bought it for them. Ex: **zapatos nuevos (Me los compró mi prima.)**

Heritage Speakers Ask heritage speakers if they or their families celebrate **el Día de los Reyes Magos** (The Feast of the Epiphany, January 6). Ask them to expand on the information given in the **Nota cultural** box and to tell whether **el Día de los Reyes** is more important for them than **la Navidad**.

NOTA CULTURAL

Las fiestas navideñas (*Christmas season*) en los países hispanos duran hasta enero. En muchos lugares celebran **la Navidad** (*Christmas*), pero no se dan los regalos hasta el seis de enero, **el Día de los Reyes Magos** (*Three Kings' Day/The Feast of the Epiphany*).

Teaching Tips
• Write **más** + [*adjective*]
+ **que** and **menos** +
[*adjective*] + **que** on the
board, explaining their
meaning. Illustrate with
examples. Ex: **Esta clase
es más grande que la
clase de la tarde. La
clase de la tarde es
menos trabajadora que
ésta.** Repeat with adverbs
and nouns.
• Point out that **que** and
what follows it are
optional if the items being
compared are evident.
Ex: **Los bistecs son más
caros (que el pollo).**

Extra Practice Ask students
questions that make
comparisons of inequality
using adjectives, adverbs,
and nouns. Ex: **¿Qué es más
sabroso que una ensalada
de frutas? ¿Quién se
despierta más tarde que
tú? ¿Quién tiene más libros
que yo?** Then ask questions
that use verbs in their
construction. Ex: **¿Quién
habla más que yo en
la clase?**

Heritage Speakers Ask
heritage speakers to give
four to five sentences
in which they compare
themselves to members of
their families. Make sure
that the comparisons are
ones of inequality. Ask
other students in the class
to report what the heritage
speakers said to verify
comprehension.

[2.3] Comparisons (SUPERSITE)

ANTE TODO Spanish and English use comparisons to indicate which of two people or things has a lesser, equal, or greater degree of a quality.

(**Comparisons**)

menos interesante   **más grande**   **tan sabroso como**
less interesting   *bigger*   *as delicious as*

Comparisons of inequality

▶ Comparisons of inequality are formed by placing **más** (*more*) or **menos** (*less*) before adjectives, adverbs, and nouns and **que** (*than*) after them.

$$\text{más/menos} + \begin{bmatrix} \textit{adjective} \\ \textit{adverb} \\ \textit{noun} \end{bmatrix} + \text{que}$$

▶ **¡Atención!** Note that while English has a comparative form for short adjectives (*tall**er***), such forms do not exist in Spanish (**más** alto).

(**adjectives**)

Los bistecs son **más caros que** el pollo. | Estas uvas son **menos ricas que** esa pera.
Steaks are more expensive than chicken. | *These grapes are less tasty than that pear.*

(**adverbs**)

Me acuesto **más tarde que** tú. | Luis se despierta **menos temprano que** yo.
I go to bed later than you (do). | *Luis wakes up less early than I (do).*

(**nouns**)

Juan prepara **más platos que** José. | Susana come **menos carne que** Enrique.
Juan prepares more dishes than José (does). | *Susana eats less meat than Enrique (does).*

Tengo más hambre que un elefante.

El lomo a la plancha es un poquito más caro pero es sabrosísimo.

▶ When the comparison involves a numerical expression, **de** is used before the number instead of **que**.

Hay más **de** cincuenta naranjas. | Llego en menos **de** diez minutos.
There are more than fifty oranges. | *I'll be there in less than ten minutes.*

▶ With verbs, this construction is used to make comparisons of inequality.

$$\begin{bmatrix} \textit{verb} \end{bmatrix} + \text{más/menos que}$$

Mis hermanos **comen más que** yo. | Arturo **duerme menos que** su padre.
My brothers eat more than I (do). | *Arturo sleeps less than his father (does).*

Comparisons of equality

▶ This construction is used to make comparisons of equality.

$$\textbf{tan} + \begin{bmatrix} \textit{adjective} \\ \textit{adverb} \end{bmatrix} + \textbf{como} \qquad \textbf{tanto/a(s)} + \begin{bmatrix} \textit{singular noun} \\ \textit{plural noun} \end{bmatrix} + \textbf{como}$$

¿Qué tal la comida?

La comida es tan buena como en España.

▶ **¡Atención!** Note that **tanto** acts as an adjective and therefore agrees in number and gender with the noun it modifies.

Tú comiste **tanta carne como** Nicolás.
You ate as much meat as Nicolás.

Yo probé **tantos platos como** él.
I tried as many dishes as he did.

▶ **Tan** and **tanto** can also be used for emphasis, rather than to compare, with these meanings: **tan** *so*, **tanto** *so much*, **tantos/as** *so many*.

¡Tu almuerzo es **tan** grande!
Your lunch is so big!

¡Comes **tantas** manzanas!
You eat so many apples!

¡Comes **tanto**!
You eat so much!

¡Preparan **tantos** platos!
They prepare so many dishes!

▶ Comparisons of equality with verbs are formed by placing **tanto como** after the verb. Note that in this construction **tanto** does not change in number or gender.

$$\begin{bmatrix} \textit{verb} \end{bmatrix} + \textbf{tanto como}$$

Tú viajas **tanto como** mi tía.
You travel as much as my aunt (does).

Ellos hablan **tanto como** mis hermanas.
They talk as much as my sisters.

Estudiamos tanto como ustedes.
We study as much as you (do).

No **descanso tanto como** Felipe.
I don't rest as much as Felipe (does).

Extra Practice Have students write three original comparative sentences that describe themselves. Ex: **Soy tan bajo como Danny DeVito.** Then collect the papers, shuffle them, and read the sentences aloud. See if the rest of the class can guess who wrote each description.

Teaching Tips
• Ask the class questions to elicit comparisons of equality. Ex: **¿Quién es tan guapa como Jennifer López? ¿Quién tiene tanto dinero como Tiger Woods?**
• Ask questions that involve comparisons with yourself. Ex: **¿Quién es tan alto/a como yo? ¿Quién se acostó tan tarde como yo?**
• Involve the class in a conversation about themselves and classroom objects. Ex: ____, **¿por qué tienes tantas plumas?** ____, **¡tu mochila es tan grande! Puedes llevar muchos libros, ¿no? ¿Quién más tiene una mochila tan grande?**

Game Divide the class into two teams, A and B. Place the names of twenty famous people into a hat. Select a member from each team to draw a name. The student from team A then has ten seconds to compare those two famous people. If the student has made a logical comparison, team A gets a point. Then it is team B's turn to make a different comparison. The team with the most points at the end wins.

Lección 2

Irregular comparisons

▶ Some adjectives have irregular comparative forms.

Irregular comparative forms

Adjective		Comparative form	
bueno/a	good	**mejor**	better
malo/a	bad	**peor**	worse
grande	big	**mayor**	bigger
pequeño/a	small	**menor**	smaller
joven	young	**menor**	younger
viejo/a	old	**mayor**	older

▶ When **grande** and **pequeño/a** refer to age, the irregular comparative forms, **mayor** and **menor**, are used. However, when these adjectives refer to size, the regular forms, **más grande** and **más pequeño/a**, are used.

Yo soy **menor** que tú.
I'm younger than you.

Pedí un plato **más pequeño**.
I ordered a smaller dish.

El médico es **mayor** que Isabel.
The doctor is older than Isabel.

La ensalada de Inés es **más grande** que ésa.
Inés's salad is bigger than that one.

▶ The adverbs **bien** and **mal** have the same irregular comparative forms as the adjectives **bueno/a** and **malo/a**.

Julio nada **mejor** que los otros chicos.
Julio swims better than the other boys.

Ellas cantan **peor** que las otras chicas.
They sing worse than the other girls.

¡INTÉNTALO! Escribe el equivalente de las palabras en inglés.

1. Ernesto mira más televisión ___que___ (*than*) Alberto.
2. Tú eres ___menos___ (*less*) simpático que Federico.
3. La camarera sirve ___tanta___ (*as much*) carne como pescado.
4. Conozco ___más___ (*more*) restaurantes que tú.
5. No estudio ___tanto como___ (*as much as*) tú.
6. ¿Sabes jugar al tenis tan bien ___como___ (*as*) tu hermana?
7. ¿Puedes beber ___tantos___ (*as many*) refrescos como yo?
8. Mis amigos parecen ___tan___ (*as*) simpáticos como ustedes.

Práctica [SUPERSITE]

1 Quickly review the use of **de** before numerals in comparisons.

1 **Escoger** Escoge la palabra correcta para comparar a dos hermanas muy diferentes. Haz los cambios necesarios.

1. Lucila es más alta y más bonita ____que____ Tita. (de, más, menos, que)
2. Tita es más delgada porque come ____más____ verduras que su hermana. (de, más, menos, que)
3. Lucila es más ____simpática____ que Tita porque es alegre. (listo, simpático, bajo)
4. A Tita le gusta comer en casa. Va a ____menos____ restaurantes que su hermana. (más, menos, que) Es tímida, pero activa. Hace ____más____ ejercicio (*exercise*) que su hermana. (más, tanto, menos) Todos los días toma más ____de____ cinco vasos (*glasses*) de agua mineral. (que, tan, de)
5. Lucila come muchas papas fritas y se preocupa ____menos____ que Tita por comer frutas. (de, más, menos) Son ____tan____ diferentes, pero se llevan (*they get along*) bien. (como, tan, tanto)

1 Ask two students a question, then have another student compare them. Ex: **¿Cuántas horas de televisión miras cada día? ¿Y tú, ____? ____ , haz una comparación.**

1 Ask several pairs of students different types of questions for later comparison. Ex: **¿Cuáles prefieres, las películas de aventuras o los dramas? ¿Estudias más para la clase de español o para la clase de matemáticas?**

2 **Emparejar** Completa las oraciones de la columna A con información de la columna B para comparar a Mario y a Luis, los novios de Lucila y Tita.

A	B
1. Mario es __tan interesante__ como Luis.	tantas
2. Mario viaja tanto __como__ Luis.	diferencia
3. Luis toma __tantas__ clases de cocina (*cooking*) como Mario.	tan interesante
4. Luis habla __francés__ tan bien como Mario.	amigos extranjeros
5. Mario tiene tantos __amigos extranjeros__ como Luis.	como
6. ¡Qué casualidad (*coincidence*)! Mario y Luis también son hermanos, pero no hay tanta __diferencia__ entre ellos como entre Lucila y Tita.	francés

2 Turn the activity statements into questions and ask them of students. Have them make up answers that involve comparisons. Ex: **¿Cómo es Mario?**

TPR Give the same types of objects to different students but in different numbers. For example, hand out three books to one student, one book to another, and four to another. Then call on individuals to make comparisons between the students based on the number of objects they have. Have students continue the activity in groups, using pens, sheets of paper, and other classroom objects.

3 **Oraciones** Combina elementos de las columnas A, B y C para hacer comparaciones. Usa oraciones completas. Answers will vary.

> **modelo**
> Arnold Schwarzenegger tiene tantos autos como Jennifer Aniston.
> Jennifer Aniston es menos musculosa que Arnold Schwarzenegger.

A	B	C
la comida japonesa	costar	la gente de Los Ángeles
el fútbol	saber	la música *country*
Arnold Schwarzenegger	ser	el brócoli
el pollo	tener	el presidente de los EE.UU.
la gente de Nueva York	¿?	la comida italiana
la primera dama (*lady*) de los EE.UU.		el hockey
las universidades privadas		Jennifer Aniston
las espinacas		las universidades públicas
la música rap		la carne de res

Large Groups Divide the class into two groups. Survey each group to get information about various topics. Ex: **¿Quiénes hacen ejercicio todos los días? ¿Quiénes van al cine cada fin de semana? ¿Quiénes comen comida rápida tres veces a la semana?** Ask for a show of hands and tally the number of hands. Then have students make comparisons between the two groups based on the information given.

3 To simplify, guide students in pairing up elements from columns A and C and brainstorming possible infinitives for each pair of elements.

Lección 2

Comunicación

4 **Intercambiar** En parejas, hagan comparaciones sobre diferentes cosas. Pueden usar las sugerencias de la lista u otras ideas. Answers will vary.

> **modelo**
> **Estudiante 1:** Los pollos de *Pollitos del Corral* son muy ricos.
> **Estudiante 2:** Pues yo creo que los pollos de *Rostipollos* son tan buenos como los pollos *de Pollitos del Corral.*
> **Estudiante 1:** Mmm… no tienen tanta mantequilla como los pollos de *Pollitos del Corral.* Tienes razón. Son muy sabrosos.

restaurantes en tu ciudad/pueblo
cafés en tu comunidad
tiendas en tu ciudad/pueblo

periódicos en tu ciudad/pueblo
revistas favoritas
libros favoritos

comidas favoritas
los profesores
los cursos que toman

4 Ask pairs of volunteers to present one of their conversations to the class. Then survey the class to see with which of the students the class agrees more.

5 **Conversar** En grupos, túrnense para hacer comparaciones entre ustedes mismos (*yourselves*) y una persona de cada categoría de la lista. Answers will vary.

▶ una persona de tu familia

▶ un(a) amigo/a especial

▶ una persona famosa

5 Model the activity by making a few comparisons between yourself and a celebrity.

Síntesis

6 **La familia López** En grupos, túrnense para hablar de Sara, Sabrina, Cristina, Ricardo y David y hacer comparaciones entre ellos. Answers will vary.

Sara　Sabrina　David　Ricardo　Cristina

> **modelo**
> **Estudiante 1:** Sara es tan alta como Sabrina.
> **Estudiante 2:** Sí, pero David es más alto que ellas.
> **Estudiante 3:** En mi opinión, él es guapo también.

6 Have students create a drawing of a family similar to the one on this page. Tell them not to let anyone see their drawings. Then pair students up and have them describe their drawings to one another. Each student must draw the family described by his or her partner.

2.4 Superlatives

ANTE TODO   Both English and Spanish use superlatives to express the highest or lowest degree of a quality.

el/la mejor	**el/la peor**	**la más alta**
the best	*the worst*	*the tallest*

▶ This construction is used to form superlatives. Note that the noun is always preceded by a definite article and that **de** is equivalent to the English *in* or *of*.

$$\textbf{el/la/los/las} + \boxed{noun} + \textbf{más/menos} + \boxed{adjective} + \textbf{de}$$

▶ The noun can be omitted if the person, place, or thing referred to is clear.

¿El restaurante El Cráter?   Recomiendo el pollo asado.
  Es **el más elegante** de la ciudad.   Es **el más sabroso** del menú.
The El Cráter restaurant?   *I recommend the roast chicken.*
  It's the most elegant (one) in the city.   *It's the most delicious on the menu.*

▶ Here are some irregular superlative forms.

Irregular superlatives

Adjective		Superlative form	
bueno/a	*good*	**el/la mejor**	*(the) best*
malo/a	*bad*	**el/la peor**	*(the) worst*
grande	*big*	**el/la mayor**	*(the) biggest*
pequeño/a	*small*	**el/la menor**	*(the) smallest*
joven	*young*	**el/la menor**	*(the) youngest*
viejo/a	*old*	**el/la mayor**	*(the) eldest*

▶ The absolute superlative is equivalent to *extremely, super,* or *very*. To form the absolute superlative of most adjectives and adverbs, drop the final vowel, if there is one, and add **-ísimo/a(s)**.

malo ⟶ mal- ⟶ **malísimo**   mucho ⟶ much- ⟶ **muchísimo**

¡El bistec está **malísimo**!   Comes **muchísimo**.

▶ Note these spelling changes.

rico ⟶ **riquísimo**   largo ⟶ **larguísimo**   feliz ⟶ **felicísimo**

fácil ⟶ **facilísimo**   joven ⟶ **jovencísimo**   trabajador ⟶ **trabajadorcísimo**

¡INTÉNTALO!   Escribe el equivalente de las palabras en inglés.

1. Marisa es ___la más inteligente___ (*the most intelligent*) de todas.
2. Ricardo y Tomás son ___los menos aburridos___ (*the least boring*) de la fiesta.
3. Miguel y Antonio son ___los peores___ (*the worst*) estudiantes de la clase.
4. Mi profesor de biología es ___el mayor___ (*the oldest*) de la universidad.

Teaching Tips
Practice superlative questions by asking for students' opinions. Ex: ¿Cuál es la clase más difícil de esta universidad? ¿Y la más fácil? Include a mix of regular and irregular forms.

¡ATENCIÓN!

While **más** alone means *more*, after **el, la, los** or **las**, it means *most*. Likewise, **menos** can mean *less* or *least*.
Es **el café más rico del** país.
It's the most delicious coffee in the country.
Es **el menú menos caro de** todos éstos.
It is the least expensive menu of all of these.

CONSULTA

The rule you learned in **Estructura 2.3** (p. 97) regarding the use of **mayor/menor** with age, but not with size, is also true with superlative forms.

Heritage Speakers Ask heritage speakers to discuss whether absolute superlatives are common in their culture (some regions use them less frequently than others).

recursos

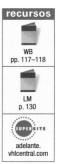

WB
pp. 117–118

LM
p. 130

SUPERSITE
adelante.
vhlcentral.com

Práctica y Comunicación   SUPERSITE

Lección 2

1   **El más...** Responde a las preguntas afirmativamente. Usa las palabras en paréntesis.

> **modelo**
>
> El cuarto está sucísimo, ¿no? (residencia)
> *Sí, es el más sucio de la residencia.*

1. El almacén Velasco es buenísimo, ¿no? (centro comercial)   Sí, es el mejor del centro comercial.
2. La silla de tu madre es comodísima, ¿no? (casa)   Sí, es la más cómoda de la casa.
3. Ángela y Julia están nerviosísimas por el examen, ¿no? (clase)   Sí, son las más nerviosas de la clase.
4. Jorge es jovencísimo, ¿no? (mis amigos)   Sí, es el menor de mis amigos.

2   **Completar** Tu profesor(a) te va a dar una hoja de actividades con descripciones de José Valenzuela Carranza y Ana Orozco Hoffman. Completa las oraciones con las palabras de la lista. Answers will vary.

altísima	del	mejor	peor
atlética	la	menor	periodista
bajo	más	guapísimo	trabajadorcísimo
de	mayor	Orozco	Valenzuela

1. José tiene 22 años; es el ____menor____ y el más ____bajo____ de su familia. Es ____guapísimo____ y ____trabajadorcísimo____. Es el mejor ____periodista____ de la ciudad y el ____peor____ jugador de baloncesto.
2. Ana es la más ____atlética____ y ____la____ mejor jugadora de baloncesto del estado. Es la ____mayor____ de sus hermanos (tiene 28 años) y es ____altísima____. Estudió la profesión ____más____ difícil ____de____ todas: medicina.
3. Jorge es el ____mejor____ jugador de videojuegos de su familia.
4. Mauricio es el menor de la familia ____Orozco____.
5. El abuelo es el ____mayor____ de todos los miembros de la familia Valenzuela.
6. Fifí es la perra más antipática ____del____ mundo.

3   **Superlativos** Trabajen en parejas para hacer comparaciones. Usen superlativos. Answers will vary.

> **modelo**
>
> Angelina Jolie, Bill Gates, Jimmy Carter
> **Estudiante 1:** *Bill Gates es el más rico de los tres.*
> **Estudiante 2:** *Sí, ¡es riquísimo! Y Jimmy Carter es el mayor de los tres.*

1. Guatemala, Argentina, España
2. Jaguar, Hummer, Mini Cooper
3. la comida mexicana, la comida francesa, la comida árabe
4. Paris Hilton, Meryl Streep, Katie Holmes
5. Ciudad de México, Buenos Aires, Nueva York
6. *Don Quijote de la Mancha, Cien años de soledad, Como agua para chocolate*
7. el fútbol americano, el golf, el béisbol
8. las películas románticas, las películas de acción, las películas cómicas

3 For item 6, briefly describe these novels for students who are not familiar with them.

Recapitulación

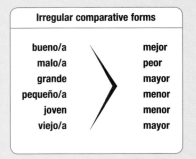

SUPERSITE For self-scoring and diagnostics, go to **adelante.vhlcentral.com**.

Completa estas actividades para repasar los conceptos de gramática que aprendiste en esta lección.

1   **Completar** Completa la tabla con la forma correcta del pretérito. **9 pts.**

Infinitive	yo	usted	ellos
dormir	dormí	durmió	durmieron
servir	serví	sirvió	sirvieron
vestirse	me vestí	se vistió	se vistieron

2   **La cena** Completa la conversación con el pretérito de los verbos. **7 pts.**

PAULA ¡Hola, Daniel! ¿Qué tal el fin de semana?

DANIEL Muy bien. Marta y yo (1) <u>conseguimos</u> (conseguir) hacer muchas cosas, pero lo mejor fue la cena del sábado.

PAULA Ah, ¿sí? ¿Adónde fueron?

DANIEL Al restaurante Vistahermosa. Es elegante, así que (nosotros) (2) <u>nos vestimos</u> (vestirse) bien.

PAULA Y, ¿qué platos (3) <u>pidieron</u> (pedir, ustedes)?

DANIEL Yo (4) <u>pedí</u> (pedir) camarones y Marta (5) <u>prefirió</u> (preferir) el pollo. Y al final, el camarero nos (6) <u>sirvió</u> (servir) flan.

PAULA ¡Qué rico!

DANIEL Sí. Pero después de la cena Marta no (7) <u>se sintió</u> (sentirse) bien.

3   **Camareros** Genaro y Úrsula son camareros en un restaurante. Completa la conversación que tienen con su jefe usando pronombres. **8 pts.**

JEFE Úrsula, ¿le ofreciste agua fría al cliente de la mesa 22?

ÚRSULA Sí, (1) <u>se la ofrecí</u> de inmediato.

JEFE Genaro, ¿los clientes de la mesa 5 te pidieron ensaladas?

GENARO Sí, (2) <u>me las pidieron</u>.

ÚRSULA Genaro, ¿recuerdas si ya me mostraste los vinos nuevos?

GENARO Sí, ya (3) <u>te los mostré</u>.

JEFE Genaro, ¿van a pagarte la cuenta (*bill*) los clientes de la mesa 5?

GENARO Sí, (4) <u>me la van a pagar/
van a pagármela</u> ahora mismo.

3 Remind students that indirect object pronouns always precede direct object pronouns.

RESUMEN GRAMATICAL

2.1   **Preterite of stem-changing verbs**   *p. 88*

servir	dormir
serví	dormí
serviste	dormiste
sirvió	durmió
servimos	dormimos
servisteis	dormisteis
sirvieron	durmieron

2.2   **Double object pronouns**   *pp. 91–92*

Indirect object pronouns: me, te, le (se), nos, os, les (se)

Direct object pronouns: lo, la, los, las

Le escribí la carta. → Se la escribí.

Nos van a servir los platos. → Nos los van a servir./
Van a servírnoslos.

2.3   **Comparisons**   *pp. 95–97*

Comparisons of inequality		
más/menos +	*adj., adv., n.*	**+ que**
verb + **más/menos + que**		

Comparisons of equality		
tan +	*adj., adv.*	**+ como**
tanto/a(s) +	*noun*	**+ como**
verb + **tanto como**		

Irregular comparative forms	
bueno/a	mejor
malo/a	peor
grande	mayor
pequeño/a	menor
joven	menor
viejo/a	mayor

Teaching Tip Remind students that the comparative **tanto/a** must agree in gender and number with the noun it modifies.

TPR Have students write a celebrity's name, a place, and a thing on separate slips of paper. Collect the papers in three envelopes, separated by category. Then divide the class into two teams, **comparativos** and **superlativos**, and have them line up. Draw out two or three slips of paper (alternate randomly) and read the terms aloud. The corresponding team member has five seconds to step forward and create a logical comparison or superlative statement.

Pairs Have pairs imagine they went to a restaurant where the server mixed up all the orders. Call on pairs to share their experiences, using **pedir** and **servir** as well as double object pronouns. Ex: **Fui a un restaurante italiano. Pedí la pasta primavera. ¡El camarero me sirvió la sopa de mariscos! ¡Y me la sirvió fría! Mi compañero pidió langosta, pero el camarero no se la sirvió. ¡Le sirvió una chuleta de cerdo!**

5 To help students organize their ideas, have them divide their paper into two columns: **mejor** and **peor**. Under each category, have students list the different reasons why their chosen restaurants are the best or worst.

6 Have students work in groups of three or four to create an original riddle related to food. Have groups read their riddles for the class to guess.

4

El menú Observa el menú y sus características. Completa las oraciones basándote en los elementos dados. Usa comparativos y superlativos. (14 pts.)

Ensaladas	Precio	Calorías
Ensalada de tomates	$9.00	170
Ensalada de mariscos	$12.99	325
Ensalada de zanahorias	$9.00	200

Platos principales		
Pollo con champiñones	$13.00	495
Cerdo con papas	$10.50	725
Atún con espárragos	$18.95	495

2.4 Superlatives *p. 100*

el/la/ los/las +	noun	+ más/ menos +	adjective	+ de

▶ Irregular superlatives follow the same pattern as irregular comparatives.

4 To challenge students, have pairs ask each other questions about the menu using comparatives and superlatives. Ex: **¿Qué ensalada cuesta tanto como la ensalada de tomates?**

1. ensalada de mariscos / otras ensaladas / costar
   La ensalada de mariscos ___cuesta más que___ las otras ensaladas.
2. pollo con champiñones / cerdo con papas / calorías
   El pollo con champiñones tiene ___menos calorías que___ el cerdo con papas.
3. atún con espárragos / pollo con champiñones / calorías
   El atún con espárragos tiene ___tantas calorías como___ el pollo con champiñones.
4. ensalada de tomates / ensalada de zanahorias / caro
   La ensalada de tomates es ___tan cara como___ la ensalada de zanahorias.
5. cerdo con papas / platos principales / caro
   El cerdo con papas es ___el menos caro de___ los platos principales.
6. ensalada de zanahorias / ensalada de tomates / costar
   La ensalada de zanahorias ___cuesta tanto como___ la ensalada de tomates.
7. ensalada de mariscos / ensaladas / caro
   La ensalada de mariscos es ___la más cara de___ las ensaladas.

5

Dos restaurantes ¿Cuál es el mejor restaurante que conoces? ¿Y el peor? Escribe un párrafo de por lo menos (*at least*) seis oraciones donde expliques por qué piensas así. Puedes hablar de la calidad de la comida, el ambiente, los precios, el servicio, etc. (12 pts.) Answers will vary.

6

Adivinanza Completa la adivinanza y adivina la respuesta. (¡2 puntos EXTRA!)

❝ En el campo yo nací°,
mis hermanos son
los ___ajos___ (*garlic, pl.*),
y aquél que llora° por mí
me está partiendo°
en pedazos°. ❞
¿Quién soy? ___La cebolla___

nací *was born* **llora** *cries* **partiendo** *cutting* **pedazos** *pieces*

Lectura

Antes de leer

Estrategia
Reading for the main idea

As you know, you can learn a great deal about a reading selection by looking at the format and looking for cognates, titles, and subtitles. You can skim to get the gist of the reading selection and scan it for specific information. Reading for the main idea is another useful strategy; it involves locating the topic sentences of each paragraph to determine the author's purpose for writing a particular piece. Topic sentences can provide clues about the content of each paragraph, as well as the general organization of the reading. Your choice of which reading strategies to use will depend on the style and format of each reading selection.

Examinar el texto

En esta sección tenemos dos textos diferentes. ¿Qué estrategias puedes usar para leer la crítica culinaria (*restaurant review*)? ¿Cuáles son las apropiadas para familiarizarte con el menú? Utiliza las estrategias más eficaces (*efficient*) para cada texto. ¿Qué tienen en común? ¿Qué tipo de comida sirven en el restaurante?

Identificar la idea principal

Lee la primera frase de cada párrafo de la crítica culinaria del restaurante **La feria del maíz**. Apunta (*Jot down*) el tema principal de cada párrafo. Luego lee todo el primer párrafo. ¿Crees que el restaurante le gustó al autor de la crítica culinaria? ¿Por qué? Ahora lee la crítica entera. En tu opinión, ¿cuál es la idea principal de la crítica? ¿Por qué la escribió el autor? Compara tus opiniones con las de un(a) compañero/a.

recursos

SUPERSITE

adelante.vhlcentral.com

Teaching Tips
- Review previous reading strategies: have students scan the text for cognates; ask how the title and format give clues to the content; and have students skim the article.
- Ask groups to create a dinner menu featuring their favorite dishes, including lists of ingredients similar to those in the menu above. Have groups present their menus to the class.

MENÚ

Entremeses

Tortilla servida con
- Ajiaceite (chile, aceite)   • Ajicomino (chile, comino)

Pan tostado servido con
- Queso frito a la pimienta   • Salsa de ajo y mayonesa

Sopas

- Tomate   • Cebolla   • Verduras   • Pollo y huevo
- Carne de res   • Mariscos

Entradas

Tomaticán
(tomate, papas, maíz, chile, arvejas y zanahorias)

Tamales
(maíz, azúcar, ajo, cebolla)

Frijoles enchilados
(frijoles negros, carne de cerdo o de res, arroz, chile)

Chilaquil
(tortilla de maíz, queso, hierbas y chile)

Tacos
(tortillas, pollo, verduras y salsa)

Cóctel de mariscos
(camarones, langosta, vinagre, sal, pimienta, aceite)

Postres°

- Plátanos caribeños   • Cóctel de frutas al ron°
- Uvate (uvas, azúcar de caña y ron)   • Flan napolitano
- Helado° de piña y naranja   • Pastel° de yogur

Después de leer

Preguntas

En parejas, contesten estas preguntas sobre la crítica culinaria de **La feria del maíz**.

1. ¿Quién es el dueño y chef de **La feria del maíz**?
   Ernesto Sandoval
2. ¿Qué tipo de comida se sirve en el restaurante?
   tradicional
3. ¿Cuál es el problema con el servicio?
   Se necesitan más camareros.
4. ¿Cómo es el ambiente del restaurante?
   agradable
5. ¿Qué comidas probó el autor? las tortillas, el ajiaceite, la sopa de mariscos, los tamales, los tacos de pollo y los plátanos caribeños
6. ¿Quieren ir ustedes al restaurante **La feria del maíz**? ¿Por qué? Answers will vary.

Teaching Tip Ask additional comprehension questions. Ex: **¿Cómo fue el camarero que atendió al crítico? ¿Cuál fue la opinión del crítico con respecto a la comida? ¿Cómo son los precios de La feria del maíz?**

23F

Gastronomía
Por Eduardo Fernández

La feria del maíz

Sobresaliente°. En el nuevo restaurante **La feria del maíz** va a encontrar la perfecta combinación entre la comida tradicional y el encanto° de la vieja ciudad de Antigua. Ernesto Sandoval, antiguo jefe de cocina° del famoso restaurante **El fogón**, está teniendo mucho éxito° en su nueva aventura culinaria.

El gerente°, el experimentado José Sierra, controla a la perfección la calidad del servicio. El camarero que me atendió esa noche fue muy amable en todo momento. Sólo hay que comentar que,

La feria del maíz
13 calle 4-41 Zona 1
La Antigua, Guatemala
2329912

lunes a sábado
10:30am-11:30pm
domingo 10:00am-10:00pm

Comida ¦¦¦¦¦

Servicio ¦¦¦

Ambiente ¦¦¦¦

Precio ¦¦¦

debido al éxito inmediato de **La feria del maíz**, se necesitan más camareros para atender a los clientes de una forma más eficaz.

En esta ocasión, el mesero se tomó unos veinte minutos en traerme la bebida.

Afortunadamente, no me importó mucho la espera entre plato y plato, pues el ambiente es tan agradable que me sentí como en casa. El restaurante mantiene el estilo colonial de Antigua. Por dentro°, el estilo es elegante y rústico a la vez. Cuando el tiempo lo permite, se puede comer también en el patio, donde hay muchas flores.

El servicio de camareros y el ambiente agradable del local pasan a un segundo plano cuando llega la comida, de una calidad extraordinaria. Las tortillas

de casa se sirven con un ajiaceite delicioso. La sopa de mariscos es excelente, y los tamales, pues, tengo que confesar que son mejores que los de mi abuelita. También recomiendo los tacos de pollo, servidos con un mole buenísimo. De postre, don Ernesto me preparó su especialidad, unos plátanos caribeños sabrosísimos.

Los precios pueden parecer altos° para una comida tradicional, pero la calidad de los productos con que se cocinan los platos y el exquisito ambiente de **La feria del maíz** le garantizan° una experiencia inolvidable°.

Bebidas

- Cerveza negra
- Chilate (bebida de maíz, chile y cacao)
- Jugos de fruta
- Agua mineral
- Té helado
- Vino tinto/blanco
- Ron

Postres *Desserts* ron *rum* Helado *Ice cream* Pastel *Cake* Sobresaliente *Outstanding* encanto *charm* jefe de cocina *head chef* éxito *success* gerente *manager* Por dentro *Inside* altos *high* garantizan *guarantee* inolvidable *unforgettable*

Lección 2

Un(a) guía turístico/a 🌐

Tú eres un(a) guía turístico/a en Guatemala. Estás en el restaurante **La feria del maíz** con un grupo de turistas norteamericanos. Ellos no hablan español y quieren pedir de comer, pero necesitan tu ayuda. Lee nuevamente el menú e indica qué error comete cada turista.

1. La señora Johnson es diabética y no puede comer azúcar. Pide sopa de verdura y tamales. No pide nada de postre.
   No debe pedir los tamales porque tienen azúcar.

2. Los señores Petit son vegeterianos y piden sopa de tomate, frijoles enchilados y plátanos caribeños.
   No deben pedir los frijoles enchilados porque tienen carne.

3. El señor Smith, que es alérgico al chocolate, pide tortilla servida con ajiaceite, chilaquil y chilate para beber.
   No debe pedir chilate porque tiene cacao.

4. La adorable hija del señor Smith tiene sólo cuatro años y le gustan mucho las verduras y las frutas naturales. Su papá le pide tomaticán y un cóctel de frutas.
   No debe pedir el cóctel de frutas porque tiene ron.

5. La señorita Jackson está a dieta y pide uvate, flan napolitano y helado.
   No debe pedir postres porque está a dieta.

Large Groups In groups of eight, have students role-play the situation depicted in the activity. Assign these roles: **camarero/a, guía turístico/a, la señora Jackson, los señores Petit, el señor Smith, la hija del señor Smith**, and **la señorita Jackson**. Have groups perform their skits for the class.

Heritage Speakers Ask a heritage speaker of Guatemalan origin or a student who has visited Guatemala and dined in restaurants or cafés to prepare a short presentation about his or her experiences there. Of particular interest would be a comparison and contrast of city vs. small-town restaurants. If possible, the presentation should be illustrated with menus from the restaurants, advertisements, or photos of and articles about the country.

Guatemala

National Standards connections cultures

El país en cifras

- ▶ **Área:** 108.890 km^2 (42.042 millas^2), *un poco más pequeño que Tennessee*
- ▶ **Población:** 14.213.000
- ▶ **Capital:** Ciudad de Guatemala—1.103.000
- ▶ **Ciudades principales:** Quetzaltenango, Escuintla, Mazatenango, Puerto Barrios

SOURCE: Population Division, UN Secretariat

- ▶ **Moneda:** quetzal
- ▶ **Idiomas:** español (oficial), lenguas mayas

El español es la lengua de un 60 por ciento° de la población; el otro 40 por ciento tiene una de las lenguas mayas (cakchiquel, quiché y kekchícomo, entre otras) como lengua materna. Una palabra que las lenguas mayas tienen en común es ixim, que significa maíz, un cultivo° de mucha importancia en estas culturas.

Bandera de Guatemala

Guatemaltecos célebres

- ▶ **Carlos Mérida,** pintor (1891–1984)
- ▶ **Miguel Ángel Asturias,** escritor (1899–1974)
- ▶ **Margarita Carrera,** poeta y ensayista (1929–)
- ▶ **Rigoberta Menchú Tum,** activista (1959–), premio Nobel de la Paz° en 1992

por ciento *percent*   cultivo *crop*   Paz *Peace*   telas *fabrics*   tinte *dye*
aplastados *crushed*   hace... destiñan *keeps the colors from running*

ESTADOS UNIDOS

OCÉANO ATLÁNTICO

GUATEMALA

OCÉANO PACÍFICO

AMÉRICA DEL SUR

Vista de una calle céntrica en la Ciudad de Guatemala

MÉXICO

Sierra de Lacandón

Río Usumacinta

Lago Petén Itzá

Río de la Pasión

BELICE

Mujeres indígenas limpiando cebollas

Lago de Izabal

Sierra Madre

Quetzaltenango

Lago de Atitlán

Sierra de las Minas

Río Motagua

★ Guatemala

Antigua Guatemala

Mazatenango

Escuintla

Iglesia de la Merced en Antigua Guatemala

EL SALVADOR

Océano Pacífico

recursos

WB pp. 119–120	VM pp. 123–124	adelante. vhlcentral.com

¡Increíble pero cierto!

¿Qué ingrediente secreto se encuentra en las telas° tradicionales de Guatemala? ¡El mosquito! El excepcional tinte° de estas telas es producto de una combinación de flores y de mosquitos aplastados°. El insecto hace que los colores no se destiñan°. Quizás es por esto que los artesanos representan la figura del mosquito en muchas de sus telas.

Ciudades • Antigua Guatemala

Antigua Guatemala fue fundada en 1543. Fue una capital de gran importancia hasta 1773, cuando un terremoto° la destruyó. Sin embargo, conserva el carácter original de su arquitectura y hoy es uno de los centros turísticos del país. Su celebración de la Semana Santa° es, para muchas personas, la más importante del hemisferio.

Naturaleza • El quetzal

El quetzal simbolizó la libertad para los antiguos° mayas porque creían° que este pájaro° no podía° vivir en cautividad°. Hoy el quetzal es el símbolo nacional. El pájaro da su nombre a la moneda nacional y aparece también en los billetes° del país. Desafortunadamente, está en peligro° de extinción. Para su protección, el gobierno mantiene una reserva biológica especial.

Historia • Los mayas

Desde 1500 a.C. hasta 900 d.C., los mayas habitaron gran parte de lo que ahora es Guatemala. Su civilización fue muy avanzada. Los mayas fueron arquitectos y constructores de pirámides, templos y observatorios. También descubrieron° y usaron el cero antes que los europeos, e inventaron un calendario complejo° y preciso.

Artesanía • La ropa tradicional

La ropa tradicional de los guatemaltecos se llama *huipil* y muestra el amor° de la cultura maya por la naturaleza. Ellos se inspiran en las flores°, plantas y animales para crear sus diseños° de colores vivos° y formas geométricas. El diseño y los colores de cada *huipil* indican el pueblo de origen y a veces también el sexo y la edad° de la persona que lo lleva.

Mar Caribe

Golfo de Honduras

Puerto Barrios

HONDURAS

¿Qué aprendiste? Responde a cada pregunta con una oración completa.

1. ¿Qué significa la palabra *ixim*?
   La palabra *ixim* significa maíz.
2. ¿Quién es Rigoberta Menchú?
   Rigoberta Menchú es una activista de Guatemala.
3. ¿Qué pájaro representa a Guatemala?
   El quetzal representa a Guatemala.
4. ¿Qué simbolizó el quetzal para los mayas?
   El quetzal simbolizó la libertad para los mayas.
5. ¿Cuál es la moneda nacional de Guatemala?
   La moneda nacional de Guatemala es el quetzal.
6. ¿De qué fueron arquitectos los mayas?
   Los mayas fueron arquitectos de pirámides, templos y observatorios.

7. ¿Qué celebración de la Antigua Guatemala es la más importante del hemisferio para muchas personas? La celebración de la Semana Santa de la Antigua Guatemala es la más importante del hemisferio.
8. ¿Qué descubrieron los mayas antes que los europeos? Los mayas descubrieron el cero antes que los europeos.
9. ¿Qué muestra la ropa tradicional de los guatemaltecos? La ropa muestra el amor a la naturaleza.
10. ¿Qué indica un *huipil* con su diseño y sus colores? Con su diseño y colores, un *huipil* indica el pueblo de origen, el sexo y la edad de la persona.

Conexión Internet Investiga estos temas en **adelante.vhlcentral.com**.

1. Busca información sobre Rigoberta Menchú. ¿De dónde es? ¿Qué libros publicó? ¿Por qué es famosa?
2. Estudia un sitio arqueológico en Guatemala para aprender más sobre los mayas, y prepara un breve informe para tu clase.

terremoto *earthquake* Semana Santa *Holy Week* antiguos *ancient* creían *they believed* pájaro *bird* no podía *couldn't* cautividad *captivity* los billetes *bills* peligro *danger* descubrieron *they discovered* complejo *complex* amor *love* flores *flowers* diseños *designs* vivos *bright* edad *age*

Las comidas

el/la camarero/a	waiter/waitress
la comida	food; meal
el/la dueño/a	owner; landlord
el menú	menu
la sección de (no) fumar	(non) smoking section
el almuerzo	lunch
la cena	dinner
el desayuno	breakfast
los entremeses	hors d'oeuvres; appetizers
el plato (principal)	(main) dish
delicioso/a	delicious
rico/a	tasty; delicious
sabroso/a	tasty; delicious

Las frutas

la banana	banana
las frutas	fruits
el limón	lemon
la manzana	apple
el melocotón	peach
la naranja	orange
la pera	pear
la uva	grape

Las verduras

las arvejas	peas
la cebolla	onion
el champiñón	mushroom
la ensalada	salad
los espárragos	asparagus
los frijoles	beans
la lechuga	lettuce
el maíz	corn
las papas/patatas (fritas)	(fried) potatoes; French fries
el tomate	tomato
las verduras	vegetables
la zanahoria	carrot

Supersite/IRCD: MP3 Audio Files, Testing Program, *Vocabulario adicional*

recursos

LM p. 130

adelante. vhlcentral.com

La carne y el pescado

el atún	tuna
el bistec	steak
los camarones	shrimp
la carne	meat
la carne de res	beef
la chuleta (de cerdo)	(pork) chop
la hamburguesa	hamburger
el jamón	ham
la langosta	lobster
los mariscos	shellfish
el pavo	turkey
el pescado	fish
el pollo (asado)	(roast) chicken
la salchicha	sausage
el salmón	salmon

Otras comidas

el aceite	oil
el ajo	garlic
el arroz	rice
el azúcar	sugar
los cereales	cereal; grains
el huevo	egg
la mantequilla	butter
la margarina	margarine
la mayonesa	mayonnaise
el pan (tostado)	(toasted) bread
la pimienta	black pepper
el queso	cheese
la sal	salt
el sándwich	sandwich
la sopa	soup
el vinagre	vinegar
el yogur	yogurt

Las bebidas

el agua (mineral)	(mineral) water
la bebida	drink
el café	coffee
la cerveza	beer
el jugo (de fruta)	(fruit) juice
la leche	milk
el refresco	soft drink
el té (helado)	(iced) tea
el vino (blanco/tinto)	(white/red) wine

Verbos

escoger	to choose
merendar (e:ie)	to snack
morir (o:ue)	to die
pedir (e:i)	to order (food)
probar (o:ue)	to taste; to try
recomendar (e:ie)	to recommend
saber	to taste; to know
saber a	to taste like
servir (e:i)	to serve

Las comparaciones

como	like; as
más de (+ number)	more than
más... que	more ... than
menos de (+ number)	fewer than
menos... que	less ... than
tan... como	as ... as
tantos/as... como	as many... as
tanto... como	as much... as
el/la mayor	the eldest
el/la mejor	the best
el/la menor	the youngest
el/la peor	the worst
mejor	better
peor	worse

Expresiones útiles	See page 83.

contextos

1 **¿Qué comida es?** Read the descriptions and write the names of the food in the blanks.

1. Son rojos y se sirven (*they are served*) en las ensaladas. los tomates _____

2. Se come (*It is eaten*) antes del plato principal; es líquida y caliente (*hot*). la sopa _____

3. Son unas verduras anaranjadas, largas y delgadas. las zanahorias _____

4. Hay de naranja y de manzana; se bebe en el desayuno. el jugo _____

5. Son dos rebanadas (*slices*) de pan con queso y jamón. el sándwich _____

6. Es comida rápida; se sirven con hamburguesas y se les pone sal. las papas fritas _____

7. Son pequeños y rosados; viven en el mar. los camarones _____

8. Son frutas amarillas; con agua y azúcar se hace una bebida de verano. los limones _____

2 **Categorías** Categorize the foods listed in the word bank.

aceite	cebollas	jamón	mantequilla	peras	salmón
arvejas	champiñones	langosta	manzanas	pimienta	tomates
atún	chuletas de	leche	margarina	pollo	uvas
azúcar	cerdo	lechuga	melocotones	queso	vinagre
bananas	espárragos	limones	naranjas	sal	yogur
bistec	hamburguesas	maíz	papas	salchichas	zanahorias
camarones					

Verduras	Productos lácteos (*dairy*)	Condimentos	Carnes y aves (*poultry*)	Pescados y mariscos	Frutas
arvejas	leche	aceite	bistec	atún	bananas
cebollas	mantequilla	azúcar	chuletas de cerdo	camarones	limones
champiñones	margarina	pimienta	hamburguesas	langosta	manzanas
espárragos	queso	sal	jamón	salmón	melocotones
lechuga	yogur	vinagre	pollo		naranjas
maíz			salchichas		peras
papas					tomates
tomates					uvas
zanahorias					

3 **¿Qué es?** Label the food item shown in each drawing. Suggested answer:

1. _____ el vino tinto _____   2. _____ las zanahorias _____

3. _____ los camarones _____   4. _____ las uvas _____

4 **¿Cuándo lo comes?** Read the lists of meals, then categorize when the meals would be eaten.

1. un sándwich de jamón y queso, unas chuletas de cerdo con arroz y frijoles, un yogur y un café con leche

Desayuno _un yogur y un café con leche_

Almuerzo _un sándwich de jamón y queso_

Cena _unas chuletas de cerdo con arroz y frijoles_

2. una langosta con papas y espárragos, huevos fritos y jugo de naranja, una hamburguesa y un refresco

Desayuno _huevos fritos y jugo de naranja_

Almuerzo _una hamburguesa y un refresco_

Cena _una langosta con papas y espárragos_

3. pan tostado con mantequilla, un sándwich de atún y té helado, un bistec con cebolla y arroz

Desayuno _pan tostado con mantequilla_

Almuerzo _un sándwich de atún y té helado_

Cena _un bistec con cebolla y arroz_

4. una sopa y una ensalada, cereales con leche, pollo asado con ajo y champiñones

Desayuno _cereales con leche_

Almuerzo _una sopa y una ensalada_

Cena _pollo asado con ajo y champiñones_

estructura

2.1 Preterite of stem-changing verbs

1   **En el pasado**   Rewrite each sentence, conjugating the verbs into the preterite tense.

1. Ana y Enrique piden unos resfrescos fríos.

   Ana y Enrique pidieron unos refrescos fríos.

2. Mi mamá nos sirve arroz con frijoles y carne.

   Mi mamá nos sirvió arroz con frijoles y carne.

3. Tina y Linda duermen en un hotel de Lima.

   Tina y Linda durmieron en un hotel de Lima.

4. Las flores (*flowers*) de mi tía mueren durante el otoño.

   Las flores de mi tía murieron durante el otoño.

5. Ustedes se sienten bien porque ayudan a las personas.

   Ustedes se sintieron bien porque ayudaron a las personas.

2   **¿Qué hicieron?**   For each sentence, choose the correct verb from those in parentheses. Then complete the sentence by writing the preterite form of the verb.

1. Rosana y Héctor _____repitieron_____ las palabras del profesor. (repetir, dormir, morir)

2. El abuelo de Luis _____murió_____ el año pasado. (despedirse, morir, servir)

3. (yo) _____Serví_____ camarones y salmón de cena en mi casa. (morir, conseguir, servir)

4. Lisa y tú _____pidieron_____ pan tostado con queso y huevo. (sentirse, seguir, pedir)

5. Elena _____durmió_____ en casa de su prima el sábado. (dormir, pedir, repetir)

6. Gilberto y su familia _____prefirieron_____ ir al restaurante francés. (servir, preferir, vestirse)

3   **No pasó así**   Your brother is very confused today. Correct his mistakes by rewriting each sentence, using the subject in parentheses.

1. Anoche nos despedimos de nuestros abuelos en el aeropuerto. (mis primos)

   Anoche mis primos se despidieron de nuestros abuelos en el aeropuerto.

2. Melinda y Juan siguieron a Camelia por la ciudad en el auto. (yo)

   Seguí a Camelia por la ciudad en el auto.

3. Alejandro prefirió quedarse en casa. (ustedes)

   Ustedes prefirieron quedarse en casa.

4. Pedí un plato de langosta con salsa de mantequilla. (ellas)

   Ellas pidieron un plato de langosta con salsa de mantequilla.

5. Los camareros les sirvieron una ensalada con atún y espárragos. (tu esposo)

   Tu esposo les sirvió una ensalada con atún y espárragos.

4 **En el restaurante** Create sentences from the elements provided. Use the preterite form of the verbs.

1. (nosotros) / preferir / este restaurante al restaurante italiano

   Preferimos este restaurante al restaurante italiano.

2. mis amigos / seguir / a Gustavo para encontrar el restaurante

   Mis amigos siguieron a Gustavo para encontrar el restaurante.

3. la camarera / servirte / huevos fritos y café con leche

   La camarera te sirvió huevos fritos y café con leche.

4. ustedes / pedir / ensalada de mariscos y vino blanco

   Ustedes pidieron ensalada de mariscos y vino blanco.

5. Carlos / preferir / las papas fritas

   Carlos prefirió las papas fritas.

6. (yo) / conseguir / el menú del restaurante

   Conseguí el menú del restaurante.

5 **La planta de la abuela** Complete the letter with the preterite form of the verbs from the word bank. Use each verb only once.

conseguir	dormir	pedir	repetir	servir
despedirse	morir	preferir	seguir	vestirse

Querida mamá:

El fin de semana pasado fui a visitar a mi abuela Lilia en el campo. (Yo) Le (1) **conseguí** unos libros de la librería de la universidad porque ella me los (2) **pidió**. Cuando llegué, mi abuela me (3) **sirvió** un plato sabroso de arroz con frijoles. La encontré triste porque la semana pasada su planta de tomates (4) **murió**, y ahora tiene que comprar los tomates en el mercado. Me invitó a quedarme, y yo (5) **dormí** en su casa. Por la mañana, abuela Lilia se despertó temprano, (6) **se vistió** y salió a comprar huevos para el desayuno. Me levanté inmediatamente y la (7) **seguí** porque quería ir con ella al mercado. En el mercado, ella me (8) **repitió** que estaba triste por la planta de tomates. Le pregunté: ¿Debemos comprar otra planta de tomates?, pero ella (9) **prefirió** esperar hasta el verano. Después del desayuno (10) **me despedí** de ella y volví a la universidad. Quiero mucho a la abuela. ¿Cuándo la vas a visitar?

Chau,

Mónica

2.2 Double object pronouns

1 **Buena gente** Rewrite each sentence, replacing the direct objects with direct object pronouns.

1. La camarera te sirvió el plato de pasta con mariscos.

   La camarera te lo sirvió.

2. Isabel nos trajo la sal y la pimienta a la mesa.

   Isabel nos las trajo a la mesa.

3. Javier me pidió el aceite y el vinagre anoche.

   Javier me los pidió anoche.

4. El dueño nos busca una mesa para seis personas.

   El dueño nos la busca (para seis personas).

5. Tu madre me consigue unos melocotones deliciosos.

   Tu madre me los consigue.

6. ¿Te recomendaron este restaurante Lola y Paco?

   ¿Te lo recomendaron Lola y Paco?

2 **En el restaurante** Last night, you and some friends ate in a popular new restaurant. Rewrite what happened there, using double object pronouns in each sentence.

1. La dueña nos abrió la sección de no fumar.

   La dueña nos la abrió.

2. Le pidieron los menús al camarero.

   Se los pidieron.

3. Nos buscaron un lugar cómodo y nos sentamos.

   Nos lo buscaron y nos sentamos.

4. Les sirven papas fritas con el pescado a los clientes.

   Se las sirven.

5. Le llevaron unos entremeses a la mesa a Marcos.

   Se los llevaron.

6. Me trajeron una ensalada de lechuga y tomate.

   Me la trajeron.

7. El dueño le compró la carne al señor Gutiérrez.

   El dueño se la compró.

8. Ellos te mostraron los vinos antes de servirlos.

   Ellos te los mostraron.

3 **¿Quiénes son?** Answer the questions, using double object pronouns.

1. ¿A quiénes les escribiste las cartas? (a ellos) _Se las escribí a ellos._

2. ¿Quién le recomendó ese plato? (su tío) _Se lo recomendó su tío./Su tío se lo recomendó._

3. ¿Quién nos va a abrir la puerta a esta hora? (Sonia) _Nos la va a abrir Sonia./Sonia nos la va a abrir._

4. ¿Quién les sirvió el pescado asado? (Miguel) _Se lo sirvió Miguel./Miguel se lo sirvió._

5. ¿Quién te llevó los entremeses? (mis amigas) _Me los llevaron mis amigas./Mis amigas me los llevaron._

6. ¿A quién le ofrece frutas Roberto? (a su familia) _Se las ofrece a su familia./Roberto se las ofrece a su familia._

4 **La cena** Read the two conversations. Then answer the questions, using double object pronouns.

CELIA *(A Tito)* Rosalía me recomendó este restaurante.

DUEÑO Buenas noches, señores. Les traigo unos entremeses, cortesía del restaurante.

CAMARERO Buenas noches. ¿Quieren ver el menú?

TITO Sí, por favor. ¿Está buena la langosta?

CAMARERO Sí, es la especialidad del restaurante.

TITO Entonces queremos pedir dos langostas.

CELIA Y yo quiero una copa *(glass)* de vino tinto, por favor.

CAMARERO Tenemos flan y fruta de postre *(for dessert)*.

CELIA Perdón, ¿me lo puede repetir?

CAMARERO Tenemos flan y fruta.

CELIA Yo no quiero nada de postre, gracias.

DUEÑO ¿Les gustó la cena?

TITO Sí, nos encantó. Muchas gracias. Fue una cena deliciosa.

1. ¿Quién le recomendó el restaurante a Celia? _Se lo recomendó Rosalía./Rosalía se lo recomendó._

2. ¿Quién les sirvió los entremeses a Celia y a Tito? _Se los sirvió el dueño./El dueño se los sirvió._

3. ¿Quién les trajo los menús a Celia y a Tito? _Se los trajo el camarero./El camarero se los trajo._

4. ¿A quién le preguntó Tito cómo está la langosta? _Se lo preguntó al camarero._

5. ¿Quién le pidió las langostas al camarero? _Se las pidió Tito./Tito se las pidió._

6. ¿Quién le pidió un vino tinto al camarero? _Se lo pidió Celia./Celia se lo pidió._

7. ¿Quién le repitió a Celia la lista de postres? _Se la repitió el camarero./El camarero se la repitió._

8. ¿A quién le dio las gracias Tito cuando se fueron? _Se las dio al dueño._

2.3 Comparisons

1 **¿Cómo se comparan?** Complete the sentences with the Spanish of the comparison in parentheses.

1. Puerto Rico es _____más pequeño que_____ (*smaller than*) Guatemala.

2. Álex corre _____más rápido que_____ (*faster than*) su amigo Ricardo.

3. Los champiñones son _____tan ricos/deliciosos/sabrosos como_____ (*as tasty as*) los espárragos.

4. Los jugadores de baloncesto son _____más altos que_____ (*taller than*) los otros estudiantes.

5. Jimena es _____más trabajadora que_____ (*more hard-working than*) su novio Pablo.

6. Marisol es _____menos inteligente que_____ (*less intelligent than*) su hermana mayor.

7. La nueva novela de ese escritor es _____tan mala como_____ (*as bad as*) su primera novela.

8. Agustín y Mario están _____menos gordos que_____ (*less fat than*) antes.

2 **Lo obvio** Your friend Francisco is always sharing his opinions with you, even though his comparisons are always painfully obvious. Write sentences that express his opinions, using the adjectives in parentheses.

> **modelo**
> (inteligente) Albert Einstein / Homer Simpson
> **Albert Einstein es más inteligente que Homer Simpson.**

1. (famoso) Gloria Estefan / mi hermana

   Gloria Estefan es más famosa que mi hermana.

2. (difícil) estudiar química orgánica / leer una novela

   Estudiar química orgánica es más difícil que leer una novela.

3. (malo) el tiempo en Boston / el tiempo en Florida

   El tiempo en Boston es peor que el tiempo en Florida.

4. (barato) los restaurantes elegantes / los restaurantes de comida rápida

   Los restaurantes elegantes son menos baratos que los restaurantes de comida rápida.

5. (viejo) mi abuelo / mi sobrino

   Mi abuelo es mayor que mi sobrino.

3 **¿Por qué?** Complete the sentences with the correct comparisons.

> **modelo**
> Darío juega mejor al fútbol que tú.
> **Es porque Darío practica más que tú.**

1. Mi hermano es más gordo que mi padre. Es porque mi hermano come _____más que mi padre/más que él_____.

2. Natalia conoce más países que tú. Es porque Natalia viaja _____más que tú_____.

3. Estoy más cansado que David. Es porque duermo _____menos que David/menos que él_____.

4. Rolando tiene más hambre que yo. Va a comer _____más que yo_____.

5. Mi vestido favorito es más barato que el tuyo. Voy a pagar _____menos que tú_____.

6. Julia gana más dinero que Lorna. Es porque Julia trabaja _____más que Lorna/más que ella_____.

4   **Comparaciones**   Form complete sentences using one word from each column. Answers will vary.

la carne	bueno	el aceite
la comida rápida	caro	el almuerzo
el desayuno	malo	las chuletas de cerdo
la fruta	pequeño	la ensalada
la mantequilla	rico	los entremeses
el pollo	sabroso	el pescado

> **modelo**
> La carne es más cara que el pescado.

1. _____ 4. _____

2. _____ 5. _____

3. _____ 6. _____

5   **Tan...como**   Compare Jorge and Marcos using comparisons of equality and the following words. Be creative in your answers. Answers will vary.

alto	delgado	inteligente
bueno	guapo	joven

> **modelo**
> Marcos no es tan inteligente como Jorge.

1. _____ 4. _____

2. _____ 5. _____

3. _____ 6. _____

6   **¿Más o menos?**   Read the pairs of sentences. Then write a new sentence that compares them.

> **modelo**
> Ese hotel tiene cien habitaciones. El otro hotel tiene cuarenta habitaciones.
> Ese hotel tiene más habitaciones que el otro.

1. La biblioteca tiene ciento cincuenta sillas. El laboratorio de lenguas tiene treinta sillas.

   La biblioteca tiene más sillas que el laboratorio de lenguas.

2. Ramón compró tres corbatas. Roberto compró tres corbatas.

   Ramón compró tantas corbatas como Roberto.

3. Yo comí un plato de pasta. Mi hermano comió dos platos de pasta.

   Yo comí menos que mi hermano./Yo comí menos pasta que mi hermano.

4. Anabel durmió ocho horas. Amelia durmió ocho horas.

   Anabel durmió tanto como Amelia./Anabel durmió tantas horas como Amelia.

5. Mi primo toma seis clases. Mi amiga Tere toma ocho clases.

   Mi primo toma menos clases que mi amiga Tere.

2.4 Superlatives

1 **El mejor...** Complete with the appropriate information in each case. Form complete sentences using the superlatives. Answers will vary. Sample answers:

> **modelo**
>
> el restaurante _____ / mejor / ciudad
> **El restaurante Dalí es el mejor restaurante de mi ciudad**

1. la película _____ / mala / la historia del cine

   La película *Cobardes* es la peor de la historia del cine.

2. la comida _____ / sabrosa / todas

   La comida mexicana es la más sabrosa de todas.

3. mi _____ / joven / mi familia

   Mi sobrino es el más joven de mi familia.

4. el libro _____ / interesante / biblioteca

   El libro *El Quijote* es el más interesante de la biblioteca.

5. las vacaciones de _____ / buenas / año

   Las vacaciones de verano son las mejores del año.

2 **Facilísimo** Rewrite each sentence, using absolute superlatives.

1. Javier y Maite están muy cansados. Javier y Maite están cansadísimos.

2. Álex es muy joven. Álex es jovencísimo.

3. Inés es muy inteligente. Inés es inteligentísima.

4. La madre de Inés está muy contenta. La madre de Inés está contentísima.

5. Estoy muy aburrido. Estoy aburridísimo.

3 **Compárate** Compare yourself with the members of your family and the students in your class. Form complete sentences using comparisons of equality and inequality, superlatives, and absolute superlatives. Answers will vary.

> **modelo**
>
> En mi familia... yo soy más bajo que mi hermano.

_____

_____

> **modelo**
>
> En mi clase... mi amigo Evan es tan inteligente como yo.

_____

_____

Síntesis

Interview a friend or a relative and ask him or her to describe two restaurants where he or she recently ate.

- How was the quality of the food at each restaurant?
- How was the quality of the service at each restaurant?
- How did the prices of the two restaurants compare?
- What did his or her dining companions think about the restaurants?
- How was the ambience different at each restaurant?
- How convenient are the restaurants? Are they centrally located? Are they accessible by public transportation? Do they have parking?

When you are finished with the interview, write up a comparison of the two restaurants based on the information you collected. Use as many different types of comparisons and superlative phrases as possible in your report. Answers will vary.

panorama

Guatemala

1 **Guatemala** Complete the sentences with the correct words.

1. La _____moneda_____ de Guatemala recibe su nombre de un pájaro que simboliza la libertad.

2. Un _____cuarenta_____ por ciento de la población guatemalteca tiene una lengua maya como materna.

3. El _____diseño_____ y los colores de cada *huipil* indican el pueblo de origen de la persona que lo lleva.

4. El _____quetzal_____ es un pájaro en peligro de extinción.

5. La civilización maya inventó un _____calendario_____ complejo y preciso.

6. La ropa tradicional refleja el amor a la _____naturaleza_____ de la cultura maya.

2 **Preguntas** Answer the questions with complete sentences. Answers will vary. Sample answers:

1. ¿Cuál es un cultivo de mucha importancia en la cultura maya?

El maíz es un cultivo de mucha importancia en la cultura maya.

2. ¿Quién es Miguel Ángel Asturias?

Miguel Ángel Asturias es un escritor guatemalteco célebre.

3. ¿Qué países limitan con (*border*) Guatemala?

México, Belice, El Salvador y Honduras limitan con Guatemala.

4. ¿Hasta cuándo fue la Antigua Guatemala una capital importante? ¿Por qué?

La Antigua Guatemala fue una capital importante hasta 1773, cuando un terremoto la destruyó.

5. ¿Por qué simbolizaba el quetzal la libertad para los mayas?

El quetzal simboliza la libertad para los mayas porque creían que este pájaro no podía vivir en cautividad.

6. ¿Qué hace el gobierno para proteger al quetzal?

El gobierno mantiene una reserva biológica especial para proteger al quetzal.

3 **Fotos de Guatemala** Label each photo.

1. _____el quetzal_____

2. _____los huipiles_____

4 **Comparar** Read the sentences about Guatemala. Then rewrite them, using comparisons and superlatives.

> modelo
>
> Guatemala no tiene doce millones de habitantes.
> *Guatemala tiene más de doce millones de habitantes.*

1. El área de Guatemala no es más grande que la de Tennessee.

   El área de Guatemala es más pequeña que la de Tennessee.

2. Un ingrediente muy interesante de las telas (*fabrics*) de Guatemala es el mosquito.

   Un ingrediente interesantísimo de las telas de Guatemala es el mosquito.

3. Las lenguas mayas no se hablan tanto como el español.

   Las lenguas mayas se hablan menos que el español.

4. Rigoberta Menchú no es mayor que Margarita Carrera.

   Rigoberta Menchú es menor que Margarita Carrera.

5. La celebración de la Semana Santa en la Antigua Guatemala es importantísima para muchas personas.

   La celebración de la Semana Santa en la Antigua Guatemala es la más importante del hemisferio para muchas personas.

5 **¿Cierto o falso?** Indicate whether the statements about Guatemala are **cierto** or **falso.** Correct the false statements.

1. Rigoberta Menchú ganó el premio Nobel de la Paz en 1992.

   Cierto.

2. La lengua materna de muchos guatemaltecos es una lengua inca.

   Falso. La lengua materna de muchos guatemaltecos es una lengua maya.

3. La civilización de los mayas no era avanzada.

   Falso. La civilización de los mayas era muy avanzada.

4. Guatemala es un país que tiene costas en dos océanos.

   Cierto.

5. Hay muchísimos quetzales en los bosques de Guatemala.

   Falso. Los quetzales están en peligro de extinción.

6. La civilización maya descubrió y usó el cero antes que los europeos.

   Cierto.

¿Qué tal la comida?

Lección 2
Fotonovela

Antes de ver el video

1 | **En un restaurante** What kinds of things do you do and say when you have lunch at a restaurant?
Answers will vary.

Mientras ves el video

2 | **¿Quién?** Watch the **¿Qué tal la comida?** segment of this video module and write the name of the person who says each of the following lines.

Afirmación	Nombre
1. ¡Tengo más hambre que un elefante!	Javier
2. Pero si van a ir de excursión deben comer bien.	señora Perales
3. Y de tomar, les recomiendo el jugo de piña, frutilla y mora.	señora Perales
4. Hoy es el cumpleaños de Maite.	don Francisco
5. ¡Rico, rico!	Maite

3 | **Los restaurantes de Madrid** Watch Maite's flashback about restaurants in Madrid and place a check mark beside the sentence that best summarizes the flashback.

_____ 1. Es muy caro salir a cenar en Madrid.

_____ 2. A Maite no le gustan los restaurantes de Madrid.

_✓_ 3. Hay una gran variedad de restaurantes en Madrid.

_____ 4. Los restaurantes de Madrid son muy elegantes.

4 | **Resumen** Watch the **Resumen** segment of this video module and fill in the missing words in these sentences.

1. **JAVIER** ¿Qué nos _____recomienda_____ usted?

2. **DON FRANCISCO** Debo _____visitarla_____ más a menudo.

3. **DOÑA RITA** ¿_____Se_____ lo traigo a todos?

4. **DON FRANCISCO** Es bueno _____conocer_____ a la dueña del mejor restaurante de la ciudad.

5. **JAVIER** Para mí las _____tortillas_____ de maíz y un ceviche de _____camarón_____.

Después de ver el video

5 **Opiniones** Write the names of the video characters who expressed the following opinions, either verbally or through body language.

señora Perales _____ 1. Don Francisco es un conductor excelente.

Álex; don Francisco _____ 2. El servicio en este restaurante es muy eficiente.

señora Perales _____ 3. Nuestros pasteles son exquisitos.

Álex _____ 4. ¡Caldo de patas! Suena (*It sounds*) como un plato horrible.

señora Perales _____ 5. Las tortillas de maíz son muy sabrosas. Se las recomiendo.

señora Perales _____ 6. Las montañas de nuestro país son muy hermosas.

6 **Corregir** Correct these false statements about the **¿Qué tal la comida?** video episode.

1. El Cráter es un mercado al aire libre.

   El Cráter es un restaurante. _____

2. La señora Perales trabaja en El Cráter. Es camarera.

   La señora Perales es la dueña del restaurante. _____

3. Maite pide las tortillas de maíz y la fuente de fritada.

   Maite pide un caldo de patas y lomo a la plancha. _____

4. Álex pide el caldo de patas y una ensalada.

   Álex pide las tortillas de maíz y el ceviche de camarón. _____

5. De beber, todos piden té.

   De beber, todos piden jugo de piña, frutilla y mora. _____

6. La señora Perales dice (*says*) que los pasteles de El Cráter son muy caros.

   La señora Perales dice que los pasteles de El Cráter son muy ricos. _____

7 **Preguntas personales** Answer these questions in Spanish. Answers will vary.

1. ¿Almuerzas en la cafetería de tu universidad? ¿Por qué? _____

   _____

2. ¿Cuál es tu plato favorito? ¿Por qué? _____

   _____

3. ¿Cuál es el mejor restaurante de tu comunidad? Explica (*Explain*) tu opinión. _____

   _____

4. ¿Cuál es tu restaurante favorito? ¿Cuál es la especialidad de ese restaurante? _____

   _____

5. ¿Sales mucho a cenar con tus amigos/as? ¿Adónde van a cenar? _____

   _____

Panorama: Guatemala

Antes de ver el video

1 **Más vocabulario** Look over these useful words and expressions before you watch the video.

Vocabulario útil		
alfombra *rug*	destruir *to destroy*	ruinas *ruins*
artículos *items*	época colonial *colonial times*	sobrevivir *to survive*
calle *street*	indígenas *indigenous people*	terremoto *earthquake*

2 **Describir** In this video you are going to learn about an open-air market that take place in Guatemala. In Spanish, describe one open-air market that you know. Answers will vary.

mercado: _____

_____

_____

_____

_____

3 **Categorías** Categorize the words listed in the word bank.

bonitas	espectaculares	indígenas	quieres
calles	grandes	mercado	región
colonial	habitantes	monasterios	sentir
conocer	iglesias	mujeres	vieja

Lugares	Personas	Verbos	Adjetivos
calles	habitantes	conocer	bonitas
iglesia	indígenas	quieres	colonial
mercado	mujeres	sentir	espectaculares
monasterios			grandes
región			vieja

Mientras ves el video

4 **Marcar** Check off what you see while watching the video.

✓ 1. fuente (*fountain*)

✓ 2. hombres con vestidos morados

____ 3. mujer bailando

✓ 4. mujer llevando bebé en el mercado

✓ 5. mujeres haciendo alfombras de flores

✓ 6. niñas sonriendo

____ 7. niño dibujando

✓ 8. personas hablando

✓ 9. ruinas

____ 10. turista mirando el paisaje

Después de ver el video

5 **Completar** Complete the sentences with words from the word bank.

| aire libre | alfombras | atmósfera | fijo | indígenas | regatear |

1. En Semana Santa las mujeres hacen _____alfombras_____ con miles de flores.

2. En Chichicastenango hay un mercado al _____aire libre_____ los jueves y domingos.

3. En el mercado los artículos no tienen un precio _____fijo_____.

4. Los clientes tienen que _____regatear_____ cuando hacen sus compras.

5. En las calles de Antigua, los turistas pueden sentir la _____atmósfera_____ del pasado.

6. Muchos _____indígenas_____ de toda la región vienen al mercado a vender sus productos.

6 **¿Cierto o falso?** Indicate whether each statement is **cierto** or **falso**. Correct the false statements.

1. Antigua fue la capital de Guatemala hasta 1773.

Cierto.

2. Una de las celebraciones más importantes de Antigua es la de la Semana Santa.

Cierto.

3. En esta celebración, muchas personas se visten con ropa de color verde.

Falso. En esta celebración muchas personas se visten con ropa de color morado.

4. Antigua es una ciudad completamente moderna. Falso. En Antigua todavía hay ruinas de la vieja capital, hay

muchas iglesias y monasterios de arquitectura colonial y se puede sentir la atmósfera del pasado.

5. Chichicastenango es una ciudad mucho más grande que Antigua.

Falso. Chichicastenango es más pequeña que Antigua.

6. El terremoto de 1773 destruyó todas las iglesias y monasterios en Antigua.

Falso. Muchas iglesias y monasterios sobrevivieron al terremoto.

7 **Escribir** Write four sentences comparing the cities Antigua and Chichicastenango. Answers will vary.

_____

_____

_____

_____

1   **Identificar**   Listen to each question and mark an **X** in the appropriate category.

> **modelo**
>
> *You hear:* ¿Qué es la piña?
> *You mark:* an **X** under **fruta**.

	carne	pescado	verdura	fruta	bebida
Modelo	____	____	____	**X**	____
1.	____	X	____	____	____
2.	____	____	____	____	X
3.	____	____	X	____	____
4.	____	X	____	____	____
5.	X	____	____	____	____
6.	____	____	____	X	____
7.	X	____	____	____	____
8.	____	____	____	____	X

2   **Describir**   Listen to each sentence and write the number of the sentence below the drawing of the food or drink mentioned.

a. _____ 4 _____   b. _____ 6 _____   c. _____ 9 _____   d. _____ 1 _____

e. _____ 7 _____   f. _____ 3 _____   g. _____ 10 _____   h. _____ 2 _____

i. _____ 8 _____   j. _____ 5 _____

3   **En el restaurante**   You will hear a couple ordering a meal in a restaurant. Write the items they order in the appropriate categories.

	SEÑORA	**SEÑOR**
Primer plato	ensalada de lechuga y tomate	sopa de verduras
Plato principal	hamburguesa con queso	pollo asado
Verdura	papas fritas	arvejas y zanahorias
Bebida	agua mineral	agua mineral

pronunciación

ll, ñ, c, and z

Most Spanish speakers pronounce the letter **ll** like the *y* in *yes*.

| pollo | llave | ella | cebolla |

The letter **ñ** is pronounced much like the *ny* in *canyon*.

| mañana | señor | baño | niña |

Before **a, o,** or **u,** the Spanish **c** is pronounced like the *c* in *car*.

| café | colombiano | cuando | rico |

Before **e** or **i,** the Spanish **c** is pronounced like the *s* in *sit*. In parts of Spain, **c** before **e** or **i** is pronounced like the *th* in *think*.

| cereales | delicioso | conducir | conocer |

The Spanish **z** is pronounced like the *s* in *sit*. In parts of Spain, **z** before a vowel is pronounced like the *th* in *think*.

| zeta | zanahoria | almuerzo | cerveza |

---

1 **Práctica** Repeat each word after the speaker to practice pronouncing **ll, ñ, c,** and **z**.

1. mantequilla	5. español	9. quince
2. cuñado	6. cepillo	10. compañera
3. aceite	7. zapato	11. almorzar
4. manzana	8. azúcar	12. calle

---

2 **Oraciones** When the speaker pauses, repeat the corresponding sentence or phrase, focusing on **ll, ñ, c,** and **z**.

1. Mi compañero de cuarto se llama Toño Núñez. Su familia es de la ciudad de Guatemala y de Quetzaltenango.
2. Dice que la comida de su mamá es deliciosa, especialmente su pollo al champiñón y sus tortillas de maíz.
3. Creo que Toño tiene razón porque hoy cené en su casa y quiero volver mañana para cenar allí otra vez.

---

3 **Refranes** Repeat each saying after the speaker to practice pronouncing **ll, ñ, c,** and **z**.

1. Las aparencias engañan.
2. Panza llena, corazón contento.

---

4 **Dictado** You will hear five sentences. Each will be said twice. Listen carefully and write what you hear.

1. Catalina compró mantequilla, chuletas de cerdo, refrescos y melocotones en el mercado.

2. Ese señor español quiere almorzar en un restaurante francés.

3. El mozo le recomendó los camarones con arroz.

4. En mi casa empezamos la comida con una sopa.

5. Guillermo llevó a Alicia al Café Azul anoche.

estructura

2.1 Preterite of stem-changing verbs

1 **Identificar** Listen to each sentence and decide whether the verb is in the present or the preterite tense. Mark an **X** in the appropriate column.

> **modelo**
> *You hear:* Pido bistec con papas fritas.
> *You mark:* an **X** under *Present*.

	Present	*Preterite*
Modelo	**X**	
1.	X	
2.	X	
3.		X
4.	X	
5.	X	
6.		X
7.		X
8.		X

2 **Cambiar** Change each sentence you hear substituting the new subject given. Repeat the correct response after the speaker. (*6 items*)

> **modelo**
> Tú no dormiste bien anoche. (Los niños)
> *Los niños no durmieron bien anoche.*

3 **Preguntas** Answer each question you hear using the cue in your lab manual. Repeat the correct response after the speaker.

> **modelo**
> *You hear:* ¿Qué pediste?
> *You see:* pavo asado con papas y arvejas
> *You say:* Pedí pavo asado con papas y arvejas.

1. Sí	3. leche	5. No
2. No	4. Sí	6. la semana pasada

4 **Un día largo** Listen as Ernesto describes what he did yesterday. Then read the statements in your lab manual and decide whether they are **cierto** or **falso**.

	Cierto	Falso
1. Ernesto se levantó a las seis y media de la mañana.	○	⊘
2. Se bañó y se vistió.	⊘	○
3. Los clientes empezaron a llegar a la una.	○	⊘
4. Almorzó temprano.	○	⊘
5. Pidió pollo asado con papas.	⊘	○
6. Después de almorzar, Ernesto y su primo siguieron trabajando.	⊘	○

2.2 Double object pronouns

1 **Escoger** The manager of **El Gran Pavo** Restaurant wants to know what items the chef is going to serve to the customers today. Listen to each question and choose the correct response.

1. a. Sí, se las voy a servir.   (b.) No, no se los voy a servir.

2. (a.) Sí, se la voy a servir.   b. No, no se lo voy a servir.

3. (a.) Sí, se los voy a servir.   b. No, no se las voy a servir.

4. a. Sí, se los voy a servir.   (b.) No, no se las voy a servir.

5. a. Sí, se la voy a servir.   (b.) No, no se lo voy a servir.

6. (a.) Sí, se lo voy a servir.   b. No, no se la voy a servir.

2 **Cambiar** Repeat each statement, replacing the direct object noun with a pronoun. (*6 items*)

> **modelo**
> María te hace ensalada.
> María te la hace.

3 **Preguntas** Answer each question using the cue you hear and object pronouns. Repeat the correct response after the speaker. (*5 items*)

> **modelo**
> ¿Me recomienda usted los mariscos? (sí)
> Sí, se los recomiendo.

4 **Una fiesta** Listen to this conversation between Eva and Marcela. Then read the statements in your lab manual and decide whether they are **cierto** or **falso**.

	Cierto	Falso
1. Le van a hacer una fiesta a Sebastián.	✓	○
2. Le van a preparar langosta.	○	✓
3. Le van a preparar una ensalada de mariscos.	✓	○
4. Van a tener vino tinto, cerveza, agua mineral y té helado.	○	✓
5. Clara va a comprar cerveza.	○	✓
6. Le compraron un cinturón.	○	✓

2.3 Comparisons

1 **Escoger** You will hear a series of descriptions. Choose the statement in your lab manual that expresses the correct comparison.

1. a. Yo tengo más dinero que Rafael.
   b. Yo tengo menos dinero que Rafael.
2. a. Elena es mayor que Juan.
   b. Elena es menor que Juan.
3. a. Enrique come más hamburguesas que José.
   b. Enrique come tantas hamburguesas como José.
4. a. La comida de la Fonda es mejor que la comida del Café Condesa.
   b. La comida de la Fonda es peor que la comida del Café Condesa.
5. a. Las langostas cuestan tanto como los camarones.
   b. Los camarones cuestan menos que las langostas.

2 **Comparar** Look at each drawing and answer the question you hear with a comparative statement. Repeat the correct response after the speaker.

1. Ricardo   Sara

2. Héctor   Alejandro

3. Leonor   Melissa

3 **Al contrario** You are babysitting Anita, a small child, who starts boasting about herself and her family. Respond to each statement using a comparative of equality. Then repeat the correct answer after the speaker. (*6 items*)

modelo
Mi mamá es más bonita que tu mamá.
Al contrario, mi mamá es tan bonita como tu mamá.

2.4 Superlatives

1 **Superlativos** You will hear a series of descriptions. Choose the statement in your lab manual that expresses the correct superlative.

1. a. Tus pantalones no son los más grandes de la tienda.
   (b.) Tus pantalones son los más grandes de la tienda.
2. (a.) La camisa blanca es la más bonita del centro comercial.
   b. La camisa blanca no es tan bonita como otras camisas de la tienda.
3. a. Las rebajas del centro comercial son peores que las rebajas de la tienda.
   (b.) En el centro comercial puedes encontrar las mejores rebajas.
4. (a.) El vestido azul es el más caro de la tienda.
   b. El vestido azul es el más barato de la tienda.
5. (a.) Sebastián es el mejor vendedor de la tienda.
   b. Sebastián es el peor vendedor de la tienda.

2 **Preguntas** Answer each question you hear using the absolute superlative. Repeat the correct response after the speaker. (*6 items*)

> **modelo**
> La comida de la cafetería es mala, ¿no?
> Sí, *es* malísima.

3 **Anuncio** Listen to this advertisement. Then read the statements and decide whether they are **cierto** or **falso**.

	Cierto	Falso
1. El Corte Inglés es el almacén más pequeño de la ciudad.	○	⊘
2. La mejor ropa es siempre carísima.	○	⊘
3. Los zapatos de El Corte Inglés son muy elegantes.	⊘	○
4. En El Corte Inglés gastas menos dinero y siempre tienes muy buena calidad.	⊘	○
5. El horario de El Corte Inglés es tan flexible como el horario de las tiendas.	○	⊘

vocabulario

You will now hear the vocabulary found in your worktext on the last page of this lesson. Listen and repeat each Spanish word or phrase after the speaker.

Additional Vocabulary

Additional Vocabulary

Notes

Notes

Las fiestas

3

Communicative Goals

You will learn how to:
- Express congratulations
- Express gratitude
- Ask for and pay the bill at a restaurant

Las fiestas

Más vocabulario

la alegría	happiness
la amistad	friendship
el amor	love
el beso	kiss
la sorpresa	surprise
el aniversario (de bodas)	(wedding) anniversary
la boda	wedding
el cumpleaños	birthday
el día de fiesta	holiday
el divorcio	divorce
el matrimonio	marriage
la Navidad	Christmas
el/la recién casado/a	newlywed
la quinceañera	young woman's fifteenth birthday celebration
cambiar (de)	to change
celebrar	to celebrate
divertirse (e:ie)	to have fun
graduarse (de/en)	to graduate (from/in)
invitar	to invite
jubilarse	to retire (from work)
nacer	to be born
odiar	to hate
pasarlo bien/mal	to have a good/bad time
regalar	to give (a gift)
reírse (e:i)	to laugh
relajarse	to relax
sorprender	to surprise
sonreír (e:i)	to smile
juntos/as	together

Variación léxica

pastel ⟷ torta (*Arg., Venez.*)

comprometerse ⟷ prometerse (*Esp.*)

Supersite/IRCD: Lesson Plans, MP3 Audio Files and Listening Scripts, Overheads, *Vocabulario adicional*

recursos

| WB pp. 159–160 | LM p. 173 | adelante. vhlcentral.com |

la pareja

el pastel de chocolate

la botella de vino

el flan de caramelo

las galletas

los postres

el champán

los dulces

FELIZ CUMPLEAÑOS

brindar

el invitado

regalar

el helado

Relaciones personales

casarse (con)	*to get married (to)*
comprometerse (con)	*to get engaged (to)*
divorciarse (de)	*to get divorced (from)*
enamorarse (de)	*to fall in love (with)*
llevarse bien/mal (con)	*to get along well/ badly (with)*
romper (con)	*to break up (with)*
salir (con)	*to go out (with); to date*
separarse (de)	*to separate (from)*
tener una cita	*to have a date; to have an appointment*

Práctica

 1 2 Supersite/IRCD: MP3 Audio Files, Scripts

1 **Escuchar** Escucha la conversación e indica si las oraciones son **ciertas** o **falsas**.

1. A Silvia no le gusta mucho el chocolate. Falsa.
2. Silvia sabe que sus amigos le van a hacer una fiesta. Falsa.
3. Los amigos de Silvia le compraron un pastel de chocolate. Cierta.
4. Los amigos brindan por Silvia con refrescos. Falsa.
5. Silvia y sus amigos van a comer helado. Cierta.
6. Los amigos de Silvia le van a servir flan y galletas. Falsa.

2 **Ordenar** Escucha la narración y ordena las oraciones de acuerdo con los eventos de la vida de Beatriz.

 5 a. Beatriz se compromete con Roberto.
 4 b. Beatriz se gradúa.
 3 c. Beatriz sale con Emilio.
 2 d. Sus padres le hacen una gran fiesta.
 6 e. La pareja se casa.
 1 f. Beatriz nace en Montevideo.

3 **Emparejar** Indica la letra de la frase que mejor completa cada oración.

a. **cambió de**	d. **nos divertimos**	g. **se llevan bien**
b. **lo pasaron mal**	e. **se casaron**	h. **sonrió**
c. **nació**	f. **se jubiló**	i. **tenemos una cita**

1. María y sus compañeras de cuarto _g_. Son buenas amigas.
2. Pablo y yo _d_ en la fiesta. Bailamos y comimos mucho.
3. Manuel y Felipe _b_ en el cine. La película fue muy mala.
4. ¡Tengo una nueva sobrina! Ella _c_ ayer por la mañana.
5. Mi madre _a_ profesión. Ahora es artista.
6. Mi padre _f_ el año pasado. Ahora no trabaja.
7. Jorge y yo _i_ esta noche. Vamos a ir a un restaurante muy elegante.
8. Jaime y Laura _e_ el septiembre pasado. La boda fue maravillosa.

4 **Definiciones** En parejas, definan las palabras y escriban una oración para cada ejemplo. Answers will vary. Suggested answers below.

> **modelo**
>
> **romper (con)** una pareja termina la relación
>
> *Marta rompió con su novio.*

1. regalar dar un regalo
2. helado una comida fría y dulce
3. pareja dos personas enamoradas
4. invitado una persona que va a una fiesta
5. casarse ellos deciden estar juntos para siempre
6. pasarlo bien divertirse
7. sorpresa la persona no sabe lo que va a pasar
8. quinceañera la fiesta de cumpleaños de una chica de 15 años

Heritage Speakers Ask heritage speakers to describe Hispanic holidays or other celebrations that their families celebrate. Ex: **el Cinco de Mayo, la quinceañera**

Las etapas de la vida de Sergio

el nacimiento

la niñez

la adolescencia

la juventud

la madurez

la vejez

Más vocabulario	
la edad	*age*
el estado civil	*marital status*
las etapas de la vida	*the stages of life*
la muerte	*death*
casado/a	*married*
divorciado/a	*divorced*
separado/a	*separated*
soltero/a	*single*
viudo/a	*widower/widow*

5   **Las etapas de la vida** Identifica las etapas de la vida que se describen en estas oraciones.

1. Mi abuela se jubiló y se mudó (*moved*) a Viña del Mar.   la vejez
2. Mi padre trabaja para una compañía grande en Santiago.   la madurez
3. ¿Viste a mi nuevo sobrino en el hospital? Es precioso y ¡tan pequeño! · el nacimiento
4. Mi abuelo murió este año.   la muerte
5. Mi hermana se enamoró de un chico nuevo en la escuela.   la adolescencia
6. Mi hermana pequeña juega con muñecas (*dolls*).   la niñez

6   **Cambiar** Tu hermano/a menor no entiende nada de las etapas de la vida. En parejas, túrnense para decir que las afirmaciones son falsas y corríjanlas (*correct them*) cambiando las expresiones subrayadas (*underlined*).

> **modelo**
> **Estudiante 1:** La <u>niñez</u> es cuando trabajamos mucho.
> **Estudiante 2:** No, te equivocas (*you're wrong*). La madurez es cuando trabajamos mucho.

1. <u>El nacimiento</u> es el fin de la vida.   La muerte
2. <u>La juventud</u> es la etapa cuando nos jubilamos.   La vejez
3. A los sesenta y cinco años, muchas personas <u>comienzan a trabajar.</u>   se jubilan
4. Julián y nuestra prima <u>se divorcian</u> mañana.   se casan
5. Mamá <u>odia</u> a su hermana.   quiere / se lleva bien con
6. El abuelo murió, por eso la abuela es <u>separada</u>.   viuda
7. Cuando te gradúas de la universidad, estás en la etapa de <u>la adolescencia</u>.   la juventud
8. Mi tío nunca se casó; es <u>viudo</u>.   soltero

SUPERSITE

5 Ask students to create five sentences using words from the **Más vocabulario** box on this page.

NOTA CULTURAL

Viña del Mar es una ciudad en la costa de Chile, situada al oeste de Santiago. Tiene playas hermosas, excelentes hoteles, casinos y buenos restaurantes. El poeta Pablo Neruda pasó muchos años allí.

AYUDA

Other ways to contradict someone:
No es verdad.
It's not true.
Creo que no.
I don't think so.
¡Claro que no!
Of course not!
¡Qué va!
No way!

6 Explain that students are to give the opposite of the underlined words in their answers.

Comunicación

7

Una fiesta Trabaja con dos compañeros/as para planear una fiesta. Recuerda incluir la siguiente información.   Answers will vary.

1. ¿Qué tipo de fiesta es? ¿Dónde va a ser? ¿Cuándo va a ser?
2. ¿A quiénes van a invitar?
3. ¿Qué van a comer? ¿Quiénes van a llevar o a preparar la comida?
4. ¿Qué van a beber? ¿Quiénes van a llevar las bebidas?
5. ¿Qué van a hacer todos durante la fiesta?

7 To simplify, create a six-column chart on the board, with the headings **Lugar, Fecha y hora, Invitados, Comida, Bebidas,** and **Actividades**. Have groups brainstorm a few items for each category.

7 Have students make invitations for their party. Ask the class to judge which invitation is the cleverest, funniest, most elegant, and so forth.

Lección 3

8

Encuesta Tu profesor(a) va a darte una hoja de actividades. Haz las preguntas de la hoja a dos o tres compañeros/as de clase para saber qué actitudes tienen en sus relaciones personales. Luego comparte los resultados de la encuesta con la clase y comenta tus conclusiones.

Answers will vary.   Supersite/IRCD: *Hojas de actividades*

Preguntas	Nombres	Actitudes
1. ¿Te importa la amistad? ¿Por qué?		
2. ¿Es mejor tener un(a) buen(a) amigo/a o muchos/as amigos/as?		
3. ¿Cuáles son las características que buscas en tus amigos/as?		
4. ¿Tienes novio/a? ¿A qué edad es posible enamorarse?		
5. ¿Deben las parejas hacer todo juntos? ¿Deben tener las mismas opiniones? ¿Por qué?		

¡LENGUA VIVA!

While a **buen(a) amigo/a** is a *good friend*, the term **amigo/a íntimo/a** refers to a *close friend*, or a *very good friend*, without any romantic overtones.

Extra Practice Add a visual aspect to this vocabulary practice. Using magazine pictures, display images that pertain to parties or celebrations, stages of life, or interpersonal relations. Have students describe the pictures and make guesses about who the people are, how they are feeling, etc.

9

Minidrama En parejas, consulten la ilustración en la página 134, y luego, usando las palabras de la lista, preparen un minidrama para representar las etapas de la vida de Sergio. Pueden ser creativos e inventar más información sobre su vida.   Answers will vary.

amor	celebrar	enamorarse	romper
boda	comprometerse	graduarse	salir
cambiar	cumpleaños	jubilarse	separarse
casarse	divorciarse	nacer	tener una cita

9 To simplify, read through the word list as a class and have students name the stage(s) of life that correspond to each word.

¡Feliz cumpleaños, Maite!

Don Francisco y los estudiantes celebran el cumpleaños de Maite en el restaurante El Cráter.

PERSONAJES

MAITE

INÉS

DON FRANCISCO

ÁLEX

JAVIER

DOÑA RITA

CAMARERO

INÉS A mí me encantan los dulces. Maite, ¿tú qué vas a pedir?

MAITE Ay, no sé. Todo parece tan delicioso. Quizás el pastel de chocolate.

JAVIER Para mí el pastel de chocolate con helado. Me encanta el chocolate. Y tú, Álex, ¿qué vas a pedir?

ÁLEX Generalmente prefiero la fruta, pero hoy creo que voy a probar el pastel de chocolate.

DON FRANCISCO Yo siempre tomo un flan y un café.

DOÑA RITA ¡Feliz cumpleaños, Maite!

INÉS ¿Hoy es tu cumpleaños, Maite?

MAITE Sí, el 22 de junio. Y parece que vamos a celebrarlo.

TODOS MENOS MAITE ¡Felicidades!

ÁLEX Yo también acabo de cumplir los veintitrés años.

MAITE ¿Cuándo?

ÁLEX El cuatro de mayo.

DOÑA RITA Aquí tienen un flan, pastel de chocolate con helado... y una botella de vino para dar alegría.

MAITE ¡Qué sorpresa! ¡No sé qué decir! Muchísimas gracias.

DON FRANCISCO El conductor no puede tomar vino. Doña Rita, gracias por todo. ¿Puede traernos la cuenta?

DOÑA RITA Enseguida, Paco.

Video Synopsis While the travelers are looking at the dessert menu, **Doña Rita** and the waiter bring in some flan, a cake, and some wine to celebrate **Maite's** birthday. The group leaves **Doña Rita** a nice tip, thanks her, and says goodbye.

Preview Before playing the video segment, ask questions to review the previous episode. Ex: **¿Quién es doña Rita? ¿Qué platos sirven en El Cráter?** Then have students read the first line of dialogue in each caption and predict what happens in this episode.

recursos

VM pp. 169–170

adelante. vhlcentral.com

Expresiones útiles Draw attention to the forms **dijo** and **supe**. Explain that these are irregular preterite forms of the verbs **decir** and **saber**. Point out the phrase **no quisiste decírmelo** under video still 5 of the **Fotonovela**. Explain that **quisiste** is an irregular preterite form of the verb **querer**. Tell the class that **no querer** in the preterite means *to refuse*. Tell students that they will learn more about these concepts in **Estructura**.

Lección 3

MAITE ¡Gracias! Pero, ¿quién le dijo que es mi cumpleaños?

DOÑA RITA Lo supe por don Francisco.

ÁLEX Ayer te lo pregunté, ¡y no quisiste decírmelo! ¿Eh? ¡Qué mala eres!

JAVIER ¿Cuántos años cumples?

MAITE Veintitrés.

INÉS Creo que debemos dejar una buena propina. ¿Qué les parece?

MAITE Sí, vamos a darle una buena propina a la señora Perales. Es simpatiquísima.

DON FRANCISCO Gracias una vez más. Siempre lo paso muy bien aquí.

MAITE Muchísimas gracias, señora Perales. Por la comida, por la sorpresa y por ser tan amable con nosotros.

Expresiones útiles

Celebrating a birthday party

- **¡Feliz cumpleaños!**
  Happy birthday!
- **¡Felicidades!/¡Felicitaciones!**
  Congratulations!

- **¿Quién le dijo que es mi cumpleaños?**
  Who told you (form.) *that it's my birthday?*
  Lo supe por don Francisco.
  I found out through Don Francisco.

- **¿Cuántos años cumples/ cumple Ud.?**
  How old are you now?
  Veintitrés.
  Twenty-three.

Asking for and getting the bill

- **¿Puede traernos la cuenta?**
  Can you bring us the bill?
- **La cuenta, por favor.**
  The bill, please.
  Enseguida, señor/señora/señorita.
  Right away, sir/ma'am/miss.

Expressing gratitude

- **¡(Muchas) gracias!**
  Thank you (very much)!
- **Muchísimas gracias.**
  Thank you very, very much.
- **Gracias por todo.**
  Thanks for everything.
- **Gracias una vez más.**
  Thanks again. (lit. Thanks one more time.)

Leaving a tip

- **Creo que debemos dejar una buena propina. ¿Qué les parece?**
  I think we should leave a good tip. What do you guys think?
  Sí, vamos a darle/dejarle una buena propina.
  Yes, let's give her/leave her a good tip.

Teaching Tip Ask a group of volunteers to ad-lib the **Fotonovela** episode for the class. Assure them that it is not necessary to memorize the episode or stick strictly to its content. They should try to get the general meaning across with the vocabulary and expressions they know, and they should also feel free to be creative.

Game Divide the class into two teams, A and B. Give a member from team A a card with the name of an item from the **Fotonovela** or **Expresiones útiles** (Ex: **helado, propina, botella de vino**). He or she has thirty seconds to draw the item, while team A has to guess what it is. Award one point per correct answer. If team A cannot guess the item within the time limit, team B may try to "steal" the point.

¿Qué paso?

1 Have students work in pairs or small groups and write questions that would have elicited these statements

1 Completar Completa las oraciones con la información correcta, según la **Fotonovela**.

1. De postre, don Francisco siempre pide ___un café y un flan___.
2. A Javier le encanta ___el chocolate___.
3. Álex cumplió los ___veintitrés___ años ___el cuatro de mayo___.
4. Hoy Álex quiere tomar algo diferente. De postre, quiere pedir ___un pastel de chocolate___.
5. Los estudiantes le van a dejar ___una buena propina___ a doña Rita.

2 Identificar Identifica quién puede decir estas oraciones.

1. Gracias, doña Rita, pero no puedo tomar vino. don Francisco
2. ¡Qué simpática es doña Rita! Fue tan amable conmigo. Maite
3. A mí me encantan los dulces y los pasteles, ¡especialmente si son de chocolate! Javier
4. Mi amigo acaba de informarme que hoy es el cumpleaños de Maite. doña Rita
5. ¿Tienen algún postre de fruta? Los postres de fruta son los mejores. Álex
6. Me parece una buena idea dejarle una buena propina a la dueña. ¿Qué piensan ustedes? Inés

JAVIER **ÁLEX** **INÉS** **MAITE** **DON FRANCISCO** **DOÑA RITA**

NOTA CULTURAL

En los países hispanos los camareros no dependen tanto de **las propinas** como en los EE.UU. Por eso, en estos países no es común dejar propina, pero siempre es buena idea dejar una buena propina cuando el grupo es grande o el servicio es excepcional.

3 Seleccionar Selecciona algunas de las opciones de la lista para completar las oraciones.

el amor	la cuenta	la galleta	la quinceañera
una botella de champán	día de fiesta	pedir	¡Qué sorpresa!
celebrar	el divorcio	un postre	una sorpresa

1. Maite no sabe que van a celebrar su cumpleaños porque es ___una sorpresa___.
2. Cuando una pareja celebra su aniversario y quiere tomar algo especial, compra ___una botella de champán___
3. Después de una cena o un almuerzo, es normal pedir ___un postre/la cuenta___.
4. Inés y Maite no saben exactamente lo que van a ___pedir___ de postre.
5. Después de comer en un restaurante, tienes que pagar ___la cuenta___.
6. Una pareja de enamorados nunca piensa en ___el divorcio___.
7. Hoy no trabajamos porque es un ___día de fiesta___.

CONSULTA

En algunos países hispanos, el cumpleaños número quince de una chica se celebra haciendo una **quinceañera**. Ésta es una fiesta en su honor y en la que es "presentada" a la sociedad. Para conocer más sobre este tema, ve a **Lectura**, p. 155.

4 Un cumpleaños Trabajen en grupos para representar una conversación en la que uno/a de ustedes está celebrando su cumpleaños en un restaurante.

- Una persona le desea feliz cumpleaños a su compañero/a y le pregunta cuántos años cumple.
- Cada persona del grupo le pide al/a la camarero/a un postre y algo de beber.
- Después de terminar los postres, una persona pide la cuenta.
- Otra persona habla de dejar una propina.
- Los amigos que no cumplen años dicen que quieren pagar la cuenta.
- El/La que cumple años les da las gracias por todo.

Pairs Have students tell each other about their last birthday celebration, using new vocabulary from **Fotonovela** and **Contextos**.

Supersite/IRCD: MP3 Audio Files, Listening Scripts

Pronunciación

The letters h, j, and g

Lección 3

helado	hombre	hola	hermosa

The Spanish **h** is always silent.

José	jubilarse	dejar	pareja

The letter **j** is pronounced much like the English *h* in *his*.

agencia	general	Gil	Gisela

The letter **g** can be pronounced three different ways. Before **e** or **i**, the letter **g** is pronounced much like the English *h*.

Gustavo, gracias por llamar el domingo.

At the beginning of a phrase or after the letter **n**, the Spanish **g** is pronounced like the English *g* in *girl*.

Me gradué en agosto.

In any other position, the Spanish **g** has a somewhat softer sound.

Guerra	conseguir	guantes	agua

In the combinations **gue** and **gui**, the **g** has a hard sound and the **u** is silent. In the combination **gua**, the **g** has a hard sound and the **u** is pronounced like the English *w*.

Práctica Lee las palabras en voz alta, prestando atención a la **h,** la **j** y la **g**.

1. hamburguesa	5. geografía	9. seguir	13. Jorge
2. jugar	6. magnífico	10. gracias	14. tengo
3. oreja	7. espejo	11. hijo	15. ahora
4. guapa	8. hago	12. galleta	16. guantes

Oraciones Lee las oraciones en voz alta, prestando atención a la **h,** la **j** y la **g**.

1. Hola. Me llamo Gustavo Hinojosa Lugones y vivo en Santiago de Chile.
2. Tengo una familia grande; somos tres hermanos y tres hermanas.
3. Voy a graduarme en mayo.
4. Para celebrar mi graduación mis padres van a regalarme un viaje a Egipto.
5. ¡Qué generosos son!

Refranes Lee los refranes en voz alta, prestando atención a la **h,** la **j** y la **g**.

A la larga, lo más dulce amarga.[1]

El hábito no hace al monje.[2]

2 *The clothes don't make the man.*
1 *Too much of a good thing.*

Teaching Tips
- As you model the pronunciation of these sounds with the class, write additional words on the board and have students repeat.
- Contrast the pronunciations of the English *hotel* and the Spanish **hotel**. Repeat with *Julia* and **Julia**, *Gilbert* and **Gilberto**.
- Have students use the English words *guess* and *Guinness* to help them remember the silent **u** in the Spanish combinations **gue** and **gui**.
- For additional auditory practice, say several words with **h, j,** and **g** aloud. Have the class repeat and then write down the words. Go over as a class to check spelling.

Video Photocopy the *Fotonovela* script (Supersite/IRCD) and white out words with **h, j,** and **g** to create a cloze activity. Play the video again and have students fill in the words as they watch the episode. Have volunteers write answers on the board to check spelling and repeat as a class.

Heritage Speakers Provide heritage speakers with several words and phrases containing the letter **g** and ask them to read them aloud. Have the class underline the words with a hard **g** sound, circle the words with a softer **g** sound, and put an X on words with the English *h* sound.

recursos

LM p. 174

adelante. vhlcentral.com

EN DETALLE

Semana Santa: vacaciones y tradición

¿Te imaginas pasar veinticuatro horas tocando un tambor° entre miles de personas? Así es como mucha gente celebra el Viernes Santo° en el pequeño pueblo de **Calanda**, España. De todas las celebraciones hispanas, la **Semana Santa°** es una de las más espectaculares y únicas.

Procesión en Sevilla, España

Semana Santa es la semana antes de Pascua°, una celebración religiosa que conmemora la Pasión de Jesucristo. Generalmente, la gente tiene unos días de vacaciones en esta semana. Algunas personas aprovechan° estos días para viajar, pero otras prefieren participar en las tradicionales celebraciones religiosas en las calles. En **Antigua**, Guatemala, hacen alfombras° de flores° y altares; también organizan Vía Crucis° y danzas. En las famosas procesiones y desfiles° religiosos de **Sevilla**, España, los fieles°

sacan a las calles imágenes religiosas. Las imágenes van encima de plataformas ricamente decoradas con abundantes flores y velas°. En la procesión, los penitentes llevan túnicas y unos sombreros cónicos que les cubren° la cara°. En sus manos llevan faroles° o velas encendidas.

Si visitas algún país hispano durante la Semana Santa, debes asistir a un desfile. Las playas pueden esperar hasta la semana siguiente.

Alfombra de flores en Antigua, Guatemala

Otras celebraciones famosas

Ayacucho, Perú: Además de alfombras de flores y procesiones, aquí hay una antigua tradición llamada "quema de la chamiza"°.

Iztapalapa, Ciudad de México: Es famoso el Vía Crucis del cerro° de la Estrella. Es una representación del recorrido° de Jesucristo con la cruz°.

Popayán, Colombia: En las procesiones "chiquitas" los niños llevan imágenes que son copias pequeñas de las que llevan los mayores.

tocando un tambor *playing a drum* Viernes Santo *Good Friday* Semana Santa *Holy Week* Pascua *Easter Sunday* aprovechan *take advantage of* alfombras *carpets* flores *flowers* Vía Crucis *Stations of the Cross* desfiles *parades* fieles *faithful* velas *candles* cubren *cover* cara *face* faroles *lamps* quema de la chamiza *burning of brushwood* cerro *hill* recorrido *route* cruz *cross*

ACTIVIDADES

1 **¿Cierto o falso?** Indica si lo que dicen estas oraciones es **cierto** o **falso**. Corrige la información falsa.

1. La Semana Santa se celebra después de Pascua. Falso. La Semana Santa es la semana antes de Pascua.
2. En los países hispanos, las personas tienen días libres durante la Semana Santa. Cierto.
3. En los países hispanos, todas las personas asisten a las celebraciones religiosas. Falso. Algunas personas aprovechan estos días para viajar.

4. En los países hispanos, las celebraciones se hacen en las calles. Cierto.
5. El Vía Crucis de Iztapalapa es en el interior de una iglesia. Falso. Es en el cerro de la Estrella.
6. En Antigua y en Ayacucho es típico hacer alfombras de flores en Semana Santa. Cierto.
7. Las procesiones "chiquitas" son famosas en Sevilla, España. Falso. Son famosas en Popayán, Colombia.
8. En Sevilla, sacan imágenes religiosas a las calles. Cierto.

Supersite/DVD: To expand on the material presented here, show the *Flash cultura* episode.

ciento cuarenta y uno **141**

Lección 3

ASÍ SE DICE

Fiestas y celebraciones

la despedida de soltero/a	*bachelor(ette) party*
el día feriado/festivo	el día de fiesta
disfrutar	*to enjoy*
festejar	celebrar
los fuegos artificiales	*fireworks*
pasarlo en grande	divertirse mucho
la vela	*candle*

EL MUNDO HISPANO

Celebraciones latinoamericanas

○ **Oruro, Bolivia** Durante el carnaval de Oruro se realiza la famosa Diablada, una antigua danza° que muestra la lucha° entre el bien y el mal: ángeles contra° demonios.

○ **Panchimalco, El Salvador** La primera semana de mayo, Panchimalco se cubre de flores y de color. También hacen el Desfile de las palmas° y bailan danzas antiguas.

○ **Quito, Ecuador** El mes de agosto es el Mes de las Artes. Danza, teatro, música, cine, artesanías° y otros eventos culturales inundan la ciudad.

○ **San Pedro Sula, Honduras** En junio se celebra la Feria Juniana. Hay comida típica, bailes, desfiles, conciertos, rodeos, exposiciones ganaderas° y eventos deportivos y culturales.

danza *dance* lucha *fight* contra *versus* palmas *palm leaves* artesanías *handcrafts* exposiciones ganaderas *cattle shows*

PERFIL

Festival de Viña del Mar

En 1959 unos estudiantes de **Viña del Mar,** Chile, celebraron una fiesta en una casa de campo conocida como la Quinta Vergara donde hubo° un espectáculo° musical. En 1960 repitieron el evento. Asistió tanta gente que muchos vieron el espectáculo parados° o sentados en el suelo°. Algunos se subieron a los árboles°.

Años después, se convirtió en el **Festival Internacional de la Canción**. Este evento se celebra en febrero, en el mismo lugar donde empezó. ¡Pero ahora nadie necesita subirse a un árbol para verlo! Hay un anfiteatro con capacidad para quince mil personas.

En el festival hay concursos° musicales y conciertos de artistas famosos como Daddy Yankee y Paulina Rubio.

Daddy Yankee

hubo *there was* **espectáculo** *show* **parados** *standing* **suelo** *floor* **se subieron a los árboles** *climbed trees* **concursos** *competitions*

SUPERSITE **Conexión Internet**

¿Qué celebraciones hispanas hay en los Estados Unidos y Canadá?	Go to **adelante.vhlcentral.com** to find more cultural information related to this **Cultura** section.

ACTIVIDADES

2 **Comprensión** Responde a las preguntas.

1. ¿Cuántas personas pueden asistir al Festival de Viña del Mar hoy día? quince mil

2. ¿Qué es la Diablada? Es una antigua danza que muestra la lucha entre el bien y el mal.

3. ¿Qué celebran en Quito en agosto? Celebran el Mes de las Artes.

4. Nombra dos atracciones en la Feria Juniana de San Pedro Sula. Answers will vary.

5. ¿Qué es la Quinta Vergara? una casa de campo donde empezó el Festival de Viña del Mar

3 **¿Cuál es tu celebración favorita?** Escribe un pequeño párrafo sobre la celebración que más te gusta de tu comunidad. Explica cómo se llama, cuándo ocurre y cómo es. Answers will vary.

3 Have students exchange papers with a classmate for peer editing.

recursos

SUPERSITE

adelante.vhlcentral.com

3.1 Irregular preterites

ANTE TODO You already know that the verbs **ir** and **ser** are irregular in the preterite. You will now learn other verbs whose preterite forms are also irregular.

Preterite of **tener, venir,** and **decir**			
		tener (**u**-stem)	**venir** (**i**-stem)	**decir** (**j**-stem)

		tener (**u**-stem)	**venir** (**i**-stem)	**decir** (**j**-stem)
SINGULAR FORMS	yo	tuv**e**	vin**e**	dij**e**
	tú	tuv**iste**	vin**iste**	dij**iste**
	Ud./él/ella	tuv**o**	vin**o**	dij**o**
PLURAL FORMS	nosotros/as	tuv**imos**	vin**imos**	dij**imos**
	vosotros/as	tuv**isteis**	vin**isteis**	dij**isteis**
	Uds./ellos/ellas	tuv**ieron**	vin**ieron**	dij**eron**

▶ **¡Atención!** The endings of these verbs are the regular preterite endings of **-er/-ir** verbs, except for the **yo** and **usted** forms. Note that these two endings are unaccented.

▶ These verbs observe similar stem changes to **tener, venir,** and **decir.**

INFINITIVE	U-STEM	PRETERITE FORMS
poder	pud-	pude, pudiste, pudo, pudimos, pudisteis, pudieron
poner	pus-	puse, pusiste, puso, pusimos, pusisteis, pusieron
saber	sup-	supe, supiste, supo, supimos, supisteis, supieron
estar	estuv-	estuve, estuviste, estuvo, estuvimos, estuvisteis, estuvieron

INFINITIVE	I-STEM	PRETERITE FORMS
querer	quis-	quise, quisiste, quiso, quisimos, quisisteis, quisieron
hacer	hic-	hice, hiciste, hizo, hicimos, hicisteis, hicieron

INFINITIVE	J-STEM	PRETERITE FORMS
traer	traj-	traje, trajiste, trajo, trajimos, trajisteis, trajeron
conducir	conduj-	conduje, condujiste, condujo, condujimos, condujisteis, condujeron
traducir	traduj-	traduje, tradujiste, tradujo, tradujimos, tradujisteis, tradujeron

▶ **¡Atención!** Most verbs that end in **-cir** are **j**-stem verbs in the preterite. For example, **producir → produje, produjiste,** etc.

> **Produjimos** un documental sobre los accidentes en la casa.
> *We produced a documentary about accidents in the home.*

▶ Notice that the preterites with **j**-stems omit the letter **i** in the **ustedes/ellos/ellas** form.

> Mis amigos **trajeron** comida a la fiesta.   Ellos **dijeron** la verdad.

Game Divide the class into two teams. Indicate one team member at a time, alternating between teams. Give a verb in its infinitive form and a subject pronoun (Ex: **querer/tú**). The team member should give the correct preterite form (Ex: **quisiste**). Give one point per correct answer. Deduct one point for each wrong answer. The team with the most points at the end wins.

Lección 3

Teaching Tips
• Point out that **dar** has the same preterite endings as **ver**.
• Drill the preterite of **dar** by asking students about what they gave their family members for their last birthdays or other special occasion. Ex: **¿Qué le diste a tu hermano para su cumpleaños?** Then ask what other family members gave them. Ex: **¿Qué te dio tu padre? ¿Y tu madre?**

The preterite of dar

	SINGULAR FORMS		PLURAL FORMS
yo	d**i**	nosotros/as	d**imos**
tú	d**iste**	vosotros/as	d**isteis**
Ud./él/ella	d**io**	Uds./ellos/ellas	d**ieron**

▶ The endings for **dar** are the same as the regular preterite endings for **-er** and **-ir** verbs, except that there are no accent marks.

La camarera me **dio** el menú.
The waitress gave me the menu.

Le **di** a Juan algunos consejos.
I gave Juan some advice.

Los invitados le **dieron** un regalo.
The guests gave him/her a gift.

Nosotros **dimos** una gran fiesta.
We gave a great party.

▶ The preterite of **hay** (*inf.* **haber**) is **hubo** (*there was; there were*).

CONSULTA

Note that there are other ways to say *there was* or *there were* in Spanish. See **Estructura 4.1**, p. 190.

Video Show the *Fotonovela* again to give students more input containing irregular preterite forms. Stop the video where appropriate to discuss how certain verbs were used and to ask comprehension questions.

Doña Rita les dio una botella de vino a los viajeros.

Hubo una fiesta en el restaurante El Cráter.

¡INTÉNTALO! Escribe la forma correcta del pretérito de cada verbo que está entre paréntesis.

1. (querer) tú _quisiste_
2. (decir) usted _dijo_
3. (hacer) nosotras _hicimos_
4. (traer) yo _traje_
5. (conducir) ellas _condujeron_
6. (estar) ella _estuvo_
7. (tener) tú _tuviste_
8. (dar) ella y yo _dimos_
9. (traducir) yo _traduje_
10. (haber) ayer _hubo_
11. (saber) usted _supo_
12. (poner) ellos _pusieron_

13. (venir) yo _vine_
14. (poder) tú _pudiste_
15. (querer) ustedes _quisieron_
16. (estar) nosotros _estuvimos_
17. (decir) tú _dijiste_
18. (saber) ellos _supieron_
19. (hacer) él _hizo_
20. (poner) yo _puse_
21. (traer) nosotras _trajimos_
22. (tener) yo _tuve_
23. (dar) tú _diste_
24. (poder) ustedes _pudieron_

Extra Practice Ask personalized questions to elicit irregular preterite forms. Ex: _____, ¿qué hiciste el sábado? Ah, hubo una fiesta para tu hermano. ¿Le dieron muchos regalos?

recursos

WB pp. 161–162

LM p. 175

SUPERSITE
adelante.
vhlcentral.com

Práctica SUPERSITE

1

Completar Completa estas oraciones con el pretérito de los verbos entre paréntesis.

1. El sábado ____hubo____ (haber) una fiesta sorpresa para Elsa en mi casa.
2. Sofía ____hizo____ (hacer) un pastel para la fiesta y Miguel ____trajo____ (traer) un flan.
3. Los amigos y parientes de Elsa ____vinieron____ (venir) y ____trajeron____ (traer) regalos.
4. El hermano de Elsa no ____vino____ (venir) porque ____tuvo____ (tener) que trabajar.
5. Su tía María Dolores tampoco ____pudo____ (poder) venir.
6. Cuando Elsa abrió la puerta, todos gritaron: "¡Feliz cumpleaños!" y su esposo le ____dio____ (dar) un beso.
7. Al final de la fiesta, todos ____dijeron____ (decir) que se divirtieron mucho.
8. La historia (*story*) le ____dio____ (dar) a Elsa tanta risa (*laughter*) que no ____pudo____ (poder) dejar de reírse (*stop laughing*) durante toda la noche.

2

Describir En parejas, usen verbos de la lista para describir lo que estas personas hicieron. Deben dar por lo menos dos oraciones por cada dibujo. Some answers will vary.

dar	hacer	tener	traer
estar	poner	traducir	venir

1. el señor López
El señor López le dio dinero a su hijo.

2. Norma
Norma puso el pavo en la mesa.

3. anoche nosotros
Anoche nosotros tuvimos (hicimos/dimos) una fiesta de Navidad./Anoche nosotros estuvimos en una fiesta de Navidad.

4. Roberto y Elena
Roberto y Elena le trajeron/dieron un regalo a su amigo.

2 To challenge students, have them see how many sentences they can come up with to describe each drawing using the target verbs.

Comunicación

3

Heritage Speakers Ask if any heritage speakers celebrate **el Día de los Muertos** or **el Día de todos los Santos**. Have them describe these celebrations and encourage the class to ask questions.

Preguntas En parejas, túrnense para hacerse y responder a estas preguntas. Answers will vary.

1. ¿Fuiste a una fiesta de cumpleaños el año pasado? ¿De quién?
2. ¿Quiénes fueron a la fiesta?
3. ¿Quién condujo el auto?
4. ¿Cómo estuvo la fiesta?
5. ¿Quién llevó regalos, bebidas o comida? ¿Llevaste algo especial?
6. ¿Hubo comida? ¿Quién la hizo? ¿Hubo champán?
7. ¿Qué regalo diste tú? ¿Qué otros regalos dieron los invitados?
8. ¿Cuántos invitados hubo en la fiesta?
9. ¿Qué tipo de música hubo?
10. ¿Qué dijeron los invitados de la fiesta?

3 To practice the formal register, call on different students to ask you the questions in the activity.

4

Encuesta Tu profesor(a) va a darte una hoja de actividades. Para cada una de las actividades de la lista, encuentra a alguien que hizo esa actividad en el tiempo indicado. Answers will vary.

modelo   Supersite/IRCD: *Hoja de actividades*

> traer dulces a clase
> **Estudiante 1:** ¿Trajiste dulces a clase?
> **Estudiante 2:** Sí, traje galletas y helado a la fiesta del fin del semestre.

NOTA CULTURAL

Halloween es una fiesta que también se celebra en algunos países hispanos, como México, por su proximidad con los Estados Unidos, pero no es parte de la cultura hispana. El Día de todos los Santos (1 de noviembre) y el Día de los Muertos (2 de noviembre) sí son celebraciones muy arraigadas (*deeply rooted*) entre los hispanos.

▶

Actividades

Nombres

1. ponerse un disfraz (*costume*) de Halloween
2. traer dulces a clase
3. conducir su auto a clase
4. estar en la biblioteca ayer
5. dar un regalo a alguien ayer
6. poder levantarse temprano esta mañana
7. hacer un viaje a un país hispano en el verano
8. tener una cita anoche
9. ir a una fiesta el fin de semana pasado
10. tener que trabajar el sábado pasado

Síntesis

5

Large Groups Divide the class into two groups. Give each member of the first group a strip of paper with a question. Ex: **¿Quién me trajo el pastel de cumpleaños?** Give each member of the second group a strip of paper with an answer. Ex: **Marta te lo trajo.** Students must find their partners.

Conversación En parejas, preparen una conversación en la que uno/a de ustedes va a visitar a su hermano/a para explicarle por qué no fue a su fiesta de graduación y para saber cómo estuvo la fiesta. Incluyan esta información en la conversación: Answers will vary.

- cuál fue el menú
- quiénes vinieron a la fiesta y quiénes no pudieron venir
- quiénes prepararon la comida o trajeron algo
- si él/ella tuvo que preparar algo
- lo que la gente hizo antes y después de comer
- cómo lo pasaron, bien o mal

5 Have pairs work in groups of four to write a paragraph combining the most interesting or unusual aspects of each pair's conversation. Ask a group representative to read the paragraph to the class, who will vote for the most creative or funniest paragraph.

[3.2] Verbs that change meaning in the preterite

ANTE TODO The verbs **conocer, saber, poder,** and **querer** change meanings when used in the preterite. Because of this, each of them corresponds to more than one verb in English, depending on its tense.

Verbs that change meaning in the preterite

Present	Preterite
conocer	
to know; to be acquainted with	*to meet*
Conozco a esa pareja.	**Conocí** a esa pareja ayer.
I know that couple.	*I met that couple yesterday.*
saber	
to know information; to know how to do something	*to find out; to learn*
Sabemos la verdad.	**Supimos** la verdad anoche.
We know the truth.	*We found out (learned) the truth last night.*
poder	
to be able; can	*to manage; to succeed (could and did)*
Podemos hacerlo.	**Pudimos** hacerlo ayer.
We can do it.	*We managed to do it yesterday.*
querer	
to want; to love	*to try*
Quiero ir pero tengo que trabajar.	**Quise** evitarlo pero fue imposible.
I want to go but I have to work.	*I tried to avoid it, but it was impossible.*

¡ATENCIÓN!

In the preterite, the verbs **poder** and **querer** have different meanings, depending on whether they are used in affirmative or negative sentences.
pude *I succeeded*
no pude *I failed (to)*
quise *I tried (to)*
no quise *I refused (to)*

 **¡INTÉNTALO!** Elige la respuesta más lógica.

1. Yo no hice lo que me pidieron mis padres. ¡Tengo mis principios! a
   a. No quise hacerlo.   b. No supe hacerlo.

2. Hablamos por primera vez con Nuria y Ana en la boda. a
   a. Las conocimos en la boda.   b. Las supimos en la boda.

3. Por fin hablé con mi hermano después de llamarlo siete veces. b
   a. No quise hablar con él.   b. Pude hablar con él.

4. Josefina se acostó para relajarse. Se durmió inmediatamente. a
   a. Pudo relajarse.   b. No pudo relajarse.

5. Después de mucho buscar, encontraste la definición en el diccionario. b
   a. No supiste la respuesta.   b. Supiste la respuesta.

6. Las chicas fueron a la fiesta. Cantaron y bailaron mucho. a
   a. Ellas pudieron divertirse.   b. Ellas no supieron divertirse.

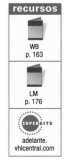

Práctica

1

Carlos y Eva Forma oraciones con los siguientes elementos. Usa el pretérito y haz todos los cambios necesarios. Al final, inventa la razón del divorcio de Carlos y Eva.

1. anoche / mi esposa y yo / saber / que / Carlos y Eva / divorciarse
   Anoche mi esposa y yo supimos que Carlos y Eva se divorciaron.
2. los / conocer / viaje / isla de Pascua
   Los conocimos en un viaje a la isla de Pascua.
3. no / poder / hablar / mucho / con / ellos / ese día
   No pudimos hablar mucho con ellos ese día.
4. pero / ellos / ser / simpático / y / nosotros / hacer planes / vernos / con más / frecuencia
   Pero ellos fueron simpáticos y nosotros hicimos planes para vernos con más frecuencia.
5. yo / poder / encontrar / su / número / teléfono / páginas / amarillo
   Yo pude encontrar su número de teléfono en las páginas amarillas.
6. (yo) querer / llamar / les / ese día / pero / no / tener / tiempo
   Quise llamarles ese día pero no tuve tiempo.
7. cuando / los / llamar / nosotros / poder / hablar / Eva
   Cuando los llamé, nosotros pudimos hablar con Eva.
8. nosotros / saber / razón / divorcio / después / hablar / ella
   Nosotros supimos la razón del divorcio después de hablar con ella.

NOTA CULTURAL

La isla de Pascua es un remoto territorio chileno situado en el océano Pacífico Sur. Sus inmensas estatuas son uno de los mayores misterios del mundo: nadie sabe cómo o por qué se construyeron. Para más información, puedes ir a **Panorama**, p. 157.

2 Preview the activity by describing some recent things you found out, tried to do, failed to do, etc.

2

Completar Completa estas frases de una manera lógica. Answers will vary.

1. Ayer mi compañero/a de cuarto supo…
2. Esta mañana no pude…
3. Conocí a mi mejor amigo/a en…
4. Mis padres no quisieron…
5. Mi mejor amigo/a no pudo…
6. Mi novio/a y yo nos conocimos en…
7. La semana pasada supe…
8. Ayer mis amigos quisieron…

Comunicación

3

Pairs In pairs, have students write three sentences using verbs that change meaning in the preterite. Two of the sentences should be true and the third should be false. Their partner has to guess which of the sentences is the false one.

3 Point out that unlike their U.S. counterparts, Hispanic soap operas run for a limited period of time, like a miniseries.

Telenovela (*Soap opera*) En parejas, escriban el diálogo para una escena de una telenovela. La escena trata de una situación amorosa entre tres personas: Mirta, Daniel y Raúl. Usen el pretérito de **conocer, poder, querer** y **saber** en su diálogo. Answers will vary.

Síntesis

4 Have pairs repeat the activity, this time describing another person. Ask students to share their descriptions with the class, who will guess the person being described.

4

Conversación En una hoja de papel, escribe dos listas: las cosas que hiciste durante el fin de semana y las cosas que quisiste hacer pero no pudiste. Luego, compara tu lista con la de un(a) compañero/a, y expliquen por qué no pudieron hacer esas cosas. Answers will vary.

3.3 ¿Qué? and ¿cuál? SUPERSITE

ANTE TODO You've already learned how to use interrogative words and phrases. As you know, **¿qué?** and **¿cuál?** or **¿cuáles?** mean *what?* or *which?* However, they are not interchangeable.

▶ **¿Qué?** followed by a verb is used to ask for a definition or an explanation.

¿Qué es el flan?	**¿Qué** estudias?
What is flan?	*What do you study?*

▶ **¿Cuál(es)?** is used when there is a choice among several possibilities.

¿Cuál de los dos prefieres, el vino o el champán?	**¿Cuáles** son tus medias, las negras o las blancas?
Which of these (two) do you prefer, wine or champagne?	*Which ones are your socks, the black ones or the white ones?*

▶ **¿Cuál?** cannot be used before a noun; in this case, **¿qué?** is used.

¿Qué sorpresa te dieron tus amigos?	**¿Qué** colores te gustan?
What surprise did your friends give you?	*What colors do you like?*

▶ **¿Qué?** used before a noun has the same meaning as **¿cuál?**

¿Qué regalo te gusta?	**¿Qué dulces** quieren ustedes?
What (Which) gift do you like?	*What (Which) sweets do you want?*

Review of interrogative words and phrases

¿a qué hora?	at what time?	**¿cuánto/a?**	how much?
¿adónde?	(to) where?	**¿cuántos/as?**	how many?
¿cómo?	how?	**¿de dónde?**	from where?
¿cuál(es)?	what?; which?	**¿dónde?**	where?
¿cuándo?	when?	**¿qué?**	what?; which?
		¿quién(es)?	who?

 **¡INTÉNTALO!** Completa las preguntas con **¿qué?** o **¿cuál(es)?**, según el contexto.

1. ¿ _Cuál_ de los dos te gusta más?
2. ¿ _Cuál_ es tu teléfono?
3. ¿ _Qué_ tipo de pastel pediste?
4. ¿ _Qué_ es una quinceañera?
5. ¿ _Qué_ haces ahora?
6. ¿ _Cuáles_ son tus platos favoritos?
7. ¿ _Qué_ bebidas te gustan más?
8. ¿ _Qué_ es esto?
9. ¿ _Cuál_ es el mejor?
10. ¿ _Cuál_ es tu opinión?
11. ¿ _Qué_ fiestas celebras tú?
12. ¿ _Qué_ botella de vino prefieres?
13. ¿ _Cuál_ es tu helado favorito?
14. ¿ _Qué_ pones en la mesa?
15. ¿ _Qué_ restaurante prefieres?
16. ¿ _Qué_ estudiantes estudian más?
17. ¿ _Qué_ quieres comer esta noche?
18. ¿ _Cuál_ es la sorpresa mañana?
19. ¿ _Qué_ postre prefieres?
20. ¿ _Qué_ opinas?

Extra Practice Ask students to write one question using each of the interrogative words or phrases in the chart on this page. Then have them ask those questions of a partner, who must answer in complete sentences.

Teaching Tips
• Write incomplete questions on the board and ask students which interrogative word best completes each sentence. Ex: 1. ¿_____ es tu número de teléfono? (Cuál) 2. ¿_____ es esto? (Qué)
• Give students pairs of questions and have them explain the difference in meaning. Ex: **¿Qué es tu número de teléfono? ¿Cuál es tu número de teléfono?** Emphasize that the first question would be asked by someone who has no idea what a phone number is (asking for a definition) and, in the second question, someone wants to know *which* number (out of all the phone numbers in the world) is yours.
• Review the chart of interrogative words and phrases. Ask personalized questions (Ex: **¿Cuál es tu película favorita? ¿Adónde vas después de la clase?**) and call on volunteers to ask you questions.

recursos

WB p. 164

LM p. 177

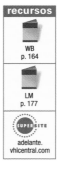

adelante. vhlcentral.com

Lección 3

Práctica

1

Completar Tu clase de español va a crear un sitio web. Completa estas preguntas con alguna(s) palabra(s) interrogativa(s). Luego, con un(a) compañero/a, hagan y contesten las preguntas para obtener la información para el sitio web.

1. ¿___Cuál___ es la fecha de tu cumpleaños?
2. ¿___Dónde___ naciste?
3. ¿___Cuál___ es tu estado civil?
4. ¿___Cómo/Cuándo/Dónde___ te relajas?
5. ¿___Quién___ es tu mejor amigo/a?
6. ¿___Qué___ cosas te hacen reír?
7. ¿___Qué___ postres te gustan? ¿___Cuál___ te gusta más?
8. ¿___Qué___ problemas tuviste en la primera cita con alguien?

1 Conduct a conversation with the whole class to find consensus on some of the questions.

2 For expansion, have students ask additional questions using the interrogative words and phrases on p. 148. Ex: **¿A qué hora es la ceremonia?**

Comunicación

2

Una invitación En parejas, lean esta invitación. Luego, túrnense para hacer y contestar preguntas con **qué** y **cuál** basadas en la información de la invitación. Answers will vary.

modelo

> **Estudiante 1:** ¿Cuál es el nombre del padre de la novia?
> **Estudiante 2:** Su nombre es Fernando Sandoval Valera.

¡LENGUA VIVA!

The word **invitar** is not always used exactly like *invite*. Sometimes, if you say **Te invito a un café**, it means that you are offering to buy that person a coffee.

> Fernando Sandoval Valera   Lorenzo Vásquez Amaral
> Isabel Arzipe de Sandoval   Elena Soto de Vásquez
>
> tienen el agrado de invitarlos
> a la boda de sus hijos
>
> María Luisa y José Antonio
>
> La ceremonia religiosa tendrá lugar
> el sábado 10 de junio a las dos de la tarde
> en el Templo de Santo Domingo
> (Calle Santo Domingo, 961).
>
> Después de la ceremonia sírvanse pasar a la recepción en el salón
> de baile del Hotel Metrópoli (Sotero del Río, 465).

Game Play a *Jeopardy*-style game with the class. Select one team member from each of three teams and read an answer. The first team member to come up with an appropriate question wins the point. Ex: **Prefiero la blusa azul. (¿Cuál prefieres?)**

Supersite/IRCD: Information Gap Activities

3

Quinceañera Trabaja con un(a) compañero/a. Uno/a de ustedes es el/la director(a) del salón de fiestas "Renacimiento". La otra persona es el padre/la madre de Ana María, quien quiere hacer la fiesta de quinceañera de su hija sin gastar más de $25 por invitado. Su profesor(a) va a darles la información necesaria para confirmar la reservación. Answers will vary.

modelo

> **Estudiante 1:** ¿Cuánto cuestan los entremeses?
> **Estudiante 2:** Depende. Puede escoger champiñones por 50 centavos o camarones por dos dólares.
> **Estudiante 1:** ¡Uf! A mi hija le gustan los camarones, pero son muy caros.
> **Estudiante 2:** Bueno, también puede escoger quesos por un dólar por invitado.

3.4 Pronouns after prepositions

ANTE TODO In Spanish, as in English, the object of a preposition is the noun or pronoun that follows a preposition. Observe the following diagram.

PREPOSITION	NOUN	PREPOSITION	PRONOUN
La sopa es para	Alicia	y para	él.

Prepositional pronouns

	Singular			Plural	
	mí	me		**nosotros/as**	us
	ti	you (fam.)		**vosotros/as**	you (fam.)
preposition +	**Ud.**	you (form.)		**Uds.**	you (form.)
	él	him		**ellos**	them (m.)
	ella	her		**ellas**	them (f.)

▶ Note that, except for **mí** and **ti,** these pronouns are the same as the subject pronouns. **¡Atención! Mí** (*me*) has an accent mark to distinguish it from the possessive adjective **mi** (*my*).

▶ The preposition **con** combines with **mí** and **ti** to form **conmigo** and **contigo,** respectively.

—¿Quieres venir **conmigo** a Concepción?   —Sí, gracias, me gustaría ir **contigo.**
Do you want to come with me to Concepción?   *Yes, thanks, I would like to go with you.*

▶ The preposition **entre** is followed by **tú** and **yo** instead of **ti** and **mí.**

Papá va a sentarse **entre tú y yo**.
Dad is going to sit between you and me.

¡INTÉNTALO! Completa estas oraciones con las preposiciones y los pronombres apropiados.

1. *(with him)* No quiero ir ___con él___.
2. *(for her)* Las galletas son ___para ella___.
3. *(for me)* Los mariscos son ___para mí___.
4. *(with you,* pl. form.*)* Preferimos estar ___con ustedes___.
5. *(with you,* sing. fam.*)* Me gusta salir ___contigo___.
6. *(with me)* ¿Por qué no quieres tener una cita ___conmigo___?
7. *(for her)* La cuenta es ___para ella___.
8. *(for them,* m.*)* La habitación es muy pequeña ___para ellos___.
9. *(with them,* f.*)* Anoche celebré la Navidad ___con ellas___.
10. *(for you,* sing. fam.*)* Este beso es ___para ti___.
11. *(with you,* sing. fam.*)* Nunca me aburro ___contigo___.
12. *(with you,* pl. form.*)* ¡Qué bien que vamos ___con ustedes___!
13. *(for you,* sing. fam.*)* ___Para ti___ la vida es muy fácil.
14. *(for them,* f.*)* ___Para ellas___ no hay sorpresas.

Teaching Tips
• Review previously learned prepositions before beginning this grammar presentation.
• Ask personalized questions to elicit prepositional pronouns. Ex: _____, ¿quién está detrás de ti? ¿Quién está delante de ella? ¿Ese libro es para mí?
• Point out that students have already been using prepositional pronouns after **a** with verbs like **gustar** and to clarify indirect object pronouns.

CONSULTA

For more prepositions, you can refer to **¡ADELANTE! UNO**, **Estructura 2.3,** p. 76.

Video Show the *Fotonovela* again to give students more input containing prepositional pronouns. Stop the video where appropriate to discuss how certain pronouns were used and to ask comprehension questions.

Game Divide the class into two teams. One student from the first team chooses an item in the classroom and writes it down. Call on five students from the other team to ask questions about the item's location. Ex: **¿Está cerca de mí?** The first student can respond with **sí, no, caliente,** or **frío**. If a team guesses the item within five tries, give them a point. If not, give the other team a point. The team with the most points wins.

recursos

WB
pp. 165–166

LM
p. 178

adelante.
vhlcentral.com

Lección 3

Práctica SUPERSITE

1

Completar David sale con sus amigos a comer. Para saber quién come qué, lee el mensaje electrónico que David le envió (*sent*) a Cecilia dos días después y completa el diálogo en el restaurante con los pronombres apropiados.

1 Remind students that they are to fill in the blanks with prepositional pronouns, not names of the characters in the conversation.

> **modelo**
> **Camarero:** Los camarones en salsa verde, ¿para quién son?
> **David:** Son para _____ella_____.

Para: Cecilia	Asunto: El menú

Hola, Cecilia:

¿Recuerdas la comida del viernes? Quiero repetir el menú en mi casa el miércoles. Ahora voy a escribir lo que comimos, luego me dices si falta algún plato. Yo pedí el filete de pescado y Maribel camarones en salsa verde. Tatiana pidió un plato grandísimo de machas a la parmesana. Diana y Silvia pidieron langostas, ¿te acuerdas? Y tú, ¿qué pediste? Ah, sí, un bistec grande con papas. Héctor también pidió un bistec, pero más pequeño. Miguel pidió pollo y vino tinto para todos. Y la profesora comió ensalada verde porque está a dieta. ¿Falta algo? Espero tu mensaje. Hasta pronto. David.

CAMARERO	El filete de pescado, ¿para quién es?
DAVID	Es para (1)____mí____.
CAMARERO	Aquí está. ¿Y las machas a la parmesana y las langostas?
DAVID	Las machas son para (2)____ella____.
SILVIA Y DIANA	Las langostas son para (3)____nosotras____.
CAMARERO	Tengo un bistec grande...
DAVID	Cecilia, es para (4)____ti____, ¿no es cierto? Y el bistec más pequeño es para (5)____él____.
CAMARERO	¿Y la botella de vino?
MIGUEL	Es para todos (6)____nosotros____, y el pollo es para (7)____mí____.
CAMARERO	(*a la profesora*) Entonces la ensalada verde es para (8)____usted____.

Comunicación

NATIONAL communication STANDARDS

Supersite/IRCD: Information Gap Activities

2

Compartir Tu profesor(a) va a darte una hoja de actividades en la que hay un dibujo. En parejas, hagan preguntas para saber dónde está cada una de las personas en el dibujo. Ustedes tienen dos versiones diferentes de la ilustración. Al final deben saber dónde está cada persona. Answers will vary.

2 Using both versions of the drawing as a guide, ask questions of the class to find out where the people are.
Ex: **¿Quién sabe dónde está la señora Blanco?**

> **modelo**
> **Estudiante 1:** ¿Quién está al lado de Óscar?
> **Estudiante 2:** Alfredo está al lado de él.

Alfredo	Dolores	Graciela	Raúl
Sra. Blanco	Enrique	Leonor	Rubén
Carlos	Sra. Gómez	Óscar	Yolanda

2 Verify that all students labeled the characters correctly by suggesting changes to the drawing and using prepositions to ask about their new locations. Ex: **Yolanda y Carlos cambian de lugar. ¿Quién está al lado de Yolanda ahora? (Rubén)**

Recapitulación

SUPER SITE For self-scoring and diagnostics, go to **adelante.vhlcentral.com**.

Completa estas actividades para repasar los conceptos de gramática que aprendiste en esta lección.

1 **Completar** Completa la tabla con el pretérito de los verbos. **9 pts.**

Infinitive	yo	ella	nosotros
conducir	conduje	condujo	condujimos
hacer	hice	hizo	hicimos
saber	supe	supo	supimos

2 **Mi fiesta** Completa este mensaje electrónico con el pretérito de los verbos de la lista. Vas a usar cada verbo sólo una vez. **10 pts.**

dar	haber	tener
decir	hacer	traer
estar	poder	venir
	poner	

Hola, Omar:

Como tú no (1) ___pudiste___ venir a mi fiesta de cumpleaños, quiero contarte cómo fue. El día de mi cumpleaños muy temprano por la mañana mis hermanos me (2) ___dieron___ una gran sorpresa: ellos (3) ___pusieron___ un regalo delante de la puerta de mi habitación: ¡una bicicleta roja preciosa! Mi madre nos preparó un desayuno riquísimo. Después de desayunar, mis hermanos y yo (4) ___tuvimos___ que limpiar toda la casa, así que (*therefore*) no (5) ___hubo___ más celebración hasta la tarde. A las seis y media (nosotros) (6) ___hicimos___ una barbacoa en el patio de la casa. Todos los invitados (7) ___trajeron___ bebidas y regalos. (8) ___Vinieron___ todos mis amigos, excepto tú, ¡qué pena! :-(La fiesta (9) ___estuvo___ muy animada hasta las diez de la noche, cuando mis padres (10) ___dijeron___ que los vecinos (*neighbors*) iban a (*were going to*) protestar y entonces todos se fueron a sus casas.

2 Have students work in pairs to write a response e-mail from **Omar**. Tell them to use the preterite tense to ask for more details about the party.

RESUMEN GRAMATICAL

3.1 **Irregular preterites** *pp. 142–143*

u-stem	estar poder poner saber tener	estuv- pud- pus- sup- tuv-	
i-stem	hacer querer venir	hic- quis- vin-	-e, -iste, -o, -imos, -isteis, -(i)eron
j-stem	conducir decir traducir traer	conduj- dij- traduj- traj-	

▶ Preterite of **dar**: di, diste, dio, dimos, disteis, dieron

▶ Preterite of **hay** (*inf.* haber): hubo

3.2 **Verbs that change meaning in the preterite** *p. 146*

Present	Preterite
conocer	
to know; to be acquainted with	to meet
saber	
to know info.; to know how to do something	to find out; to learn
poder	
to be able; can	to manage; to succeed
querer	
to want; to love	to try

3.3 **¿Qué? and ¿cuál?** *p. 148*

▶ Use **¿qué?** to ask for a definition or an explanation.

▶ Use **¿cuál(es)?** when there is a choice among several possibilities.

▶ **¿Cuál?** cannot be used before a noun; use **¿qué?** instead.

▶ **¿Qué?** used before a noun has the same meaning as **¿cuál?**

TPR Have students stand and form a circle. Call out an infinitive from **Resumen gramatical** and a subject pronoun (Ex: **poder/nosotros**) and toss a foam or paper ball to a student, who will give the correct preterite form (Ex: **pudimos**). He or she then tosses the ball to another student, who must use the verb correctly in a sentence before throwing the ball back to you. Ex: **No pudimos comprar los regalos.**

Lección 3

3

¿Presente o pretérito? Escoge la forma correcta de los verbos en paréntesis. **6 pts.**

1. Después de muchos intentos (*tries*), (podemos/ (pudimos)) hacer una piñata.
2. —¿Conoces a Pepe?
   —Sí, lo (conozco/(conocí)) en tu fiesta.
3. Como no es de aquí, Cristina no ((sabe)/supo) mucho de las celebraciones locales.
4. Yo no ((quiero)/quise) ir a un restaurante grande, pero tú decides.
5. Ellos (quieren/(quisieron)) darme una sorpresa, pero Nina me lo dijo todo.
6. Mañana se terminan las clases; por fin ((podemos)/pudimos) divertirnos.

3.4 **Pronouns after prepositions**   *p. 150*

Prepositional pronouns

	Singular	**Plural**
Preposition +	mí	nosotros/as
	ti	vosotros/as
	Ud.	Uds.
	él	ellos
	ella	ellas

► **Exceptions: conmigo, contigo, entre tú y yo**

4

Preguntas Escribe una pregunta para cada respuesta con los elementos dados. Empieza con **qué**, **cuál** o **cuáles** de acuerdo con el contexto y haz los cambios necesarios. **8 pts.**

1. —¿? / pastel / querer —Quiero el pastel de chocolate. 1. ¿Qué pastel quieres?
2. —¿? / ser / sangría —La sangría es una bebida típica española. 2. ¿Qué es la sangría?
3. —¿? / ser / restaurante favorito —Mis restaurantes favoritos son Dalí y Jaleo. 3. ¿Cuáles son tus restaurantes favoritos?
4. —¿? / ser / dirección electrónica —Mi dirección electrónica es paco@email.com. 4. ¿Cuál es tu dirección electrónica?

5

¿Dónde me siento? Completa la conversación con los pronombres apropiados. **7 pts.**

JUAN A ver, te voy a decir dónde te vas a sentar. Manuel, ¿ves esa silla? Es para ____ti____. Y esa otra silla es para tu novia, que todavía no está aquí.

MANUEL Muy bien, yo la reservo para ____ella____.

HUGO ¿Y esta silla es para ____mí____?

JUAN No, Hugo. No es para ____ti____. Es para Carmina, que viene con Julio.

HUGO No, Carmina y Julio no pueden venir. Hablé con ____ellos____ y me lo dijeron.

JUAN Pues ellos se lo pierden (*it's their loss*). ¡Más comida para ____nosotros____ (*us*)!

CAMARERO Aquí tienen el menú. Les doy un minuto y enseguida estoy con ____ustedes____.

6

Cumpleaños feliz Escribe cinco oraciones describiendo cómo celebraste tu último cumpleaños. Usa el pretérito y los pronombres que aprendiste en esta lección. **10 pts.** Answers will vary.

7

Poema Completa este fragmento del poema *Elegía nocturna* de Carlos Pellicer con el pretérito de los verbos entre paréntesis. **¡2 puntos EXTRA!**

❝ Ay de mi corazón° que nadie ____quiso____ (querer)
tomar de entre mis manos desoladas.
Tú ____viniste____ (venir) a mirar sus llamaradas°
y le miraste arder° claro° y sereno. ❞

corazón *heart* **llamaradas** *flames* **arder** *to burn* **claro** *clear*

Lectura

Antes de leer

Estrategia
Recognizing word families

Recognizing root words can help you guess the meaning of words in context, ensuring better comprehension of a reading selection. Using this strategy will enrich your Spanish vocabulary as you will see below.

Examinar el texto

Familiarízate con el texto usando las estrategias de lectura más efectivas para ti. ¿Qué tipo de documento es? ¿De qué tratan (*What are... about?*) las cuatro secciones del documento? Explica tus respuestas.

Raíces (*Roots*)

Completa el siguiente cuadro (*chart*) para ampliar tu vocabulario. Usa palabras de la lectura de esta lección y el vocabulario de las lecciones anteriores. ¿Qué significan las palabras que escribiste en el cuadro? Answers will vary.

Verbo	Sustantivos	Otras formas
1. agradecer	agradecimiento/ gracias	agradecido
2. estudiar	estudiante / *student*	estudiado / *studied*
3. celebrar / *to celebrate*	celebración / *celebration*	celebrado
4. bailar / *to dance*	baile	bailable / *danceable*
5. bautizar	bautismo / *baptism*	bautizado / *baptized*

Teaching Tips
- Have students fill in the chart after they have read **Vida social**.
- Write **conocer** (*to know*) on the board. Next to it, write **conocimiento** and **conocido** and guide students to recognize their meanings (*knowledge* and *known*). Explain that recognizing word families will help students infer the meaning of new words.

recursos

SUPERSITE

adelante.vhlcentral.com

Extra Practice Write additional related words on the board and ask students to guess their meanings. Ex: **hablar, hablador, hablante, hablado; ideal, idealizar, idealista**

Teaching Tips Divide the class into groups of three and assign each one a section of the article (Ex: **Matrimonio**). Group members should take turns reading aloud, then write three comprehension questions about their section for the class to answer.

Vida social

Matrimonio
Espinoza Álvarez- Reyes Salazar

El día sábado 17 de junio de 2008 a las 19 horas, se celebró el matrimonio de Silvia Reyes y Carlos Espinoza en la catedral de Santiago. La ceremonia fue oficiada por el pastor Federico Salas y participaron los padres de los novios, el señor Jorge Espinoza y señora y el señor José Alfredo

Reyes y señora. Después de la ceremonia, los padres de los recién casados ofrecieron una fiesta bailable en el restaurante La Misión.

Bautismo

José María recibió el bautismo el 26 de junio de 2008.

Sus padres, don Roberto Lagos Moreno y doña María Angélica Sánchez, compartieron la alegría de la fiesta con todos sus parientes y amigos. La ceremonia religiosa tuvo lugar° en la catedral de Aguas Blancas. Después de la ceremonia, padres, parientes y amigos celebraron una fiesta en la residencia de la familia Lagos.

32B

Fiesta quinceañera

El doctor don Amador Larenas Fernández y la señora Felisa Vera de Larenas celebraron los quince años de su hija Ana Ester junto a sus parientes y amigos. La quinceañera° reside en la ciudad de Valparaíso y es estudiante del Colegio Francés. La fiesta de presentación en sociedad de la señorita Ana Ester fue el día viernes 2 de mayo a las 19 horas, en el Club Español. Entre los invitados especiales asistieron el alcalde° de la ciudad, don Pedro Castedo, y su esposa. La música estuvo a cargo de la Orquesta Americana. ¡Feliz cumpleaños le deseamos a la señorita Ana Ester en su fiesta bailable!

Expresión de gracias
Carmen Godoy Tapia

Agradecemos° sinceramente a todas las personas que nos acompañaron en el último adiós a nuestra apreciada esposa, madre, abuela y tía, la señora Carmen Godoy Tapia. El funeral tuvo lugar el día 28 de junio de 2008 en la ciudad de Viña del Mar. La vida de Carmen Godoy fue un ejemplo de trabajo, amistad, alegría y amor para todos nosotros. La familia agradece de todo corazón° su asistencia° al funeral a todos los parientes y amigos. Su esposo, hijos y familia.

---

tuvo lugar *took place* quinceañera *fifteen year-old girl* alcalde *mayor*
Agradecemos *We thank* **de todo corazón** *sincerely* **asistencia** *attendance*

Después de leer

Corregir
Escribe estos comentarios otra vez para corregir la información errónea.

1. El alcalde y su esposa asistieron a la boda de Silvia y Carlos. El alcalde y su esposa asistieron a la fiesta de quinceañera de Ana Ester.
2. Todos los anuncios (*announcements*) describen eventos felices. Tres de los anuncios tratan de eventos felices. Uno trata de una muerte.
3. Ana Ester Larenas cumple dieciséis años. Ana Ester Larenas cumple quince años.
4. Roberto Lagos y María Angélica Sánchez son hermanos. Roberto Lagos y María Angélica Sánchez están casados/son esposos.
5. Carmen Godoy Tapia les dio las gracias a las personas que asistieron al funeral. La familia de Carmen Godoy Tapia les dio las gracias a las personas que asistieron al funeral.

Identificar
Escribe el nombre de la(s) persona(s) descrita(s) (*described*).

1. Dejó viudo a su esposo en junio de 2008. Carmen Godoy Tapia
2. Sus padres y todos los invitados brindaron por él, pero él no entendió por qué. José María
3. El Club Español les presentó una cuenta considerable para pagar. don Amador Larenas Fernández y doña Felisa Vera de Larenas
4. Unió a los novios en santo matrimonio. el pastor Federico Salas
5. La celebración de su cumpleaños marcó el comienzo de su vida adulta. Ana Ester

Un anuncio
Trabaja con dos o tres compañeros/as de clase e inventen un anuncio breve sobre una celebración importante. Esta celebración puede ser una graduación, un matrimonio o una gran fiesta en la que ustedes participan. Incluyan la siguiente información. Answers will vary.

1. nombres de los participantes
2. la fecha, la hora y el lugar
3. qué se celebra
4. otros detalles de interés

Lección 3

Chile

connections cultures NATIONAL STANDARDS

El país en cifras

▶ **Área:** 756.950 km² (292.259 millas²), *dos veces el área de Montana*

▶ **Población:** 17.134.000
Aproximadamente el 80 por ciento de la población del país es urbana.

▶ **Capital:** Santiago de Chile—5.982.000

▶ **Ciudades principales:** Concepción, Viña del Mar, Valparaíso, Temuco

SOURCE: Population Division, UN Secretariat

▶ **Moneda:** peso chileno

▶ **Idiomas:** español (oficial), mapuche

Bandera de Chile

Chilenos célebres

▶ **Bernardo O'Higgins,** militarº y héroe nacional (1778–1842)

▶ **Gabriela Mistral,** Premio Nobel de Literatura, 1945; poeta y diplomática (1889–1957)

▶ **Pablo Neruda,** Premio Nobel de Literatura, 1971; poeta (1904–1973)

▶ **Isabel Allende,** novelista (1942–)

Pablo Neruda

militar *soldier*   terremoto *earthquake*   heridas *wounded*
hogar *home*

PERÚ

Pampa del Tamarugal

Cordillera de los Andes

Océano Pacífico

Viña del Mar
Valparaíso

★ Santiago de Chile

Concepción

Temuco

Lago Buenos Aires

Punta Arenas

Estrecho de Magallanes

Isla Grande de Tierra del Fuego

Palacio de la Moneda en Santiago

BOLIVIA

Una calle de Santiago

ARGENTINA

Una celebración en Temuco

Océano Atlántico

Vista de la costa de Viña del Mar

Pescadores de Valparaíso

recursos

WB pp. 167–168	VM pp. 171–172	adelante. vhlcentral.com

¡Increíble pero cierto!

El terremotoº de mayor intensidad registrado tuvo lugar en Chile el 22 de mayo de 1960. Registró una intensidad récord de 9.5 en la escala de Richter. Murieron 2.000 personas, 3.000 resultaron heridasº y 2.000.000 perdieron su hogarº. La geografía del país se modificó notablemente.

Lugares • La isla de Pascua

La isla de Pascua° recibió ese nombre porque los exploradores holandeses° llegaron a la isla por primera vez el día de Pascua de 1722. Ahora es parte del territorio de Chile. La isla de Pascua es famosa por los *moai,* estatuas enormes que representan personas con rasgos° muy exagerados. Estas estatuas las construyeron los *rapa nui,* los antiguos habitantes de la zona. Todavía no se sabe mucho sobre los *rapa nui,* ni tampoco se sabe por qué decidieron abandonar la isla.

Deportes • Los deportes de invierno

Hay muchos lugares para practicar los deportes de invierno en Chile porque las montañas nevadas de los Andes ocupan gran parte del país. El Parque Nacional de Villarrica, por ejemplo, situado al pie de un volcán y junto a° un lago, es un sitio popular para el esquí y el *snowboard.* Para los que prefieren deportes más extremos, el centro de esquí Valle Nevado organiza excursiones para practicar el heliesquí.

Ciencias • Astronomía

Los observatorios chilenos, situados en los Andes, son lugares excelentes para las observaciones astronómicas. Científicos° de todo el mundo van a Chile para estudiar las estrellas° y otros cuerpos celestes. Hoy día Chile está construyendo nuevos observatorios y telescopios para mejorar las imágenes del universo.

Economía • El vino

La producción de vino comenzó en Chile en el siglo° XVI. Ahora la industria del vino constituye una parte importante de la actividad agrícola del país y la exportación de sus productos está subiendo° cada vez más. Los vinos chilenos reciben el aprecio internacional por su gran variedad, sus ricos y complejos sabores° y su precio moderado. Los más conocidos internacionalmente son los vinos de Aconcagua, de Santiago y de Huasco.

 ¿Qué aprendiste? Responde a cada pregunta con una oración completa.

1. ¿Qué porcentaje (*percentage*) de la población chilena es urbana?
   El 80 por ciento de la población chilena es urbana.

2. ¿Qué son los *moai*? ¿Dónde están? Los *moai* son estatuas enormes. Están en la isla de Pascua.

3. ¿Qué deporte extremo ofrece el centro de esquí Valle Nevado?
   Ofrece la práctica de heliesquí.

4. ¿Por qué van a Chile científicos de todo el mundo? Porque los observatorios chilenos son excelentes para las observaciones astronómicas.

5. ¿Cuándo comenzó la producción de vino en Chile?
   Comenzó en el siglo XVI.

6. ¿Por qué reciben los vinos chilenos el aprecio internacional? Lo reciben por su variedad, sus ricos y complejos sabores y su precio moderado.

 Conexión Internet Investiga estos temas en **adelante.vhlcentral.com.**

1. Busca información sobre Pablo Neruda e Isabel Allende. ¿Dónde y cuándo nacieron? ¿Cuáles son algunas de sus obras (*works*)? ¿Cuáles son algunos de los temas de sus obras?

2. Busca información sobre sitios donde los chilenos y los turistas practican deportes de invierno en Chile. Selecciona un sitio y descríbeselo a tu clase.

··

La isla de Pascua *Easter Island*   holandeses *Dutch*   rasgos *features*   junto a *beside*   Científicos *Scientists*   estrellas *stars*
siglo *century*   subiendo *increasing*   complejos sabores *complex flavors*

Supersite/DVD: You may want to wrap up this section by playing the *Panorama cultural* video footage for this lesson.

Las celebraciones

el aniversario (de bodas)	(wedding) anniversary
la boda	wedding
el cumpleaños	birthday
el día de fiesta	holiday
la fiesta	party
el/la invitado/a	guest
la Navidad	Christmas
la quinceañera	young woman's fifteenth birthday celebration
la sorpresa	surprise
brindar	to toast (drink)
celebrar	to celebrate
divertirse (e:ie)	to have fun
invitar	to invite
pasarlo bien/mal	to have a good/bad time
regalar	to give (a gift)
reírse (e:i)	to laugh
relajarse	to relax
sonreír (e:i)	to smile
sorprender	to surprise

Los postres y otras comidas

la botella (de vino)	bottle (of wine)
el champán	champagne
los dulces	sweets; candy
el flan (de caramelo)	baked (caramel) custard
la galleta	cookie
el helado	ice cream
el pastel (de chocolate)	(chocolate) cake; pie
el postre	dessert

Las relaciones personales

la amistad	friendship
el amor	love
el divorcio	divorce
el estado civil	marital status
el matrimonio	marriage
la pareja	(married) couple; partner
el/la recién casado/a	newlywed
casarse (con)	to get married (to)
comprometerse (con)	to get engaged (to)
divorciarse (de)	to get divorced (from)
enamorarse (de)	to fall in love (with)
llevarse bien/mal (con)	to get along well/badly (with)
odiar	to hate
romper (con)	to break up (with)
salir (con)	to go out (with); to date
separarse (de)	to separate (from)
tener una cita	to have a date; to have an appointment
casado/a	married
divorciado/a	divorced
juntos/as	together
separado/a	separated
soltero/a	single
viudo/a	widower/widow

Las etapas de la vida

la adolescencia	adolescence
la edad	age
el estado civil	marital status
las etapas de la vida	the stages of life
la juventud	youth
la madurez	maturity; middle age
la muerte	death
el nacimiento	birth
la niñez	childhood
la vejez	old age
cambiar (de)	to change
graduarse (de/en)	to graduate (from/in)
jubilarse	to retire (from work)
nacer	to be born

Palabras adicionales

la alegría	happiness
el beso	kiss
conmigo	with me
contigo	with you

Expresiones útiles	See page 137.

Supersite/IRCD: MP3 Audio Files, Testing Program, *Vocabulario adicional*

recursos

LM p. 178

adelante. vhlcentral.com

contextos

Lección 3

1 **Identificar** Label the following terms as **estado civil, fiesta,** or **etapa de la vida.**

1. casada _____estado civil_____

2. adolescencia _____etapa de la vida_____

3. viudo _____estado civil_____

4. juventud _____etapa de la vida_____

5. quinceañera _____fiesta_____

6. niñez _____etapa de la vida_____

7. vejez _____etapa de la vida_____

8. aniversario de bodas _____fiesta_____

9. divorciado _____estado civil_____

10. madurez _____etapa de la vida_____

11. cumpleaños _____fiesta_____

12. soltera _____estado civil_____

2 **Las etapas de la vida** Label the stages of life on the timeline.

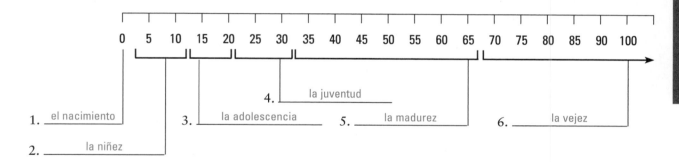

1. el nacimiento
2. la niñez
3. la adolescencia
4. la juventud
5. la madurez
6. la vejez

3 **Escribir** Fill in the blanks with the stage of life in which these events would normally occur.

1. jubilarse _____la vejez_____

2. graduarse en la universidad _____la juventud_____

3. cumplir nueve años _____la niñez_____

4. conseguir el primer trabajo _____la juventud_____

5. graduarse de la escuela secundaria _____la adolescencia_____

6. morir o quedar viudo _____la vejez_____

7. casarse (por primera vez) _____la juventud_____

8. tener un hijo _____la juventud_____

9. celebrar el cincuenta aniversario de bodas _____la vejez_____

10. tener la primera cita _____la adolescencia_____

4 **Información personal** Read the descriptions and answer the questions.

"Me llamo Jorge Rosas. Nací el 26 de enero de 1938. Mi esposa murió el año pasado. Tengo dos hijos: Marina y Daniel. Terminé mis estudios de sociología en la Universidad Interamericana en 1960. Me voy a jubilar este año. Voy a celebrar este evento con una botella de champán."

1. ¿Cuál es la fecha de nacimiento de Jorge? _el 26 de enero de 1938_

2. ¿Cuál es el estado civil de Jorge? _viudo_

3. ¿En qué etapa de la vida está Jorge? _en la vejez_

4. ¿Cuándo es el cumpleaños de Jorge? _el 26 de enero_

5. ¿Cuándo se graduó Jorge? _en 1960_

6. ¿Cómo va a celebrar la jubilación (*retirement*) Jorge? _con una botella de champán_

"Soy Julia Jiménez. Nací el 11 de marzo de 1973. Me comprometí a los veinte años, pero rompí con mi novio antes de casarme. Ahora estoy saliendo con un músico cubano. Soy historiadora del arte desde que terminé mi carrera (*degree*) en la Universidad de Salamanca en 1995. Mi postre favorito es el flan de caramelo."

7. ¿Cuál es la fecha de nacimiento de Julia? _el 11 de marzo de 1973_

8. ¿Cuál es el estado civil de Julia? _soltera_

9. ¿En qué etapa de la vida está Julia? _en la juventud_

10. ¿Cuándo es el cumpleaños de Julia? _el 11 de marzo_

11. ¿Cuándo se graduó Julia? _en 1995_

12. ¿Qué postre le gusta a Julia? _el flan de caramelo_

"Me llamo Manuel Blanco y vivo en Caracas. Mi esposa y yo nos comprometimos a los veintiséis años, y la boda fue dos años después. Pasaron quince años y tuvimos tres hijos. Me gustan mucho los dulces."

13. ¿Dónde vive Manuel? _en Caracas_

14. ¿En qué etapa de la vida se comprometió Manuel? _en la juventud_

15. ¿A qué edad se casó Manuel? _a los veintiocho años_

16. ¿Cuál es el estado civil de Manuel? _casado_

17. ¿Cuántos hijos tiene Manuel? _tres_

18. ¿Qué postre le gusta a Manuel? _los dulces_

estructura

3.1 Irregular preterites

1 **¿Hay o hubo?** Complete these sentences with the correct tense of **haber**.

1. Ahora _____ hay _____ una fiesta de graduación en el patio de la universidad.

2. _____ Hubo _____ muchos invitados en la fiesta de aniversario anoche.

3. Ya _____ hubo _____ una muerte en su familia el año pasado.

4. Siempre _____ hay _____ galletas y dulces en esas conferencias.

5. _____ Hubo _____ varias botellas de vino, pero los invitados se las tomaron.

6. Por las mañanas _____ hay _____ unos postres deliciosos en esa tienda.

2 **¿Cómo fue?** Complete these sentences with the preterite of the verb in parentheses.

1. Cristina y Lara _____ estuvieron _____ (estar) en la fiesta anoche.

2. (yo) _____ Tuve _____ (Tener) un problema con mi pasaporte y lo pasé mal en la aduana.

3. Rafaela _____ vino _____ (venir) temprano a la fiesta y conoció a Humberto.

4. El padre de la novia _____ hizo _____ (hacer) un brindis por los novios.

5. Román _____ puso _____ (poner) las maletas en el auto antes de salir.

3 **¿Qué hicieron?** Complete these sentences, using the preterite of **decir, conducir, traducir,** and **traer**.

1. Felipe y Silvia _____ dijeron _____ que no les gusta ir a la playa.

2. Claudia le _____ tradujo _____ unos papeles al inglés a su hermano.

3. David _____ condujo _____ su motocicleta nueva durante el fin de semana.

4. Rosario y Pepe me _____ trajeron _____ un pastel de chocolate de regalo.

5. Cristina y yo les _____ dijimos _____ a nuestras amigas que vamos a bailar.

4 **Es mejor dar...** Rewrite these sentences in the preterite tense.

1. Antonio le da un beso a su madre.

Antonio le dio un beso a su madre.

2. Los invitados le dan las gracias a la familia.

Los invitados le dieron las gracias a la familia.

3. Tú les traes una sorpresa a tus padres.

Tú les trajiste una sorpresa a tus padres.

4. Rosa y yo le damos un regalo al profesor.

Rosa y yo le dimos un regalo al profesor.

5. Carla nos da muchos consejos para el viaje.

Carla nos dio muchos consejos para el viaje.

5 **Combinar** Create logical sentences in the preterite using one element from each column. Notice that there is only one correct match between second and third columns. Answers will vary. Suggested answers:

Rita y Sara	decir	una cámara
ellos	estar	a este lugar
tú	hacer	un examen
mi tía	poner	galletas
ustedes	producir	una película
Rosa	tener	en el Perú
nosotras	traer	la televisión
yo	venir	la verdad

1. Rosa hizo galletas.

2. Mi tía estuvo en el Perú.

3. Yo vine a este lugar.

4. Rita y Sara dijeron la verdad.

5. Ustedes pusieron la televisión.

6. Ellos produjeron una película.

7. Nosotras trajimos una cámara.

8. Tú tuviste un examen.

6 **Ya lo hizo** Your friend Miguel is very forgetful. Answer his questions negatively, indicating that the action has already occurred. Use the verbs in parentheses.

> **modelo**
> ¿Quiere Pepe cenar en el restaurante japonés? (restaurante chino)
> **No, Pepe ya cenó en el restaurante chino.**

1. ¿Vas a estar en la biblioteca hoy? (ayer)

No, ya estuve en la biblioteca ayer.

2. ¿Quieren dar una fiesta Elena y Miguel este fin de semana? (el sábado pasado)

No, Elena y Miguel ya dieron una fiesta el sábado pasado.

3. ¿Debe la profesora traducir esa novela este semestre? (el año pasado)

No, la profesora ya tradujo esa novela el año pasado.

4. ¿Va a haber un pastel de limón en la cena de hoy? (anoche)

No, ya hubo un pastel de limón anoche./ en la cena de anoche.

5. ¿Deseas poner los abrigos en la silla? (sobre la cama)

No, ya puse los abrigos sobre la cama.

6. ¿Van ustedes a tener un hijo? (tres hijos)

No, ya tuvimos/tenemos tres hijos.

3.2 Verbs that change meaning in the preterite

1 **Completar** Complete these sentences with the preterite tense of the verbs in parentheses.

1. Liliana no _____pudo_____ (poder) llegar a la fiesta de cumpleaños de Esteban.

2. Las chicas _____conocieron_____ (conocer) a muchos estudiantes en la biblioteca.

3. Raúl y Marta no _____quisieron_____ (querer) invitar al padre de Raúl a la boda.

4. Lina _____supo_____ (saber) ayer que sus tíos se van a divorciar.

5. (nosotros) _____Pudimos_____ (poder) regalarle una bicicleta a Marina.

6. María _____quiso_____ (querer) cortar con su novio antes del verano.

2 **Traducir** Use these verbs to write sentences in Spanish.

conocer	querer
poder	saber

1. I failed to finish the book on Wednesday.

   No pude terminar el libro el miércoles.

2. Inés found out last week that Vicente is divorced.

   Inés supo la semana pasada que Vicente es divorciado.

3. Her girlfriends tried to call her, but they failed to.

   Sus amigas quisieron llamarla (por teléfono), pero no pudieron.

4. Susana met Alberto's parents last night.

   Susana conoció a los padres de Alberto anoche.

5. The waiters managed to serve dinner at eight.

   Los camareros pudieron servir la cena a las ocho.

6. Your mother refused to go to your brother's house.

   Tu madre no quiso ir a la casa de tu hermano.

3 **Raquel y Ronaldo** Complete the paragraph with the preterite of the verbs in the word bank.

conocer	querer
poder	saber

El año pasado Raquel (1) _____conoció_____ al muchacho que ahora es su esposo, Ronaldo. Primero, Raquel no (2) _____quiso_____ salir con él porque él vivía (*was living*) en una ciudad muy lejos de ella. Ronaldo (3) _____quiso_____ convencerla durante muchos meses, pero no (4) _____pudo_____ hacerlo. Finalmente, Raquel decidió darle una oportunidad a Ronaldo. Cuando empezaron a salir, Raquel y Ronaldo (5) _____supieron_____ inmediatamente que eran el uno para el otro (*they were made for each other*). Raquel y Ronaldo (6) _____pudieron_____ comprar una casa en la misma ciudad y se casaron ese verano.

Nombre

Fecha

3.3 ¿Qué? and ¿cuál?

1 **¿Qué o cuál?** Complete these sentences with **qué, cuál,** or **cuáles.**

1. ¿_____Qué_____ estás haciendo ahora?

2. ¿_____Qué_____ gafas te gustan más?

3. ¿_____Cuál_____ prefieres, el vestido largo o el corto?

4. ¿Sabes _____cuál_____ de éstos es mi disco favorito?

5. ¿_____Qué_____ es un departamento de hacienda?

6. ¿_____Cuáles_____ trajiste, las de chocolate o las de limón?

7. ¿_____Qué_____ auto compraste este año?

8. ¿_____Cuál_____ es la tienda más elegante del centro?

2 **¿Cuál es la pregunta?** Write questions that correspond to these responses. Use each word or phrase from the word bank only once.

¿a qué hora?	¿cuál?	¿cuándo?	¿de dónde?	¿qué?
¿adónde?	¿cuáles?	¿cuántos?	¿dónde?	¿quién?

1. ¿Cuál es la camisa que más te gusta?

La camisa que más me gusta es ésa.

2. ¿Qué quieres hacer hoy?

Hoy quiero descansar durante el día.

3. ¿Quién es tu profesora de matemáticas?

Mi profesora de matemáticas es la señora Aponte.

4. ¿De dónde eres?/¿De dónde es usted?

Soy de Buenos Aires, Argentina.

5. ¿Cuáles son tus gafas favoritas?

Mis gafas favoritas son las azules.

6. ¿Dónde está el pastel de cumpleaños?

El pastel de cumpleaños está en el refrigerador.

7. ¿A qué hora empieza la fiesta sorpresa?

La fiesta sorpresa empieza a las ocho en punto de la noche.

8. ¿Cuándo cierra el restaurante?

El restaurante cierra los lunes.

9. ¿Cuántos invitados hay en la lista?

Hay ciento cincuenta invitados en la lista.

10. ¿Adónde van ustedes?

Vamos a la fiesta de cumpleaños de Inés.

3.4 Pronouns after prepositions

1 **Antes de la fiesta** Complete the paragraph with the correct pronouns.

Hoy voy al mercado al aire libre cerca de mi casa con mi tía Carmen. Me gusta ir con

(1) _____ella_____ porque sabe escoger las mejores frutas y verduras del mercado. Y a ella le gusta

venir (2) _____conmigo_____ porque sé regatear mejor que nadie.

—Entre (3) _____tú_____ y yo, debes saber que a (4) _____mí_____ no me gusta gastar mucho

dinero. Me gusta venir (5) _____contigo_____ porque me ayudas a ahorrar (*save*) dinero— me confesó

un día. Hoy la vienen a visitar sus hijos porque es su cumpleaños, y ella quiere hacer una ensalada de

frutas para (6) _____ellos_____.

—Estas peras son para (7) _____ti_____, por venir conmigo al mercado. También me llevo unos

hermosos melocotones para el novio de Verónica, que viene con (8) _____nosotros_____. Siempre

compro frutas para (9) _____él_____ porque le encantan y no consigue muchas frutas en el lugar

donde vive —dice (*says*) mi tía.

—¿Voy a conocer al novio de Verónica?

—Sí, ¡queremos invitarte a (10) _____ti_____ a la fiesta de cumpleaños!

2 **El pastel de Maite** The video characters are having Maite's birthday cake. Complete the conversation with the correct pronouns.

DON FRANCISCO Chicos, voy a hablar con la señora Perales, en un momento estoy con

(1) _____ustedes_____.

JAVIER Sí, don Efe, no se preocupe por (2) _____nosotros_____.

INÉS ¡Qué rico está el pastel! A (3)_____mí_____ me encantan los pasteles.

Javier, ¿quieres compartir un pedazo (*slice*) (4) _____conmigo_____?

JAVIER ¡Claro! Para (5) _____mí_____ el chocolate es lo más delicioso.

MAITE Pero no se lo terminen... Álex, quiero compartir el último (*last*) pedazo

(6) _____contigo_____.

ÁLEX Mmmh, está bien; sólo por (7) _____ti_____ hago este sacrificio.

MAITE Toma, Álex, este pedazo es especial para (8) _____ti_____.

JAVIER Oh no. Mira Inés; hay más miel (*honey*) en (9) _____ellos/él_____ que en

cien pasteles.

Síntesis

Research the life of a famous person who has had a stormy personal life, such as Elizabeth Taylor or Henry VIII. Write a brief biography of the person, including the following information:

- When was the person born?
- What was that person's childhood like?
- With whom did the person fall in love?
- Who did the person marry?
- Did he or she have children?

- Did the person get divorced?
- Did the person go to school, and did he or she graduate?
- How did his or her career or lifestyle vary as the person went through different stages in life?

Answers will vary.

_____

_____

_____

_____

_____

_____

_____

_____

_____

_____

_____

_____

_____

_____

_____

_____

_____

panorama

Chile

1 **Datos chilenos** Complete the chart with the correct information about Chile.

Ciudades más grandes	Deportes de invierno	Países fronterizos (*bordering*)	Escritores chilenos
Santiago de Chile	el esquí	Perú	Gabriela Mistral
Concepción	el snowboard	Bolivia	Pablo Neruda
Viña del Mar	el heliesquí	Argentina	Isabel Allende

2 **¿Cierto o falso?** Indicate whether the sentences are **cierto** or **falso.** Correct the false sentences.

1. Una quinta parte de los chilenos vive en Santiago de Chile.

   Falso. Una tercera parte de los chilenos vive en Santiago de Chile.

2. En Chile se hablan el idioma español y el mapuche.

   Cierto.

3. La mayoría (*most*) de las playas de Chile están en la costa del océano Atlántico.

   Falso. La mayoría de las playas de Chile están en la costa del océano Pacífico.

4. El terremoto más grande de la historia tuvo lugar en Chile.

   Cierto.

5. La isla de Pascua es famosa por sus observatorios astronómicos.

   Falso. La isla de Pascua es famosa por los moai, unas estatuas enormes.

6. El Parque Nacional de Villarica está situado al pie de un volcán y junto a un lago.

   Cierto.

7. Se practican deportes de invierno en los Andes chilenos.

   Cierto.

8. La exportación de vinos chilenos se redujo en los últimos años.

   Falso. La exportación de vinos está subiendo cada vez más.

3 **Información de Chile** Complete the sentences with the correct words.

1. La moneda de Chile es el _____peso chileno_____.

2. Bernardo O'Higgins fue un militar y _____héroe_____ nacional de Chile.

3. Los exploradores _____holandeses_____ descubrieron la isla de Pascua.

4. Desde los _____observatorios_____ chilenos de los Andes, los científicos estudian las estrellas.

5. La producción de _____vino_____ es una parte importante de la actividad agrícola de Chile.

6. El país al este de Chile es _____Argentina_____.

4 **Fotos de Chile** Label the photos.

1. _____Pablo Neruda_____

2. _____Moais de la isla de Pascua_____

5 **El pasado de Chile** Complete the sentences with the preterite of the correct words from the word bank.

comenzar	escribir
decidir	recibir

1. Pablo Neruda _____escribió_____ muchos poemas románticos durante su vida.

2. La isla de Pascua _____recibió_____ su nombre porque la descubrieron el Día de Pascua.

3. No se sabe por qué los *rapa nui* _____decidieron_____ abandonar la isla de Pascua.

4. La producción de vino en Chile _____comenzó_____ en el siglo XVI.

6 **Preguntas chilenas** Write questions that correspond to the answers below. Vary the interrogative words you use.

1. ¿Cuántos habitantes hay en Chile? _____

Hay más de dieciséis millones de habitantes en Chile.

2. ¿Cuál es la capital chilena? _____

Santiago de Chile es la capital chilena.

3. ¿Qué idiomas se hablan en Chile?/¿Cuáles son los idiomas que se hablan en Chile? _____

Los idiomas que se hablan en Chile son el español y el mapuche.

4. ¿Quiénes descubrieron la isla de Pascua?/¿Qué descubrieron los exploradores holandeses? _____

Los exploradores holandeses descubrieron la isla de Pascua.

5. ¿Dónde se puede practicar el heliesquí?/¿Qué (deporte) se puede practicar en el centro de esquí Valle Nevado? _____

El centro de esquí Valle Nevado organiza excursiones de heliesquí.

6. ¿Cuándo comenzó la producción de vino en Chile? _____

La producción de vino en Chile comenzó en el siglo XVI.

¡Feliz cumpleaños, Maite!

Antes de ver el video

1 **Una fiesta** In this video episode, Señora Perales and Don Francisco surprise Maite with a birthday party. Based on this information, what kinds of things do you expect to see in this episode? Answers will vary.

_____
_____
_____
_____
_____
_____
_____
_____
_____

Mientras ves el video

2 **Ordenar** Watch the **¡Feliz cumpleaños, Maite!** segment of this video module and put the following events in the correct order.

__4__ a. Álex recuerda la quinceañera de su hermana.

__1__ b. Los estudiantes miran el menú.

__2__ c. Javier pide un pastel de chocolate.

__3__ d. La señora Perales trae un flan, un pastel y una botella de vino.

__5__ e. Los estudiantes deciden dejarle una buena propina a la señora Perales.

3 **La quinceañera** Watch Álex's flashback about his sister's **quinceañera**. Place a check mark in the **Sí** column if the following actions occurred in the flashback; place a check mark in the **No** column if the actions did *not* occur.

Acción	Sí	No
1. Álex canta para su hermana.		X
2. Todos se sientan a cenar.		X
3. Todos nadan en la piscina.		X
4. Varias personas bailan.	X	

4 **Resumen** Watch the **Resumen** segment of this video module and indicate who says the following lines.

_____Javier_____ 1. Señora Perales, mi cumpleaños es el primero de octubre...

_____Maite_____ 2. Dicen que las fiestas son mejores cuando son una sorpresa.

_____Inés_____ 3. ¿Hoy es tu cumpleaños, Maite?

_____Álex_____ 4. Ayer te lo pregunté, ¡y no quisiste decírmelo!

Después de ver el video

5 **Corregir** All of the following statements about this video episode are false. Rewrite them so that they will be correct.

1. Álex le sirve un pastel de cumpleaños a Maite.

   La señora Perales y el camarero le sirven un pastel de cumpleaños a Maite.

2. Don Francisco le deja una buena propina a la señora Perales.

   Los estudiantes le dejan una buena propina a la señora Perales.

3. Maite cumple diecinueve años.

   Maite cumple veintitrés años.

4. Don Francisco toma una copa de vino.

   Los estudiantes toman vino. El conductor no puede tomar vino.

5. El cumpleaños de Javier es el quince de diciembre.

   El cumpleaños de Javier es el primero de octubre.

6. El cumpleaños de Maite es el primero de octubre.

   El cumpleaños de Maite es el 22 de junio.

6 **Eventos importantes** In Spanish, list the three events from this video episode that you consider to be the most important, and explain your choices. Answers will vary.

_____

_____

_____

_____

_____

_____

_____

7 **Preguntas personales** Answer these questions in Spanish. Answers will vary.

1. ¿Vas a muchas fiestas? ¿Qué haces en las fiestas? _____

   _____

2. ¿Qué haces antes de ir a una fiesta? ¿Y después? _____

   _____

3. ¿Cuándo es tu cumpleaños? ¿Cómo vas a celebrarlo? _____

   _____

4. ¿Te gusta recibir regalos en tu cumpleaños? ¿Qué tipo de regalos? _____

   _____

Panorama: Chile	**Lección 3**
	Panorama cultural

Antes de ver el video

1 **Más vocabulario** Look over these useful words and expressions before you watch the video.

Vocabulario útil	
disfrutar (de) *to take advantage (of)*	**isla** *island*
grados *degrees*	**recursos naturales** *natural resources*
hace miles de años *thousands of years ago*	**repartidas** *spread throughout, distributed*
indígena *indigenous*	**vista** *view*

2 **Escribir** This video talks about Chile's Easter Island. In preparation for watching the video, answer the following questions. Answers will vary.

1. ¿Has estado en una isla o conoces alguna? ¿Cómo se llama?

_____

2. ¿Dónde está? ¿Cómo es?

_____

Mientras ves el video

3 **Fotos** Describe the video stills. Write at least three sentences in Spanish for each still. Answers will vary.

_____
_____
_____
_____
_____

_____
_____
_____
_____
_____

Después de ver el video

4 **Completar** Complete the sentences with words from the word bank.

atracción	indígena
característico	llega
diferente	recursos
difícil	remoto
escalan	repartidas

1. Rapa Nui es el nombre de la isla de Pascua en la lengua _____ indígena _____ de la región.

2. Esta isla está en un lugar _____ remoto _____.

3. Los habitantes de esta isla no tenían muchos _____ recursos _____ naturales.

4. En un día de verano la temperatura _____ llega _____ a los noventa grados.

5. Las esculturas moai son el elemento más _____ característico _____ de esta isla.

6. Hay más de novecientas esculturas _____ repartidas _____ por toda la isla.

7. Otra gran _____ atracción _____ de la isla es el gran cráter Rano Kau.

8. Los visitantes _____ escalan _____ el cráter para disfrutar de la espectacular vista.

5 **Preferencias** In Spanish, list at least two things you like about this video and explain your choices. Answers will vary.

_____

_____

_____

_____

_____

_____

_____

_____

_____

_____

_____

_____

_____

contextos

1 **¿Lógico o ilógico?** You will hear some statements. Decide if they are **lógico** or **ilógico**.

1. Lógico   (Ilógico)
2. (Lógico)   Ilógico
3. (Lógico)   Ilógico
4. Lógico   (Ilógico)

5. Lógico   (Ilógico)
6. (Lógico)   Ilógico
7. (Lógico)   Ilógico
8. Lógico   (Ilógico)

2 **Escoger** For each drawing, you will hear three statements. Choose the one that corresponds to the drawing.

1. a.   b.   (c.)

2. a.   (b.)   c.

3. (a.)   b.   c.

4. a.   b.   (c.)

3 **Una celebración** Listen as señora Jiménez talks about a party she has planned. Then answer the questions in your lab manual.

1. ¿Para quién es la fiesta?

   La fiesta es para Martín, su hijo.

2. ¿Cuándo es la fiesta?

   La fiesta es el viernes a las ocho y media.

3. ¿Por qué hacen la fiesta?

   Porque él se gradúa.

4. ¿Quiénes van a la fiesta?

   La familia y los amigos de Martín van a la fiesta.

5. ¿Qué van a hacer los invitados en la fiesta?

   Los invitados van a cenar, a bailar y a comer pastel.

Lab Manual

pronunciación

The letters **h**, **j**, and **g**

The Spanish **h** is always silent.

| **h**elado | **h**ombre | **h**ola | **h**ermosa |

The letter **j** is pronounced much like the English *h* in *his*.

| **J**osé | **j**ubilarse | de**j**ar | pare**j**a |

The letter **g** can be pronounced three different ways. Before **e** or **i**, the letter **g** is pronounced much like the English *h*.

| a**g**encia | **g**eneral | **G**il | **G**isela |

At the beginning of a phrase or after the letter **n**, the Spanish **g** is pronounced like the English *g* in *girl*.

Gustavo, **g**racias por llamar el domin**g**o.

In any other position, the Spanish **g** has a somewhat softer sound.

Me **g**radué en a**g**osto.

In the combinations **gue** and **gui**, the **g** has a hard sound and the **u** is silent. In the combination **gua**, the **g** has a hard sound and the **u** is pronounced like the English *w*.

| **Gue**rra | conse**gui**r | **gua**ntes | a**gua** |

---

1 **Práctica** Repeat each word after the speaker to practice pronouncing **h**, **j**, and **g**.

1. hamburguesa	4. guapa	7. espejo	10. gracias	13. Jorge
2. jugar	5. geografía	8. hago	11. hijo	14. tengo
3. oreja	6. magnífico	9. seguir	12. galleta	15. ahora

---

2 **Oraciones** When you hear the number, read the corresponding sentence aloud. Then listen to the speaker and repeat the sentence.

1. Hola. Me llamo Gustavo Hinojosa Lugones y vivo en Santiago de Chile.
2. Tengo una familia grande; somos tres hermanos y tres hermanas.
3. Voy a graduarme en mayo.
4. Para celebrar mi graduación mis padres van a regalarme un viaje a Egipto.
5. ¡Qué generosos son!

---

3 **Refranes** Repeat each saying after the speaker to practice pronouncing **h**, **j**, and **g**.

1. A la larga, lo más dulce amarga.   2. El hábito no hace al monje.

---

4 **Dictado** Victoria is talking to her friend Mirta on the phone. Listen carefully and during the pauses write what she says. The entire passage will then be repeated so that you can check your work.

Mirta, sabes que el domingo es el aniversario de bodas de Héctor y Ángela, ¿no? Sus hijos quieren hacerles una fiesta

grande e invitar a todos sus amigos. Pero a Ángela y a Héctor no les gusta la idea. Ellos quieren salir juntos a algún

restaurante y después relajarse en casa.

estructura

3.1 Irregular preterites

1 **Escoger** Listen to each question and choose the most logical response.

1. (a.) No, no conduje hoy.
2. a. Te dije que tengo una cita con Gabriela esta noche.
3. (a.) Estuvimos en la casa de Marta.
4. (a.) Porque tuvo que estudiar.
5. a. Lo supe la semana pasada.
6. (a.) Los pusimos en la mesa.
7. a. No, sólo tradujimos un poco.
8. (a.) Sí, le di $20.000.

b. No, no condujo hoy.
(b.) Me dijo que tiene una cita con Gabriela esta noche.
b. Estuvieron en la casa de Marta.
b. Porque tiene que estudiar.
(b.) Lo supimos la semana pasada.
b. Los pusiste en la mesa.
(b.) No, sólo traduje un poco.
b. Sí, le dio $20.000.

2 **Cambiar** Change each sentence from the present to the preterite. Repeat the correct answer after the speaker. (*8 items*)

> **modelo**
> Él pone el flan sobre la mesa.
> Él puso el flan sobre la mesa.

3 **Preguntas** Answer each question you hear using the cue in your lab manual. Substitute object pronouns for the direct object when possible. Repeat the correct answer after the speaker.

> **modelo**
> You hear: ¿Quién condujo el auto?
> You see: yo
> You say: Yo lo conduje.

1. Gerardo
2. Mateo y Yolanda
3. nosotros
4. muy buena
5. ¡Felicitaciones!
6. mi papá

4 **Completar** Listen to the dialogue and write the missing words in your lab manual.

(1) _____Supe_____ por un amigo que los Márquez (2) _____vinieron_____ a visitar a su hija. Me (3) _____dijo_____ que (4) _____condujeron_____ desde Antofagasta y que se (5) _____quedaron_____ en el Hotel Carrera. Les (6) _____hice_____ una llamada (*call*) anoche pero no (7) _____contestaron_____ el teléfono. Sólo (8) _____pude_____ dejarles un mensaje. Hoy ellos me (9) _____llamaron_____ y me (10) _____preguntaron_____ si mi esposa y yo teníamos tiempo para almorzar con ellos. Claro que les (11) _____dije_____ que sí.

3.2 Verbs that change meaning in the preterite

1 **Identificar** Listen to each sentence and mark and **X** in the column for the subject of the verb.

> **modelo**
> *You hear:* ¿Cuándo lo supiste?
> *You mark:* an **X** under **tú.**

	yo	tú	él/ella	nosotros	ellos/ellas
Modelo		**X**			
1.				X	
2.			X		
3.	X				
4.		X			
5.					X
6.	X				
7.					X
8.			X		

2 **Preguntas** Answer each question you hear using the cue in your lab manual. Substitute object pronouns for the direct object when possible. Repeat the correct response after the speaker.

> **modelo**
> *You hear:* ¿Conocieron ellos a Sandra?
> *You see:* sí
> *You say:* Sí, la conocieron.

1. sí   2. en la casa de Ángela   3. el viernes   4. no   5. no   6. anoche

3 **¡Qué lástima! (*What a shame!*)** Listen as José talks about some news he recently received. Then read the statements and decide whether they are **cierto** or **falso**.

	Cierto	Falso
1. Supieron de la muerte ayer.	○	⊘
2. Se sonrieron cuando oyeron las noticias (*news*).	○	⊘
3. Carolina no se pudo comunicar con la familia.	⊘	○
4. Francisco era (*was*) joven.	⊘	○
5. Mañana piensan llamar a la familia de Francisco.	○	⊘

4 **Relaciones amorosas** Listen as Susana describes what happened between her and Pedro. Then answer the questions in your lab manual.

1. ¿Por qué no pudo salir Susana con Pedro? No pudo salir con Pedro porque pasó toda la noche estudiando.

2. ¿Qué supo por su amiga? Supo que Pedro salió con Mónica anoche.

3. ¿Cómo se puso ella cuando Pedro llamó? Se puso muy enojada.

4. ¿Qué le dijo Susana a Pedro? Le dijo que supo que el domingo salió con Mónica.

3.3 ¿Qué? and ¿cuál?

1 **¿Lógico o ilógico?** You will hear some questions and the responses. Decide if they are **lógico** or **ilógico**.

1. Lógico   (Ilógico)   5. Lógico   (Ilógico)
2. (Lógico)   Ilógico   6. Lógico   (Ilógico)
3. Lógico   (Ilógico)   7. (Lógico)   Ilógico
4. (Lógico)   Ilógico   8. (Lógico)   Ilógico

2 **Preguntas** You will hear a series of responses to questions. Using **¿qué?** or **¿cuál?**, form the question that prompted each response. Repeat the correct answer after the speaker. (8 items)

> **modelo**
> Santiago de Chile es la capital de Chile.
> *¿Cuál es la capital de Chile?*

3 **De compras** Look at Marcela's shopping list for Christmas and answer each question you hear. Repeat the correct response after the speaker. (6 items)

Raúl	2 camisas, talla 17
Cristina	blusa, color azul
Pepe	bluejeans y tres pares de calcetines blancos
Abuelo	cinturón
Abuela	suéter blanco

4 **Escoger** Listen to this radio commercial and choose the most logical response to each question.

1. ¿Qué hace Fiestas Mar?

(a.) Organiza fiestas.   b. Es una tienda que vende cosas para fiestas.   c. Es un club en el mar.

2. ¿Para qué tipo de fiesta no usaría Fiestas Mar?

a. Para una boda.   b. Para una fiesta de sorpresa.   (c.) Para una cena con los suegros.

3. ¿Cuál de estos servicios no ofrece Fiestas Mar?

a. Poner las decoraciones.   b. Proveer (*Provide*) el lugar.   (c.) Proveer los regalos.

4. ¿Qué tiene que hacer el cliente si usa Fiestas Mar?

(a.) Tiene que preocuparse por la lista de invitados.   b. Tiene que preocuparse por la música.
c. Tiene que preparar la comida.

5. Si uno quiere contactar Fiestas Mar, ¿qué debe hacer?

a. Debe escribirles un mensaje electrónico.   (b.) Debe llamarlos.   c. Debe ir a Casa Mar.

3.4 Pronouns after prepositions

1 **Cambiar** Listen to each statement and say that the feeling is not mutual. Use a pronoun after the preposition in your response. Then repeat the correct answer after the speaker. (*6 items*)

> **modelo**
>
> Carlos quiere desayunar con nosotros.
> *Pero nosotros no queremos desayunar con él.*

2 **Preguntas** Answer each question you hear using the appropriate pronoun after the preposition and the cue in your lab manual. Repeat the correct response after the speaker.

> **modelo**
>
> *You hear:* ¿Almuerzas con Alberto hoy?
> *You see:* No
> *You say:* No, no almuerzo con él hoy.

1. Sí
2. Luis
3. Sí
4. Sí
5. No
6. Francisco

3 **Preparativos (*Preparations*)** Listen to this conversation between David and Andrés. Then answer the questions in your lab manual.

1. ¿Qué necesitan comprar para la fiesta?

   Necesitan comprar jamón, pan, salchicha y queso.

2. ¿Con quién quiere Alfredo ir a la fiesta?

   Alfredo quiere ir a la fiesta con Sara.

3. ¿Por qué ella no quiere ir con él?

   Ella no quiere ir con él porque está muy enojada.

4. ¿Con quién va Sara?

   Sara va con Andrés.

5. ¿Para quién quieren comprar algo especial?

   Quieren comprar algo especial para Alfredo.

vocabulario

You will now hear the vocabulary found in your worktext on the last page of this lesson. Listen and repeat each Spanish word or phrase after the speaker.

Additional Vocabulary

Additional Vocabulary

Notes

Notes

En el consultorio

Communicative Goals

You will learn how to:

- **Describe how you feel physically**
- **Talk about health and medical conditions**

En el consultorio

Más vocabulario

la clínica	clinic
el consultorio	doctor's office
el/la dentista	dentist
el examen médico	physical exam
la farmacia	pharmacy
el hospital	hospital
la operación	operation
la sala de emergencia(s)	emergency room
el cuerpo	body
el oído	(sense of) hearing; inner ear
el accidente	accident
la salud	health
el síntoma	symptom
caerse	to fall (down)
darse con	to bump into; to run into
doler (o:ue)	to hurt
enfermarse	to get sick
estar enfermo/a	to be sick
poner una inyección	to give an injection
recetar	to prescribe
romperse (la pierna)	to break (one's leg)
sacar(se) un diente	to have a tooth removed
sufrir una enfermedad	to suffer an illness
torcerse (o:ue) (el tobillo)	to sprain (one's ankle)
toser	to cough

Variación léxica

gripe ⟷ gripa (*Col., Gua., Méx.*)

resfriado ⟷ catarro (*Cuba, Esp., Gua.*)

sala de emergencia(s) ⟷ sala de urgencias (*Arg., Esp., Méx.*)

romperse ⟷ quebrarse (*Arg., Gua.*)

Supersite/IRCD: Lesson Plans, MP3 Audio Files and Listening Scripts, Overheads, *Vocabulario adicional*

recursos

WB pp. 211–212

LM p. 229

SUPERSITE adelante. vhlcentral.com

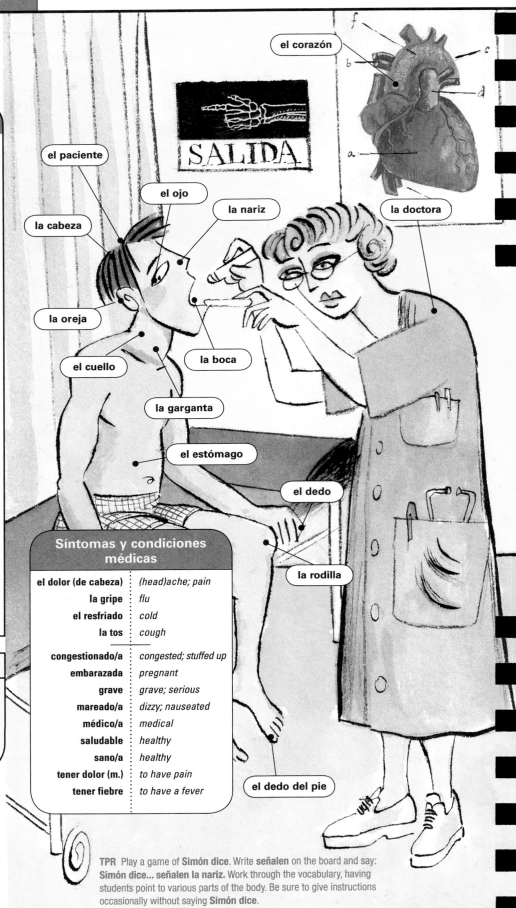

el corazón

el paciente

SALIDA

el ojo

la nariz

la doctora

la cabeza

la oreja

la boca

el cuello

la garganta

el estómago

el dedo

la rodilla

el dedo del pie

Síntomas y condiciones médicas

el dolor (de cabeza)	(head)ache; pain
la gripe	flu
el resfriado	cold
la tos	cough
congestionado/a	congested; stuffed up
embarazada	pregnant
grave	grave; serious
mareado/a	dizzy; nauseated
médico/a	medical
saludable	healthy
sano/a	healthy
tener dolor (m.)	to have pain
tener fiebre	to have a fever

TPR Play a game of **Simón dice**. Write **señalen** on the board and say: **Simón dice... señalen la nariz.** Work through the vocabulary, having students point to various parts of the body. Be sure to give instructions occasionally without saying **Simón dice**.

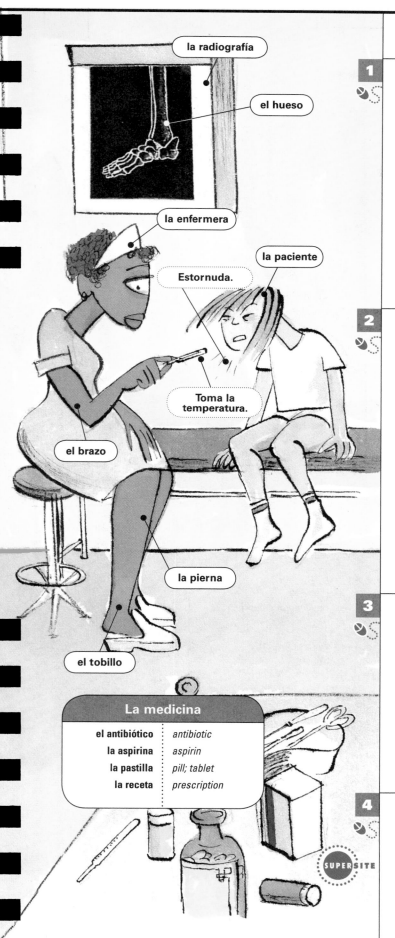

la radiografía

el hueso

la enfermera

la paciente

Estornuda.

Toma la temperatura.

el brazo

la pierna

el tobillo

La medicina

el antibiótico	*antibiotic*
la aspirina	*aspirin*
la pastilla	*pill; tablet*
la receta	*prescription*

Práctica

1 **2** Supersite/IRCD: MP3 Audio Files, Scripts

1

Escuchar 🎧 Escucha las preguntas y selecciona la respuesta más adecuada.

a. Tengo dolor de cabeza y fiebre.
b. No fui a la clase porque estaba (*I was*) enfermo.
c. Me caí la semana pasada jugando al tenis.
d. Debes ir a la farmacia.
e. Porque tengo gripe.
f. Sí, tengo mucha tos por las noches.
g. Lo llevaron directamente a la sala de emergencia.
h. No sé. Todavía tienen que tomarme la temperatura.

1. __c__   3. __g__   5. __f__   7. __a__
2. __e__   4. __d__   6. __h__   8. __b__

2

Seleccionar 🎧 Escucha la conversación entre Daniel y su doctor y selecciona la respuesta que mejor complete cada oración.

1. Daniel cree que tiene __a__.
   a. gripe   b. un resfriado   c. la temperatura alta
2. A Daniel le duele la cabeza, estornuda, tose y __c__.
   a. se cae   b. tiene fiebre   c. está congestionado
3. El doctor le __b__.
   a. pone una inyección   b. toma la temperatura
   c. mira el oído
4. A Daniel no le gustan __a__.
   a. las inyecciones   b. los antibióticos   c. las visitas al doctor
5. El doctor dice que Daniel tiene __b__.
   a. gripe   b. un resfriado   c. fiebre
6. Después de la consulta Daniel va a __c__.
   a. la sala de emergencia   b. la clínica   c. la farmacia

3

Completar Completa las oraciones con una palabra de la misma familia de la palabra subrayada. Usa la forma correcta de cada palabra.

1. Cuando <u>oyes</u> algo, usas el ___oído___.
2. Cuando te <u>enfermas</u>, te sientes ___enfermo/a___ y necesitas ir al consultorio para ver a la ___enfermera___.
3. ¿Alguien ___estornudó___? Creo que oí un <u>estornudo</u> (*sneeze*).
4. No puedo <u>arrodillarme</u> (*kneel down*) porque me lastimé la ___rodilla___ en un accidente de coche.
5. ¿Vas al ___consultorio___ para <u>consultar</u> al médico?
6. Si te rompes un <u>diente</u>, vas al ___dentista___.

4

Contestar Mira el dibujo y contesta las preguntas. Answers will vary.

1. ¿Qué hace la doctora?
2. ¿Qué hay en la pared (*wall*)?
3. ¿Qué hace la enfermera?
4. ¿Qué hace el paciente?
5. ¿A quién le duele la garganta?
6. ¿Qué tiene la paciente?

SUPERSITE

4 Ask additional questions about the doctor's office scene. Ex: **¿Qué hace la chica? (Estornuda.)**

5

Asociaciones Trabajen en parejas para identificar las partes del cuerpo que ustedes asocian con estas actividades. Sigan el modelo. Answers will vary.

> modelo
> nadar
> **Estudiante 1:** Usamos los brazos para nadar.
> **Estudiante 2:** Usamos las piernas también.

1. hablar por teléfono
2. tocar el piano
3. correr en el parque
4. escuchar música
5. ver una película
6. toser
7. llevar zapatos
8. comprar perfume
9. estudiar biología
10. comer lomo a la plancha

5 For each item, encourage students to list as many parts of the body as they can. For variation, say parts of the body and have students associate each one with at least five activities.

6

Cuestionario Contesta el cuestionario seleccionando las respuestas que reflejen mejor tus experiencias. Suma (*Add*) los puntos de cada respuesta y anota el resultado. Después, con el resto de la clase, compara y analiza los resultados del cuestionario y comenta lo que dicen de la salud y de los hábitos de todo el grupo. Answers will vary.

¿Tienes buena salud?

27–30 puntos	Salud y hábitos excelentes
23–26 puntos	Salud y hábitos buenos
22 puntos o menos	Salud y hábitos problemáticos

1. ¿Con qué frecuencia te enfermas? (resfriados, gripe, etc.)
Cuatro veces por año o más. (1 punto)
Dos o tres veces por año. (2 puntos)
Casi nunca. (3 puntos)

2. ¿Con qué frecuencia tienes dolores de estómago o problemas digestivos?
Con mucha frecuencia. (1 punto)
A veces. (2 puntos)
Casi nunca. (3 puntos)

3. ¿Con qué frecuencia sufres de dolores de cabeza?
Frecuentemente. (1 punto)
A veces. (2 puntos)
Casi nunca. (3 puntos)

4. ¿Comes verduras y frutas?
No, casi nunca como verduras ni frutas. (1 punto)
Sí, a veces. (2 puntos)
Sí, todos los días. (3 puntos)

5. ¿Eres alérgico/a a algo?
Sí, a muchas cosas. (1 punto)
Sí, a algunas cosas. (2 puntos)
No. (3 puntos)

6. ¿Haces ejercicios aeróbicos?
No, casi nunca hago ejercicios aeróbicos. (1 punto)
Sí, a veces. (2 puntos)
Sí, con frecuencia. (3 puntos)

7. ¿Con qué frecuencia te haces un examen médico?
Nunca o casi nunca. (1 punto)
Cada dos años. (2 puntos)
Cada año y/o antes de practicar un deporte. (3 puntos)

8. ¿Con qué frecuencia vas al dentista?
Nunca voy al dentista. (1 punto)
Sólo cuando me duele un diente. (2 puntos)
Por lo menos una vez por año. (3 puntos)

9. ¿Qué comes normalmente por la mañana?
No como nada por la mañana. (1 punto)
Tomo una bebida dietética. (2 puntos)
Como cereal y fruta. (3 puntos)

10. ¿Con qué frecuencia te sientes mareado/a?
Frecuentemente. (1 punto)
A veces. (2 puntos)
Casi nunca. (3 puntos)

6 Write the three categories with their point totals on the board. Ask for a show of hands for those who fall into each group. Analyze the trends of the class—are your students healthy or unhealthy?

6 Ask for volunteers from each of the three groups to explain whether they think the results of the survey are accurate or not. Ask them to give examples based on their own eating, exercise, and other health habits.

Game Play a modified version of **20 Preguntas**. Ask a volunteer to think of a part of the body. Other students get one chance each to ask a yes-no question until someone guesses the item correctly. Limit attempts to ten questions per item. Encourage students to guess by associating activities with various parts of the body.

Supersite/IRCD: At this point you may want to present *Vocabulario adicional: Más vocabulario para el consultorio.*

6 For expansion, have students brainstorm a few additional health-related questions and responses, and adjust the point totals accordingly. Ex: **¿Con qué frecuencia te lavas las manos? ¿Con qué frecuencia usas seda dental? ¿Tomas el sol sin bloqueador solar? ¿Comes comida rápida (McDonald's, etc.)? ¿Fumas cigarros? ¿Consumes mucha cafeína?**

Lección 4

Comunicación

7

7 Ask students to list the various possibilities of what happened to these people and how they feel. Have them name possible treatments for each.

7 Bring in magazine pictures related to illness, medicine, and medical appointments. Have students describe what is going on in the images.

¿Qué le pasó? Trabajen en grupos de dos o tres personas. Hablen de lo que les pasó y de cómo se sienten las personas que aparecen en los dibujos. Answers will vary.

1. Adela

2. Francisco

3. Pilar

4. Pedro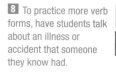

5. Cristina

6. Félix

8

8 To practice more verb forms, have students talk about an illness or accident that someone they know had.

Pairs For homework, ask students to draw an alien or other fantastic being. In the next class period, have students describe the alien to a classmate, who will draw it according to the description. Ex: **Tiene una cabeza grande y tres piernas delgadas con pelo en las rodillas. Encima de la cabeza tiene ocho ojos pequeños y uno grande…** Then have students compare the drawings for accuracy.

Un accidente Cuéntale a la clase de un accidente o una enfermedad que tuviste. Incluye información que conteste estas preguntas. Answers will vary.

8 Model this activity by talking about an illness or accident you had.

✓ ¿Qué ocurrió?
✓ ¿Dónde ocurrió?
✓ ¿Cuándo ocurrió?
✓ ¿Cómo ocurrió?
✓ ¿Quién te ayudó y cómo?
✓ ¿Tuviste algún problema después del accidente o después de la enfermedad?
✓ ¿Cuánto tiempo tuviste el problema?

9

Supersite/IRCD: Information Gap Activities

Crucigrama (*Crossword*) Tu profesor(a) les va a dar a ti y a tu compañero/a un crucigrama incompleto. Tú tienes las palabras que necesita tu compañero/a y él/ella tiene las palabras que tú necesitas. Tienen que darse pistas para completarlo. No pueden decir la palabra necesaria; deben utilizar definiciones, ejemplos y frases. Answers will vary.

9 Have pairs use words from the crossword to role-play a visit to a doctor's office.

modelo
10 horizontal: La usamos para hablar.
14 vertical: Es el médico que examina los dientes.

Extra Practice Write **Mido _____ pies y _____ pulgadas** on the board and explain what it means. Have students write physical descriptions of themselves. Students should use as much vocabulary from this lesson as they can. Collect the papers, shuffle them, and read the descriptions aloud. The rest of the class has to guess who is being described.

¡Uf! ¡Qué dolor!

communication cultures NATIONAL STANDARDS

Don Francisco y Javier van a la clínica de la doctora Márquez.

PERSONAJES

INÉS

DON FRANCISCO

JAVIER

DRA. MÁRQUEZ

JAVIER Estoy aburrido…
tengo ganas de dibujar.
Con permiso.

INÉS ¡Javier! ¿Qué te pasó?

JAVIER ¡Ay! ¡Uf! ¡Qué dolor!
¡Creo que me rompí el
tobillo!

DON FRANCISCO No te preocupes,
Javier. Estamos cerca de la
clínica donde trabaja la
doctora Márquez, mi amiga.

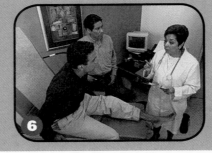

DRA. MÁRQUEZ ¿Cuánto tiempo
hace que se cayó?

JAVIER Ya se me olvidó… déjeme
ver… este… eran más o menos
las dos o dos y media cuando
me caí… o sea hace más de
una hora. ¡Me duele mucho!

DRA. MÁRQUEZ Bueno, vamos a
sacarle una radiografía.

DON FRANCISCO Sabes, Javier,
cuando era chico yo les tenía
mucho miedo a los médicos.
Visitaba mucho al doctor
porque me enfermaba con
mucha frecuencia y tenía
muchas infecciones de la
garganta. No me gustaban las
inyecciones ni las pastillas.
Una vez me rompí la pierna
jugando al fútbol…

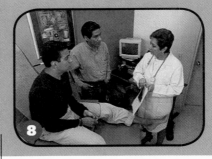

JAVIER ¡Doctora! ¿Qué dice?
¿Está roto el tobillo?

DRA. MÁRQUEZ Tranquilo, le
tengo buenas noticias,
Javier. No está roto el tobillo.
Apenas está torcido.

recursos

VM
pp. 225–226

adelante.
vhlcentral.com

Video Synopsis While on the bus, **Javier** injures his ankle. **Don Francisco** takes him to the clinic of his friend, **Dra. Márquez**. **Dra. Márquez** determines that **Javier** has twisted his ankle. She prescribes some pain medication and sends them on their way.

Preview Ask students to read the **Fotonovela** captions in groups of four. Ask one or two groups to role-play the dialogue for the class.

Expresiones útiles Point out the verb forms **enfermaba, enfermabas,** and **tenía.** Explain that these are imperfect tense forms, used here to talk about habitual events in the past. Point out the adverb **frecuentemente** and tell the class that many adverbs end in -**mente.** Under video still 6, point out the phrase **se me olvidó** and inform the class that **se** constructions are often used to talk about unplanned events. Tell students that they will learn more about these concepts in **Estructura.**

JAVIER ¿Tengo dolor? Sí, mucho. ¿Dónde? En el tobillo. ¿Tengo fiebre? No lo creo. ¿Estoy mareado? Un poco. ¿Soy alérgico a algún medicamento? No. ¿Embarazada? Definitivamente NO.

DRA. MÁRQUEZ ¿Cómo se lastimó el pie?

JAVIER Me caí cuando estaba en el autobús.

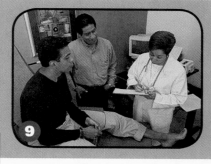

JAVIER Pero, ¿voy a poder ir de excursión con mis amigos?

DRA. MÁRQUEZ Creo que sí. Pero debe descansar y no caminar mucho durante un par de días. Le receto unas pastillas para el dolor.

DRA. MÁRQUEZ Adiós, Francisco. Adiós, Javier. ¡Cuidado! ¡Buena suerte en las montañas!

Expresiones útiles

Discussing medical conditions

- **¿Cómo se lastimó el pie? (lastimarse)**
  How did you hurt your foot?
  Me caí en el autobús.
  I fell when I was on the bus.

- **¿Te duele el tobillo?**
  Does your ankle hurt? (fam.)
- **¿Le duele el tobillo?**
  Does your ankle hurt? (form.)
  Sí, (me duele) mucho.
  Yes, (it hurts) a lot.

- **¿Es usted alérgico/a a algún medicamento?**
  Are you allergic to any medication?
  Sí, soy alérgico/a a la penicilina.
  Yes, I'm allergic to penicillin.

- **¿Está roto el tobillo?**
  Is my ankle broken?
  No está roto. Apenas está torcido.
  It's not broken. It's just twisted.

- **¿Te enfermabas frecuentemente?**
  Did you get sick frequently? (fam.)
  Sí, me enfermaba frecuentemente.
  Yes, I used to get sick frequently.
  Tenía muchas infecciones.
  I used to get a lot of infections.

Other expressions

- **hace +** [*period of time*] **+ que +** [*present tense*]:
- **¿Cuánto tiempo hace que te duele?**
  How long has it been hurting?
  Hace una hora que me duele.
  It's been hurting for an hour.

- **hace +** [*period of time*] **+ que +** [*preterite*]:
- **¿Cuánto tiempo hace que se cayó?**
  How long ago did you fall?
  Me caí hace más de una hora./ Hace más de una hora que me caí.
  I fell more than an hour ago.

Teaching Tips
- Photocopy the ***Fotonovela*** Videoscript (Supersite/IRCD) and white out words related to injuries and illnesses in order to make a master for a cloze activity. Have students fill in the missing words as they watch the episode.
- Tell students that before traveling to a Spanish-speaking country, they should make a list of their allergies and medical needs and learn how to say them in Spanish.
- On the board, write the paradigms for **hace** + [*time period*] + **que** + [*present*] and **hace** + [*time period*] + **que** + [*preterite*]. Ask a few comprehension questions to contrast their uses. Ex: **¿Cuánto tiempo hace que te graduaste de la escuela secundaria? ¿Cuánto tiempo hace que eres estudiante universitario?**

¿Qué pasó?

1 ¿Cierto o falso? Decide si lo que dicen estas oraciones sobre Javier es **cierto**
o **falso**. Corrige las oraciones falsas.

1 Ask students to create three additional true-false statements and exchange with a partner.

	Cierto	Falso	
1. Está aburrido y tiene ganas de hacer algo creativo.	⊘	○	
2. Cree que se rompió la rodilla.	○	⊘	Cree que se rompió el tobillo.
3. Se lastimó cuando se cayó en el autobús.	⊘	○	
4. Es alérgico a dos medicamentos.	○	⊘	No es alérgico a ningún medicamento.
5. No está mareado pero sí tiene un poco de fiebre.	○	⊘	Está un poco mareado pero no tiene fiebre.

2 Identificar Identifica quién puede decir estas oraciones.

1. Hace años me rompí la pierna cuando estaba jugando al fútbol. don Francisco
2. Hace más de una hora que me lastimé el pie. Me duele muchísimo. Javier
3. Tengo que sacarle una radiografía. No sé si se rompió uno de los huesos del pie. Dra. Márquez
4. No hay problema, vamos a ver a mi amiga, la doctora Márquez. don Francisco
5. Bueno, parece que el tobillo no está roto. Qué bueno, ¿no? Dra. Márquez
6. No sé si voy a poder ir de excursión con el grupo. Javier

DRA. MÁRQUEZ

DON FRANCISCO

JAVIER

2 Give students these additional items: **7. Le voy a recetar unas pastillas para el dolor.** (Dra. Márquez)
8. Cuando era niño, no me gustaba mucho ir al doctor. (don Francisco)

4 Possible conversation:
E1: Buenos días. ¿Cómo se lastimó?
E2: Doctor, me caí en casa.
E1: ¿Y cuánto tiempo hace que se cayó?
E2: Hace más de dos horas. Creo que me rompí el dedo.
E1: ¿Ah, sí? ¿Le duele mucho?
E2: Me duele muchísimo, doctor. Y estoy mareada.
E1: Bueno, le voy a sacar una radiografía primero.
E2: ¿Está roto el dedo?
E1: No se preocupe. No está roto el dedo. Como le duele mucho, le receto unas pastillas para el dolor.
E2: Sí, doctor. Gracias.

3 Ordenar Pon estos eventos en el orden correcto.

a. La doctora le saca una radiografía. __4__
b. La doctora le receta unas pastillas para el dolor. __6__
c. Javier se lastima el tobillo en el autobús. __2__
d. Don Francisco le habla a Javier de cuando era chico. __5__
e. Javier quiere dibujar un rato (*a while*). __1__
f. Don Francisco lo lleva a una clínica. __3__

4 En el consultorio Trabajen en parejas para representar los papeles de un(a) médico/a y su paciente. Usen las instrucciones como guía. ◄

NATIONAL communication STANDARDS

AYUDA

Here are some useful expressions:

¿Cómo se lastimó...?
¿Le duele...?
¿Cuánto tiempo hace que...?
Tengo...
Estoy...
¿Es usted alérgico/a a algún medicamento?
Usted debe...

El/La médico/a	El/La paciente
Pregúntale al/a la paciente si le duele. →	Te caíste en casa. Describe tu dolor.
Pregúntale cuánto tiempo hace que se cayó. →	Describe la situación. Piensas que te rompiste el dedo.
Mira el dedo. Debes recomendar un tratamiento (*treatment*) al/a la paciente. →	Debes hacer preguntas al/a la médico/a sobre el tratamiento (*treatment*).

Heritage Speakers Ask heritage speakers to prepare a poster about the health-care system of their families' countries of origin or other Spanish-speaking countries they have visited. Have them present their posters to the class, who can ask questions about the information.

NATIONAL comparisons STANDARDS

Teaching Tips
• You may want to explain that all words in which the spoken stress falls on the antepenultimate syllable or one before will carry a written accent, regardless of the letter they end in.
• As you go through each point in the explanation, write the example words on the board, pronounce them, and have students repeat. Then, ask students to provide words they learned in previous lessons that exemplify each point.
• For additional auditory practice, read several words aloud and have students raise their hand if the word has a written accent mark. Ask volunteers to write the words on the board.

CONSULTA

In Spanish, **a**, **e**, and **o** are considered strong vowels while **i** and **u** are weak vowels. To review this concept, see **¡ADELANTE! UNO**, **Lección 3**, **Pronunciación**, p. 119.

Ortografía

 Supersite/IRCD: MP3 Audio Files, Listening Scripts

El acento y las sílabas fuertes

In Spanish, written accent marks are used on many words. Here is a review of some of the principles governing word stress and the use of written accents.

as-pi-ri-na   gri-pe   to-man   an-tes

In Spanish, when a word ends in a vowel, **-n**, or **-s**, the spoken stress usually falls on the next-to-last syllable. Words of this type are very common and do not need a written accent.

a-sí   in-glés   in-fec-ción   hé-ro-e

When a word ends in a vowel, **-n**, or **-s**, and the spoken stress does *not* fall on the next-to-last syllable, then a written accent is needed.

hos-pi-tal   na-riz   re-ce-tar   to-ser

When a word ends in any consonant *other* than **-n** or **-s**, the spoken stress usually falls on the last syllable. Words of this type are very common and do not need a written accent.

lá-piz   fút-bol   hués-ped   sué-ter

When a word ends in any consonant *other* than **-n** or **-s** and the spoken stress does *not* fall on the last syllable, then a written accent is needed.

far-ma-cia   bio-lo-gí-a   su-cio   frí-o

Diphthongs (two weak vowels or a strong and weak vowel together) are normally pronounced as a single syllable. A written accent is needed when a diphthong is broken into two syllables.

sol   pan   mar   tos

Spanish words of only one syllable do not usually carry a written accent (unless it is to distinguish meaning: **se** and **sé**.)

Práctica Busca las palabras que necesitan acento escrito y escribe su forma correcta.

1. sal-mon salmón
2. ins-pec-tor
3. nu-me-ro número
4. fa-cil fácil
5. ju-go
6. a-bri-go
7. ra-pi-do rápido
8. sa-ba-do sábado
9. vez
10. me-nu menú
11. o-pe-ra-cion operación
12. im-per-me-a-ble
13. a-de-mas además
14. re-ga-te-ar
15. an-ti-pa-ti-co antipático
16. far-ma-cia
17. es-qui esquí
18. pen-sion pensión
19. pa-is país
20. per-don perdón

El ahorcado (*Hangman*) Juega al ahorcado para adivinar las palabras.

1. _ l _ _ _ _ _ a   Vas allí cuando estás enfermo. clínica
2. _ _ _ _ e _ c _ _ n   Se usa para poner una vacuna (*vaccination*). inyección
3. _ _ d _ o _ _ _ _ _ a   Ves los huesos. radiografía
4. _ _ _ _ i _ o   Trabaja en un hospital. médico
5. a _ _ _ b _ _ _ _ _ _   Es una medicina. antibiótico

recursos

LM p. 230   adelante. vhlcentral.com

SUPERSITE · Flash CULTURA

EN DETALLE

Servicios de salud

¿Pensaste alguna vez en visitar un país hispano? Si lo haces, vas a encontrar algunas diferencias respecto a la vida en los Estados Unidos. Una de ellas está en los servicios de salud.

En la mayor parte de los países hispanos, el gobierno ofrece servicios médicos muy baratos o gratuitos° a sus ciudadanos°. Los turistas y extranjeros también pueden tener acceso a los servicios médicos a bajo° costo. La Seguridad Social y organizaciones similares son las responsables de gestionar° estos servicios.

Naturalmente, esto no funciona igual° en todos los países. En Colombia, Ecuador, México y Perú, la situación varía según las regiones. Los habitantes de las ciudades y pueblos grandes tienen acceso a más servicios médicos, mientras que quienes viven en pueblos remotos sólo cuentan con° pequeñas clínicas.

Cruz verde de farmacia en Madrid, España

Por su parte, Argentina, Costa Rica, Cuba, Uruguay y España tienen sistemas de salud muy desarrollados°. Toda la población tiene acceso a ellos y en muchos casos son completamente gratuitos. Costa Rica ofrece servicios gratuitos también a los extranjeros.

¡Así que ya lo sabes! Si vas a viajar a otro país, antes de ir debes obtener información sobre los servicios médicos en el lugar de destino°. Prepara todos los documentos necesarios. ¡Y disfruta° tu estadía° en el extranjero sin problemas!

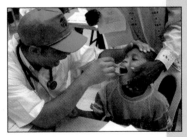

Consulta médica en la República Dominicana

Las farmacias

Farmacia de guardia: Las farmacias generalmente tienen un horario comercial. Sin embargo°, en cada barrio° hay una farmacia de guardia que abre las veinticuatro horas del día.

Productos farmacéuticos: Todavía hay muchas farmacias tradicionales que están más especializadas en medicinas y productos farmacéuticos. No venden una gran variedad de productos.

Recetas: Muchos medicamentos se venden sin receta médica. Los farmacéuticos aconsejan° a las personas sobre problemas de salud y les dan las medicinas.

Cruz° verde: En muchos países, las farmacias tienen el signo de una cruz verde. Cuando la cruz verde está encendida°, la farmacia está abierta.

gratuitos *free (of charge)* ciudadanos *citizens* bajo *low* gestionar *to manage* igual *in the same way* cuentan con *have* desarrollados *developed* destino *destination* disfruta *enjoy* estadía *stay* Sin embargo *However* barrio *neighborhood* aconsejan *advise* Cruz *Cross* encendida *lit (up)*

ACTIVIDADES

1 **¿Cierto o falso?** Indica si lo que dicen las oraciones es **cierto** o **falso**. Corrige la información falsa.

1. En los países hispanos los gobiernos ofrecen servicios de salud accesibles a sus ciudadanos. Cierto.

2. En los países hispanos los extranjeros tienen que pagar mucho dinero por los servicios médicos. Falso. Los extranjeros tienen acceso a los servicios médicos a bajo costo.

3. En Costa Rica los extranjeros pueden recibir servicios médicos gratuitos. Cierto.

4. Las farmacias de guardia abren sólo los sábados y domingos. Falso. Las farmacias de guardia abren las 24 horas del día.

5. En los países hispanos las farmacias venden una gran variedad de productos. Falso. En los países hispanos las farmacias están más especializadas en medicinas y productos farmacéuticos.

6. Los farmacéuticos de los países hispanos aconsejan a los enfermos y venden algunas medicinas sin necesidad de receta. Cierto.

7. En México y otros países, los pueblos remotos cuentan con grandes centros médicos. Falso. Cuentan con pequeñas clínicas.

8. Muchas farmacias usan una cruz verde como símbolo. Cierto.

ASÍ SE DICE

La salud

el chequeo (Esp., Méx.)	el examen médico
la droguería (Col.)	la farmacia
la herida	*injury; wound*
la píldora	la pastilla
los primeros auxilios	*first aid*
la sangre	*blood*

EL MUNDO HISPANO

Remedios caseros° y plantas medicinales

○ **Achiote°** En Suramérica se usa para curar inflamaciones de garganta. Las hojas° de achiote se cuecen° en agua, se cuelan° y se hacen gargarismos° con esa agua.

○ **Ají** En Perú se usan cataplasmas° de las semillas° de ají para aliviar los dolores reumáticos y la tortícolis°.

○ **Azúcar** En Nicaragua y otros países centroamericanos se usa el azúcar para detener° la sangre en pequeñas heridas.

○ **Sábila (aloe vera)** En Latinoamérica, el jugo de las hojas de sábila se usa para reducir cicatrices°. Se recomienda aplicarlo sobre la cicatriz dos veces al día, durante varios meses.

Remedios caseros *Home remedies* Achiote *Annatto* hojas *leaves* se cuecen *are cooked* se cuelan *they are drained* gargarismos *gargles* cataplasmas *pastes* semillas *seeds* tortícolis *stiff neck* detener *to stop* cicatrices *scars*

PERFILES

Curanderos° y chamanes

¿Quieres ser doctor(a), juez(a)°, político/a o psicólogo/a? En algunas sociedades de las Américas **los curanderos** y **los chamanes** no tienen que escoger entre estas profesiones porque ellos son mediadores de conflictos y dan consejos a la comunidad. Su opinión es muy respetada.

Códice Florentino, México, siglo XVI

Desde las culturas antiguas° de las Américas muchas personas piensan que la salud del cuerpo y de la mente sólo puede existir si hay un equilibrio entre el ser humano y la naturaleza. Los curanderos y los chamanes son quienes cuidan este equilibrio.

Los curanderos se especializan más en enfermedades físicas, mientras que los chamanes están más relacionados

con los males° de la mente y el alma°. Ambos° usan plantas, masajes y rituales, y sus conocimientos se basan en la tradición, la experiencia, la observación y la intuición.

Cuzco, Perú

Curanderos *Healers* juez(a) *judge* antiguas *ancient* males *illnesses* alma *soul* Ambos *Both*

Conexión Internet

¿Cuáles son algunos hospitales importantes del mundo hispano?

Go to **adelante.vhlcentral.com** to find more cultural information related to this **Cultura** section.

Lección 4

ACTIVIDADES

2 **Comprensión** Responde a las preguntas.

1. ¿Cómo se les llama a las farmacias en Colombia? *droguerías*
2. ¿Qué parte del achiote se usa para curar la garganta? *las hojas*
3. ¿Cómo se aplica la sábila para reducir cicatrices? *Se aplica sobre la cicatriz dos veces al día.*
4. En algunas partes de las Américas, ¿quiénes mantienen el equilibrio entre el ser humano y la naturaleza? *los chamanes y curanderos*
5. ¿Qué usan los curanderos y chamanes para curar? *Usan plantas, masajes y rituales.*

3 **¿Qué haces cuando tienes gripe?** Escribe cuatro oraciones sobre las cosas que haces cuando tienes gripe. Explica si vas al médico, si tomas medicamentos o si sigues alguna dieta especial. Después, comparte tu texto con un(a) compañero/a. *Answers will vary.*

Heritage Speakers Ask heritage speakers to describe home remedies used in their families.

recursos

adelante.vhlcentral.com

4.1 The imperfect tense

ANTE TODO You have already learned the preterite tense. You will now learn the imperfect, which describes past activities in a different way.

The imperfect of regular verbs

		cantar	beber	escribir
SINGULAR FORMS	yo	cant**aba**	beb**ía**	escrib**ía**
	tú	cant**abas**	beb**ías**	escrib**ías**
	Ud./él/ella	cant**aba**	beb**ía**	escrib**ía**
PLURAL FORMS	nosotros/as	cant**ábamos**	beb**íamos**	escrib**íamos**
	vosotros/as	cant**abais**	beb**íais**	escrib**íais**
	Uds./ellos/ellas	cant**aban**	beb**ían**	escrib**ían**

Sabes, Javier, cuando era chico yo les tenía mucho miedo a los médicos.

De niño tenía que ir mucho a una clínica en Quito. ¡No me gustaban nada las inyecciones!

▶ There are no stem changes in the imperfect.

entender (e:ie)	**Entendíamos** japonés. *We used to understand Japanese.*
servir (e:i)	El camarero les **servía** el café. *The waiter was serving them coffee.*
doler (o:ue)	A Javier le **dolía** el tobillo. *Javier's ankle was hurting.*

▶ The imperfect form of **hay** is **había** *(there was; there were; there used to be)*.

▶ **¡Atención!** **Ir, ser,** and **ver** are the only verbs that are irregular in the imperfect.

The imperfect of irregular verbs

		ir	ser	ver
SINGULAR FORMS	yo	ib**a**	er**a**	ve**ía**
	tú	ib**as**	er**as**	ve**ías**
	Ud./él/ella	ib**a**	er**a**	ve**ía**
PLURAL FORMS	nosotros/as	**íb**amos	**ér**amos	ve**íamos**
	vosotros/as	ib**ais**	er**ais**	ve**íais**
	Uds./ellos/ellas	ib**an**	er**an**	ve**ían**

Lección 4

Teaching Tips
• Ask students to compare and contrast a home video with a snapshot in the family picture album. Then call their attention to the brief description of uses of the imperfect. Which actions would be best captured by a home video? (Continuing actions; incomplete actions; what was happening; how things used to be.) Which actions are best captured in a snapshot? (A completed action.)
• Ask students to answer questions about themselves in the past. Ex: **Y tú, _____ , ¿ibas al parque los domingos cuando eras niño/a? ¿Qué hacías mientras tu madre preparaba la comida? ¿Cómo eras de niño/a?**

Extra Practice Ask students to write a description of their first-grade classroom and teacher, using the imperfect. Ex: **En la sala de clases había… La maestra se llamaba… Ella era…** Have students share their descriptions with a classmate.

Uses of the imperfect

▶ As a general rule, the imperfect is used to describe actions which are seen by the speaker as incomplete or "continuing," while the preterite is used to describe actions which have been completed. The imperfect expresses what was happening at a certain time or how things used to be. The preterite, in contrast, expresses a completed action.

—¿Qué te **pasó**?
What happened to you?

—¿Dónde **vivías** de niño?
Where did you live as a child?

—Me **torcí** el tobillo.
I sprained my ankle.

—**Vivía** en San José.
I lived in San José.

▶ These expressions are often used with the imperfect because they express habitual or repeated actions: **de niño/a** (*as a child*), **todos los días** (*every day*), **mientras** (*while*).

Uses of the imperfect

1. **Habitual or repeated actions** . . . .
Íbamos al parque los domingos.
We used to go to the park on Sundays.

2. **Events or actions that were in progress**
Yo **leía** mientras él **estudiaba**.
I was reading while he was studying.

3. **Physical characteristics** . . . .
Era alto y guapo.
He was tall and handsome.

4. **Mental or emotional states** . . . .
Quería mucho a su familia.
He loved his family very much.

5. **Telling time** . . . .
Eran las tres y media.
It was 3:30.

6. **Age** . . . .
Los niños **tenían** seis años.
The children were six years old.

¡INTÉNTALO! Indica la forma correcta de cada verbo en el imperfecto.

1. Mis hermanos ___veían___ (ver) la televisión.
2. Yo ___viajaba___ (viajar) a la playa.
3. ¿Dónde ___vivía___ (vivir) Samuel de niño?
4. Tú ___hablabas___ (hablar) con Javier.
5. Leonardo y yo ___corríamos___ (correr) por el parque.
6. Ustedes ___iban___ (ir) a la clínica.
7. Nadia ___bailaba___ (bailar) merengue.
8. ¿Cuándo ___asistías___ (asistir) tú a clase de español?
9. Yo ___era___ (ser) muy feliz.
10. Nosotras ___comprendíamos___ (comprender) las preguntas.

Large Group Write a list of activities on the board. Ex: **1. tenerle miedo a la oscuridad 2. ir a la escuela en autobús 3. llevar el almuerzo a la escuela 4. creer en Santa Claus**. Have students copy the list and write sentences for each item they used to do when they were in the second grade. Then have them circulate around the room and find other students that used to do the same activities. Ask volunteers to report back to the class. Ex: **Mark y yo creíamos en Santa Claus.**

Extra Practice For additional oral practice, call out a new subject for each activity item and have students restate the sentence.

Práctica · SUPERSITE

1

Completar Primero, completa las oraciones con el imperfecto de los verbos. Luego, pon las oraciones en orden lógico y compáralas con las de un(a) compañero/a.

_7_ a. El doctor dijo que no ___era___ (ser) nada grave.

_6_ b. El doctor ___quería___ (querer) ver la nariz del niño.

_3_ c. Su mamá ___estaba___ (estar) dibujando cuando Miguelito entró llorando.

_4_ d. Miguelito ___tenía___ (tener) la nariz hinchada (*swollen*). Fueron al hospital.

_8_ e. Miguelito no ___iba___ (ir) a jugar más. Ahora quería ir a casa a descansar.

_2_ f. Miguelito y sus amigos ___jugaban___ (jugar) al béisbol en el patio.

_1_ g. ___Eran___ (Ser) las dos de la tarde.

_5_ h. Miguelito le dijo a la enfermera que ___le dolía___ (dolerle) la nariz.

2

Transformar Forma oraciones completas para describir lo que hacían Julieta y César. Usa las formas correctas del imperfecto y añade todas las palabras necesarias.

1. Julieta y César / ser / paramédicos
   Julieta y César eran paramédicos.
2. trabajar / juntos y / llevarse / muy bien
   Trabajaban juntos y se llevaban muy bien.
3. cuando / haber / accidente, / siempre / analizar / situación / con cuidado
   Cuando había un accidente, siempre analizaban la situación con cuidado.
4. preocuparse / mucho / por / pacientes
   Se preocupaban mucho por los pacientes.
5. si / paciente / tener / mucho / dolor, / ponerle / inyección
   Si el paciente tenía mucho dolor, le ponían una inyección.

3

En la escuela de medicina Usa los verbos de la lista para completar las oraciones con las formas correctas del imperfecto. Algunos verbos se usan más de una vez. Some answers will vary.

caerse	enfermarse	ir	querer	tener
comprender	estornudar	pensar	sentirse	tomar
doler	hacer	poder	ser	toser

1. Cuando Javier y Victoria ___eran___ estudiantes de medicina, siempre ___tenían___ que ir al médico.
2. Cada vez que él ___tomaba___ un examen, a Javier le ___dolía___ mucho la cabeza.
3. Cuando Victoria ___hacía___ ejercicios aeróbicos, siempre ___se sentía___ mareada.
4. Todas las primaveras, Javier ___estornudaba/tosía___ mucho porque es alérgico al polen.
5. Victoria también ___se caía___ de su bicicleta en camino a clase.
6. Después de comer en la cafetería, a Victoria siempre le ___dolía___ el estómago.
7. Javier ___quería/pensaba___ ser médico para ayudar a los demás.
8. Pero no ___comprendía___ por qué él ___se enfermaba___ con tanta frecuencia.
9. Cuando Victoria ___tenía___ fiebre, no ___podía___ ni leer el termómetro.
10. A Javier ___le dolían___ los dientes, pero nunca ___quería___ ir al dentista.
11. Victoria ___tosía/estornudaba___ mucho cuando ___se sentía___ congestionada.
12. Javier y Victoria ___pensaban___ que nunca ___iban___ a graduarse.

1 Before assigning the activity, review the forms of the imperfect by calling out an infinitive and a series of subject pronouns. Ask volunteers to give the corresponding forms. Ex: **querer: usted (quería); yo (quería); nosotras (queríamos).** Include irregular verbs.

1 Have students write a conversation between **Miguelito** and his friends in which he relates what happened after the accident.

2 To challenge students, ask them to identify the reason the imperfect was necessary in each sentence.

3 For expansion, write these sentences on the board and have students complete them in pairs.
1. Fui al doctor porque _____. 2. Tuvo que ir al dentista porque _____. 3. El médico le dio unas pastillas porque _____. 4. La enfermera le tomó la temperatura porque _____.

Small Groups Ask students to write about a favorite or least favorite doctor or dentist from the past. They should use at least five verbs in the imperfect. Then have them read, compare, and discuss the descriptions in groups of four.

Comunicación

4

Entrevista Trabajen en parejas. Un(a) estudiante usa estas preguntas para entrevistar a su compañero/a. Luego compartan los resultados de la entrevista con la clase. Answers will vary.

1. Cuando eras estudiante de primaria, ¿te gustaban tus profesores/as?
2. ¿Veías mucha televisión cuando eras niño/a?
3. Cuando tenías diez años, ¿cuál era tu programa de televisión favorito?
4. Cuando eras niño/a, ¿qué hacía tu familia durante las vacaciones?
5. ¿Cuántos años tenías en 2002?
6. Cuando estabas en el quinto año escolar, ¿qué hacías con tus amigos/as?
7. Cuando tenías once años, ¿cuál era tu grupo musical favorito?
8. Antes de tomar esta clase, ¿sabías hablar español?

5 After students present their partner's descriptions, call on volunteers to ask one additional question about each student's childhood.

5 You may want to assign this activity as a short written composition.

5

Describir En parejas, túrnense para describir cómo eran sus vidas cuando eran niños. Pueden usar las sugerencias de la lista u otras ideas. Luego informen a la clase sobre la vida de su compañero/a.
Answers will vary.

NOTA CULTURAL

El Parque Nacional Tortuguero está en la costa del Caribe, al norte de la ciudad de Limón, en Costa Rica. Varias especies de tortuga (*turtle*) utilizan las playas del parque para poner (*lay*) sus huevos. Esto ocurre de noche, y hay guías que llevan pequeños grupos de turistas a observar este fenómeno biológico.

modelo

▶   Cuando yo era niña, mi familia y yo siempre íbamos a Tortuguero.
Tomábamos un barco desde Limón, y por las noches mirábamos
las tortugas (*turtles*) en la playa. Algunas veces teníamos suerte,
porque las tortugas venían a poner (*lay*) huevos. Otras veces,
volvíamos al hotel sin ver ninguna tortuga.

- las vacaciones
- ocasiones especiales
- qué hacías durante el verano
- celebraciones con tus amigos/as
- celebraciones con tu familia

- cómo era tu escuela
- cómo eran tus amigos/as
- los viajes que hacías
- a qué jugabas
- qué hacías cuando te sentías enfermo/a

Síntesis

6

Supersite/IRCD:
Information Gap Activities

Game Divide the class into teams of three. Each team should choose a historical or fictional villain. When it is their turn, they will use the imperfect to give the class one hint. The other teams are allowed three questions. At the end of the question/ answer session, teams must guess the identity. Award one point for each correct guess and two to any team able to stump the class.

En el consultorio Tu profesor(a) te va a dar una lista incompleta con los pacientes que fueron al consultorio del doctor Donoso ayer. En parejas, conversen para completar sus listas y saber a qué hora llegaron las personas al consultorio y cuáles eran sus problemas. Answers will vary.

6 Have pairs write **Dr. Donoso's** advice for three of the patients. Then have them read the advice to the class and compare it with what other pairs wrote for the same patients.

4.2 The preterite and the imperfect

ANTE TODO   Now that you have learned the forms of the preterite and the imperfect, you will learn more about how they are used. The preterite and the imperfect are not interchangeable. In Spanish, the choice between these two tenses depends on the context and on the point of view of the speaker.

> *De niño jugaba mucho al fútbol. Una vez me rompí la pierna.*

> *Me caí cuando estaba en el autobús.*

Teaching Tip Give examples as you contrast the preterite and the imperfect. Ex: **La semana pasada fui al dentista porque me dolía mucho el diente.** Then ask personalized questions. Ex: _____, ¿**paseabas en bicicleta cuando eras niño/a? Te caíste alguna vez?**

COMPARE & CONTRAST

Use the preterite to...

1. Express actions that are viewed by the speaker as completed

Don Francisco **se rompió** la pierna.
Don Francisco broke his leg.

Fueron a Buenos Aires ayer.
They went to Buenos Aires yesterday.

2. Express the beginning or end of a past action

La película **empezó** a las nueve.
The movie began at nine o'clock.

Ayer **terminé** el proyecto para la clase de química.
Yesterday I finished the project for chemistry class.

3. Narrate a series of past actions or events

La doctora me **miró** los oídos, me **hizo** unas preguntas y **escribió** la receta.
The doctor looked in my ears, asked me some questions, and wrote the prescription.

Me di con la mesa, **me caí** y **me lastimé** el pie.
I bumped into the table, I fell, and I injured my foot.

Use the imperfect to...

1. Describe an ongoing past action with no reference to its beginning or end

Don Francisco **esperaba** a Javier.
Don Francisco was waiting for Javier.

El médico **se preocupaba** por sus pacientes.
The doctor worried about his patients.

2. Express habitual past actions and events

Cuando **era** joven, **jugaba** al tenis.
When I was young, I used to play tennis.

De niño, don Francisco **se enfermaba** con mucha frecuencia.
As a child, Don Francisco used to get sick very frequently.

3. Describe physical and emotional states or characteristics

La chica **quería** descansar. **Se sentía** mal y **tenía** dolor de cabeza.
The girl wanted to rest. She felt ill and had a headache.

Ellos **eran** altos y **tenían** ojos verdes.
They were tall and had green eyes.

Estábamos felices de ver a la familia.
We were happy to see the family.

AYUDA

These words and expressions, as well as similar ones, commonly occur with the preterite: **ayer, anteayer, una vez, dos veces, tres veces, el año pasado, de repente.**

They usually imply that an action has happened at a specific point in time. For a review, see **¡ADELANTE! UNO, Estructura 6.3,** p. 293.

AYUDA

These words and expressions, as well as similar ones, commonly occur with the imperfect: **de niño/a, todos los días, mientras, siempre, con frecuencia, todas las semanas.** They usually express habitual or repeated actions in the past.

Lección 4

▶ The preterite and the imperfect often appear in the same sentence. In such cases the imperfect describes what *was happening*, while the preterite describes the action that "interrupted" the ongoing activity.

Miraba la tele cuando **sonó** el teléfono.
I was watching TV when the phone rang.

Maite **leía** el periódico cuando **llegó** Álex.
Maite was reading the newspaper when Álex arrived.

▶ You will also see the preterite and the imperfect together in narratives such as fiction, news, and retelling of events. The imperfect provides background information, such as time, weather, and location, while the preterite indicates the specific events that occurred.

Eran las dos de la mañana y el detective ya no **podía** mantenerse despierto. **Se bajó** lentamente del coche, **estiró** las piernas y **levantó** los brazos hacia el cielo oscuro.
It was two in the morning, and the detective could no longer stay awake. He slowly stepped out of the car, stretched his legs, and raised his arms toward the dark sky.

La luna **estaba** llena y no **había** en el cielo ni una sola nube. De repente, el detective **escuchó** un grito espeluznante proveniente del parque.
The moon was full and there wasn't a single cloud in the sky. Suddenly, the detective heard a piercing scream coming from the park.

Un médico colombiano descubrió la vacuna contra la malaria

El doctor colombiano Manuel Elkin Patarroyo descubrió una vacuna contra la malaria. Esta enfermedad se erradicó hace décadas en muchas partes del mundo. Sin embargo, los casos de malaria empezaban a aumentar otra vez, justo cuando salió la vacuna de Patarroyo. En mayo de 1993, el doctor Patarroyo donó la vacuna, a nombre de Colombia, a la Organización Mundial de la Salud. Los grandes laboratorios farmacéuticos presionaron a la OMS porque querían la vacuna. Pero en 1995 las dos partes, el doctor Patarroyo y la OMS, ratificaron el pacto original.

¡INTÉNTALO! Elige el pretérito o el imperfecto para completar la historia. Explica por qué se usa ese tiempo verbal en cada ocasión.

1. ___Eran___ (Fueron/Eran) las doce.
2. ___Había___ (Hubo/Había) mucha gente en la calle.
3. A las doce y media, Tomás y yo ___entramos___ (entramos/entrábamos) en el restaurante Tárcoles.
4. Todos los días yo ___almorzaba___ (almorcé/almorzaba) con Tomás al mediodía.
5. El camarero ___llegó___ (llegó/llegaba) inmediatamente, para darnos el menú.
6. Nosotros ___empezamos___ (empezamos/empezábamos) a leerlo.
7. Yo ___pedí___ (pedí/pedía) el pescado.
8. De repente, el camarero ___volvió___ (volvió/volvía) a nuestra mesa.
9. Y nos ___dio___ (dio/daba) una mala noticia.
10. Desafortunadamente, no ___tenían___ (tuvieron/tenían) más pescado.
11. Por eso Tomás y yo ___decidimos___ (decidimos/decidíamos) comer en otro lugar.
12. ___Llovía___ (Llovió/Llovía) mucho cuando ___salimos___ (salimos/salíamos) del restaurante.
13. Así que ___regresamos___ (regresamos/regresábamos) al restaurante Tárcoles.
14. Esta vez, ___pedí___ (pedí/pedía) el arroz con pollo.

Práctica

1 To simplify, begin by reading through the items as a class. Have students label each blank with an *I* for *imperfect* or *P* for *preterite*.

1 Have volunteers explain why they chose the preterite or imperfect in each case. Ask them to point out any words or expressions that triggered one tense or the other.

1   **Seleccionar** Utiliza el tiempo verbal adecuado, según el contexto.

1. La semana pasada, Manolo y Aurora __querían__ (querer) dar una fiesta. __Decidieron__ (Decidir) invitar a seis amigos y servirles mucha comida.

2. Manolo y Aurora __estaban__ (estar) preparando la comida cuando Elena __llamó__ (llamar). Como siempre, __tenía__ (tener) que estudiar para un examen.

3. A las seis, __volvió__ (volver) a sonar el teléfono. Su amigo Francisco tampoco __podía__ (poder) ir a la fiesta, porque __tenía__ (tener) fiebre. Manolo y Aurora __se sentían__ (sentirse) muy tristes, pero __tenían__ (tener) que preparar la comida.

4. Después de otros 15 minutos, __sonó__ (sonar) el teléfono. Sus amigos, los señores Vega, __estaban__ (estar) en camino (*en route*) al hospital: a su hijo le __dolía__ (doler) mucho el estómago. Sólo dos de los amigos __podían__ (poder) ir a la cena.

5. Por supuesto, __iban__ (ir) a tener demasiada comida. Finalmente, cinco minutos antes de las ocho, __llamaron__ (llamar) Ramón y Javier. Ellos __pensaban__ (pensar) que la fiesta __era__ (ser) la próxima semana.

6. Tristes, Manolo y Aurora __se sentaron__ (sentarse) a comer solos. Mientras __comían__ (comer), pronto __llegaron__ (llegar) a la conclusión de que __era__ (ser) mejor estar solos: ¡La comida __estaba__ (estar) malísima!

2   **En el periódico** Completa esta noticia con la forma correcta del pretérito o el imperfecto.

AYUDA

Reading Spanish-language newspapers is a good way to practice verb tenses. You will find that both the imperfect and the preterite occur with great regularity. Many newsstands carry international papers, and many Spanish-language newspapers (such as Spain's *El País*, Mexico's *Reforma*, and Argentina's *Clarín*) are on the Web.

Un accidente trágico

Ayer temprano por la mañana (1)__hubo__ (haber) un trágico accidente en el centro de San José cuando el conductor de un autobús no (2)__vio__ (ver) venir un carro. La mujer que (3)__manejaba__ (manejar) el carro (4)__murió__ (morir) al instante y los paramédicos (5)__tuvieron__ (tener) que llevar al pasajero al hospital porque (6)__sufrió__ (sufrir) varias fracturas. El conductor del autobús (7)__dijo__ (decir) que no (8)__vio__ (ver) el carro hasta el último momento porque (9)__estaba__ (estar) muy nublado y (10)__llovía__ (llover). Él (11)__intentó__ (intentar) (*to attempt*) dar un viraje brusco (*to swerve*), pero (12)__perdió__ (perder) el control del autobús y no (13)__pudo__ (poder) evitar (*to avoid*) el accidente. Según nos informaron, no (14)__se lastimó__ (lastimarse) ningún pasajero del autobús.

2 Follow up with comprehension questions. Ex: **¿Qué pasó ayer? (Hubo un accidente.) ¿Qué tiempo hacía? (Estaba muy nublado y llovía.) ¿Qué le pasó a la mujer que manejaba? (Murió al instante.)**

3   **Completar** Completa las frases de una manera lógica. Usa el pretérito o el imperfecto. En parejas, comparen sus respuestas.   Answers will vary.

1. De niño/a, yo...
2. Yo conducía el auto mientras...
3. Anoche mi novio/a...
4. Ayer el/la profesor(a)...
5. La semana pasada un(a) amigo/a...
6. Con frecuencia mis padres...
7. Esta mañana en la cafetería...
8. Hablábamos con el doctor cuando...

3 To challenge students, ask them to expand on one of their sentences, creating a paragraph about an imaginary or actual past experience.

NATIONAL communication STANDARDS

4

4 Have students write a summary of their partners' responses, omitting all names. Collect the summaries, then read them to the class. Have students guess who had the relationship described in the summary.

Comunicación

Entrevista Usa estas preguntas para entrevistar a un(a) compañero/a acerca de su primer(a) novio/a. Si quieres, puedes añadir otras preguntas. Answers will vary.

1. ¿Quién fue tu primer(a) novio/a?
2. ¿Cuántos años tenían ustedes cuando se conocieron?
3. ¿Cómo era él/ella?
4. ¿Qué le gustaba hacer? ¿Le interesaban los deportes?
5. ¿Por cuánto tiempo salieron ustedes?
6. ¿Qué hacían ustedes cuando salían?
7. ¿Pensaban casarse?
8. ¿Cuándo y por qué rompieron ustedes?

5 Remind students that the 24-hour clock is often used for schedules. Go through a few of the times and ask volunteers to provide the equivalent in the 12-hour clock.

5 Have pairs share their answers with the class, but without mentioning the patient's name. The class must guess who is being described.

5

La sala de emergencias En parejas, miren la lista e inventen qué les pasó a estas personas que están en la sala de emergencias. Answers will vary.

modelo

Eran las tres de la tarde. Como todos los días, Pablo jugaba al fútbol con sus amigos. Estaba muy contento. De repente, se cayó y se rompió el brazo. Después fue a la sala de emergencias.

Paciente	Edad	Hora	Condición
1. Pablo Romero	9 años	15:20	hueso roto (el brazo)
2. Estela Rodríguez	45 años	15:25	tobillo torcido
3. Lupe Quintana	29 años	15:37	embarazada, dolores
4. Manuel López	52 años	15:45	infección de garganta
5. Marta Díaz	3 años	16:00	temperatura muy alta, fiebre
6. Roberto Salazar	32 años	16:06	dolor de oído
7. Marco Brito	18 años	16:18	daño en el cuello, posible fractura
8. Ana María Ortiz	66 años	16:29	reacción alérgica a un medicamento

6 Have students decide who in their group would be the most likely thief based on his or her responses. Ask the group to prepare a police report explaining why they believe their suspect is the culprit.

6

Situación Anoche alguien robó (*stole*) el examen de la **Lección 4** de la oficina de tu profesor(a) y tú tienes que averiguar quién lo hizo. Pregúntales a tres compañeros dónde estaban, con quién estaban y qué hicieron entre las ocho y las doce de la noche. Answers will vary.

NATIONAL communication STANDARDS

Síntesis

7

La primera vez En grupos, cuéntense cómo fue la primera vez que les pusieron una inyección, se rompieron un hueso, pasaron la noche en un hospital, estuvieron mareados/as, etc. Incluyan estos puntos en su conversación: una descripción del tiempo que hacía, sus edades, qué pasó y cómo se sentían. Answers will vary.

Lección 4

4.3 Constructions with se

ANTE TODO In **Lección 1,** you learned how to use **se** as the third-person reflexive pronoun (**Él se despierta. Ellos se visten. Ella se baña.**). **Se** can also be used to form constructions in which the person performing the action is not expressed or is de-emphasized.

Impersonal constructions with se

▶ In Spanish, verbs that are not reflexive can be used with **se** to form impersonal constructions. These are statements in which the person performing the action is not defined.

Se habla español en Costa Rica.
Spanish is spoken in Costa Rica.

Se puede leer en la sala de espera.
You can read in the waiting room.

Se hacen operaciones aquí.
They perform operations here.

Se necesitan medicinas enseguida.
They need medicine right away.

▶ **¡Atención!** Note that the third person singular verb form is used with singular nouns and the third person plural form is used with plural nouns.

Se vende ropa.   **Se venden** camisas.

▶ You often see the impersonal **se** in signs, advertisements, and directions.

**SE PROHÍBE
NADAR**

**Se necesitan
programadores**
GRUPO TECNO
Tel. 778-34-34

ENTRADA ←
Se entra por la
izquierda

Se for unplanned events

¿Cuánto
tiempo hace que
se cayó?

Ya se
me olvidó.

Bueno, vamos
a sacarle una radiografía
para ver si se le rompió
el hueso.

▶ **Se** also describes accidental or unplanned events. In this construction, the person who performs the action is de-emphasized, implying that the accident or unplanned event is not his or her direct responsibility. Note this construction.

$$\textbf{se} + \begin{bmatrix} \text{INDIRECT} \\ \text{OBJECT} \\ \text{PRONOUN} \end{bmatrix} + \begin{bmatrix} \text{VERB} \end{bmatrix} + \begin{bmatrix} \text{SUBJECT} \end{bmatrix}$$

Se   me   cayó   la pluma.

▶ In this type of construction, what would normally be the direct object of the sentence becomes the subject, and it agrees with the verb, not with the indirect object pronoun.

I.O. PRONOUN	VERB		SUBJECT
Se	me, te, le	quedó / cayó / dañó	SINGULAR: la receta. / la taza. / el radio.
	nos, os, les	rompieron / olvidaron / perdieron	PLURAL: las botellas. / las pastillas. / las llaves.

▶ These verbs are the ones most frequently used with **se** to describe unplanned events.

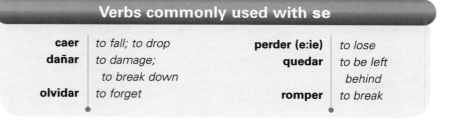

Verbs commonly used with se

caer	to fall; to drop	**perder (e:ie)**	to lose
dañar	to damage; to break down	**quedar**	to be left behind
olvidar	to forget	**romper**	to break

Se me perdió el teléfono de la farmacia.
I lost the pharmacy's phone number.

Se nos olvidaron los pasajes.
We forgot the tickets.

▶ **¡Atención!** While Spanish has a verb for *to fall* (**caer**), there is no direct translation for *to drop*. **Dejar caer** (*To let fall*) or a **se** construction is often used to mean *to drop*.

El médico **dejó caer** la aspirina.
The doctor dropped the aspirin.

A mí **se me cayeron** los cuadernos.
I dropped the notebooks.

▶ To clarify or emphasize who the person involved in the action is, this construction commonly begins with the preposition **a** + [*noun*] or **a** + [*prepositional pronoun*].

Al paciente se le perdió la receta.
The patient lost his prescription.

A ustedes se les quedaron los libros en casa.
You left the books at home.

 **¡INTÉNTALO!** Completa las oraciones con **se** impersonal y los verbos en presente.

A

1. <u>Se enseñan</u> (enseñar) cinco lenguas en esta universidad.
2. <u>Se come</u> (comer) muy bien en El Cráter.
3. <u>Se venden</u> (vender) muchas camisetas allí.
4. <u>Se sirven</u> (servir) platos exquisitos cada noche.

Completa las oraciones con **se** y los verbos en pretérito.

B

1. <u>Se me rompieron</u> (*I broke*) las gafas.
2. <u>Se te cayeron</u> (*You* (fam., sing.) *dropped*) las pastillas.
3. <u>Se les perdió</u> (*They lost*) la receta.
4. <u>Se le quedó</u> (*You* (form., sing.) *left*) aquí la radiografía.

Práctica

1 **¿Cierto o falso?** Lee estas oraciones sobre la vida en 1901. Indica si lo que dice cada oración es **cierto** o **falso**. Luego corrige las oraciones falsas.

1. Se veía mucha televisión. Falso. No se veía televisión. Se leía mucho.
2. Se escribían muchos libros. Cierto.
3. Se viajaba mucho en tren. Cierto.
4. Se montaba a caballo. Cierto.
5. Se mandaba mucho correo electrónico.   Falso. No se mandaba correo electrónico. Se mandaban muchas cartas y postales.
6. Se preparaban muchas comidas en casa. Cierto.
7. Se llevaban minifaldas.   Falso. No se llevaban minifaldas. Se llevaban faldas largas.
8. Se pasaba mucho tiempo con la familia. Cierto.

1 Change the date from 1901 to 2005 and go through the exercise again orally.

1 Have students work in pairs and, using constructions with **se**, write a description of a period in history such as the French or American Revolution, the Sixties, Prohibition, and so forth. Then have pairs form groups of six and read their descriptions aloud to their group.

Extra Practice Have students use **se** constructions to compare cultural differences between Spanish-speaking countries and their own. Ex: **Aquí se habla inglés, pero en _____ se habla español.**

2 **Traducir** Traduce estos letreros *(signs)* y anuncios al español.

1. Nurses needed   Se necesitan enfermeros/as
2. Eating and drinking prohibited   Se prohíbe comer y beber
3. Programmers sought   Se buscan programadores
4. English is spoken   Se habla inglés
5. Computers sold   Se venden computadoras
6. No talking   Se prohíbe hablar
7. Teacher needed   Se necesita profesor(a)
8. Books sold   Se venden libros
9. Do not enter   Se prohíbe entrar
10. Spanish is spoken   Se habla español

2 For expansion, ask students to find three signs on campus and translate them using the impersonal **se**.

3 **¿Qué pasó?** Mira los dibujos e indica lo que pasó en cada uno. Some answers will vary.

1. camarero / pastel

Al camarero se le cayó el pastel.

2. Sr. Álvarez / espejo

Al señor Álvarez se le rompió el espejo.

3. Arturo / tarea

A Arturo se le olvidó la tarea.

4. Sra. Domínguez / llaves

A la Sra. Domínguez se le perdieron las llaves.

5. Carla y Lupe / botellas de vino

A Carla y a Lupe se les rompieron dos botellas de vino.

6. Juana / platos

A Juana se le rompieron los platos.

3 To simplify, have students work in pairs to brainstorm verbs that could be used to complete this activity.

3 Add another visual aspect to this activity. Use magazine pictures to have students continue describing past events using constructions with **se**.

Extra Practice Have students imagine that they have just seen a movie about the future. Have them work in groups to prepare a description of the way of life portrayed in the movie using the imperfect tense and constructions with **se**. Ex: **No se necesitaba trabajar. Se usaban robots para hacer todo. Se viajaba por telepatía. No se comía nada sino en los fines de semana.**

Lección 4

Comunicación

4 Have each pair decide on the most unusual answer to the questions. Ask the student who gave it to describe the event to the class.

4

Preguntas Trabajen en parejas y usen estas preguntas para entrevistarse. Answers will vary.

1. ¿Qué comidas se sirven en tu restaurante favorito?
2. ¿Se te olvidó invitar a alguien a tu última fiesta o comida? ¿A quién?
3. ¿A qué hora se abre la cafetería de tu universidad?
4. ¿Alguna vez se te quedó algo importante en la casa? ¿Qué?
5. ¿Alguna vez se te perdió algo importante durante un viaje? ¿Qué?
6. ¿Qué se vende en una farmacia?
7. ¿Sabes si en la farmacia se aceptan cheques?
8. ¿Alguna vez se te rompió algo muy caro? ¿Qué?

5

Opiniones En parejas, terminen cada oración con ideas originales. Después, comparen los resultados con la clase para ver qué pareja tuvo las mejores ideas. Answers will vary.

1. No se tiene que dejar propina cuando…
2. Antes de viajar, se debe…
3. Si se come bien,…
4. Para tener una vida sana, se debe…
5. Se sirve la mejor comida en…
6. Se hablan muchas lenguas en…

5 Ask pairs to write similar beginnings to three different statements using **se** constructions. Have pairs exchange papers and finish each other's sentences.

Síntesis

6

Anuncios En grupos, preparen dos anuncios de televisión para presentar a la clase. Usen el imperfecto y por lo menos dos construcciones con **se** en cada uno. Answers will vary.

modelo

> Se me cayeron unos libros en el pie y me dolía mucho. Pero ahora no, gracias a SuperAspirina 500. ¡Dos pastillas y se me fue el dolor! Se puede comprar SuperAspirina 500 en todas las farmacias Recetamax.

Extra Practice Write these sentence fragments on the board and ask students to supply several logical endings using a construction with **se**. **1. Cuando ella subía al avión, _____.** (se le cayó la maleta; se le torció el pie) **2. Una vez, cuando yo comía en un restaurante elegante, _____.** (se me rompió un vaso; se me perdió la tarjeta de crédito) **3. Ayer cuando yo venía a clase, _____.** (se me dañó la bicicleta; me caí y se me rompió el brazo) **4. Cuando era niño/a, siempre _____.** (se me olvidaban las cosas; se me perdían las cosas) **5. El otro día cuando yo lavaba los platos, _____.** (se me rompieron tres vasos; se me terminó el detergente)

6 After all the groups have presented their ads, have each group write a letter of complaint. Their letter should be directed to one of the other groups, claiming false advertising.

4.4 Adverbs

ANTE TODO   Adverbs are words that describe how, when, and where actions take place. They can modify verbs, adjectives, and even other adverbs. In previous lessons, you have already learned many Spanish adverbs, such as the ones below.

aquí	hoy	nunca
ayer	mal	siempre
bien	muy	temprano

▶ The most common adverbs end in **-mente**, equivalent to the English ending *-ly*.

verdaderamente *truly, really*   **generalmente** *generally*   **simplemente** *simply*

▶ To form these adverbs, add **-mente** to the feminine form of the adjective. If the adjective does not have a special feminine form, just add **-mente** to the standard form. **¡Atención!** Adjectives do not lose their accents when adding **-mente**.

ADJECTIVE	FEMININE FORM	SUFFIX	ADVERB
seguro	segura	-mente	seguramente
fabuloso	fabulosa	-mente	fabulosamente
enorme		-mente	enormemente
fácil		-mente	fácilmente

▶ Adverbs that end in **-mente** generally follow the verb, while adverbs that modify an adjective or another adverb precede the word they modify.

Javier dibuja **maravillosamente**.   Inés está **casi siempre** ocupada.
Javier draws wonderfully.   *Inés is almost always busy.*

Common adverbs and adverbial expressions

a menudo	often	**así**	like this; so	**menos**	less
a tiempo	on time	**bastante**	enough; rather	**muchas veces**	a lot; many times
a veces	sometimes	**casi**	almost		
además (de)	furthermore; besides	**con frecuencia**	frequently	**poco**	little
				por lo menos	at least
apenas	hardly; scarcely	**de vez en cuando**	from time to time	**pronto**	soon
		despacio	slowly	**rápido**	quickly

Teaching Tips
• Use magazine pictures to review known adverbs. Ex: *Hoy* esta chica se siente *bien*, pero *ayer* se sentía *mal*.

¡ATENCIÓN!
When a sentence contains two or more adverbs in sequence, the suffix **-mente** is dropped from all but the last adverb. Ex: **El médico nos habló simple y abiertamente.** *The doctor spoke to us simply and openly.*

• Ask volunteers to use **-mente** to convert known adjectives into adverbs. Ex: **cómodo/cómodamente**.

¡ATENCIÓN!
Rápido functions as an adjective (**Ella tiene una computadora rápida.**) as well as an adverb (**Ella corre rápido.**). Note that as an adverb, **rápido** does not need to agree with any other word in the sentence. You can also use the adverb **rápidamente** (**Ella corre rápidamente**).

recursos

WB pp. 221–222

LM p. 234

SUPERSITE
adelante.
vhlcentral.com

¡INTÉNTALO!   Transforma los adjetivos en adverbios.

1. alegre _alegremente_
2. constante _constantemente_
3. gradual _gradualmente_
4. perfecto _perfectamente_
5. real _realmente_
6. frecuente _frecuentemente_
7. tranquilo _tranquilamente_
8. regular _regularmente_
9. maravilloso _maravillosamente_
10. normal _normalmente_
11. básico _básicamente_
12. afortunado _afortunadamente_

Extra Practice Name celebrities and have students create sentences about them, using adverbs. Ex: **Shakira (Shakira baila maravillosamente)**.

Lección 4

Práctica

1 To simplify, use a three-column chart (**¿Cómo?**, **¿Cuándo?**, and **¿Dónde?**) to review adverbs and adverbial expressions.

1

Escoger Completa las oraciones con los adverbios adecuados.

1. La cita era a las dos, pero llegamos _____tarde_____. (mientras, nunca, tarde)
2. El problema fue que _____ayer_____ se nos dañó el despertador. (aquí, ayer, despacio)
3. La recepcionista no se enojó porque sabe que normalmente llego _____a tiempo_____. (a veces, a tiempo, poco)
4. _____Por lo menos_____ el doctor estaba listo. (Por lo menos, Muchas veces, Casi)
5. _____Apenas_____ tuvimos que esperar cinco minutos. (Así, Además, Apenas)
6. El doctor dijo que nuestra hija Irene necesitaba cambiar su rutina diaria _____inmediatamente_____. (temprano, menos, inmediatamente)
▶ 7. El doctor nos explicó _____bien_____ las recomendaciones del Cirujano General (*Surgeon General*) sobre la salud de los jóvenes. (de vez en cuando, bien, apenas)
8. _____Afortunadamente_____ nos dijo que Irene estaba bien, pero tenía que hacer más ejercicio y comer mejor. (Bastante, Afortunadamente, A menudo)

Comunicación

2

Aspirina Lee el anuncio y responde a las preguntas con un(a) compañero/a. Answers will vary.

Game Divide the class into teams of three. Each team should have a piece of paper or a transparency. Say the name of a historical figure and give teams three minutes to write down as many facts as they can about that person, using adverbs and adverbial expressions. At the end of each round, have teams project their answers or read them aloud. Award one point to the team with the most correct answers for each historical figure.

No Hay Tiempo Para el Dolor de Cabeza

Si tienes prisa, o simplemente quieres que tu dolor de cabeza se vaya muy pronto, piensa en Bayer. Se asimila mejor y actúa rápidamente. Ya no se puede perder tiempo por un dolor de cabeza.

ASPIRINA

Bayer
Siempre a tu lado.

2 Before assigning the activity, ask some general questions about the ad. Ex: **¿Qué producto se vende?** (aspirina) **¿Dónde se encuentra un anuncio de este tipo?** (en una revista)

1. ¿Cuáles son los adverbios que aparecen en el anuncio?
2. Según el anuncio, ¿cuáles son las ventajas (*advantages*) de este tipo de aspirina?
3. ¿Tienen ustedes muchos dolores de cabeza? ¿Qué toman para curarlos?
4. ¿Qué medicamentos ven con frecuencia en los anuncios de televisión? Escriban descripciones de varios de estos anuncios. Usen adverbios en sus descripciones.

2 For expansion, have pairs create a similar ad for a different product, using at least four adverbs. Collect the ads and read the descriptions aloud. The class should identify the adverbs and then guess what product is being advertised.

Recapitulación

For self-scoring and diagnostics, go to **adelante.vhlcentral.com**.

Completa estas actividades para repasar los conceptos de gramática que aprendiste en esta lección.

1 Completar Completa el cuadro con la forma correspondiente del imperfecto. **12 pts.**

yo/Ud./él/ella	tú	nosotros	Uds./ellos/ellas
era	eras	éramos	eran
cantaba	**cantabas**	cantábamos	cantaban
venía	venías	**veníamos**	venían
quería	querías	queríamos	**querían**

2 Adverbios Escoge el adverbio correcto de la lista para completar estas oraciones. Lee con cuidado las oraciones; los adverbios sólo se usan una vez. No vas a usar uno de los adverbios. **8 pts.**

a menudo	apenas	fácilmente
a tiempo	casi	maravillosamente
además	despacio	por lo menos

1. Pablito se cae __a menudo__; cuatro veces por semana en promedio (*average*).

2. No me duele nada y no sufro de ninguna enfermedad; me siento __maravillosamente__ bien.

3. —Doctor, ¿cómo supo que tuve una operación de garganta?
   —Muy __fácilmente__, lo leí en su historial médico.

4. ¿Le duele mucho la espalda? Entonces tiene que levantarse __despacio__.

5. Ya te sientes mucho mejor, ¿verdad? Mañana puedes volver al trabajo; tu temperatura es __casi__ normal.

6. Es importante hacer ejercicio con regularidad, __por lo menos__ tres veces a la semana.

7. El examen médico no comenzó ni tarde ni temprano. Comenzó __a tiempo__, a las tres de la tarde.

8. Parece que ya te estás curando del resfriado. __Apenas__ estás congestionada.

RESUMEN GRAMATICAL

4.1 The imperfect tense *pp. 190–191*

The imperfect of regular verbs

cantar	beber	escribir
cantaba	bebía	escribía
cantabas	bebías	escribías
cantaba	bebía	escribía
cantábamos	bebíamos	escribíamos
cantabais	bebíais	escribíais
cantaban	bebían	escribían

► There are no stem changes in the imperfect:
   entender (e:ie) → entendía; servir (e:i) → servía;
   doler (o:ue) → dolía

► The imperfect of **hay** is **había**.

► Only three verbs are irregular in the imperfect.
   ir: iba, ibas, iba, íbamos, ibais, iban
   ser: era, eras, era, éramos, erais, eran
   ver: veía, veías, veía, veíamos, veíais, veían

4.2 The preterite and the imperfect *pp. 194–195*

Preterite	Imperfect
1. Completed actions	1. Ongoing past action
Fueron a **Buenos Aires** el mes pasado.	De niño, usted jugaba al fútbol.
2. Beginning or end of past action	2. Habitual past actions
La película empezó a las nueve.	Todos los días yo jugaba al tenis.
3. Series of past actions or events	3. Description of states or characteristics
Me caí y me lastimé el pie.	Ella era alta. Quería descansar.

4.3 Constructions with se *pp. 198–199*

	Impersonal constructions with **se**	
	prohíbe fumar.	
Se	habla español.	
	hablan varios idiomas.	

TPR Divide the class into three groups: **-ar** verbs, **-er** verbs, and **-ir** verbs. Read a series of sentences that contain the imperfect tense. Have groups stand up when their verb form is used. Ex: **Mi escuela primaria tenía un patio grande.** (**-er** verb group stands)

3

Un accidente Escoge el imperfecto o el pretérito según el contexto para completar esta conversación. **10 pts.**

NURIA Hola, Felipe. ¿Estás bien? ¿Qué es eso? ¿(1) (Te lastimaste/Te lastimabas) el pie?

FELIPE Ayer (2) (tuve/tenía) un pequeño accidente.

NURIA Cuéntame. ¿Cómo (3) (pasó/pasaba)?

FELIPE Bueno, (4) (fueron/eran) las cinco de la tarde y (5) (llovió/llovía) mucho cuando (6) (salí/salía) de la casa en mi bicicleta. No (7) (vi/veía) a una chica que (8) (caminó/caminaba) en mi dirección, y los dos (9) (nos caímos/nos caíamos) al suelo (*ground*).

NURIA Y la chica, ¿está bien ella?

FELIPE Sí. Cuando llegamos al hospital, ella sólo (10) (tuvo/tenía) dolor de cabeza.

Se for unplanned events		
Se	me, te, le, nos, os, les	cayó la taza.
		dañó el radio.
		rompieron las botellas.
		olvidaron las llaves.

4.4 Adverbs *p. 202*

Formation of adverbs
fácil → fácilmente
seguro → seguramente
verdadero → verdaderamente

Lección 4

4

Oraciones Escribe oraciones con **se** a partir de los elementos dados (*given*). Usa el tiempo especificado entre paréntesis y añade pronombres cuando sea necesario. **10 pts.**

> **modelo**
> Carlos / quedar / la tarea en casa (pretérito)
> A Carlos se le quedó la tarea en casa.

1. en la farmacia / vender / medicamentos (presente)   En la farmacia se venden medicamentos.

2. ¿(tú) / olvidar / las llaves / otra vez? (pretérito)   ¿Se te olvidaron las llaves otra vez?

3. (yo) / dañar / la computadora (pretérito)   Se me dañó la computadora.

4. en esta clase / prohibir / hablar inglés (presente)   En esta clase se prohíbe hablar inglés.

5. ellos / romper / las gafas / en el accidente (pretérito)   A ellos se les rompieron las gafas en el accidente.

5

En la consulta Escribe al menos cinco oraciones describiendo tu última visita al médico. Incluye cinco verbos en pretérito y cinco en imperfecto. Habla de qué te pasó, cómo te sentías, cómo era el/la doctor(a), qué te dijo, etc. Usa tu imaginación. **10 pts.**   Answers will vary.

6

Refrán Completa el refrán con las palabras que faltan. **¡2 puntos EXTRA!**

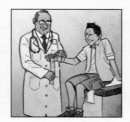

❝ Lo que ___bien___ (*well*) se aprende, nunca ___se___ pierde. ❞

Lectura

Antes de leer

Estrategia

Activating background knowledge

Using what you already know about a particular subject will often help you better understand a reading selection. For example, if you read an article about a recent medical discovery, you might think about what you already know about health in order to understand unfamiliar words or concepts.

Examinar el texto

Utiliza las estrategias de lectura que tú consideras más efectivas para hacer unas observaciones preliminares acerca del texto. Después trabajen en parejas para comparar sus observaciones acerca del texto. Luego contesten estas preguntas:

- Analicen el formato del texto. ¿Qué tipo de texto es? ¿Dónde creen que se publicó este artículo?
- ¿Quiénes son Carla Baron y Tomás Monterrey?
- Miren la foto del libro. ¿Qué sugiere el título del libro sobre su contenido?

Conocimiento previo (*Background knowledge*)

Ahora piensen en su conocimiento previo sobre el cuidado de la salud en los viajes. Consideren estas preguntas:

- ¿Viajaron alguna vez a otro estado o a otro país?
- ¿Tuvieron algunos problemas durante sus viajes con el agua, la comida o el clima del lugar?
- ¿Olvidaron poner en su maleta algún medicamento que después necesitaron?
- Imaginen que su amigo/a se va de viaje. Díganle por lo menos cinco cosas que debe hacer para prevenir cualquier problema de salud.

Libro de la semana

Cómo hacer un viaje saludable y feliz

Carla Baron

Después de leer

Correspondencias

Busca las correspondencias entre los problemas y las recomendaciones.

Problemas

1. el agua ___b___
2. el sol ___d___
3. la comida ___a___
4. la identificación ___e___
5. el clima ___c___

Recomendaciones

a. Hay que adaptarse a los ingredientes no familiares.
b. Toma sólo productos purificados (*purified*).
c. Es importante llevar ropa adecuada cuando viajas.
d. Lleva loción o crema con alta protección solar.
e. Lleva tu pasaporte.

Entrevista a Carla Baron
por Tomás Monterrey

Teaching Tip After reading the selection, call on pairs of students to role-play additional interview questions and answers.

Tomás: ¿Por qué escribió su libro *Cómo hacer un viaje saludable y feliz?*

Carla: Me encanta viajar, conocer otras culturas y escribir. Mi primer viaje lo hice cuando era estudiante universitaria. Todavía recuerdo el día en que llegamos a San Juan, Puerto Rico. Era el panorama ideal para unas vacaciones maravillosas, pero al llegar a la habitación del hotel, bebí mucha agua de la llave° y luego pedí un jugo de frutas con mucho hielo°. El clima en San Juan es tropical y yo tenía mucha sed y calor. Los síntomas llegaron en menos de media hora: pasé dos días con dolor de estómago y corriendo al cuarto de baño cada diez minutos. Desde entonces, siempre que viajo sólo bebo agua mineral y llevo un pequeño bolso con medicinas necesarias como pastillas para el dolor y también bloqueador solar, una crema repelente de mosquitos y un desinfectante.

Tomás: ¿Son reales° las situaciones que se narran en su libro?

Carla: Sí, son reales y son mis propias° historias°. A menudo los autores crean caricaturas divertidas de un turista en dificultades. ¡En mi libro la turista en dificultades soy yo!

Tomás: ¿Qué recomendaciones puede encontrar el lector en su libro?

Carla: Bueno, mi libro es anecdótico y humorístico, pero el tema de la salud se trata° de manera seria. En general, se dan recomendaciones sobre ropa adecuada para cada sitio, consejos para protegerse del sol, y comidas y bebidas adecuadas para el turista que viaja al Caribe o Suramérica.

Tomás: ¿Tiene algún consejo para las personas que se enferman cuando viajan?

Carla: Muchas veces los turistas toman el avión sin saber nada acerca del país que van a visitar. Ponen toda su ropa en la maleta, toman el pasaporte, la cámara fotográfica y ¡a volar°! Es necesario tomar precauciones porque nuestro cuerpo necesita adaptarse al clima, al sol, a la humedad, al agua y a la comida. Se trata de° viajar, admirar las maravillas del mundo y regresar a casa con hermosos recuerdos. En resumen, el secreto es "prevenir en vez de° curar".

llave *faucet* **hielo** *ice* **reales** *true* **propias** *own* **historias** *stories* **se trata** *is treated* **¡a volar!** *Off they go!* **Se trata de** *It's a question of* **en vez de** *instead of*

Lección 4

Seleccionar
Selecciona la respuesta correcta.

1. El tema principal de este libro es __d__.
   a. Puerto Rico b. la salud y el agua c. otras culturas
   d. el cuidado de la salud en los viajes

2. Las situaciones narradas en el libro son __a__.
   a. autobiográficas b. inventadas c. ficticias
   d. imaginarias

3. ¿Qué recomendaciones no vas a encontrar en este libro? __d__
   a. cómo vestirse adecuadamente
   b. cómo prevenir las quemaduras solares
   c. consejos sobre la comida y la bebida
   d. cómo dar propina en los países del Caribe o de Suramérica

4. En opinión de la señorita Baron, __b__.
   a. es bueno tomar agua de la llave y beber jugo de frutas con mucho hielo
   b. es mejor tomar solamente agua embotellada (*bottled*)
   c. los minerales son buenos para el dolor abdominal
   d. es importante visitar el cuarto de baño cada diez minutos

5. ¿Cuál de estos productos no lleva la autora cuando viaja a otros países? __c__
   a. desinfectante
   b. crema repelente
   c. detergente
   d. pastillas medicinales

Small Groups Have groups of three select a country they would like to visit, then research specific precautions that should be taken by visitors.
Heritage Speakers Ask heritage speakers to prepare a short presentation on health and travel tips for visitors to their families' countries of origin.

Costa Rica

El país en cifras

▶ **Área:** 51.100 km^2 (19.730 millas^2), *aproximadamente el área de Virginia Occidental°*

▶ **Población:** 4.665.000

Costa Rica es el país de Centroamérica con la población más homogénea. El 98% de sus habitantes es blanco y mestizo°. Más del 50% de la población es de ascendencia° española y un alto porcentaje tiene sus orígenes en otros países europeos.

▶ **Capital:** San José —1.374.000

▶ **Ciudades principales:** Alajuela, Cartago, Puntarenas, Heredia

SOURCE: Population Division, UN Secretariat

▶ **Moneda:** colón costarricense°

▶ **Idioma:** español (oficial)

Bandera de Costa Rica

Costarricenses célebres

▶ **Carmen Lyra,** escritora (1888–1949)
▶ **Chavela Vargas,** cantante (1919–)
▶ **Óscar Arias Sánchez,** presidente de Costa Rica (1949–)
▶ **Claudia Poll,** nadadora° olímpica (1972–)

Óscar Arias recibió el Premio Nobel de la Paz en 1987.

Virginia Occidental *West Virginia* **mestizo** *of indigenous and white parentage* **ascendencia** *descent* **costarricense** *Costa Rican* **nadadora** *swimmer* **ejército** *army* **gastos** *expenditures* **invertir** *to invest* **cuartel** *barracks*

Carreta pintada a mano

Volcán Arenal

NICARAGUA

Río San Juan

Río Tempisque

Cordillera de Guanacaste

Cordillera de Tilarán

Volcán Arenal

Cordillera Central

Alajuela

Puntarenas

Heredia

Río Grande de Tárcoles

San José

Volcán Irazú

Cartago

Cordillera de

Edificio Metálico en San José

Océano Pacífico

ESTADOS UNIDOS

OCÉANO ATLÁNTICO

COSTA RICA

OCÉANO PACÍFICO

AMÉRICA DEL SUR

Basílica de Nuestra Señora de los Ángeles en Cartago

recursos

WB pp. 223–224	VM pp. 227–228	adelante. vhlcentral.com

¡Increíble pero cierto!

Costa Rica es el único país latinoamericano que no tiene ejército°. Sin gastos° militares, el gobierno puede invertir° más dinero en la educación y las artes. En la foto aparece el Museo Nacional de Costa Rica, antiguo cuartel° del ejército.

Lugares • Los parques nacionales

El sistema de parques nacionales de Costa Rica ocupa el 9,3% de su territorio y fue establecido° para la protección de su biodiversidad. En los parques, los ecoturistas pueden admirar montañas, cataratas° y una gran variedad de plantas exóticas. Algunos ofrecen también la oportunidad de ver quetzales°, monos°, jaguares, armadillos y serpientes° en su hábitat natural.

Mar Caribe

Economía • Las plantaciones de café

Costa Rica fue el primer país centroamericano en desarrollar° la industria del café. En el siglo° XIX, los costarricenses empezaron a exportar esta semilla a Inglaterra°, lo que significó una contribución importante a la economía de la nación. Actualmente, más de 50.000 costarricenses trabajan en el cultivo del café. Este producto representa cerca del 15% de sus exportaciones anuales.

Limón

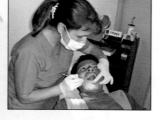

Sociedad • Una nación progresista

Costa Rica es un país progresista. Tiene un nivel de alfabetización° del 96%, uno de los más altos de Latinoamérica. En 1870, esta nación centroamericana abolió la pena de muerte° y en 1948 eliminó el ejército e hizo obligatoria y gratuita° la educación para todos sus ciudadanos.

Talamanca

PANAMÁ

¿Qué aprendiste? Responde cada pregunta con una oración completa.

1. ¿Cómo se llama la capital de Costa Rica? La capital de Costa Rica se llama San José.
2. ¿Quién es Claudia Poll?
   Claudia Poll es una nadadora olímpica.
3. ¿Qué porcentaje del territorio de Costa Rica ocupan los parques nacionales? Los parques nacionales ocupan el 9,3% del territorio de Costa Rica.
4. ¿Para qué se establecen los parques nacionales? Los parques nacionales se establecen para proteger los ecosistemas de la región y su biodiversidad.
5. ¿Qué pueden ver los turistas en los parques nacionales? En los parques nacionales, los turistas pueden ver cataratas, montañas y muchas plantas exóticas.
6. ¿Cuántos costarricenses trabajan en las plantaciones de café hoy día?
   Más de 50.000 costarricenses trabajan en las plantaciones de café hoy día.
7. ¿Cuándo eliminó Costa Rica la pena de muerte?
   Costa Rica eliminó la pena de muerte en 1870.

Bañistas en Limón

Conexión Internet Investiga estos temas en **adelante.vhlcentral.com**.

1. Busca información sobre Óscar Arias Sánchez. ¿Quién es? ¿Por qué se le considera (*is he considered*) un costarricense célebre?
2. Busca información sobre los artistas de Costa Rica. ¿Qué artista, escritor o cantante te interesa más? ¿Por qué?

establecido *established* cataratas *waterfalls* quetzales *type of tropical bird* monos *monkeys* serpientes *snakes* en desarrollar *to develop* siglo *century* Inglaterra *England* nivel de alfabetización *literacy rate* pena de muerte *death penalty* gratuita *free*

El cuerpo

la boca	mouth
el brazo	arm
la cabeza	head
el corazón	heart
el cuello	neck
el cuerpo	body
el dedo	finger
el dedo del pie	toe
el estómago	stomach
la garganta	throat
el hueso	bone
la nariz	nose
el oído	(sense of) hearing; inner ear
el ojo	eye
la oreja	(outer) ear
el pie	foot
la pierna	leg
la rodilla	knee
el tobillo	ankle

La salud

el accidente	accident
el antibiótico	antibiotic
la aspirina	aspirin
la clínica	clinic
el consultorio	doctor's office
el/la dentista	dentist
el/la doctor(a)	doctor
el dolor (de cabeza)	(head)ache; pain
el/la enfermero/a	nurse
el examen médico	physical exam
la farmacia	pharmacy
la gripe	flu
el hospital	hospital
la infección	infection
el medicamento	medication
la medicina	medicine
la operación	operation
el/la paciente	patient
la pastilla	pill; tablet
la radiografía	X-ray
la receta	prescription
el resfriado	cold (illness)
la sala de emergencia(s)	emergency room
la salud	health
el síntoma	symptom
la tos	cough

Verbos

caerse	to fall (down)
dañar	to damage; to break down
darse con	to bump into; to run into
doler (o:ue)	to hurt
enfermarse	to get sick
estar enfermo/a	to be sick
estornudar	to sneeze
lastimarse (el pie)	to injure (one's foot)
olvidar	to forget
poner una inyección	to give an injection
prohibir	to prohibit
recetar	to prescribe
romper	to break
romperse (la pierna)	to break (one's leg)
sacar(se) un diente	to have a tooth removed
ser alérgico/a (a)	to be allergic (to)
sufrir una enfermedad	to suffer an illness
tener dolor (m.)	to have a pain
tener fiebre	to have a fever
tomar la temperatura	to take someone's temperature
torcerse (o:ue) (el tobillo)	to sprain (one's ankle)
toser	to cough

Adjetivos

congestionado/a	congested; stuffed-up
embarazada	pregnant
grave	grave; serious
mareado/a	dizzy; nauseated
médico/a	medical
saludable	healthy
sano/a	healthy

Supersite/IRCD: MP3 Audio Files, Testing Program, *Vocabulario adicional*

Adverbios

a menudo	often
a tiempo	on time
a veces	sometimes
además (de)	furthermore; besides
apenas	hardly; scarcely
así	like this; so
bastante	enough; rather
casi	almost
con frecuencia	frequently
de niño/a	as a child
de vez en cuando	from time to time
despacio	slowly
menos	less
mientras	while
muchas veces	a lot; many times
poco	little
por lo menos	at least
pronto	soon
rápido	quickly
todos los días	every day

Expresiones útiles	See page 185.

recursos

LM
p. 234

adelante.
vhlcentral.com

contextos

Lección 4

1 **El cuerpo humano** Label the parts of the body.

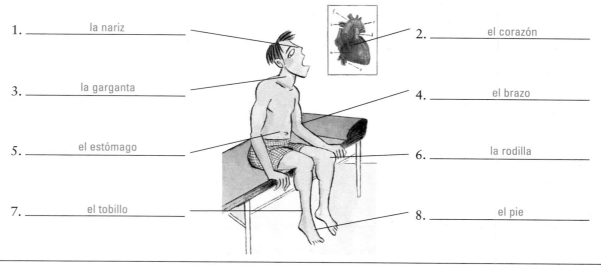

1. _la nariz_

2. _el corazón_

3. _la garganta_

4. _el brazo_

5. _el estómago_

6. _la rodilla_

7. _el tobillo_

8. _el pie_

2 **¿Adónde vas?** Indicate where you would go in each of the following situations.

| la clínica | el dentista | el hospital |
| el consultorio | la farmacia | la sala de emergencia |

1. tienes que comprar aspirinas _la farmacia_

2. te duele un diente _el dentista_

3. te rompes una pierna _la sala de emergencia_

4. te debes hacer un examen médico _la clínica/el consultorio_

5. te van a hacer una operación _el hospital_

6. te van a poner una inyección _la clínica/el consultorio_

3 **Las categorías** List these terms under the appropriate category.

antibiótico	gripe	receta
aspirina	operación	resfriado
estornudos	pastilla	tomar la temperatura
fiebre	radiografía	tos

Síntoma: _fiebre, tos, estornudos_

Enfermedad: _resfriado, gripe_

Diagnóstico: _radiografía, tomar la temperatura_

Tratamiento (*Treatment*): _receta, pastilla, operación, antibiótico, aspirina_

4 **En el consultorio** Complete the sentences with the correct words.

1. La señora Gandía va a tener un hijo en septiembre. Está _____embarazada_____.

2. Manuel tiene la temperatura muy alta. Tiene _____fiebre_____.

3. A Rosita le recetaron un antibiótico y le van a poner una _____inyección_____.

4. A Pedro le cayó una mesa en el pie. El pie le _____duele_____ mucho.

5. Durante la primavera, mi tía estornuda mucho y está muy _____congestionada_____.

6. Tienes que llevar la _____receta_____ a la farmacia para que te vendan (*in order for them to sell you*) la medicina.

7. Le tomaron una _____radiografía_____ de la pierna para ver si se le rompió.

8. Los _____síntomas_____ de un resfriado son los estornudos y la tos.

5 **Doctora y paciente** Choose the logical sentences to complete the conversation between Doctora Márquez and Don Francisco.

DOCTORA ¿Qué síntomas tiene?

DON FRANCISCO (1) _____a_____
a. Tengo tos y me duele la cabeza.
b. Soy muy saludable.
c. Me recetaron un antibiótico.

DOCTORA (2) _____b_____
a. ¿Cuándo fue el accidente?
b. ¿Le dio fiebre ayer?
c. ¿Dónde está la sala de emergencia?

DON FRANCISCO (3) _____c_____
a. Fue a la farmacia.
b. Me torcí el tobillo.
c. Sí, mi esposa me tomó la temperatura.

DOCTORA (4) _____a_____
a. ¿Está muy congestionado?
b. ¿Está embarazada?
c. ¿Le duele el dedo del pie?

DON FRANCISCO (5) _____c_____
a. Sí, me hicieron una operación.
b. Sí, estoy mareado.
c. Sí, y también me duele la garganta.

DOCTORA (6) _____b_____
a. Tiene que ir al consultorio.
b. Es una infección de garganta.
c. La farmacia está muy cerca.

DON FRANCISCO (7) _____a_____
a. ¿Tengo que tomar un antibiótico?
b. ¿Debo ir al dentista?
c. ¿Qué indican las radiografías?

DOCTORA (8) _____c_____
a. Sí, es usted una persona saludable.
b. Sí, se lastimó el pie.
c. Sí, ahora se lo voy a recetar.

estructura

4.1 The imperfect tense

1 **¿Cómo eran las cosas?** Complete the sentences with the imperfect forms of the verbs in parentheses.

1. Antes, la familia Álvarez _____ cenaba _____ (cenar) a las ocho de la noche.

2. De niña, yo _____ cantaba _____ (cantar) en el Coro de Niños de San Juan.

3. Cuando vivían en la costa, ustedes _____ nadaban _____ (nadar) por las mañanas.

4. Mis hermanas y yo _____ jugábamos _____ (jugar) en un equipo de béisbol.

5. La novia de Raúl _____ tenía _____ (tener) el pelo rubio en ese tiempo.

6. Antes de tener la computadora, (tú) _____ escribías _____ (escribir) a mano (*by hand*).

7. (nosotros) _____ Creíamos _____ (creer) que el concierto era el miércoles.

8. Mientras ellos lo _____ buscaban _____ (buscar) en su casa, él se fue a la universidad.

2 **Oraciones imperfectas** Create sentences with the elements provided and the imperfect tense.

1. mi abuela / ser / muy trabajadora y amable
Mi abuela era muy trabajadora y amable.

2. tú / ir / al teatro / cuando vivías en Nueva York
Tú ibas al teatro cuando vivías en Nueva York.

3. ayer / haber / muchísimos pacientes en el consultorio
Ayer había muchísimos pacientes en el consultorio.

4. (nosotros) / ver / tu casa desde allí
Veíamos tu casa desde allí.

5. ser / las cinco de la tarde / cuando llegamos a San José
Eran las cinco de la tarde cuando llegamos a San José.

6. ella / estar / muy nerviosa durante la operación
Ella estaba muy nerviosa durante la operación.

3 **No, pero antes...** Your nosy friend Cristina is asking you many questions. Answer her questions negatively, using the imperfect tense.

modelo

¿Juega Daniel al fútbol?
No, *pero antes jugaba.*

1. ¿Hablas por teléfono? No, pero antes hablaba.

2. ¿Fue a la playa Susana? No, pero antes iba.

3. ¿Come carne Benito? No, pero antes (la) comía.

4. ¿Te trajo muchos regalos tu novio? No, pero antes me traía.

5. ¿Conduce tu mamá? No, pero antes conducía.

4 **¿Qué hacían?** Write sentences that describe what the people in the drawings were doing yesterday at three o'clock in the afternoon. Use the subjects provided and the imperfect tense.

1. tú

Tú escribías cartas/postales. _____

_____

_____

2. Rolando

Rolando buceaba en el mar. _____

_____

3. Pablo y Elena

Pablo y Elena jugaban a las _____

cartas. _____

_____

4. Lilia y yo

Lilia y yo tomábamos el sol. _____

_____

5 **Antes y ahora** Javier is thinking about his childhood—how things were then and how they are now. Write two sentences comparing what Javier used to do and what he does now.

> **modelo**
>
> vivir en casa / vivir en la residencia estudiantil
> **Antes vivía en casa.**
> **Ahora vivo en la residencia estudiantil.**

1. jugar al fútbol con mis primos / jugar en el equipo de la universidad

Antes jugaba al fútbol con mis primos. Ahora juego en el equipo de la universidad. _____

_____

2. escribir las cartas a mano / escribir el correo electrónico con la computadora

Antes escribía las cartas a mano. Ahora escribo el correo electrónico con la computadora. _____

_____

3. ser gordito (*chubby*) / ser delgado

Antes era gordito. Ahora soy delgado. _____

_____

4. tener a mi familia cerca / tener a mi familia lejos

Antes tenía a mi familia cerca. Ahora tengo a mi familia lejos. _____

_____

5. estudiar en mi habitación / estudiar en la biblioteca

Antes estudiaba en mi habitación. Ahora estudio en la biblioteca. _____

_____

6. conocer personas de mi ciudad / conocer personas de todo el (*the whole*) país

Antes conocía a personas de mi ciudad. Ahora conozco a personas de todo el país. _____

_____

4.2 The preterite and the imperfect

1 **Los accidentes** Complete the sentences correctly with imperfect or preterite forms of the verbs in parentheses.

1. Claudia _____celebraba_____ (celebrar) su cumpleaños cuando se torció el tobillo.

2. Ramiro tenía fiebre cuando _____llegó_____ (llegar) a la clínica.

3. Mientras el doctor _____miraba_____ (mirar) la radiografía, yo llamé por teléfono a mi novia.

4. (yo) _____Estaba_____ (estar) mirando la televisión cuando mi mamá se lastimó la mano con la puerta.

5. Cuando Sandra llegó a la universidad, _____tenía_____ (tener) un dolor de cabeza terrible.

6. ¿De niño (tú) _____te enfermabas_____ (enfermarse) con frecuencia?

7. El verano pasado, Luis y Olivia _____sufrieron_____ (sufrir) una enfermedad exótica.

8. Anoche, mi primo y yo _____perdimos_____ (perder) la receta de mi tía.

2 **Antes y ayer** Complete each pair of sentences by using the imperfect and preterite forms of the verbs in parentheses.

(bailar)

1. Cuando era pequeña, Sara _____bailaba_____ ballet todos los lunes y miércoles.

2. Ayer Sara _____bailó_____ ballet en el recital de la universidad.

(escribir)

3. La semana pasada, (yo) le _____escribí_____ un correo electrónico a mi papá.

4. Antes (yo) _____escribía_____ las cartas a mano o con una máquina de escribir.

(ser)

5. El novio de María _____era_____ delgado y deportista.

6. El viaje de novios _____fue_____ una experiencia inolvidable (*unforgettable*).

(haber)

7. _____Hubo_____ una fiesta en casa de Maritere el viernes pasado.

8. Cuando llegamos a la fiesta, _____había_____ mucha gente.

(ver)

9. El lunes _____vi_____ a mi prima Lisa en el centro comercial.

10. De niña, yo _____veía_____ a Lisa todos los días.

3 **¿Qué pasaba?** Look at the drawings, then complete the sentences, using the preterite or imperfect.

1. Cuando llegué a casa anoche, las

niñas _____dormían_____

_____.

2. Cuando empezó a llover, Sara

_____cerró la ventana_____

_____.

3. Antes de irse de vacaciones, la señora

García _____compró una maleta_____

_____.

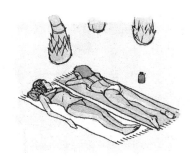

4. Cada verano, las chicas

_____tomaban el sol_____

_____.

4 **El pasado** Decide whether the verbs in parentheses should be in the preterite or the imperfect. Then rewrite the sentences.

1. Ayer Clara (ir) a casa de sus primos, (saludar) a su tía y (comer) con ellos.

   Ayer Clara fue a casa de sus primos, saludó a su tía y comió con ellos.

2. Cuando Manuel (vivir) en San José, (conducir) muchos kilómetros todos los días.

   Cuando Manuel vivía en San José, conducía muchos kilómetros todos los días.

3. Mientras Carlos (leer) las traducciones (*translations*), Blanca (traducir) otros textos.

   Mientras Carlos leía las traducciones, Blanca traducía otros textos.

4. El doctor (terminar) el examen médico y me (recetar) un antibiótico.

   El doctor terminó el examen médico y me recetó un antibiótico.

5. La niña (tener) ocho años y (ser) inteligente y alegre.

   La niña tenía ocho años y era inteligente y alegre.

6. Rafael (cerrar) todos los programas, (apagar) la computadora y (irse).

   Rafael cerró todos los programas, apagó la computadora y se fue.

5 **¡Qué diferencia!** Complete this paragraph with the preterite or the imperfect of the verbs in parentheses.

La semana pasada (yo) (1) _____ llegué _____ (llegar) a la universidad y me di cuenta

(*realized*) de que este año iba ser muy diferente a los anteriores. Todos los años Laura y yo

(2) _____ vivíamos _____ (vivir) con Regina, pero la semana pasada (nosotras)

(3) _____ conocimos _____ (conocer) a nuestra nueva compañera de cuarto, Gisela. Antes Laura,

Regina y yo (4) _____ teníamos _____ (tener) un apartamento muy pequeño, pero al llegar la

semana pasada, (nosotras) (5) _____ vimos _____ (ver) el apartamento nuevo: es enorme y

tiene mucha luz. Antes de vivir con Gisela, Laura y yo no (6) _____ podíamos _____ (poder) leer

el correo electrónico desde la casa, pero ayer Gisela (7) _____ conectó _____ (conectar) su

computadora a Internet y todas (8) _____ miramos _____ (mirar) nuestros mensajes. Antes

(nosotras) siempre (9) _____ caminábamos _____ (caminar) hasta la biblioteca para ver el correo,

pero anoche Gisela nos (10) _____ dijo _____ (decir) que podemos compartir su

computadora. ¡Qué diferencia!

6 **¿Dónde estabas?** Write questions and answers with the words provided. Ask where these people were when something happened.

> **modelo**
>
> Maite ⟶ Inés / salir a bailar // cuarto / dormir la siesta
> ¿Dónde estaba Maite cuando Inés salió a bailar?
> Maite estaba en el cuarto. Dormía la siesta.

1. Javier ⟶ (yo) / llamar por teléfono // cocina / lavar los platos

   ¿Dónde estaba Javier cuando llamé por teléfono? Javier estaba en la cocina. Lavaba los platos.

   _____

2. (tú) ⟶ don Francisco y yo / ir al cine // casa / leer una revista

   ¿Dónde estabas cuando don Francisco y yo fuimos al cine? Estaba en casa. Leía una revista.

   _____

3. tu hermano ⟶ empezar a llover // calle / pasear en bicicleta

   ¿Dónde estaba tu hermano cuando empezó a llover? Mi hermano estaba en la calle. Paseaba en bicicleta.

   _____

4. ustedes ⟶ Álex / venir a casa // estadio / jugar al fútbol

   ¿Dónde estaban ustedes cuando Álex vino a casa? Estábamos en el estadio. Jugábamos al fútbol.

   _____

5. Álex y Javier ⟶ (tú) / saludarlos // supermercado / hacer la compra

   ¿Dónde estaban Álex y Javier cuando los saludaste? Estaban en el supermercado. Hacían la compra.

   _____

7   **El diario de Laura** Laura has just found a page from her old diary. Rewrite the page in the past tense, using the preterite and imperfect forms of the verbs as appropriate.

Querido diario:

Estoy pasando el verano en Alajuela, y es un lugar muy divertido. Salgo con mis amigas todas las noches hasta tarde. Bailo con nuestros amigos y nos divertimos mucho. Durante la semana trabajo: doy clases de inglés. Los estudiantes son alegres y se interesan mucho por aprender. El día de mi cumpleaños conocí a un chico muy simpático que se llama Francisco. Me llamó al día siguiente (*next*) y nos vemos todos los días. Me siento enamorada de él.

Estaba pasando el verano en Alajuela, y era un lugar muy divertido. Salía con mis amigas todas las noches hasta

tarde. Bailaba con nuestros amigos y nos divertíamos mucho. Durante la semana, trabajaba: daba clases de inglés. Los

estudiantes eran alegres y se interesaban mucho por aprender. El día de mi cumpleaños conocí a un chico muy simpático

que se llamaba Francisco. Me llamó al día siguiente y nos veíamos todos los días. Me sentía enamorada de él.

_____

_____

_____

_____

_____

_____

8   **Un día en la playa** Laura is still reading her old diary. Rewrite this paragraph, using the preterite or imperfect forms of the verbs in parentheses as appropriate.

Querido diario:

Ayer mi hermana y yo (ir) a la playa. Cuando llegamos, (ser) un día despejado (*clear*) con mucho sol, y nosotras (estar) muy contentas. A las doce (comer) unos sándwiches de almuerzo. Los sándwiches (ser) de jamón y queso. Luego (descansar) y entonces (nadar) en el mar. Mientras (nadar), (ver) a las personas que (practicar) el esquí acuático. (Parecer) muy divertido, así que (decidir) probarlo. Mi hermana (ir) primero, mientras yo la (mirar). Luego (ser) mi turno. Las dos (divertirse) mucho esa tarde.

Ayer mi hermana y yo fuimos a la playa. Cuando llegamos, era un día despejado con mucho sol, y nosotras estábamos

muy contentas. A las doce comimos unos sándwiches de almuerzo. Los sándwiches eran de jamón y queso. Luego

descansamos y entonces nadamos en el mar. Mientras nadábamos, vimos a las personas que practicaban el esquí

acuático. Parecía muy divertido, así que decidimos probarlo. Mi hermana fue primero, mientras yo la miraba. Luego fue mi

turno. Las dos nos divertimos mucho esa tarde.

_____

_____

_____

4.3 Constructions with se

1 **¿Qué se hace?** Complete the sentences with verbs from the word bank. Use impersonal constructions with **se** in the present tense.

caer	hablar	recetar	vender
dañar	poder	servir	vivir

1. En Costa Rica _____se habla_____ español.

2. En las librerías _____se venden_____ libros y revistas.

3. En los restaurantes _____se sirve_____ comida.

4. En los consultorios _____se recetan_____ medicinas.

5. En el campo _____se vive_____ muy bien.

6. En el mar _____se puede_____ nadar y pescar.

2 **Los anuncios** Write advertisements or signs for the situations described. Use impersonal constructions with **se**.

1. "Está prohibido fumar."

Se prohíbe fumar.

2. "Vendemos periódicos."

Se venden periódicos.

3. "Hablamos español."

Se habla español.

4. "Necesitamos enfermeras."

Se necesitan enfermeras.

5. "No debes nadar."

No se debe nadar./Se prohíbe nadar.

6. "Estamos buscando un auto usado."

Se busca un auto usado.

3 **¿Qué les pasó?** Complete the sentences with the correct indirect object pronouns.

1. Se _____le_____ perdieron las maletas a Roberto.

2. A mis hermanas se _____les_____ cayó la mesa.

3. A ti se _____te_____ olvidó venir a buscarme ayer.

4. A mí se _____me_____ quedó la ropa nueva en mi casa.

5. A las tías de Ana se _____les_____ rompieron los vasos.

6. A Isabel y a mí se _____nos_____ dañó el auto.

4 **Los accidentes** Your classmates are very unlucky. Rewrite what happened to them, using the correct form of the verb in parentheses.

1. A Marina se le (cayó, cayeron) la bolsa.

 A Marina se le cayó la bolsa. _____

2. A ti se te (olvidó, olvidaron) comprarme la medicina.

 A ti se te olvidó comprarme la medicina. _____

3. A nosotros se nos (quedó, quedaron) los libros en el auto.

 A nosotros se nos quedaron los libros en el auto. _____

4. A Ramón y a Pedro se les (dañó, dañaron) el proyecto.

 A Ramón y a Pedro se les dañó el proyecto. _____

5 **Mala suerte** You and your friends are trying to go on vacation, but everything is going wrong. Use the elements provided, the preterite tense, and constructions with **se** to write sentences.

> **modelo**
>
> (a Raquel) / olvidar / traer su pasaporte
> *Se le olvidó traer su pasaporte.*

1. (a nosotros) / perder / las llaves del auto

 Se nos perdieron las llaves del auto. _____

2. (a ustedes) / olvidar / ponerse las inyecciones

 Se les olvidó ponerse las inyecciones. _____

3. (a ti) / caer / los papeles del médico

 Se te cayeron los papeles del médico. _____

4. (a Marcos) / romper / la pierna cuando esquiaba

 Se le rompió la pierna cuando esquiaba. _____

5. (a mí) / dañar / la cámara durante el viaje

 Se me dañó la cámara durante el viaje. _____

6 **¿Qué pasó?** As the vacation goes on, you and your friends have more bad luck. Answer the questions, using the phrases in parentheses and the preterite tense.

> **modelo**
>
> ¿Qué le pasó a Roberto? (quedar la cámara nueva en casa)
> *Se le quedó la cámara nueva en casa.*

1. ¿Qué les pasó a Pilar y a Luis? (dañar el coche)

 Se les dañó el coche. _____

2. ¿Qué les pasó a los padres de Sara? (romper la botella de vino)

 Se les rompió la botella de vino. _____

3. ¿Qué te pasó a ti? (perder las llaves del hotel)

 Se me perdieron las llaves del hotel. _____

4. ¿Qué les pasó a ustedes? (quedar las toallas en la playa)

 Se nos quedaron las toallas en la playa. _____

5. ¿Qué le pasó a Hugo? (olvidar estudiar para el examen en el avión)

 Se le olvidó estudiar para el examen en el avión. _____

4.4 Adverbs

1 **En mi ciudad** Complete the sentences by changing the adjectives in the first sentences into adverbs in the second.

1. Los conductores son lentos. Conducen _lentamente_.

2. Esa doctora es amable. Siempre nos saluda _amablemente_.

3. Los autobuses de mi ciudad son frecuentes. Pasan por la parada _frecuentemente_.

4. Rosa y Julia son chicas muy alegres. Les encanta bailar y cantar _alegremente_.

5. Mario y tú hablan un español perfecto. Hablan español _perfectamente_.

6. Los pacientes visitan al doctor de manera constante. Lo visitan _constantemente_.

7. Llegar tarde es normal para David. Llega tarde _normalmente_.

8. Me gusta trabajar de manera independiente. Trabajo _independientemente_.

2 **Completar** Complete the sentences with adverbs and adverbial expressions from the word bank. Use each term once.

a menudo	así	por lo menos
a tiempo	bastante	pronto
apenas	casi	

1. Tito no es un niño muy sano. Se enferma _a menudo_.

2. El doctor Garrido es muy puntual. Siempre llega al consultorio _a tiempo_.

3. Mi madre visita al doctor con frecuencia. Se chequea _por lo menos_ una vez cada año.

4. Fui al doctor el año pasado. Tengo que volver _pronto_.

5. Llegué tarde al autobús, y _casi_ tengo que ir al centro caminando.

6. El examen fue _bastante_ difícil.

3 **Traducir** Complete the sentences with the adverbs or adverbial phrases that correspond to the words in parentheses.

1. Llegaron temprano al concierto; _así_ (so), consiguieron asientos muy buenos.

2. El accidente fue _bastante_ (rather) grave, pero al conductor no se le rompió ningún hueso.

3. Irene y Vicente van a comer _menos_ (less) porque quieren estar más delgados.

4. Silvia y David _casi_ (almost) se cayeron de la motocicleta cerca de su casa.

5. Para aprobar (pass) el examen, tienes que contestar _por lo menos_ (at least) el 75% de las preguntas.

6. Mi mamá _a veces_ (sometimes) se tuerce el tobillo cuando camina mucho.

4 **Háblame de ti** Answer the questions using the adverbs and adverbial phrases that you learned in this lesson. Do not repeat the adverb or adverbial phrase of the question. Then, say how long ago you last did each activity. Answers will vary.

> **modelo**
>
> ¿Vas a la playa siempre?
> No, voy a la playa a veces. Hace cuatro meses que no voy a la playa.

1. ¿Tú y tus amigos van al cine con frecuencia?

_____

2. ¿Comes comida china?

_____

3. ¿Llegas tarde a tu clase de español?

_____

4. ¿Te enfermas con frecuencia?

_____

5. ¿Comes carne?

_____

Síntesis

Think of a summer in which you did a lot of different things on vacation or at home. State exceptional situations or activities that you did just once. Then state the activities that you used to do during that summer; mention which of those things you still do in the present. How often did you do those activities then? How often do you do them now? How long ago did you do some of those things? Create a "photo album" of that summer, using actual photographs if you have them, or drawings that you make. Use your writing about the summer as captions for the photo album.

Answers will vary.

_____

_____

_____

_____

_____

_____

_____

_____

_____

_____

panorama

Costa Rica

1 **El mapa de Costa Rica** Label the map of Costa Rica.

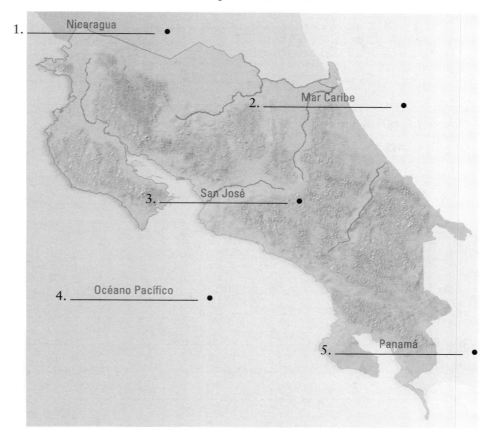

1. _____ Nicaragua

2. _____ Mar Caribe

3. _____ San José

4. _____ Océano Pacífico

5. _____ Panamá

2 **¿Cierto o falso?** Indicate whether the statements are **cierto** or **falso**. Correct the false statements.

1. Los parques nacionales costarricenses se establecieron para el turismo.

Falso. Los parques nacionales costarricenses se establecieron para la protección de los delicados ecosistemas de la región y la biodiversidad.

2. Costa Rica fue el primer país centroamericano en desarrollar la industria del café.

Cierto.

3. El café representa más del 50% de las exportaciones anuales de Costa Rica.

Falso. El café representa cerca del 15% de las exportaciones anuales de Costa Rica.

4. Costa Rica tiene un nivel de alfabetización del 96%.

Cierto.

5. El ejército de Costa Rica es uno de los más grandes y preparados de Latinoamérica.

Falso. Costa Rica eliminó el ejército en 1948.

6. En Costa Rica se eliminó la educación gratuita para los costarricenses.

Falso. En 1948 Costa Rica hizo obligatoria y gratuita la educación para todos los costarricenses.

3 **Costa Rica** Complete the sentences with the correct words.

1. Costa Rica es el país de Centroamérica con la población más _____homogénea_____.

2. La moneda que se usa en Costa Rica es _____el colón costarricense_____.

3. Costa Rica es el único país latinoamericano que no tiene _____ejército_____.

4. En el siglo XIX los costarricenses empezaron a exportar su café a _____Inglaterra_____.

5. Hoy día más de 50.000 costarricenses trabajan _____cultivando/en el cultivo de_____ el café.

6. Costa Rica es un modelo de _____democracia,_____ y de _____estabilidad_____.

4 **Datos costarricenses** Fill in the blanks with the correct information.

En los parques nacionales de Costa Rica los ecoturistas pueden ver: Order of answers will vary.

1. _____cataratas_____   5. _____monos_____

2. _____montañas_____   6. _____jaguares_____

3. _____plantas exóticas_____   7. _____armadillos_____

4. _____quetzales_____   8. _____serpientes_____

Costa Rica es uno de los países más progresistas del mundo porque:

9. _Tiene un nivel de alfabetización del 96%._

10. _En 1870 eliminó la pena de muerte._

11. _En 1948 eliminó el ejército._

12. _En 1948 hizo obligatoria y gratuita la educación para todos los costarricenses._

5 **Completar** Use impersonal constructions with **se** to complete the sentences. Be sure to use the correct tense of the verbs in the word bank.

> **modelo**
> En Costa Rica ahora *se pone* más dinero en la educación y las artes.

eliminar	establecer	mantener	poder
empezar	invertir	ofrecer	proveer

1. En Costa Rica _____se mantiene_____ una democracia estable.

2. El sistema de parques nacionales _____se estableció_____ para la protección de los ecosistemas.

3. En los parques _____se pueden_____ ver animales en su hábitat natural.

4. En el siglo XIX _____se empezó_____ a exportar el café costarricense.

5. En Costa Rica _____se ofrece_____ educación gratuita a todos los ciudadanos.

6. En 1870 _____se eliminó_____ la pena de muerte en Costa Rica.

¡Uf! ¡Qué dolor!

Lección 4
Fotonovela

Antes de ver el video

1 **Un accidente** Look at the video still. Where do you think Javier and Don Francisco are? What is happening in this scene? Answers will vary.

_____
_____
_____
_____
_____
_____
_____
_____

Mientras ves el video

2 **¿Quién?** Watch the **¡Uf! ¡Qué dolor!** segment of this video module and place a check mark in the correct column to indicate who said each expression.

Expresión	Javier	don Francisco	Dra. Márquez
1. ¡Creo que me rompí el tobillo!	✓		
2. ¿Cómo se lastimó el pie?			✓
3. ¿Embarazada? Definitivamente NO.	✓		
4. ¿Está roto el tobillo?	✓		
5. No te preocupes, Javier.		✓	

3 **Clínicas y hospitales** Watch Javier's flashback about medical facilities in Puerto Rico and place a check mark beside the things you see.

✓ 1. una paciente
✓ 2. una computadora
✓ 3. enfermeras
___ 4. un termómetro
✓ 5. una radiografía

✓ 6. letreros (*signs*)
✓ 7. unos edificios
___ 8. unas pastillas
✓ 9. un microscopio
___ 10. una inyección

4 **Resumen** Watch the **Resumen** segment of this video module. Then write the name of the person who said each sentence and fill in the missing words.

Javier 1. De niño tenía que ir mucho a una ___clínica___ en San Juan.

doctora Márquez 2. ¿Cuánto tiempo ___hace___ que se cayó?

Javier 3. Tengo que descansar durante dos o tres días porque me ___duele___ el tobillo.

doctora Márquez 4. No está ___roto___ el tobillo.

Javier 5. Pero por lo menos no necesito el ___tobillo___ para dibujar.

Después de ver el video

5   **Seleccionar** Write the letter of the word or words that best completes each sentence in the spaces provided.

1. _____ conoce a una doctora que trabaja en una clínica cercana (*nearby*).

   a. Don Francisco   b. Maite   c. Álex   d. Inés

2. La doctora Márquez le va a _____ unas pastillas a Javier.

   a. vender   b. comprar   c. recetar   d. romper

3. Cuando era _____, _____ se enfermaba mucho de la garganta.

   a. niña; la doctora Márquez   b. niño; Javier   c. niño; Álex   d. niño; don Francisco

4. La doctora Márquez quiere ver si Javier se rompió uno de los huesos _____.

   a. de la pierna   b. del pie   c. del tobillo   d. de la rodilla

5. Una vez _____ se rompió la pierna jugando al _____.

   a. don Francisco; fútbol   b. Javier; béisbol   c. la doctora Márquez; baloncesto   d. Álex; fútbol

6. _____ se cayó cuando estaba en _____.

   a. Álex; el parque   b. Javier; el autobús   c. Don Francisco; la clínica   d. Javier; el restaurante

6   **Preguntas** Answer the following questions in Spanish.

1. ¿Tiene fiebre Javier? ¿Está mareado?

   No, Javier no tiene fiebre. Sí, está un poco mareado.

2. ¿Cuánto tiempo hace que se cayó Javier?

   Hace más de una hora que se cayó Javier.

3. ¿Cómo se llama la clínica donde trabaja la doctora Márquez?

   La clínica donde trabaja la doctora Márquez se llama Clínica Villa Flora./Se llama Clínica Villa Flora.

4. ¿A quién no le gustaban mucho ni las inyecciones ni las pastillas?

   No le gustaban mucho a don Francisco las inyecciones ni las pastillas./A don Francisco no le gustaban mucho
   las inyecciones ni las pastillas.

5. ¿Va a poder ir Javier de excursión con sus amigos?

   Sí, Javier va a poder ir de excursión con sus amigos.

7   **Preguntas personales** Answer these questions in Spanish.   Answers will vary.

1. ¿Te gusta ir al médico? ¿Por qué? _____

   _____

2. ¿Tienes muchas alergias? ¿Eres alérgico/a a algún medicamento? _____

   _____

3. ¿Cuándo es importante ir a la sala de emergencias? _____

   _____

4. ¿Qué haces cuando tienes fiebre y te duele la garganta? _____

   _____

Panorama: Costa Rica

Antes de ver el video

1 **Más vocabulario** Look over these useful words and expressions before you watch the video.

Vocabulario útil		
bosque *forest*	guía certificado *certified guide*	riqueza *wealth*
conservar *to preserve*	nuboso *cloudy*	tiendas de campaña *camping tents*
cubierto *covered*	permitir *to allow*	tocar *to touch*
entrar *to enter*	regla *rule*	tortugas marinas *sea turtles*

2 **Foto** Describe the video still. Write at least three sentences in Spanish. Answers will vary.

3 **Categorías** Categorize the words listed in the word bank.

bosque	guía	pedir	sacar
diferentes	hermosos	permite	Tortuguero
entrar	Monteverde	playa	turistas
exóticas	nuboso	pueblos	visitantes
frágil			

Lugares	Personas	Verbos	Adjetivos
bosque	guía	entrar	diferentes
Monteverde	turistas	pedir	exóticas
playa	visitantes	permite	frágil
pueblos		sacar	hermosos
Tortuguero			nuboso

Mientras ves el video

4 **Marcar** While watching the video, check off the rules that have been put in place to protect nature.

___✓___ 1. En el parque Monteverde no pueden entrar más de 150 personas al mismo tiempo.

_____ 2. Los turistas tienen que dormir en tiendas de campaña.

_____ 3. Los turistas no pueden visitar Tortuguero en febrero.

___✓___ 4. Después de la seis no se permite ir a la playa sin un guía certificado.

___✓___ 5. Los turistas no pueden tocar las tortugas.

___✓___ 6. En Tortuguero está prohibido tomar fotografías.

Después de ver el video

5 **Completar** Complete the sentences with words from the word bank.

> acampan   entrar   pasan   prohíbe
> conservan   estudiar   prefieren transportan

1. En Monteverde se _____ conservan _____ más de dos mil especies diferentes de animales.

2. En este parque no pueden _____ entrar _____ más de 150 personas al mismo tiempo.

3. Algunos turistas _____ acampan _____ en Monteverde.

4. Otros _____ prefieren _____ ir a los hoteles de los pueblos que están cerca de Monteverde.

5. Se _____ prohíbe _____ sacar fotografías.

6 **Preferencias** Write a brief paragraph in Spanish where you describe which place(s) you would like to visit in Costa Rica and why. Answers will vary.

_____

_____

_____

_____

_____

_____

_____

_____

_____

contextos

Lección 4

1 **Identificar** You will hear a series of words. Write each one in the appropriate category.

> **modelo**
> *You hear:* el hospital
> *You write:* **el hospital** under **Lugares**

Lugares	Medicinas	Condiciones y síntomas médicos
el hospital	la aspirina	la tos
la sala de emergencia	la pastilla	el resfriado
la farmacia	el antibiótico	la gripe
el consultorio		la fiebre

2 **Describir** For each drawing, you will hear two statements. Choose the one that corresponds to the drawing.

1. a. (b.)

2. a. (b.)

3. (a.) b.

4. a. (b.)

pronunciación

c (before a consonant) and q

You learned that, in Spanish, the letter **c** before the vowels **a, o,** and **u** is pronounced like the *c* in the English word *car*. When the letter **c** appears before any consonant except **h,** it is also pronounced like the *c* in *car*.

| **cl**ínica | bici**cl**eta | **cr**ema | do**ct**ora | o**ct**ubre |

In Spanish, the letter **q** is always followed by an **u,** which is silent. The combination **qu** is pronounced like the *k* sound in the English word *kitten*. Remember that the sounds **kwa, kwe, kwi, kwo,** and **koo** are always spelled with the combination **cu** in Spanish, never with **qu**.

| **qu**erer | par**qu**e | **qu**eso | **qu**ímica | mante**qu**illa |

---

1 **Práctica** Repeat each word after the speaker, focusing on the **c** and **q** sounds.

1. quince	5. conductor	9. aquí
2. querer	6. escribir	10. ciclismo
3. pequeño	7. contacto	11. electrónico
4. equipo	8. increíble	12. quitarse

---

2 **Oraciones** When you hear the number, read the corresponding sentence aloud. Then listen to the speaker and repeat the sentence.

1. El doctor Cruz quiso sacarle un diente.
2. Clara siempre se maquilla antes de salir de casa.
3. ¿Quién perdió su equipaje?
4. Pienso comprar aquella camisa porque me queda bien.
5. La chaqueta cuesta quinientos cuarenta dólares, ¿no?
6. Esa clienta quiere pagar con tarjeta de crédito.

---

3 **Refranes** Repeat each saying after the speaker to practice the **c** and the **q** sounds.

1. Ver es creer. [1]
2. Quien mal anda, mal acaba. [2]

---

4 **Dictado** You will hear five sentences. Each will be said twice. Listen carefully and write what you hear.

1. Esta mañana Cristina se despertó enferma.

2. Le duele todo el cuerpo y no puede levantarse de la cama.

3. Cree que es la gripe y va a tener que llamar a la clínica de la universidad.

4. Cristina no quiere perder otro día de clase, pero no puede ir porque está muy mareada.

5. Su compañera de cuarto va a escribirle un mensaje electrónico a la profesora Crespo porque hoy tienen un examen en su clase.

Seeing is believing. [1]
He who lives badly, ends badly. [2]

estructura

4.1 The imperfect tense

1 **Identificar** Listen to each sentence and circle the verb tense you hear.

1. a. present   b. preterite   (c.) imperfect
2. a. present   (b.) preterite   c. imperfect
3. a. present   b. preterite   (c.) imperfect
4. (a.) present   b. preterite   c. imperfect
5. a. present   (b.) preterite   c. imperfect

6. a. present   b. preterite   (c.) imperfect
7. a. present   (b.) preterite   c. imperfect
8. a. present   b. preterite   (c.) imperfect
9. (a.) present   b. preterite   c. imperfect
10. a. present   (b.) preterite   c. imperfect

2 **Cambiar** Form a new sentence using the cue you hear. Repeat the correct answer after the speaker. (6 items)

> **modelo**
> Iban a casa. (Eva)
> *Eva iba a casa.*

3 **Preguntas** A reporter is writing an article about funny things people used to do when they were children. Answer her questions, using the cues in your lab manual. Then repeat the correct response after the speaker.

> **modelo**
> *You hear:* ¿Qué hacía Miguel de niño?
> *You see:* ponerse pajitas (*straws*) en la nariz
> *You say:* Miguel se ponía pajitas en la nariz.

1. quitarse los zapatos en el restaurante
2. vestirnos con la ropa de mamá
3. sólo querer comer dulces
4. jugar con un amigo invisible
5. usar las botas de su papá
6. comer con las manos

4 **Completar** Listen to this description of Ángela's medical problem and write the missing words in your lab manual.

(1) _____Sufría_____ Ángela porque (2) _____estornudaba_____ día y noche.

(3) _____Pensaba_____ que (4) _____tenía_____ un resfriado, pero se

(5) _____sentía_____ bastante saludable. Se (6) _____iba_____ de la biblioteca después

de poco tiempo porque les (7) _____molestaba_____ a los otros estudiantes. Sus amigas, Laura y

Petra, siempre le (8) _____decían_____ que (9) _____tenía_____ alguna alergia. Por fin,

decidió hacerse un examen médico. La doctora le dijo que ella (10) _____era_____

alérgica y que (11) _____había_____ muchas medicinas para las alergias. Finalmente, le

recetó unas pastillas. Al día siguiente (*following*), Ángela se (12) _____sentía_____ mejor

porque (13) _____sabía_____ cuál era el problema y ella dejó de estornudar después de

tomar las pastillas.

4.2 The preterite and the imperfect

1 **Identificar** Listen to each statement and identify the verbs in the preterite and the imperfect. Write them in the appropriate column.

> **modelo**
>
> *You hear:* Cuando llegó la ambulancia, el esposo estaba mareado.
> *You write:* **llegó** under *Preterite*, and **estaba** under *Imperfect*.

	Preterite	Imperfect
Modelo	llegó	estaba
1.	tomó	estaba
2.	lastimé	jugaba
3.		tenía, estudiaba
4.	llegó	estábamos
5.	dolió, sacó	
6.	fuí, recetó	
7.		dolían, era
8.	llevó	dolía

2 **Responder** Answer the questions using the cues in your lab manual. Substitute direct object pronouns for the direct object nouns when appropriate. Repeat the correct response after the speaker.

> **modelo**
>
> *You hear:* ¿Por qué no llamaste al médico la semana pasada?
> *You see:* perder su número de teléfono
> *You say:* Porque perdí su número de teléfono.

1. en la mesa de la cocina
2. tener ocho años
3. lastimarse el tobillo
4. no, ponerla en la mochila
5. tomarse las pastillas
6. No, pero tener una grave infección de garganta.
7. toda la mañana
8. necesitar una radiografía de la boca

3 **¡Qué nervios!** Listen as Sandra tells a friend about her day. Then read the statements in your lab manual and decide whether they are **cierto** or **falso**.

	Cierto	Falso
1. Sandra tenía mucha experiencia poniendo inyecciones.	○	☑
2. La enfermera tenía un terrible dolor de cabeza.	○	☑
3. La enfermera le dio una pastilla a Sandra.	☑	○
4. El paciente trabajaba en el hospital con Sandra.	○	☑
5. El paciente estaba muy nervioso.	○	☑
6. Sandra le puso la inyección mientras él hablaba.	☑	○

4.3 Constructions with se

1 **Escoger** Listen to each question and choose the most logical response.

1. a. Ay, se te quedó en casa.
   (b.) Ay, se me quedó en casa.
2. (a.) No, se le olvidó llamarlo.
   b. No, se me olvidó llamarlo.
3. (a.) Se le rompieron jugando al fútbol.
   b. Se les rompieron jugando al fútbol.

4. a. Ay, se les olvidaron.
   (b.) Ay, se nos olvidaron.
5. (a.) No, se me perdió.
   b. No, se le perdió.
6. (a.) Se nos rompió.
   b. Se le rompieron.

2 **Preguntas** Answer each question you hear using the cue in your lab manual and the impersonal **se**. Repeat the correct response after the speaker.

> **modelo**
> *You hear:* ¿Qué lengua se habla en Costa Rica?
> *You see:* español
> *You say:* Se habla español.

1. a las seis
2. gripe
3. en la farmacia

4. en la caja
5. en la Oficina de Turismo
6. tomar el autobús #3

3 **Letreros (Signs)** Some or all of the type is missing on the signs in your lab manual. Listen to the speaker and write the appropriate text below each sign. The text for each sign will be repeated.

(3.) Se sale por la derecha.

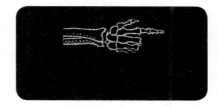

(4.) No se puede hacer radiografías a mujeres embarazadas. Favor de informar a la enfermera si piensa que está embarazada.

(1.) Se venden casas y apartamentos. Precios razonables.

(2.) Nos preocupamos por su salud. Se prohíbe fumar en el hospital.

Lab Manual

4.4 Adverbs

1 **Completar** Listen to each statement and circle the word or phrase that best completes it.

1. a. casi   b. mal   c. ayer
2. a. con frecuencia   b. además   c. ayer
3. a. poco   b. tarde   c. bien
4. a. a menudo   b. muy   c. menos
5. a. así   b. apenas   c. tranquilamente
6. a. bastante   b. a tiempo   c. normalmente

2 **Cambiar** Form a new sentence by changing the adjective in your lab manual to an adverb. Repeat the correct answer after the speaker.

> **modelo**
> *You hear:* Juan dibuja.
> *You see:* fabuloso
> *You say:* Juan dibuja fabulosamente.

1. regular   4. constante
2. rápido   5. general
3. feliz   6. fácil

3 **Preguntas** Answer each question you hear in the negative, using the cue in your lab manual. Repeat the correct response after the speaker.

> **modelo**
> *You hear:* ¿Salió bien la operación?
> *You see:* mal
> *You say:* No, la operación salió mal.

1. lentamente   4. nunca
2. tarde   5. tristemente
3. muy   6. poco

4 **Situaciones** You will hear four brief conversations. Choose the phrase that best completes each sentence in your lab manual.

1. Mónica…
   a. llegó tarde al aeropuerto.
   b. casi perdió el avión a San José.
   c. decidió no ir a San José.

2. Pilar…
   a. se preocupa por la salud de Tomás.
   b. habla con su médico.
   c. habla con Tomás sobre un problema médico.

3. La señora Blanco…
   a. se rompió la pierna hoy.
   b. va a correr mañana.
   c. se lastimó el tobillo hoy.

4. María está enojada porque Vicente…
   a. no va a recoger (*to pick up*) su medicina.
   b. no recogió su medicina ayer.
   c. no debe tomar antibióticos.

vocabulario

You will now hear the vocabulary found in your worktext on the last page of this lesson. Listen and repeat each Spanish word or phrase after the speaker.

Additional Vocabulary

Additional Vocabulary

Notes

Notes

La tecnología

5

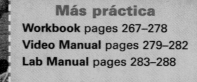

La tecnología

Más vocabulario

la calculadora	calculator
la cámara de video, digital	video, digital camera
el canal	(TV) channel
la contestadora	answering machine
el estéreo	stereo
el *fax*	fax (machine)
la televisión por cable	cable television
el tocadiscos compacto	compact disc player
el video(casete)	video(cassette)
el archivo	file
arroba	@ symbol
la dirección electrónica	e-mail address
Internet	Internet
el mensaje de texto	text message
la página principal	home page
el programa de computación	software
la red	network; Web
el sitio web	website
apagar	to turn off
borrar	to erase
descargar	to download
funcionar	to work
grabar	to record
guardar	to save
imprimir	to print
llamar	to call
navegar (en Internet)	to surf (the Internet)
poner, prender	to turn on
quemar	to burn (a CD)
sonar (o:ue)	to ring
descompuesto/a	not working; out of order
lento/a	slow
lleno/a	full

Variación léxica

computadora ⟷ ordenador (*Esp.*), computador (*Col.*)

descargar ⟷ bajar (*Esp., Col., Arg., Ven.*)

Supersite/IRCD: Lesson Plans, MP3 Audio Files and Listening Scripts, Overheads, *Vocabulario adicional*

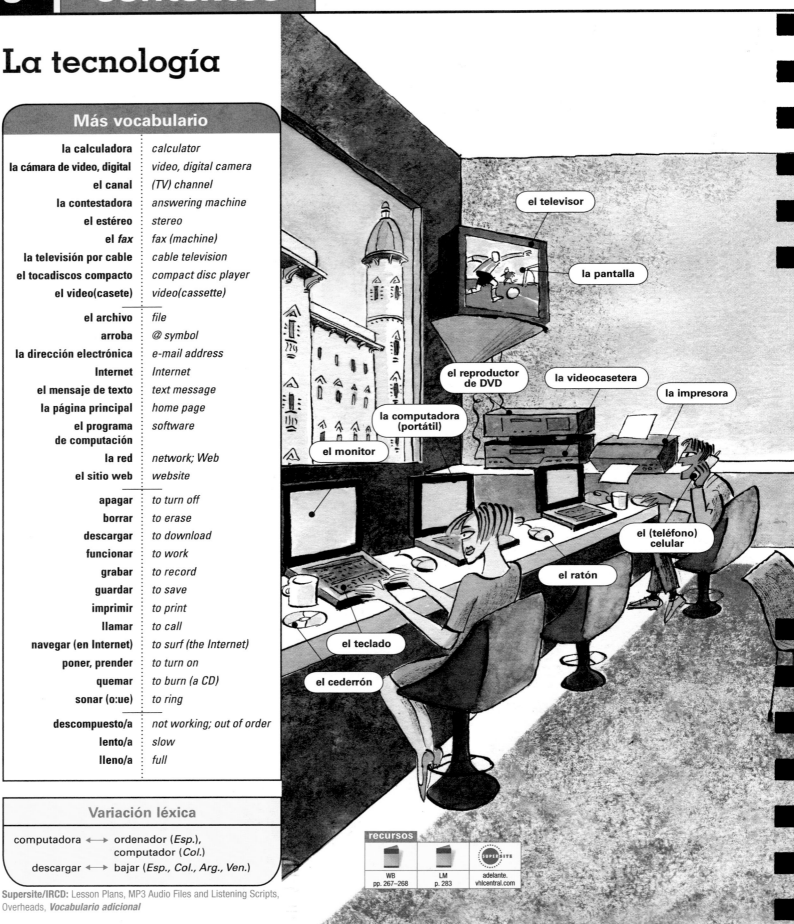

el televisor

la pantalla

el reproductor de DVD

la videocasetera

la impresora

la computadora (portátil)

el monitor

el (teléfono) celular

el ratón

el teclado

el cederrón

recursos

WB pp. 267–268

LM p. 283

SUPERSITE adelante. vhlcentral.com

Práctica  **1 2** Supersite/IRCD: MP3 Audio Files, Scripts

1

Escuchar 🎧 Escucha la conversación entre dos amigas. Después completa las oraciones.

1. María y Ana están en _____b_____.
   a. una tienda   b. un cibercafé   c. un restaurante
2. A María le encantan _____b_____.
   a. los celulares   b. las cámaras digitales   c. los cibercafés
3. Ana prefiere guardar las fotos en _____c_____.
   a. la pantalla   b. un archivo   c. un cederrón
4. María quiere tomar un café y _____c_____.
   a. poner la computadora   b. sacar fotos digitales
   c. navegar en Internet
5. Ana paga por el café y _____a_____.
   a. el uso de Internet   b. la impresora   c. el cederrón

2

¿Cierto o falso? 🎧 Escucha las oraciones e indica si lo que dice cada una es **cierto** o **falso**, según el dibujo.

1	cierto	5.	cierto
2.	falso	6.	falso
3.	falso	7.	cierto
4.	cierto	8.	falso

2 To challenge students, have them provide the correct information.

3

Oraciones Escribe oraciones usando estos elementos. Usa el pretérito y añade las palabras necesarias.

1. yo / descargar / fotos digitales / Internet
   Yo descargué las fotos digitales por Internet.
2. tú / apagar / televisor / diez / noche
   Tú apagaste el televisor a las diez de la noche.
3. Daniel y su esposa / comprar / computadora portátil / ayer
   Daniel y su esposa compraron una computadora portátil ayer.
4. Sara y yo / ir / cibercafé / para / navegar en Internet
   Sara y yo fuimos al cibercafé para navegar en Internet.
5. Jaime / decidir / comprar / reproductor de MP3
   Jaime decidió comprar un reproductor de MP3.
6. teléfono celular / sonar / pero / yo / no contestar
   El teléfono celular sonó, pero yo no contesté.

4

Preguntas Mira el dibujo y contesta las preguntas. Answers will vary.

1. ¿Qué tipo de café es?
2. ¿Cuántas impresoras hay? ¿Cuántos ratones?
3. ¿Por qué vinieron estas personas al café?
4. ¿Qué hace el camarero?
5. ¿Qué hace la mujer en la computadora? ¿Y el hombre?
6. ¿Qué máquinas están cerca del televisor?
7. ¿Dónde hay un cibercafé en tu comunidad?
8. ¿Por qué puedes tú necesitar un cibercafé?

Heritage Speakers Ask heritage speakers to describe their experiences with Spanish-language Web applications, such as e-mail or websites. Do they or their families regularly visit Spanish-language websites? Which ones?

Cibercafé CORRIENTES

el control remoto

el reproductor de MP3

el disco compacto

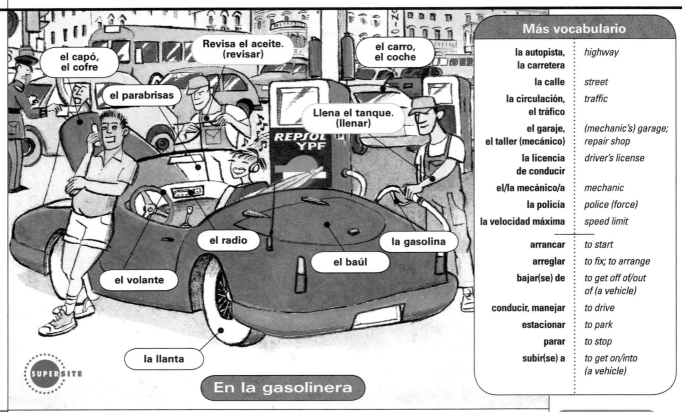

Más vocabulario

la autopista, la carretera	*highway*
la calle	*street*
la circulación, el tráfico	*traffic*
el garaje, el taller (mecánico)	*(mechanic's) garage; repair shop*
la licencia de conducir	*driver's license*
el/la mecánico/a	*mechanic*
la policía	*police (force)*
la velocidad máxima	*speed limit*
arrancar	*to start*
arreglar	*to fix; to arrange*
bajar(se) de	*to get off of/out of (a vehicle)*
conducir, manejar	*to drive*
estacionar	*to park*
parar	*to stop*
subir(se) a	*to get on/into (a vehicle)*

Labels in illustration: el capó, el cofre · Revisa el aceite. (revisar) · el carro, el coche · el parabrisas · Llena el tanque. (llenar) · REPSOL YPF · el radio · la gasolina · el baúl · el volante · la llanta · SUPERSITE · **En la gasolinera**

---

5   **Completar** Completa estas oraciones con las palabras correctas.

1. Para poder conducir legalmente, necesitas… una licencia de conducir.
2. Puedes poner las maletas en… el baúl.
3. Si tu carro no funciona, debes llevarlo a… un mecánico/taller.
4. Para llenar el tanque de tu coche, necesitas ir a… la gasolinera.
5. Antes de un viaje largo, es importante revisar… el aceite.
6. Otra palabra para autopista es… carretera.
7. Mientras hablas por teléfono celular, no es buena idea… manejar/conducir.
8. Otra palabra para coche es… carro.

¡LENGUA VIVA!

Aunque **carro** es el término que se usa en la mayoría de los países hispanos, no es el único. En España, por ejemplo, se dice **coche**, y en Argentina, Chile y Uruguay se dice **auto**.

5 Have students create three similar sentence starters for a partner to complete. Write some on the board and have the class complete them.

---

6   **Conversación** Completa la conversación con las palabras de la lista.

el aceite	la gasolina	llenar	revisar	el taller
el baúl	las llantas	manejar	el parabrisas	el volante

EMPLEADO   Bienvenido al (1)____taller____ mecánico Óscar. ¿En qué le puedo servir?

JUAN   Buenos días. Quiero (2)___llenar___ el tanque y revisar (3)__el aceite__, por favor.

EMPLEADO   Con mucho gusto. Si quiere, también le limpio (4)_el parabrisas_.

JUAN   Sí, gracias. Está un poquito sucio. La próxima semana tengo que (5)__manejar__ hasta Buenos Aires. ¿Puede cambiar (6)_las llantas_? Están gastadas (*worn*).

EMPLEADO   Claro que sí, pero voy a tardar (*it will take me*) un par de horas.

JUAN   Mejor regreso mañana. Ahora no tengo tiempo. ¿Cuánto le debo por (7)_la gasolina_?

EMPLEADO   Sesenta pesos. Y veinticinco por (8)__revisar__ y cambiar el aceite.

CONSULTA

For more information about **Buenos Aires**, see **Panorama**, p. 264.

6 Ask groups to discuss car troubles they have had. Possible subjects are: a visit to the mechanic, a car accident, getting a speeding ticket, etc. Write helpful vocabulary on the board. Ex: **ponerle una multa, exceder la velocidad máxima,** etc. Have each group pick the strangest or funniest story to share with the class.

Lección 5

Comunicación

7

Preguntas Trabajen en grupos para contestar estas preguntas. Después compartan sus respuestas con la clase. Answers will vary.

1. a. ¿Tienes un teléfono celular? ¿Para qué lo usas?
   b. ¿Qué utilizas más: el teléfono o el correo electrónico? ¿Por qué?
   c. En tu opinión, ¿cuáles son las ventajas (*advantages*) y desventajas de los diferentes modos de comunicación?
2. a. ¿Con qué frecuencia usas la computadora?
   b. ¿Para qué usas Internet?
   c. ¿Tienes tu propio sitio web? ¿Cómo es?
3. a. ¿Miras la televisión con frecuencia? ¿Qué programas ves?
   b. ¿Tienes televisión por cable? ¿Por qué?
   c. ¿Tienes una videocasetera? ¿Un reproductor de DVD? ¿Un reproductor de DVD en la computadora?
   d. ¿A través de (*By*) qué medio escuchas música? ¿Radio, estéreo, tocadiscos compacto, reproductor de MP3 o computadora?
4. a. ¿Tienes licencia de conducir?
   b. ¿Cuánto tiempo hace que la conseguiste?
   c. ¿Tienes carro? Descríbelo.
   d. ¿Llevas tu carro al taller? ¿Para qué?

NOTA CULTURAL

Algunos sitios web utilizan códigos para identificar su país de origen. Éstos son los códigos para algunos países hispanohablantes.

Argentina .ar
Colombia .co
España .es
México .mx
Venezuela .ve

CONSULTA

To review expressions like **hace…que**, see **Lección 4, Expresiones útiles**, p. 185.

8

Postal En parejas, lean la tarjeta postal. Después contesten las preguntas. Answers will vary.

19 de julio de 1979

Hola, Paco:

¡Saludos! Estamos de viaje por unas semanas. La Costa del Sol es muy bonita. No hemos encontrado (we haven't found) a tus amigos porque nunca están en casa cuando llamamos. El teléfono suena y suena y nadie contesta. Vamos a seguir llamando.

Sacamos muchas fotos muy divertidas. Cuando regresemos y las revelemos (get them developed), te las voy a enseñar. Las playas son preciosas. Hasta ahora el único problema fue que la oficina en la cual reservamos un carro perdió nuestros papeles y tuvimos que esperar mucho tiempo.

También tuvimos un pequeño problema con el hotel. La agencia de viajes nos reservó una habitación en un hotel que está muy lejos de todo. No podemos cambiarla, pero no me importa mucho. A pesar de eso, estamos contentos.

Tu hermana, Gabriela

Francisco Jiménez
San Lorenzo 3250
Rosario, Argentina 2000

8 For expansion, ask groups to write a postcard in which the problems are a direct result of the existence of technology, not its absence.

8 Possible answers:
1. Gabriela no encuentra a los amigos de Paco porque nunca están en casa, tuvo que esperar mucho por el carro y su hotel estaba muy lejos de todo. 2. No existen los mismos problemas porque existen las contestadoras y los teléfonos celulares, se puede reservar un carro en Internet y se puede buscar información sobre un hotel en la red antes del viaje.

Large Groups Stage a debate about the role of technology in today's world. Divide the class into two groups and assign each side a position. Propose this debate topic: **La tecnología: ¿beneficio o no?** Allow groups time to plan their arguments before staging the debate.

Supersite/IRCD: At this point you may want to present *Vocabulario adicional: Más vocabulario para el carro y la tecnología*.

1. ¿Cuáles son los problemas que ocurren en el viaje de Gabriela?
2. Con la tecnología de hoy, ¿existen los mismos problemas cuando se viaja? ¿Por qué?
3. Hagan una comparación entre la tecnología de los años 70 y 80 y la de hoy.
4. Imaginen que la hija de Gabriela escribe un correo electrónico sobre el mismo tema con fecha de hoy. Escriban ese correo, incorporando la tecnología de hoy (teléfonos celulares, Internet, cámaras digitales, etc.). Inventen nuevos problemas.

Tecnohombre, ¡mi héroe!

communication
cultures
NATIONAL
STANDARDS

El autobús se daña.

PERSONAJES

MAITE

INÉS

DON FRANCISCO

ÁLEX

JAVIER

SR. FONSECA

ÁLEX ¿Bueno? ... Con él habla... Ah, ¿cómo estás? ... Aquí, yo muy bien. Vamos para Ibarra. ¿Sabes lo que pasó? Esta tarde íbamos para Ibarra cuando Javier tuvo un accidente en el autobús. Se cayó y tuvimos que llevarlo a una clínica.

JAVIER Episodio veintiuno: Tecnohombre y los superamigos suyos salvan el mundo una vez más.

INÉS Oh, Tecnohombre, ¡mi héroe!

MAITE ¡Qué cómicos! Un día de éstos, ya van a ver...

ÁLEX Van a ver quién es realmente Tecnohombre. Mis superamigos y yo nos hablamos todos los días por el teléfono Internet, trabajando para salvar el mundo. Pero ahora, con su permiso, quiero escribirle un mensaje electrónico a mi mamá y navegar en la red un ratito.

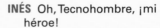

INÉS Pues... no sé... creo que es el alternador. A ver... sí... Mire, don Francisco... está quemado el alternador.

DON FRANCISCO Ah, sí. Pero aquí no podemos arreglarlo. Conozco a un mecánico pero está en Ibarra, a veinte kilómetros de aquí.

ÁLEX ¡Tecnohombre, a sus órdenes!

DON FRANCISCO ¡Eres la salvación, Álex! Llama al Sr. Fonseca al cinco, treinta y dos, cuarenta y siete, noventa y uno. Nos conocemos muy bien. Seguro que nos ayuda.

ÁLEX Buenas tardes. ¿Con el Sr. Fonseca por favor? ... Soy Álex Morales, cliente de Ecuatur. Le hablo de parte del señor Francisco Castillo... Es que íbamos para Ibarra y se nos dañó el autobús. ... Pensamos que es el... el alternador... Estamos a veinte kilómetros de la ciudad...

recursos

SUPERSITE

VM
pp. 279–280

adelante.
vhlcentral.com

Video Synopsis On the way to Ibarra, the bus breaks down. **Don Francisco** cannot locate the problem, but **Inés,** an experienced mechanic, diagnoses it as a burned-out alternator. **Álex** uses his cell phone to call **Don Francisco's** friend, **Sr. Fonseca,** who is a mechanic. **Maite** and **Don Francisco** praise **Inés** and **Álex** for saving the day.

Preview Show the **Tecnohombre, ¡mi héroe!** episode once without sound and have the class create a plot summary based on the visual cues. Then show the episode with sound and have the class make corrections and fill in any gaps in the plot summary.

Expresiones útiles Write some phone call scenarios on the board. Ex: **1. Llamas a la casa de tu mejor amigo/a, pero no está. 2. Llamas a tu profesor(a) de español para explicarle por qué no fuiste a clase.** Ask students to sit or stand in twos, back-to-back, and have them role-play the conversations, using phrases from **Expresiones útiles**. To simplify, you may want to have students brainstorm phrases for each situation. If nearly all students have cell phones, have them use the phones as props for this activity.

DON FRANCISCO Chicos, creo que tenemos un problema con el autobús. ¿Por qué no se bajan?

DON FRANCISCO Mmm, no veo el problema.

INÉS Cuando estaba en la escuela secundaria, trabajé en el taller de mi tío. Me enseñó mucho sobre mecánica. Por suerte, arreglé unos autobuses como éste.

DON FRANCISCO ¡No me digas!

SR. FONSECA Creo que va a ser mejor arreglar el autobús allí mismo. Tranquilo, enseguida salgo.

ÁLEX Buenas noticias. El señor Fonseca viene enseguida. Piensa que puede arreglar el autobús aquí mismo.

MAITE ¡La Mujer Mecánica y Tecnohombre, mis héroes!

DON FRANCISCO ¡Y los míos también!

Teaching Tip Draw attention to the phrases **nos hablamos** (video still 3), **llama al Sr. Fonseca** (video still 7), and **los míos** (video still 10). Provide one or two additional examples of reciprocal reflexive constructions, **tú** commands, and stressed possessive pronouns. Tell students they will learn more about these concepts in **Estructura**.

Extra Practice Make a photocopy of the **Fotonovela** Videoscript (Supersite/IRCD) and white out lesson vocabulary. Have students fill in the missing words as they watch the episode.

Expresiones útiles

Talking on the telephone

- **Aló./¿Bueno?/Diga.**
  Hello.
- **¿Quién habla?**
  Who is speaking?
- **¿De parte de quién?**
  Who is calling?
  Con él/ella habla.
  This is he/she.
  Le hablo de parte de Francisco Castillo.
  I'm speaking to you on behalf of Francisco Castillo.
- **¿Puedo dejar un recado?**
  May I leave a message?
  Está bien. Llamo más tarde.
  That's fine. I'll call later.

Talking about bus or car problems

- **¿Qué pasó?**
  What happened?
  Se nos dañó el autobús.
  The bus broke down.
  Se nos pinchó una llanta.
  We had a flat tire.
  Está quemado el alternador.
  The alternator is burned out.

Saying how far away things are

- **Está a veinte kilómetros de aquí.**
  It's twenty kilometers from here.
- **Estamos a veinte millas de la ciudad.**
  We're twenty miles from the city.

Expressing surprise

- **¡No me digas!**
  You don't say! (fam.)
- **¡No me diga!**
  You don't say! (form.)

Offering assistance

- **A sus órdenes.**
  At your service.

Additional vocabulary

- **aquí mismo**
  right here

¿Qué pasó?

1

Seleccionar Selecciona las respuestas que completan correctamente estas oraciones.

1. Álex quiere __b__.
   a. llamar a su mamá por teléfono celular b. escribirle a su mamá y navegar en la red
   c. hablar por teléfono Internet y navegar en la red
2. Se les dañó el autobús. Inés dice que __a__.
   a. el alternador está quemado b. se pinchó una llanta c. el taller está lejos
3. Álex llama al mecánico, el señor __c__.
   a. Castillo b. Ibarra c. Fonseca
4. Maite llama a Inés la "Mujer Mecánica" porque antes __a__.
   a. trabajaba en el taller de su tío b. arreglaba computadoras
   c. conocía a muchos mecánicos
5. El grupo está a __c__ de la ciudad.
   a. veinte millas b. veinte grados centígrados c. veinte kilómetros

2

Identificar Identifica quién puede decir estas oraciones.

1. Gracias a mi tío tengo un poco de experiencia
   arreglando autobuses. Inés
2. Sé manejar un autobús pero no sé arreglarlo.
   ¿Por qué no llamamos a mi amigo? don Francisco
3. Sabes, admiro mucho a la Mujer Mecánica y
   a Tecnohombre. Maite
4. Aló... Sí, ¿de parte de quién? Álex
5. El nombre de Tecnohombre fue idea mía.
   ¡Qué cómico!, ¿no? Javier

 JAVIER   ÁLEX

 MAITE

 INÉS   DON FRANCISCO

3

Problema mecánico Trabajen en parejas para representar los papeles de un(a) mecánico/a y un(a) cliente/a que está llamando al taller porque su carro está descompuesto. Usen las instrucciones como guía. Answers will vary.

Mecánico/a	Cliente/a
Contesta el teléfono con un saludo y el nombre del taller.	→ Saluda y explica que tu carro está descompuesto.
Pregunta qué tipo de problema tiene exactamente.	→ Explica que tu carro no arranca cuando hace frío.
Di que debe traer el carro al taller.	→ Pregunta cuándo puedes llevarlo.
Ofrece una hora para revisar el carro.	→ Acepta la hora que ofrece el/la mecánico/a.
Da las gracias y despídete.	→ Despídete y cuelga (*hang up*) el teléfono.

Ahora cambien los papeles y representen otra conversación. Ustedes son un(a) técnico/a y un(a) cliente/a. Usen estas ideas:

el celular no guarda mensajes   la impresora imprime muy lentamente
la computadora no descarga fotos   el reproductor de DVD está descompuesto

3 Have students sit back-to-back to simulate a real phone conversation. Remind students that speaking on the phone requires practice because one cannot see the speaker's facial expressions. Encourage students to listen for the gist and for key information, rather than trying to understand every word.

3 Possible conversation:
E1: ¿Bueno? Taller Mendoza.
E2: Buenos días. Tengo un problema con mi carro.
E1: ¿Qué pasó? ¿Cuál es el problema exactamente?
E2: El carro no arranca cuando hace frío. No sé si es el alternador.
E1: Tengo que revisarlo. ¿Puede venir al taller?
E2: Creo que sí. ¿A qué hora debo pasar?
E1: Tengo tiempo esta tarde a las tres.
E2: Muy bien. Es buena hora para mí también.
E1: Nos vemos a las tres. Gracias, y hasta esta tarde.
E2: Hasta luego.

Small Groups Have the class work in small groups to write questions about the **Fotonovela**. Have each group hand its questions to another group, which will write the answers. Ex: **G1: ¿A quién llamó Álex? G2: Álex llamó al señor Fonseca, el mecánico**.

Extra Practice Have each student choose one of the **Fotonovela** characters and prepare a five- to six-sentence summary of the day's events from that person's point of view. Have a few volunteers read their summaries to the class; the class will guess which character would have given each summary.

NATIONAL STANDARDS · comparisons

Heritage Speakers Ask heritage speakers to come up with additional sentences to exemplify each point in the chart. Have them write their sentences on the board without accent marks. Call on volunteers to determine which words, if any, require written accents.

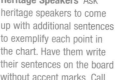

Teaching Tips
• If necessary, briefly review the information about written accents in **Lección 4**, p. 187.
• Emphasize the difference in stress between **por qué** and **porque**.
• Have students work in pairs to explain which words in the **Práctica** activity need written accents and why.

Extra Practice Add an auditory aspect to this **Ortografía** section. Prepare a series of mini-dialogues. Slowly read each one aloud, pausing to allow students to write. Then, in pairs, have students check their work. Ex: 1. —¿**Ésta** es tu cámara? —Sí, papá la trajo de **Japón** para mí. 2. —¿**Dónde** encontraste mi mochila? —¡Pues, donde la dejaste! 3. —¿**Cuándo** visitó Buenos Aires Mario? —Yo sé que Laura fue **allí** el año pasado, ¿pero cuándo fue él? ¡Ni idea! 4. —¿Me quieres explicar por qué llegas tarde? —Porque mi carro está descompuesto.

Ortografía
La acentuación de palabras similares

 SUPERSITE Supersite/IRCD: MP3 Audio Files, Listening Scripts

Although accent marks usually indicate which syllable in a word is stressed, they are also used to distinguish between words that have the same or similar spellings.

Lección 5

Él maneja el coche.   **Sí, voy** si quieres.

Although one-syllable words do not usually carry written accents, some *do* have accent marks to distinguish them from words that have the same spelling but different meanings.

Sé cocinar.   Se baña.   ¿Tomas té?   Te duermes.

Sé (*I know*) and **té** (*tea*) have accent marks to distinguish them from the pronouns **se** and **te**.

para mí   mi cámara   Tú lees.   tu estéreo

Mí (*Me*) and **tú** (*you*) have accent marks to distinguish them from the possessive adjectives **mi** and **tu**.

¿Por qué vas?   Voy porque quiero.

Several words of more than one syllable also have accent marks to distinguish them from words that have the same or similar spellings.

Éste es rápido.   Este módem es rápido.

Demonstrative pronouns have accent marks to distinguish them from demonstrative adjectives.

¿Cuándo fuiste?   Fui cuando me llamó.
¿Dónde trabajas?   Voy al taller donde trabajo.

Adverbs have accent marks when they are used to convey a question.

Práctica Marca los acentos en las palabras que los necesitan.

ANA   Alo, soy Ana. ¿Que tal? Aló/¿Qué?
JUAN Hola, pero... ¿por que me llamas tan tarde? ¿por qué?
ANA   Porque mañana tienes que llevarme a la universidad. Mi auto esta dañado. está
JUAN ¿Como se daño? ¿Cómo?/dañó
ANA   Se daño el sabado. Un vecino (*neighbor*) choco con (*crashed into*) el. dañó/sábado/chocó/él

Crucigrama Utiliza las siguientes pistas (*clues*) para completar el crucigrama. ¡Ojo con los acentos!

Horizontales
1. Él _____ levanta.
4. No voy _____ no puedo.
7. Tú _____ acuestas.
9. ¿_____ es el examen?
10. Quiero este video y _____.

Verticales
2. ¿Cómo _____ usted?
3. Eres _____ mi hermano.
5. ¿_____ tal?
6. Me gusta _____ suéter.
8. Navego _____ la red.

	¹S	²E			³C			
		S		⁴P	O	R	⁵Q	⁶E
		⁷T	⁸E	M	U		S	
⁹C	U	Á	N	D	O		¹⁰É	S	E

Game Divide the class into two teams. Assign a member of each team one of two similar words (Ex: **se/sé**). Provide one minute for students to write a sentence using the word. Award one point for each correct usage. Continue until all students have had a turn.

El teléfono celular

¿Cómo te comunicas con tus amigos y familia? En países como Argentina y España, el servicio de teléfono común° es bastante caro, por lo que el **teléfono celular**, más accesible y barato, es el favorito de mucha gente.

El servicio más popular entre los jóvenes es el sistema de tarjetas prepagadas°, porque no requiere de un contrato ni de cuotas° extras. En muchas ciudades puedes encontrar estas tarjetas en cualquier° tienda. Para tener un servicio todavía más económico, mucha gente usa el mensaje de texto en sus teléfonos celulares. Un mensaje típico de un joven frugal podría° ser, por ejemplo: **N LLMS X TL. ¡S MY KRO!** (No llames por teléfono. ¡Es muy caro!)

Los celulares de la década de 1980 eran grandes e incómodos, y estaban limitados al uso de la voz°. Los celulares de hoy tienen muchas funciones más. Se pueden usar como despertadores, como cámara de fotos y hasta para leer y escribir correo electrónico. Sin embargo°, la función favorita de muchos jóvenes es la de poder descargar música de Internet en sus teléfonos para poder escucharla cuando lo deseen°, es decir, ¡casi todo el tiempo!

Mensajes de texto en español

¿K TL?	¿Qué tal?	**CONT, XFA**	Contesta, por favor.
STY S3A2	Estoy estresado°.	**TB**	también
TQ MXO.	Te quiero mucho.	**¿A K ORA S**	¿A qué hora es
A2	Adiós.	**L FSTA?**	la fiesta?
¿XQ?	¿Por qué?	**M DBS $**	Me debes dinero.
GNL	genial	**5MNTRIOS**	Sin comentarios.
¡K RSA!	¡Qué risa!°	**¿K ACS?**	¿Qué haces?
¡QT 1 BD!	¡Que tengas un buen día!°	**STY N L BBLIOTK**	Estoy en la biblioteca.
		1 BSO	Un beso.
SALU2, PP	Saludos, Pepe.	**NS VMS + TRD**	Nos vemos más tarde.

común *ordinary* prepagadas *prepaid* cuotas *fees* cualquier *any* podría *could* voz *voice* Sin embargo *However* cuando lo deseen *whenever they wish* estresado *stressed out* ¡Qué risa! *So funny!* ¡Que tengas un buen día! *Have a nice day!*

1 **¿Cierto o falso?** Indica si lo que dicen estas oraciones es **cierto** o **falso**. Corrige la información falsa.

1. El teléfono común es un servicio caro en Argentina. Cierto.

2. Muchas personas usan más el teléfono celular que el teléfono común. Cierto.

3. Es difícil encontrar tarjetas prepagadas en las ciudades hispanas. Falso. Puedes encontrar tarjetas prepagadas en cualquier tienda.

4. Los jóvenes suelen (*tend to*) usar el mensaje de texto para pagar menos por el servicio de teléfono celular. Cierto.

5. Los primeros teléfonos celulares eran muy cómodos y pequeños. Falso. Los primeros teléfonos celulares eran incómodos y grandes.

6. En la década de 1980, los teléfonos celulares tenían muchas funciones. Falso. En la década de 1980, los celulares estaban limitados al uso de la voz.

7. **STY S3A2** significa "Te quiero mucho". Falso. **STY S3A2** significa "Estoy estresado".

Lección 5

ASÍ SE DICE
La tecnología

los audífonos (Méx., Col.), los auriculares (Arg.), los cascos (Esp.)	*headset; earphones*
el móvil (Esp.)	**el celular**
(teléfono) deslizable	*slider (phone)*
inalámbrico/a	*cordless; wireless*
el manos libres (Amér. S.)	*hands-free system*
(teléfono) plegable	*flip (phone)*

EL MUNDO HISPANO
Las bicimotos

○ **Argentina** El ciclomotor se usa mayormente° para repartir a domicilio° comidas y medicinas.

○ **Perú** La motito se usa mucho para el reparto a domicilio de pan fresco todos los días.

○ **México** La *Vespa* se usa para evitar° el tráfico en grandes ciudades.

○ **España** La población usa el *Vespino* para ir y volver al trabajo cada día.

○ **Puerto Rico** Una *scooter* es el medio de transporte favorito en las zonas rurales.

○ **República Dominicana** Las moto-taxis son el medio de transporte más económico, ¡pero no olvides el casco°!

mayormente *mainly* repartir a domicilio *home delivery of* evitar *to avoid* casco *helmet*

PERFIL
Los cibercafés

Hoy día, en casi cualquier ciudad grande latinoamericana te puedes encontrar en cada esquina° un nuevo tipo de café: **el cibercafé**. Allí uno puede disfrutar de° un refresco o un café mientras navega en Internet, escribe correo electrónico o chatea° en múltiples foros virtuales.

De hecho°, el negocio° del cibercafé está mucho más desarrollado° en Latinoamérica que en los Estados Unidos. En una ciudad hispana, es común ver varios en una misma cuadra°. Los extranjeros piensan que no puede haber

suficientes clientes para todos, pero los cibercafés ofrecen servicios especializados que permiten su coexistencia. Por ejemplo, mientras que el cibercafé Videomax atrae° a los niños con videojuegos, el Conécta-T ofrece servicio de chat con cámara para jóvenes, y el Mundo° Ejecutivo atrae a profesionales, todo en la misma calle.

esquina *corner* disfrutar de *enjoy* chatea *chat (from the English verb to chat)* De hecho *In fact* negocio *business* desarrollado *developed* cuadra *(city) block* atrae *attracts* Mundo *World*

Conexión Internet

¿Qué sitios web son populares entre los jóvenes hispanos?	Go to **adelante.vhlcentral.com** to find more cultural information related to this **Cultura** section.

ACTIVIDADES

2 **Comprensión** Responde a las preguntas.

1. ¿Cuáles son tres formas de decir *headset*? los audífonos, los auriculares, los cascos
2. ¿Para qué se usan las bicimotos en Argentina? para repartir a domicilio comidas y medicinas
3. ¿Qué puedes hacer mientras tomas un refresco en un cibercafé? Puedes navegar en Internet, escribir correo electrónico o chatear.
4. ¿Qué tienen de especial los cibercafés en Latinoamérica? Ofrecen servicios especializados.

3 **¿Cómo te comunicas?** Escribe un párrafo breve en donde expliques qué utilizas para comunicarte con tus amigos/as (correo electrónico, teléfono, etc.) y de qué hablan cuando se llaman por teléfono. Answers will vary.

3 Have students exchange their paragraphs with a partner for peer editing.

recursos

adelante.vhlcentral.com

5.1 Familiar commands (SUPERSITE)

ANTE TODO In Spanish, the command forms are used to give orders or advice. You use **tú** commands (**mandatos familiares**) when you want to give an order or advice to someone you normally address with the familiar **tú**.

Affirmative tú commands

Infinitive	Present tense él/ella form	Affirmative tú command
hablar	habla	**habla** (tú)
guardar	guarda	**guarda** (tú)
prender	prende	**prende** (tú)
volver	vuelve	**vuelve** (tú)
pedir	pide	**pide** (tú)
imprimir	imprime	**imprime** (tú)

▶ Affirmative **tú** commands usually have the same form as the **él/ella** form of the present indicative.

Guarda el documento antes de cerrarlo.
Save the document before closing it.

Imprime tu tarea para la clase de inglés.
Print your homework for English class.

▶ There are eight irregular affirmative **tú** commands.

Irregular affirmative tú commands

decir	**di**	salir	**sal**
hacer	**haz**	ser	**sé**
ir	**ve**	tener	**ten**
poner	**pon**	venir	**ven**

¡**Sal** de aquí ahora mismo!
Leave here at once!

Haz los ejercicios.
Do the exercises.

▶ Since **ir** and **ver** have the same **tú** command (**ve**), context will determine the meaning.

Ve al cibercafé con Yolanda.
Go to the cybercafé with Yolanda.

Ve ese programa... es muy interesante.
See that program... it's very interesting.

> Apaga ese walkman y contesta el teléfono.

> ¡No me digas!

Lección 5

Teaching Tip Contrast the negative forms of **tú** commands by giving an affirmative command followed by a negative command. Ex: _____, **camina a la puerta. No camines rápidamente.** Write the examples on the board as you go along.

Negative tú commands

Infinitive	Present tense yo form	Negative tú command
hablar	hablo	**no hables** (tú)
guardar	guardo	**no guardes** (tú)
prender	prendo	**no prendas** (tú)
volver	vuelvo	**no vuelvas** (tú)
pedir	pido	**no pidas** (tú)

▶ The negative **tú** commands are formed by dropping the final **-o** of the **yo** form of the present tense. For **-ar** verbs, add **-es**. For **-er** and **-ir** verbs, add **-as**.

> Héctor, **no pares** el carro aquí.
> _Héctor, don't stop the car here._

> **No prendas** la computadora todavía.
> _Don't turn on the computer yet._

▶ Verbs with irregular **yo** forms maintain the same irregularity in their negative **tú** commands. These verbs include **conducir, conocer, decir, hacer, ofrecer, oír, poner, salir, tener, traducir, traer, venir,** and **ver**.

> **No pongas** el cederrón en la computadora.
> _Don't put the CD-ROM in the computer._

> **No conduzcas** tan rápido.
> _Don't drive so fast._

▶ Note also that stem-changing verbs keep their stem changes in negative **tú** commands.

> No p**ie**rdas tu celular.
> _Don't lose your cell phone._

> No v**ue**lvas a esa gasolinera.
> _Don't go back to that gas station._

> No rep**i**tas las instrucciones.
> _Don't repeat the instructions._

▶ Verbs ending in **-car, -gar,** and **-zar** have a spelling change in the negative **tú** commands.

sa**car**	c → **qu**	no sa**qu**es
apa**gar**	g → **gu**	no apa**gu**es
almor**zar**	z → **c**	no almuer**c**es

▶ The following verbs have irregular negative **tú** commands.

Irregular negative tú commands

dar	**no des**
estar	**no estés**
ir	**no vayas**
saber	**no sepas**
ser	**no seas**

¡ATENCIÓN!

In affirmative commands, reflexive, indirect, and direct object pronouns are always attached to the end of the verb. In negative commands, these pronouns always precede the verb.

Bórralos./No los borres.

Escríbeles un correo electrónico./**No les escribas** un correo electrónico.

• • •

When a pronoun is attached to an affirmative command that has two or more syllables, an accent mark is added to maintain the original stress:

borra → bórralos

prende → préndela

imprime → imprímelo

---

recursos

WB pp. 269–270

LM p. 285

SUPERSITE
adelante.
vhlcentral.com

¡INTÉNTALO! Indica los mandatos familiares afirmativos y negativos de estos verbos.

1. correr — _Corre_ más rápido. — No _corras_ más rápido.
2. llenar — _Llena_ el tanque. — No _llenes_ el tanque.
3. salir — _Sal_ ahora. — No _salgas_ ahora.
4. descargar — _Descarga_ ese documento. — No _descargues_ ese documento.
5. levantarse — _Levántate_ temprano. — No _te levantes_ temprano.
6. hacerlo — _Hazlo_ ya. — No _lo hagas_ ahora.

Extra Practice Ask volunteers to convert affirmative **tú** commands with reflexive and object pronouns into negative commands, and vice versa. Ex: **Imprímelo. (No lo imprimas.)**

Práctica

1 **Completar** Tu mejor amigo no entiende nada de tecnología y te pide ayuda. Completa los comentarios de tu amigo con el mandato de cada verbo.

1. No ___vengas___ en una hora. ___Ven___ ahora mismo. (venir)
2. ___Haz___ tu tarea después. No la ___hagas___ ahora. (hacer)
3. No ___vayas___ a la tienda a comprar papel para la impresora. ___Ve___ a la cafetería a comprarme algo de comer. (ir)
4. No ___me digas___ que no puedes abrir un archivo. ___Dime___ que el programa de computación funciona sin problemas. (decirme)
5. ___Sé___ generoso con tu tiempo, y no ___seas___ antipático si no entiendo fácilmente. (ser)
6. ___Ten___ mucha paciencia y no ___tengas___ prisa. (tener)
7. ___Apaga___ tu teléfono celular, pero no ___apagues___ la computadora. (apagar)

2 **Cambiar** Pedro y Marina no pueden ponerse de acuerdo (*agree*) cuando viajan en su carro. Cuando Pedro dice que algo es necesario, Marina expresa una opinión diferente. Usa la información entre paréntesis para formar las órdenes que Marina le da a Pedro.

> **modelo**
> **Pedro:** Necesito revisar el aceite del carro. (seguir hasta el próximo pueblo)
> **Marina:** *No revises el aceite del carro. Sigue hasta el próximo pueblo.*

1. Necesito conducir más rápido. (parar el carro) No conduzcas más rápido. Para el carro.
2. Necesito poner el radio. (hablarme) No pongas el radio. Háblame.
3. Necesito almorzar ahora. (comer más tarde) No almuerces ahora. Come más tarde.
4. Necesito sacar los discos compactos. (manejar con cuidado) No saques… Maneja…
5. Necesito estacionar el carro en esta calle. (pensar en otra opción) No estaciones… Piensa…
6. Necesito volver a esa gasolinera. (arreglar el carro en un taller) No vuelvas… Arregla…
7. Necesito leer el mapa. (pedirle ayuda a aquella señora) No leas… Pídele…
8. Necesito dormir en el carro. (acostarse en una cama) No duermas… Acuéstate…

3 **Problemas** Tú y tu compañero/a trabajan en el centro de computadoras de la universidad. Muchos estudiantes están llamando con problemas. Denles órdenes para ayudarlos a resolverlos.
Answers will vary. Suggested answers:

> **modelo**
> **Problema:** No veo nada en la pantalla.
> **Tu respuesta:** Prende la pantalla de tu computadora.

| apagar… | descargar… | grabar… | imprimir… | prender… |
| borrar… | funcionar… | guardar… | navegar… | quemar… |

1. No me gusta este programa de computación. Descarga otro.
2. Tengo miedo de perder mi documento. Guárdalo.
3. Prefiero leer este sitio web en papel. Imprímelo.
4. Mi correo electrónico funciona muy lentamente. Borra los mensajes más viejos.
5. Busco información sobre los gauchos de Argentina. Navega en Internet. ◄
6. Tengo demasiados archivos en mi computadora. Borra algunos archivos.
7. Mi computadora se congeló (*froze*). Apaga la computadora y luego préndela.
8. Quiero ver las fotos del cumpleaños de mi hermana. Descárgalas.

3 To simplify, review the vocabulary in the word bank by asking students to make associations with each word. Ex: **imprimir** (documento), **descargar** (programa)

1 Continue this activity orally with the class, using regular verbs. Call out a negative command and designate individuals to make corresponding affirmative commands. Ex: **No sirvas la comida ahora. (Sirve la comida ahora./Sírvela ahora.)**

TPR Have the class stand in a circle. Name an infinitive and toss a foam or paper ball to a student. He or she will give the affirmative **tú** command and throw the ball to another student, who will provide the negative form.

Pairs Have pairs imagine that they are in charge of a computer lab at a university in a Spanish-speaking country. Have them make a handout of four things students must do and four things they must not do while in the lab. Instruct them to use **tú** commands throughout. Then, write **Mandatos afirmativos** and **Mandatos negativos** on the board and ask individuals to write one of their commands in the appropriate column.

NOTA CULTURAL

Los gauchos (*nomadic cowboys*), conocidos por su habilidad (*skill*) para montar caballos y utilizar lazos, viven en la región más extensa de Argentina, la Patagonia. Esta región ocupa casi la mitad (*half*) de la superficie (*land area*) del país.

Comunicación

4 Have volunteers report to the class what they were asked to do, what they did, and what they did not do.

4 **Órdenes** Circula por la clase e intercambia mandatos negativos y afirmativos con tus compañeros/as. Debes seguir las órdenes que ellos te dan o reaccionar apropiadamente. Answers will vary.

4 To simplify, ask students to brainstorm a list of what they might ask their classmates to do.

> **modelo**
>
> **Estudiante 1:** Dame todo tu dinero.
> **Estudiante 2:** No, no quiero dártelo. Muéstrame tu cuaderno.
> **Estudiante 1:** Aquí está.
> **Estudiante 3:** Ve a la pizarra y escribe tu nombre.
> **Estudiante 4:** No quiero. Hazlo tú.

5 Ask comprehension questions about the ad. **¿Qué se anuncia? (cursos de informática) ¿Cómo puedes informarte? (llamar por teléfono) ¿Dónde se encuentra este tipo de anuncio? (en periódicos y revistas)**

5 **Anuncios** Miren este anuncio. Luego, en grupos pequeños, preparen tres anuncios adicionales para tres escuelas que compiten (*compete*) con ésta. Answers will vary.

INFORMÁTICA ARGENTINA

Toma nuestros cursos y aprende a usar la computadora

abre y lee tus archivos

imprime tus documentos

entra al campo de la tecnología

¡Ponte en contacto con nosotros llamando al **11-4-129-1508** HOY!

Síntesis

6 **¡Tanto que hacer!** Tu profesor(a) te va a dar una lista de diligencias (*errands*). Algunas las hiciste tú y algunas las hizo tu compañero/a. Las diligencias que ya hicieron tienen esta marca ✔. Pero quedan cuatro diligencias por hacer. Dale mandatos a tu compañero/a, y él/ella responde para confirmar si hay que hacerla o si ya la hizo. Answers will vary.

Supersite/IRCD: Information Gap Activities

Pairs Have pairs prepare a conversation between two roommates who are getting ready for a party. Students should use affirmative and negative **tú** commands. Ex: **E1: ¡Sal del baño ya! E2: ¡No me grites!**

> **modelo**
>
> **Estudiante 1:** Llena el tanque.
> **Estudiante 2:** Ya llené el tanque. / ¡Ay, no! Tenemos que
> llenar el tanque.

Extra Practice Add an auditory aspect to this grammar practice. Prepare series of commands that would be said to certain individuals. Write the names on the board and read each series aloud. Have students match the commands to each name. Ex: **No comas eso. Dame el periódico. No te subas al sofá. Tráeme las pantuflas. (un perro)**

5.2 | Por and para SUPERSITE

ANTE TODO   Unlike English, Spanish has two words that mean *for*: **por** and **para**. These two prepositions are not interchangeable. Study the following charts to see how they are used.

TPR Label one half of the classroom **por**, the other half **para**. Write a sentence on the board, omitting the preposition, and ask students to go to the appropriate half of the classroom.

Es para usted. Es un cliente de don Paco.

Álex habla por teléfono.

Ex: **Tengo que leer la lección 5 _____ mañana.** (para); **Jimena trabaja _____ la noche.** (por) Avoid cases where either **por** or **para** could be used.

Por is used to indicate...

1. Motion or a general location . . . .
(around, through, along, by)

La excursión nos llevó **por** el centro.
The tour took us through downtown.

Pasamos **por** el parque y **por** el río.
We passed by the park and along the river.

2. Duration of an action . . . .
(for, during, in)

Estuve en la Patagonia **por** un mes.
I was in Patagonia for a month.

Ana navegó la red **por** la tarde.
Ana surfed the net in the afternoon.

3. Reason or motive for an action . . . .
(because of, on account of, on behalf of)

Lo hizo **por** su familia.
She did it on behalf of her family.

Papá llegó a casa tarde **por** el tráfico.
Dad arrived home late because of the traffic.

4. Object of a search . . . .
(for, in search of)

Vengo **por** ti a las ocho.
I'm coming for you at eight.

Javier fue **por** su cámara digital.
Javier went in search of his digital camera.

5. Means by which something is done . . .
(by, by way of, by means of)

Ellos viajan **por** la autopista.
They travel by (by way of) the highway.

¿Hablaste con la policía **por** teléfono?
Did you talk to the police by (on the) phone?

6. Exchange or substitution . . . .
(for, in exchange for)

Le di dinero **por** la videocasetera.
I gave him money for the VCR.

Muchas gracias **por** el cederrón.
Thank you very much for the CD-ROM.

7. Unit of measure . . . .
(per, by)

José manejaba a 120 kilómetros **por** hora.
José was driving 120 kilometers per hour.

¡ATENCIÓN!

Por is also used in several idiomatic expressions, including:
por aquí *around here*
por ejemplo *for example*
por eso *that's why; therefore*
por fin *finally*

AYUDA

Remember that when giving an exact time, **de** is used instead of **por** before **la mañana, la tarde,** or **la noche**.
La clase empieza a las nueve **de** la mañana.

• • •

In addition to **por**, **durante** is also commonly used to mean *for* when referring to time.
Esperé al mecánico **durante** cincuenta minutos.

Video Replay the *Fotonovela* episode and pause to discuss each example of **por** and **para**. Ask students to determine the corresponding use in the charts on pp. 250-251.

Lección 5

Teaching Tip Create a matching activity for the uses of **para**. Write sentences exemplifying each use of **para** listed, but not in the order they are given in the text. Ex: **1. El señor López compró el Ferrari para Mariana. 2. Este autobús va para Corrientes. 3. Para don Francisco, conducir un autobús no es nada difícil. 4. Don Francisco trabaja para Ecuatur. 5. Estudia para llegar a ser ingeniero. 6. El baúl es para las maletas. 7. Tengo que pagar la multa para el lunes.** Call on individual students to match each sentence with its usage.

Game Play **Concentración**. Create one card for each use of **por** and **para**, and one card with a sentence illustrating each use, for a total of 28 cards. Shuffle the cards and lay them face down. Then, taking turns, students uncover two cards at a time, trying to match a use to a sentence. The student with the most matches wins.

Para is used to indicate...

1. **Destination** . . . .
   (*toward, in the direction of*)

   Salimos **para** Córdoba el sábado.
   We are leaving for Córdoba on Saturday.

2. **Deadline or a specific time in the future** . . .
   (*by, for*)

   Él va a arreglar el carro **para** el viernes.
   He will fix the car by Friday.

3. **Purpose or goal** + [*infinitive*] . . . .
   (*in order to*)

   Juan estudia **para** (ser) mecánico.
   Juan is studying to be a mechanic.

4. **Purpose** + [*noun*] . . . .
   (*for, used for*)

   Es una llanta **para** el carro.
   It's a tire for the car.

5. **The recipient of something** . . . .
   (*for*)

   Compré una impresora **para** mi hijo.
   I bought a printer for my son.

6. **Comparison with others or an opinion** . .
   (*for, considering*)

   Para un joven, es demasiado serio.
   For a young person, he is too serious.

   Para mí, esta lección no es difícil.
   For me, this lesson isn't difficult.

7. **In the employ of** . . . .
   (*for*)

   Sara trabaja **para** Telecom Argentina.
   Sara works for Telecom Argentina.

► In many cases it is grammatically correct to use either **por** or **para** in a sentence. The meaning of the sentence is different, however, depending on which preposition is used.

Caminé **por** el parque.
I walked through the park.

Caminé **para** el parque.
I walked to (toward) the park.

Trabajó **por** su padre.
He worked for (in place of) his father.

Trabajó **para** su padre.
He worked for his father('s company).

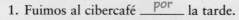

¡INTÉNTALO! Completa estas oraciones con las preposiciones **por** o **para.**

1. Fuimos al cibercafé __por__ la tarde.
2. Necesitas un módem __para__ navegar en la red.
3. Entraron __por__ la puerta.
4. Quiero un pasaje __para__ Buenos Aires.
5. __Para__ arrancar el carro, necesito la llave.
6. Arreglé el televisor __para__ mi amigo.
7. Estuvieron nerviosos __por__ el examen.
8. ¿No hay una gasolinera __por__ aquí?
9. El reproductor de MP3 es __para__ usted.
10. Juan está enfermo. Tengo que trabajar __por__ él.
11. Estuvimos en Canadá __por__ dos meses.
12. __Para__ mí, el español es fácil.
13. Tengo que estudiar la lección __para__ el lunes.
14. Voy a ir __por__ la carretera.
15. Compré dulces __para__ mi novia.
16. Compramos el auto __por__ un buen precio.

recursos

WB
pp. 271–272

LM
p. 286

SUPERSITE
adelante.
vhlcentral.com

Extra Practice For visual learners, bring in magazine pictures and have students write sentences about them using **por** and **para**. Ex: **Este señor hace la cena para su esposa.**

Práctica

1

Completar Completa este párrafo con las preposiciones **por** o **para**.

El mes pasado mi esposo y yo hicimos un viaje a Buenos Aires y sólo pagamos dos mil dólares (1)__por__ los pasajes. Estuvimos en Buenos Aires (2)__por__ una semana y paseamos por toda la ciudad. Durante el día caminamos (3)__por__ la plaza San Martín, el microcentro y el barrio de La Boca, donde viven muchos artistas. (4)__Por__ la noche fuimos a una tanguería, que es una especie de teatro, (5)__para__ mirar a la gente bailar tango. Dos días después decidimos hacer una excursión (6)__por__ las pampas (7)__para__ ver el paisaje y un rodeo con gauchos. Alquilamos (*We rented*) un carro y manejamos (8)__por__ todas partes y pasamos unos días muy agradables. El último día que estuvimos en Buenos Aires fuimos a Galerías Pacífico (9)__para__ comprar recuerdos (*souvenirs*) (10)__para__ nuestros hijos y nietos. Compramos tantos regalos que tuvimos que pagar impuestos (*duties*) en la aduana al regresar.

> **1** Have students refer to the charts on pp. 250–251 to identify each use of **por** and **para** in the paragraph. In pairs, have them write additional sentences for the remaining uses (**por:** reason or motive, object of search, means, unit of measure / **para:** destination, deadline, purpose + [*noun*], comparison, employment).

2

Oraciones Crea oraciones originales con los elementos de las columnas. Une los elementos usando **por** o **para**.   Answers will vary.

> **2** Model the activity by creating a sentence with an element from each column. Emphasize that the columns can be combined in several ways. Ex: **Fueron a Buenos Aires por tres días para divertirse.**

modelo
> Fuimos a Mar del Plata por razones de salud para visitar a un especialista. ◀

(no) fuimos al mercado	por/para	comprar frutas	por/para	¿?
(no) fuimos a las montañas	por/para	tres días	por/para	¿?
(no) fuiste a Mar del Plata	por/para	razones de salud	por/para	¿?
(no) fueron a Buenos Aires	por/para	tomar el sol	por/para	¿?

3

Describir Usa **por** o **para** y el tiempo presente para describir estos dibujos.   Answers will vary.

1. _____   2. _____   3. _____

4. _____   5. _____   6. _____

> **Large Group** Have students use **por** and **para** to create ten questions for a survey about technology. Ex: **¿Por cuántos minutos al día hablas por teléfono?** Have students administer their survey to five different people in the room. Follow up with class discussion.

> **3** Have students take turns with a partner to expand their descriptions to a short oral narrative. After each drawing has been described, ask students to pick two or three of their narratives and link them into a story.

Comunicación

4 Have students create new sentences, employing additional uses of **por** and **para**.

4

Descripciones Usa **por** o **para** y completa estas frases de manera lógica. Luego, compara tus respuestas con las de un(a) compañero/a. Answers will vary.

1. En casa, hablo con mis amigos…
2. Mi padre/madre trabaja…
3. Ayer fui al taller…
4. Los miércoles tengo clases…
5. A veces voy a la biblioteca…

6. Esta noche tengo que estudiar…
7. Necesito… dólares…
8. Compré un regalo…
9. Mi mejor amigo/a estudia…
10. Necesito hacer la tarea…

5

Situación En parejas, dramaticen esta situación. Utilicen muchos ejemplos de **por** y **para**.

Answers will vary.

5 Ask students about the car in the picture. Ex: ¿Te gusta este carro? ¿Cuánto se paga por un carro así? ¿A cuántas millas por hora corre este carro?

5 Show a picture of an old used car and ask students to create a new conversation. The parents are offering to buy their son/daughter this car instead of the one shown in the activity.

Hijo/a		**Padre/Madre**
Pídele dinero a tu padre/madre.	→	Pregúntale a tu hijo/a para qué lo necesita.
Dile que quieres comprar un carro.	→	Pregúntale por qué necesita un carro.
Explica tres razones por las que necesitas un carro.	→	Explica por qué sus razones son buenas o malas.
Dile que por no tener un carro tu vida es muy difícil.	→	Decide si vas a darle el dinero y explica por qué.

Síntesis

6

Una subasta (*auction*) Cada estudiante debe traer a la clase un objeto o una foto del objeto para vender. En grupos, túrnense para ser el/la vendedor(a) y los postores (*bidders*). Para empezar, el/la vendedor(a) describe el objeto y explica para qué se usa y por qué alguien debe comprarlo. Answers will vary.

modelo

Vendedora: Aquí tengo una videocasetera Sony. Pueden usar esta videocasetera para ver películas en su casa o para grabar sus programas favoritos. Sólo hace un año que la compré y todavía funciona perfectamente. ¿Quién ofrece $ 1.500 para empezar?

Postor(a) 1: Pero las videocaseteras son anticuadas y no tienen buena imagen. Te doy $ 5,00.

Vendedora: Ah, pero ésta es muy especial porque viene con el video de mi fiesta de quinceañera.

Postor(a) 2: ¡Yo te doy $ 2.000!

Extra Practice For students still having trouble distinguishing between **por** and **para**, have them create a mnemonic device, like a story or chant, for remembering the different uses. Ex: **Vine por la tarde y busqué por el parque, por el río y por el centro. Busqué por horas. Viajé por carro, por tren y por avión.** Do the same for **para**.

Lección 5

5.3 Reciprocal reflexives

ANTE TODO   In **Lección 1**, you learned that reflexive verbs indicate that the subject of a sentence does the action to itself. Reciprocal reflexives, on the other hand, express a shared or reciprocal action between two or more people or things. In this context, the pronoun means *(to) each other* or *(to) one another*.

Luis y Marta **se** miran en el espejo.
Luis and Marta look at themselves in the mirror.

Luis y Marta **se** miran.
Luis and Marta look at each other.

▶ Only the plural forms of the reflexive pronouns (**nos, os, se**) are used to express reciprocal actions because the action must involve more than one person or thing.

Cuando **nos vimos** en la calle, **nos abrazamos**.
When we saw each other on the street, we hugged one another.

Ustedes **se** van a **encontrar** en el cibercafé, ¿no?
You are meeting each other at the cybercafé, right?

Nos ayudamos cuando usamos la computadora.
We help each other when we use the computer.

Las amigas **se saludaron** y **se besaron**.
The friends greeted each other and kissed one another.

¡ATENCIÓN!

Here is a list of common verbs that can express reciprocal actions:
abrazar(se) *to hug; to embrace (each other)*
ayudar(se) *to help (each other)*
besar(se) *to kiss (each other)*
encontrar(se) *to meet (each other); to run into (each other)*
saludar(se) *to greet (each other)*

¡INTÉNTALO!   Indica el reflexivo recíproco adecuado y el presente o el pretérito de estos verbos.

presente

1. (escribir) Los novios __se escriben__.
   Nosotros __nos escribimos__.
   Ana y Ernesto __se escriben__.
2. (escuchar) Mis tíos __se escuchan__.
   Nosotros __nos escuchamos__.
   Ellos __se escuchan__.
3. (ver) Nosotros __nos vemos__.
   Fernando y Tomás __se ven__.
   Ustedes __se ven__.
4. (llamar) Ellas __se llaman__.
   Mis hermanos __se llaman__.
   Pepa y yo __nos llamamos__.

pretérito

1. (saludar) Nicolás y tú __se saludaron__.
   Nuestros vecinos __se saludaron__.
   Nosotros __nos saludamos__.
2. (hablar) Los amigos __se hablaron__.
   Elena y yo __nos hablamos__.
   Nosotras __nos hablamos__.
3. (conocer) Alberto y yo __nos conocimos__.
   Ustedes __se conocieron__.
   Ellos __se conocieron__.
4. (encontrar) Ana y Javier __se encontraron__.
   Los primos __se encontraron__.
   Mi hermana y yo __nos encontramos__.

recursos

WB pp. 273–274

LM p. 287

SUPERSITE adelante. vhlcentral.com

Lección 5

Práctica

1 **Un amor recíproco** Describe a Laura y a Elián usando los verbos recíprocos.

> **modelo**
>
> Laura veía a Elián todos los días. Elián veía a Laura todos los días.
> *Laura y Elián se veían todos los días.*

1. Laura conocía bien a Elián. Elián conocía bien a Laura.
   Laura y Elián se conocían bien.
2. Laura miraba a Elián con amor. Elián la miraba con amor también.
   Laura y Elián se miraban con amor.
3. Laura entendía bien a Elián. Elián entendía bien a Laura.
   Laura y Elián se entendían bien.
4. Laura hablaba con Elián todas las noches por teléfono. Elián hablaba
   con Laura todas las noches por teléfono.
   Laura y Elián se hablaban todas las noches por teléfono.
5. Laura ayudaba a Elián con sus problemas. Elián la ayudaba también
   con sus problemas.
   Laura y Elián se ayudaban con sus problemas.

2 **Describir** Mira los dibujos y describe lo que estas personas hicieron.

1. Las hermanas __se abrazaron__.

2. Ellos __se besaron__.

3. Gilberto y Mercedes __no se miraron__ /
   __no se hablaron__ / __se enojaron__.

4. Tú y yo __nos saludamos__ /
   __nos encontramos en la calle__.

Comunicación

3 **Preguntas** En parejas, túrnense para hacerse estas preguntas. Answers will vary.

1. ¿Se vieron tú y tu mejor amigo/a ayer? ¿Cuándo se ven ustedes normalmente?
2. ¿Dónde se encuentran tú y tus amigos?
3. ¿Se ayudan tú y tu mejor amigo/a con sus problemas?
4. ¿Se entienden bien tú y tu novio/a?
5. ¿Dónde se conocieron tú y tu novio/a? ¿Cuánto tiempo hace que se conocen ustedes?
6. ¿Cuándo se dan regalos tú y tu novio/a?
7. ¿Se escriben tú y tus amigos mensajes de texto o prefieren llamarse por teléfono?
8. ¿Siempre se llevan bien tú y tu compañero/a de cuarto? Explica.

5.4 Stressed possessive adjectives and pronouns

ANTE TODO   Spanish has two types of possessive adjectives: the unstressed (or short) forms you learned in *¡ADELANTE! UNO*, **Lección 3** and the stressed (or long) forms. The stressed forms are used for emphasis or to express *of mine, of yours,* and so on.

Stressed possessive adjectives

Masculine singular	Feminine singular	Masculine plural	Feminine plural	
mío	**mía**	**míos**	**mías**	*my; (of) mine*
tuyo	**tuya**	**tuyos**	**tuyas**	*your; (of) yours (fam.)*
suyo	**suya**	**suyos**	**suyas**	*your; (of) yours (form.); his; (of) his; her; (of) hers; its*
nuestro	**nuestra**	**nuestros**	**nuestras**	*our; (of) ours*
vuestro	**vuestra**	**vuestros**	**vuestras**	*your; (of) yours (fam.)*
suyo	**suya**	**suyos**	**suyas**	*your; (of) yours (form.); their; (of) theirs*

▶ **¡Atención!** Used with **un/una**, these possessives are similar in meaning to the English expression *of mine/yours/etc.*

> Juancho es **un** amigo **mío**.
> *Juancho is a friend of mine.*

> Ella es **una** compañera **nuestra**.
> *She is a classmate of ours.*

▶ Stressed possessive adjectives agree in gender and number with the nouns they modify. Stressed possessive adjectives are placed after the noun they modify, while unstressed possessive adjectives are placed before the noun.

> **su** impresora
> *her printer*

> la impresora **suya**
> *her printer*

> **nuestros** televisores
> *our television sets*

> los televisores **nuestros**
> *our television sets*

▶ A definite article, an indefinite article, or a demonstrative adjective usually precedes a noun modified by a stressed possessive adjective.

Me encantan { **unos** discos compactos **tuyos**.   *I love some of your CDs.*
{ **los** discos compactos **tuyos**.   *I love your CDs.*
{ **estos** discos compactos **tuyos**.   *I love these CDs of yours.*

▶ Since **suyo, suya, suyos,** and **suyas** have more than one meaning, you can avoid confusion by using the construction: [*article*] + [*noun*] + **de** + [*subject pronoun*].

> **el** teclado **suyo**

> el teclado **de él/ella**   *his/her keyboard*
> el teclado **de ustedes**   *your keyboard*

Teaching Tip Write the masculine forms of the stressed possessive adjectives/pronouns on the board, and ask volunteers to give the feminine and plural forms. Emphasize that when a stressed possessive adjective is used, the word it modifies is preceded by an article.

Pairs Tell students that their laundry has gotten mixed up with their roommate's and since they are the same size and have the same tastes in clothing, they cannot tell what belongs to whom. Have them ask each other questions about different articles of clothing. Ex: —¿Son tuyos estos pantalones de rayas? —Sí, son míos. —Y, ¿estos calcetines rojos son tuyos? —Sí, son míos, pero esta camisa grandísima no es mía.

Video Replay the *Fotonovela* episode. Have students listen for each use of an unstressed possessive adjective and write down the sentence. Next, have students rewrite those sentences using a stressed possessive adjective. Discuss how the use of stressed possessive adjectives affected the meaning or fluidity of the sentences.

CONSULTA

This is the same construction you learned in *¡ADELANTE! UNO*, **Lección 3** for clarifying **su** and **sus**. To review unstressed possessive adjectives, see *¡ADELANTE! UNO*, **Estructura 3.2,** p. 127.

Lección 5

Possessive pronouns

▶ Possessive pronouns are used to replace a noun + [*possessive adjective*]. In Spanish, the possessive pronouns have the same forms as the stressed possessive adjectives, and they are preceded by a definite article.

la calculadora **nuestra**   ▶   **la nuestra**
el *fax* **tuyo**   **el tuyo**
los archivos **suyos**   **los suyos**

▶ A possessive pronoun agrees in number and gender with the noun it replaces.

—Aquí está **mi coche**. ¿Dónde está **el tuyo**?
Here's my car. Where is yours?

—**El mío** está en el taller de mi hermano.
Mine is at my brother's garage.

—¿Tienes **las revistas** de Carlos?
Do you have Carlos' magazines?

—No, pero tengo **las nuestras**.
No, but I have ours.

Teaching Tips
• Ask students questions using unstressed possessive adjectives or the [*article*] + [*noun*] + **de** construction before a name, having them answer with a possessive pronoun. Ex: **Es tu cuaderno, ¿verdad? (Sí, es el mío.) Clase, ¿son éstos sus exámenes? (Sí, son los nuestros.) Ésta es la mochila negra de _____, ¿no? (No, no es la suya. La mochila roja es la suya.)**
• Point out that the function of the stressed possessives is to give emphasis. They are often used to point out contrasts. Ex: ¿**Tu carro es azul? Pues, el carro mío es rojo. ¿Tu cámara digital no es buena? La mía es excelente.**

Episodio veintiuno: Tecnohombre y los superamigos suyos salvan el mundo una vez más.

La Mujer Mecánica y Tecnohombre, ¡mis héroes!

¡Y los míos también!

¡INTÉNTALO!   Indica las formas tónicas (*stressed*) de estos adjetivos posesivos y los pronombres posesivos correspondientes.

		adjetivos	**pronombres**
1.	su videocasetera	la videocasetera suya	la suya
2.	mi televisor	el televisor mío	el mío
3.	nuestros discos compactos	los discos compactos nuestros	los nuestros
4.	tus calculadoras	las calculadoras tuyas	las tuyas
5.	su monitor	el monitor suyo	el suyo
6.	mis videos	los videos míos	los míos
7.	nuestra impresora	la impresora nuestra	la nuestra
8.	tu estéreo	el estéreo tuyo	el tuyo
9.	nuestro cederrón	el cederrón nuestro	el nuestro
10.	mi computadora	la computadora mía	la mía

recursos

WB pp. 275–276

LM p. 288

SUPERSITE
adelante. vhlcentral.com

Extra Practice Call out a noun and subject, then ask students to say which stressed possessive adjective they would use. Ex: **discos compactos, ustedes (suyos)**

Práctica

1 **Oraciones** Forma oraciones con estas palabras. Usa el presente y haz los cambios necesarios.

1. un / amiga / suyo / vivir / Mendoza   Una amiga suya vive en Mendoza.
2. ¿me / prestar / calculadora / tuyo?   ¿Me prestas la calculadora tuya?
3. el / coche / suyo / nunca / funcionar / bien   El coche suyo nunca funciona bien.
4. no / nos / interesar / problemas / suyo   No nos interesan los problemas suyos.
5. yo / querer / cámara digital / mío / ahora mismo   Yo quiero la cámara digital mía ahora mismo.
6. un / amigos / nuestro / manejar / como / loco   Unos amigos nuestros manejan como locos.

2 **¿Es suyo?** Un policía ha capturado (*has captured*) al hombre que robó (*robbed*) en tu casa. Ahora quiere saber qué cosas son tuyas. Túrnate con un(a) compañero/a para hacer el papel del policía y usa las pistas para contestar las preguntas.

> **modelo**
> no/viejo
> **Policía:** Esta calculadora, ¿es suya?
> **Estudiante:** No, no es mía. La mía era más vieja.

1. sí   Este estéreo, ¿es suyo?/Sí, es mío.

2. sí   Esta computadora portátil, ¿es suya?/Sí, es mía.

3. sí   Este radio, ¿es suyo?/Sí, es mío.

4. no/grande   Este televisor, ¿es suyo?/ No, no es mío. El mío era más grande.

5. no/pequeño   Esta cámara de video, ¿es suya?/ No, no es mía. La mía era más pequeña.

6. no/de Shakira   Estos discos compactos, ¿son suyos?/ No, no son míos. Los míos eran de Shakira.

3 **Conversaciones** Completa estas conversaciones con las formas adecuadas de los pronombres posesivos.

1. —La casa de ellos estaba en la Avenida Borges. ¿Dónde estaba la casa de ustedes?
   —__La nuestra__ estaba en la calle Bolívar.
2. —A Carmen le encanta su monitor nuevo.
   —¿Sí? A José no le gusta ___el suyo___.
3. —Puse mis discos aquí. ¿Dónde pusiste ___los tuyos___, Alfonso?
   —Puse ___los míos___ en el escritorio.
4. —Se me olvidó traer mis llaves. ¿Trajeron ustedes ___las suyas___?
   —No, dejamos ___las nuestras___ en casa.
5. —Yo compré mi computadora en una tienda y Marta compró ___la suya___ en Internet. Y ___la tuya___, ¿dónde la compraste?
   —___La mía___ es de Cíbermax.

1 Have students write four additional dehydrated sentences that use stressed possessive adjectives or pronouns. Have them exchange papers with a classmate, who will "rehydrate" them.

2 Have students continue the activity, using these items: **la impresora, el teléfono celular, la videocasetera, el reproductor de DVD, la contestadora,** and **el reproductor de MP3.**

3 To simplify, have students begin by scanning the conversations and writing the English translation of the word for each blank. Ex: 1. *Ours.* Then have them underline the noun that the pronoun refers to and state its gender and number. Ex: 1. **la casa**; feminine singular.

3 Have students create conversations modeled after the ones in the activity and perform them for the class. Each one should consist of at least six lines and use as many stressed possessive adjectives and pronouns as possible.

Comunicación

4 **Identificar** Trabajen en grupos. Cada estudiante da tres objetos. Pongan todos los objetos juntos. Luego, un(a) estudiante escoge uno o dos objetos y le pregunta a otro/a si esos objetos son suyos. Usen los adjetivos posesivos en sus preguntas. Answers will vary.

> **modelo**
>
> **Estudiante 1:** *Felipe, ¿son tuyos estos discos compactos?*
> **Estudiante 2:** *Sí, son míos.*
> *No, no son míos. Son los discos compactos de Bárbara.*

4 If students cannot bring in three objects, have them either find photos of objects or draw them. Students should find one feminine, one masculine, and one plural object to do the activity.

5 **Comparar** Trabajen en parejas. Intenta (*Try to*) convencer a tu compañero/a de que algo que tú tienes es mejor que el que él/ella tiene. Pueden hablar de sus carros, estéreos, discos compactos, clases, horarios o trabajos. Answers will vary.

> **modelo**
>
> **Estudiante 1:** *Mi computadora tiene una pantalla de quince pulgadas (inches). ¿Y la tuya?*
> **Estudiante 2:** *La mía es mejor porque tiene una pantalla de diecisiete pulgadas.*
> **Estudiante 1:** *Pues la mía…*

5 Before beginning the activity, have students make a list of objects to compare. Then have them brainstorm as many different qualities or features of those objects as they can. Finally, have them list adjectives that they might use to compare the objects they have chosen.

Síntesis

Supersite/IRCD: See the Information Gap Activities for an additional activity to practice the material presented in this section.

6 **Inventos locos** En grupos pequeños, lean la descripción de este invento fantástico. Después diseñen su propio invento y expliquen por qué es mejor que el de los demás grupos. Utilicen los posesivos, **por** y **para** y el vocabulario de **Contextos**. Answers will vary.

Nuestro celular tiene conexión a Internet, ¿y el tuyo?

Este teléfono celular es mucho mejor que el tuyo por estas razones:

- El nuestro tiene capacidad para guardar un millón de mensajes electrónicos.
- El celular nuestro toma video.
- Da la temperatura.
- Funciona como control remoto para la tele.
- También arranca el coche y tiene reproductor de MP3.

Sirve para todo.

Oferta: $45 dólares por mes (con un contrato mínimo de dos años)

Para más información, llama al 607-362-1990 o visita nuestro sitio web **www.telefonoloco.com**

Extra Practice Have students imagine that they are salespersons at a car dealership and they are writing a letter to a customer explaining why their cars are better than those of the other two dealerships in town. Students should compare several attributes of the cars and use stressed possessive adjectives and pronouns when appropriate.

Lección 5

Recapitulación

SUPERSITE For self-scoring and diagnostics, go to **adelante.vhlcentral.com.**

Completa estas actividades para repasar los conceptos de gramática que aprendiste en esta lección.

1 **Completar** Completa la tabla con las formas de los mandatos familiares. `8 pts.`

	Mandato	
Infinitivo	**Afirmativo**	**Negativo**
comer	**come**	**no comas**
hacer	haz	no hagas
sacar	saca	no saques
venir	ven	no vengas
ir	ve	no vayas

2 **Por y para** Completa el diálogo con **por** o **para**. `10 pts.`

MARIO Hola, yo trabajo (1) ___para___ el periódico de la universidad. ¿Puedo hacerte unas preguntas?

INÉS Sí, claro.

MARIO ¿Navegas mucho (2) ___por___ la red?

INÉS Sí, todos los días me conecto a Internet (3) ___para___ leer mi correo y navego (4) ___por___ una hora. También me gusta hablar (5) ___por___ el *messenger* con mis amigos. Es barato y, (6) ___para___ mí, es divertido.

MARIO ¿Y qué piensas sobre hacer la tarea en la computadora?

INÉS En general, me parece bien, pero (7) ___por___ ejemplo, anoche hice unos ejercicios (8) ___para___ la clase de álgebra y al final me dolieron los ojos. (9) ___Por___ eso a veces prefiero hacer la tarea a mano.

MARIO Muy bien. Muchas gracias (10) ___por___ tu ayuda.

3 **Posesivos** Completa las oraciones y confirma de quién son las cosas. `6 pts.`

1. —¿Éste es mi bolígrafo? —Sí, es el ___tuyo___ (*fam.*).
2. —¿Ésta es la cámara de tu papá? —Sí, es la ___suya___.
3. —¿Ese teléfono es de Pilar? —Sí, es el ___suyo___.
4. —¿Éstos son los cederrones de ustedes? —No, no son ___nuestros___.
5. —¿Ésta es tu computadora portátil? —No, no es ___mía___.
6. —¿Ésas son mis calculadoras? —Sí, son las ___suyas___ (*form.*).

5.1 **Familiar commands** *pp. 246–247*

tú commands		
Infinitive	**Affirmative**	**Negative**
guardar	**guard**a	**no guard**es
volver	**vuelv**e	**no vuelv**as
imprimir	**imprim**e	**no imprim**as

Irregular tú command forms

dar → **no des**	saber → **no sepas**
decir → **di**	salir → **sal**
estar → **no estés**	ser → **sé, no seas**
hacer → **haz**	tener → **ten**
ir → **ve, no vayas**	venir → **ven**
poner → **pon**	

► Verbs ending in **-car, -gar, -zar** have a spelling change in the negative **tú** commands:

sacar → **no sa**qu**es**
apagar → **no apa**gu**es**
almorzar → **no almuer**c**es**

5.2 **Por and para** *pp. 250–251*

► Uses of **por:**

motion or general location; duration; reason or motive; object of a search; means by which something is done; exchange or substitution; unit of measure

► Uses of **para:**

destination; deadline; purpose or goal; recipient of something; comparison or opinion; in the employ of

5.3 **Reciprocal reflexives** *p. 254*

► Reciprocal reflexives express a shared or reciprocal action between two or more people or things. Only the plural forms (**nos, os, se**) are used.

Cuando **nos vimos** en la calle, **nos abrazamos.**

► Common verbs that can express reciprocal actions:

abrazar(se), ayudar(se), besar(se), conocer(se), encontrar(se), escribir(se), escuchar(se), hablar(se), llamar(se), mirar(se), saludar(se), ver(se)

Small Groups As a class, brainstorm a list of infinitives that can be made reciprocal (**llamar, abrazar, conocer,** etc.) and write them on the board. In small groups, have students create a dialogue using at least six of these infinitives. Then have students act out their dialogues for the class. Encourage students to use lesson vocabulary.

Lección 5

5.4 Stressed possessive adjectives and pronouns

pp. 256–257

| Stressed possessive adjectives | |
Masculine	Feminine
mío(s)	mía(s)
tuyo(s)	tuya(s)
suyo(s)	suya(s)
nuestro(s)	nuestra(s)
vuestro(s)	vuestra(s)
suyo(s)	suya(s)

la impresora suya → la suya

las llaves mías → las mías

4

Ángel y diablito A Juan le gusta pedir consejos a su ángel y a su diablito imaginarios. Completa las respuestas con mandatos familiares desde las dos perspectivas. **8 pts.**

1. Estoy manejando. ¿Voy más rápido?

   Á No, no ___vayas___ más rápido.

   D Sí, ___ve___ más rápido.

2. Es el disco compacto favorito de mi hermana.
   ¿Lo pongo en mi mochila?

   Á No, no ___lo pongas___ en tu mochila.

   D Sí, ___ponlo___ en tu mochila.

3. Necesito estirar (*to stretch*) las piernas.
   ¿Doy un paseo?

   Á Sí, ___da___ un paseo.

   D No, no ___des___ un paseo.

4. Mi amigo necesita imprimir algo. ¿Apago la impresora?

   Á No, no ___apagues___ la impresora.

   D Sí, ___apaga___ la impresora.

5

Oraciones Forma oraciones para expresar acciones recíprocas con el tiempo indicado. **6 pts.**

> **modelo**
>
> tú y yo / conocer / bien (presente) *Tú y yo nos conocemos bien.*

1. José y Paco / llamar / una vez por semana (imperfecto)
   José y Paco se llamaban una vez por semana.
2. mi novia y yo / ver / todos los días (presente)
   Mi novia y yo nos vemos todos los días.
3. los compañeros de clase / ayudar / con la tarea (pretérito)
   Los compañeros de clase se ayudaron con la tarea.
4. tú y tu mamá / escribir / por correo electrónico / cada semana (imperfecto)
   Tú y tu mamá se escribían por correo electrónico cada semana.
5. mis hermanas y yo / entender / perfectamente (presente)
   Mis hermanas y yo nos entendemos perfectamente.
6. los profesores / saludar / con mucho respeto (pretérito)
   Los profesores se saludaron con mucho respeto.

6

La tecnología Escribe al menos seis oraciones diciéndole a un(a) amigo/a qué hacer para tener "una buena relación" con la tecnología. Usa mandatos familiares afirmativos y negativos. **12 pts.**

Answers will vary.

7

Saber compartir Completa la expresión con los dos pronombres posesivos que faltan.

¡2 puntos EXTRA!

" Lo que° es ___mío___
es ___tuyo___. "

Lo que *What*

Heritage Speakers Ask heritage speakers to come up with additional popular expressions using grammar from this lesson (**tú** commands, **por** and **para**, reciprocal reflexives, stressed possessives). Have them write the expressions on the board, leaving key words blank for classmates to guess.

Sidebar (left column):

4 Give students these situations as items 5–8: 5. Mi amigo tiene las respuestas del examen final de historia. ¿Se las pido? (No, no se las pidas.; Sí, pídeselas.) 6. Es el cumpleaños de mi compañero de cuarto. ¿Le compro algo? (Sí, cómprale algo.; No, no le compres nada.) 7. Rompí la computadora portátil de mi padre. ¿Se lo digo? (Sí, díselo.; No, no se lo digas.) 8. No tengo nada de dinero. ¿Busco trabajo? (Sí, búscalo.; No, no lo busques.)

5 Have students create two additional dehydrated sentences. Then have them exchange papers with a classmate and complete the exercise.

6 To challenge students, have them first write a letter from the point of view of the friend who needs help with technology. Then have students write their suggestions according to the problems outlined in the letter.

7 Explain that this expression takes the masculine possessive form because it does not refer to anything specific, as denoted by **lo que**.

recursos

SUPERSITE

adelante.vhlcentral.com

Lectura

Antes de leer

Estrategia
Recognizing borrowed words

One way languages grow is by borrowing words from each other. English words that relate to technology often are borrowed by Spanish and other languages throughout the world. Sometimes the words are modified slightly to fit the sounds of the languages that borrow them. When reading in Spanish, you can often increase your understanding by looking for words borrowed from English or other languages you know.

Examinar el texto

Mira brevemente (*briefly*) la selección. ¿De qué trata? (*What is it about?*) ¿Cómo lo sabes? Answers will vary.

Buscar

Esta lectura contiene varias palabras tomadas (*taken*) del inglés. Trabaja con un(a) compañero/a para encontrarlas. Internet, *fax*, Deep Blue

Predecir

Trabaja con un(a) compañero/a para contestar estas preguntas. Answers will vary.

1. En la foto, ¿quiénes participan en el juego?
2. ¿Jugabas en una computadora cuando eras niño/a? ¿Juegas ahora?
3. ¿Cómo cambiaron las computadoras y la tecnología en los años 80? ¿En los años 90? ¿En los principios del siglo XXI?
4. ¿Qué tipo de "inteligencia" tiene una computadora?
5. ¿Qué significa "inteligencia artificial" para ti?

Teaching Tips
• Call on volunteers to help you list additional borrowed words from current or previously learned vocabulary (Ex: **cederrón, DVD, sitio web**).
• For expansion, list common English words that have been borrowed from Spanish (Ex: *adobe, canyon, salsa*). Point out that many words related to North American plants, animals, and geography entered English through the Spanish language (sometimes already borrowed from indigenous languages).

recursos
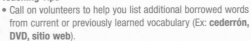
adelante.vhlcentral.com

Inteligencia y memoria: **la inteligencia artificial** por Alfonso Santamaría

Una de las principales características de la película de ciencia ficción *2001: una odisea del espacio*, es la gran inteligencia de su protagonista no humano, la computadora HAL-9000. Para muchas personas, la genial película de Stanley Kubrick es una reflexión sobre la evolución de la inteligencia, desde que el hombre utilizó por primera vez un hueso como herramienta° hasta la llegada de la inteligencia artificial (I.A.).

Ahora que vivimos en el siglo XXI, un mundo en el que Internet y el *fax* son ya comunes, podemos preguntarnos: ¿consiguieron los científicos especialistas en I.A. crear una computadora como HAL? La respuesta es no. Hoy día no existe una computadora con las capacidades intelectuales de HAL porque todavía no existen *inteligencias*

---

herramienta *tool*

Después de leer

¿Cierto o falso? 🔊

Indica si cada oración es **cierta** o **falsa**. Corrige las falsas.

Cierta	1.	La computadora HAL-9000 era muy inteligente.
Falsa	2.	Deep Blue es un buen ejemplo de la inteligencia artificial general. Deep Blue es un buen ejemplo de la inteligencia artificial especializada.
Falsa	3.	El maestro de ajedrez Garry Kasparov le ganó a Deep Blue en 1997. Deep Blue le ganó a Garry Kasparov en 1997.
Cierta	4.	Las computadoras no tienen la creatividad de Mozart o Picasso.
Falsa	5.	Hoy hay computadoras como HAL-9000. Las computadoras con la inteligencia de HAL-9000 son pura ciencia ficción.

Thomas J. Watson de Nueva York para desarrollar Deep Blue, la computadora que en 1997 derrotó° al campeón mundial de ajedrez, Garry Kasparov. Esta extraordinaria computadora pudo ganarle al maestro ruso de ajedrez porque estaba diseñada para procesar 200 millones de jugadas° por segundo. Además, Deep Blue guardaba en su memoria una recopilación de los movimientos de ajedrez más brillantes de toda la historia, entre ellos los que Kasparov efectuó en sus competiciones anteriores.

Para muchas personas, la victoria de Deep Blue sobre Kasparov simbolizó la victoria de la inteligencia artificial sobre la del ser humano°. Debemos reconocer los grandes avances científicos en el área de las computadoras y las ventajas° que pueden traernos en un futuro, pero también tenemos que entender sus limitaciones. Las computadoras generan nuevos modelos con conocimientos° muy definidos, pero todavía no tienen sentido común: una computadora como Deep Blue puede ganar una partida° de ajedrez, pero no puede explicar la diferencia entre una reina° y un peón°. Tampoco puede crear algo nuevo y original a partir de lo establecido, como hicieron Mozart o Picasso.

Las inteligencias artificiales especializadas son una realidad. ¿Pero una inteligencia como la de HAL-9000? Pura ciencia ficción. ■

artificiales generales que demuestren lo que llamamos "sentido común"°. Sin embargo, la I.A. está progresando mucho en el desarrollo° de las inteligencias especializadas. El ejemplo más famoso es Deep Blue, la computadora de IBM especializada en jugar al ajedrez°.

La idea de crear una máquina con capacidad para jugar al ajedrez se originó en 1950. En esa década, el científico Claude Shannon desarrolló una teoría que se convirtió en realidad en 1967, cuando apareció el primer programa que permitió a una computadora competir, aunque sin éxito°, en un campeonato° de ajedrez. Más de veinte años después, un grupo de expertos en I.A. fue al centro de investigación

---

sentido común *common sense* desarrollo *development* ajedrez *chess* éxito *success* campeonato *championship* derrotó *defeated* jugadas *moves* la del ser humano *that of the human being* ventajas *advantages* conocimientos *knowledge* partida *match* reina *queen* peón *pawn*

Preguntas

Contesta las preguntas.

1. ¿Qué tipo de inteligencia se relaciona con HAL-9000?
   La inteligencia artificial general se relaciona con HAL-9000.
2. ¿Qué tipo de inteligencia tienen las computadoras como Deep Blue? Las computadoras como Deep Blue tienen una inteligencia especializada.
3. ¿Cuándo se originó la idea de crear una máquina para jugar al ajedrez? La idea de crear una máquina para jugar al ajedrez se originó en 1950.
4. ¿Qué compañía inventó Deep Blue? IBM inventó Deep Blue.
5. ¿Por qué Deep Blue le pudo ganar a Garry Kasparov? Deep Blue le ganó a Garry Kasparov porque podía procesar 200 millones de jugadas por segundo.

Conversar

En grupos pequeños, hablen de estos temas.
Answers will vary.

1. ¿Son las computadoras más inteligentes que los seres humanos?

2. ¿Para qué cosas son mejores las computadoras, y para qué cosas son mejores los seres humanos? ¿Por qué?

3. En el futuro, ¿van a tener las computadoras la inteligencia de los seres humanos? ¿Cuándo?

SUPERSITE

Argentina

NATIONAL STANDARDS connections cultures

El país en cifras

▶ **Área:** 2.780.400 km² (1.074.000 millas²)
*Argentina es el país de habla española más
grande del mundo. Su territorio es dos veces
el tamaño° de Alaska.*

▶ **Población:** 40.738.000

▶ **Capital:** Buenos Aires —13.067.000
*En Buenos Aires vive más del
treinta por ciento de la población
total del país. La ciudad es
conocida° como el "París de
Suramérica" por el estilo parisino°
de muchas de sus calles y edificios.*

Buenos Aires

▶ **Ciudades principales:** Córdoba —1.492.000,
Rosario —1.231.000, Mendoza —917.000

SOURCE: Population Division, UN Secretariat

▶ **Moneda:** peso argentino

▶ **Idiomas:** español (oficial), guaraní

Bandera de Argentina

Argentinos célebres

▶ **Jorge Luis Borges,** escritor (1899–1986)
▶ **María Eva Duarte de Perón ("Evita"),**
primera dama° (1919–1952)
▶ **Mercedes Sosa,** cantante (1935–)
▶ **Gato Barbieri,** saxofonista (1935–)

tamaño *size* conocida *known* parisino *Parisian* primera dama *First Lady*
ancha *wide* mide *it measures* campo *field*

Gaucho

BOLIVIA

PARAGUAY

Las cataratas
de Iguazú

San Miguel
de Tucumán

ESTADOS UNIDOS

OCÉANO
ATLÁNTICO

OCÉANO
PACÍFICO

AMÉRICA DEL SUR

ARGENTINA

La Cordillera
de los Andes

Córdoba

Aconcagua

Mendoza

Rosario

Río Paraná

URUGUAY

CHILE

Buenos Aires

Mar
del Plata

La Pampa

Océano
Atlántico

San Carlos
de Bariloche

Montañas de Patagonia

Patagonia

Vista de San Carlos
de Bariloche

recursos

WB
pp. 277–278

VM
pp. 281–282

SUPERSITE
adelante.
vhlcentral.com

Tierra del Fuego

¡Increíble pero cierto!

La Avenida 9 de Julio en Buenos Aires es
la calle más ancha° del mundo. De lado a
lado mide° cerca de 140 metros, lo que es
equivalente a un campo° y medio de fútbol.
Su nombre conmemora el Día de la
Independencia de Argentina.

BRASIL

Historia • Inmigración europea

Se dice que Argentina es el país más "europeo" de toda Latinoamérica. Después del año 1880, inmigrantes italianos, alemanes, españoles e ingleses llegaron para establecerse en esta nación. Esta diversidad cultural ha dejado° una profunda huella° en la música, el cine y la arquitectura argentinos.

Artes • El tango

El tango es uno de los símbolos culturales más importantes de Argentina. Este género° musical es una mezcla de ritmos de origen africano, italiano y español, y se originó a finales del siglo XIX entre los porteños°. Poco después se hizo popular entre el resto de los argentinos y su fama llegó hasta París. Como baile, el tango en un principio° era provocativo y violento, pero se hizo más romántico durante los años 30. Hoy día, este estilo musical es popular en muchas partes del mundo°.

Lugares • Las cataratas de Iguazú

Las famosas cataratas° de Iguazú se encuentran entre las fronteras de Argentina, Paraguay y Brasil, al norte de Buenos Aires. Cerca de ellas confluyen° los ríos Iguazú y Paraná. Estas extensas caídas de agua tienen unos 70 metros (230 pies) de altura° y en época° de lluvias llegan a medir 4 kilómetros (2,5 millas) de ancho. Situadas en el Parque Nacional Iguazú, las cataratas son un destino° turístico muy visitado.

 ¿Qué aprendiste? Responde a cada pregunta con una oración completa.

1. ¿Qué porcentaje de la población de Argentina vive en la capital?
   Más del treinta por ciento de la población de Argentina vive en la capital.

2. ¿Quién es Mercedes Sosa?
   Mercedes Sosa es una cantante argentina.

3. Se dice que Argentina es el país más europeo de Latinoamérica.
   ¿Por qué? Se dice que Argentina es el país más europeo de Latinoamérica porque muchos inmigrantes europeos se establecieron allí.

4. ¿Qué tipo de baile es uno de los símbolos culturales más importantes de Argentina?
   El tango es uno de los símbolos culturales más importantes de Argentina.

5. ¿Dónde y cuándo se originó el tango?
   El tango se originó entre los porteños en la década de 1880.

6. ¿Cómo era el tango originalmente?
   El tango era un baile provocativo y violento.

7. ¿En qué parque nacional están las cataratas de Iguazú?
   Las cataratas de Iguazú están en el Parque Nacional Iguazú.

Artesano en
Buenos Aires

 Conexión Internet Investiga estos temas en **adelante.vhlcentral.com**.

1. Busca información sobre el tango. ¿Te gustan los ritmos y sonidos del tango? ¿Por qué? ¿Se baila el tango en tu comunidad?

2. ¿Quiénes fueron Juan y Eva Perón y qué importancia tienen en la historia de Argentina?

....

ha dejado *has left* **huella** *mark* **género** *genre* **porteños** *people of Buenos Aires* **en un principio** *at first* **mundo** *world*
cataratas *waterfalls* **confluyen** *converge* **altura** *height* **época** *season* **destino** *destination*

Supersite/DVD: You may want to wrap up this section by playing the ***Panorama cultural*** video footage for this lesson.

Heritage Speakers If applicable, ask heritage speakers who use **vos** instead of **tú** to provide examples for the class.

La tecnología

la calculadora	calculator
la cámara digital, de video	digital, video camera
el canal	(TV) channel
el cibercafé	cybercafé
la contestadora	answering machine
el control remoto	remote control
el disco compacto	compact disc
el estéreo	stereo
el fax	fax (machine)
el radio	radio (set)
el reproductor de MP3	MP3 player
el (teléfono) celular	(cell) telephone
la televisión por cable	cable television
el televisor	televison set
el tocadiscos compacto	compact disc player
el video(casete)	video(cassette)
la videocasetera	VCR
apagar	to turn off
funcionar	to work
llamar	to call
poner, prender	to turn on
sonar (o:ue)	to ring
descompuesto/a	not working; out of order
lento/a	slow
lleno/a	full

La computadora

el archivo	file
arroba	@ symbol
el cederrón	CD-ROM
la computadora (portátil)	(portable) computer; (laptop)
la dirección electrónica	e-mail address
el disco compacto	compact disc
la impresora	printer
Internet	Internet
el mensaje de texto	text message
el monitor	(computer) monitor
la página principal	home page
la pantalla	screen
el programa de computación	software
el ratón	mouse
la red	network; Web
el reproductor de DVD	DVD player
el sitio web	website
el teclado	keyboard
borrar	to erase
descargar	to download
grabar	to record
guardar	to save
imprimir	to print
navegar (en Internet)	to surf (the Internet)
quemar	to burn (a CD)

El carro

la autopista, la carretera	highway
el baúl	trunk
la calle	street
el capó, el cofre	hood
el carro, el coche	car
la circulación, el tráfico	traffic
el garaje, el taller (mecánico)	garage; (mechanic's) repair shop
la gasolina	gasoline
la gasolinera	gas station
la licencia de conducir	driver's license
la llanta	tire
el/la mecánico/a	mechanic
el parabrisas	windshield
la policía	police (force)
la velocidad máxima	speed limit
el volante	steering wheel
arrancar	to start
arreglar	to fix; to arrange
bajar(se) de	to get off of/out of (a vehicle)
conducir, manejar	to drive
estacionar	to park
llenar (el tanque)	to fill (the tank)
parar	to stop
revisar (el aceite)	to check (the oil)
subir(se) a	to get on/into (a vehicle)

Verbos

abrazar(se)	to hug; to embrace (each other)
ayudar(se)	to help (each other)
besar(se)	to kiss (each other)
encontrar(se) (o:ue)	to meet (each other); to run into (each other)
saludar(se)	to greet (each other)

Supersite/IRCD: MP3 Audio Files, Testing Program, *Vocabulario adicional*

Otras palabras y expresiones

por aquí	around here
por ejemplo	for example
por eso	that's why; therefore
por fin	finally

Por and **para**	See pages 250–251.
Stressed possessive adjectives and pronouns	See pages 256–257.
Expresiones útiles	See page 241.

recursos

LM
p. 288

adelante.
vhlcentral.com

contextos

Lección 5

1 **La tecnología** Fill in the blanks with the correct terms.

1. Para multiplicar y dividir puedes usar _la/una calculadora_.

2. Para hacer videos de tu familia puedes usar _una cámara de video_.

3. Cuando vas a un sitio web, lo primero (*the first thing*) que ves es _la página principal_.

4. Cuando no estás en casa y alguien te llama, te deja un mensaje en _la contestadora_.

5. La red de computadoras y servidores más importante del mundo es _Internet_.

6. Para poder ver muchos canales, tienes que tener _la televisión por cable_.

2 **Eso hacían** Match a subject from the word bank to each verb phrase. Then write complete sentences for the pairs using the imperfect.

algunos jóvenes estadounidenses	el conductor del autobús	el mecánico de Jorge
el carro viejo	la impresora nueva	el teléfono celular

1. manejar lentamente por la nieve

   El conductor del autobús manejaba lentamente por la nieve.

2. imprimir los documentos muy rápido

   La impresora nueva imprimía los documentos muy rápido.

3. revisarle el aceite al auto todos los meses

   El mecánico de Jorge le revisaba el aceite al auto todos los meses.

4. sonar en la casa pero nadie contestarlo

   El teléfono celular sonaba en la casa pero nadie lo contestaba.

5. no arrancar cuando llover

   El carro viejo no arrancaba cuando llovía.

6. navegar en Internet de niños

   Algunos jóvenes estadounidenses navegaban en Internet de niños.

3 **La computadora** Label the drawing with the correct terms.

1. _el monitor_

2. _la pantalla_

3. _el teclado_

4. _el ratón_

5. _la impresora_

6. _la calculadora_

7. _el disco compacto/el cederrón_

4   **Preguntas** Answer the questions with complete sentences.

1. ¿Para qué se usa la impresora?

La impresora se usa para imprimir.

2. ¿Para qué se usan los frenos (*brakes*) del coche?

Los frenos del coche se usan para parar.

3. ¿Qué se usa para enviar documentos?

El *fax* se usa para enviar documentos.

4. ¿Qué se usa para manejar el carro?

El volante se usa para manejar el carro.

5. ¿Qué se usa para cambiar los canales del televisor?

El control remoto se usa para cambiar los canales del televisor.

6. ¿Para qué se usan las llaves del carro?

Las llaves del carro se usan para arrancar el carro.

5   **Mi primer día en la carretera** Complete the paragraph with terms from the word bank.

accidente	estacionar	policía
aceite	lento	revisar
arrancar	licencia de conducir	subir
autopista	llanta	taller mecánico
calle	lleno	tráfico
descargar	parar	velocidad máxima

Después de dos exámenes, conseguí mi (1) ___licencia de conducir___ para poder manejar legalmente

por primera vez. Estaba muy emocionado cuando (2) ___subí___ al carro de mi papá.

El tanque estaba (3) ___lleno___, el (4) ___aceite___ lo revisaron el día

anterior (*previous*) en el (5) ___taller mecánico___. El carro y yo estábamos listos para

(6) ___arrancar___. Primero salí por la (7) ___calle___ en donde está mi

casa. Luego llegué a un área de la ciudad donde había mucha gente y también mucho

(8) ___tráfico___. Se me olvidó (9) ___parar___ en el semáforo (*light*), que

estaba amarillo, y estuve cerca de tener un (10) ___accidente___. Sin saberlo, entré en la

(11) ___autopista___ interestatal (*interstate*). La (12) ___velocidad máxima___ era de 70

millas (*miles*) por hora, pero yo estaba tan nervioso que iba mucho más (13) ___lento___,

a 10 millas por hora. Vi un carro de la (14) ___policía___ y tuve miedo. Por eso volví a

casa y (15) ___estacioné___ el carro en la calle. ¡Qué aventura!

estructura

5.1 Familiar commands

1

Cosas por hacer Read the list of things to do. Then use familiar commands to finish the e-mail from Ana to her husband, Eduardo, about the things that he has to do before their vacation.

comprar un paquete de papel para la impresora	revisar el aceite del carro
ir al sitio web de la agencia de viajes y pedir la información sobre nuestro hotel	comprobar que tenemos una llanta extra
	limpiar el parabrisas
imprimir la información	llenar el tanque de gasolina
terminar de hacer las maletas	venir a buscarme a la oficina

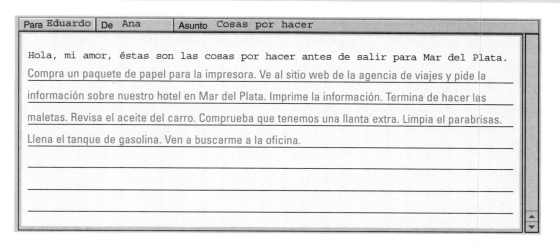

Para Eduardo	De Ana	Asunto Cosas por hacer

Hola, mi amor, éstas son las cosas por hacer antes de salir para Mar del Plata.

Compra un paquete de papel para la impresora. Ve al sitio web de la agencia de viajes y pide la

información sobre nuestro hotel en Mar del Plata. Imprime la información. Termina de hacer las

maletas. Revisa el aceite del carro. Comprueba que tenemos una llanta extra. Limpia el parabrisas.

Llena el tanque de gasolina. Ven a buscarme a la oficina.

_____

_____

_____

2

Díselo You're feeling bossy today. Give your friends instructions based on the cues provided using familiar commands.

> **modelo**
>
> Ramón / comprarte un disco compacto en Mendoza
> *Ramón, cómprame un disco compacto en Mendoza.*

1. Mario / traerte la cámara digital que le regaló Gema

   Mario, tráeme la cámara digital que te regaló Gema.

2. Natalia / escribirle un mensaje de texto a su hermana

   Natalia, escríbele un mensaje de texto a tu hermana.

3. Martín / llamarlos por teléfono celular

   Martín, llámalos por teléfono celular.

4. Gloria / hacer la cama antes de salir

   Gloria, haz la cama antes de salir.

5. Carmen / no revisar el aceite hasta la semana que viene

   Carmen, no revises el aceite hasta la semana que viene.

6. Lilia / enseñarte a manejar

   Lilia, enséñame a manejar.

3   **Planes para el invierno** Rewrite this paragraph from a travel website. Use informal commands instead of the infinitives you see.

Este invierno, (decir) adiós al frío y a la nieve. (Descubrir) una de las más grandes maravillas (*marvels*) naturales del mundo (*world*). (Ir) al Parque Nacional Iguazú en Argentina y (visitar) las hermosas cascadas. (Explorar) el parque y (mirar) las más de 400 especies de pájaros y animales que viven ahí. (Visitar) este santuario de la naturaleza en los meses de enero a marzo y (disfrutar) de una temperatura promedio de 77° F. Para unas vacaciones de aventura, (hacer) un safari por la selva (*jungle*) o (reservar) una excursión por el río Iguazú. De noche, (dormir) en uno de nuestros exclusivos hoteles en medio de la selva. (Respirar) el aire puro y (probar) la deliciosa comida de la región.

Invierno en Argentina

Este invierno, dile adiós al frío y a la nieve. Descubre una de las más grandes maravillas naturales del mundo. Ve al

Parque Nacional Iguazú en Argentina y visita las hermosas cascadas. Explora el parque y mira las más de 400 especies de

pájaros y animales que viven ahí. Visita este santuario de la naturaleza en los meses de enero a marzo y disfruta de una

temperatura promedio de 77° F. Para unas vacaciones de aventura, haz un safari por la selva o reserva una excursión por

el río Iguazú. De noche, duerme en uno de nuestros exclusivos hoteles en medio de la selva. Respira el aire puro y prueba

la deliciosa comida de la región.

4   **¿Qué hago?** Clara's brother Miguel is giving her a driving lesson, and Clara has a lot of questions. Write Miguel's answers to her questions in the form of positive or negative familiar commands.

> **modelo**
>
> ¿Tengo que comprar gasolina?
> *Sí, compra gasolina./No, no compres gasolina.*

1. ¿Puedo hablar por teléfono celular con mis amigos?
   Sí, habla por teléfono celular con tus amigos./No, no hables por teléfono celular con tus amigos.

2. ¿Puedo manejar en la autopista?
   Sí, maneja en la autopista./No, no manejes en la autopista.

3. ¿Debo estacionar por aquí?
   Sí, estaciona por aquí./No, no estaciones por aquí.

4. ¿Debo sacar mi licencia de conducir?
   Sí, saca tu licencia de conducir./No, no saques tu licencia de conducir.

5. ¿Puedo bajar por esta calle?
   Sí, baja por esta calle./No, no bajes por esta calle.

6. ¿Tengo que seguir el tráfico?
   Sí, sigue el tráfico./No, no sigas el tráfico.

5.2 Por and para

1 **Para éste o por aquello** Complete the sentences with **por** or **para** as appropriate.

1. Pudieron terminar el trabajo _____ por _____ haber empezado (*having begun*) a tiempo.

2. Ese *fax* es _____ para _____ enviar y recibir documentos de la compañía.

3. Elsa vivió en esa ciudad _____ por _____ algunos meses hace diez años.

4. Mi mamá compró esta computadora portátil _____ para _____ mi papá.

5. Sales _____ para _____ Argentina mañana a las ocho y media.

6. Rosaura cambió el estéreo _____ por _____ el reproductor de MP3.

7. El señor López necesita el informe _____ para _____ el 2 de agosto.

8. Estuve estudiando toda la noche _____ para _____ el examen.

9. Los turistas fueron de excursión _____ por _____ las montañas.

10. Mis amigos siempre me escriben _____ por _____ correo electrónico.

2 **Por muchas razones** Complete the sentences with the expressions in the word bank. Note that you will use two of them twice.

> por aquí   por eso
> por ejemplo   por fin

1. Ramón y Sara no pudieron ir a la fiesta anoche; _____ por eso _____ no los viste.

2. Buscaron el vestido perfecto por mucho tiempo, y _____ por fin _____ lo encontraron en esa tienda.

3. Creo que va a ser difícil encontrar un teclado y un monitor _____ por aquí _____.

4. Pídele ayuda a uno de tus amigos, _____ por ejemplo _____, Miguel, Carlos o Francisco.

5. Miguel y David no saben si podemos pasar _____ por aquí _____ en bicicleta.

6. La videocasetera no está conectada, y _____ por eso _____ no funciona.

3 **Por y para** Complete the sentences with **por** or **para**.

1. Fui a comprar frutas _____ por _____ (*instead of*) mi madre.

2. Fui a comprar frutas _____ para _____ (*to give to*) mi madre.

3. Rita le dio dinero _____ para _____ (*in order to buy*) la computadora portátil.

4. Rita le dio dinero _____ por _____ (*in exchange for*) la computadora portátil.

5. La familia los llevó _____ por _____ (*through*) los Andes.

6. La familia los llevó _____ para _____ (*to*) los Andes.

4 **Escribir oraciones** Write sentences in the preterite, using the elements provided and **por** or **para**.

> **modelo**
> (tú) / salir en el auto / ¿? / Córdoba
> *Saliste en el auto para Córdoba.*

1. Ricardo y Emilia / traer un pastel / ¿? / su prima

   Ricardo y Emilia trajeron un pastel para su prima.

2. los turistas / llegar a las ruinas / ¿? / barco

   Los turistas llegaron a las ruinas por barco.

3. (yo) / tener resfriado / ¿? / el frío

   Tuve resfriado por el frío.

4. mis amigas / ganar dinero / ¿? / viajar a Suramérica

   Mis amigas ganaron dinero para viajar a Suramérica.

5. ustedes / buscar a Teresa / ¿? / toda la playa

   Ustedes buscaron a Teresa por toda la playa.

6. el avión / salir a las doce / ¿? / Buenos Aires

   El avión salió a las doce para Buenos Aires.

5 **Para Silvia** Complete the paragraph with **por** and **para**.

Fui a la agencia de viajes porque quería ir (1) _____ para _____ Mendoza

(2) _____ para _____ visitar a mi novia, Silvia. Entré (3) _____ por _____ la

puerta y Marta, la agente de viajes, me dijo: "¡Tengo una oferta excelente (4) _____ para _____

ti!". Me explicó que podía viajar en avión (5) _____ para _____ Buenos Aires

(6) _____ por _____ seiscientos dólares. Podía salir un día de semana,

(7) _____ por _____ ejemplo lunes o martes. Me podía quedar en un hotel en Buenos Aires

(8) _____ por _____ quince dólares (9) _____ por _____ noche. Luego viajaría

(10) _____ por _____ tren a Mendoza (11) _____ para _____ encontrarme con

Silvia. "Debes comprar el pasaje (12) _____ para _____ el fin de mes", me recomendó

Marta. Fue la oferta perfecta (13) _____ para _____ mí. Llegué a Mendoza y Silvia vino a la

estación (14) _____ por _____ mí. Traje unas flores (15) _____ para _____ ella.

Estuve en Mendoza (16) _____ por _____ un mes y (17) _____ por _____ fin

Silvia y yo nos comprometimos. Estoy loco (18) _____ por _____ ella.

5.3 Reciprocal reflexives

1 **Se conocen** Complete the sentences with the reciprocal reflexives of the verbs in parentheses. Use the present tense.

1. Álex y don Francisco _____ se ven _____ (ver) todos los días.

2. Los amigos _____ se encuentran _____ (encontrar) en el centro de la ciudad.

3. El padre y la madre de Maite _____ se quieren _____ (querer) mucho.

4. Javier y yo _____ nos saludamos _____ (saludar) por las mañanas.

5. Los compañeros de clase _____ se ayudan _____ (ayudar) con las tareas.

6. Inés y su mamá _____ se llaman _____ (llamar) por teléfono todos los días.

2 **Nos vemos** Complete the sentences with the reciprocal reflexives of the verbs in the word bank.

abrazar	besar	encontrar	mirar	saludar
ayudar	despedir	llamar	querer	ver

1. Cuando los estudiantes llegan a clase, todos _____ se saludan _____.

2. Hace seis meses que Ricardo no ve a su padre. Cuando se ven, _____ se abrazan _____.

3. Los buenos amigos _____ se ayudan _____ cuando tienen problemas.

4. Es el final de la boda. El novio y la novia _____ se besan _____.

5. Mi novia y yo nos vamos a casar porque _____ nos queremos _____ mucho.

6. Antes de irse a sus casas, todos los amigos de Irene y Vicente _____ se despiden _____.

7. Hablo todos los días con mi hermana. Nosotras _____ nos llamamos _____ todos los días.

8. Cuando Sandra sale a comer con sus amigas, ellas _____ se encuentran _____ en el restaurante.

3 **Así fue** Write sentences from the elements provided. Use reciprocal reflexives and the preterite of the verbs.

1. ayer / Felipe y Lola / enviar / mensajes por correo electrónico

   Ayer Felipe y Lola se enviaron mensajes por correo electrónico.

2. Raúl y yo / encontrar / en el centro de computación

   Raúl y yo nos encontramos en el centro de computación.

3. mis abuelos / querer / mucho toda la vida

   Mis abuelos se quisieron mucho toda la vida.

4. los protagonistas de la película / abrazar y besar / al final

   Los protagonistas de la película se abrazaron y se besaron al final.

5. esos hermanos / ayudar / a conseguir trabajo

   Esos hermanos se ayudaron a conseguir trabajo.

4 **Noticias (*News*) de Alma** Read the letter from Alma, then complete the sentences about the letter with reciprocal reflexive forms of the correct verbs.

Querida Claudia:

Conocí a Manolo el mes pasado en Buenos Aires. Desde el día en que lo conocí, lo veo todos los días. Cuando salgo de la universidad me encuentro con él en algún lugar de la ciudad. Nuestro primer beso fue en el parque. Anoche Manolo me dijo que me quiere a mí y yo le dije que lo quiero mucho a él. Siempre nos ayudamos mucho con las tareas de la universidad. Llamo mucho a mi hermana y ella me llama a mí para hablar de nuestras cosas. Mi hermana me entiende muy bien y viceversa.

Hasta luego,
Alma

1. Manolo y Alma _____se conocieron_____ el mes pasado en Buenos Aires.

2. Ellos _____se ven_____ todos los días desde que se conocieron.

3. Manolo y Alma _____se encuentran_____ después de clase en algún lugar de la ciudad.

4. La primera vez que _____se besaron_____, Manolo y Alma estaban en el parque.

5. Anoche Manolo y Alma _____se dijeron_____ que se quieren mucho.

6. Manolo y Alma siempre _____se ayudan_____ mucho con las tareas de la universidad.

7. Alma y su hermana _____se llaman_____ mucho para hablar de sus cosas.

8. Alma y su hermana _____se entienden_____ muy bien.

5 **Completar** Complete each pair of sentences with the preterite of the verbs in parentheses. Use the reciprocal reflexive verb in only one sentence in each pair.

(conocer)

1. Ricardo y Juan _____conocieron_____ a Cristina el año pasado.

2. Los González _____se conocieron_____ en un viaje por Europa.

(saludar)

3. Los chicos _____se saludaron_____ cuando llegaron al restaurante.

4. La camarera _____saludó_____ a los chicos cuando les trajo el menú.

(ayudar)

5. Las enfermeras _____ayudaron_____ al paciente a levantarse.

6. Los niños _____se ayudaron_____ para terminar la tarea más temprano.

(ver)

7. Los mecánicos _____vieron_____ los coches descompuestos.

8. El profesor y los estudiantes _____se vieron_____ por primera vez en clase.

5.4 Stressed possesive adjectives and pronouns

1 **Esas cosas tuyas** Fill in the blanks with the possessive adjectives as indicated.

1. Ana nos quiere mostrar unas fotos _____ suyas _____ (*of hers*).

2. A Lorena le encanta la ropa _____ nuestra _____ (*of ours*).

3. Los turistas traen las toallas _____ suyas _____ (*of theirs*).

4. El mecánico te muestra unos autos _____ suyos _____ (*of his*).

5. El sitio web _____ suyo _____ (*of his*) es espectacular.

6. ¿Quieres probar el programa de computación _____ nuestro _____ (*of ours*)?

7. Roberto prefiere usar la computadora _____ mía _____ (*of mine*).

8. Ese ratón _____ tuyo _____ (*of yours*) es el más moderno que existe.

2 **¿De quién es?** Complete the sentences with possessive adjectives.

1. Ésa es mi computadora. Es la computadora mía _____.

2. Vamos a ver su sitio web. Vamos a ver el sitio web suyo _____.

3. Aquéllos son mis archivos. Son los archivos míos _____.

4. Quiero usar el programa de él. Quiero usar el programa suyo _____.

5. Buscamos nuestra impresora. Buscamos la impresora nuestra _____.

6. Ésos son los discos compactos de ella. Son los discos compactos suyos _____.

7. Tienen que arreglar tu teclado. Tienen que arreglar el teclado tuyo _____.

8. Voy a usar el teléfono celular de ustedes. Voy a usar el teléfono celular suyo _____.

3 **Los suyos** Answer the questions. Follow the model.

> **modelo**
> ¿Vas a llevar tu cámara de video?
> Sí, voy a llevar la mía.

1. ¿Prefieres usar tu calculadora? Sí, prefiero usar la mía.

2. ¿Quieres usar nuestra cámara digital? Sí, quiero usar la suya./Sí, quiero usar la nuestra.

3. ¿Guardaste mis archivos? Sí, guardé los tuyos.

4. ¿Llenaste el tanque de su carro? Sí, llené el suyo.

5. ¿Manejó Sonia nuestro carro? Sí, manejó el nuestro./ Sí, manejó el suyo.

6. ¿Vas a comprar mi televisor? Sí, voy a comprar el tuyo.

7. ¿Tienes el teclado de ellos? Sí, tengo el suyo.

8. ¿Quemaste tus discos compactos? Sí, quemé los míos.

4 **¿De quién son?** Replace the question with one using **de** to clarify the possession. Then answer the question affirmatively, using a possessive pronoun.

> *modelo*
>
> ¿Es suyo el teléfono celular? (de ella)
>
> *¿Es de ella el teléfono celular? Sí, es suyo.*

1. ¿Son suyas las gafas? (de usted)

   ¿Son de usted las gafas? Sí, son mías.

2. ¿Es suyo el estéreo? (de Joaquín)

   ¿Es de Joaquín el estéreo? Sí, es suyo.

3. ¿Es suya la impresora? (de ellos)

   ¿Es de ellos la impresora? Sí, es suya.

4. ¿Son suyos esos reproductores de DVD? (de Susana)

   ¿Son de Susana esos reproductores de DVD? Sí, son suyos.

5. ¿Es suyo el coche? (de tu mamá)

   ¿Es de tu mamá el coche? Sí, es suyo.

6. ¿Son suyas estas calculadoras? (de ustedes)

   ¿Son de ustedes estas calculadoras? Sí, son nuestras.

Síntesis

Tell the story of a romantic couple you know. Use reciprocal reflexive forms of verbs to tell what happened between them and when. Use stressed possessive adjectives and pronouns as needed to talk about their families and their difficulties. Use familiar commands to give examples of advice you give to each member of the couple on important issues. Answers will vary.

_____

_____

_____

_____

_____

_____

_____

_____

_____

_____

_____

_____

panorama

Argentina

1 **Argentina** Fill in the blanks with the correct terms.

1. La ciudad de Buenos Aires se conoce como el _____"París de Suramérica"_____.

2. Se dice que Argentina es el país más _____europeo_____ de toda Latinoamérica.

3. Después de 1880, muchos _____inmigrantes_____ se establecieron en Argentina.

4. Los sonidos y ritmos del tango tienen raíces _____africanas_____,
_____italianas_____ y _____españolas_____.

5. A los habitantes de Buenos Aires se les llama _____porteños_____.

6. El nombre de la Avenida 9 de Julio conmemora la _____independencia_____ de Argentina.

2 **Palabras desordenadas** Unscramble the words about Argentina, using the clues.

1. URGAÍNA _____guaraní_____
(idioma que se habla en Argentina además del español)

2. ESEDREMC _____Mercedes_____
(nombre de una cantante argentina)

3. GAIOATNAP _____Patagonia_____
(región fría que está en la parte sur (*south*) de Argentina)

4. REGTARLNIA _____Inglaterra_____
(uno de los países de origen de muchos inmigrantes a Argentina)

5. OTÑSOERP _____porteños_____
(personas de Buenos Aires)

6. TOORVPOAVCI _____provocativo_____
(una característica del tango en un principio)

3 **Datos argentinos** Fill in the blanks with the aspects of Argentina described.

1. saxofonista argentino _Gato Barbieri_

2. las tres mayores ciudades de Argentina _Buenos Aires, Córdoba y Rosario_

3. países de origen de muchos inmigrantes argentinos _Italia, Alemania, España e Inglaterra_

4. escritor argentino célebre _Jorge Luis Borges_

5. países que comparten las cataratas de Iguazú _Argentina, Paraguay y Brasil_

6. primera dama argentina; nació en 1919 _Evita Perón/María Eva Duarte de Perón_

4   **Fotos de Argentina**   Label the photographs from Argentina.

1. _____ el tango _____   2. _____ las cataratas de Iguazú _____

5   **¿Cierto o falso?**   Indicate whether the statements are **cierto** or **falso**. Correct the false statements.

1. Argentina es el país más grande del mundo.

    Falso. Argentina es el país de habla hispana más grande del mundo.

2. La Avenida 9 de Julio en Buenos Aires es la calle más ancha del mundo.

    Cierto.

3. Los idiomas que se hablan en Argentina son el español y el inglés.

    Falso. Los idiomas que se hablan en Argentina son el español y el guaraní.

4. Los inmigrantes argentinos venían principalmente de Europa.

    Cierto.

5. El tango es un baile con raíces indígenas y africanas.

    Falso. El tango es un baile con raíces africanas, italianas y españolas.

6. Las cataratas de Iguazú están cerca de la confluencia de los ríos Iguazú y Paraná.

    Cierto.

6   **Preguntas argentinas**   Answer the questions with complete sentences.   Answers will vary. Suggested answers:

1. ¿Por qué se conoce a Buenos Aires como el "París de Suramérica"?

    Buenos Aires se conoce como el "París de Suramérica" por el estilo parisino de sus calles y edificios.

2. ¿Quién fue la primera dama de Argentina hasta 1952?

    La primera dama de Argentina hasta 1952 fue María Eva Duarte de Perón./La primera dama de Argentina hasta 1952 fue Evita Perón.

3. ¿Qué dejaron las diferentes culturas de los inmigrantes a Argentina?

    Las diferentes culturas de los inmigrantes dejaron una huella profunda en la música, el cine, el arte y la arquitectura de Argentina.

4. ¿Cómo cambió el tango desde su origen hasta la década de 1940?

    En un principio, el tango era un baile provocativo y violento, pero se hizo más romántico durante los 1940.

Tecnohombre, ¡mi héroe!

Antes de ver el video

1 **¿Qué pasa?** Look at the video still. Where do you think Inés and don Francisco are? What do you think they are doing, and why? Answers will vary.

_____

_____

_____

_____

_____

_____

_____

Mientras ves el video

2 **¿Qué oíste?** Watch the **Tecnohombre, ¡mi héroe!** segment of this video module and place a check mark beside the items you hear.

___ 1. Lo siento. No está.

✔ 2. ¿Quién habla?

✔ 3. Con el señor Fonseca, por favor.

___ 4. ¡A sus órdenes!

___ 5. ¡Uy! ¡Qué dolor!

✔ 6. ¡No me digas!

___ 7. Estamos en Ibarra.

✔ 8. Viene enseguida.

___ 9. No puede venir hoy.

✔ 10. No veo el problema.

3 **Madrid** Watch Maite's flashback about getting around in Madrid and place a check mark beside the things you see.

✔ 1. calles

___ 2. bicicletas

✔ 3. carros

✔ 4. una motocicleta

✔ 5. monumentos

✔ 6. taxis

___ 7. un *walkman*

___ 8. un taller

✔ 9. una ambulancia

___ 10. una gasolinera

4 **Resumen** Watch the **Resumen** segment of this video module. Then write the name of the person who said each line.

_____Inés_____ 1. Cuando estaba en la escuela secundaria, trabajé en el taller de mi tío.

_____Javier_____ 2. Y Álex (...) usó su teléfono celular para llamar a un mecánico.

_____Javier_____ 3. Al salir de Quito los otros viajeros y yo no nos conocíamos muy bien.

_____Álex_____ 4. Piensa que puede arreglar el autobús aquí mismo.

_____Javier_____ 5. Es bueno tener superamigos, ¿no?

Después de ver el video

5   **Corregir** All of these statements about the video episode are false. Rewrite them so that they will be true.

1. Don Francisco llamó al señor Fonseca, el mecánico.
   Álex llamó al señor Fonseca.

2. Maite aprendió a arreglar autobuses en el taller de su tío.
   Inés aprendió a arreglar autobuses en el taller de su tío.

3. Don Francisco descubre que el problema está en el alternador.
   Inés descubre que el problema está en el alternador.

4. El mecánico saca una foto de Tecnohombre y la Mujer Mecánica con Maite y don Francisco.
   Javier saca la foto.

5. El asistente del señor Fonseca está mirando la televisión.
   El asistente del señor Fonseca está escuchando la radio.

6. El autobús está a unos treinta y cinco kilómetros de la ciudad.
   El autobús está a unos veinte kilómetros de la ciudad.

6   **Una carta** Imagine that Maite is writing a short letter to a friend about today's events. In Spanish, write what you think Maite would say in her letter. Answers will vary.

_____

_____

_____

_____

_____

_____

_____

_____

7   **Preguntas personales** Answer these questions in Spanish. Answers will vary.

1. Cuando tu carro está descompuesto, ¿lo llevas a un(a) mecánico/a o lo arreglas tú mismo/a?
   ¿Por qué? _____

_____

_____

2. ¿Conoces a un(a) buen(a) mecánico/a? ¿Cómo se llama? _____

_____

_____

3. ¿Tienes un teléfono celular? ¿Para qué lo usas? _____

_____

_____

Panorama: Argentina

Antes de ver el video

1 **Más vocabulario** Look over these useful words and expressions before you watch the video.

Vocabulario útil		
actualmente *nowadays*	**gaucho** *cowboy*	**pintura** *paint*
barrio *neighborhood*	**género** *genre*	**salón de baile** *ballroom*
cantante *singer*	**homenaje** *tribute*	**suelo** *floor*
exponer *to exhibit*	**pareja** *partner*	**surgir** *to emerge*
extrañar *to miss*	**paso** *step*	**tocar** *to play*

2 **Completar** The previous vocabulary will be used in this video. In preparation for watching the video, complete the sentences using words from the vocabulary list. Conjugate the verbs as necessary. Some words will not be used.

1. Los artistas _____exponen_____ sus pinturas en las calles.

2. Beyoncé es una _____cantante_____ famosa.

3. El tango tiene _____pasos_____ muy complicados.

4. El jazz es un _____género_____ musical que se originó en los Estados Unidos.

5. El tango _____surgió_____ en Buenos Aires, Argentina.

6. La gente va a los _____salones de baile_____ a divertirse.

7. Las personas _____extrañan_____ mucho a su país cuando tienen que vivir en el extranjero.

Mientras ves el video

3 **Marcar** Check off the cognates you hear while watching the video.

__✔__ 1. adultos __✔__ 7. dramático

__✔__ 2. aniversario __✔__ 8. exclusivamente

____ 3. arquitectura __✔__ 9. famosos

__✔__ 4. artistas __✔__ 10. gráfica

____ 5. demostración ____ 11. impacto

__✔__ 6. conferencia __✔__ 12. musical

Después de ver el video

4 **¿Cierto o falso?** Indicate whether each statement is **cierto** or **falso**. Correct the false statements.

1. Guillermo Alio dibuja en el suelo una gráfica para enseñar a cantar.

Falso. Alio dibuja una gráfica en el suelo para enseñar a bailar.

2. El tango es música, danza, poesía y pintura.

Cierto.

3. Alio es un artista que baila y canta al mismo tiempo.

Falso. Alio es un artista que baila y pinta al mismo tiempo.

4. Alio y su pareja se ponen pintura verde en los zapatos.

Falso. Alio pone pintura negra y su pareja pone pintura roja en sus zapatos.

5. Ahora los tangos son historias de hombres que sufren por amor.

Cierto.

6. El tango tiene un tono dramático y nostálgico.

Cierto.

5 **Completar** Complete the sentences with words from the word bank.

actualmente	compositor	fiesta	género	homenaje	pintor	surgió	toca

1. El tango es un _____ género _____ musical que se originó en Argentina en 1880.

2. El tango _____ surgió _____ en el barrio La Boca.

3. _____ Actualmente _____ este barrio se considera un museo al aire libre.

4. En la calle Caminito se _____ toca _____ y se baila el tango.

5. Carlos Gardel fue el _____ compositor _____ de varios de los tangos más famosos.

6. En el aniversario de su muerte, sus aficionados le hacen un _____ homenaje _____.

6 **Responder** Answer the questions in Spanish. Use complete sentences. Answers will vary.

1. ¿Por qué crees que el tango es tan famoso en todo el mundo?

2. ¿Te gustaría (*Would you like*) aprender a bailar tango? ¿Por qué?

3. ¿Qué tipo de música te gusta? Explica tu respuesta.

contextos

1 **Asociaciones** Circle the word or words that are not logically associated with each word you hear.

1. la impresora — (la velocidad) — el *fax*
2. guardar — imprimir — (funcionar)
3. la carretera — el motor — (el sitio web)
4. el tanque — (el ratón) — el aceite
5. conducir — (el cibercafé) — (el reproductor de MP3)
6. (el archivo) — la televisión — (la llanta)

2 **¿Lógico o ilógico?** You will hear some statements. Decide if they are **lógico** or **ilógico**.

	Lógico	Ilógico		Lógico	Ilógico
1.	○	◉	4.	◉	○
2.	◉	○	5.	◉	○
3.	○	◉	6.	○	◉

3 **Identificar** For each drawing in your lab manual, you will hear two statements. Choose the statement that best corresponds to the drawing.

1. (a.)   b.   2. a.   (b.)

3. (a.)   b.   4. (a.)   b.

pronunciación

c (before e or i), s, and z

In Latin America, **c** before **e** or **i** sounds much like the *s* in *sit*.

medi**c**ina	**c**elular	cono**c**er	pa**c**iente

In parts of Spain, **c** before **e** or **i** is pronounced like the *th* in *think*.

condu**c**ir	poli**c**ía	**c**ederrón	velo**c**idad

The letter **s** is pronounced like the *s* in *sit*.

subir	be**s**ar	**s**onar	impre**s**ora

In Latin America, the Spanish **z** is pronounced like the **s**.

cabe**z**a	nari**z**	abra**z**ar	embara**z**ada

The **z** is pronounced like the *th* in *think* in parts of Spain.

zapatos	**z**ona	pla**z**a	bra**z**o

---

1 **Práctica** Repeat each word after the speaker to practice pronouncing **s, z**, and **c** before **i** and **e**.

1. funcionar	4. sitio	7. zanahoria	10. perezoso
2. policía	5. disco	8. marzo	11. quizás
3. receta	6. zapatos	9. comenzar	12. operación

---

2 **Oraciones** When you hear each number, read the corresponding sentence aloud. Then listen to the speaker and repeat the sentence.

1. Vivió en Buenos Aires en su niñez pero siempre quería pasar su vejez en Santiago.
2. Cecilia y Zulaima fueron al centro a cenar al restaurante Las Delicias.
3. Sonó el despertador a las seis y diez pero estaba cansado y no quiso oírlo.
4. Zacarías jugaba al baloncesto todas las tardes después de cenar.

---

3 **Refranes** Repeat each saying after the speaker to practice pronouncing **s, z**, and **c** before **i** and **e**.

1. Zapatero, a tus zapatos.[1]
2. Primero es la obligación que la devoción.[2]

---

4 **Dictado** You will hear a friend describing Azucena's weekend experiences. Listen carefully and write what you hear during the pauses. The entire passage will be repeated so that you can check your work.

El sábado pasado Azucena iba a salir con Francisco. Se subió al carro e intentó arrancarlo, pero no funcionaba. El carro

tenía gasolina y, como revisaba el aceite con frecuencia, sabía que tampoco era eso. Decidió tomar un autobús cerca

de su casa. Se subió al autobús y comenzó a relajarse. Debido a la circulación llegó tarde, pero se alegró de ver que

Francisco estaba esperándola.

_____

_____

_____

Mind your P's and Q's. (lit. Shoemaker, to your shoes.)[1]
Business before pleasure.[2]

estructura

5.1 Familiar commands

1 **Identificar** You will hear some sentences. If the verb is a **tú** command, circle **Sí** in your lab manual. If the verb is not a **tú** command, circle **No**.

> **modelo**
>
> *You hear:* Ayúdanos a encontrar el control remoto.
> *You circle:* **Sí** because **Ayúdanos** is a **tú** command.

1. Sí   (No)
2. Sí   (No)
3. (Sí)   No
4. (Sí)   No
5. (Sí)   No

6. Sí   (No)
7. Sí   (No)
8. (Sí)   No
9. Sí   (No)
10. (Sí)   No

2 **Cambiar** Change each command you hear to the negative. Repeat the correct answer after the speaker. (*8 items*)

> **modelo**
>
> Cómprame un reproductor de DVD.
> **No me compres un reproductor de DVD.**

3 **Preguntas** Answer each question you hear using an affirmative **tú** command. Repeat the correct response after the speaker. (*7 items*)

> **modelo**
>
> ¿Estaciono aquí?
> **Sí, estaciona aquí.**

4 **Consejos prácticos** You will hear a conversation among three friends. Using **tú** commands and the ideas presented, write six pieces of advice that Mario can follow to save some money.

1. Usa el transporte público. _____

2. Compra un carro más pequeño. _____

3. Habla menos por teléfono. _____

4. Cancela la televisión por cable. _____

5. Vende tu teléfono celular. _____

6. Apaga las luces, la televisión y la computadora. _____

5.2 Por and para

1 **Escoger** You will hear some sentences with a beep in place of a preposition. Decide if **por** or **para** should complete each sentence.

> **modelo**
>
> *You hear:* El teclado es (*beep*) la computadora de Nuria.
> *You mark:* an **X** under **para**.

	por	para
Modelo		X
1.		X
2.		X
3.	X	
4.	X	
5.	X	
6.	X	
7.		X
8.	X	

2 **La aventura** Complete each phrase about Jaime with **por** or **para** and the cue in your lab manual. Repeat each correct response after the speaker.

> **modelo**
>
> *You hear:* Jaime estudió
> *You see:* médico
> *You say:* Jaime estudió para médico.

1. unos meses
2. hacer sus planes
3. mil dólares
4. ver a sus padres
5. la ciudad
6. su mamá
7. pesos
8. las montañas

3 **Los planes** Listen to the telephone conversation between Antonio and Sonia and then select the best response for the questions in your lab manual.

1. ¿Por dónde quiere ir Sonia para ir a Bariloche?
   a. Quiere ir por Santiago de Chile.
   b. Quiere ir por avión.

2. ¿Para qué va Sonia a Bariloche?
   a. Va para esquiar.
   b. Va para comprar esquíes.

3. ¿Por qué tiene que ir de compras Sonia?
   a. Para comprar una bolsa.
   b. Necesita un abrigo por el frío.

4. ¿Por qué quiere ir Antonio con ella hoy?
   a. Quiere ir para estar con ella.
   b. Quiere ir para comprar un regalo.

5.3 Reciprocal reflexives

1 **Escoger** Listen to each question and, in your lab manual, choose the most logical response.

1. a. Hace cuatro años que nos conocimos.
   b. Se vieron todos los fines de semana.
2. a. Nos besamos antes de salir a trabajar.
   b. No, creo que se besaron en la segunda.
3. a. Nos llevamos mal sólo el último año.
   b. Se llevaron mal siempre.
4. a. Sí, se saludan con un abrazo y también con un beso.
   b. Nos saludamos desde lejos.
5. a. Casi nunca me miraban.
   b. Creo que se miraban con mucho amor.
6. a. Sólo nos ayudamos para el examen.
   b. Se ayudan a menudo.
7. a. Creo que se hablan todas las noches.
   b. Le hablan mucho porque tienen celulares.
8. a. Cuando se casaron se querían mucho.
   b. Cada día nos queremos más.

2 **Responder** Answer each question in the affirmative. Repeat the correct answer after the speaker.
(6 *items*)

> **modelo**
>
> ¿Se abrazaron tú y Carolina en la primera cita?
> Sí, nos abrazamos en la primera cita.

3 **Los amigos** Listen to a description of a friendship and then, in your lab manual, choose the phrase that best completes each sentence.

1. Desde los once años, los chicos _____ con frecuencia.
   a. se veían   b. se ayudaban   c. se besaban
2. Samuel y Andrea _____ por la amistad (*friendship*) de sus madres.
   a. se escribían   b. se entendían   c. se conocieron
3. Las madres de Andrea y Samuel...
   a. se ayudaban.   b. se conocían bien.   c. se odiaban.
4. Andrea y Samuel no _____ por un tiempo por un problema.
   a. se conocieron   b. se hablaron   c. se ayudaron
5. Después de un tiempo,...
   a. se besaron.   b. se pidieron perdón.   c. se odiaron.
6. La separación sirvió para enseñarles que...
   a. se querían.   b. se hablaban mucho.   c. se conocían bien.
7. No es cierto. Andrea y Samuel no...
   a. se casaron.   b. se entendían bien.   c. se querían.
8. Los dos amigos _____ por un tiempo.
   a. se besaban   b. se comprometieron   c. se llevaron mal

5.4 Stressed possessive adjectives and pronouns

1 **Identificar** Listen to each statement and mark an **X** in the column identifying the possessive pronoun you hear.

> **modelo**
>
> *You hear:* Ya arreglaron todos los coches pero el tuyo no.
> *You write: an* **X** *under yours.*

	mine	*yours*	*his/hers*	*ours*	*theirs*
Modelo		**X**			
1.	X				
2.		X			
3.			X		
4.					X
5.				X	
6.	X				
7.		X			
8.			X		

2 **Transformar** Restate each sentence you hear, using the cues in your lab manual. Repeat the correct answer after the speaker.

> **modelo**
>
> *You hear:* ¿De qué año es el carro suyo?
> *You see: mine*
> *You say:* ¿De qué año es el carro mío?

1. *his*	3. *yours (fam.)*	5. *mine*
2. *ours*	4. *theirs*	6. *hers*

3 **¿Cierto o falso?** You will hear two brief conversations. Listen carefully and then indicate whether the statements in your lab manual are **cierto** or **falso**.

	Cierto	Falso
Conversación 1		
1. Pablo dice que el carro es de Ana.	○	⊘
2. Ana necesita la computadora para su trabajo.	○	⊘
3. Los discos compactos de Ana son mejores que los de Pablo.	⊘	○
Conversación 2		
4. La computadora de Adela tiene un módem muy rápido.	○	⊘
5. La calculadora de la prima de Adela es muy buena.	○	⊘
6. La calculadora es más de Adela que de ellos dos.	⊘	○

vocabulario

You will now hear the vocabulary found in your worktext on the last page of this lesson. Listen and repeat each Spanish word or phrase after the speaker.

Additional Vocabulary

Additional Vocabulary

Notes

Notes

La vivienda

6

Communicative Goals

You will learn how to:

- **Welcome people to your home**
- **Describe your house or apartment**
- **Talk about household chores**
- **Give instructions**

La vivienda

Más vocabulario

las afueras	suburbs; outskirts
el alquiler	rent (payment)
el ama (*m., f.*) de casa	housekeeper; caretaker
el barrio	neighborhood
el edificio de apartamentos	apartment building
el/la vecino/a	neighbor
la vivienda	housing
el balcón	balcony
la entrada	entrance
la escalera	stairs; stairway
el garaje	garage
el jardín	garden; yard
el patio	patio; yard
el sótano	basement; cellar
la cafetera	coffee maker
el electrodoméstico	electrical appliance
el horno (de microondas)	(microwave) oven
la lavadora	washing machine
la luz	light; electricity
la secadora	clothes dryer
la tostadora	toaster
el cartel	poster
la mesita de noche	night stand
los muebles	furniture
alquilar	to rent
mudarse	to move (from one house to another)

Variación léxica

dormitorio ⟷	aposento (*Rep. Dom.*); recámara (*Méx.*)
apartamento ⟷	departamento (*Arg., Chile*); piso (*Esp.*)
lavar los platos ⟷	lavar/fregar los trastes (*Amér. C., Rep. Dom.*)

recursos

WB pp. 323–324	LM p. 339	SUPERSITE adelante. vhlcentral.com

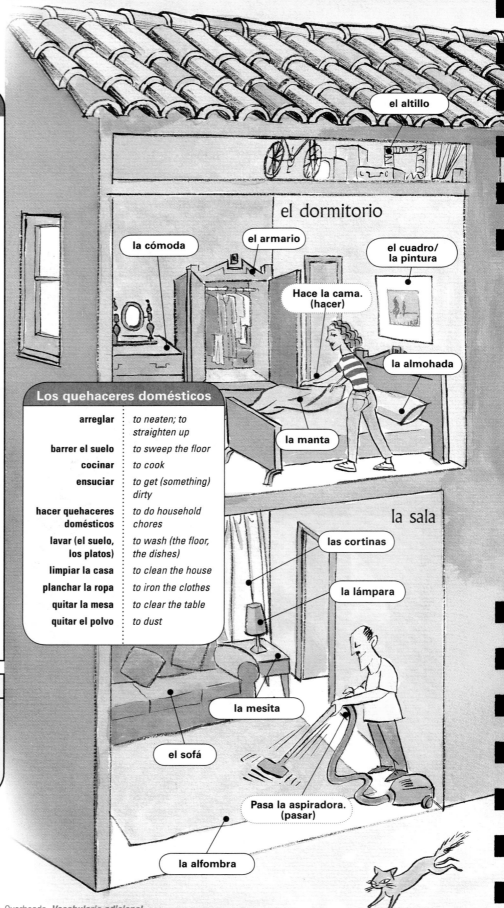

el altillo

el dormitorio

la cómoda

el armario

el cuadro/ la pintura

Hace la cama. (hacer)

la almohada

la manta

Los quehaceres domésticos

arreglar	to neaten; to straighten up
barrer el suelo	to sweep the floor
cocinar	to cook
ensuciar	to get (something) dirty
hacer quehaceres domésticos	to do household chores
lavar (el suelo, los platos)	to wash (the floor, the dishes)
limpiar la casa	to clean the house
planchar la ropa	to iron the clothes
quitar la mesa	to clear the table
quitar el polvo	to dust

la sala

las cortinas

la lámpara

la mesita

el sofá

Pasa la aspiradora. (pasar)

la alfombra

la oficina

el sillón

la pared

el estante

Sacude los muebles.
(sacudir)

la cocina

el refrigerador

el congelador

la cocina, la estufa

el horno

el lavaplatos

Saca la basura.
(sacar)

Supersite/IRCD: MP3 Audio Files, Scripts

Práctica

1 Escuchar Escucha la conversación y completa las oraciones.

1. Pedro va a limpiar primero _____la sala_____.
2. Paula va a comenzar en _____la cocina_____.
3. Pedro va a __planchar la ropa__ en el sótano.
4. Pedro también va a limpiar _____la oficina_____.
5. Ellos están limpiando la casa porque
   __la madre de Pedro viene a visitarlos__.

2 Respuestas Escucha las preguntas y selecciona la respuesta más adecuada. Una respuesta no se va a usar.

2 Before listening, have students read through the items and brainstorm possible questions.

__3__ a. Sí, la alfombra estaba muy sucia.
__5__ b. No, porque todavía se están mudando.
__1__ c. Sí, sacudí la mesa y el estante.
____ d. Sí, puse el pollo en el horno.
__2__ e. Hice la cama, pero no limpié los muebles.
__4__ f. Sí, después de sacarla de la secadora.

3 Escoger Escoge la letra de la respuesta correcta.

1. Cuando quieres tener una lámpara y un despertador cerca de tu cama, puedes ponerlos en __c__.
   a. el barrio   b. el cuadro   c. la mesita de noche
2. Si no quieres vivir en el centro de la ciudad, puedes mudarte __b__.
   a. al alquiler   b. a las afueras   c. a la vivienda
3. Guardamos (*We keep*) los pantalones, las camisas y los zapatos en __b__.
   a. la secadora   b. el armario   c. el patio
4. Para subir de la planta baja al primer piso, usamos __c__.
   a. la entrada   b. el cartel   c. la escalera
5. Ponemos cuadros y pinturas en __a__.
   a. las paredes   b. los quehaceres   c. los jardines

4 Definiciones En parejas, identifiquen cada cosa que se describe. Luego inventen sus propias descripciones de algunas palabras y expresiones de **Contextos**.

modelo
Estudiante 1: *Es donde pones los libros.*
Estudiante 2: *el estante*

1. Es donde pones la cabeza cuando duermes. una almohada
2. Es el quehacer doméstico que haces después de comer. lavar los platos/ quitar la mesa
3. Algunos de ellos son las cómodas y los sillones. los muebles
4. Son las personas que viven en tu barrio. los vecinos

Lección 6

el comedor

Supersite/IRCD: At this point you may want to present *Vocabulario adicional: Más vocabulario para el hogar*.

Teaching Tip Add a visual aspect to this vocabulary presentation. Bring in silverware, plates, and glasses. As you hold up each item, have students name it and guide you in setting the table. Ex: **¿Dónde pongo el tenedor, a la derecha o a la izquierda del plato?**

5 **Completar** Completa estas frases con la palabra más adecuada.

1. Para tomar vino necesitas... una copa
2. Para comer una ensalada necesitas... un tenedor/un plato
3. Para tomar café necesitas... una taza
4. Para poner la comida en la mesa necesitas... un plato/poner la mesa
5. Para limpiarte la boca después de comer necesitas... una servilleta
6. Para cortar (*to cut*) un bistec necesitas... un cuchillo (y un tenedor)
7. Para tomar agua necesitas... un vaso/una copa
8. Para tomar sopa necesitas... una cuchara/un plato

5 Ask volunteers to answer questions modeled on the sentence starters. Ex: **¿Qué se necesita para comer la carne?**

6 **Los quehaceres** Trabajen en grupos para indicar quién hace estos quehaceres domésticos en sus casas. Luego contesten las preguntas. Answers will vary.

> **modelo**
>
> **Estudiante 1:** ¿Quién pasa la aspiradora en tu casa?
> **Estudiante 2:** Mi hermano y yo pasamos la aspiradora.

barrer el suelo	lavar los platos	planchar la ropa
cocinar	lavar la ropa	sacar la basura
hacer las camas	pasar la aspiradora	sacudir los muebles

1. ¿Quién hace más quehaceres, tú o tus compañeros/as?
2. ¿Quiénes hacen la mayoría de los quehaceres, los hombres o las mujeres?
3. ¿Piensas que debes hacer más quehaceres? ¿Por qué?

Extra Practice Ask students to complete these analogies.
1. aspiradora : _____ :: *lavadora* : ropa (alfombra) (*Aspiradora es a alfombra como lavadora es a ropa.*)
2. frío : calor :: congelador : _____ (horno)
3. cama : alcoba :: _____ : oficina (escritorio)
4. platos : cocina :: carro : _____ (garaje)

6 Before breaking the class into groups, model the activity using your own situation. Ex: **En casa, mi esposa siempre pasa la aspiradora, pero yo sacudo los muebles. Mi hijo...**

Game Have students bring in real estate ads. Ask teams of three to write a description of a property. Teams then take turns reading their descriptions aloud. Other teams guess the price. The team that guesses the amount closest to the real price without going over scores one point.

Comunicación

7

La vida doméstica En parejas, describan las habitaciones que ven en estas fotos. Identifiquen y describan cinco muebles o adornos (*accessories*) de cada foto y digan dos quehaceres que se pueden hacer en cada habitación. Answers will vary.

7 Model the activity using a magazine picture. Ex: **¡Qué comedor más desordenado! ¡Es un desastre! Alguien debe quitar los platos sucios de la mesa. También es necesario sacudir los muebles y pasar la aspiradora. La mesa y las sillas son muy bonitas, pero el comedor está muy sucio.**

7 To simplify, give students three minutes to look at the pictures and brainstorm possible answers.

8 Draw a floor plan of a three-room apartment on the board. Ask volunteers to describe it.

CONSULTA

To review bathroom-related vocabulary, see **Lección 1, Contextos,** p. 22.

8

Mi apartamento Dibuja el plano (*floor plan*) de un apartamento amueblado (*furnished*) imaginario y escribe los nombres de las habitaciones y de los muebles. En parejas, pónganse espalda contra espalda (*sit back to back*). Uno/a de ustedes describe su apartamento mientras su compañero/a lo dibuja según la descripción. Cuando terminen, miren el segundo dibujo. ¿Es similar al dibujo original? Hablen de los cambios que se necesitan hacer para mejorar el dibujo. Repitan la actividad intercambiando los papeles. Answers will vary.

9

¡Corre, corre! Tu profesor(a) va a darte una serie incompleta de dibujos que forman una historia. Tú y tu compañero/a tienen dos series diferentes. Descríbanse los dibujos para completar la historia. Answers will vary.

> **modelo**
>
> **Estudiante 1:** Marta quita la mesa.
> **Estudiante 2:** Francisco...

Supersite/IRCD: Information Gap Activities

9 Have pairs tell each other about an occasion when they have had to clean up their home for a particular reason. Ask them to share their stories with the class.

Extra Practice Have students complete this cloze activity. **La vida doméstica de un estudiante universitario puede ser un desastre, ¿no? Nunca hay tiempo para hacer los _____ (quehaceres) domésticos. Sólo _____ (pasa) la aspiradora una vez al semestre y nunca _____ (sacude) los muebles. Los _____ (platos) sucios se acumulan en la _____ (cocina). Saca la ropa de la _____ (secadora) y se la pone sin _____ (planchar). Y, ¿por qué hacer la _____ (cama)? Se va a acostar en ella de nuevo este mismo día, ¿no?**

Lección 6

¡Les va a encantar la casa!

Don Francisco y los estudiantes llegan a Ibarra.

communication cultures
NATIONAL STANDARDS

PERSONAJES

INÉS

DON FRANCISCO

ÁLEX

JAVIER

SRA. VIVES

SRA. VIVES ¡Hola, bienvenidos!

DON FRANCISCO Señora Vives, le presento a los chicos. Chicos, ésta es la señora Vives, el ama de casa.

SRA. VIVES Encantada. Síganme que quiero mostrarles la casa. ¡Les va a encantar!

SRA. VIVES Esta alcoba es para los chicos. Tienen dos camas, una mesita de noche, una cómoda… En el armario hay más mantas y almohadas por si las necesitan.

SRA. VIVES Ésta es la sala. El sofá y los sillones son muy cómodos. Pero, por favor, ¡no los ensucien!

SRA. VIVES Allí están la cocina y el comedor. Al fondo del pasillo hay un baño.

DON FRANCISCO Chicos, a ver… ¡atención! La señora Vives les va a preparar las comidas. Pero quiero que ustedes la ayuden con los quehaceres domésticos. Quiero que arreglen sus alcobas, que hagan las camas, que pongan la mesa… ¿entendido?

JAVIER No se preocupe… la vamos a ayudar en todo lo posible.

ÁLEX Sí, cuente con nosotros.

recursos

VM pp. 335–336

SUPERSITE adelante. vhlcentral.com

Video Synopsis **Don Francisco** and the students go to the house where they will stay before their hike. The housekeeper shows the students around the house. **Don Francisco** tells the students to help with the chores, and he advises them that their guide for the hike will arrive at seven the next morning.

Preview In pairs, have students cover the captions and look at the video stills. Using vocabulary from **Contextos**, have students describe the rooms, furniture, and appliances.

Expresiones útiles Point out the verbs **Síganme** and **Cuente** and have students guess which is an **usted** command and which is an **ustedes** command. Point out the sentences that begin with **Quiero que...**, **Insistimos en que...**, and **Le(s) aconsejo que....** Explain that these sentences contain examples of the present subjunctive. Tell students that they will learn more about these concepts in **Estructura**.

Lección 6

SRA. VIVES Javier, no ponga las maletas en la cama. Póngalas en el piso, por favor.

SRA. VIVES Tomen ustedes esta alcoba, chicas.

INÉS Insistimos en que nos deje ayudarla a preparar la comida.

SRA. VIVES No, chicos, no es para tanto, pero gracias por la oferta. Descansen un rato que seguramente están cansados.

ÁLEX Gracias. A mí me gustaría pasear por la ciudad.

INÉS Perdone, don Francisco, ¿a qué hora viene el guía mañana?

DON FRANCISCO ¿Martín? Viene temprano, a las siete de la mañana. Les aconsejo que se acuesten temprano esta noche. ¡Nada de televisión ni de conversaciones largas!

ESTUDIANTES ¡Ay, don Francisco!

Expresiones útiles

Welcoming people
- **¡Bienvenido(s)/a(s)!**
  Welcome!

Showing people around the house
- **Síganme... que quiero mostrarles la casa.**
  Follow me... I want to show you the house.
- **Esta alcoba es para los chicos.**
  This bedroom is for the guys.
- **Ésta es la sala.**
  This is the living room.
- **Allí están la cocina y el comedor.**
  The kitchen and dining room are over there.
- **Al fondo del pasillo hay un baño.**
  At the end of the hall there is a bathroom.

Telling people what to do
- **Quiero que la ayude(n) con los quehaceres domésticos.**
  I want you to help her with the household chores.
- **Quiero que arregle(n) su(s) alcoba(s).**
  I want you to straighten your room(s).
- **Quiero que haga(n) las camas.**
  I want you to make the beds.
- **Quiero que ponga(n) la mesa.**
  I want you to set the table.
- **Cuente con nosotros.**
  (You can) count on us.
- **Insistimos en que nos deje ayudarla a preparar la comida.**
  We insist that you let us help you make the food.
- **Le (Les) aconsejo que se acueste(n) temprano.**
  I recommend that you go to bed early.

Other expressions
- **No es para tanto.**
  It's not a big deal.
- **Gracias por la oferta.**
  Thanks for the offer.

Teaching Tip Photocopy the *Fotonovela* Videoscript (Supersite/IRCD) and white out words related to houses and household chores. Have students fill in the missing words as they watch the episode. Then ask them to circle any words they had already used in the Preview activity (p. 294).

Pairs Ask students to imagine this house is for sale and create a brief conversation between the real estate agent and a prospective buyer.

¿Qué pasó? SUPERSITE

1 Give students these additional items: **6. Álex quiere descansar. (Falso. Álex quiere pasear por la ciudad.) 7. Martín va a llegar mañana a las cuatro de la tarde. (Falso. Martín va a llegar a las siete de la mañana.)**

1 **¿Cierto o falso?** Indica si lo que dicen estas oraciones es **cierto** o **falso**. Corrige las oraciones falsas.

	Cierto	Falso
1. Las alcobas de los estudiantes tienen dos camas, dos mesitas de noche y una cómoda. Tienen sólo una mesita de noche.	○	☑
2. La señora Vives no quiere que Javier ponga las maletas en la cama.	☑	○
3. El sofá y los sillones están en la sala.	☑	○
4. Los estudiantes tienen que sacudir los muebles y sacar la basura. Tienen que arreglar las alcobas, hacer las camas y poner la mesa.	○	☑
5. Los estudiantes van a preparar las comidas. La señora Vives va a preparar las comidas.	○	☑

2 **Identificar** Identifica quién puede decir estas oraciones.

1. Nos gustaría preparar la comida esta noche. ¿Le parece bien a usted? Inés
2. Miren, si quieren otra almohada o manta, hay más en el armario. Sra. Vives
3. Tranquilo, tranquilo, que nosotros vamos a ayudarla muchísimo. Javier
4. Tengo ganas de caminar un poco por la ciudad. Álex
5. No quiero que nadie mire la televisión esta noche. ¡Tenemos que levantarnos temprano mañana! don Francisco

ÁLEX

JAVIER

INÉS

DON FRANCISCO

SRA. VIVES

2 Give students these additional items: **6. Ésta es la alcoba de las chicas. (Sra. Vives) 7. El guía va a llegar a las siete de la mañana. (don Francisco) 8. ¿Quieren descansar un rato? (Sra. Vives) 9. Chicos, les presento a la señora Vives. (don Francisco)**

3 **Completar** Los estudiantes y la señora Vives están haciendo los quehaceres. Adivina en qué cuarto está cada uno de ellos.

1. Inés limpia el congelador. Inés está en __la cocina__.
2. Javier limpia el escritorio. Javier está en __la oficina__.
3. Álex pasa la aspiradora debajo de la mesa y las sillas. Álex está en __el comedor__.
4. La señora Vives sacude el sillón. La señora Vives está en __la sala__.
5. Don Francisco no está haciendo nada. Él está dormido en __el dormitorio/ la alcoba__.

3 Ask pairs to come up with lists of other household chores that can be done in each of the rooms. Have them share their answers with the class. Keep count of the items on their lists to find out which pair came up with the most correct possibilities.

4 **Mi casa** Dibuja el plano de una casa o de un apartamento. Puede ser el plano de la casa o del apartamento donde vives o de donde te gustaría (*you would like*) vivir. Después, trabajen en parejas y describan lo que se hace en cuatro de las habitaciones. Para terminar, pídanse (*ask for*) ayuda para hacer dos quehaceres domésticos. Pueden usar estas frases en su conversación. Answers will vary.

> Quiero mostrarte...
> Ésta es (la cocina).
> Allí yo (preparo la comida).
>
> Al fondo hay...
> Quiero que me ayudes a (sacar la basura).
> Por favor, ayúdame con...

Small Groups Ask small groups to write four comprehension questions about the *Fotonovela*, then exchange with another group to complete the activity.

4 To simplify, draw your own floor plan on the board and model the activity. Ex: **Ésta es la sala. Me gusta mirar la televisión allí. Aquí está la oficina. Allí hablo por teléfono y trabajo en la computadora. Ésta es la cocina, donde preparo las comidas... _____, quiero que me ayudes a sacudir los muebles. _____, por favor, ayúdame a pasar la aspiradora.**

Teaching Tips
- Explain that in a few Spanish city and country names the definite article is considered part of the name, and is thus capitalized. Ex: **La Habana, La Coruña, La Haya, El Salvador.**
- Spanish treatment of titles of books, film, and works of art differs from English. In Spanish, only the first word and any proper noun gets an initial capital. Spanish treatment of the names of newspapers and magazines is the same as in English. Tell students that *El País* is a newspaper and *Muy Interesante* is a magazine. All the items mentioned are italicized in print.

Ortografía Supersite/IRCD: MP3 Audio Files, Listening Scripts

Mayúsculas y minúsculas

Here are some of the rules that govern the use of capital letters (**mayúsculas**) and lowercase letters (**minúsculas**) in Spanish.

Los estudiantes llegaron al aeropuerto a las dos. Luego fueron al hotel.

In both Spanish and English, the first letter of every sentence is capitalized.

Rubén Blades   Panamá   Colón   los Andes

The first letter of all proper nouns (names of people, countries, cities, geographical features, etc.) is capitalized.

Cien años de soledad   Don Quijote de la Mancha
El País   Muy Interesante

The first letter of the first word in titles of books, films, and works of art is generally capitalized, as well as the first letter of any proper names. In newspaper and magazine titles, as well as other short titles, the initial letter of each word is often capitalized.

---

la señora Ramos   don Francisco
el presidente   Sra. Vives

Titles associated with people are *not* capitalized unless they appear as the first word in a sentence. Note, however, that the first letter of an abbreviated title is capitalized.

Último   Álex   MENÚ   PERDÓN

Accent marks should be retained on capital letters. In practice, however, this rule is often ignored.

---

lunes   viernes   marzo   primavera

The first letter of days, months, and seasons is <u>not</u> capitalized.

---

español   estadounidense   japonés   panameños

The first letter of nationalities and languages is <u>not</u> capitalized.

Profesor Herrera, ¿es cierto que somos venenosas°?

Sí, Pepito. ¿Por qué lloras?

Extra Practice Write additional titles, names, sentences, etc., all in lowercase on the board. Ask volunteers to decide which letters should be capitalized.

Pairs In pairs, have students scan the reading on the next page, circle all the capital letters, and explain why each is capitalized. Point out the words **árabe, españoles,** and **islámica** and have students explain why they are not capitalized.

Práctica Corrige las mayúsculas y minúsculas incorrectas.

1. soy lourdes romero. Soy Colombiana.
   Soy Lourdes Romero. Soy colombiana.
2. éste Es mi Hermano álex.
   Éste es mi hermano Álex.
3. somos De panamá. Somos de Panamá.
4. ¿es ud. La sra. benavides?
   ¿Es Ud. la Sra. Benavides?
5. ud. Llegó el Lunes, ¿no?
   Ud. llegó el lunes, ¿no?

Palabras desordenadas Lee el diálogo de las serpientes. Ordena las letras para saber de qué palabras se trata. Después escribe las letras indicadas para descubrir por qué llora Pepito.

m n a a P á ⬭⬜⬜⬜⬜⬜⬜

s t e m r a ⬭⬜⬜⬜⬜⬜⬜

i g s l é n ⬜⬜⬜⬭⬜⬜⬜

y a U r u g u ⬜⬜⬜⬭⬜⬜⬜

r o ñ e s a ⬜⬜⬜⬜⬜⬭

¡ _orque _e acabo de morder° la _en _u_!

Respuestas: Panamá, martes, inglés, Uruguay, señora.
¡Porque me acabo de morder la lengua!

venenosas *venomous*   morder *to bite*

recursos

LM p. 340

adelante. vhlcentral.com

EN DETALLE

El patio central

En las tardes cálidas° de Oaxaca, México; Córdoba, España, o Popayán, Colombia, es un placer sentarse en **el patio central** de una casa y tomar un refresco disfrutando de° una buena conversación. De influencia árabe, esta característica arquitectónica° fue traída° a las Américas por los españoles. En la época° colonial, se construyeron casas, palacios, monasterios, hospitales y escuelas con patio central. Éste es un espacio privado e íntimo en donde se puede disfrutar del sol y de la brisa° estando aislado° de la calle.

El centro del patio es un espacio abierto. Alrededor de° él, separado por columnas, hay un pasillo cubierto°. Así, en el patio hay zonas de sol y de sombra°. El patio es una parte importante de la vivienda familiar y su decoración se cuida° mucho. En el centro del patio muchas veces hay una fuente°, plantas e incluso árboles°. El agua es un elemento muy importante en la ideología islámica porque simboliza la purificación del cuerpo y del alma°. Por esta razón y para disminuir° la temperatura, el agua en estas construcciones es muy importante. El agua y la vegetación ayudan a mantener la temperatura fresca y el patio proporciona° luz y ventilación a todas las habitaciones.

La distribución

Las casas con patio central eran usualmente las viviendas de familias adineradas°. Son casas de dos o tres pisos. Los cuartos de la planta baja son las áreas comunes: cocina, comedor, sala, etc., y tienen puertas al patio. En los pisos superiores están las habitaciones privadas de la familia.

---

cálidas *hot* disfrutando de *enjoying* arquitectónica *architectural* traída *brought* época *era* brisa *breeze* aislado *isolated* Alrededor de *Surrounding* cubierto *covered* sombra *shade* se cuida *is looked after* fuente *fountain* árboles *trees* alma *soul* disminuir *lower* proporciona *provides* adineradas *wealthy*

ACTIVIDADES

1 **¿Cierto o falso?** Indica si lo que dicen estas oraciones es **cierto** o **falso**. Corrige la información falsa.

1. Los patios centrales de Latinoamérica tienen su origen en la tradición indígena. Falso. Los patios tienen su origen en la arquitectura árabe.

2. En la época colonial las casas eran las únicas construcciones con patio central. Falso. Se construyeron casas, palacios, monasterios, hospitales y escuelas.

3. El patio es una parte importante en estas construcciones. Cierto.

4. El patio central es un lugar de descanso que da luz y ventilación a las habitaciones. Cierto.

5. Las casas con patio central eran para personas adineradas. Cierto.

6. Los cuartos de la planta baja son privados. Falso. Los cuartos de la planta baja son las áreas comunes.

7. Las fuentes en los patios tienen importancia por razones ideológicas y porque bajan la temperatura. Cierto.

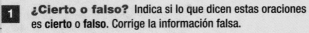

Lección 6

ASÍ SE DICE

La vivienda

el ático, el desván	el altillo
la cobija (Méx.), la frazada (Arg., Cuba, Ven.)	la manta
el escaparate (Cuba, Ven.), el ropero (Méx.)	el armario
el fregadero	*kitchen sink*
el frigidaire (Perú); el frigorífico (Esp.), la nevera	el refrigerador
el lavavajillas (Arg., Esp., Méx.)	el lavaplatos

EL MUNDO HISPANO

Los muebles

○ **Mecedora°** La mecedora es un mueble típico de Latinoamérica, especialmente de la zona del Caribe. A las personas les gusta relajarse mientras se mecen° en el patio.

○ **Mesa camilla** Era un mueble popular en España hasta hace algunos años. Es una mesa con un bastidor° en la parte inferior° para poner un brasero°. En invierno, las personas se sentaban alrededor de la mesa camilla para conversar, jugar a las cartas o tomar café.

○ **Hamaca** Se cree que los taínos hicieron las primeras hamacas con fibras vegetales. Su uso es muy popular en toda Latinoamérica para dormir y descansar.

Mecedora *Rocking chair* **se mecen** *they rock themselves*
bastidor *frame* **inferior** *bottom* **brasero** *container for hot coals*

PERFIL

Las islas flotantes del lago Titicaca

Bolivia y Perú comparten **el lago Titicaca**, donde viven **los uros**, uno de los pueblos indígenas más antiguos de América. Hace muchos años, los uros fueron a vivir al lago escapando de **los incas**. Hoy en día, siguen viviendo allí en cuarenta **islas flotantes** que ellos mismos hacen con unos juncos° llamados **totora**. Primero tejen° grandes plataformas. Luego, con el mismo material, construyen sus casas sobre las plataformas. La totora es resistente, pero con el tiempo el agua la pudre°. Los habitantes de las islas

necesitan renovar continuamente las plataformas y las casas. Sus muebles y sus barcos también están hechos° de juncos. Los uros viven de la pesca y del turismo; en las islas hay unas tiendas donde venden artesanías° hechas con totora.

PERÚ

Lago Titicaca

BOLIVIA

juncos *reeds* **tejen** *they weave* **la pudre** *rots it* **hechos** *made* **artesanías** *handcrafts*

SUPERSITE **Conexión Internet**

¿Cómo son las casas modernas en los países hispanos?

Go to **adelante.vhlcentral.com** to find more cultural information related to this **Cultura** section.

ACTIVIDADES

2 **Comprensión** Responde a las preguntas.

1. Tu amigo mexicano te dice: "La **cobija** azul está en el **ropero**". ¿Qué quiere decir? La manta azul está en en el armario.

2. ¿Quiénes hicieron las primeras hamacas? ¿Qué material usaron? los taínos; fibras vegetales

3. ¿Qué grupo indígena vive en el lago Titicaca? Los uros viven en el lago Titicaca.

4. ¿Qué pueden comprar los turistas en las islas flotantes del lago Titicaca? Pueden comprar artesanías hechas con totora.

3 **Viviendas tradicionales** Escribe cuatro oraciones sobre una vivienda tradicional que conoces. Explica en qué lugar se encuentra, de qué materiales está hecha y cómo es. Answers will vary.

3 To add a visual aspect, have students find a photo of a traditional dwelling to use as the basis for the written description.

recursos

adelante.vhlcentral.com

6.1 Relative pronouns

ANTE TODO In both English and Spanish, relative pronouns are used to combine two sentences or clauses that share a common element, such as a noun or pronoun. Study this diagram.

> Mis padres me regalaron **la aspiradora**.
> *My parents gave me the vacuum cleaner.*

> **La aspiradora** funciona muy bien.
> *The vacuum cleaner works really well.*

> La aspiradora **que** me regalaron mis padres funciona muy bien.
> *The vacuum cleaner that my parents gave me works really well.*

> **Lourdes** es muy inteligente.
> *Lourdes is very intelligent.*

> **Lourdes** estudia español.
> *Lourdes is studying Spanish.*

> Lourdes, **quien** estudia español, es muy inteligente.
> *Lourdes, who studies Spanish, is very intelligent.*

> *Pueden usar las almohadas que están en el armario.*

> *Chicos, ésta es la señora Vives, quien les va a mostrar la casa.*

▶ Spanish has three frequently-used relative pronouns. **¡Atención!** Interrogative words (**qué**, **quién**, etc.) always carry an accent. Relative pronouns, however, never carry a written accent.

que	*that; which; who*
quien(es)	*who; whom; that*
lo que	*that which; what*

▶ **Que** is the most frequently used relative pronoun. It can refer to things or to people. Unlike its English counterpart, *that*, **que** is never omitted.

> ¿Dónde está la cafetera **que** compré?
> *Where is the coffee maker (that) I bought?*

> El hombre **que** limpia es Pedro.
> *The man who is cleaning is Pedro.*

▶ The relative pronoun **quien** refers only to people, and is often used after a preposition or the personal **a. Quien** has only two forms: **quien** (singular) and **quienes** (plural).

> ¿Son las chicas **de quienes** me hablaste la semana pasada?
> *Are they the girls (that) you told me about last week?*

> Eva, **a quien** conocí anoche, es mi nueva vecina.
> *Eva, whom I met last night, is my new neighbor.*

Lección 6

Teaching Tips
- Test comprehension as you proceed by asking volunteers to answer questions about students and objects in the classroom. Ex: ¿Cómo se llama la estudiante que se sienta detrás de ____? ¿Cómo se llaman los estudiantes a quienes acabo de hacer esta pregunta? ¿Dónde está la tarea que ustedes hicieron para hoy?
- Add a visual aspect to this grammar presentation. Line up four to five pictures. Ask questions that use relative pronouns or elicit them in student answers. Ex: ¿Quién está comiendo una hamburguesa? (El muchacho que está sentado en la playa está comiendo una hamburguesa.) ¿Quién sabe lo que está haciendo esta muchacha? (Está quitando la mesa.)

▶ **Quien(es)** is occasionally used instead of **que** in clauses set off by commas.

Lola, **quien** es cubana, es médica.
Lola, who is Cuban, is a doctor.

Su tía, **que** es alemana, ya llegó.
His aunt, who is German, already arrived.

▶ Unlike **que** and **quien(es)**, **lo que** doesn't refer to a specific noun. It refers to an idea, a situation, or a past event and means *what, that which,* or *the thing that.*

Este mercado tiene todo lo que Inés necesita.

A la señora Vives no le gustó lo que hizo Javier.

Lo que me molesta es el calor.
What bothers me is the heat.

Lo que quiero es una casa.
What I want is a house.

¡INTÉNTALO! Completa estas oraciones con pronombres relativos.

1. Voy a utilizar los platos ___que___ me regaló mi abuela.
2. Ana comparte un apartamento con la chica a ___quien___ conocimos en la fiesta de Jorge.
3. Esta oficina tiene todo ___lo que___ necesitamos.
4. Puedes estudiar en el dormitorio ___que___ está a la derecha de la cocina.
5. Los señores ___que___ viven en esa casa acaban de llegar de Centroamérica.
6. Los niños a ___quienes___ viste en nuestro jardín son mis sobrinos.
7. La piscina ___que___ ves desde la ventana es la piscina de mis vecinos.
8. Fue Úrsula ___quien___ ayudó a mamá a limpiar el refrigerador.
9. Ya te dije que fue mi padre ___quien___ alquiló el apartamento.
10. ___Lo que___ te dijo Pablo no es cierto.
11. Tengo que sacudir los muebles ___que___ están en el altillo una vez al mes.
12. No entiendo por qué no lavaste los vasos ___que___ te dije.
13. La mujer a ___quien___ saludaste vive en las afueras.
14. ¿Sabes ___lo que___ necesita este dormitorio? ¡Unas cortinas!
15. No quiero volver a hacer ___lo que___ hice ayer.
16. No me gusta vivir con personas a ___quienes___ no conozco.

Extra Practice Ask students to make two short lists: **Lo que tengo en mi dormitorio** and **Lo que quiero tener en mi dormitorio**. Ask volunteers to read part of their lists to the class. Encourage a conversation by asking questions such as: **¿Es esto lo que tienes en tu dormitorio? ¿Es un ____ lo que quieres tú?**

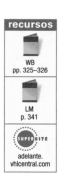

Práctica

NOTA CULTURAL

Rubén Blades es
un cantante y actor
panameño muy
famoso. Ha grabado
más de veinte
álbumes y ha actuado
en más de treinta
películas. En sus
canciones expresa su
amor por la literatura
y la política.

1 **Combinar** Combina elementos de la columna A y la columna B para formar oraciones lógicas.

A

1. Ése es el hombre ___d___.
2. Rubén Blades, ___c___.
3. No traje ___e___.
4. ¿Te gusta la manta ___b___?
5. ¿Cómo se llama el programa ___g___?
6. La mujer ___a___.

B

a. con quien bailaba es mi vecina
b. que te compró Cecilia ◀
c. quien es de Panamá, es un cantante muy bueno
d. que arregló mi lavadora
e. lo que necesito para la clase de matemáticas
f. que comiste en el restaurante
g. que escuchaste en la radio anoche

2 **Completar** Completa la historia sobre la casa que Jaime y Tina quieren comprar, usando los pronombres relativos **que, quien, quienes** o **lo que**.

1. Jaime y Tina son los chicos a ___quienes___ conocí la semana pasada.
2. Quieren comprar una casa ___que___ está en las afueras de la ciudad.
3. Es una casa ___que___ era de una artista famosa.
4. La artista, a ___quien___ yo conocía, murió el año pasado y no tenía hijos.
5. Ahora se vende la casa con todos los muebles ___que___ ella tenía.
6. La sala tiene una alfombra ___que___ ella trajo de Kuwait.
7. La casa tiene muchos estantes, ___lo que___ a Tina le encanta.

2 Ask questions about the
content of the activity.
Ex: 1. ¿Quiénes quieren
comprar una casa? (Jaime
y Tina) 2. ¿Qué casa
quieren comprar? (una casa
que está en las afueras de
la ciudad) 3. ¿De quién era
la casa? (de una artista
famosa) 4. ¿Cómo venden
la casa? (con todos los
muebles que tenía) 5. ¿Qué
tipo de alfombra tiene la
sala? (una alfombra que la
artista trajo de Kuwait)

Extra Practice Have
students use relative
pronouns to complete this
series. 1. _____ tenemos
que hacer es buscar otro
apartamento. (Lo que) 2. El
apartamento _____ tenemos
sólo tiene dos alcobas.
(que) 3. Ayer hablamos con
un compañero _____ alquila
una casa cerca de aquí.
(que) 4. Buscamos algo
similar a _____ él tiene: tres
alcobas, dos cuartos de
baño, una cocina, una sala,
un comedor... ¡y un alquiler
bajo! (lo que) 5. Nos dio el
nombre de unos agentes a
_____ podemos contactar.
(quienes)

Pairs Ask pairs of students
to write a description of a
new household gadget, using
relative pronouns. Their
descriptions should include
the purpose of the gadget and
how it is used.

3 **Oraciones** Javier y Ana acaban de casarse y han comprado (*they have bought*) una casa y muchas otras cosas. Combina sus declaraciones para formar una sola oración con los pronombres relativos **que, quien(es)** y **lo que**.

> **modelo**
>
> Vamos a usar los vasos nuevos mañana. Los pusimos en el comedor.
> *Mañana vamos a usar los vasos nuevos que pusimos en el comedor.*

3 Ask a volunteer to read
the **modelo** aloud. Ask
another volunteer to explain
what word is replaced by the
relative pronoun **que**.

3 Have pairs write two
more sentences that contain
relative pronouns and refer to
Javier and **Ana's** new home.

1. Tenemos una cafetera nueva. Mi prima nos la regaló.
   Tenemos una cafetera nueva que mi prima nos regaló.
2. Tenemos una cómoda nueva. Es bueno porque no hay espacio en el armario.
   Tenemos una cómoda nueva, lo que es bueno porque no hay espacio en el armario.
3. Esos platos no nos costaron mucho. Están encima del horno.
   Esos platos que están encima del horno no nos costaron mucho.
4. Esas copas me las regaló mi amiga Amalia. Ella viene a visitarme mañana.
   Esas copas me las regaló mi amiga Amalia, quien viene a visitarme mañana.
5. La lavadora está casi nueva. Nos la regalaron mis suegros.
   La lavadora que nos regalaron mis suegros está casi nueva.
6. La vecina nos dio una manta de lana. Ella la compró en México.
   La vecina nos dio una manta de lana que compró en México.

Comunicación

4

Entrevista En parejas, túrnense para hacerse estas preguntas. Answers will vary.

1. ¿Qué es lo que más te gusta de vivir en las afueras o en la ciudad?
2. ¿Cómo son las personas que viven en tu barrio?
3. ¿Cuál es el quehacer doméstico que menos te gusta? ¿Y el que más te gusta?
4. ¿Quién es la persona que hace los quehaceres domésticos en tu casa?
5. ¿Quiénes son las personas con quienes más sales los fines de semana? ¿Quién es la persona a quien más llamas por teléfono?
6. ¿Cuál es el deporte que más te gusta? ¿Cuál es el que menos te gusta?
7. ¿Cuál es el barrio de tu ciudad que más te gusta y por qué?
8. ¿Quién es la persona a quien más llamas cuando tienes problemas?
9. ¿Quién es la persona a quien más admiras? ¿Por qué?
10. ¿Qué es lo que más te gusta de tu casa?
11. ¿Qué es lo que más te molesta de tus amigos?
12. ¿Qué es lo que menos te gusta de tu barrio?

5

Adivinanza En grupos, túrnense para describir distintas partes de una vivienda usando pronombres relativos. Los demás compañeros tienen que hacer preguntas hasta que adivinen la palabra.
Answers will vary.

modelo

> **Estudiante 1:** Es lo que tenemos en el dormitorio.
> **Estudiante 2:** ¿Es el mueble que usamos para dormir?
> **Estudiante 1:** No. Es lo que usamos para guardar la ropa.
> **Estudiante 3:** Lo sé. Es la cómoda.

Síntesis

6

Definir En parejas, definan las palabras. Usen los pronombres relativos **que, quien(es)** y **lo que.** Luego compartan sus definiciones con la clase. Answers will vary.

modelo

> lavadora   Es lo que se usa para lavar la ropa.
> pastel   Es un postre que comes en tu cumpleaños.

alquiler	flan	patio	tenedor
amigos	guantes	postre	termómetro
aspiradora	jabón	sillón	vaso
enfermera	manta	sótano	vecino

6.2 Formal commands

ANTE TODO As you learned in **Lección 5**, the command forms are used to give orders or advice. Formal commands are used with people you address as **usted** or **ustedes.** Observe these examples, then study the chart.

Hable con ellos, don Francisco.
Talk with them, Don Francisco.

Coma frutas y verduras.
Eat fruits and vegetables.

Laven los platos ahora mismo.
Wash the dishes right now.

Beban menos té y café.
Drink less tea and coffee.

AYUDA

By learning formal commands, it will be easier for you to learn the subjunctive forms that are presented in **Estructura 6.3**, p. 308.

Formal commands (Ud. and Uds.)

Infinitive	Present tense **yo** form	**Ud.** command	**Uds.** command
limpiar	limp**io**	limp**ie**	limp**ien**
barrer	barr**o**	barr**a**	barr**an**
sacudir	sacud**o**	sacud**a**	sacud**an**
decir (e:i)	dig**o**	dig**a**	dig**an**
pensar (e:ie)	piens**o**	piens**e**	piens**en**
volver (o:ue)	vuelv**o**	vuelv**a**	vuelv**an**
servir (e:i)	sirv**o**	sirv**a**	sirv**an**

▶ The **usted** and **ustedes** commands, like the negative **tú** commands, are formed by dropping the final **-o** of the **yo** form of the present tense. For **-ar** verbs, add **-e** or **-en.** For **-er** and **-ir** verbs, add **-a** or **-an.**

No se preocupe... La vamos a ayudar en todo lo posible.

Sí, cuente con nosotros.

▶ Verbs with irregular **yo** forms maintain the same irregularity in their formal commands. These verbs include **conducir, conocer, decir, hacer, ofrecer, oír, poner, salir, tener, traducir, traer, venir,** and **ver.**

Oiga, don Francisco...
Listen, Don Francisco...

¡Salga inmediatamente!
Leave immediately!

Ponga la mesa, por favor.
Set the table, please.

Hagan la cama antes de salir.
Make the bed before leaving.

▶ Note also that verbs maintain their stem changes in **usted** and **ustedes** commands.

e:ie	o:ue	e:i
No **pierda** la llave.	**Vuelva** temprano, joven.	**Sirva** la sopa, por favor.
Cierren la puerta.	**Duerman** bien, chicos.	**Repitan** las frases.

Teaching Tips
• Model the use of formal commands with simple examples using TPR and gestures. Ex: **Levántense. Siéntense.** Then point to individual students and give commands in an exaggerated formal tone. Ex: **Señor(ita) ____, levántese.** Give other commands using **salga/ salgan, vuelva/vuelvan,** and **venga/vengan.**
• Write a list of verbs on the board and have volunteers give commands, first to you, then to the class. Respond with humor to any impossible or inappropriate requests. Ex: **¡Ni loco/a!**

Video Replay the *Fotonovela* episode and have students write down each formal command that they hear. Have students compare their lists with a partner.

Extra Practice Describe situations and have students call out **ustedes** commands that would be used. Ex: A mother sending her kids off to overnight camp. (**Cepíllense los dientes antes de dormir.**) An aerobics class. (**Levanten los brazos.**)

Lección 6

Teaching Tips
• Ask volunteers to write formal command forms of other verbs with spelling changes on the board. Ex: **empezar (empiece); comenzar (comience); buscar (busque); pagar (pague); llegar (llegue).**
• Test comprehension as you proceed by asking volunteers to supply the correct form of other infinitives you name.
• Point out that the written accent mark on **dé** serves to distinguish the verb form from the preposition **de**.

▶ Verbs ending in **-car, -gar,** and **-zar** have a spelling change in the command forms.

sa**car**	c ⟶ qu	sa**que**, sa**qu**en
ju**gar**	g ⟶ gu	jue**gue**, jue**gu**en
almor**zar**	z ⟶ c	almuer**ce**, almuer**c**en

▶ These verbs have irregular formal commands.

Infinitive	Ud. command	Uds. command
dar	**dé**	**den**
estar	**esté**	**estén**
ir	**vaya**	**vayan**
saber	**sepa**	**sepan**
ser	**sea**	**sean**

▶ To make a formal command negative, simply place **no** before the verb.

No ponga las maletas en la cama.   **No ensucien** los sillones.
Don't put the suitcases on the bed.   *Don't dirty the armchairs.*

▶ In affirmative commands, reflexive, indirect and direct object pronouns are always attached to the end of the verb.

Siénten**se**, por favor.   Acuésten**se** ahora.
Síga**me**, Laura.   Póngan**las** en el suelo, por favor.

▶ **¡Atención!** When a pronoun is attached to an affirmative command that has two or more syllables, an accent mark is added to maintain the original stress.

limpie ⟶ **límpielo**   **lean** ⟶ **léanlo**
diga ⟶ **dígamelo**   **sacudan** ⟶ **sacúdanlos**

▶ In negative commands, these pronouns always precede the verb.

No **se** preocupe.   No **los** ensucien.
No **me lo** dé.   No **nos las** traigan.

▶ **Usted** and **ustedes** can be used with the command forms to strike a more formal tone. In such instances they follow the command form.

Muéstrele usted la foto a su amigo.   **Tomen ustedes** esta alcoba.
Show the photo to your friend.   *Take this bedroom.*

recursos

WB
pp. 327–328

LM
p. 342

SUPERSITE
adelante.
vhlcentral.com

¡INTÉNTALO! Indica los mandatos (*commands*) afirmativos y negativos correspondientes.

1. escucharlo (Ud.) _Escúchelo_ . _No lo escuche_ .
2. decírmelo (Uds.) _Díganmelo_ . _No me lo digan_ .
3. salir (Ud.) _Salga_ . _No salga_ .
4. servírnoslo (Uds.) _Sírvannoslo_ . _No nos lo sirvan_ .
5. barrerla (Ud.) _Bárrala_ . _No la barra_ .
6. hacerlo (Ud.) _Hágalo_ . _No lo haga_ .

Extra Practice Write a list of situations on the board using singular and plural forms. Ex: **La cocina está sucia. Mis amigos y yo tenemos hambre. Tenemos miedo.** Then have students write responses in the form of commands. Ex: **Límpiela. Hagan la cena. No tengan miedo.**

Teaching Tip Point out the double n in item 4: **Sírvannoslo.**

Práctica

1 **Completar** La señora González quiere mudarse de casa. Ayúdala a organizarse. Indica el mandato formal de cada verbo.

1. _____Lea_____ los anuncios del periódico y ___guárdelos___. (Leer, guardarlos)
2. _____Vaya_____ personalmente y _____vea_____ las casas usted misma. (Ir, ver)
3. Decida qué casa quiere y ___llame___ al agente. ___Pídale___ un contrato de alquiler. (llamar, Pedirle)
4. ___Contrate___ un camión *(truck)* para ese día y ___pregúnteles___ la hora exacta de llegada. (Contratar, preguntarles)
5. El día de la mudanza *(On moving day)* ___esté___ tranquila. ___Vuelva___ a revisar su lista para completar todo lo que tiene que hacer. (estar, Volver)
6. Primero, ___dígales___ a todos en casa que usted va a estar ocupada. No ___les diga___ que usted va a hacerlo todo. (decirles, decirles)
7. ___Saque___ tiempo para hacer las maletas tranquilamente. No ___les haga___ las maletas a los niños más grandes. (Sacar, hacerles)
8. No ___se preocupe___. ___Sepa___ que todo va a salir bien. (preocuparse, Saber)

2 **¿Qué dicen?** Mira los dibujos y escribe un mandato lógico para cada uno. Usa palabras que aprendiste en **Contextos**.   Answers will vary. Suggested answers:

1. _____Abran sus libros, por favor._____

2. _____Cierre la puerta. ¡Hace frío!_____

3. _____Traiga usted la cuenta, por favor._____

4. _La cocina está sucia. Bárranla, por favor._

5. _____Duerma bien, niña._____

6. _Arreglen el cuarto, por favor. Está desordenado._

Lección 6

Comunicación

3 Ask volunteers to offer other suggestions for the problem in the **modelo**. Ex: **Tenga usted más cuidado. Compre nuevos zapatos de tenis.**

3 Ask pairs to pick their most humorous or unusual response to present to the class.

3 **Solucionar** Trabajen en parejas para presentar estos problemas. Un(a) estudiante presenta los problemas de la columna A y el/la otro/a los de la columna B. Usen mandatos formales y túrnense para ofrecer soluciones. Answers will vary.

> **modelo**
>
> **Estudiante 1:** Vilma se torció un tobillo jugando al tenis. Es la tercera vez.
> **Estudiante 2:** No juegue más al tenis. / Vaya a ver a un especialista.

A

1. Se me perdió el libro de español con todas mis notas.
2. A Vicente se le cayó la botella de vino para la cena.
3. ¿Cómo? ¿Se le olvidó traer el traje de baño a la playa?
4. Se nos quedaron los boletos en la casa. El avión sale en una hora.

B

1. Mis hijas no se levantan temprano. Siempre llegan tarde a la escuela.
2. A mi abuela le robaron (*stole*) las maletas. Era su primer día de vacaciones.
3. Nuestra casa es demasiado pequeña para nuestra familia.
4. Me preocupo constantemente por Roberto. Trabaja demasiado.

4 Have pairs write another scenario on a sheet of paper. Then ask them to exchange papers with another pair and give them two minutes to prepare another dialogue. Have them act out their dialogues for the authors.

4 **Conversaciones** En parejas, escojan dos situaciones y preparen conversaciones para presentar a la clase. Usen mandatos formales. Answers will vary.

> **modelo**
>
> **Lupita:** Señor Ramírez, siento mucho llegar tan tarde. Mi niño se enfermó. ¿Qué debo hacer?
> **Sr. Ramírez:** No se preocupe. Siéntese y descanse un poco.

SITUACIÓN 1 Profesor Rosado, no vine la semana pasada porque el equipo jugaba en Boquete. ¿Qué debo hacer para ponerme al día *(catch up)*?

SITUACIÓN 2 Los invitados de la boda llegan a las cuatro de la tarde, las mesas están sin poner y el champán sin servir. Los camareros apenas están llegando. ¿Qué deben hacer los camareros?

SITUACIÓN 3 Mi novio es un poco aburrido. No le gustan ni el cine, ni los deportes, ni salir a comer. Tampoco habla mucho. ¿Qué puedo hacer?

▶ **SITUACIÓN 4** Tengo que preparar una presentación para mañana sobre el Canal de Panamá. ¿Por dónde comienzo?

NOTA CULTURAL

El 31 de diciembre de 1999, los Estados Unidos cedió el control del **Canal de Panamá** al gobierno de Panamá, terminando así con casi 100 años de administración estadounidense.

Síntesis

5 **Presentar** En grupos, preparen un anuncio de televisión para presentar a la clase. El anuncio debe tratar de un detergente, un electrodoméstico o una agencia inmobiliaria (*real estate agency*). Usen mandatos, los pronombres relativos (**que, quien(es)** o **lo que**) y el **se** impersonal. Answers will vary.

> **modelo**
>
> Compre el lavaplatos Siglo XXI. Tiene todo lo que usted desea. Es el lavaplatos que mejor funciona. Venga a verlo ahora mismo… No pierda ni un minuto más. Se aceptan tarjetas de crédito.

Supersite/IRCD: See the Information Gap Activities for an additional activity to practice the material presented in this section.

6.3 The present subjunctive

ANTE TODO With the exception of commands, all the verb forms you have been using have been in the indicative mood. The indicative is used to state facts and to express actions or states that the speaker considers to be real and definite. In contrast, the subjunctive mood expresses the speaker's attitudes toward events, as well as actions or states the speaker views as uncertain or hypothetical.

> Quiero que ustedes ayuden con los quehaceres domésticos.

> Insistimos en que nos deje ayudarla a preparar la comida.

Present subjunctive of regular verbs

		hablar	**comer**	**escribir**
SINGULAR FORMS	yo	hable	coma	escriba
	tú	hables	comas	escribas
	Ud./él/ella	hable	coma	escriba
PLURAL FORMS	nosotros/as	hablemos	comamos	escribamos
	vosotros/as	habléis	comáis	escribáis
	Uds./ellos/ellas	hablen	coman	escriban

▶ The present subjunctive is formed very much like **usted** and **ustedes** and *negative* **tú** commands. From the **yo** form of the present indicative, drop the **-o** ending, and replace it with the subjunctive endings.

INFINITIVE	PRESENT INDICATIVE	VERB STEM	PRESENT SUBJUNCTIVE
hablar	hablo	habl-	hable
comer	como	com-	coma
escribir	escribo	escrib-	escriba

▶ The present subjunctive endings are:

-ar verbs		-er and -ir verbs	
-e	-emos	-a	-amos
-es	-éis	-as	-áis
-e	-en	-a	-an

Teaching Tip Write sentences like these on the board in two columns labeled *Indicative* and *Subjunctive*. Column 1: **Mi esposo lava los platos. Mi esposo barre el suelo. Mi esposo cocina.**

Column 2: **Mi esposo quiere que yo lave los platos. Mi esposo quiere que yo barra el suelo. Mi esposo quiere que yo cocine.** Underline **yo lave**, asking students what the indicative form would be. Do the same for the other sentences.

¡LENGUA VIVA!

You may think that English has no subjunctive, but it does! While once common, it now survives mostly in set expressions such as *if I were you* and *be that as it may.*

AYUDA

Note that, in the present subjunctive, **-ar** verbs use endings normally associated with present tense **-er** and **-ir** verbs. Likewise, **-er** and **-ir** verbs in the present subjunctive use endings normally associated with **-ar** verbs in the present tense. Note also that, in the present subjunctive, the **yo** form is the same as the **Ud./él/ella** form.

Teaching Tips
• Provide additional examples of the subjunctive mood in English. Ex: *I wish she were here. I insist that he take notes. I suggest you be there tomorrow.*
• Emphasize the stem changes that occur in the **nosotros/as** and **vosotros/as** forms of **-ir** stem-changing verbs.

Extra Practice Create sentences that use the subjunctive. Say the sentence, and have students repeat. Then call out a different subject for the subordinate clause. Have students then say the sentence with the new subject, making all other necessary changes. Ex: **Quiero que ustedes trabajen mucho. Javier. (Quiero que Javier trabaje mucho.) Quiero que lleguen temprano. Nosotras. (Quiero que lleguemos temprano.)**

▶ Verbs with irregular **yo** forms show the same irregularity in all forms of the present subjunctive.

Infinitive	Present indicative	Verb stem	Present subjunctive
conducir	conduzco	**conduzc-**	**conduzca**
conocer	conozco	**conozc-**	**conozca**
decir	digo	**dig-**	**diga**
hacer	hago	**hag-**	**haga**
ofrecer	ofrezco	**ofrezc-**	**ofrezca**
oír	oigo	**oig-**	**oiga**
parecer	parezco	**parezc-**	**parezca**
poner	pongo	**pong-**	**ponga**
tener	tengo	**teng-**	**tenga**
traducir	traduzco	**traduzc-**	**traduzca**
traer	traigo	**traig-**	**traiga**
venir	vengo	**veng-**	**venga**
ver	veo	**ve-**	**vea**

▶ To maintain the **-c, -g,** and **-z** sounds, verbs ending in **-car, -gar,** and **-zar** have a spelling change in all forms of the present subjunctive.

sacar:	sa**que**, sa**que**s, sa**que**, sa**que**mos, sa**qué**is, sa**que**n
jugar:	jue**gue**, jue**gue**s, jue**gue**, ju**gue**mos, ju**gué**is, jue**gue**n
almorzar:	almuer**ce**, almuer**ce**s, almuer**ce**, almor**ce**mos, almor**cé**is, almuer**ce**n

Present subjunctive of stem-changing verbs

AYUDA

Note that stem-changing verbs and verbs that have a spelling change have the same ending as regular verbs in the present subjunctive.

▶ **-Ar** and **-er** stem-changing verbs have the same stem changes in the subjunctive as they do in the present indicative.

pensar (e:ie):	p**ie**nse, p**ie**nses, p**ie**nse, pensemos, penséis, p**ie**nsen
mostrar (o:ue):	m**ue**stre, m**ue**stres, m**ue**stre, mostremos, mostréis, m**ue**stren
entender (e:ie):	ent**ie**nda, ent**ie**ndas, ent**ie**nda, entendamos, entendáis, ent**ie**ndan
volver (o:ue):	v**ue**lva, v**ue**lvas, v**ue**lva, volvamos, volváis, v**ue**lvan

TPR Call out an infinitive verb and a subject pronoun (Ex: **alquilar/yo**). Toss a foam or paper ball to a student. He or she must provide the correct subjunctive phrase (**que yo alquile**), then toss the ball to another student. Avoid verbs with irregular subjunctive forms.

▶ **-Ir** stem-changing verbs have the same stem changes in the subjunctive as they do in the present indicative, but in addition, the **nosotros/as** and **vosotros/as** forms undergo a stem change. The unstressed **e** changes to **i,** while the unstressed **o** changes to **u.**

pedir (e:i):	p**i**da, p**i**das, p**i**da, p**i**damos, p**i**dáis, p**i**dan
sentir (e:ie):	s**ie**nta, s**ie**ntas, s**ie**nta, s**i**ntamos, s**i**ntáis, s**ie**ntan
dormir (o:ue):	d**ue**rma, d**ue**rmas, d**ue**rma, d**u**rmamos, d**u**rmáis, d**ue**rman

Extra Practice Ask students to compare family members' attitudes toward domestic life using the subjunctive. Ex: **Los padres quieren que los hijos... Los hijos insisten en que...**

Irregular verbs in the present subjunctive

▶ These five verbs are irregular in the present subjunctive.

Irregular verbs in the present subjunctive

		dar	estar	ir	saber	ser
SINGULAR FORMS	yo	dé	esté	vaya	sepa	sea
	tú	des	estés	vayas	sepas	seas
	Ud./él/ella	dé	esté	vaya	sepa	sea
PLURAL FORMS	nosotros/as	demos	estemos	vayamos	sepamos	seamos
	vosotros/as	deis	estéis	vayáis	sepáis	seáis
	Uds./ellos/ellas	den	estén	vayan	sepan	sean

▶ **¡Atención!** The subjunctive form of **hay** (*there is, there are*) is also irregular: **haya.**

General uses of the subjunctive

▶ The subjunctive is mainly used to express: 1) will and influence, 2) emotion, 3) doubt, disbelief, and denial, and 4) indefiniteness and nonexistence.

▶ The subjunctive is most often used in sentences that consist of a main clause and a subordinate clause. The main clause contains a verb or expression that triggers the use of the subjunctive. The conjunction **que** connects the subordinate clause to the main clause.

Main clause	Connector	Subordinate clause
Es muy importante	que	**vayas** al hotel ahora mismo.

▶ These impersonal expressions are always followed by clauses in the subjunctive:

Es bueno que...	**Es mejor que...**	**Es malo que...**
It's good that...	*It's better that...*	*It's bad that...*
Es importante que...	**Es necesario que...**	**Es urgente que...**
It's important that...	*It's necessary that...*	*It's urgent that...*

 **¡INTÉNTALO!**   Indica el presente de subjuntivo de estos verbos.

1. (alquilar, beber, vivir)   que yo <u>alquile, beba, viva</u>
2. (estudiar, aprender, asistir)   que tú <u>estudies, aprendas, asistas</u>
3. (encontrar, poder, dormir)   que él <u>encuentre, pueda, duerma</u>
4. (hacer, tener, venir)   que nosotras <u>hagamos, tengamos, vengamos</u>
5. (dar, hablar, escribir)   que ellos <u>den, hablen, escriban</u>
6. (pagar, empezar, buscar)   que ustedes <u>paguen, empiecen, busquen</u>
7. (ser, ir, saber)   que yo <u>sea, vaya, sepa</u>
8. (estar, dar, oír)   que tú <u>estés, des, oigas</u>

Teaching Tips
• Point out that, in order to use the subjunctive in the subordinate clause, the conjunction **que** must be present and there must be a change of subject. Write these sentences on the board: **Es importante que limpies la cocina. Es importante limpiar la cocina.** Have a volunteer explain why the subjunctive is used only in the first sentence. Emphasize that, while the first example states one person's responsibility, the second is a broad statement about the importance of cleaning kitchens.
• Reiterate that, whereas the word *that* is usually optional in English, **que** is required in Spanish.

Extra Practice Call on two volunteers at a time. The first student writes a main clause on the board that requires the subjunctive (Ex: **Es importante que**). The second student writes an ending for the sentence (Ex: **aprendamos español.**).

Video Replay the *Fotonovela* episode and pause where appropriate to discuss each use of the subjunctive.

recursos

WB
pp. 329–330

LM
p. 343

SUPERSITE
adelante.
vhlcentral.com

Práctica

1

Completar Completa las oraciones con el presente de subjuntivo de los verbos entre paréntesis. Luego empareja las oraciones del primer grupo con las del segundo grupo.

A

1. Es mejor que ___cenemos___ en casa. (nosotros, cenar) b
2. Es importante que ___visites___ las casas colgantes de Cuenca. (tú, visitar) c
3. Señora, es urgente que le ___saque___ el diente. Tiene una infección. (yo, sacar) e
4. Es malo que Ana les ___dé___ tantos dulces a los niños. (dar) a
5. Es necesario que ___lleguen___ a la una de la tarde. (ustedes, llegar) f
6. Es importante que ___nos acostemos___ temprano. (nosotros, acostarse) d

B

a. Es importante que ___coman___ más verduras. (ellos, comer)
b. No, es mejor que ___salgamos___ a comer. (nosotros, salir)
c. Y yo creo que es bueno que ___vaya___ a Madrid después. (yo, ir)
d. En mi opinión, no es necesario que ___durmamos___ tanto. (nosotros, dormir)
e. ¿Ah, sí? ¿Es necesario que me ___tome___ un antibiótico también? (yo, tomar)
f. Para llegar a tiempo, es necesario que ___almorcemos___ temprano. (nosotros, almorzar)

NOTA CULTURAL ▶

Las casas colgantes (*hanging*) de Cuenca, España, son muy famosas. Situadas en un acantilado (*cliff*), forman parte del paisaje de la ciudad.

Comunicación

2

Minidiálogos En parejas, completen los minidiálogos con expresiones impersonales de una manera lógica. Answers will vary.

> **modelo**
>
> **Miguelito:** Mamá, no quiero arreglar mi cuarto.
> **Sra. Casas:** Es necesario que lo arregles. Y es importante que sacudas los muebles también.

1. **MIGUELITO** Mamá, no quiero estudiar. Quiero salir a jugar con mis amigos.
   SRA. CASAS

2. **MIGUELITO** Mamá, es que no me gustan las verduras. Prefiero comer pasteles.
   SRA. CASAS

3. **MIGUELITO** ¿Tengo que poner la mesa, mamá?
   SRA. CASAS

4. **MIGUELITO** No me siento bien, mamá. Me duele todo el cuerpo y tengo fiebre.
   SRA. CASAS

2 Ask questions about **Miguelito** and **señora Casas** to elicit the subjunctive. Ex: **¿En qué insiste la señora Casas?** (Insiste en que Miguelito arregle su cuarto, que coma verduras y que ponga la mesa.) **¿Qué quiere Miguelito?** (Quiere salir a jugar y comer pasteles.)

3

Entrevista Trabajen en parejas. Entrevístense usando estas preguntas. Expliquen sus respuestas.
Answers will vary.

1. ¿Es importante que los niños ayuden con los quehaceres domésticos?
2. ¿Es urgente que los estadounidenses aprendan otras lenguas?
3. Si un(a) estadounidense quiere aprender francés, ¿es mejor que lo aprenda en Francia?
4. En su universidad, ¿es necesario que los estudiantes vivan en residencias estudiantiles?
5. ¿Es importante que todas las personas asistan a la universidad?

3 Ask students to report on their partner's answers using complete sentences and explanations. Ex: **¿Qué opina ____ sobre los quehaceres de los niños? ¿Cree que es importante que ayuden?**

Extra Practice Ask students to write ten statements using the subjunctive to describe their dream house (**la casa de mis sueños**). Ex: **Para mí es importante que haya una piscina de tamaño olímpico en la casa de mis sueños. Es mejor que la cocina sea grande porque me gusta cocinar. Es necesario que tenga varios dormitorios porque siempre tengo huéspedes.** Have students share their sentences with a partner.

Lección 6

Subjunctive with verbs of will and influence

ANTE TODO You will now learn how to use the subjunctive with verbs and expressions of will and influence.

Quiero que tengas dientes más blancos.

▶ Verbs of will and influence are often used when someone wants to affect the actions or behavior of other people.

Enrique **quiere** que salgamos a cenar.
Enrique wants us to go out to dinner.

Paola **prefiere** que cenemos en casa.
Paola prefers that we have dinner at home.

▶ Here is a list of widely used verbs of will and influence.

Verbs of will and influence

aconsejar	to advise	**pedir** (e:i)	to ask (for)
desear	to wish; to desire	**preferir** (e:ie)	to prefer
importar	to be important; to matter	**prohibir**	to prohibit
		querer (e:ie)	to want
insistir (en)	to insist (on)	**recomendar** (e:ie)	to recommend
mandar	to order	**rogar** (o:ue)	to beg; to plead
necesitar	to need	**sugerir** (e:ie)	to suggest

▶ Some impersonal expressions, such as **es necesario que, es importante que, es mejor que,** and **es urgente que,** are considered expressions of will or influence.

▶ When the main clause contains an expression of will or influence, the subjunctive is required in the subordinate clause, provided that the two clauses have different subjects.

Main clause	Connector	Subordinate clause
VERB OF WILL		SUBJUNCTIVE
Mi mamá **prefiere**	que	yo **saque** la basura.

Lección 6

Quiero que arreglen sus alcobas, que hagan las camas, que pongan la mesa…

…y les aconsejo que se acuesten temprano esta noche.

▶ Indirect object pronouns are often used with the verbs **aconsejar, importar, mandar, pedir, prohibir, recomendar, rogar,** and **sugerir.**

Te aconsejo que estudies.
I advise you to study.

Le sugiero que vaya a casa.
I suggest that he go home.

Les recomiendo que barran el suelo.
I recommend that you sweep the floor.

Le ruego que no venga.
I beg him not to come.

▶ Note that all the forms of **prohibir** in the present tense carry a written accent, except for the **nosotros/as** form: **prohíbo, prohíbes, prohíbe, prohibimos, prohibís, prohíben.**

Ella les **prohíbe** que miren la televisión.
She prohibits them from watching television.

Nos **prohíben** que nademos en la piscina.
They prohibit that we swim in the swimming pool.

▶ The infinitive is used with words or expressions of will and influence, if there is no change of subject in the sentence.

No quiero **sacudir** los muebles.
I don't want to dust the furniture.

Paco prefiere **descansar.**
Paco prefers to rest.

Es importante **sacar** la basura.
It's important to take out the trash.

No es necesario **quitar** la mesa.
It's not necessary to clear the table.

¡INTÉNTALO!   Completa cada oración con la forma correcta del verbo entre paréntesis.

1. Te sugiero que __vayas__ (ir) con ella al supermercado.
2. Él necesita que yo le __preste__ (prestar) dinero.
3. No queremos que tú __hagas__ (hacer) nada especial para nosotros.
4. Mis papás quieren que yo __limpie__ (limpiar) mi cuarto.
5. Nos piden que la __ayudemos__ (ayudar) a preparar la comida.
6. Quieren que tú __saques__ (sacar) la basura todos los días.
7. Quiero __descansar__ (descansar) esta noche.
8. Es importante que ustedes __limpien__ (limpiar) los estantes.
9. Su tía les manda que __pongan__ (poner) la mesa.
10. Te aconsejo que no __salgas__ (salir) con él.
11. Mi tío insiste en que mi prima __haga__ (hacer) la cama.
12. Prefiero __ir__ (ir) al cine.
13. Es necesario __estudiar__ (estudiar).
14. Recomiendo que ustedes __pasen__ (pasar) la aspiradora.

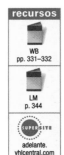

Práctica SUPERSITE

1 Completar Completa el diálogo con palabras de la lista.

cocina	haga	quiere	sea
comas	ponga	saber	ser
diga	prohíbe	sé	vaya

IRENE Tengo problemas con Vilma. Sé que debo hablar con ella. ¿Qué me recomiendas que le (1)___diga___?

JULIA Pues, necesito (2)___saber___ más antes de darte consejos.

IRENE Bueno, para empezar me (3)___prohíbe___ que traiga dulces a la casa.

JULIA Pero chica, tiene razón. Es mejor que tú no (4)___comas___ cosas dulces.

IRENE Sí, ya lo sé. Pero quiero que (5)___sea___ más flexible. Además, insiste en que yo (6)___haga___ todo en la casa.

JULIA Yo (7)___sé___ que Vilma (8)___cocina___ y hace los quehaceres todos los días.

IRENE Sí, pero siempre que hay fiesta me pide que (9)___ponga___ los cubiertos y las copas en la mesa y que (10)___vaya___ al sótano por las servilletas y los platos. ¡Es lo que más odio: ir al sótano!

JULIA Mujer, ¡Vilma sólo (11)___quiere___ que ayudes en la casa!

2 Aconsejar En parejas, lean lo que dice cada persona. Luego den consejos lógicos usando verbos como **aconsejar, recomendar** y **prohibir**. Sus consejos deben ser diferentes de lo que la persona quiere hacer. Answers will vary.

> **modelo**
>
> **Isabel:** Quiero conseguir un comedor con los muebles más caros del mundo.
>
> **Consejo:** *Te aconsejamos que consigas unos muebles menos caros.*

1. **DAVID** Pienso poner el cuadro del lago de Maracaibo en la cocina.
2. **SARA** Voy a ir a la gasolinera para comprar unas copas de cristal elegantes.
3. **SR. ALARCÓN** Insisto en comenzar a arreglar el jardín en marzo.
4. **SRA. VILLA** Quiero ver las tazas y los platos de la tienda El Ama de Casa Feliz.
5. **DOLORES** Voy a poner servilletas de tela (*cloth*) para los cuarenta invitados.
6. **SR. PARDO** Pienso poner todos mis muebles nuevos en el altillo.
7. **SRA. GONZÁLEZ** Hay una fiesta en casa esta noche pero no quiero limpiarla.
8. **CARLITOS** Hoy no tengo ganas de hacer las camas ni de quitar la mesa.

3 Preguntas En parejas, túrnense para contestar las preguntas. Usen el subjuntivo.
Answers will vary.

1. ¿Te dan consejos tus amigos/as? ¿Qué te aconsejan? ¿Aceptas sus consejos? ¿Por qué?
2. ¿Qué te sugieren tus profesores que hagas antes de terminar los cursos que tomas?
3. ¿Insisten tus amigos/as en que salgas mucho con ellos?
4. ¿Qué quieres que te regalen tu familia y tus amigos/as en tu cumpleaños?
5. ¿Qué le recomiendas tú a un(a) amigo/a que no quiere salir los sábados con su novio/a?
6. ¿Qué les aconsejas a los nuevos estudiantes de tu universidad?

3 Follow up the activity with class discussion. Ex: **¿Quiénes siempre les dan consejos a sus amigos? ¿Que tipo de cosas aconsejan?**

1 Before beginning the activity, ask a volunteer to read the first line of dialogue aloud. Guide students to see that the subject of the verb in the blank is **yo**, which is implied by **me** in the main clause.

1 Have pairs write a summary of the dialogue in the third person. Ask one or two volunteers to read their summaries to the class.

2 Have students create two suggestions for each person. In the second they should use one of the impersonal expressions listed on page 312.

NOTA CULTURAL

En el **lago de Maracaibo,** en Venezuela, hay casas suspendidas sobre el agua que se llaman palafitos. Los palafitos son reminiscencias de Venecia, Italia, de donde viene el nombre "Venezuela", que significa "pequeña Venecia".

Large Group Write the names of famous historical figures on individual sticky notes and place them on the students' backs. Have students circulate around the room, giving each other advice that will help them guess their "identity."

Comunicación

4

4 Ask each pair to pick their favorite response and share it with the class, who will vote for the most clever, most shocking, or funniest suggestion.

Inventar En parejas, preparen una lista de seis personas famosas. Un(a) estudiante da el nombre de una persona famosa y el/la otro/a le da un consejo. Answers will vary.

> **modelo**
>
> **Estudiante 1:** *Judge Judy.*
> **Estudiante 2:** *Le recomiendo que sea más simpática con la gente.*
> **Estudiante 2:** *Orlando Bloom.*
> **Estudiante 1:** *Le aconsejo que haga más películas.*

5 Before beginning the activity, ask volunteers to describe the drawing, naming everything they see and all the chores that need to be done.

5

Hablar En parejas, miren la ilustración. Imaginen que Gerardo necesita ayuda para arreglar su casa y resolver sus problemas románticos y económicos. Usen expresiones impersonales y verbos como **aconsejar**, **sugerir** y **recomendar**. Answers will vary.

> **modelo**
>
> *Es mejor que arregles el apartamento más a menudo.*
> *Te aconsejo que no dejes para mañana lo que puedes hacer hoy.*

6 Have pairs compare their responses in groups of four. Ask groups to choose which among all of the suggestions are the most likely to work for **Hernán** and have them share these with the class.

Síntesis

6

6 Have pairs choose a famous couple in history or fiction. Ex: Romeo and Juliet or Napoleon and Josephine. Then have them write a letter from one of the couples to **doctora Salvamórez**. Finally, have them exchange their letters with another pair and write the corresponding responses from the doctor.

La doctora Salvamórez Hernán tiene problemas con su novia y le escribe a la doctora Salvamórez, columnista del periódico *Panamá y su gente*. Ella responde a las cartas de personas con problemas románticos. En parejas, lean la carta de Hernán y después usen el subjuntivo para escribir los consejos de la doctora. Answers will vary.

> Estimada doctora Salvamórez:
>
> Mi novia nunca quiere que yo salga de casa. No le molesta que vengan mis amigos a visitarme. Pero insiste en que nosotros sólo miremos los programas de televisión que ella quiere. Necesita saber dónde estoy en cada momento, y yo necesito que ella me dé un poco de independencia. ¿Qué hago?
>
> Hernán

Recapitulación

SUPERSITE For self-scoring and diagnostics, go to **adelante.vhlcentral.com.**

Completa estas actividades para repasar los conceptos de gramática que aprendiste en esta lección.

1   **Completar** Completa el cuadro con la forma correspondiente del presente de subjuntivo. **12 pts.**

yo/él/ella	tú	nosotros/as	Uds./ellos/ellas
limpie	limpies	limpiemos	limpien
venga	**vengas**	vengamos	vengan
quiera	quieras	**queramos**	quieran
ofrezca	ofrezcas	ofrezcamos	**ofrezcan**

2   **El apartamento ideal** Completa este folleto (*brochure*) informativo con las formas correctas del presente de subjuntivo. **8 pts.**

> *A los jóvenes que buscan su primera vivienda, les ofrecemos estos consejos:*
>
> - Te sugiero que primero (tú) (1) ___escribas___ (escribir) una lista de las cosas que quieres en un apartamento.
> - Quiero que después (2) ___pienses___ (pensar) muy bien cuáles son tus prioridades. Es necesario que cada persona (3) ___tenga___ (tener) sus prioridades claras, porque el hogar (*home*) perfecto no existe.
> - Antes de decidir en qué área quieren vivir, les aconsejo a ti y a tu futuro/a compañero/a de apartamento que (4) ___salgan___ (salir) a ver la ciudad y que (5) ___conozcan___ (conocer) los distintos barrios y las afueras.
> - Pidan que el agente les (6) ___muestre___ (mostrar) todas las partes de cada casa.
> - Finalmente, como consumidores, es importante que nosotros (7) ___sepamos___ (saber) bien nuestros derechos (*rights*); por eso, deben insistir en que todos los puntos del contrato (8) ___estén___ (estar) muy claros antes de firmarlo (*signing it*).
>
> *¡Buena suerte!*

Teaching Tip Review verbs with stem changes and spelling changes in the subjunctive.

RESUMEN GRAMATICAL

6.1 Relative pronouns   *pp. 300–301*

Relative pronouns	
que	*that; which; who*
quien(es)	*who; whom; that*
lo que	*that which; what*

6.2 Formal commands   *pp. 304–305*

Formal commands (Ud. and Uds.)		
Infinitive	**Present tense yo form**	**Ud(s). command**
limpiar	limpi**o**	limpi**e(n)**
barrer	barr**o**	barr**a(n)**
sacudir	sacud**o**	sacud**a(n)**

▶ Verbs with stem changes or irregular **yo** forms maintain the same irregularity in the formal commands:

hacer: yo ha**g**o → Ha**g**an la cama.

Irregular formal commands	
dar	**dé (Ud.); den (Uds.)**
estar	**esté(n)**
ir	**vaya(n)**
saber	**sepa(n)**
ser	**sea(n)**

6.3 The present subjunctive   *pp. 308–310*

Present subjunctive of regular verbs		
hablar	**comer**	**escribir**
habl**e**	com**a**	escrib**a**
habl**es**	com**as**	escrib**as**
habl**e**	com**a**	escrib**a**
habl**emos**	com**amos**	escrib**amos**
habl**éis**	com**áis**	escrib**áis**
habl**en**	com**an**	escrib**an**

Extra Practice Call out verbs and have volunteers give the singular and plural command forms Ex: **barrer (barra, barran)** Repeat the drill with the subjunctive, varying the subject pronouns. Ex: **dormir/nosotros (que nosotros durmamos).**

3 Have students circle the noun or idea to which each relative pronoun refers.

3 Have students work in pairs to create four additional sentences using relative pronouns.

3

Relativos Completa las oraciones con **lo que**, **que** o **quien**. **8 pts.**

1. Me encanta la alfombra ___que___ está en el comedor.
2. Mi amiga Tere, con ___quien___ trabajo, me regaló ese cuadro.
3. Todas las cosas ___que___ tenemos vienen de la casa de mis abuelos.
4. Hija, no compres más cosas. ___Lo que___ debes hacer ahora es organizarlo todo.
5. La agencia de decoración de ___que___ le hablé se llama Casabella.
6. Esas flores las dejaron en la puerta mis nuevos vecinos, a ___quienes___ aún (*yet*) no conozco.
7. Leonor no compró nada, porque ___lo que___ le gustaba era muy caro.
8. Mi amigo Aldo, a ___quien___ visité ayer, es un cocinero excelente.

Irregular verbs in the present subjunctive		
dar		dé, des, dé, demos, deis, den
estar	est- +	-é, -és, -é, -emos, -éis, -én
ir	vay- +	
saber	sep- +	-a, -as, -a, -amos, -áis, -an
ser	se- +	

6.4 **Subjunctive with verbs of will and influence**

pp. 312–313

▶ Verbs of will and influence: **aconsejar, desear, importar, insistir (en), mandar, necesitar, pedir** (e:i), **preferir** (e:ie), **prohibir, querer** (e:ie), **recomendar** (e:ie), **rogar** (o:ue), **sugerir** (e:ie)

4 To simplify, have students begin by scanning the paragraph and identifying which blanks call for **usted** commands and which call for **ustedes** commands.

4 Tell students that some answers will contain object pronouns (items 2 and 10).

4

Preparando la casa Martín y Ángela van a hacer un curso de verano en Costa Rica y una vecina va a cuidarles (*take care of*) la casa mientras ellos no están. Completa las instrucciones de la vecina con mandatos formales. Usa cada verbo una sola vez y agrega pronombres de objeto directo o indirecto si es necesario. **10 pts.**

arreglar	dejar	hacer	pedir	sacudir
barrer	ensuciar	limpiar	poner	tener

Primero, (1) ___hagan___ ustedes las maletas. Las cosas que no se llevan a Costa Rica, (2) ___pónganlas___ en el altillo. Ángela, (3) ___arregle/limpie___ las habitaciones y Martín, (4) ___limpie/arregle___ usted la cocina y el baño. Después, los dos (5) ___barran___ el suelo y (6) ___sacudan___ los muebles de toda la casa. Ángela, no (7) ___deje___ sus joyas (*jewelry*) en el apartamento. (8) ___Tengan___ cuidado ¡y (9) ___no ensucien___ nada antes de irse! Por último, (10) ___pídanle___ a alguien que recoja (*pick up*) su correo.

5 Before beginning this activity, have pairs discuss their own habits regarding chores.

5 Have students imagine they have two roommates and ask them to rewrite their sentences using **ustedes** commands.

5

Los quehaceres A tu compañero/a de cuarto no le gusta ayudar con los quehaceres. Escribe al menos seis oraciones dándole consejos para hacer los quehaceres más divertidos. **12 pts.**

Answers will vary.

modelo

Te sugiero que pongas música mientras lavas los platos....

6

El circo (*circus*) Completa esta famosa frase que tiene su origen en el circo. **¡2 puntos EXTRA!**

"¡ ___Pasen___ (Pasar) ustedes y ___vean___ (ver)! El espectáculo va a comenzar."

Heritage Speakers Ask heritage speakers to think of other popular phrases or quotes that use formal command forms. Have them write the phrases on the board, leaving blanks for classmates to guess the commands.

Lectura

communication cultures NATIONAL STANDARDS

Antes de leer

Estrategia
Locating the main parts of a sentence

Did you know that a text written in Spanish is an average of 15% longer than the same text written in English? Because the Spanish language tends to use more words to express ideas, you will often encounter long sentences when reading in Spanish. Of course, the length of sentences varies with genre and with authors' individual styles. To help you understand long sentences, identify the main parts of the sentence before trying to read it in its entirety. First locate the main verb of the sentence, along with its subject, ignoring any words or phrases set off by commas. Then reread the sentence, adding details like direct and indirect objects, transitional words, and prepositional phrases.

Examinar el texto
Mira el formato de la lectura. ¿Qué tipo de documento es? ¿Qué cognados encuentras en la lectura? ¿Qué te dicen sobre el tema de la selección?

¿Probable o improbable?
Mira brevemente el texto e indica si estas oraciones son probables o improbables.

1. Este folleto (*brochure*) es de interés turístico. probable
2. Describe un edificio moderno cubano. improbable
3. Incluye algunas explicaciones de arquitectura. probable
4. Espera atraer (*to attract*) a visitantes al lugar. probable

Oraciones largas
Mira el texto y busca algunas oraciones largas. Con un(a) compañero/a, identifiquen las partes principales de la oración y después examinen las descripciones adicionales. ¿Qué significan las oraciones?

Teaching Tips
• Students should see from the layout (cover page with title, photo, and phone numbers; interior pages with an introduction and several headings followed by short paragraphs) that this is a brochure. Revealing cognates are: **información** (cover) and **residencia oficial del Presidente de Panamá** (introduction).

recursos

SUPERSITE

adelante.vhlcentral.com

Bienvenidos al Palacio de Las Garzas

**El palacio está abierto de martes a domingo.
Para más información,
llame al teléfono 507-226-7000.
También puede solicitar° un folleto
a la casilla° 3467,
Ciudad de Panamá, Panamá.**

Después de leer

Ordenar
Pon estos eventos en el orden cronológico adecuado.

___3___ El palacio se convirtió en residencia presidencial.

___2___ Durante diferentes épocas (*time periods*), maestros, médicos y banqueros practicaron su profesión en el palacio.

___4___ El Dr. Belisario Porras ocupó el palacio por primera vez.

___1___ Los españoles construyeron el palacio.

___5___ Se renovó el palacio.

___6___ Los turistas pueden visitar el palacio de martes a domingo.

• Ask pairs to suggest a couple of long sentences. Have them point out the main verb and subject.

Variación léxica Point out that in Spanish, **planta baja** means *ground floor*. The second story is called **el primer piso**, *the third story* is **el segundo piso**, and so forth. In the **Palacio de Las Garzas**, **el segundo piso** is also **la planta alta** (*top floor*).

trescientos diecinueve   **319**

El Palacio de Las Garzas° es la residencia oficial del Presidente de Panamá desde 1903. Fue construido en 1673 para ser la casa de un gobernador español. Con el paso de los años fue almacén, escuela, hospital, aduana, banco y por último, palacio presidencial.

En la actualidad el edificio tiene tres pisos, pero los planos originales muestran una construcción de un piso con un gran patio en el centro. La restauración del palacio comenzó en el año 1922 y los trabajos fueron realizados por el arquitecto Villanueva-Myers y el pintor Roberto Lewis. El palacio, un monumento al estilo colonial, todavía conserva su elegancia y buen gusto, y es una de las principales atracciones turísticas del barrio Casco Viejo°.

Planta baja

EL PATIO DE LAS GARZAS

Una antigua puerta de hierro° recibe a los visitantes. El patio interior todavía conserva los elementos originales de la construcción: piso de mármol°, columnas cubiertas° de nácar° y una magnífica fuente° de agua en el centro. Aquí están las nueve garzas que le dan el nombre al palacio y que representan las nueve provincias de Panamá.

Primer piso

EL SALÓN AMARILLO

Aquí el turista puede visitar una galería de cuarenta y un retratos° de gobernadores y personajes ilustres de Panamá. La principal atracción de este salón es el sillón presidencial, que se usa especialmente cuando hay cambio de presidente. Otros atractivos de esta área son el comedor de Los Tamarindos, que se destaca° por la elegancia de sus muebles y sus lámparas de cristal, y el patio andaluz, con sus coloridos mosaicos que representan la unión de la cultura indígena y la española.

EL SALÓN DR. BELISARIO PORRAS

Este elegante y majestuoso salón es uno de los lugares más importantes del Palacio de Las Garzas. Lleva su nombre en honor al Dr. Belisario Porras, quien fue tres veces presidente de Panamá (1912–1916, 1918–1920 y 1920–1924).

Segundo piso

Es el área residencial del palacio y el visitante no tiene acceso a ella. Los armarios, las cómodas y los espejos de la alcoba fueron comprados en Italia y Francia por el presidente Porras, mientras que las alfombras, cortinas y frazadas° son originarias de España.

solicitar *request* **casilla** *post office box* **Garzas** *Herons* **Casco Viejo** *Old Quarter*
hierro *iron* **mármol** *marble* **cubiertas** *covered* **nácar** *mother-of-pearl* **fuente**
fountain **retratos** *portraits* **se destaca** *stands out* **frazadas** *blankets*

Lección 6

Preguntas

Contesta las preguntas.

1. ¿Qué sala es notable por sus muebles elegantes y sus lámparas de cristal? el comedor de Los Tamarindos
2. ¿En qué parte del palacio se encuentra la residencia del presidente? en el segundo piso
3. ¿Dónde empiezan los turistas su visita al palacio? en el patio de las Garzas
4. ¿En qué lugar se representa artísticamente la rica herencia cultural de Panamá? en el patio andaluz
5. ¿Qué salón honra la memoria de un gran panameño? el salón Dr. Belisario Porras
6. ¿Qué partes del palacio te gustaría (*would you like*) más visitar? ¿Por qué? Explica tu respuesta. Answers will vary.

Small Groups In small groups, ask students to compare the **Palacio de las Garzas** to other official residences, historic homes, or government buildings they have visited.

Conversación

En grupos de tres o cuatro estudiantes, hablen sobre lo siguiente: Answers will vary.

1. ¿Qué tiene en común el Palacio de Las Garzas con otras residencias presidenciales u otras casas muy grandes?
2. ¿Te gustaría vivir en el Palacio de Las Garzas? ¿Por qué?
3. Imagina que puedes diseñar tu palacio ideal. Describe los planos para cada piso del palacio.

Heritage Speakers Ask heritage speakers to give a brief presentation about the official residence of the president of their parents' home country. Tell them to include in their description recommendations to visitors about what rooms and objects are particularly noteworthy and should not be missed. If possible, they should illustrate their presentation with photographs or brochures.

Panamá

NATIONAL connections cultures STANDARDS

El país en cifras

▶ **Área:** 78.200 km² (30.193 millas²), *aproximadamente el área de Carolina del Sur*

▶ **Población:** 3.509.000

▶ **Capital:** La Ciudad de Panamá —1.379.000

▶ **Ciudades principales:** Colón, David

SOURCE: Population Division, UN Secretariat

▶ **Moneda:** balboa; Es equivalente al dólar estadounidense.

En Panamá circulan los billetes de dólar estadounidense. El país centroamericano, sin embargo, acuña° sus propias monedas. "El peso" es una moneda grande equivalente a cincuenta centavos°. La moneda de cinco centavos es llamada frecuentemente "real".

▶ **Idiomas:** español (oficial), chibcha, inglés

La mayoría de los panameños es bilingüe. La lengua materna del 14% de los panameños es el inglés.

Bandera de Panamá

Panameños célebres

▶ **Rod Carew,** beisbolista (1945–)

▶ **Mireya Moscoso,** política (1947–)

▶ **Rubén Blades,** músico y político (1948–)

acuña *mints* centavos *cents*
Actualmente *Currently*
peaje *toll* promedio *average*

Mujer kuna lavando una mola

Un turista disfruta del bosque tropical colgado de un cable.

COSTA RICA

Lago Gatún · Canal de Panamá

Islas San Blas

Bocas del Toro
Mar Caribe
Colón
Cordillera de San Blas
Río Chepo

Serranía de Tabasará

Ciudad de Panamá

David

Río Cobre

Isla del Rey

Océano Pacífico

Golfo de Panamá

ESTADOS UNIDOS

OCÉANO ATLÁNTICO

PANAMÁ

AMÉRICA DEL SUR

Isla de Coiba

recursos

WB
pp. 333–334

VM
pp. 337–338

SUPERSITE
adelante.
vhlcentral.com

Ruinas de un fuerte panameño

¡Increíble pero cierto!

¿Conocías estos datos sobre el Canal de Panamá?

• Gracias al Canal de Panamá, el viaje en barco de Nueva York a Tokio es 3.000 millas más corto.

• Su construcción costó 639 millones de dólares.

• Actualmente° lo usan 38 barcos al día.

• El peaje° promedio° cuesta 40.000 dólares.

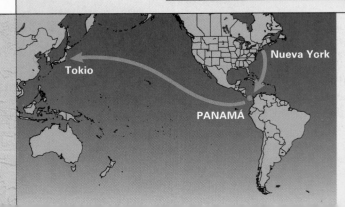

Tokio

Nueva York

PANAMÁ

Lugares • El Canal de Panamá

El Canal de Panamá conecta el océano Pacífico con el océano Atlántico. La construcción de este cauce° artificial empezó en 1903 y concluyó diez años después. Es la fuente° principal de ingresos° del país, gracias al dinero que aportan los más de 12.000 buques° que transitan anualmente por esta ruta.

Artes • La mola

La mola es una forma de arte textil de los kunas, una tribu indígena que vive en las islas San Blas. Esta pieza artesanal se confecciona con fragmentos de tela° de colores vivos. Algunos de sus diseños representan plantas o animales, otros son abstractos, inspirados en las formas del coral, y otros son geométricos, como en las molas más tradicionales. Antiguamente, estos tejidos se usaban como ropa, pero hoy día también sirven para decorar las casas.

Naturaleza • El mar

Panamá, cuyo° nombre significa "lugar de muchos peces°", es un país muy frecuentado por los aficionados del buceo y la pesca. El territorio panameño cuenta con una gran variedad de playas en los dos lados del istmo°, con el mar Caribe a un lado y el océano Pacífico al otro. Algunas de las zonas costeras de esta nación están destinadas al turismo y otras son protegidas por la diversidad de su fauna marina, en la que abundan los arrecifes° de coral. En la playa Bluff, por ejemplo, se pueden observar cuatro especies de tortugas° en peligro° de extinción.

COLOMBIA

Vista de la Ciudad de Panamá

¿Qué aprendiste? Responde a cada pregunta con una oración completa.

1. ¿Cuál es la lengua materna del catorce por ciento de los panameños?
   El inglés es la lengua materna del catorce por ciento de los panameños.
2. ¿A qué unidad monetaria (*monetary unit*) es equivalente el balboa?
   El balboa es equivalente al dólar estadounidense.
3. ¿Qué océanos une el Canal de Panamá?
   El Canal de Panamá une los océanos Atlántico y Pacífico.
4. ¿Quién es Rod Carew?
   Rod Carew es un beisbolista panameño.
5. ¿Qué son las molas?
   Las molas son una forma de arte textil común entre los kunas.
6. ¿Cómo son los diseños de las molas?
   Sus diseños son abstractos.
7. ¿Para qué se usaban las molas antes?
   Las molas se usaban como ropa.
8. ¿Cómo son las playas de Panamá?
   Son muy variadas; unas están destinadas al turismo, otras tienen valor ecológico.
9. ¿Qué significa "Panamá"?
   "Panamá" significa "lugar de muchos peces".

Conexión Internet Investiga estos temas en **adelante.vhlcentral.com**.

1. Investiga la historia de las relaciones entre Panamá y los Estados Unidos y la decisión de devolver (*give back*) el Canal de Panamá. ¿Estás de acuerdo con la decisión? Explica tu opinión.
2. Investiga sobre los kunas u otro grupo indígena de Panamá. ¿En qué partes del país viven? ¿Qué lenguas hablan? ¿Cómo es su cultura?

....

cauce *channel* **fuente** *source* **ingresos** *income* **buques** *ships* **tela** *fabric* **cuyo** *whose* **peces** *fish* **istmo** *isthmus*
arrecifes *reefs* **tortugas** *turtles* **peligro** *danger*

Supersite/DVD: You may want to wrap up this section by playing the *Panorama cultural* video footage for this lesson.

Las viviendas

las afueras	suburbs; outskirts
el alquiler	rent (payment)
el ama (m., f.) de casa	housekeeper; caretaker
el barrio	neighborhood
el edificio de apartamentos	apartment building
el/la vecino/a	neighbor
la vivienda	housing
alquilar	to rent
mudarse	to move (from one house to another)

Los cuartos y otros lugares

el altillo	attic
el balcón	balcony
la cocina	kitchen
el comedor	dining room
el dormitorio	bedroom
la entrada	entrance
la escalera	stairs; stairway
el garaje	garage
el jardín	garden; yard
la oficina	office
el pasillo	hallway
el patio	patio; yard
la sala	living room
el sótano	basement; cellar

Supersite/IRCD: MP3 Audio Files, Testing Program, *Vocabulario adicional*

Los muebles y otras cosas

la alfombra	carpet; rug
la almohada	pillow
el armario	closet
el cartel	poster
la cómoda	chest of drawers
las cortinas	curtains
el cuadro	picture
el estante	bookcase; bookshelves
la lámpara	lamp
la luz	light; electricity
la manta	blanket
la mesita	end table
la mesita de noche	night stand
los muebles	furniture
la pared	wall
la pintura	painting; picture
el sillón	armchair
el sofá	couch; sofa

Los electrodomésticos

la cafetera	coffee maker
la cocina, la estufa	stove
el congelador	freezer
el electrodoméstico	electric appliance
el horno (de microondas)	(microwave) oven
la lavadora	washing machine
el lavaplatos	dishwasher
el refrigerador	refrigerator
la secadora	clothes dryer
la tostadora	toaster

La mesa

la copa	wineglass; goblet
la cuchara	(table or large) spoon
el cuchillo	knife
el plato	plate
la servilleta	napkin
la taza	cup
el tenedor	fork
el vaso	glass

Los quehaceres domésticos

arreglar	to neaten; to straighten up
barrer el suelo	to sweep the floor
cocinar	to cook
ensuciar	to get (something) dirty
hacer la cama	to make the bed
hacer quehaceres domésticos	to do household chores
lavar (el suelo, los platos)	to wash (the floor, the dishes)
limpiar la casa	to clean the house
pasar la aspiradora	to vacuum
planchar la ropa	to iron the clothes
poner la mesa	to set the table
quitar la mesa	to clear the table
quitar el polvo	to dust
sacar la basura	to take out the trash
sacudir los muebles	to dust the furniture

Verbos y expresiones verbales

aconsejar	to advise
insistir (en)	to insist (on)
mandar	to order
recomendar (e:ie)	to recommend
rogar (o:ue)	to beg; to plead
sugerir (e:ie)	to suggest
Es bueno que…	It's good that…
Es importante que…	It's important that…
Es malo que…	It's bad that…
Es mejor que…	It's better that…
Es necesario que…	It's necessary that…
Es urgente que…	It's urgent that…

Relative pronouns	See page 300.
Expresiones útiles	See page 295.

contextos

Lección 6

1 **Los aparatos domésticos** Answer the questions with complete sentences.

> **modelo**
> Julieta quiere comer pan tostado. ¿Qué tiene que usar Julieta?
> Julieta tiene que usar una tostadora.

1. La ropa de Joaquín está sucia. ¿Qué necesita Joaquín?

   Joaquín necesita una lavadora.

2. Clara lavó la ropa. ¿Qué necesita Clara ahora?

   Clara necesita una secadora ahora.

3. Los platos de la cena están sucios. ¿Qué se necesita?

   Se necesita un lavaplatos.

4. Rita quiere hacer hielo. ¿Dónde debe poner el agua?

   Rita debe poner el agua en el congelador.

2 **¿En qué habitación?** Label these items as belonging to **la cocina, la sala,** or **el dormitorio**.

1. el lavaplatos _la cocina_

2. el sillón _la sala_

3. la cama _el dormitorio_

4. el horno _la cocina_

5. la almohada _el dormitorio_

6. la cafetera _la cocina_

7. la mesita de noche _el dormitorio_

8. la cómoda _el dormitorio_

3 **¿Qué hacían?** Complete the sentences, describing the domestic activity in each drawing. Use the imperfect tense.

1. Ramón _Ramón sacaba la basura._

2. Rebeca _Rebeca hacía la cama._

3. Mi tío Juan _Mi tío Juan pasaba la aspiradora._

4. Isabel _Isabel sacudía los muebles._

4 **Una es diferente** Fill in the blank with the word that doesn't belong in each group.

1. sala, plato, copa, vaso, taza ___sala___

2. cuchillo, altillo, plato, copa, tenedor ___altillo___

3. cocina, balcón, patio, jardín, garaje ___cocina___

4. cartel, estante, pintura, lavadora, cuadro ___lavadora___

5. dormitorio, sala, comedor, cafetera, oficina ___cafetera___

6. lavadora, escalera, secadora, lavaplatos, tostadora ___escalera___

5 **Crucigrama** Complete the crossword puzzle.

Horizontales

4. el hombre que vive al lado de tu casa
5. Julieta habló con Romeo desde su _____.
6. sillón, mesa, cama o silla
8. lo que pones cuando necesitas luz
10. lo que usas para tomar vino
11. Usas estas cosas para tomar agua o soda.
14. lo que usas cuando hace frío de noche

Verticales

1. lo que usas para ir de un piso a otro
2. obras (*works*) de Picasso, de Goya, etc.
3. pagar dinero cada mes por vivir en un lugar
7. _____ de microondas
9. Si vas a vivir en otro lugar, vas a _____.
12. donde se pueden sentar tres o cuatro personas
13. lo que usas para tomar el café

estructura

6.1 Relative pronouns

1 **Relativamente** Complete the sentences with **que**, **quien**, or **quienes**.

1. La persona a _____quien_____ debes conocer es Marta.

2. El restaurante _____que_____ más me gusta es Il Forno.

3. Los amigos a _____quienes_____ fue a visitar son Ana y Antonio.

4. Doña María, _____quien/que_____ me cuidaba cuando yo era niña, vino a verme.

5. El estudiante _____que_____ mejor conozco de la clase es Gustavo.

6. La habitación _____que_____ tiene las paredes azules es la tuya.

7. Los primos con _____quienes_____ mejor me llevo son Pedro y Natalia.

8. El profesor _____que_____ sabe la respuesta está en la biblioteca ahora.

2 **Conversación telefónica** You're talking on the phone with your mother, who wants to catch up on everything in your life. Answer her questions using the words in parentheses.

> **modelo**
>
> ¿Qué es lo que encontraste en el altillo? (un álbum de fotos)
> **Lo que encontré en el altillo fue un álbum de fotos.**

1. ¿Qué es lo que preparas en la cocina? (el almuerzo)

   Lo que preparo en la cocina es el almuerzo.

2. ¿Qué es lo que buscas en el estante? (mi libro favorito)

   Lo que busco en el estante es mi libro favorito.

3. ¿Qué es lo que te gusta hacer en verano? (ir al campo)

   Lo que me gusta hacer en verano es ir al campo.

4. ¿Qué es lo que vas a poner en el balcón? (un sofá)

   Lo que voy a poner en el balcón es un sofá.

5. ¿Qué es lo que tienes en el armario? (mucha ropa)

   Lo que tengo en el armario es mucha ropa.

6. ¿Qué es lo que le vas a regalar a tu hermana? (una cafetera)

   Lo que le voy a regalar a mi hermana es una cafetera.

3 **¿Que o lo que?** Complete the sentences with **que** or **lo que**.

1. El pastel de cumpleaños _____que_____ me trajo mi abuela estuvo delicioso.

2. _____Lo que_____ más les gusta a Pedro y Andrés es jugar baloncesto.

3. Miguel perdió las llaves, _____lo que_____ le hizo llegar tarde al dentista.

4. Ricardo y Ester querían los muebles _____que_____ vieron en la tienda.

4 **Pronombres relativos** Complete the sentences with **que, quien, quienes,** or **lo que**.

1. Los vecinos _____que_____ viven frente a mi casa son muy simpáticos.

2. Rosa y Pepe viajan mucho, _____lo que_____ los expone a muchas culturas.

3. Las amigas con _____quienes_____ estudias en la universidad son de varias ciudades.

4. El apartamento _____que_____ Rebeca y Jorge alquilaron está cerca del centro.

5. Adrián y Daniel, _____que/quienes_____ estudian física, son expertos en computación.

6. Rubén debe pedirle la aspiradora a Marcos, a _____quien_____ le regalaron una.

5 **Mi prima Natalia** Complete the paragraph with **que, quien, quienes,** or **lo que**.

Natalia, (1) _____que/quien_____ es mi prima, tiene un problema. Natalia es la prima

(2) _____que_____ más quiero de todas las que tengo. (3) _____Lo que_____ le pasa a

Natalia es que siempre está muy ocupada. Su novio, a (4) _____quien_____ conoció hace dos

años, quiere pasar más tiempo con ella. La clase (5) _____que_____ más le gusta a Natalia es la

clase de francés. Natalia, (6) _____que/quien_____ ya habla inglés y español, quiere aprender el

francés muy bien. Tiene dos amigos franceses con (7) _____quienes_____ practica el idioma. Natalia

también está en el equipo de natación, (8) _____lo que_____ le toma dos horas todas las mañanas.

Pero las otras nadadoras (9) _____que_____ están en el equipo la necesitan. Además, a Natalia

le gusta visitar a sus padres, a (10) _____quienes_____ ve casi todos los fines de semana. También ve

con frecuencia a los parientes y amigos (11) _____que_____ viven en su ciudad. ¡Este verano

(12) _____lo que_____ Natalia necesita son unas vacaciones!

6 **Lo que me parece** Rewrite each sentence using **lo que**.

> **modelo**
> A mí me gusta comer en restaurantes.
> *Lo que a mí me gusta es comer en restaurantes.*

1. Raúl dijo una mentira.

   Lo que Raúl dijo fue una mentira.

2. Conseguiste enojar a Victoria.

   Lo que conseguiste fue enojar a Victoria.

3. Lilia va a comprar una falda.

   Lo que Lilia va a comprar es una falda.

4. Ellos preparan una sorpresa.

   Lo que ellos preparan es una sorpresa.

5. A Teo y a mí nos gusta la nieve.

   Lo que a Teo y a mí nos gusta es la nieve.

6.2 Formal commands

1

Háganlo así Complete the commands, using the verbs in parentheses.

Usted

1. (lavar) _____Lave_____ la ropa con el nuevo detergente.

2. (salir) _____Salga_____ de su casa y disfrute del aire libre.

3. (decir) _____Diga_____ todo lo que piensa hacer hoy.

4. (beber) No _____beba_____ demasiado en la fiesta.

5. (venir) _____Venga_____ preparado para pasarlo bien.

6. (irse) No _____se vaya_____ sin probar la langosta de Maine.

Ustedes

7. (comer) No _____coman_____ con la boca abierta.

8. (oír) _____Oigan_____ música clásica en casa.

9. (poner) No _____pongan_____ los codos (*elbows*) en la mesa.

10. (traer) _____Traigan_____ un regalo a la fiesta de cumpleaños.

11. (ver) _____Vean_____ programas de televisión educativos.

12. (conducir) _____Conduzcan_____ con precaución (*caution*) por la ciudad.

2

Por favor Give instructions to people cleaning a house by changing the verb phrases into formal commands.

> **modelo**
> sacudir la alfombra
> *Sacuda la alfombra, por favor.*

1. traer la aspiradora

   Traiga la aspiradora, por favor.

2. arreglar el coche

   Arregle el coche, por favor.

3. bajar al sótano

   Baje al sótano, por favor.

4. apagar la cafetera

   Apague la cafetera, por favor.

5. venir a la casa

   Venga a la casa, por favor.

3 · **Para emergencias** Rewrite this hotel's emergency instructions, replacing each **debe** + (*infinitive*) with formal commands.

Querido huésped:

Debe leer estas instrucciones para casos de emergencia. Si ocurre (*occurs*) una emergencia, debe tocar la puerta antes de abrirla. Si la puerta no está caliente, debe salir de la habitación con cuidado (*carefully*). Al salir, debe doblar a la derecha por el pasillo y debe bajar por la escalera de emergencia. Debe mantener la calma y debe caminar lentamente. No debe usar el ascensor durante una emergencia. Debe dejar su equipaje en la habitación en caso de emergencia. Al llegar a la planta baja, debe salir al patio o a la calle. Luego debe pedir ayuda a un empleado del hotel.

Querido huésped:

Lea estas instrucciones para casos de emergencia. Si ocurre una emergencia, toque la puerta antes de abrirla. Si la puerta

no está caliente, salga de la habitación con cuidado. Al salir, doble a la derecha por el pasillo y baje por la escalera de

emergencia. Mantenga la calma y camine lentamente. No use el ascensor durante una emergencia. Deje su equipaje en la

habitación en caso de emergencia. Al llegar a la planta baja, salga al patio o a la calle. Luego pida ayuda a un empleado

del hotel.

_____

_____

_____

_____

_____

4 · **Lo opuesto** Change each command to express the opposite sentiment.

> **modelo**
> Recéteselo a mi hija.
> **No se lo recete a mi hija.**

1. Siéntense en la cama. No se sienten en la cama.

2. No lo limpie ahora. Límpielo ahora.

3. Lávenmelas mañana. No me las laven mañana.

4. No nos los sirvan. Sírvannoslos.

5. Sacúdalas antes de ponerlas. No las sacuda antes de ponerlas.

6. No se las busquen. Búsquenselas.

7. Despiértenlo a las ocho. No lo despierten a las ocho.

8. Cámbiesela por otra. No se la cambie por otra.

9. Pídanselos a Martín. No se los pidan a Martín.

10. No se lo digan hoy. Díganselo hoy.

6.3 The present subjunctive

1 **Oraciones** Complete the sentences with the present subjunctive of the verb in parentheses.

1. Es bueno que ustedes _____coman_____ (comer) frutas, verduras y yogures.

2. Es importante que Laura y yo _____estudiemos_____ (estudiar) para el examen de física.

3. Es urgente que el doctor te _____mire_____ (mirar) la rodilla y la pierna.

4. Es malo que los niños no _____lean_____ (leer) mucho de pequeños (*when they are little*).

5. Es mejor que (tú) les _____escribas_____ (escribir) una carta antes de llamarlos.

6. Es necesario que (yo) _____pase_____ (pasar) por la casa de Mario por la mañana.

2 **El verbo correcto** Complete the sentences with the present subjunctive of the verbs from the word bank.

almorzar	hacer	oír	poner	traducir	venir
conducir	ofrecer	parecer	sacar	traer	ver

1. Es necesario que (yo) _____venga_____ a casa temprano para ayudar a mi mamá.

2. Es bueno que (la universidad) _____ofrezca_____ muchos cursos por semestre.

3. Es malo que (ellos) _____almuercen_____ justo antes de ir a nadar a la piscina.

4. Es urgente que (Lara) _____traduzca_____ estos documentos legales.

5. Es mejor que (tú) _____conduzcas_____ más lento para evitar (*avoid*) accidentes.

6. Es importante que (ella) no _____ponga_____ la cafetera en la mesa.

7. Es bueno que (tú) _____traigas_____ las fotos para verlas en la fiesta.

8. Es necesario que (él) _____vea_____ la casa antes de comprarla.

9. Es malo que (nosotros) no _____saquemos_____ la basura todas las noches.

10. Es importante que (ustedes) _____hagan_____ los quehaceres domésticos.

3 **Opiniones** Rewrite these sentences using the present subjunctive of the verbs in parentheses.

1. Mi padre dice que es importante que yo (estar) contenta con mi trabajo.

   Mi padre dice que es importante que yo esté contenta con mi trabajo.

2. Rosario cree que es bueno que la gente (irse) de vacaciones más a menudo.

   Rosario cree que es bueno que la gente se vaya de vacaciones más a menudo.

3. Creo que es mejor que Elsa (ser) la encargada del proyecto.

   Creo que es mejor que Elsa sea la encargada del proyecto.

4. Es importante que les (dar) las gracias por el favor que te hicieron.

   Es importante que les des las gracias por el favor que te hicieron.

5. Él piensa que es malo que muchos estudiantes no (saber) otras lenguas.

   Él piensa que es malo que muchos estudiantes no sepan otras lenguas.

6. El director dice que es necesario que (haber) una reunión de la facultad.

   El director dice que es necesario que haya una reunión de la facultad.

4 **Es necesario** Write sentences using the elements provided and the present subjunctive of the verbs.

> *modelo*
>
> malo / Roberto / no poder / irse de vacaciones
> Es malo que Roberto no pueda irse de vacaciones.

1. importante / Nora / pensar / las cosas antes de tomar la decisión

   Es importante que Nora piense en las cosas antes de tomar la decisión.

2. necesario / (tú) / entender / la situación de esas personas

   Es necesario que entiendas la situación de esas personas.

3. bueno / Clara / sentirse / cómoda en el apartamento nuevo

   Es bueno que Clara se sienta cómoda en el apartamento nuevo.

4. urgente / mi madre / mostrarme / los papeles que llegaron

   Es urgente que mi madre me muestre los papeles que llegaron.

5. mejor / David / dormir / antes de conducir la motocicleta

   Es mejor que David duerma antes de conducir la motocicleta.

6. malo / los niños / pedirles / tantos regalos a los abuelos

   Es malo que los niños (les) pidan tantos regalos a sus abuelos.

5 **Sí, es bueno** Answer the questions using the words in parentheses and the present subjunctive.

> *modelo*
>
> ¿Tiene Álex que terminar ese trabajo hoy? (urgente)
> Sí, es urgente que Álex termine ese trabajo hoy.

1. ¿Debemos traer el pasaporte al aeropuerto? (necesario)

   Sí, es necesario que traigan el pasaporte al aeropuerto./Sí, es necesario que traigamos el pasaporte al aeropuerto.

2. ¿Tienes que hablar con don Francisco? (urgente)

   Sí, es urgente que hable con don Francisco.

3. ¿Debe Javier ir a visitar a su abuela todas las semanas? (bueno)

   Sí, es bueno que Javier vaya a visitar a su abuela todas las semanas.

4. ¿Puede Maite llamar a Inés para darle las gracias? (importante)

   Sí, es importante que Maite llame a Inés para darle las gracias.

5. ¿Va Álex a saber lo que le van a preguntar en el examen? (mejor)

   Sí, es mejor que Álex sepa lo que le van a preguntar en el examen.

6.4 Subjunctive with verbs of will and influence

1 **Preferencias** Complete the sentences with the present subjuntive of the verbs in parentheses.

1. Rosa quiere que tú _____escojas_____ (escoger) el sofá para la sala.

2. La mamá de Susana prefiere que ella _____estudie_____ (estudiar) medicina.

3. Miranda insiste en que Luisa _____sea_____ (ser) la candidata a vicepresidenta.

4. Rita y yo deseamos que nuestros padres _____viajen_____ (viajar) a Panamá.

5. A Eduardo no le importa que nosotros _____salgamos_____ (salir) esta noche.

6. La agente de viajes nos recomienda que _____nos quedemos_____ (quedarnos) en ese hotel.

2 **Comprar una casa** Read the following suggestions for buying a house. Then write a note to a friend, repeating the advice and using the present subjunctive of the verbs.

Antes de comprar una casa:
- Se aconseja tener un agente inmobiliario (*real estate*).
- Se sugiere buscar una casa en un barrio seguro (*safe*).
- Se insiste en mirar los baños, la cocina y el sótano.
- Se recomienda comparar precios de varias casas antes de decidir.
- Se aconseja hablar con los vecinos del barrio.

Te aconsejo que tengas un agente inmobiliario. _Te sugiero que_ busques una casa en un barrio seguro. Te insisto en que mires los baños, la cocina y el sótano. Te recomiendo que compares los precios de varias casas antes de decidir. Te aconsejo que hables con los vecinos del barrio.

_____

_____

_____

_____

3 **Instrucciones** Write sentences using the elements provided and the present subjunctive. Replace the indirect objects with indirect object pronouns.

> **modelo**
> (a ti) / Simón / sugerir / terminar la tarea luego
> *Simón te sugiere que termines la tarea luego.*

1. (a Daniela) / José / rogar / escribir esa carta de recomendación

   José le ruega que escriba esa carta de recomendación.

2. (a ustedes) / (yo) / aconsejar / vivir en las afueras de la ciudad

   Les aconsejo que vivan en las afueras de la ciudad.

3. (a ellos) / la directora / prohibir / estacionar frente a la escuela

   La directora les prohíbe que estacionen frente a la escuela.

4. (a mí) / (tú) / sugerir / alquilar un apartamento en el barrio

   Me sugieres que alquile un apartamento en el barrio.

4 **¿Subjuntivo o infinitivo?** Write sentences using the elements provided. Use the subjunctive of the verbs when required.

1. Marina / querer / yo / traer / la compra a casa

   Marina quiere que yo traiga la compra a casa.

2. Sonia y yo / preferir / buscar / la información en Internet

   Sonia y yo preferimos buscar la información por Internet.

3. el profesor / desear / nosotros / usar / el diccionario

   El profesor desea que nosotros usemos el diccionario.

4. ustedes / necesitar / escribir / una carta al consulado

   Ustedes necesitan escribir una carta al consulado.

5. (yo) / preferir / Manuel / ir / al apartamento por mí

   Prefiero que Manuel vaya al apartamento por mí.

6. Ramón / insistir en / buscar / las alfombras de la casa

   Ramón insiste en buscar las alfombras de la casa.

Síntesis

Imagine that you are going away for the weekend and you are letting some of your friends stay in your house. Write instructions for your houseguests asking them how to take care of the house. Use formal commands, the phrases **Es bueno, Es mejor, Es importante, Es necesario,** and **Es malo,** and the verbs **aconsejar, pedir, necesitar, prohibir, recomendar, rogar,** and **sugerir** to describe how to make sure that your house is in perfect shape when you get home. Answers will vary.

panorama

Panamá

1 **Datos panameños** Complete the sentences with the correct information.

1. _____ Rubén Blades _____ es un músico y político célebre de Panamá.

2. La fuente principal de ingresos de Panamá es _____ el Canal de Panamá _____.

3. Las _____ molas _____ son una forma de arte textil de la tribu indígena kuna.

4. Los diseños de las molas se inspiran en las formas del _____ coral _____.

2 **Relativamente** Rewrite each pair of sentences as one sentence. Use relative pronouns to combine the sentences.

> **modelo**
>
> La Ciudad de Panamá es la capital de Panamá. Tiene más de un millón de habitantes.
> La Ciudad de Panamá, que tiene más de un millón de habitantes, es la capital de Panamá.

1. La moneda de Panamá es equivalente al dólar estadounidense. Se llama el balboa.

   La moneda de Panamá, que se llama el balboa, es equivalente al dólar estadounidense.

2. El Canal de Panamá se empezó a construir en 1903. Éste une a los océanos Atlántico y Pacífico.

   El Canal de Panamá, que une a los océanos Atlántico y Pacífico, se empezó a construir en 1903.

3. La tribu indígena de los kuna es de las islas San Blas. Ellos hacen molas.

   La tribu indígena de los kuna, que hace molas, es de las islas San Blas.

4. Panamá es un sitio excelente para el buceo. Panamá significa "lugar de muchos peces".

   Panamá, que significa "lugar de muchos peces", es un sitio excelente para el buceo.

3 **Geografía panameña** Fill in the blanks with the correct geographical name.

1. la capital de Panamá la Ciudad de Panamá

2. ciudades principales de Panamá la Ciudad de Panamá, Colón y David

3. países que limitan (*border*) con Panamá Costa Rica y Colombia

4. mar al norte (*north*) de Panamá el Mar Caribe

5. océano al sur (*south*) de Panamá el océano Pacífico

6. por donde pasan más de 12.000 buques por año el Canal de Panamá

7. en donde vive la tribu indígena de los kuna las islas San Blas

8. donde se pueden observar tortugas en peligro de extinción la playa Bluff

4 **Viaje a Panamá** Complete the phrases with the correct information. Then write a paragraph of a tourist brochure about Panama. Use formal commands in the paragraph. The first sentence is done for you.

1. viajar en avión la ____Ciudad de Panamá____, capital de Panamá

2. visitar el país centroamericano, donde circulan los billetes de ____dólar estadounidense____

3. conocer a los panameños; la lengua natal del 14% de ellos es ____el inglés____

4. ir al Canal de Panamá, que une los océanos ____Atlántico____ y ____Pacífico____

5. ver las ____molas____ que hace la tribu indígena kuna y decorar la casa con ellas

6. bucear en las playas de gran valor ____ecológico____ por la riqueza y diversidad de su vida marina

Viaje en avión a la Ciudad de Panamá, capital de Panamá. Visite el país centroamericano, donde

circulan los billetes de dólar estadounidense. Conozca a los panameños; la lengua natal del 14% de ellos es el inglés. Vaya

al Canal de Panamá, que une los océanos Atlántico y Pacífico. Vea las molas que hace la tribu indígena kuna y decore la

casa con ellas. Bucee en las playas de gran valor ecológico por la riqueza y diversidad de su vida marina.

5 **¿Cierto o falso?** Indicate whether the statements are **cierto** or **falso**. Correct the false statements.

1. Panamá es aproximadamente del tamaño de California.

Falso. El área de Panamá es aproximada al tamaño de Carolina del Sur.

2. La moneda panameña, que se llama el balboa, es equivalente al dólar estadounidense.

Cierto.

3. La lengua natal de todos los panameños es el español.

Falso. La lengua natal del 14% de los panameños es el inglés.

4. El Canal de Panamá une los océanos Pacífico y Atlántico.

Cierto.

5. Las molas tradicionales siempre se usaron para decorar las casas.

Falso. Las molas tradicionales antes sólo se usaban como ropa pero hoy día también se usan para decorar las casas.

¡Les va a encantar la casa!

Lección 6
Fotonovela

Antes de ver el video

1 **En la casa** In this lesson, the students arrive at the house in Ibarra near the area where they will go on their hiking excursion. Keeping this information in mind, look at the video still and describe what you think is going on. Answers will vary.

_____

_____

_____

_____

_____

_____

Mientras ves el video

2 **¿Cierto o falso?** Watch the **¡Les va a encantar la casa!** segment of this video module and indicate whether each statement is **cierto** or **falso**.

	Cierto	Falso
1. La señora Vives es la hermana de don Francisco.	○	☑
2. Hay mantas y almohadas en el armario de la alcoba de los chicos.	☑	○
3. El guía llega mañana a las siete y media de la mañana.	○	☑
4. Don Francisco va a preparar todas las comidas.	○	☑
5. La señora Vives cree que Javier debe poner las maletas en la cama.	○	☑

3 **En México** Watch Álex's flashback about lodgings in Mexico and place a check mark beside the things you see.

✓ 1. balcones

✓ 2. puertas

✓ 3. apartamentos

✓ 4. una bicicleta

____ 5. un perro (_dog_)

✓ 6. una vaca (_cow_)

4 **Resumen** Watch the **Resumen** segment of this video module. Then place a check mark beside each event that occurred in the **Resumen**.

____ 1. La señora Vives les dice a los estudiantes que deben descansar.

✓ 2. Inés habla de la llegada de los estudiantes a la casa.

✓ 3. Inés dice que va a acostarse porque el guía llega muy temprano mañana.

____ 4. Don Francisco les dice a los estudiantes que les va a encantar la casa.

✓ 5. Javier dice que los estudiantes van a ayudar a la señora Vives con los quehaceres domésticos.

Video Manual

Nombre _____

Fecha _____

Después de ver el video

5 **Seleccionar** Write the letter of the words that best complete each sentence.

1. Don Francisco dice que la casa es _____.
   a. pequeña pero bonita   b. pequeña pero cómoda   (c.) cómoda y grande

2. La habitación de los chicos tiene dos camas, una _____ y una _____.
   (a.) mesita de noche; cómoda b. cafetera; lavadora   c. cómoda; tostadora

3. El sofá y los sillones _____ son muy cómodos.
   a. del jardín   (b.) de la sala   c. de las alcobas

4. Al fondo del _____ hay un _____.
   a. apartamento; comedor b. edificio; baño   (c.) pasillo; baño

5. Inés le dice a _____ que los estudiantes quieren ayudarla a _____ la comida.
   a. Maite; comprar   (b.) la señora Vives; preparar   c. don Francisco; comprar

6 **Preguntas** Answer the following questions about this video episode in Spanish.

1. ¿Cómo se llama el guía que viene mañana?

   El guía se llama Martín.

2. ¿Quién puso su maleta en la cama?

   Javier puso su maleta en la cama.

3. ¿Cómo se llama el ama de casa?

   La señora Vives es el ama de casa.

4. ¿Quién quiere que los estudiantes hagan sus camas?

   Don Francisco quiere que los estudiantes hagan sus camas.

5. Según don Francisco, ¿por qué deben acostarse temprano los estudiantes?

   Según don Francisco, los estudiantes deben acostarse temprano porque el guía viene muy temprano.

7 **Escribir** Imagine that you are one of the characters you saw in this video episode. Write a paragraph from that person's point of view, summarizing what happened in this episode. Answers will vary.

_____

_____

_____

_____

Panorama: Panamá

Antes de ver el video

1 **Más vocabulario** Look over these useful words before you watch the video.

Vocabulario útil		
anualmente *annually*	impresionante *incredible*	según *according to*
arrecife *reef*	lado *side*	sitio *site*
disfrutar *to enjoy*	peces *fish*	torneo *tournament*
especies *species*	precioso *beautiful*	

2 **Responder** This video talks about the best places to dive and surf in Panama. In preparation for watching this video, answer these questions about surfing. Answers will vary.

1. ¿Te gusta el *surf*? ¿Por qué?

_____

2. ¿Practicas este deporte? ¿Conoces a alguien que lo practique? ¿Dónde lo practica/s?

_____

Mientras ves el video

3 **Ordenar** Number the items in the order in which they appear in the video.

1

3

2

Después de ver el video

4 **Emparejar** Find the items in the second column that correspond to the ones in the first.

1. La isla Contadora es la más grande ___b___
2. Allí siempre hace calor ___d___
3. En Panamá, los visitantes pueden bucear en el océano Pacífico por la mañana, ___f___
4. Las islas de San Blas son 365, ___e___
5. En Santa Catarina los deportistas disfrutan de ___c___

a. por la noche.
b. del archipiélago.
c. la playa blanca y el agua color turquesa.
d. por eso se puede bucear en todas las estaciones.
e. una para cada día del año.
f. y en el mar Caribe por la tarde.

5 **Responder** Answer the questions in Spanish. Use complete sentences.

1. ¿Qué país centroamericano tiene costas en el océano Pacífico y en el mar Caribe?

Panamá tiene costas en el mar Caribe y en el océano Pacífico.

2. ¿Por qué Las Perlas es un buen lugar para bucear?

Las Perlas es un buen lugar para bucear porque allí hay miles de especies tropicales de peces y muchos arrecifes de

corales y siempre hace mucho calor.

3. ¿Cómo llegan los turistas a la isla Contadora?

Los turistas llegan a la isla Contadora por barco o por avión.

4. ¿Cómo se llaman los indígenas que viven en las islas San Blas?

Los indígenas kuna viven en las islas de San Blas.

5. ¿Adónde van los mejores deportistas de *surfing* del mundo?

Los mejores deportistas de *surfing* del mundo van a Santa Catarina.

6 **Pasatiempos** Complete this chart in Spanish. Answers will vary.

Mis deportes/ pasatiempos favoritos	Por qué me gustan	Dónde/Cuándo los practico

contextos

Lección 6

1 **Describir** Listen to each sentence and write the number of the sentence below the drawing of the household item mentioned.

a. _____ 3 _____

b. _____ 7 _____

c. _____ 2 _____

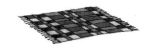

d. _____ 8 _____

e. _____ 6 _____

f. _____ 1 _____

g. _____ 4 _____

h. _____ 5 _____

2 **Identificar** You will hear a series of words. Write the word that does not belong in each series.

1. _____ el armario _____

2. _____ el tenedor _____

3. _____ el cartel _____

4. _____ la pared _____

5. _____ el alquiler _____

6. _____ el cubierto _____

7. _____ la servilleta _____

8. _____ la vivienda _____

3 **Quehaceres domésticos** Your children are complaining about the state of things in your house. Respond to their complaints by telling them what household chores they should do to correct the situation. Repeat the correct response after the speaker. (*6 items*)

> **modelo**
>
> La ropa está arrugada (*wrinkled*).
> *Debes planchar la ropa.*

4 **En la oficina de la agente inmobiliaria** Listen to this conversation between Mr. Fuentes and a real estate agent. Then read the statements in your lab manual and decide whether they are **cierto** or **falso**.

	Cierto	Falso
1. El señor Fuentes quiere alquilar una casa.	○	◉
2. El señor Fuentes quiere vivir en las afueras.	◉	○
3. Él no quiere pagar más de 900 balboas al mes.	○	◉
4. Él vive solo (*alone*).	○	◉
5. El edificio de apartamentos tiene ascensor.	◉	○
6. El apartamento tiene lavadora.	○	◉

Lab Manual

pronunciación

The letter x

In Spanish, the letter **x** has several sounds. When the letter **x** appears between two vowels, it is usually pronounced like the *ks* sound in *eccentric* or the *gs* sound in *egg salad*.

con**exi**ón   **exa**men   **saxo**fón

If the letter **x** is followed by a consonant, it is pronounced like *s* or *ks*.

e**xp**licar   se**xt**o   e**xc**ursión

In Old Spanish, the letter **x** had the same sound as the Spanish **j**. Some proper names and some words from native languages like Náhuatl and Maya have retained this pronunciation.

Don Qui**x**ote   Oa**x**aca   Te**x**as

---

1 **Práctica** Repeat each word after the speaker, focusing on the **x** sound.

1. éxito
2. reflexivo
3. exterior
4. excelente
5. expedición
6. mexicano
7. expresión
8. examinar
9. excepto
10. exagerar
11. contexto
12. Maximiliano

---

2 **Oraciones** When you hear the number, read the corresponding sentence aloud. Then listen to the speaker and repeat the sentence.

1. Xavier Ximénez va de excursión a Ixtapa.
2. Xavier es una persona excéntrica y se viste de trajes extravagantes.
3. Él es un experto en lenguas extranjeras.
4. Hoy va a una exposición de comidas exóticas.
5. Prueba algunos platos exquisitos y extraordinarios.

---

3 **Refranes** Repeat each saying after the speaker to practice the **x** sound.

1. Ir por extremos no es de discretos.[1]
2. El que de la ira se deja vencer, se expone a perder. [2]

---

4 **Dictado** You will hear five sentences. Each will be said twice. Listen carefully and write what you hear.

1. Doña Ximena vive en un edificio de apartamentos en el extremo de la Ciudad de México.

2. Su apartamento está en el sexto piso.

3. Ella es extranjera.

4. Viene de Extremadura, España.

5. A doña Ximena le gusta ir de excursión y le fascina explorar lugares nuevos.

Prudent people don't go to extremes. [1]

He who allows anger to overcome him, risks losing. [2]

estructura

6.1 Relative pronouns

1 **Escoger** You will hear some sentences with a beep in place of the relative pronoun. Decide whether **que**, **quien**, or **lo que** should complete each sentence and circle it.

> **modelo**
>
> You hear: (Beep) me gusta de la casa es el jardín.
> You circle: **Lo que** because the sentence is **Lo que me gusta de la casa es el jardín**.

1. (que)   quien   lo que
2. que   (quien)   lo que
3. (que)   quien   lo que
4. que   quien   (lo que)
5. que   (quien)   lo que

6. (que)   quien   lo que
7. Que   Quien   (Lo que)
8. (que)   quien   lo que
9. que   (quien)   lo que
10. que   quien   (lo que)

2 **Completar** You will hear some incomplete sentences. Choose the correct ending for each sentence.

1. a. con que trabaja tu amiga.
   (b.) que se mudó a Portobelo.
2. (a.) que vende muebles baratos.
   b. que trabajábamos.
3. (a.) a quienes escribí son mis primas.
   b. de quien te escribí.

4. a. con que barres el suelo.
   (b.) que queremos vender.
5. (a.) lo que deben.
   b. que deben.
6. a. que te hablo es ama de casa.
   (b.) en quien pienso es ama de casa.

3 **Preguntas** Answer each question you hear using a relative pronoun and the cues in your lab manual. Repeat the correct response after the speaker.

> **modelo**
>
> You hear: ¿Quiénes son los chicos rubios?
> You see: mis primos / viven en Colón
> You say: Son mis primos que viven en Colón.

1. chica / conocí en el café
2. el cliente / llamó ayer
3. chico / se casa Patricia

4. agente / nos ayudó
5. vecinos / viven en la casa azul
6. chica / trabajo

4 **Un robo (break-in)** There has been a theft at the Rivera's house. The detective they have hired has gathered all the family members in the living room to reveal the culprit. Listen to his conclusions. Then complete the list of clues (**pistas**) in your lab manual and answer the question.

Pistas

1. El reloj que _estaba roto_
2. La taza que _estaba sucia (estaba en el lavaplatos)_
3. La almohada que _tenía dos pelos (pelirrojos)_

Pregunta

¿Quién se llevó las cucharas de la abuela y por qué se las llevó? _La tía Matilde se llevó las cucharas de la abuela porque necesitaba dinero._

6.2 Formal commands

1 **Identificar** You will hear some sentences. If the verb is a formal command, circle **Sí**. If the verb is not a command, circle **No**.

> **modelo**
>
> *You hear:* Saque la basura.
> *You circle:* **Sí** because **Saque** is a formal command.

1. Sí (No) 6. (Sí) No
2. (Sí) No 7. Sí (No)
3. (Sí) No 8. Sí (No)
4. Sí (No) 9. Sí (No)
5. (Sí) No 10. (Sí) No

2 **Cambiar** A physician is giving a patient advice. Change each sentence you hear from an indirect command to a formal command. Repeat the correct answer after the speaker. *(6 items)*

> **modelo**
>
> Usted tiene que dormir ocho horas cada noche.
> **Duerma** *ocho horas cada noche.*

3 **Preguntas** Answer each question you hear in the affirmative using a formal command and a direct object pronoun. Repeat the correct response after the speaker. *(8 items)*

> **modelo**
>
> ¿Cerramos las ventanas?
> *Sí, ciérrenlas.*

4 **Más preguntas** Answer each question you hear using a formal command and the cue in your lab manual. Repeat the correct response after the speaker.

> **modelo**
>
> *You hear:* ¿Debo llamar al señor Rodríguez?
> *You see:* no / ahora
> *You say:* No, no lo llame ahora.

1. no 4. no
2. a las cinco 5. el primer día del mes
3. sí / aquí 6. que estamos ocupados

5 **Direcciones** Julia is going to explain how to get to her home. Listen to her instructions, then number the instructions in your lab manual in the correct order. Two items will not be used.

____2____ a. entrar al edificio que está al lado del Banco Popular

_____ b. tomar el ascensor al cuarto piso

____5____ c. buscar la llave debajo de la alfombra

_____ d. ir detrás del edificio

____1____ e. bajarse del metro en la estación Santa Rosa

____3____ f. subir las escaleras al tercer piso

____4____ g. caminar hasta el final del pasillo

6.3 The present subjunctive

1 **Escoger** You will hear some sentences with a beep in place of a verb. Decide which verb should complete each sentence and circle it.

> **modelo**
> *You hear:* Es urgente que (*beep*) al médico.
> *You see:* vas vayas
> *You circle:* **vayas** *because the sentence is* **Es urgente que vayas al médico.**

1. tomamos — (tomemos)
2. (conduzcan) — conducen
3. (aprenda) — aprende
4. arreglas — (arregles)

5. se acuestan — (se acuesten)
6. sabes — (sepas)
7. (almorcemos) — almorzamos
8. (se mude) — se muda

2 **Cambiar** You are a Spanish instructor, and it's the first day of class. Tell your students what is important for them to do using the cues you hear. (*8 items*)

> **modelo**
> hablar español en la clase
> **Es importante que ustedes hablen español en la clase.**

3 **Transformar** Change each sentence you hear to the subjunctive mood using the expression in your lab manual. Repeat the correct answer after the speaker.

> **modelo**
> *You hear:* Pones tu ropa en el armario.
> *You see:* Es necesario
> *You say:* **Es necesario que pongas tu ropa en el armario.**

1. Es mejor
2. Es urgente
3. Es malo
4. Es importante
5. Es bueno
6. Es necesario

4 **¿Qué pasa aquí?** Listen to this conversation. Then choose the phrase that best completes each sentence in your lab manual.

1. Esta conversación es entre…
   a. un empleado y una clienta.
   b. un hijo y su madre.
   c. un camarero y la dueña de un restaurante.
2. Es necesario que Mario…
   a. llegue temprano.
   b. se lave las manos.
   c. use la lavadora.
3. Es urgente que Mario…
   a. ponga las mesas.
   b. quite las mesas.
   c. sea listo.

6.4 Subjunctive with verbs of will and influence

1 **Identificar** Listen to each sentence. If you hear a verb in the subjunctive, mark **Sí**. If you don't hear the subjunctive, mark **No**.

1. (Sí) No
2. Sí (No)
3. (Sí) No

4. Sí (No)
5. Sí (No)
6. (Sí) No

2 **Transformar** Some people are discussing what they or their friends want to do. Say that you don't want them to do those things. Repeat the correct response after the speaker. (6 *items*)

> **modelo**
> Esteban quiere invitar a tu hermana a una fiesta.
> **No quiero que Esteban invite a mi hermana a una fiesta.**

3 **Situaciones** Listen to each situation and make a recommendation using the cues in your lab manual. Repeat the correct response after the speaker.

> **modelo**
> *You hear:* Sacamos una "F" en el examen de química.
> *You see:* estudiar más
> *You say:* **Les recomiendo que estudien más.**

1. ponerte un suéter
2. quedarse en la cama
3. regalarles una tostadora

4. no hacerlo
5. comprarlas en La Casa Bonita
6. ir a La Cascada

4 **¿Qué hacemos?** Listen to this conversation and answer the questions in your lab manual.

1. ¿Qué quiere el señor Barriga que hagan los chicos?

   El señor Barriga quiere que los chicos le paguen el alquiler.

2. ¿Qué le pide el chico?

   Le pide que les dé más tiempo.

3. ¿Qué les sugiere el señor a los chicos?

   Les sugiere que pidan dinero a sus padres y que Juan Carlos encuentre otro trabajo pronto.

4. ¿Qué tienen que hacer los chicos si no consiguen el dinero?

   Los chicos tienen (van a tener) que mudarse.

5. Al final, ¿en qué insiste el señor Barriga?

   Al final, el señor Barriga insiste en que le paguen el alquiler mañana por la mañana.

vocabulario

You will now hear the vocabulary found in your worktext on the last page of this lesson. Listen and repeat each Spanish word or phrase after the speaker.

Additional Vocabulary

Additional Vocabulary

Notes

Notes

Plan de escritura

1 ### Ideas y organización

Begin by organizing your writing materials. If you prefer to write by hand, you may want to have a few spare pens and pencils on hand, as well as an eraser or correction fluid. If you prefer to use a word-processing program, make sure you know how to type Spanish accent marks, the **tilde,** and Spanish punctuation marks. Then make a list of the resources you can consult while writing. Finally, make a list of the basic ideas you want to cover. Beside each idea, jot down a few Spanish words and phrases you may want to use while writing.

2 ### Primer borrador

Write your first draft, using the resources and ideas you gathered in **Ideas y organización.**

3 ### Comentario

Exchange papers with a classmate and comment on each other's work, using these questions as a guide. Begin by mentioning what you like about your classmate's writing.

a. How can your classmate make his or her writing clearer, more logical, or more organized?

b. What suggestions do you have for making the writing more interesting or complete?

c. Do you see any spelling or grammatical errors?

4 ### Redacción

Revise your first draft, keeping in mind your classmate's comments. Also, incorporate any new information you may have. Before handing in the final version, review your work using these guidelines:

a. Make sure each verb agrees with its subject. Then check the gender and number of each article, noun, and adjective.

b. Check your spelling and punctuation.

c. Consult your **Anotaciones para mejorar la escritura** (see description below) to avoid repetition of previous errors.

5 ### Evaluación y progreso

You may want to share what you've written with a classmate, a small group, or the entire class. After your instructor has returned your paper, review the comments and corrections. On a separate sheet of paper, write the heading **Anotaciones para mejorar** (*Notes for improving*) **la escritura** and list your most common errors. Place this list and your corrected document in your writing portfolio (**Carpeta de trabajos**) and consult it from time to time to gauge your progress.

Spanish Terms for Direction Lines and Classroom Use

Below is a list of useful terms that you might hear your instructor say in class. It also includes Spanish terms that appear in the direction lines of your textbook.

En las instrucciones · *In direction lines*

Cambia/Cambien...	*Change...*
Camina/Caminen por la clase.	*Walk around the classroom.*
Ciertas o falsas	*True or false*
Cierto o falso	*True or false*
Circula/Circulen por la clase.	*Walk around the classroom.*
Completa las oraciones de una manera lógica.	*Complete the sentences logically.*
Con un(a) compañero/a...	*With a classmate...*
Contesta las preguntas.	*Answer the questions.*
Corrige las oraciones falsas.	*Correct the false statements.*
Cuenta/Cuenten...	*Tell...*
Di/Digan...	*Say...*
Discute/Discutan...	*Discuss...*
En grupos...	*In groups...*
En parejas...	*In pairs...*
Entrevista...	*Interview...*
Escúchala	*Listen to it*
Forma oraciones completas.	*Create/Make complete sentences.*
Háganse preguntas.	*Ask each other questions.*
Haz el papel de...	*Play the role of...*
Haz los cambios necesarios.	*Make the necessary changes.*
Indica/Indiquen si las oraciones...	*Indicate if the sentences...*
Intercambia/Intercambien...	*Exchange...*
Lee/Lean en voz alta.	*Read aloud.*
Pon/Pongan...	*Put...*
...que mejor completa...	*...that best completes...*
Reúnete...	*Get together...*
...se da/dan como ejemplo.	*...is/are given as a model.*
Toma nota...	*Take note...*
Tomen apuntes.	*Take notes.*
Túrnense...	*Take turns...*

Palabras útiles · *Useful words*

la adivinanza	*riddle*
el anuncio	*advertisement/ad*
los apuntes	*notes*
el borrador	*draft*
la canción	*song*
la concordancia	*agreement*
el contenido	*contents*
eficaz	*efficient*
la encuesta	*survey*
el equipo	*team*
el esquema	*outline*
el folleto	*brochure*
las frases	*statements*
la hoja de actividades	*activity sheet/handout*
la hoja de papel	*piece of paper*
la información errónea	*incorrect information*
el/la lector(a)	*reader*
la lectura	*reading*
las oraciones	*sentences*
la ortografía	*spelling*
las palabras útiles	*useful words*
el papel	*role*
el párrafo	*paragraph*
el paso	*step*
la(s) persona(s) descrita(s)	*the person (people) described*
la pista	*clue*
por ejemplo	*for example*
el propósito	*purpose*
los recursos	*resources*
el reportaje	*report*
los resultados	*results*
según	*according to*
siguiente	*following*
la sugerencia	*suggestion*
el sustantivo	*noun*
el tema	*topic*
último	*last*
el último recurso	*last resort*

Verbos útiles *Useful verbs*

adivinar	to guess
anotar	to jot down
añadir	to add
apoyar	to support
averiguar	to find out
cambiar	to change
combinar	to combine
compartir	to share
comprobar (o:ue)	to check
corregir (e:i)	to correct
crear	to create
devolver (o:ue)	to return
doblar	to fold
dramatizar	to act out
elegir (e:i)	to choose/select
emparejar	to match
entrevistar	to interview
escoger	to choose
identificar	to identify
incluir	to include
informar	to report
intentar	to try
intercambiar	to exchange
investigar	to research
marcar	to mark
preguntar	to ask
recordar (o:ue)	to remember
responder	to answer
revisar	to revise
seguir (e:i)	to follow
seleccionar	to select
subrayar	to underline
traducir	to translate
tratar de	to be about

Expresiones útiles *Useful expressions*

Ahora mismo.	Right away.
¿Cómo no?	But of course.
¿Cómo se dice _____ en español?	How do you say _____ in Spanish?
¿Cómo se escribe _____?	How do you spell _____?
¿Comprende(n)?	Do you understand?
Con gusto.	With pleasure.
Con permiso.	Excuse me.
De acuerdo.	Okay.
De nada.	You're welcome.
¿De veras?	Really?
¿En qué página estamos?	What page are we on?
¿En serio?	Seriously?
Enseguida.	Right away.
hoy día	nowadays
Más despacio, por favor.	Slower, please.
Muchas gracias.	Thanks a lot.
No entiendo.	I don't understand.
No hay de qué.	Don't mention it.
No importa.	No problem./It doesn't matter.
¡No me digas!	You don't say!
No sé.	I don't know.
¡Ojalá!	Hopefully!
Perdone.	Pardon me.
Por favor.	Please.
Por supuesto.	Of course.
¡Qué bien!	Great!
¡Qué gracioso!	How funny!
¡Qué pena!	What a shame/pity!
¿Qué significa _____?	What does _____ mean?
Repite, por favor.	Please repeat.
Tengo una pregunta.	I have a question.
¿Tiene(n) alguna pregunta?	Do you have any questions?
Vaya(n) a la página dos.	Go to page 2.

Glossary of Grammatical Terms

ADJECTIVE A word that modifies, or describes, a noun or pronoun.

muchos libros
many books

un hombre **rico**
*a **rich** man*

las mujeres **altas**
*the **tall** women*

Demonstrative adjective An adjective that specifies which noun a speaker is referring to.

esta fiesta
this party

ese chico
that boy

aquellas flores
those flowers

Possessive adjective An adjective that indicates ownership or possession.

mi mejor vestido
my best dress

Éste es **mi** hermano.
*This is **my** brother.*

Stressed possessive adjective A possessive adjective that emphasizes the owner or possessor.

Es un libro **mío**.
*It's **my** book./It's a book **of mine**.*

Es amiga **tuya**; yo no la conozco.
*She's a friend **of yours**; I don't know her.*

ADVERB A word that modifies, or describes, a verb, adjective, or other adverb.

Pancho escribe **rápidamente**.
*Pancho writes **quickly**.*

Este cuadro es **muy** bonito.
*This picture is **very** pretty.*

ARTICLE A word that points out a noun in either a specific or a non-specific way.

Definite article An article that points out a noun in a specific way.

el libro
the book

la maleta
the suitcase

los diccionarios
the dictionaries

las palabras
the words

Indefinite article An article that points out a noun in a general, non-specific way.

un lápiz
a pencil

una computadora
a computer

unos pájaros
some birds

unas escuelas
some schools

CLAUSE A group of words that contains both a conjugated verb and a subject, either expressed or implied.

Main (or Independent) clause A clause that can stand alone as a complete sentence.

Pienso ir a cenar pronto.
I plan to go to dinner soon.

Subordinate (or Dependent) clause A clause that does not express a complete thought and therefore cannot stand alone as a sentence.

Trabajo en la cafetería **porque necesito dinero para la escuela.**
*I work in the cafeteria **because I need money for school.***

COMPARATIVE A construction used with an adjective or adverb to express a comparison between two people, places, or things.

Este programa es **más interesante que** el otro.
*This program is **more interesting than** the other one.*

Tomás no es **tan alto como** Alberto.
*Tomás is not **as tall as** Alberto.*

CONJUGATION A set of the forms of a verb for a specific tense or mood or the process by which these verb forms are presented.

Preterite conjugation of **cantar:**

cant**é**	cant**amos**
cant**aste**	cant**asteis**
cant**ó**	cant**aron**

CONJUNCTION A word used to connect words, clauses, or phrases.

Susana es de Cuba **y** Pedro es de España.
*Susana is from Cuba **and** Pedro is from Spain.*

No quiero estudiar **pero** tengo que hacerlo.
*I don't want to study, **but** I have to.*

CONTRACTION The joining of two words into one. The only contractions in Spanish are **al** and **del**.

Mi hermano fue **al** concierto ayer.
*My brother went **to the** concert yesterday.*

Saqué dinero **del** banco.
*I took money **from the** bank.*

DIRECT OBJECT A noun or pronoun that directly receives the action of the verb.

Tomás lee **el libro**.   **La** pagó ayer.
*Tomás reads **the book**.   She paid **it** yesterday.*

GENDER The grammatical categorizing of certain kinds of words, such as nouns and pronouns, as masculine, feminine, or neuter.

Masculine
articles el, un
pronouns él, lo, mío, éste, ése, aquél
adjective simpático

Feminine
articles la, una
pronouns ella, la, mía, ésta, ésa, aquélla
adjective simpática

IMPERSONAL EXPRESSION A third-person expression with no expressed or specific subject.

Es muy importante.   **Llueve** mucho.
It's very important.   It's raining hard.

Aquí se **habla** español.
*Spanish **is spoken** here.*

INDIRECT OBJECT A noun or pronoun that receives the action of the verb indirectly; the object, often a living being, to or for whom an action is performed.

Eduardo **le** dio un libro **a Linda**.
*Eduardo gave a book **to Linda**.*

La profesora **me** dio una C en el examen.
*The professor gave **me** a C on the test.*

INFINITIVE The basic form of a verb. Infinitives in Spanish end in -ar, -er, or -ir.

hablar   correr   abrir
to speak   to run   to open

INTERROGATIVE An adjective or pronoun used to ask a question.

¿Quién habla?   **¿Cuántos** compraste?
Who is speaking?   How many did you buy?

¿Qué piensas hacer hoy?
What do you plan to do today?

INVERSION Changing the word order of a sentence, often to form a question.

Statement: Elena pagó la cuenta del restaurante.

Inversion: ¿Pagó Elena la cuenta del restaurante?

MOOD A grammatical distinction of verbs that indicates whether the verb is intended to make a statement or command or to express a doubt, emotion, or condition contrary to fact.

Imperative mood Verb forms used to make commands.

Di la verdad.   **Caminen** ustedes conmigo.
Tell the truth.   Walk with me.

¡Comamos ahora!
Let's eat now!

Indicative mood Verb forms used to state facts, actions, and states considered to be real.

Sé que **tienes** el dinero.
I know that you have the money.

Subjunctive mood Verb forms used principally in subordinate (dependent) clauses to express wishes, desires, emotions, doubts, and certain conditions, such as contrary-to-fact situations.

Prefieren que **hables** en español.
*They prefer that **you speak** in Spanish.*

Dudo que Luis **tenga** el dinero necesario.
*I doubt that Luis **has** the necessary money.*

NOUN A word that identifies people, animals, places, things, and ideas.

hombre   gato
man   cat

México   casa
Mexico   house

libertad   libro
freedom   book

NUMBER A grammatical term that refers to singular or plural. Nouns in Spanish and English have number. Other parts of a sentence, such as adjectives, articles, and verbs, can also have number.

Singular	Plural
una cosa	**unas** cosas
a thing	*some things*
el profesor	**los** profesores
the professor	*the professors*

NUMBERS Words that represent amounts.

Cardinal numbers Words that show specific amounts.

cinco minutos
five minutes

el año **dos mil siete**
the year 2007

Ordinal numbers Words that indicate the order of a noun in a series.

el **cuarto** jugador	la **décima** hora
*the **fourth** player*	*the **tenth** hour*

PAST PARTICIPLE A past form of the verb used in compound tenses. The past participle may also be used as an adjective, but it must then agree in number and gender with the word it modifies.

Han **buscado** por todas partes.
*They have **searched** everywhere.*

Yo no había **estudiado** para el examen.
*I hadn't **studied** for the exam.*

Hay una **ventana abierta** en la sala.
*There is an **open window** in the living room.*

PERSON The form of the verb or pronoun that indicates the speaker, the one spoken to, or the one spoken about. In Spanish, as in English, there are three persons: first, second, and third.

Person	Singular	Plural
1st	**yo** *I*	**nosotros/as** *we*
2nd	**tú, Ud.** *you*	**vosotros/as, Uds.** *you*
3rd	**él, ella** *he, she*	**ellos, ellas** *they*

PREPOSITION A word or words that describe(s) the relationship, most often in time or space, between two other words.

Anita es **de** California.
*Anita is **from** California.*

La chaqueta está **en** el carro.
*The jacket is **in** the car.*

Marta se peinó **antes de** salir.
*Marta combed her hair **before** going out.*

PRESENT PARTICIPLE In English, a verb form that ends in *-ing*. In Spanish, the present participle ends in **-ndo**, and is often used with **estar** to form a progressive tense.

Mi hermana está **hablando** por teléfono ahora mismo.
*My sister is **talking** on the phone right now.*

PRONOUN A word that takes the place of a noun or nouns.

Demonstrative pronoun A pronoun that takes the place of a specific noun.

Quiero **ésta**.
*I want **this one**.*

¿Vas a comprar **ése**?
*Are you going to buy **that one**?*

Juan prefirió **aquéllos**.
*Juan preferred **those** (over there).*

Object pronoun A pronoun that functions as a direct or indirect object of the verb.

Te digo la verdad.
*I'm telling **you** the truth.*

Me lo trajo Juan.
*Juan brought **it** to **me**.*

Reflexive pronoun A pronoun that indicates that the action of a verb is performed by the subject on itself. These pronouns are often expressed in English with *-self: myself, yourself*, etc.

Yo **me** bañé antes de salir.
*I bathed (**myself**) before going out.*

Elena **se** acostó a las once y media.
*Elena **went to bed** at eleven-thirty.*

Glossary

Relative pronoun A pronoun that connects a subordinate clause to a main clause.

El chico **que** nos escribió viene de visita mañana.
*The boy **who** wrote us is coming to visit tomorrow.*

Ya sé **lo que** tenemos que hacer.
*I already know **what** we have to do.*

Subject pronoun A pronoun that replaces the name or title of a person or thing, and acts as the subject of a verb.

Tú debes estudiar más.
***You** should study more.*

Él llegó primero.
***He** arrived first.*

SUBJECT A noun or pronoun that performs the action of a verb and is often implied by the verb.

María va al supermercado.
***María** goes to the supermarket.*

(Ellos) Trabajan mucho.
***They** work hard.*

Esos **libros** son muy caros.
*Those **books** are very expensive.*

SUPERLATIVE A word or construction used with an adjective or adverb to express the highest or lowest degree of a specific quality among three or more people, places, or things.

De todas mis clases, ésta es la **más interesante**.
*Of all my classes, this is the **most interesting**.*

Raúl es el **menos simpático** de los chicos.
*Raúl is the **least pleasant** of the boys.*

TENSE A set of verb forms that indicates the time of an action or state: past, present, or future.

Compound tense A two-word tense made up of an auxiliary verb and a present or past participle. In Spanish, there are two auxiliary verbs: **estar** and **haber**.

En este momento, **estoy estudiando**.
*At this time, **I am studying**.*

El paquete no **ha llegado** todavía.
*The package **has** not **arrived** yet.*

Simple tense A tense expressed by a single verb form.

María **estaba** mal anoche.
*María **was** ill last night.*

Juana **hablará** con su mamá mañana.
*Juana **will speak** with her mom tomorrow.*

VERB A word that expresses actions or states-of-being.

Auxiliary verb A verb used with a present or past participle to form a compound tense. **Haber** is the most commonly used auxiliary verb in Spanish.

Los chicos **han** visto los elefantes.
*The children **have** seen the elephants.*

Espero que **hayas** comido.
*I hope you **have** eaten.*

Reflexive verb A verb that describes an action performed by the subject on itself and is always used with a reflexive pronoun.

Me compré un carro nuevo.
*I **bought myself** a new car.*

Pedro y Adela **se levantan** muy temprano.
*Pedro and Adela **get (themselves) up** very early.*

Spelling change verb A verb that undergoes a predictable change in spelling, in order to reflect its actual pronunciation in the various conjugations.

practicar	c→qu	practico	practiqué
dirigir	g→j	dirigí	dirijo
almorzar	z→c	almorzó	almorcé

Stem-changing verb A verb whose stem vowel undergoes one or more predictable changes in the various conjugations.

entender (e:ie)	entiendo
pedir (e:i)	piden
dormir (o:ue, u)	duermo, durmieron

Verb Conjugation Tables

The verb lists

The list of verbs below, and the model-verb tables that start on page 355 show you how to conjugate every verb taught in **¡ADELANTE!** Each verb in the list is followed by a model verb conjugated according to the same pattern. The number in parentheses indicates where in the verb tables you can find the conjugated forms of the model verb. If you want to find out how to conjugate **divertirse**, for example, look up number 33, **sentir**, the model for verbs that follow the **e:ie** stem-change pattern.

How to use the verb tables

In the tables you will find the infinitive, present and past participles, and all the simple forms of each model verb. The formation of the compound tenses of any verb can be inferred from the table of compound tenses, pages 355–356, either by combining the past participle of the verb with a conjugated form of **haber** or by combining the present participle with a conjugated form of **estar**.

abrazar (z:c) like cruzar (37)

abrir like vivir (3) *except* past participle is **abierto**

aburrir(se) like vivir (3)

acabar de like hablar (1)

acampar like hablar (1)

acompañar like hablar (1)

aconsejar like hablar (1)

acordarse (o:ue) like contar (24)

acostarse (o:ue) like contar (24)

adelgazar (z:c) like cruzar (37)

afeitarse like hablar (1)

ahorrar like hablar (1)

alegrarse like hablar (1)

aliviar like hablar (1)

almorzar (o:ue) like contar (24) *except* (z:c)

alquilar like hablar (1)

andar like hablar (1) *except* preterite stem is **anduv-**

anunciar like hablar (1)

apagar (g:gu) like llegar (41)

aplaudir like vivir (3)

apreciar like hablar (1)

aprender like comer (2)

apurarse like hablar (1)

arrancar (c:qu) like tocar (43)

arreglar like hablar (1)

asistir like vivir (3)

aumentar like hablar (1)

ayudar(se) like hablar (1)

bailar like hablar (1)

bajar(se) like hablar (1)

bañarse like hablar (1)

barrer like comer (2)

beber like comer (2)

besar(se) like hablar (1)

borrar like hablar (1)

brindar like hablar (1)

bucear like hablar (1)

buscar (c:qu) like tocar (43)

caber (4)

caer(se) (5)

calentarse (e:ie) like pensar (30)

calzar (z:c) like cruzar (37)

cambiar like hablar (1)

caminar like hablar (1)

cantar like hablar (1)

casarse like hablar (1)

cazar (z:c) like cruzar (37)

celebrar like hablar (1)

cenar like hablar (1)

cepillarse like hablar (1)

cerrar (e:ie) like pensar (30)

cobrar like hablar (1)

cocinar like hablar (1)

comenzar (e:ie) (z:c) like empezar (26)

comer (2)

compartir like vivir (3)

comprar like hablar (1)

comprender like comer (2)

comprometerse like comer (2)

comunicarse (c:qu) like tocar (43)

conducir (c:zc) (6)

confirmar like hablar (1)

conocer (c:zc) (35)

conseguir (e:i) (g:gu) like seguir (32)

conservar like hablar (1)

consumir like vivir (3)

contaminar like hablar (1)

contar (o:ue) (24)

controlar like hablar (1)

correr like comer (2)

costar (o:ue) like contar (24)

creer (y) (36)

cruzar (z:c) (37)

cubrir like vivir (3) *except* past participle is **cubierto**

cuidar like hablar (1)

cumplir like vivir (3)

dañar like hablar (1)

dar (7)

deber like comer (2)

decidir like vivir (3)

decir (e:i) (8)

declarar like hablar (1)

dejar like hablar (1)

depositar like hablar (1)

desarrollar like hablar (1)

desayunar like hablar (1)

descansar like hablar (1)

descargar like hablar (1)

describir like vivir (3) *except* past participle is **descrito**

descubrir like vivir (3) *except* past participle is **descubierto**

desear like hablar (1)

despedirse (e:i) like pedir (29)

despertarse (e:ie) like pensar (30)

destruir (y) (38)

dibujar like hablar (1)

dirigir (g:j) like vivir (3) *except* (g:j)

disfrutar like hablar (1)

divertirse (e:ie) like sentir (33)

divorciarse like hablar (1)

doblar like hablar (1)

doler (o:ue) like volver (34) *except* past participle is regular

dormir(se) (o:ue, u) (25)

ducharse like hablar (1)

dudar like hablar (1)

durar like hablar (1)

echar like hablar (1)

elegir (e:i) like pedir (29) *except* (g:j)

emitir like vivir (3)

empezar (e:ie) (z:c) (26)
enamorarse like hablar (1)
encantar like hablar (1)
encontrar(se) (o:ue) like contar (24)
enfermarse like hablar (1)
engordar like hablar (1)
enojarse like hablar (1)
enseñar like hablar (1)
ensuciar like hablar (1)
entender (e:ie) (27)
entrenarse like hablar (1)
entrevistar like hablar (1)
enviar (envío) (39)
escalar like hablar (1)
escoger (g:j) like proteger (42)
escribir like vivir (3) *except* past participle is escrito
escuchar like hablar (1)
esculpir like vivir (3)
esperar like hablar (1)
esquiar (esquío) like enviar (39)
establecer (c:zc) like conocer (35)
estacionar like hablar (1)
estar (9)
estornudar like hablar (1)
estudiar like hablar (1)
evitar like hablar (1)
explicar (c:qu) like tocar (43)
explorar like hablar (1)
faltar like hablar (1)
fascinar like hablar (1)
firmar like hablar (1)
fumar like hablar (1)
funcionar like hablar (1)
ganar like hablar (1)
gastar like hablar (1)
grabar like hablar (1)
graduarse (gradúo) (40)
guardar like hablar (1)
gustar like hablar (1)
haber (hay) (10)
hablar (1)
hacer (11)
importar like hablar (1)
imprimir like vivir (3)
informar like hablar (1)
insistir like vivir (3)
interesar like hablar (1)
invertir (e:ie) like sentir (33)

invitar like hablar (1)
ir(se) (12)
jubilarse like hablar (1)
jugar (u:ue) (g:gu) (28)
lastimarse like hablar (1)
lavar(se) like hablar (1)
leer (y) like creer (36)
levantar(se) like hablar (1)
limpiar like hablar (1)
llamar(se) like hablar (1)
llegar (g:gu) (41)
llenar like hablar (1)
llevar(se) like hablar (1)
llover (o:ue) like volver (34) *except* past participle is regular
luchar like hablar (1)
mandar like hablar (1)
manejar like hablar (1)
mantener(se) (e:ie) like tener (20)
maquillarse like hablar (1)
mejorar like hablar (1)
merendar (e:ie) like pensar (30)
mirar like hablar (1)
molestar like hablar (1)
montar like hablar (1)
morir (o:ue) like dormir (25) *except* past participle is muerto
mostrar (o:ue) like contar (24)
mudarse like hablar (1)
nacer (c:zc) like conocer (35)
nadar like hablar (1)
navegar (g:gu) like llegar (41)
necesitar like hablar (1)
negar (e:ie) like pensar (30) *except* (g:gu)
nevar (e:ie) like pensar (30)
obedecer (c:zc) like conocer (35)
obtener (e:ie) like tener (20)
ocurrir like vivir (3)
odiar like hablar (1)
ofrecer (c:zc) like conocer (35)
oír (13)
olvidar like hablar (1)
pagar (g:gu) like llegar (41)
parar like hablar (1)
parecer (c:zc) like conocer (35)

pasar like hablar (1)
pasear like hablar (1)
patinar like hablar (1)
pedir (e:i) (29)
peinarse like hablar (1)
pensar (e:ie) (30)
perder (e:ie) like entender (27)
pescar (c:qu) like tocar (43)
pintar like hablar (1)
planchar like hablar (1)
poder (o:ue) (14)
poner(se) (15)
practicar (c:qu) like tocar (43)
preferir (e:ie) like sentir (33)
preguntar like hablar (1)
preocuparse like hablar (1)
preparar like hablar (1)
presentar like hablar (1)
prestar like hablar (1)
probar(se) (o:ue) like contar (24)
prohibir like vivir (3)
proteger (g:j) (42)
publicar (c:qu) like tocar (43)
quedar(se) like hablar (1)
quemar like hablar (1)
querer (e:ie) (16)
quitar(se) like hablar (1)
recetar like hablar (1)
recibir like vivir (3)
reciclar like hablar (1)
recoger (g:j) like proteger (42)
recomendar (e:ie) like pensar (30)
recordar (o:ue) like contar (24)
reducir (c:zc) like conducir (6)
regalar like hablar (1)
regatear like hablar (1)
regresar like hablar (1)
reír(se) (e:i) (31)
relajarse like hablar (1)
renunciar like hablar (1)
repetir (e:i) like pedir (29)
resolver (o:ue) like volver (34)
respirar like hablar (1)
revisar like hablar (1)
rogar (o:ue) like contar (24)

except (g:gu)
romper(se) like comer (2) *except* past participle is roto
saber (17)
sacar (c:qu) like tocar (43)
sacudir like vivir (3)
salir (18)
saludar(se) like hablar (1)
secar(se) (c:qu) like tocar (43)
seguir (e:i) (32)
sentarse (e:ie) like pensar (30)
sentir(se) (e:ie) (33)
separarse like hablar (1)
ser (19)
servir (e:i) like pedir (29)
solicitar like hablar (1)
sonar (o:ue) like contar (24)
sonreír (e:i) like reír(se) (31)
sorprender like comer (2)
subir like vivir (3)
sudar like hablar (1)
sufrir like vivir (3)
sugerir (e:ie) like sentir (33)
suponer like poner (15)
temer like comer (2)
tener (e:ie) (20)
terminar like hablar (1)
tocar (c:qu) (43)
tomar like hablar (1)
torcerse (o:ue) like volver (34) *except* (c:z) and past participle is regular; e.g., yo tuerzo
toser like comer (2)
trabajar like hablar (1)
traducir (c:zc) like conducir (6)
traer (21)
transmitir like vivir (3)
tratar like hablar (1)
usar like hablar (1)
vender like comer (2)
venir (e:ie, i) (22)
ver (23)
vestirse (e:i) like pedir (29)
viajar like hablar (1)
visitar like hablar (1)
vivir (3)
volver (o:ue) (34)
votar like hablar (1)

Regular verbs: simple tenses

Infinitive	INDICATIVE						SUBJUNCTIVE		IMPERATIVE
	Present	Imperfect	Preterite	Future	Conditional		Present	Past	
hablar	hablo	hablaba	hablé	hablaré	hablaría		hable	hablara	
	hablas	hablabas	hablaste	hablarás	hablarías		hables	hablaras	habla tú (no hables)
Participles:	habla	hablaba	habló	hablará	hablaría		hable	hablara	hable Ud.
hablando	hablamos	hablábamos	hablamos	hablaremos	hablaríamos		hablemos	habláramos	hablemos
hablado	habláis	hablabais	hablasteis	hablaréis	hablaríais		habléis	hablarais	hablad (no habléis)
	hablan	hablaban	hablaron	hablarán	hablarían		hablen	hablaran	hablen Uds.
comer	como	comía	comí	comeré	comería		coma	comiera	
	comes	comías	comiste	comerás	comerías		comas	comieras	come tú (no comas)
Participles:	come	comía	comió	comerá	comería		coma	comiera	coma Ud.
comiendo	comemos	comíamos	comimos	comeremos	comeríamos		comamos	comiéramos	comamos
comido	coméis	comíais	comisteis	comeréis	comeríais		comáis	comierais	comed (no comáis)
	comen	comían	comieron	comerán	comerían		coman	comieran	coman Uds.
vivir	vivo	vivía	viví	viviré	viviría		viva	viviera	
	vives	vivías	viviste	vivirás	vivirías		vivas	vivieras	vive tú (no vivas)
Participles:	vive	vivía	vivió	vivirá	viviría		viva	viviera	viva Ud.
viviendo	vivimos	vivíamos	vivimos	viviremos	viviríamos		vivamos	viviéramos	vivamos
vivido	vivís	vivíais	vivisteis	viviréis	viviríais		viváis	vivierais	vivid (no viváis)
	viven	vivían	vivieron	vivirán	vivirían		vivan	vivieran	vivan Uds.

All verbs: compound tenses

PERFECT TENSES

INDICATIVE								SUBJUNCTIVE			
Present Perfect		Past Perfect		Future Perfect		Conditional Perfect		Present Perfect		Past Perfect	
he		había		habré		habría		haya		hubiera	
has	hablado	habías	hablado	habrás	hablado	habrías	hablado	hayas	hablado	hubieras	hablado
ha	comido	había	comido	habrá	comido	habría	comido	haya	comido	hubiera	comido
hemos	vivido	habíamos	vivido	habremos	vivido	habríamos	vivido	hayamos	vivido	hubiéramos	vivido
habéis		habíais		habréis		habríais		hayáis		hubierais	
han		habían		habrán		habrían		hayan		hubieran	

Verb tables

PROGRESSIVE TENSES

INDICATIVE				SUBJUNCTIVE	
Present Progressive	Past Progressive	Future Progressive	Conditional Progressive	Present Progressive	Past Progressive
estoy	estaba	estaré	estaría	esté	estuviera
estás	estabas	estarás	estarías	estés	estuvieras
está + hablando comiendo viviendo	estaba + hablando comiendo viviendo	estará + hablando comiendo viviendo	estaría + hablando comiendo viviendo	esté + hablando comiendo viviendo	estuviera + hablando comiendo viviendo
estamos	estábamos	estaremos	estaríamos	estemos	estuviéramos
estáis	estabais	estaréis	estaríais	estéis	estuvierais
están	estaban	estarán	estarían	estén	estuvieran

Irregular verbs

	Infinitive	INDICATIVE					SUBJUNCTIVE		IMPERATIVE
		Present	Imperfect	Preterite	Future	Conditional	Present	Past	
4	caber	**quepo**	cabía	**cupe**	**cabré**	**cabría**	**quepa**	**cupiera**	
		cabes	cabías	**cupiste**	**cabrás**	**cabrías**	**quepas**	**cupieras**	cabe tú (no **quepas**)
		cabe	cabía	**cupo**	**cabrá**	**cabría**	**quepa**	**cupiera**	**quepa** Ud.
		cabemos	cabíamos	**cupimos**	**cabremos**	**cabríamos**	**quepamos**	**cupiéramos**	**quepamos**
	Participles:	cabéis	cabíais	**cupisteis**	**cabréis**	**cabríais**	**quepáis**	**cupierais**	cabed (no **quepáis**)
	cabiendo	caben	cabían	**cupieron**	**cabrán**	**cabrían**	**quepan**	**cupieran**	**quepan** Uds.
	cabido								
5	caer(se)	**caigo**	caía	caí	caeré	caería	**caiga**	**cayera**	
		caes	caías	**caíste**	caerás	caerías	**caigas**	**cayeras**	cae tú (no **caigas**)
		cae	caía	**cayó**	caerá	caería	**caiga**	**cayera**	**caiga** Ud.
		caemos	caíamos	**caímos**	caeremos	caeríamos	**caigamos**	**cayéramos**	**caigamos**
	Participles:	caéis	caíais	**caísteis**	caeréis	caeríais	**caigáis**	**cayerais**	caed (no **caigáis**)
	cayendo	caen	caían	**cayeron**	caerán	caerían	**caigan**	**cayeran**	**caigan** Uds.
	caído								
6	conducir (c:zc)	**conduzco**	conducía	**conduje**	conduciré	conduciría	**conduzca**	**condujera**	
		conduces	conducías	**condujiste**	conducirás	conducirías	**conduzcas**	**condujeras**	conduce tú (no **conduzcas**)
		conduce	conducía	**condujo**	conducirá	conduciría	**conduzca**	**condujera**	**conduzca** Ud.
		conducimos	conducíamos	**condujimos**	conduciremos	conduciríamos	**conduzcamos**	**condujéramos**	**conduzcamos**
	Participles:	conducís	conducíais	**condujisteis**	conduciréis	conduciríais	**conduzcáis**	**condujerais**	conducid (no **conduzcáis**)
	conduciendo	conducen	conducían	**condujeron**	conducirán	conducirían	**conduzcan**	**condujeran**	**conduzcan** Uds.
	conducido								

7. dar
Participles: dando, dado

	INDICATIVE					SUBJUNCTIVE		IMPERATIVE
	Present	Imperfect	Preterite	Future	Conditional	Present	Past	
	doy	daba	di	daré	daría	dé	diera	
	das	dabas	diste	darás	darías	des	dieras	da tú (no des)
	da	daba	dio	dará	daría	dé	diera	dé Ud.
	damos	dábamos	dimos	daremos	daríamos	demos	diéramos	demos
	dais	dabais	disteis	daréis	daríais	deis	dierais	dad (no deis)
	dan	daban	dieron	darán	darían	den	dieran	den Uds.

8. decir (e:i)
Participles: diciendo, dicho

	INDICATIVE					SUBJUNCTIVE		IMPERATIVE
	Present	Imperfect	Preterite	Future	Conditional	Present	Past	
	digo	decía	dije	diré	diría	diga	dijera	
	dices	decías	dijiste	dirás	dirías	digas	dijeras	di tú (no digas)
	dice	decía	dijo	dirá	diría	diga	dijera	diga Ud.
	decimos	decíamos	dijimos	diremos	diríamos	digamos	dijéramos	digamos
	decís	decíais	dijisteis	diréis	diríais	digáis	dijerais	decid (no digáis)
	dicen	decían	dijeron	dirán	dirían	digan	dijeran	digan Uds.

9. estar
Participles: estando, estado

	INDICATIVE					SUBJUNCTIVE		IMPERATIVE
	Present	Imperfect	Preterite	Future	Conditional	Present	Past	
	estoy	estaba	estuve	estaré	estaría	esté	estuviera	
	estás	estabas	estuviste	estarás	estarías	estés	estuvieras	está tú (no estés)
	está	estaba	estuvo	estará	estaría	esté	estuviera	esté Ud.
	estamos	estábamos	estuvimos	estaremos	estaríamos	estemos	estuviéramos	estemos
	estáis	estabais	estuvisteis	estaréis	estaríais	estéis	estuvierais	estad (no estéis)
	están	estaban	estuvieron	estarán	estarían	estén	estuvieran	estén Uds.

10. haber
Participles: habiendo, habido

	INDICATIVE					SUBJUNCTIVE		IMPERATIVE
	Present	Imperfect	Preterite	Future	Conditional	Present	Past	
	he	había	hube	habré	habría	haya	hubiera	
	has	habías	hubiste	habrás	habrías	hayas	hubieras	
	ha	había	hubo	habrá	habría	haya	hubiera	
	hemos	habíamos	hubimos	habremos	habríamos	hayamos	hubiéramos	
	habéis	habíais	hubisteis	habréis	habríais	hayáis	hubierais	
	han	habían	hubieron	habrán	habrían	hayan	hubieran	

11. hacer
Participles: haciendo, hecho

	INDICATIVE					SUBJUNCTIVE		IMPERATIVE
	Present	Imperfect	Preterite	Future	Conditional	Present	Past	
	hago	hacía	hice	haré	haría	haga	hiciera	
	haces	hacías	hiciste	harás	harías	hagas	hicieras	haz tú (no hagas)
	hace	hacía	hizo	hará	haría	haga	hiciera	haga Ud.
	hacemos	hacíamos	hicimos	haremos	haríamos	hagamos	hiciéramos	hagamos
	hacéis	hacíais	hicisteis	haréis	haríais	hagáis	hicierais	haced (no hagáis)
	hacen	hacían	hicieron	harán	harían	hagan	hicieran	hagan Uds.

12. ir
Participles: yendo, ido

	INDICATIVE					SUBJUNCTIVE		IMPERATIVE
	Present	Imperfect	Preterite	Future	Conditional	Present	Past	
	voy	iba	fui	iré	iría	vaya	fuera	
	vas	ibas	fuiste	irás	irías	vayas	fueras	ve tú (no vayas)
	va	iba	fue	irá	iría	vaya	fuera	vaya Ud.
	vamos	íbamos	fuimos	iremos	iríamos	vayamos	fuéramos	vamos
	vais	ibais	fuisteis	iréis	iríais	vayáis	fuerais	id (no vayáis)
	van	iban	fueron	irán	irían	vayan	fueran	vayan Uds.

13. oír (y)
Participles: oyendo, oído

	INDICATIVE					SUBJUNCTIVE		IMPERATIVE
	Present	Imperfect	Preterite	Future	Conditional	Present	Past	
	oigo	oía	oí	oiré	oiría	oiga	oyera	
	oyes	oías	oíste	oirás	oirías	oigas	oyeras	oye tú (no oigas)
	oye	oía	oyó	oirá	oiría	oiga	oyera	oiga Ud.
	oímos	oíamos	oímos	oiremos	oiríamos	oigamos	oyéramos	oigamos
	oís	oíais	oísteis	oiréis	oiríais	oigáis	oyerais	oíd (no oigáis)
	oyen	oían	oyeron	oirán	oirían	oigan	oyeran	oigan Uds.

Verb tables

		INDICATIVE				SUBJUNCTIVE		IMPERATIVE
Infinitive	**Present**	**Imperfect**	**Preterite**	**Future**	**Conditional**	**Present**	**Past**	
14 poder (o:ue)	**puedo**	podía	**pude**	**podré**	**podría**	**pueda**	**pudiera**	
	puedes	podías	**pudiste**	**podrás**	**podrías**	**puedas**	**pudieras**	**puede** tú (no **puedas**)
Participles:	**puede**	podía	**pudo**	**podrá**	**podría**	**pueda**	**pudiera**	**pueda** Ud.
pudiendo	podemos	podíamos	**pudimos**	**podremos**	**podríamos**	podamos	**pudiéramos**	podamos
podido	podéis	podíais	**pudisteis**	**podréis**	**podríais**	podáis	**pudierais**	poded (no podáis)
	pueden	podían	**pudieron**	**podrán**	**podrían**	**puedan**	**pudieran**	**puedan** Uds.
15 poner	**pongo**	ponía	**puse**	**pondré**	**pondría**	**ponga**	**pusiera**	
	pones	ponías	**pusiste**	**pondrás**	**pondrías**	**pongas**	**pusieras**	**pon** tú (no **pongas**)
Participles:	pone	ponía	**puso**	**pondrá**	**pondría**	**ponga**	**pusiera**	**ponga** Ud.
poniendo	ponemos	poníamos	**pusimos**	**pondremos**	**pondríamos**	**pongamos**	**pusiéramos**	**pongamos**
puesto	ponéis	poníais	**pusisteis**	**pondréis**	**pondríais**	**pongáis**	**pusierais**	poned (no **pongáis**)
	ponen	ponían	**pusieron**	**pondrán**	**pondrían**	**pongan**	**pusieran**	**pongan** Uds.
16 querer (e:ie)	**quiero**	quería	**quise**	**querré**	**querría**	**quiera**	**quisiera**	
	quieres	querías	**quisiste**	**querrás**	**querrías**	**quieras**	**quisieras**	**quiere** tú (no **quieras**)
Participles:	**quiere**	quería	**quiso**	**querrá**	**querría**	**quiera**	**quisiera**	**quiera** Ud.
queriendo	queremos	queríamos	**quisimos**	**querremos**	**querríamos**	queramos	**quisiéramos**	**queramos**
querido	queréis	queríais	**quisisteis**	**querréis**	**querríais**	queráis	**quisierais**	quered (no queráis)
	quieren	querían	**quisieron**	**querrán**	**querrían**	**quieran**	**quisieran**	**quieran** Uds.
17 saber	**sé**	sabía	**supe**	**sabré**	**sabría**	**sepa**	**supiera**	
	sabes	sabías	**supiste**	**sabrás**	**sabrías**	**sepas**	**supieras**	sabe tú (no **sepas**)
Participles:	sabe	sabía	**supo**	**sabrá**	**sabría**	**sepa**	**supiera**	**sepa** Ud.
sabiendo	sabemos	sabíamos	**supimos**	**sabremos**	**sabríamos**	**sepamos**	**supiéramos**	**sepamos**
sabido	sabéis	sabíais	**supisteis**	**sabréis**	**sabríais**	**sepáis**	**supierais**	sabed (no **sepáis**)
	saben	sabían	**supieron**	**sabrán**	**sabrían**	**sepan**	**supieran**	**sepan** Uds.
18 salir	**salgo**	salía	salí	**saldré**	**saldría**	**salga**	saliera	
	sales	salías	saliste	**saldrás**	**saldrías**	**salgas**	salieras	**sal** tú (no **salgas**)
Participles:	sale	salía	salió	**saldrá**	**saldría**	**salga**	saliera	**salga** Ud.
saliendo	salimos	salíamos	salimos	**saldremos**	**saldríamos**	**salgamos**	saliéramos	**salgamos**
salido	salís	salíais	salisteis	**saldréis**	**saldríais**	**salgáis**	salierais	salid (no **salgáis**)
	salen	salían	salieron	**saldrán**	**saldrían**	**salgan**	salieran	**salgan** Uds.
19 ser	**soy**	**era**	**fui**	seré	sería	**sea**	**fuera**	
	eres	**eras**	**fuiste**	serás	serías	**seas**	**fueras**	**sé** tú (no **seas**)
Participles:	**es**	**era**	**fue**	será	sería	**sea**	**fuera**	sea Ud.
siendo	**somos**	**éramos**	**fuimos**	seremos	seríamos	**seamos**	**fuéramos**	**seamos**
sido	**sois**	**erais**	**fuisteis**	seréis	seríais	**seáis**	**fuerais**	sed (no **seáis**)
	son	**eran**	**fueron**	serán	serían	**sean**	**fueran**	**sean** Uds.
20 tener (e:ie)	**tengo**	**tenía**	**tuve**	**tendré**	**tendría**	**tenga**	**tuviera**	
	tienes	**tenías**	**tuviste**	**tendrás**	**tendrías**	**tengas**	**tuvieras**	**ten** tú (no **tengas**)
Participles:	**tiene**	**tenía**	**tuvo**	**tendrá**	**tendría**	**tenga**	**tuviera**	**tenga** Ud.
teniendo	tenemos	**teníamos**	**tuvimos**	**tendremos**	**tendríamos**	**tengamos**	**tuviéramos**	**tengamos**
tenido	tenéis	**teníais**	**tuvisteis**	**tendréis**	**tendríais**	**tengáis**	**tuvierais**	tened (no **tengáis**)
	tienen	**tenían**	**tuvieron**	**tendrán**	**tendrían**	**tengan**	**tuvieran**	**tengan** Uds.

Infinitive	INDICATIVE					SUBJUNCTIVE		IMPERATIVE
	Present	Imperfect	Preterite	Future	Conditional	Present	Past	
21 traer	traigo	traía	traje	traeré	traería	traiga	trajera	
Participles:	traes	traías	trajiste	traerás	traerías	traigas	trajeras	trae tú (no **traigas**)
trayendo	trae	traía	trajo	traerá	traería	traiga	trajera	**traiga** Ud.
traído	traemos	traíamos	trajimos	traeremos	traeríamos	traigamos	trajéramos	**traigamos**
	traéis	traíais	trajisteis	traeréis	traeríais	traigáis	trajerais	traed (no **traigáis**)
	traen	traían	trajeron	traerán	traerían	traigan	trajeran	**traigan** Uds.
22 venir (e:ie)	vengo	venía	vine	vendré	vendría	venga	viniera	
Participles:	vienes	venías	viniste	vendrás	vendrías	vengas	vinieras	**ven** tú (no **vengas**)
viniendo	viene	venía	vino	vendrá	vendría	venga	viniera	**venga** Ud.
venido	venimos	veníamos	vinimos	vendremos	vendríamos	vengamos	viniéramos	**vengamos**
	venís	veníais	vinisteis	vendréis	vendríais	vengáis	vinierais	venid (no **vengáis**)
	vienen	venían	vinieron	vendrán	vendrían	vengan	vinieran	**vengan** Uds.
23 ver	veo	**veía**	vi	veré	vería	vea	viera	
Participles:	ves	**veías**	viste	verás	verías	veas	vieras	**ve** tú (no **veas**)
viendo	ve	**veía**	vio	verá	vería	vea	viera	**vea** Ud.
visto	vemos	**veíamos**	vimos	veremos	veríamos	**veamos**	viéramos	**veamos**
	veis	**veíais**	visteis	veréis	veríais	**veáis**	vierais	ved (no **veáis**)
	ven	**veían**	vieron	verán	verían	**vean**	vieran	**vean** Uds.

Stem-changing verbs

Infinitive	INDICATIVE					SUBJUNCTIVE		IMPERATIVE
	Present	Imperfect	Preterite	Future	Conditional	Present	Past	
24 contar (o:ue)	**cuento**	contaba	conté	contaré	contaría	**cuente**	contara	
Participles:	**cuentas**	contabas	contaste	contarás	contarías	**cuentes**	contaras	**cuenta** tú (no **cuentes**)
contando	**cuenta**	contaba	contó	contará	contaría	**cuente**	contara	**cuente** Ud.
contado	contamos	contábamos	contamos	contaremos	contaríamos	contemos	contáramos	contemos
	contáis	contabais	contasteis	contaréis	contaríais	contéis	contarais	contad (no contéis)
	cuentan	contaban	contaron	contarán	contarían	**cuenten**	contaran	**cuenten** Uds.
25 dormir (o:ue)	**duermo**	dormía	dormí	dormiré	dormiría	**duerma**	durmiera	
Participles:	**duermes**	dormías	dormiste	dormirás	dormirías	**duermas**	durmieras	**duerme** tú (no **duermas**)
durmiendo	**duerme**	dormía	**durmió**	dormirá	dormiría	**duerma**	durmiera	**duerma** Ud.
dormido	dormimos	dormíamos	dormimos	dormiremos	dormiríamos	**durmamos**	durmiéramos	**durmamos**
	dormís	dormíais	dormisteis	dormiréis	dormiríais	**durmáis**	durmierais	dormid (no **durmáis**)
	duermen	dormían	**durmieron**	dormirán	dormirían	**duerman**	durmieran	**duerman** Uds.
26 empezar	**empiezo**	empezaba	**empecé**	empezaré	empezaría	**empiece**	empezara	
(e:ie) (z:c)	**empiezas**	empezabas	empezaste	empezarás	empezarías	**empieces**	empezaras	**empieza** tú (no **empieces**)
Participles:	**empieza**	empezaba	empezó	empezará	empezaría	**empiece**	empezara	**empiece** Ud.
empezando	empezamos	empezábamos	empezamos	empezaremos	empezaríamos	**empecemos**	empezáramos	**empecemos**
empezado	empezáis	empezabais	empezasteis	empezaréis	empezaríais	**empecéis**	empezarais	empezad (no **empecéis**)
	empiezan	empezaban	empezaron	empezarán	empezarían	**empiecen**	empezaran	**empiecen** Uds.

Verb tables

Infinitive	INDICATIVE					SUBJUNCTIVE		IMPERATIVE
	Present	Imperfect	Preterite	Future	Conditional	Present	Past	
27 entender (e:ie) **Participles:** entendiendo entendido	entiendo entiendes entiende entendemos entendéis entienden	entendía entendías entendía entendíamos entendíais entendían	entendí entendiste entendió entendimos entendisteis entendieron	entenderé entenderás entenderá entenderemos entenderéis entenderán	entendería entenderías entendería entenderíamos entenderíais entenderían	entienda entiendas entienda entendamos entendáis entiendan	entendiera entendieras entendiera entendiéramos entendierais entendieran	entiende tú (no entiendas) entienda Ud. entendamos entended (no entendáis) entiendan Uds.
28 jugar (u:ue) (g:gu) **Participles:** jugando jugado	juego juegas juega jugamos jugáis juegan	jugaba jugabas jugaba jugábamos jugabais jugaban	jugué jugaste jugó jugamos jugasteis jugaron	jugaré jugarás jugará jugaremos jugaréis jugarán	jugaría jugarías jugaría jugaríamos jugaríais jugarían	juegue juegues juegue juguemos juguéis jueguen	jugara jugaras jugara jugáramos jugarais jugaran	juega tú (no juegues) juegue Ud. juguemos jugad (no juguéis) jueguen Uds.
29 pedir (e:i) **Participles:** pidiendo pedido	pido pides pide pedimos pedís piden	pedía pedías pedía pedíamos pedíais pedían	pedí pediste pidió pedimos pedisteis pidieron	pediré pedirás pedirá pediremos pediréis pedirán	pediría pedirías pediría pediríamos pediríais pedirían	pida pidas pida pidamos pidáis pidan	pidiera pidieras pidiera pidiéramos pidierais pidieran	pide tú (no pidas) pida Ud. pidamos pedid (no pidáis) pidan Uds.
30 pensar (e:ie) **Participles:** pensando pensado	pienso piensas piensa pensamos pensáis piensan	pensaba pensabas pensaba pensábamos pensabais pensaban	pensé pensaste pensó pensamos pensasteis pensaron	pensaré pensarás pensará pensaremos pensaréis pensarán	pensaría pensarías pensaría pensaríamos pensaríais pensarían	piense pienses piense pensemos penséis piensen	pensara pensaras pensara pensáramos pensarais pensaran	piensa tú (no pienses) piense Ud. pensemos pensad (no penséis) piensen Uds.
31 reír(se) (e:i) **Participles:** riendo reído	río ríes ríe reímos reís ríen	reía reías reía reíamos reíais reían	reí reíste rió reímos reísteis rieron	reiré reirás reirá reiremos reiréis reirán	reiría reirías reiría reiríamos reiríais reirían	ría rías ría riamos riáis rían	riera rieras riera riéramos rierais rieran	ríe tú (no rías) ría Ud. riamos reíd (no riáis) rían Uds.
32 seguir (e:i) (gu:g) **Participles:** siguiendo seguido	sigo sigues sigue seguimos seguís siguen	seguía seguías seguía seguíamos seguíais seguían	seguí seguiste siguió seguimos seguisteis siguieron	seguiré seguirás seguirá seguiremos seguiréis seguirán	seguiría seguirías seguiría seguiríamos seguiríais seguirían	siga sigas siga sigamos sigáis sigan	siguiera siguieras siguiera siguiéramos siguierais siguieran	sigue tú (no sigas) siga Ud. sigamos seguid (no sigáis) sigan Uds.
33 sentir (e:ie) **Participles:** sintiendo sentido	siento sientes siente sentimos sentís sienten	sentía sentías sentía sentíamos sentíais sentían	sentí sentiste sintió sentimos sentisteis sintieron	sentiré sentirás sentirá sentiremos sentiréis sentirán	sentiría sentirías sentiría sentiríamos sentiríais sentirían	sienta sientas sienta sintamos sintáis sientan	sintiera sintieras sintiera sintiéramos sintierais sintieran	siente tú (no sientas) sienta Ud. sintamos sentid (no sintáis) sientan Uds.

34 volver (o:ue)

Participles: volviendo, vuelto

	INDICATIVE					SUBJUNCTIVE		IMPERATIVE
	Present	Imperfect	Preterite	Future	Conditional	Present	Past	
	vuelvo	volvía	volví	volveré	volvería	vuelva	volviera	
	vuelves	volvías	volviste	volverás	volverías	vuelvas	volvieras	vuelve tú (no vuelvas)
	vuelve	volvía	volvió	volverá	volvería	vuelva	volviera	vuelva Ud.
	volvemos	volvíamos	volvimos	volveremos	volveríamos	volvamos	volviéramos	volvamos
	volvéis	volvíais	volvisteis	volveréis	volveríais	volváis	volvierais	volved (no volváis)
	vuelven	volvían	volvieron	volverán	volverían	vuelvan	volvieran	vuelvan Uds.

Verbs with spelling changes only

35 conocer (c:zc)

Participles: conociendo, conocido

	INDICATIVE					SUBJUNCTIVE		IMPERATIVE
	Present	Imperfect	Preterite	Future	Conditional	Present	Past	
	conozco	conocía	conocí	conoceré	conocería	conozca	conociera	
	conoces	conocías	conociste	conocerás	conocerías	conozcas	conocieras	conoce tú (no conozcas)
	conoce	conocía	conoció	conocerá	conocería	conozca	conociera	conozca Ud.
	conocemos	conocíamos	conocimos	conoceremos	conoceríamos	conozcamos	conociéramos	conozcamos
	conocéis	conocíais	conocisteis	conoceréis	conoceríais	conozcáis	conocierais	conoced (no conozcáis)
	conocen	conocían	conocieron	conocerán	conocerían	conozcan	conocieran	conozcan Uds.

36 creer (y)

Participles: creyendo, creído

	INDICATIVE					SUBJUNCTIVE		IMPERATIVE
	Present	Imperfect	Preterite	Future	Conditional	Present	Past	
	creo	creía	creí	creeré	creería	crea	creyera	
	crees	creías	creíste	creerás	creerías	creas	creyeras	cree tú (no creas)
	cree	creía	creyó	creerá	creería	crea	creyera	crea Ud.
	creemos	creíamos	creímos	creeremos	creeríamos	creamos	creyéramos	creamos
	creéis	creíais	creísteis	creeréis	creeríais	creáis	creyerais	creed (no creáis)
	creen	creían	creyeron	creerán	creerían	crean	creyeran	crean Uds.

37 cruzar (z:c)

Participles: cruzando, cruzado

	INDICATIVE					SUBJUNCTIVE		IMPERATIVE
	Present	Imperfect	Preterite	Future	Conditional	Present	Past	
	cruzo	cruzaba	crucé	cruzaré	cruzaría	cruce	cruzara	
	cruzas	cruzabas	cruzaste	cruzarás	cruzarías	cruces	cruzaras	cruza tú (no cruces)
	cruza	cruzaba	cruzó	cruzará	cruzaría	cruce	cruzara	cruce Ud.
	cruzamos	cruzábamos	cruzamos	cruzaremos	cruzaríamos	crucemos	cruzáramos	crucemos
	cruzáis	cruzabais	cruzasteis	cruzaréis	cruzaríais	crucéis	cruzarais	cruzad (no crucéis)
	cruzan	cruzaban	cruzaron	cruzarán	cruzarían	crucen	cruzaran	crucen Uds.

38 destruir (y)

Participles: destruyendo, destruido

	INDICATIVE					SUBJUNCTIVE		IMPERATIVE
	Present	Imperfect	Preterite	Future	Conditional	Present	Past	
	destruyo	destruía	destruí	destruiré	destruiría	destruya	destruyera	
	destruyes	destruías	destruiste	destruirás	destruirías	destruyas	destruyeras	destruye tú (no destruyas)
	destruye	destruía	destruyó	destruirá	destruiría	destruya	destruyera	destruya Ud.
	destruimos	destruíamos	destruimos	destruiremos	destruiríamos	destruyamos	destruyéramos	destruyamos
	destruis	destruíais	destruisteis	destruiréis	destruiríais	destruyáis	destruyerais	destruid (no destruyáis)
	destruyen	destruían	destruyeron	destruirán	destruirían	destruyan	destruyeran	destruyan Uds.

39 enviar (envío)

Participles: enviando, enviado

	INDICATIVE					SUBJUNCTIVE		IMPERATIVE
	Present	Imperfect	Preterite	Future	Conditional	Present	Past	
	envío	enviaba	envié	enviaré	enviaría	envíe	enviara	
	envías	enviabas	enviaste	enviarás	enviarías	envíes	enviaras	envía tú (no envíes)
	envía	enviaba	envió	enviará	enviaría	envíe	enviara	envíe Ud.
	enviamos	enviábamos	enviamos	enviaremos	enviaríamos	enviemos	enviáramos	enviemos
	enviáis	enviabais	enviasteis	enviaréis	enviaríais	enviéis	enviarais	enviad (no enviéis)
	envían	enviaban	enviaron	enviarán	enviarían	envíen	enviaran	envíen Uds.

Verb tables

40   graduarse (gradúo) — Participles: graduando, graduado

	INDICATIVE					SUBJUNCTIVE		IMPERATIVE
	Present	Imperfect	Preterite	Future	Conditional	Present	Past	
	gradúo	graduaba	gradué	graduaré	graduaría	gradúe	graduara	
	gradúas	graduabas	graduaste	graduarás	graduarías	gradúes	graduaras	gradúa tú (no gradúes)
	gradúa	graduaba	graduó	graduará	graduaría	gradúe	graduara	gradúe Ud.
	graduamos	graduábamos	graduamos	graduaremos	graduaríamos	graduemos	graduáramos	graduemos
	graduáis	graduabais	graduasteis	graduaréis	graduaríais	graduéis	graduarais	graduad (no graduéis)
	gradúan	graduaban	graduaron	graduarán	graduarían	gradúen	graduaran	gradúen Uds.

41   llegar (g:gu) — Participles: llegando, llegado

	INDICATIVE					SUBJUNCTIVE		IMPERATIVE
	Present	Imperfect	Preterite	Future	Conditional	Present	Past	
	llego	llegaba	llegué	llegaré	llegaría	llegue	llegara	
	llegas	llegabas	llegaste	llegarás	llegarías	llegues	llegaras	llega tú (no llegues)
	llega	llegaba	llegó	llegará	llegaría	llegue	llegara	llegue Ud.
	llegamos	llegábamos	llegamos	llegaremos	llegaríamos	lleguemos	llegáramos	lleguemos
	llegáis	llegabais	llegasteis	llegaréis	llegaríais	lleguéis	llegarais	llegad (no lleguéis)
	llegan	llegaban	llegaron	llegarán	llegarían	lleguen	llegaran	lleguen Uds.

42   proteger (g:j) — Participles: protegiendo, protegido

	INDICATIVE					SUBJUNCTIVE		IMPERATIVE
	Present	Imperfect	Preterite	Future	Conditional	Present	Past	
	protejo	protegía	protegí	protegeré	protegería	proteja	protegiera	
	proteges	protegías	protegiste	protegerás	protegerías	protejas	protegieras	protege tú (no protejas)
	protege	protegía	protegió	protegerá	protegería	proteja	protegiera	proteja Ud.
	protegemos	protegíamos	protegimos	protegeremos	protegeríamos	protejamos	protegiéramos	protejamos
	protegéis	protegíais	protegisteis	protegeréis	protegeríais	protejáis	protegierais	proteged (no protejáis)
	protegen	protegían	protegieron	protegerán	protegerían	protejan	protegieran	protejan Uds.

43   tocar (c:qu) — Participles: tocando, tocado

	INDICATIVE					SUBJUNCTIVE		IMPERATIVE
	Present	Imperfect	Preterite	Future	Conditional	Present	Past	
	toco	tocaba	toqué	tocaré	tocaría	toque	tocara	
	tocas	tocabas	tocaste	tocarás	tocarías	toques	tocaras	toca tú (no toques)
	toca	tocaba	tocó	tocará	tocaría	toque	tocara	toque Ud.
	tocamos	tocábamos	tocamos	tocaremos	tocaríamos	toquemos	tocáramos	toquemos
	tocáis	tocabais	tocasteis	tocaréis	tocaríais	toquéis	tocarais	tocad (no toquéis)
	tocan	tocaban	tocaron	tocarán	tocarían	toquen	tocaran	toquen Uds.

Guide to Vocabulary

All active vocabulary in ¡ADELANTE! is presented in this glossary. The first number after an entry refers to the volume of ¡ADELANTE! where the word is activated; the second refers to the lesson number.

aceite 2.2 (Activated in *¡ADELANTE!* **DOS**, Lección 2)

posible 3.1 (Activated in *¡ADELANTE!* **TRES**, Lección 1)

Note on alphabetization

For purposes of alphabetization, **ch** and **ll** are not treated as separate letters, but **ñ** follows **n**. Therefore, in this glossary you will find that **año**, for example, appears after **anuncio**.

Abbreviations used in this glossary

adj.	adjective	*form.*	formal	*pl.*	plural
adv.	adverb	*indef.*	indefinite	*poss.*	possessive
art.	article	*interj.*	interjection	*prep.*	preposition
conj.	conjunction	*i.o.*	indirect object	*pron.*	pronoun
def.	definite	*m.*	masculine	*ref.*	reflexive
d.o.	direct object	*n.*	noun	*sing.*	singular
f.	feminine	*obj.*	object	*sub.*	subject
fam.	familiar	*p.p.*	past participle	*v.*	verb

Spanish-English

A

a *prep.* at; to 1.1
  ¿A qué hora...? At what time...? 1.1
  a bordo aboard 1.1
  a dieta on a diet 3.3
  a la derecha to the right 1.2
  a la izquierda to the left 1.2
  a la plancha grilled 2.2
  a la(s) + *time* at + *time* 1.1
  a menos que unless 3.1
  a menudo *adv.* often 2.4
  a nombre de in the name of 1.5
  a plazos in installments 3.4
  A sus órdenes. At your service. 2.5
  a tiempo *adv.* on time 2.4
  a veces *adv.* sometimes 2.4
  a ver let's see 1.2
¡Abajo! *adv.* Down! 3.3
abeja *f.* bee
abierto/a *adj.* open 1.5, 3.2
abogado/a *m., f.* lawyer 3.4
abrazar(se) *v.* to hug; to embrace (each other) 2.5
abrazo *m.* hug
abrigo *m.* coat 1.6
abril *m.* April 1.5
abrir *v.* to open 1.3
abuelo/a *m., f.* grandfather; grandmother 1.3
abuelos *pl.* grandparents 1.3

aburrido/a *adj.* bored; boring 1.5
aburrir *v.* to bore 2.1
aburrirse *v.* to get bored 3.5
acabar de (+ *inf.*) *v.* to have just done something 1.6
acampar *v.* to camp 1.5
accidente *m.* accident 2.4
acción *f.* action 3.5
  de acción action (genre) 3.5
aceite *m.* oil 2.2
ácido/a *adj.* acid 3.1
acompañar *v.* to go with; to accompany 3.2
aconsejar *v.* to advise 2.6
acontecimiento *m.* event 3.6
acordarse (de) (o:ue) *v.* to remember 2.1
acostarse (o:ue) *v.* to go to bed 2.1
activo/a *adj.* active 3.3
actor *m.* actor 3.4
actriz *f.* actor 3.4
actualidades *f., pl.* news; current events 3.6
acuático/a *adj.* aquatic 1.4
adelgazar *v.* to lose weight; to slim down 3.3
además (de) *adv.* furthermore; besides 2.4
adicional *adj.* additional
adiós *m.* good-bye 1.1
adjetivo *m.* adjective
administración de empresas *f.* business administration 1.2
adolescencia *f.* adolescence 2.3
¿adónde? *adv.* where (to)? (destination) 1.2
aduana *f.* customs 1.5

aeróbico/a *adj.* aerobic 3.3
aeropuerto *m.* airport 1.5
afectado/a *adj.* affected 3.1
afeitarse *v.* to shave 2.1
aficionado/a *adj.* fan 1.4
afirmativo/a *adj.* affirmative
afueras *f., pl.* suburbs; outskirts 2.6
agencia de viajes *f.* travel agency 1.5
agente de viajes *m., f.* travel agent 1.5
agosto *m.* August 1.5
agradable *adj.* pleasant
agua *f.* water 2.2
  agua mineral mineral water 2.2
ahora *adv.* now 1.2
  ahora mismo right now 1.5
ahorrar *v.* to save (money) 3.2
ahorros *m.* savings 3.2
aire *m.* air 1.5
ajo *m.* garlic 2.2
al (*contraction of* **a** + **el**) 1.2
  al aire libre open-air 1.6
  al contado in cash 3.2
  (al) este (to the) east 3.2
  al fondo (de) at the end (of) 2.6
  al lado de beside 1.2
  (al) norte (to the) north 3.2
  (al) oeste (to the) west 3.2
  (al) sur (to the) south 3.2
alcoba *f.* bedroom 2.6
alcohol *m.* alcohol 3.3
alcohólico/a *adj.* alcoholic 3.3
alegrarse (de) *v.* to be happy 3.1
alegre *adj.* happy; joyful 1.5
alegría *f.* happiness 2.3

alemán, alemana *adj.* German **1.3**
alérgico/a *adj.* allergic **2.4**
alfombra *f.* carpet; rug **2.6**
algo *pron.* something; anything **2.1**
algodón *m.* cotton **1.6**
alguien *pron.* someone; somebody; anyone **2.1**
algún, alguno/a(s) *adj.* any; some **2.1**
alimento *m.* food
alimentación *f.* diet
aliviar *v.* to reduce **3.3**
  aliviar el estrés/la tensión to reduce stress/tension **3.3**
allí *adv.* there **1.5**
  allí mismo right there **3.2**
almacén *m.* department store **1.6**
almohada *f.* pillow **2.6**
almorzar (o:ue) *v.* to have lunch **1.4**
almuerzo *m.* lunch **2.2**
aló *interj.* hello (*on the telephone*) **2.5**
alquilar *v.* to rent **2.6**
alquiler *m.* rent (payment) **2.6**
alternador *m.* alternator **2.5**
altillo *m.* attic **2.6**
alto/a *adj.* tall **1.3**
aluminio *m.* aluminum **3.1**
ama de casa *m., f.* housekeeper; caretaker **2.6**
amable *adj.* nice; friendly **1.5**
amarillo/a *adj.* yellow **1.6**
amigo/a *m., f.* friend **1.3**
amistad *f.* friendship **2.3**
amor *m.* love **2.3**
anaranjado/a *adj.* orange **1.6**
andar *v.* **en patineta** to skateboard **1.4**
animal *m.* animal **3.1**
aniversario (de bodas) *m.* (wedding) anniversary **2.3**
anoche *adv.* last night **1.6**
anteayer *adv.* the day before yesterday **1.6**
antes *adv.* before **2.1**
  antes (de) que *conj.* before **3.1**
  antes de *prep.* before **2.1**
antibiótico *m.* antibiotic **2.4**
antipático/a *adj.* unpleasant **1.3**
anunciar *v.* to announce; to advertise **3.6**
anuncio *m.* advertisement **3.4**
año *m.* year **1.5**
  año pasado last year **1.6**
apagar *v.* to turn off **2.5**
aparato *m.* appliance
apartamento *m.* apartment **2.6**
apellido *m.* last name **1.3**
apenas *adv.* hardly; scarcely **2.4**
aplaudir *v.* to applaud **3.5**
apreciar *v.* to appreciate **3.5**
aprender (a + *inf.*) *v.* to learn **1.3**
apurarse *v.* to hurry; to rush **3.3**
aquel, aquella *adj.* that (over there) **1.6**

aquél, aquélla *pron.* that (over there) **1.6**
aquello *neuter, pron.* that; that thing; that fact **1.6**
aquellos/as *pl. adj.* those (over there) **1.6**
aquéllos/as *pl. pron.* those (ones) (over there) **1.6**
aquí *adv.* here **1.1**
  Aquí está... Here it is... **1.5**
  Aquí estamos en... Here we are at/in... **1.2**
  aquí mismo right here **2.5**
árbol *m.* tree **3.1**
archivo *m.* file **2.5**
armario *m.* closet **2.6**
arqueólogo/a *m., f.* archaeologist **3.4**
arquitecto/a *m., f.* architect **3.4**
arrancar *v.* to start (*a car*) **2.5**
arreglar *v.* to fix; to arrange **2.5**; to neaten; to straighten up **2.6**
arriba *adv.* up
arroba *f.* @ symbol **2.5**
arroz *m.* rice **2.2**
arte *m.* art **1.2**
artes *f., pl.* arts **3.5**
artesanía *f.* craftsmanship; crafts **3.5**
artículo *m.* article **3.6**
artista *m., f.* artist **1.3**
artístico/a *adj.* artistic **3.5**
arveja *m.* pea **2.2**
asado/a *adj.* roast **2.2**
ascenso *m.* promotion **3.4**
ascensor *m.* elevator **1.5**
así *adv.* like this; so (*in such a way*) **2.4**
  así así so so **2.4**
asistir (a) *v.* to attend **1.3**
aspiradora *f.* vacuum cleaner **2.6**
aspirante *m., f.* candidate; applicant **3.4**
aspirina *f.* aspirin **2.4**
atún *m.* tuna **2.2**
aumentar *v.* **de peso** to gain weight **3.3**
aumento *m.* increase **3.4**
  aumento de sueldo pay raise **3.4**
aunque although
autobús *m.* bus **1.1**
automático/a *adj.* automatic
auto(móvil) *m.* auto(mobile) **1.5**
autopista *f.* highway **2.5**
ave *f.* bird **3.1**
avenida *f.* avenue
aventura *f.* adventure **3.5**
  de aventura adventure (genre) **3.5**
avergonzado/a *adj.* embarrassed **1.5**
avión *m.* airplane **1.5**
¡Ay! *interj.* Oh!
  ¡Ay, qué dolor! Oh, what pain!
ayer *adv.* yesterday **1.6**

ayudar(se) *v.* to help (each other) **2.5, 2.6**
azúcar *m.* sugar **2.2**
azul *adj. m., f.* blue **1.6**

B

bailar *v.* to dance **1.2**
bailarín/bailarina *m., f.* dancer **3.5**
baile *m.* dance **3.5**
bajar(se) de *v.* to get off of/out of (a vehicle) **2.5**
bajo/a *adj.* short (*in height*) **1.3**
bajo control under control **2.1**
balcón *m.* balcony **2.6**
baloncesto *m.* basketball **1.4**
banana *f.* banana **2.2**
banco *m.* bank **3.2**
banda *f.* band **3.5**
bandera *f.* flag
bañarse *v.* to bathe; to take a bath **2.1**
baño *m.* bathroom **2.1**
barato/a *adj.* cheap **1.6**
barco *m.* boat **1.5**
barrer *v.* to sweep **2.6**
  barrer el suelo to sweep the floor **2.6**
barrio *m.* neighborhood **2.6**
bastante *adv.* enough; rather **2.4**; pretty **3.1**
basura *f.* trash **2.6**
baúl *m.* trunk **2.5**
beber *v.* to drink **1.3**
bebida *f.* drink **2.2**
  bebida alcohólica *f.* alcoholic beverage **3.3**
béisbol *m.* baseball **1.4**
bellas artes *f., pl.* fine arts **3.5**
belleza *f.* beauty **3.2**
beneficio *m.* benefit **3.4**
besar(se) *v.* to kiss (each other) **2.5**
beso *m.* kiss **2.3**
biblioteca *f.* library **1.2**
bicicleta *f.* bicycle **1.4**
bien *adj.* well **1.1**
bienestar *m.* well-being **3.3**
bienvenido(s)/a(s) *adj.* welcome **2.6**
billete *m.* paper money; ticket
billón *m.* trillion
biología *f.* biology **1.2**
bisabuelo/a *m., f.* great-grandfather/great-grandmother **1.3**
bistec *m.* steak **2.2**
bizcocho *m.* biscuit
blanco/a *adj.* white **1.6**
bluejeans *m., pl.* jeans **1.6**
blusa *f.* blouse **1.6**
boca *f.* mouth **2.4**
boda *f.* wedding **2.3**
boleto *m.* ticket **3.5**
bolsa *f.* purse, bag **1.6**
bombero/a *m., f.* firefighter **3.4**
bonito/a *adj.* pretty **1.3**
borrador *m.* eraser **1.2**

borrar *v.* to erase **2.5**
bosque *m.* forest **3.1**
  bosque tropical tropical forest; rainforest **3.1**
bota *f.* boot **1.6**
botella *f.* bottle **2.3**
  botella de vino bottle of wine **2.3**
botones *m., f. sing.* bellhop **1.5**
brazo *m.* arm **2.4**
brindar *v.* to toast (*drink*) **2.3**
bucear *v.* to scuba dive **1.4**
bueno *adv.* well **1.2, 3.5**
buen, bueno/a *adj.* good **1.3, 1.6**
  ¡Buen viaje! Have a good trip! **1.1**
  buena forma good shape (*physical*) **3.3**
  Buena idea. Good idea. **1.4**
  Buenas noches. Good evening; Good night. **1.1**
  Buenas tardes. Good afternoon. **1.1**
  buenísimo/a extremely good
  ¿Bueno? Hello. (*on telephone*) **2.5**
  Buenos días. Good morning. **1.1**
bulevar *m.* boulevard
buscar *v.* to look for **1.2**
buzón *m.* mailbox **3.2**

C

caballo *m.* horse **1.5**
cabaña *f.* cabin **1.5**
cabe: no cabe duda de there's no doubt **3.1**
cabeza *f.* head **2.4**
cada *adj.* each **1.6**
caerse *v.* to fall (down) **2.4**
café *m.* café **1.4**; *adj. m., f.* brown **1.6**; *m.* coffee **2.2**
cafeína *f.* caffeine **3.2**
cafetera *f.* coffee maker **2.6**
cafetería *f.* cafeteria **1.2**
caído/a *p.p.* fallen **3.2**
caja *f.* cash register **1.6**
cajero/a *m., f.* cashier **3.2**
  cajero automático *m.* ATM **3.2**
calcetín (calcetines) *m.* sock(s) **1.6**
calculadora *f.* calculator **2.5**
caldo *m.* soup **2.2**
  caldo de patas *m.* beef soup **2.2**
calentarse (e:ie) *v.* to warm up **3.3**
calidad *f.* quality **1.6**
calle *f.* street **2.5**
calor *m.* heat **1.5**
caloría *f.* calorie **3.3**
calzar *v.* to take size... shoes **1.6**
cama *f.* bed **1.5**
cámara digital *f.* digital camera **2.5**
cámara de video *f.* video camera **2.5**
camarero/a *m., f.* waiter/ waitress **2.2**
camarón *m.* shrimp **2.2**

cambiar (de) *v.* to change **2.3**
cambio *m.* **de moneda** currency exchange
caminar *v.* to walk **1.2**
camino *m.* road
camión *m.* truck; bus
camisa *f.* shirt **1.6**
camiseta *f.* t-shirt **1.6**
campo *m.* countryside **1.5**
canadiense *adj.* Canadian **1.3**
canal *m.* (TV) channel **2.5, 3.5**
canción *f.* song **3.5**
candidato/a *m., f.* candidate **3.6**
cansado/a *adj.* tired **1.5**
cantante *m., f.* singer **3.5**
cantar *v.* to sing **1.2**
capital *f.* capital city **1.1**
capó *m.* hood **2.5**
cara *f.* face **2.1**
caramelo *m.* caramel **2.3**
carne *f.* meat **2.2**
  carne de res *f.* beef **2.2**
carnicería *f.* butcher shop **3.2**
caro/a *adj.* expensive **1.6**
carpintero/a *m., f.* carpenter **3.4**
carrera *f.* career **3.4**
carretera *f.* highway **2.5**
carro *m.* car; automobile **2.5**
carta *f.* letter **1.4**; *(playing)* card **1.5**
cartel *m.* poster **2.6**
cartera *f.* wallet **1.6**
cartero *m.* mail carrier **3.2**
casa *f.* house; home **1.2**
casado/a *adj.* married **2.3**
casarse (con) *v.* to get married (to) **2.3**
casi *adv.* almost **2.4**
catorce fourteen **1.1**
cazar *v.* to hunt **3.1**
cebolla *f.* onion **2.2**
cederrón *m.* CD-ROM **2.5**
celebrar *v.* to celebrate **2.3**
celular *adj.* cellular **2.5**
cena *f.* dinner **2.2**
cenar *v.* to have dinner **1.2**
centro *m.* downtown **1.4**
  centro comercial shopping mall **1.6**
cepillarse los dientes/el pelo *v.* to brush one's teeth/one's hair **2.1**
cerámica *f.* pottery **3.5**
cerca de *prep.* near **1.2**
cerdo *m.* pork **2.2**
cereales *m., pl.* cereal; grains **2.2**
cero *m.* zero **1.1**
cerrado/a *adj.* closed **1.5, 3.2**
cerrar (e:ie) *v.* to close **1.4**
cerveza *f.* beer **2.2**
césped *m.* grass
ceviche *m.* marinated fish dish **2.2**
  ceviche de camarón *m.* lemon-marinated shrimp **2.2**
chaleco *m.* vest
champán *m.* champagne **2.3**
champiñón *m.* mushroom **2.2**
champú *m.* shampoo **2.1**
chaqueta *f.* jacket **1.6**

chau *fam. interj.* bye **1.1**
cheque *m.* (bank) check **3.2**
  cheque (de viajero) *m.* (traveler's) check **3.2**
chévere *adj., fam.* terrific
chico/a *m., f.* boy/girl **1.1**
chino/a *adj.* Chinese **1.3**
chocar (con) *v.* to run into
chocolate *m.* chocolate **2.3**
choque *m.* collision **3.6**
chuleta *f.* chop (*food*) **2.2**
  chuleta de cerdo *f.* pork chop **2.2**
cibercafé *m.* cybercafé
ciclismo *m.* cycling **1.4**
cielo *m.* sky **3.1**
cien(to) one hundred **1.2**
ciencia *f.* science **1.2**
  de ciencia ficción *f.* science fiction (genre) **3.5**
científico/a *m., f.* scientist **3.4**
cierto *m.* certain **3.1**
  es cierto it's certain **3.1**
  no es cierto it's not certain **3.1**
cinco five **1.1**
cincuenta fifty **1.2**
cine *m.* movie theater **1.4**
cinta *f.* (audio)tape
cinta caminadora *f.* treadmill **3.3**
cinturón *m.* belt **1.6**
circulación *f.* traffic **2.5**
cita *f.* date; appointment **2.3**
ciudad *f.* city **1.4**
ciudadano/a *m., f.* citizen **3.6**
Claro (que sí). *fam.* Of course. **3.4**
clase *f.* class **1.2**
  clase de ejercicios aeróbicos *f.* aerobics class **3.3**
clásico/a *adj.* classical **3.5**
cliente/a *m., f.* customer **1.6**
clínica *f.* clinic **2.4**
cobrar *v.* to cash (a check) **3.2**
coche *m.* car; automobile **2.5**
cocina *f.* kitchen; stove **2.6**
cocinar *v.* to cook **2.6**
cocinero/a *m., f.* cook, chef **3.4**
cofre *m.* hood **3.2**
cola *f.* line **3.2**
colesterol *m.* cholesterol **3.3**
color *m.* color **1.6**
comedia *f.* comedy; play **3.5**
comedor *m.* dining room **2.6**
comenzar (e:ie) *v.* to begin **1.4**
comer *v.* to eat **1.3**
comercial *adj.* commercial; business-related **3.4**
comida *f.* food; meal **2.2**
como like; as **2.2**
¿cómo? what?; how? **1.1**
  ¿Cómo es...? What's... like? **1.3**
  ¿Cómo está usted? *form.* How are you? **1.1**
  ¿Cómo estás? *fam.* How are you? **1.1**
  ¿Cómo les fue...? *pl.* How did ... go for you? **3.3**

¿Cómo se llama (usted)?
(form.) What's your name? **1.1**
¿Cómo te llamas (tú)? (fam.)
What's your name? **1.1**
cómoda f. chest of drawers **2.6**
cómodo/a adj. comfortable **1.5**
compañero/a de clase m., f.
classmate **1.2**
compañero/a de cuarto m., f.
roommate **1.2**
compañía f. company; firm **3.4**
compartir v. to share **1.3**
completamente adv. completely **3.4**
compositor(a) m., f. composer **3.5**
comprar v. to buy **1.2**
compras f., pl. purchases **1.5**
ir de compras to go shopping **1.5**
comprender v. to understand **1.3**
comprobar v. to check
comprometerse (con) v. to get
engaged (to) **2.3**
computación f. computer
science **1.2**
computadora f. computer **1.1**
computadora portátil f. portable
computer; laptop **2.5**
comunicación f. communication **3.6**
comunicarse (con) v. to communicate (with) **3.6**
comunidad f. community **1.1**
con prep. with **1.2**
Con él/ella habla. This is
he/she. (on telephone) **2.5**
con frecuencia adv.
frequently **2.4**
Con permiso. Pardon me;
Excuse me. **1.1**
con tal (de) que provided
(that) **3.1**
concierto m. concert **3.5**
concordar v. to agree
concurso m. game show;
contest **3.5**
conducir v. to drive **1.6, 2.5**
conductor(a) m., f. driver **1.1**
confirmar v. to confirm **1.5**
confirmar v. **una reservación** f.
to confirm a reservation **1.5**
confundido/a adj. confused **1.5**
congelador m. freezer **2.6**
congestionado/a adj. congested;
stuffed-up **2.4**
conmigo pron. with me **1.4, 2.3**
conocer v. to know; to be
acquainted with **1.6**
conocido adj.; p.p. known
conseguir (e:i) v. to get; to
obtain **1.4**
consejero/a m., f. counselor;
advisor **3.4**
consejo m. advice **1.6**
conservación f. conservation **3.1**
conservar v. to conserve **3.1**
construir v. to build
consultorio m. doctor's office **2.4**
consumir v. to consume **3.3**
contabilidad f. accounting **1.2**

contador(a) m., f. accountant **3.4**
contaminación f. pollution **3.1**
**contaminación del aire/del
agua** air/water pollution **3.1**
contaminado/a adj. polluted **3.1**
contaminar v. to pollute **3.1**
contar (o:ue) v. to count; to tell **1.4**
contar (con) v. to count (on) **2.6**
contento/a adj. happy; content **1.5**
contestadora f. answering
machine **2.5**
contestar v. to answer **1.2**
contigo fam. pron. with you **2.3**
contratar v. to hire **3.4**
control m. control **2.1**
control remoto remote
control **2.5**
controlar v. to control **3.1**
conversación f. conversation **1.1**
conversar v. to converse, to chat **1.2**
copa f. wineglass; goblet **2.6**
corazón m. heart **2.4**
corbata f. tie **1.6**
corredor(a) m., f. **de bolsa**
stockbroker **3.4**
correo m. mail; post office **3.2**
correo electrónico m.
e-mail **1.4**
correr v. to run **1.3**
cortesía f. courtesy
cortinas f., pl. curtains **2.6**
corto/a adj. short (in length) **1.6**
cosa f. thing **1.1**
costar (o:ue) f. to cost **1.6**
cráter m. crater **3.1**
creer v. to believe **3.1**
creer (en) v. to believe (in) **1.3**
no creer (en) v. not to
believe (in) **3.1**
creído/a adj., p.p. believed **3.2**
crema de afeitar f. shaving
cream **2.1**
crimen m. crime; murder **3.6**
cruzar v. to cross **3.2**
cuaderno m. notebook **1.1**
cuadra f. (city) block **3.2**
¿cuál(es)? which?; which
one(s)? **1.2**
¿Cuál es la fecha de hoy?
What is today's date? **1.5**
cuadro m. picture **2.6**
cuadros m., pl. plaid **1.6**
cuando when **2.1; 3.1**
¿cuándo? when? **1.2**
¿cuánto(s)/a(s)? how much/how
many? **1.1**
¿Cuánto cuesta...? How
much does... cost? **1.6**
¿Cuántos años tienes? How
old are you? **1.3**
cuarenta forty **1.2**
cuarto de baño m. bathroom **2.1**
cuarto m. room **1.2, 2.1**
cuarto/a adj. fourth **1.5**
menos cuarto quarter to
(time) **1.1**
y cuarto quarter after (time) **1.1**

cuatro four **1.1**
cuatrocientos/as four hundred **1.2**
cubiertos m., pl. silverware
cubierto/a p.p. covered
cubrir v. to cover
cuchara f. (table or large) spoon **2.6**
cuchillo m. knife **2.6**
cuello m. neck **2.4**
cuenta f. bill **2.3**; account **3.2**
cuenta corriente f. checking
account **3.2**
cuenta de ahorros f. savings
account **3.2**
cuento m. short story **3.5**
cuerpo m. body **2.4**
cuidado m. care **1.3**
cuidar v. to take care of **3.1**
¡Cuídense! Take care! **3.2**
cultura f. culture **3.5**
cumpleaños m., sing. birthday **2.3**
cumplir años v. to have a
birthday **2.3**
cuñado/a m., f. brother-in-law;
sister-in-law **1.3**
currículum m. résumé **3.4**
curso m. course **1.2**

D

danza f. dance **3.5**
dañar v. to damage; to break
down **2.4**
dar v. to give **1.6, 2.3**
dar direcciones v. to give
directions **3.2**
dar un consejo v. to give
advice **1.6**
darse con v. to bump into; to
run into (something) **2.4**
darse prisa v. to hurry; to
rush **3.3**
de prep. of; from **1.1**
¿De dónde eres? fam.
Where are you from? **1.1**
¿De dónde es usted? form.
Where are you from? **1.1**
¿De parte de quién? Who is
calling? (on telephone) **2.5**
¿de quién...? whose...? (sing.) **1.1**
¿de quiénes...? whose...?
(pl.) **1.1**
de algodón (made) of cotton **1.6**
de aluminio (made) of
aluminum **3.1**
de buen humor in a good
mood **1.5**
de compras shopping **1.5**
de cuadros plaid **1.6**
de excursión hiking **1.4**
de hecho in fact
de ida y vuelta roundtrip **1.5**
de la mañana in the morning;
A.M. **1.1**
de la noche in the evening; at
night; P.M. **1.1**

de la tarde in the afternoon; in the early evening; P.M. **1.1**
de lana (made) of wool **1.6**
de lunares polka-dotted **1.6**
de mal humor in a bad mood **1.5**
de mi vida of my life **3.3**
de moda in fashion **1.6**
De nada. You're welcome. **1.1**
De ninguna manera. No way. **3.4**
de niño/a as a child **2.4**
de parte de on behalf of **2.5**
de plástico (made) of plastic **3.1**
de rayas striped **1.6**
de repente suddenly **1.6**
de seda (made) of silk **1.6**
de vaqueros western (genre) **3.5**
de vez en cuando from time to time **2.4**
de vidrio (made) of glass **3.1**
debajo de *prep.* below; under **1.2**
deber (+ inf.) *v.* should; must; ought to **1.3**
  Debe ser... It must be... **1.6**
deber *m.* responsibility; obligation **3.6**
debido a due to (the fact that)
débil *adj.* weak **3.3**
decidido/a *adj.* decided **3.2**
decidir (+ inf.) *v.* to decide **1.3**
décimo/a *adj.* tenth **1.5**
decir (e:i) *v.* **(que)** to say (that); to tell (that) **1.4, 2.3**
  decir la respuesta to say the answer **1.4**
  decir la verdad to tell the truth **1.4**
  decir mentiras to tell lies **1.4**
  decir que to say that **1.4**
declarar *v.* to declare; to say **3.6**
dedo *m.* finger **2.4**
dedo del pie *m.* toe **2.4**
deforestación *f.* deforestation **3.1**
dejar *v.* to let **2.6**; to quit; to leave behind **3.4**
  dejar de (+ inf.) *v.* to stop (*doing something*) **3.1**
  dejar una propina *v.* to leave a tip **2.3**
del (*contraction of* **de + el**) of the; from the **1.1**
delante de *prep.* in front of **1.2**
delgado/a *adj.* thin; slender **1.3**
delicioso/a *adj.* delicious **2.2**
demás *adj.* the rest
demasiado *adj., adv.* too much **1.6**
dentista *m., f.* dentist **2.4**
dentro de (diez años) within (ten years) **3.4**; inside
dependiente/a *m., f.* clerk **1.6**
deporte *m.* sport **1.4**
deportista *m.* sports person
deportivo/a *adj.* sports-related **1.4**
depositar *v.* to deposit **3.2**
derecha *f.* right **1.2**
derecho *adj.* straight (ahead) **3.2**

a la derecha de to the right of **1.2**
derechos *m., pl.* rights **3.6**
desarrollar *v.* to develop **3.1**
desastre (natural) *m.* (natural) disaster **3.1**
desayunar *v.* to have breakfast **1.2**
desayuno *m.* breakfast **2.2**
descafeinado/a *adj.* decaffeinated **3.3**
descansar *v.* to rest **1.2**
descargar *v.* to download **2.5**
descompuesto/a *adj.* not working; out of order **2.5**
describir *v.* to describe **1.3**
descrito/a *p.p.* described **3.2**
descubierto/a *p.p.* discovered **3.2**
descubrir *v.* to discover **3.1**
desde *prep.* from **1.6**
desear *v.* to wish; to desire **1.2**
desempleo *m.* unemployment **3.6**
desierto *m.* desert **3.1**
desigualdad *f.* inequality **3.6**
desordenado/a *adj.* disorderly **1.5**
despacio *adv.* slowly **2.4**
despedida *f.* farewell; good-bye
despedir (e:i) *v.* to fire **3.4**
despedirse (de) (e:i) *v.* to say goodbye (to) **2.1**
despejado/a *adj.* clear (*weather*)
despertador *m.* alarm clock **2.1**
despertarse (e:ie) *v.* to wake up **2.1**
después *adv.* afterwards; then **2.1**
  después de after **2.1**
  después de que *conj.* after **3.1**
destruir *v.* to destroy **3.1**
detrás de *prep.* behind **1.2**
día *m.* day **1.1**
día de fiesta holiday **2.3**
diario *m.* diary **1.1**; newspaper **3.6**
  diario/a *adj.* daily **2.1**
dibujar *v.* to draw **1.2**
dibujo *m.* drawing **3.5**
  dibujos animados *m., pl.* cartoons **3.5**
diccionario *m.* dictionary **1.1**
dicho/a *p.p.* said **3.2**
diciembre *m.* December **1.5**
dictadura *f.* dictatorship **3.6**
diecinueve nineteen **1.1**
dieciocho eighteen **1.1**
dieciséis sixteen **1.1**
diecisiete seventeen **1.1**
diente *m.* tooth **2.1**
dieta *f.* diet **3.3**
  comer una dieta equilibrada to eat a balanced diet **3.3**
diez ten **1.1**
difícil *adj.* difficult; hard **1.3**
Diga. Hello. (*on telephone*) **2.5**
diligencia *f.* errand **3.2**
dinero *m.* money **1.6**
dirección *f.* address **3.2**
  dirección electrónica *f.* e-mail address **2.5**
direcciones *f., pl.* directions **3.2**

director(a) *m., f.* director; (*musical*) conductor **3.5**
dirigir *v.* to direct **3.5**
disco compacto compact disc (CD) **2.5**
discriminación *f.* discrimination **3.6**
discurso *m.* speech **3.6**
diseñador(a) *m., f.* designer **3.4**
diseño *m.* design
disfrutar (de) *v.* to enjoy; to reap the benefits (of) **3.3**
diversión *f.* fun activity; entertainment; recreation **1.4**
divertido/a *adj.* fun **2.1**
divertirse (e:ie) *v.* to have fun **2.3**
divorciado/a *adj.* divorced **2.3**
divorciarse (de) *v.* to get divorced (from) **2.3**
divorcio *m.* divorce **2.3**
doblar *v.* to turn **3.2**
doble *adj.* double
doce twelve **1.1**
doctor(a) *m., f.* doctor **1.3, 2.4**
documental *m.* documentary **3.5**
documentos de viaje *m., pl.* travel documents
doler (o:ue) *v.* to hurt **2.4**
dolor *m.* ache; pain **2.4**
  dolor de cabeza *m.* headache **2.4**
doméstico/a *adj.* domestic **2.6**
domingo *m.* Sunday **1.2**
don/doña *title of respect used with a person's first name* **1.1**
donde *prep.* where
  ¿Dónde está...? Where is...? **1.2**
  ¿dónde? where? **1.1**
dormir (o:ue) *v.* to sleep **1.4**
dormirse (o:ue) *v.* to go to sleep; to fall asleep **2.1**
dormitorio *m.* bedroom **2.6**
dos two **1.1**
  dos veces *f.* twice; two times **1.6**
doscientos/as two hundred **1.2**
drama *m.* drama; play **3.5**
dramático/a *adj.* dramatic **3.5**
dramaturgo/a *m., f.* playwright **3.5**
droga *f.* drug **3.3**
drogadicto/a *adj.* drug addict **3.3**
ducha *f.* shower **2.1**
ducharse *v.* to shower; to take a shower **2.1**
duda *f.* doubt **3.1**
dudar *v.* to doubt **3.1**
  no dudar *v.* not to doubt **3.1**
dueño/a *m., f.* owner; landlord **2.2**
dulces *m., pl.* sweets; candy **2.3**
durante *prep.* during **2.1**
durar *v.* to last **3.6**

E

e *conj.* (*used instead of* **y** *before words beginning with* **i** *and* **hi**) and **1.4**

echar *v.* to throw
echar (una carta) al buzón *v.* to put (a letter) in the mailbox; to mail 3.2
ecología *f.* ecology 3.1
economía *f.* economics 1.2
ecoturismo *m.* ecotourism 3.1
Ecuador *m.* Ecuador 1.1
ecuatoriano/a *adj.* Ecuadorian 1.3
edad *f.* age 2.3
edificio *m.* building 2.6
edificio de apartamentos apartment building 2.6
(en) efectivo *m.* cash 1.6
ejercicio *m.* exercise 3.3
ejercicios aeróbicos aerobic exercises 3.3
ejercicios de estiramiento stretching exercises 3.3
ejército *m.* army 3.6
el *m., sing., def. art.* the 1.1
él *sub. pron.* he 1.1; *adj. pron.* him
elecciones *f., pl.* election 3.6
electricista *m., f.* electrician 3.4
electrodoméstico *m.* electric appliance 2.6
elegante *adj. m., f.* elegant 1.6
elegir (e:i) *v.* to elect 3.6
ella *sub. pron.* she 1.1; *obj. pron.* her
ellos/as *sub. pron.* they 1.1; them
embarazada *adj.* pregnant 2.4
emergencia *f.* emergency 2.4
emitir *v.* to broadcast 3.6
emocionante *adj. m., f.* exciting
empezar (e:ie) *v.* to begin 1.4
empleado/a *m., f.* employee 1.5
empleo *m.* job; employment 3.4
empresa *f.* company; firm 3.4
en *prep.* in; on; at 1.2
en casa at home 2.1
en caso (de) que in case (that) 3.1
en cuanto as soon as 3.1
en efectivo in cash 3.2
en exceso in excess; too much 3.3
en línea in-line 1.4
¡En marcha! Let's get going! 3.3
en mi nombre in my name
en punto on the dot; exactly; sharp *(time)* 1.1
en qué in what; how 1.2
¿En qué puedo servirles? How can I help you? 1.5
enamorado/a (de) *adj.* in love (with) 1.5
enamorarse (de) *v.* to fall in love (with) 2.3
encantado/a *adj.* delighted; pleased to meet you 1.1
encantar *v.* to like very much; to love *(inanimate objects)* 2.1
¡Me encantó! I loved it! 3.3
encima de *prep.* on top of 1.2
encontrar (o:ue) *v.* to find 1.4

encontrar(se) (o:ue) *v.* to meet (each other); to run into (each other) 2.5
encuesta *f.* poll; survey 3.6
energía *f.* energy 3.1
energía nuclear nuclear energy 3.1
energía solar solar energy 3.1
enero *m.* January 1.5
enfermarse *v.* to get sick 2.4
enfermedad *f.* illness 2.4
enfermero/a *m., f.* nurse 2.4
enfermo/a *adj.* sick 2.4
enfrente de *adv.* opposite; facing 3.2
engordar *v.* to gain weight 3.3
enojado/a *adj.* mad; angry 1.5
enojarse (con) *v.* to get angry (with) 2.1
ensalada *f.* salad 2.2
enseguida *adv.* right away 2.3
enseñar *v.* to teach 1.2
ensuciar *v.* to get (something) dirty 2.6
entender (e:ie) *v.* to understand 1.4
entonces *adv.* then 2.1
entrada *f.* entrance 2.6; ticket 3.5
entre *prep.* between; among 1.2
entremeses *m., pl.* hors d'oeuvres; appetizers 2.2
entrenador(a) *m., f.* trainer 3.3
entrenarse *v.* to practice; to train 3.3
entrevista *f.* interview 3.4
entrevistador(a) *m., f.* interviewer 3.4
entrevistar *v.* to interview 3.4
envase *m.* container 3.1
enviar *v.* to send; to mail 3.2
equilibrado/a *adj.* balanced 3.3
equipado/a *adj.* equipped 3.3
equipaje *m.* luggage 1.5
equipo *m.* team 1.4
equivocado/a *adj.* wrong 1.5
eres *fam.* you are 1.1
es you *(form.)* are, he/she/it is 1.1
Es bueno que... It's good that... 2.6
Es de... He/She is from... 1.1
es extraño it's strange 3.1
Es importante que... It's important that... 2.6
es imposible it's impossible 3.1
es improbable it's improbable 3.1
Es malo que... It's bad that... 2.6
Es mejor que... It's better that... 2.6
Es necesario que... It's necessary that... 2.6
es obvio it's obvious 3.1
es ridículo it's ridiculous 3.1
es seguro it's sure 3.1
es terrible it's terrible 3.1
es triste it's sad 3.1
Es urgente que... It's urgent that... 2.6

Es la una. It's one o'clock. 1.1
es una lástima it's a shame 3.1
es verdad it's true 3.1
esa(s) *f., adj.* that; those 1.6
ésa(s) *f., pron.* that (one); those (ones) 1.6
escalar *v.* to climb 1.4
escalar montañas *v.* to climb mountains 1.4
escalera *f.* stairs; stairway 2.6
escoger *v.* to choose 2.2
escribir *v.* to write 1.3
escribir un mensaje electrónico to write an e-mail message 1.4
escribir una postal to write a postcard 1.4
escribir una carta to write a letter 1.4
escrito/a *p.p.* written 3.2
escritor(a) *m., f.* writer 3.5
escritorio *m.* desk 1.2
escuchar *v.* to listen to 1.2
escuchar la radio to listen (to) the radio 1.2
escuchar música to listen (to) music 1.2
escuela *f.* school 1.1
esculpir *v.* to sculpt 3.5
escultor(a) *m., f.* sculptor 3.5
escultura *f.* sculpture 3.5
ese *m., sing., adj.* that 1.6
ése *m., sing., pron.* that one 1.6
eso *neuter, pron.* that; that thing 1.6
esos *m., pl., adj.* those 1.6
ésos *m., pl., pron.* those (ones) 1.6
España *f.* Spain 1.1
español *m.* Spanish *(language)* 1.2
español(a) *adj. m., f.* Spanish 1.3
espárragos *m., pl.* asparagus 2.2
especialización *f.* major 1.2
espectacular *adj.* spectacular 3.3
espectáculo *m.* show 3.5
espejo *m.* mirror 2.1
esperar *v.* to hope; to wish 3.1
esperar (+ infin.) *v.* to wait (for); to hope 1.2
esposo/a *m., f.* husband/wife; spouse 1.3
esquí (acuático) *m.* (water) skiing 1.4
esquiar *v.* to ski 1.4
esquina *m.* corner 3.2
está he/she/it is, you are
Está (muy) despejado. It's (very) clear. *(weather)*
Está lloviendo. It's raining. 1.5
Está nevando. It's snowing. 1.5
Está (muy) nublado. It's (very) cloudy. *(weather)* 1.5
Está bien. That's fine. 2.5
esta(s) *f., adj.* this; these 1.6
esta noche tonight 1.4
ésta(s) *f., pron.* this (one); these (ones) 1.6

Ésta es... *f.* This is...
(*introducing someone*) **1.1**
establecer *v.* to start,
to establish **3.4**
estación *f.* station; season **1.5**
  estación de autobuses
    bus station **1.5**
  estación del metro subway
    station **1.5**
  estación de tren train
    station **1.5**
estacionamiento *m.* parking
lot **3.2**
estacionar *v.* to park **2.5**
estadio *m.* stadium **1.2**
estado civil *m.* marital status **2.3**
Estados Unidos *m., pl.* (EE.UU.;
E.U.) United States **1.1**
estadounidense *adj. m., f.* from
the United States **1.3**
estampado/a *adj.* print
estampilla *f.* stamp **3.2**
estante *m.* bookcase;
bookshelves **2.6**
estar *v.* to be **1.2**
  estar a (veinte kilómetros)
    de aquí to be (20 kilometers)
    from here **2.5**
  estar a dieta to be on a diet **3.3**
  estar aburrido/a to be
    bored **1.5**
  estar afectado/a (por) to be
    affected (by) **3.1**
  estar bajo control to be under
    control **2.1**
  estar cansado/a to be tired **1.5**
  estar contaminado/a to be
    polluted **3.1**
  estar de acuerdo to agree **3.4**
    Estoy (completamente)
      de acuerdo. I agree
      (completely). **3.4**
    No estoy de acuerdo.
      I don't agree. **3.4**
  estar de moda to be in
    fashion **1.6**
  estar de vacaciones *f., pl.* to
    be on vacation **1.5**
  estar en buena forma to be
    in good shape **3.3**
  estar enfermo/a to be sick **2.4**
  estar listo/a to be ready **3.3**
  estar perdido/a to be lost **3.2**
  estar roto/a to be broken **2.4**
  estar seguro/a to be sure **1.5**
  estar torcido/a to be twisted;
    to be sprained **2.4**
  No está nada mal. It's not bad
    at all. **1.5**
estatua *f.* statue **3.5**
este *m.* east **3.2**; umm **3.5**
este *m., sing., adj.* this **1.6**
éste *m., sing., pron.* this (one) **1.6**
  Éste es... *m.* This is...
    (*introducing someone*) **1.1**
estéreo *m.* stereo **2.5**
estilo *m.* style

estiramiento *m.* stretching **3.3**
esto *neuter pron.* this; this
thing **1.6**
estómago *m.* stomach **2.4**
estornudar *v.* to sneeze **2.4**
estos *m., pl., adj.* these **1.6**
éstos *m., pl., pron.* these (ones) **1.6**
estrella *f.* star **3.1**
  estrella de cine *m., f.* movie
    star **3.5**
estrés *m.* stress **3.3**
estudiante *m., f.* student **1.1, 1.2**
estudiantil *adj. m., f.* student **1.2**
estudiar *v.* to study **1.2**
estufa *f.* stove **2.6**
estupendo/a *adj.* stupendous **1.5**
etapa *f.* stage **2.3**
evitar *v.* to avoid **3.1**
examen *m.* test; exam **1.2**
  examen médico physical
    exam **2.4**
excelente *adj. m., f.* excellent **1.5**
exceso *m.* excess; too much **3.3**
excursión *f.* hike; tour;
excursion
excursionista *m., f.* hiker
éxito *m.* success **3.4**
experiencia *f.* experience **3.6**
explicar *v.* to explain **1.2**
explorar *v.* to explore
expresión *f.* expression
extinción *f.* extinction **3.1**
extranjero/a *adj.* foreign **3.5**
extraño/a *adj.* strange **3.1**

<hr/>

F

fabuloso/a *adj* fabulous **1.5**
fácil *adj.* easy **1.3**
falda *f.* skirt **1.6**
faltar *v.* to lack; to need **2.1**
familia *f.* family **1.3**
famoso/a *adj.* famous **3.4**
farmacia *f.* pharmacy **2.4**
fascinar *v.* to fascinate **2.1**
favorito/a *adj.* favorite **1.4**
fax *m.* fax (machine) **2.5**
febrero *m.* February **1.5**
fecha *f.* date **1.5**
feliz *adj.* happy **1.5**
  ¡Felicidades! Congratulations!
    (*for an event such as a
    birthday or anniversary*) **2.3**
  ¡Felicitaciones!
    Congratulations! (*for an event
    such as an engagement or a
    good grade on a test*) **2.3**
  ¡Feliz cumpleaños! Happy
    birthday! **2.3**
fenomenal *adj.* great, phenomenal **1.5**
feo/a *adj.* ugly **1.3**
festival *m.* festival **3.5**
fiebre *f.* fever **2.4**
fiesta *f.* party **2.3**
fijo/a *adj.* fixed, set **1.6**

fin *m.* end **1.4**
  fin de semana weekend **1.4**
finalmente *adv.* finally **3.3**
firmar *v.* to sign (*a document*) **3.2**
física *f.* physics **1.2**
flan (de caramelo) *m.* baked
(caramel) custard **2.3**
flexible *adj.* flexible **3.3**
flor *f.* flower **3.1**
folklórico/a *adj.* folk; folkloric **3.5**
folleto *m.* brochure
fondo *m.* end **2.6**
forma *f.* shape **3.3**
formulario *m.* form **3.2**
foto(grafía) *f.* photograph **1.1**
francés, francesa *adj. m., f.*
French **1.3**
frecuentemente *adv.* frequently **2.4**
frenos *m., pl.* brakes
fresco/a *adj.* cool **1.5**
frijoles *m., pl.* beans **2.2**
frío/a *adj.* cold **1.5**
frito/a *adj.* fried **2.2**
fruta *f.* fruit **2.2**
frutería *f.* fruit store **3.2**
frutilla *f.* strawberry **2.2**
fuente de fritada *f.* platter of
fried food
fuera *adv.* outside
fuerte *adj. m., f.* strong **3.3**
fumar *v.* to smoke **3.3**
  (no) fumar *v.* (not) to
    smoke **3.3**
funcionar *v.* to work **2.5**; to
function
fútbol *m.* soccer **1.4**
fútbol americano *m.* football **1.4**
futuro/a *adj.* future **3.4**
  en el futuro in the future **3.4**

<hr/>

G

gafas (de sol) *f., pl.* (sun)glasses **1.6**
gafas (oscuras) *f., pl.* (sun)glasses
galleta *f.* cookie **2.3**
ganar *v.* to win **1.4**; to earn
(money) **3.4**
ganga *f.* bargain **1.6**
garaje *m.* garage; (mechanic's)
repair shop **2.5**; garage (*in a
house*) **2.6**
garganta *f.* throat **2.4**
gasolina *f.* gasoline **2.5**
gasolinera *f.* gas station **2.5**
gastar *v.* to spend (*money*) **1.6**
gato *m.* cat **3.1**
gemelo/a *m., f.* twin **1.3**
gente *f.* people **1.3**
geografía *f.* geography **1.2**
gerente *m., f.* manager **3.4**
gimnasio *m.* gymnasium **1.4**
gobierno *m.* government **3.1**
golf *m.* golf **1.4**
gordo/a *adj.* fat **1.3**
grabadora *f.* tape recorder **1.1**
grabar *v.* to record **2.5**

gracias *f., pl.* thank you; thanks **1.1**
   Gracias por todo. Thanks for everything. **2.3, 3.3**
   Gracias una vez más. Thanks again. **2.3**
graduarse (de/en) *v.* to graduate (from/in) **2.3**
gran, grande *adj.* big; large **1.3**
grasa *f.* fat **3.3**
gratis *adj. m., f.* free of charge **3.2**
grave *adj.* grave; serious **2.4**
gravísimo/a *adj.* extremely serious **3.1**
grillo *m.* cricket
gripe *f.* flu **2.4**
gris *adj. m., f.* gray **1.6**
gritar *v.* to scream **2.1**
guantes *m., pl.* gloves **1.6**
guapo/a *adj.* handsome; good-looking **1.3**
guardar *v.* to save (on a computer) **2.5**
guerra *f.* war **3.6**
guía *m., f.* guide
gustar *v.* to be pleasing to; to like **1.2**
   Me gustaría... I would like...
gusto *m.* pleasure **1.1**
   El gusto es mío. The pleasure is mine. **1.1**
   Gusto de verlo/la. *(form.)* It's nice to see you. **3.6**
   Gusto de verte. *(fam.)* It's nice to see you. **3.6**
   Mucho gusto. Pleased to meet you. **1.1**
   ¡Qué gusto volver a verlo/la! *(form.)* I'm happy to see you again! **3.6**
   ¡Qué gusto volver a verte! *(fam.)* I'm happy to see you again! **3.6**

H

haber *(auxiliar)* *v.* to have (done something) **3.3**
   Ha sido un placer. It's been a pleasure. **3.3**
habitación *f.* room **1.5**
   habitación doble double room **1.5**
   habitación individual single room **1.5**
hablar *v.* to talk; to speak **1.2**
hacer *v.* to do; to make **1.4**
   Hace buen tiempo. The weather is good. **1.5**
   Hace (mucho) calor. It's (very) hot. *(weather)* **1.5**
   Hace fresco. It's cool. *(weather)* **1.5**
   Hace (mucho) frío. It's (very) cold. *(weather)* **1.5**
   Hace mal tiempo. The weather is bad. **1.5**

Hace (mucho) sol. It's (very) sunny. *(weather)* **1.5**
Hace (mucho) viento. It's (very) windy. *(weather)* **1.5**
hacer cola to stand in line **3.2**
hacer diligencias to run errands **3.2**
hacer ejercicio to exercise **3.3**
hacer ejercicios aeróbicos to do aerobics **3.3**
hacer ejercicios de estiramiento to do stretching exercises **3.3**
hacer el papel (de) to play the role (of) **3.5**
hacer gimnasia to work out **3.3**
hacer juego (con) to match (with) **1.6**
hacer la cama to make the bed **2.6**
hacer las maletas to pack (one's) suitcases **1.5**
hacer quehaceres domésticos to do household chores **2.6**
hacer turismo to go sightseeing
hacer un viaje to take a trip **1.5**
hacer una excursión to go on a hike; to go on a tour
hacia *prep.* toward **3.2**
hambre *f.* hunger **1.3**
hamburguesa *f.* hamburger **2.2**
hasta *prep.* until **1.6**; toward
   Hasta la vista. See you later. **1.1**
   Hasta luego. See you later. **1.1**
   Hasta mañana. See you tomorrow. **1.1**
   hasta que until **3.1**
   Hasta pronto. See you soon. **1.1**
hay there is; there are **1.1**
   Hay (mucha) contaminación. It's (very) smoggy.
   Hay (mucha) niebla. It's (very) foggy.
   Hay que It is necessary that **3.2**
   No hay duda de There's no doubt **3.1**
   No hay de qué. You're welcome. **1.1**
hecho/a *p.p.* done **3.2**
heladería *f.* ice cream shop **3.2**
helado/a *adj.* iced **2.2**
helado *m.* ice cream **2.3**
hermanastro/a *m., f.* stepbrother/stepsister **1.3**
hermano/a *m., f.* brother/sister **1.3**
hermano/a mayor/menor *m., f.* older/younger brother/sister **1.3**
hermanos *m., pl.* siblings (brothers and sisters) **1.3**
hermoso/a *adj.* beautiful **1.6**
hierba *f.* grass **3.1**
hijastro/a *m., f.* stepson/stepdaughter **1.3**
hijo/a *m., f.* son/daughter **1.3**
   hijo/a único/a *m., f.* only child **1.3**
hijos *m., pl.* children **1.3**

historia *f.* history **1.2**; story **3.5**
hockey *m.* hockey **1.4**
hola *interj.* hello; hi **1.1**
hombre *m.* man **1.1**
   hombre de negocios *m.* businessman **3.4**
hora *f.* hour **1.1**; the time
horario *m.* schedule **1.2**
horno *m.* oven **2.6**
   horno de microondas *m.* microwave oven **2.6**
horror *m.* horror **3.5**
   de horror horror (genre) **3.5**
hospital *m.* hospital **2.4**
hotel *m.* hotel **1.5**
hoy *adv.* today **1.2**
   hoy día *adv.* nowadays
   Hoy es... Today is... **1.2**
huelga *f.* strike *(labor)* **3.6**
hueso *m.* bone **2.4**
huésped *m., f.* guest **1.5**
huevo *m.* egg **2.2**
humanidades *f., pl.* humanities **1.2**
huracán *m.* hurricane **3.6**

I

ida *f.* one way *(travel)*
idea *f.* idea **1.4**
iglesia *f.* church **1.4**
igualdad *f.* equality **3.6**
igualmente *adv.* likewise **1.1**
impermeable *m.* raincoat **1.6**
importante *adj. m., f.* important **1.3**
importar *v.* to be important to; to matter **2.1**
imposible *adj. m., f.* impossible **3.1**
impresora *f.* printer **2.5**
imprimir *v.* to print **2.5**
improbable *adj. m., f.* improbable **3.1**
impuesto *m.* tax **3.6**
incendio *m.* fire **3.6**
increíble *adj. m., f.* incredible **1.5**
individual *adj.* private *(room)* **1.5**
infección *f.* infection **2.4**
informar *v.* to inform **3.6**
informe *m.* report; paper *(written work)* **3.6**
ingeniero/a *m., f.* engineer **1.3**
inglés *m.* English *(language)* **1.2**
inglés, inglesa *adj.* English **1.3**
inodoro *m.* toilet **2.1**
insistir (en) *v.* to insist (on) **2.6**
inspector(a) de aduanas *m., f.* customs inspector **1.5**
inteligente *adj. m., f.* intelligent **1.3**
intercambiar *v.* to exchange
interesante *adj. m., f.* interesting **1.3**
interesar *v.* to be interesting to; to interest **2.1**
internacional *adj. m., f.* international **3.6**

Internet Internet **2.5**
inundación *f.* flood **3.6**
invertir (e:ie) *v.* to invest **3.4**
invierno *m.* winter **1.5**
invitado/a *m., f.* guest
 (*at a function*) **2.3**
invitar *v.* to invite **2.3**
inyección *f.* injection **2.4**
ir *v.* to go **1.4**
 ir a (+ *inf.*) to be going to do
  something **1.4**
 ir de compras to go shopping **1.5**
 **ir de excursión (a las
  montañas)** to go for a hike
  (in the mountains) **1.4**
 ir de pesca to go fishing
 ir de vacaciones to go on
  vacation **1.5**
 ir en autobús to go by bus **1.5**
 ir en auto(móvil) to go by
  auto(mobile); to go by car **1.5**
 ir en avión to go by plane **1.5**
 ir en barco to go by boat **1.5**
 ir en metro to go by subway
 ir en motocicleta to go by
  motorcycle **1.5**
 ir en taxi to go by taxi **1.5**
 ir en tren to go by train
irse *v.* to go away; to leave **2.1**
italiano/a *adj.* Italian **1.3**
izquierdo/a *adj.* left **1.2**
 a la izquierda de to the left
  of **1.2**

jabón *m.* soap **2.1**
jamás *adv.* never; not ever **2.1**
jamón *m.* ham **2.2**
japonés, japonesa *adj.*
 Japanese **1.3**
jardín *m.* garden; yard **2.6**
jefe, jefa *m., f.* boss **3.4**
joven *adj. m., f.* young **1.3**
 joven *m., f.* youth; young
  person **1.1**
joyería *f.* jewelry store **3.2**
jubilarse *v.* to retire (*from
 work*) **2.3**
juego *m.* game
jueves *m., sing.* Thursday **1.2**
jugador(a) *m., f.* player **1.4**
jugar (u:ue) *v.* to play **1.4**
 jugar a las cartas *f., pl.* to
  play cards **1.5**
jugo *m.* juice **2.2**
 jugo de fruta *m.* fruit juice **2.2**
julio *m.* July **1.5**
jungla *f.* jungle **3.1**
junio *m.* June **1.5**
juntos/as *adj.* together **2.3**
juventud *f.* youth **2.3**

kilómetro *m.* kilometer **1.1**

la *f., sing., def. art.* the **1.1**
 la *f., sing., d.o. pron.* her, it,
  form. you **1.5**
laboratorio *m.* laboratory **1.2**
lago *m.* lake **3.1**
lámpara *f.* lamp **2.6**
lana *f.* wool **1.6**
langosta *f.* lobster **2.2**
lápiz *m.* pencil **1.1**
largo/a *adj.* long **1.6**
las *f., pl., def. art.* the **1.1**
 las *f., pl., d.o. pron.* them; *form.*
  you **1.5**
lástima *f.* shame **3.1**
lastimarse *v.* to injure oneself **2.4**
 lastimarse el pie to injure
  one's foot **2.4**
lata *f.* (*tin*) can **3.1**
lavabo *m.* sink **2.1**
lavadora *f.* washing machine **2.6**
lavandería *f.* laundromat **3.2**
lavaplatos *m., sing.* dishwasher **2.6**
lavar *v.* to wash **2.6**
 lavar (el suelo, los platos) to
  wash (the floor, the dishes) **2.6**
lavarse *v.* to wash oneself **2.1**
 lavarse la cara to wash one's
  face **2.1**
 lavarse las manos to wash
  one's hands **2.1**
le *sing., i.o. pron.* to/for him, her,
 form. you **1.6**
 Le presento a... *form.* I would
  like to introduce... to you. **1.1**
lección *f.* lesson **1.1**
leche *f.* milk **2.2**
lechuga *f.* lettuce **2.2**
leer *v.* to read **1.3**
 leer correo electrónico
  to read e-mail **1.4**
 leer un periódico to read a
  newspaper **1.4**
 leer una revista to read a
  magazine **1.4**
leído/a *p.p.* read **3.2**
lejos de *prep.* far from **1.2**
lengua *f.* language **1.2**
 lenguas extranjeras *f., pl.*
  foreign languages **1.2**
lentes de contacto *m., pl.*
 contact lenses
 lentes (de sol) (sun)glasses
lento/a *adj.* slow **2.5**
les *pl., i.o. pron.* to/for them, *form.*
 you **1.6**
letrero *m.* sign **3.2**
levantar *v.* to lift **3.3**
 levantar pesas to lift
  weights **3.3**

levantarse *v.* to get up **2.1**
ley *f.* law **3.1**
libertad *f.* liberty; freedom **3.6**
libre *adj. m., f.* free **1.4**
librería *f.* bookstore **1.2**
libro *m.* book **1.2**
licencia de conducir *f.* driver's
 license **2.5**
limón *m.* lemon **2.2**
limpiar *v.* to clean **2.6**
limpiar la casa *v.* to clean the
 house **2.6**
limpio/a *adj.* clean **1.5**
línea *f.* line **1.4**
listo/a *adj.* ready; smart **1.5**
literatura *f.* literature **1.2**
llamar *v.* to call **2.5**
 llamar por teléfono to call on
  the phone
llamarse *v.* to be called; to be
 named **2.1**
llanta *f.* tire **2.5**
llave *f.* key **1.5**
llegada *f.* arrival **1.5**
llegar *v.* to arrive **1.2**
llenar *v.* to fill **2.5, 3.2**
 llenar el tanque to fill the
  tank **2.5**
 llenar (un formulario) to fill
  out (a form) **3.2**
lleno/a *adj.* full **2.5**
llevar *v.* to carry **1.2**; *v.* to wear;
 to take **1.6**
 llevar una vida sana to lead
  a healthy lifestyle **3.3**
 llevarse bien/mal (con) to
  get along well/badly (with) **2.3**
llover (o:ue) *v.* to rain **1.5**
 Llueve. It's raining. **1.5**
lluvia *f.* rain **3.1**
 lluvia ácida acid rain **3.1**
lo *m., sing. d.o. pron.* him, it, *form.*
 you **1.5**
 **¡Lo hemos pasado de
  película!** We've had a great
  time! **3.6**
 **¡Lo hemos pasado
  maravillosamente!** We've
  had a great time! **3.6**
 lo mejor the best (thing) **3.6**
 Lo pasamos muy bien. We
  had a good time. **3.6**
 lo peor the worst (thing) **3.6**
 lo que that which; what **2.6**
 Lo siento. I'm sorry. **1.1**
 Lo siento muchísimo. I'm so
  sorry. **1.4**
loco/a *adj.* crazy **1.6**
locutor(a) *m., f.* (TV or radio)
 announcer **3.6**
lomo a la plancha *m.* grilled
 flank steak **2.2**
los *m., pl., def. art.* the **1.1**
 los *m. pl., d.o. pron.* them, *form.*
  you **1.5**

luchar (contra/por) *v.* to fight; to struggle (against/for) **3.6**
luego; *adv.* later **1.1;** *adv.* then **2.1**
lugar *m.* place **1.4**
luna *f.* moon **3.1**
lunares *m.* polka dots **1.6**
lunes *m., sing.* Monday **1.2**
luz *f.* light; electricity **2.6**

M

madrastra *f.* stepmother **1.3**
madre *f.* mother **1.3**
madurez *f.* maturity; middle age **2.3**
maestro/a *m., f.* teacher **3.4**
magnífico/a *adj.* magnificent **1.5**
maíz *m.* corn **2.2**
mal, malo/a *adj.* bad **1.3**
maleta *f.* suitcase **1.1**
mamá *f.* mom **1.3**
mandar *v.* to order **2.6;** to send; to mail **3.2**
manejar *v.* to drive **2.5**
manera *f.* way **3.4**
mano *f.* hand **1.1**
manta *f.* blanket **2.6**
mantener (e:ie) *v.* to maintain **3.3**
  mantenerse en forma to stay in shape **3.3**
mantequilla *f.* butter **2.2**
manzana *f.* apple **2.2**
mañana *f.* morning, a.m. **1.1;** tomorrow **1.1**
mapa *m.* map **1.1, 1.2**
maquillaje *m.* makeup **2.1**
maquillarse *v.* to put on makeup **2.1**
mar *m.* sea **1.5**
maravilloso/a *adj.* marvelous **1.5**
mareado/a *adj.* dizzy; nauseated **2.4**
margarina *f.* margarine **2.2**
mariscos *m., pl.* shellfish **2.2**
marrón *adj. m., f.* brown **1.6**
martes *m., sing.* Tuesday **1.2**
marzo *m.* March **1.5**
más *pron.* more **1.2**
  más de (+ number) more than **2.2**
  más tarde later (on) **2.1**
  más... que more... than **2.2**
masaje *m.* massage **3.3**
matemáticas *f., pl.* mathematics **1.2**
materia *f.* course **1.2**
matrimonio *m.* marriage **2.3**
máximo/a *adj.* maximum **2.5**
mayo *m.* May **1.5**
mayonesa *f.* mayonnaise **2.2**
mayor *adj.* older **1.3**
  el/la mayor *adj.* eldest **2.2;** oldest
me *sing., d.o. pron.* me **1.5;** *sing. i.o. pron.* to/for me **1.6**
  Me duele mucho. It hurts me a lot. **2.4**
  Me gusta... I like... **1.2**

No me gustan nada. I don't like them at all. **1.2**
  Me gustaría(n)... I would like... **3.5**
  Me llamo... My name is... **1.1**
  Me muero por... I'm dying to (for)...
mecánico/a *m., f.* mechanic **2.5**
mediano/a *adj.* medium
medianoche *f.* midnight **1.1**
medias *f., pl.* pantyhose, stockings **1.6**
medicamento *m.* medication **2.4**
medicina *f.* medicine **2.4**
médico/a *m., f.* doctor **1.3;** *adj.* medical **2.4**
medio/a *adj.* half **1.3**
  medio ambiente *m.* environment **3.1**
  medio/a hermano/a *m., f.* half-brother/half-sister **1.3**
  mediodía *m.* noon **1.1**
  medios de comunicación *m., pl.* means of communication; media **3.6**
  y media thirty minutes past the hour (time) **1.1**
mejor *adj.* better **2.2**
  el/la mejor *m., f.* the best **2.2**
mejorar *v.* to improve **3.1**
melocotón *m.* peach **2.2**
menor *adj.* younger **1.3**
  el/la menor *m., f.* youngest **2.2**
menos *adv.* less **2.4**
  menos cuarto..., menos quince... quarter to... (time) **1.1**
  menos de (+ number) fewer than **2.2**
  menos... que less... than **2.2**
mensaje *m.* **de texto** text message **2.5**
mensaje electrónico *m.* e-mail message **1.4**
mentira *f.* lie **1.4**
menú *m.* menu **2.2**
mercado *m.* market **1.6**
  mercado al aire libre open-air market **1.6**
merendar (e:ie) *v.* to snack **2.2;** to have an afternoon snack
merienda *f.* afternoon snack **3.3**
mes *m.* month **1.5**
mesa *f.* table **1.2**
mesita *f.* end table **2.6**
  mesita de noche night stand **2.6**
metro *m.* subway **1.5**
mexicano/a *adj.* Mexican **1.3**
México *m.* Mexico **1.1**
mí *pron., obj. of prep.* me **2.2**
mi(s) *poss. adj.* my **1.3**
microonda *f.* microwave **2.6**
  horno de microondas *m.* microwave oven **2.6**
miedo *m.* fear **1.3**
mientras *adv.* while **2.4**

miércoles *m., sing.* Wednesday **1.2**
mil *m.* one thousand **1.2**
  mil millones billion
  Mil perdones. I'm so sorry. (*lit.* A thousand pardons.) **1.4**
milla *f.* mile **2.5**
millón *m.* million **1.2**
millones (de) *m.* millions (of)
mineral *m.* mineral **3.3**
minuto *m.* minute **1.1**
mío(s)/a(s) *poss.* my; (of) mine **2.5**
mirar *v.* to look (at); to watch **1.2**
  mirar (la) televisión to watch television **1.2**
mismo/a *adj.* same **1.3**
mochila *f.* backpack **1.2**
moda *f.* fashion **1.6**
módem *m.* modem
moderno/a *adj.* modern **3.5**
molestar *v.* to bother; to annoy **2.1**
monitor *m.* (computer) monitor **2.5**
  monitor(a) *m., f.* trainer
montaña *f.* mountain **1.4**
montar *v.* **a caballo** to ride a horse **1.5**
monumento *m.* monument **1.4**
mora *f.* blackberry **2.2**
morado/a *adj.* purple **1.6**
moreno/a *adj.* brunet(te) **1.3**
morir (o:ue) *v.* to die **2.2**
mostrar (o:ue) *v.* to show **1.4**
motocicleta *f.* motorcycle **1.5**
motor *m.* motor
muchacho/a *m., f.* boy; girl **1.3**
mucho/a *adj., adv.* a lot of; much **1.2;** many **1.3**
  (Muchas) gracias. Thank you (very much); Thanks (a lot). **1.1**
  muchas veces *adv.* a lot; many times **2.4**
  Muchísimas gracias. Thank you very, very much. **2.3**
  Mucho gusto. Pleased to meet you. **1.1**
muchísimo very much **1.2**
mudarse *v.* to move (from one house to another) **2.6**
muebles *m., pl.* furniture **2.6**
muela *f.* tooth
muerte *f.* death **2.3**
muerto/a *p.p.* died **3.2**
mujer *f.* woman **1.1**
  mujer de negocios *f.* business woman **3.4**
  mujer policía *f.* female police officer
multa *f.* fine
mundial *adj. m., f.* worldwide
mundo *m.* world **3.1**
municipal *adj. m., f.* municipal
músculo *m.* muscle **3.3**
museo *m.* museum **1.4**
música *f.* music **1.2, 3.5**
musical *adj. m., f.* musical **3.5**
músico/a *m., f.* musician **3.5**

muy *adv.* very **1.1**
  Muy amable. That's very kind of you. **1.5**
  (Muy) bien, gracias. (Very) well, thanks. **1.1**

N

nacer *v.* to be born **2.3**
nacimiento *m.* birth **2.3**
nacional *adj. m., f.* national **3.6**
nacionalidad *f.* nationality **1.1**
nada nothing **1.1**; not anything **2.1**
  nada mal not bad at all **1.5**
nadar *v.* to swim **1.4**
nadie *pron.* no one, nobody, not anyone **2.1**
naranja *f.* orange **2.2**
nariz *f.* nose **2.4**
natación *f.* swimming **1.4**
natural *adj. m., f.* natural **3.1**
naturaleza *f.* nature **3.1**
navegar (en Internet) *v.* to surf (the Internet) **2.5**
Navidad *f.* Christmas **2.3**
necesario/a *adj.* necessary **2.6**
necesitar (+ inf.) *v.* to need **1.2**
negar (e:ie) *v.* to deny **3.1**
  no negar (e:ie) *v.* not to deny **3.1**
negativo/a *adj.* negative
negocios *m., pl.* business; commerce **3.4**
negro/a *adj.* black **1.6**
nervioso/a *adj.* nervous **1.5**
nevar (e:ie) *v.* to snow **1.5**
  Nieva. It's snowing. **1.5**
ni...ni neither... nor **2.1**
niebla *f.* fog
nieto/a *m., f.* grandson/granddaughter **1.3**
nieve *f.* snow
ningún, ninguno/a(s) *adj.* no; none; not any **2.1**
ningún problema no problem
niñez *f.* childhood **2.3**
niño/a *m., f.* child **1.3**
no no; not **1.1**
  ¿no? right? **1.1**
  No cabe duda de... There is no doubt... **3.1**
  No es así. That's not the way it is **3.4**
  No es para tanto. It's not a big deal. **2.6**
  no es seguro it's not sure **3.1**
  no es verdad it's not true **3.1**
  No está nada mal. It's not bad at all. **1.5**
  no estar de acuerdo to disagree
  No estoy seguro. I'm not sure.
  no hay there is not; there are not **1.1**
  No hay de qué. You're welcome. **1.1**
  No hay duda de... There is no doubt... **3.1**

No hay problema. No problem. **2.1**
¡No me diga(s)! You don't say! **2.5**
No me gustan nada. I don't like them at all. **1.2**
no muy bien not very well **1.1**
No quiero. I don't want to. **1.4**
No sé. I don't know.
No se preocupe. (*form.*) Don't worry. **2.1**
No te preocupes. (*fam.*) Don't worry. **2.1**
no tener razón to be wrong **1.3**
noche *f.* night **1.1**
nombre *m.* name **1.1**
norte *m.* north **3.2**
norteamericano/a *adj.* (North) American **1.3**
nos *pl., d.o. pron.* us **1.5**; *pl., i.o. pron.* to/for us **1.6**
  Nos divertimos mucho. We had a lot of fun. **3.6**
  Nos vemos. See you. **1.1**
nosotros/as *sub. pron.* we **1.1**; *ob. pron.* us
noticias *f., pl.* news **3.6**
noticiero *m.* newscast **3.6**
novecientos/as nine hundred **1.2**
noveno/a *adj.* ninth **1.5**
noventa ninety **1.2**
noviembre *m.* November **1.5**
novio/a *m., f.* boyfriend/girlfriend **1.3**
nube *f.* cloud **3.1**
nublado/a *adj.* cloudy **1.5**
  Está (muy) nublado. It's very cloudy. **1.5**
nuclear *adj. m. f.* nuclear **3.1**
nuera *f.* daughter-in-law **1.3**
nuestro(s)/a(s) *poss. adj.* our **1.3**; (of ours) **2.5**
nueve nine **1.1**
nuevo/a *adj.* new **1.6**
número *m.* number **1.1**; (shoe) size **1.6**
nunca *adj.* never; not ever **2.1**
nutrición *f.* nutrition **3.3**
nutricionista *m., f.* nutritionist **3.3**

O

o or **2.1**
o... o; either... or **2.1**
obedecer *v.* to obey **3.6**
obra *f.* work (*of art, literature, music, etc.*) **3.5**
  obra maestra *f.* masterpiece **3.5**
obtener *v.* to obtain; to get **3.4**
obvio/a *adj.* obvious **3.1**
océano *m.* ocean
ochenta eighty **1.2**
ocho eight **1.1**
ochocientos/as eight hundred **1.2**

octavo/a *adj.* eighth **1.5**
octubre *m.* October **1.5**
ocupación *f.* occupation **3.4**
ocupado/a *adj.* busy **1.5**
ocurrir *v.* to occur; to happen **3.6**
odiar *v.* to hate **2.3**
oeste *m.* west **3.2**
oferta *f.* offer **2.6**
oficina *f.* office **2.6**
oficio *m.* trade **3.4**
ofrecer *v.* to offer **1.6**
oído *m.* (sense of) hearing; inner ear **2.4**
  oído/a *p.p.* heard **3.2**
oír *v.* to hear **1.4**
  Oiga/Oigan. *form., sing./pl.* Listen. (*in conversation*) **1.1**
  Oye. *fam., sing.* Listen. (*in conversation*) **1.1**
ojalá (que) *interj.* I hope (that); I wish (that) **3.1**
ojo *m.* eye **2.4**
olvidar *v.* to forget **2.4**
once eleven **1.1**
ópera *f.* opera **3.5**
operación *f.* operation **2.4**
ordenado/a *adj.* orderly **1.5**
ordinal *adj.* ordinal (*number*)
oreja *f.* (outer) ear **2.4**
orquesta *f.* orchestra **3.5**
ortografía *f.* spelling
ortográfico/a *adj.* spelling
os *fam., pl. d.o. pron.* you **1.5**; *fam., pl. i.o. pron.* to/for you **1.6**
otoño *m.* autumn **1.5**
otro/a *adj.* other; another **1.6**
  otra vez again

P

paciente *m., f.* patient **2.4**
padrastro *m.* stepfather **1.3**
padre *m.* father **1.3**
  padres *m., pl.* parents **1.3**
pagar *v.* to pay **1.6, 2.3**
  pagar a plazos to pay in installments **3.2**
  pagar al contado to pay in cash **3.2**
  pagar en efectivo to pay in cash **3.2**
  pagar la cuenta to pay the bill **2.3**
página *f.* page **2.5**
  página principal *f.* home page **2.5**
país *m.* country **1.1**
paisaje *m.* landscape **1.5**
pájaro *m.* bird **3.1**
palabra *f.* word **1.1**
pan *m.* bread **2.2**
  pan tostado *m.* toasted bread **2.2**
panadería *f.* bakery **3.2**
pantalla *f.* screen **2.5**
pantalones *m., pl.* pants **1.6**

pantalones cortos *m., pl.* shorts **1.6**

pantuflas *f.* slippers **2.1**

papa *f.* potato **2.2**

  papas fritas *f., pl.* fried potatoes; French fries **2.2**

papá *m.* dad **1.3**

  papás *m., pl.* parents **1.3**

papel *m.* paper **1.2**; role **3.5**

papelera *f.* wastebasket **1.2**

paquete *m.* package **3.2**

par *m.* pair **1.6**

  par de zapatos pair of shoes **1.6**

para *prep.* for; in order to; by; used for; considering **2.5**

  para que so that **3.1**

parabrisas *m., sing.* windshield **2.5**

parar *v.* to stop **2.5**

parecer *v.* to seem **1.6**

pared *f.* wall **2.6**

pareja *f.* (married) couple; partner **2.3**

parientes *m., pl.* relatives **1.3**

parque *m.* park **1.4**

párrafo *m.* paragraph

parte: de parte de on behalf of **2.5**

partido *m.* game; match (*sports*) **1.4**

pasado/a *adj.* last; past **1.6**

  pasado *p.p.* passed

pasaje *m.* ticket **1.5**

  pasaje de ida y vuelta *m.* roundtrip ticket **1.5**

pasajero/a *m., f.* passenger **1.1**

pasaporte *m.* passport **1.5**

pasar *v.* to go through **1.5**

  pasar la aspiradora to vacuum **2.6**

  pasar por el banco to go by the bank **3.2**

  pasar por la aduana to go through customs

  pasar tiempo to spend time

  pasarlo bien/mal to have a good/bad time **2.3**

pasatiempo *m.* pastime; hobby **1.4**

pasear *v.* to take a walk; to stroll **1.4**

  pasear en bicicleta to ride a bicycle **1.4**

  pasear por to walk around **1.4**

pasillo *m.* hallway **2.6**

pasta *f.* **de dientes** toothpaste **2.1**

pastel *m.* cake; pie **2.3**

  pastel de chocolate *m.* chocolate cake **2.3**

  pastel de cumpleaños *m.* birthday cake

pastelería *f.* pastry shop **3.2**

pastilla *f.* pill; tablet **2.4**

patata *f.* potato; **2.2**

  patatas fritas *f., pl.* fried potatoes; French fries **2.2**

patinar (en línea) *v.* to (in-line) skate **1.4**

patineta *f.* skateboard **1.4**

patio *m.* patio; yard **2.6**

pavo *m.* turkey **2.2**

paz *f.* peace **3.6**

pedir (e:i) *v.* to ask for; to request **1.4**; to order (*food*) **2.2**

  pedir prestado *v.* to borrow **3.2**

  pedir un préstamo *v.* to apply for a loan **3.2**

peinarse *v.* to comb one's hair **2.1**

película *f.* movie **1.4**

peligro *m.* danger **3.1**

peligroso/a *adj.* dangerous **3.6**

pelirrojo/a *adj.* red-haired **1.3**

pelo *m.* hair **2.1**

pelota *f.* ball **1.4**

peluquería *f.* beauty salon **3.2**

peluquero/a *m., f.* hairdresser **3.4**

penicilina *f.* penicillin **2.4**

pensar (e:ie) *v.* to think **1.4**

  pensar (+ *inf.*) *v.* to intend to; to plan to (*do something*) **1.4**

  pensar en *v.* to think about **1.4**

pensión *f.* boardinghouse

peor *adj.* worse **2.2**

  el/la peor *adj.* the worst **2.2**

pequeño/a *adj.* small **1.3**

pera *f.* pear **2.2**

perder (e:ie) *v.* to lose; to miss **1.4**

perdido/a *adj.* lost **3.2**

Perdón. Pardon me.; Excuse me. **1.1**

perezoso/a *adj.* lazy

perfecto/a *adj.* perfect **1.5**

periódico *m.* newspaper **1.4**

periodismo *m.* journalism **1.2**

periodista *m., f.* journalist **1.3**

permiso *m.* permission

pero *conj.* but **1.2**

perro *m.* dog **3.1**

persona *f.* person **1.3**

personaje *m.* character **3.5**

  personaje principal *m.* main character **3.5**

pesas *f. pl.* weights **3.3**

pesca *f.* fishing

pescadería *f.* fish market **3.2**

pescado *m.* fish (*cooked*) **2.2**

pescador(a) *m., f.* fisherman/fisherwoman

pescar *v.* to fish **1.5**

peso *m.* weight **3.3**

pez *m.* fish (*live*) **3.1**

pie *m.* foot **2.4**

piedra *f.* stone **3.1**

pierna *f.* leg **2.4**

pimienta *f.* black pepper **2.2**

pintar *v.* to paint **3.5**

pintor(a) *m., f.* painter **3.4**

pintura *f.* painting; picture **2.6, 3.5**

piña *f.* pineapple **2.2**

piscina *f.* swimming pool **1.4**

piso *m.* floor (*of a building*) **1.5**

pizarra *f.* blackboard **1.2**

placer *m.* pleasure **3.3**

  Ha sido un placer. It's been a pleasure. **3.3**

planchar la ropa *v.* to iron the clothes **2.6**

planes *m., pl.* plans **1.4**

planta *f.* plant **3.1**

  planta baja *f.* ground floor **1.5**

plástico *m.* plastic **3.1**

plato *m.* dish (*in a meal*) **2.2**; *m.* plate **2.6**

  plato principal *m.* main dish **2.2**

playa *f.* beach **1.5**

plaza *f.* city or town square **1.4**

plazos *m., pl.* periods; time **3.2**

pluma *f.* pen **1.2**

población *f.* population **3.1**

pobre *adj. m., f.* poor **1.6**

pobreza *f.* poverty

poco/a *adj.* little; few **1.5; 2.4**

poder (o:ue) *v.* to be able to; can **1.4**

poema *m.* poem **3.5**

poesía *f.* poetry **3.5**

poeta *m., f.* poet **3.5**

policía *f.* police (force) **2.5**

política *f.* politics **3.6**

político/a *m., f.* politician **3.4**; *adj.* political **3.6**

pollo *m.* chicken **2.2**

  pollo asado *m.* roast chicken **2.2**

ponchar *v.* to go flat

poner *v.* to put; to place **1.4**; *v.* to turn on (*electrical appliances*) **2.5**

  poner la mesa *v.* to set the table **2.6**

  poner una inyección *v.* to give an injection **2.4**

ponerse (+ *adj.*) *v.* to become (+ *adj.*) **2.1**; to put on **2.1**

por *prep.* in exchange for; for; by; in; through; around; along; during; because of; on account of; on behalf of; in search of; by way of; by means of **2.5**

  por aquí around here **2.5**

  por avión by plane

  por ejemplo for example **2.5**

  por eso that's why; therefore **2.5**

  por favor please **1.1**

  por fin finally **2.5**

  por la mañana in the morning **2.1**

  por la noche at night **2.1**

  por la tarde in the afternoon **2.1**

  por lo menos *adv.* at least **2.4**

  ¿por qué? why? **1.2**

  Por supuesto. Of course. **3.4**

  por teléfono by phone; on the phone

  por último finally **2.1**

porque *conj.* because **1.2**

portátil *m.* portable **2.5**

porvenir *m.* future **3.4**
  ¡Por el porvenir! Here's to the future! **3.4**
posesivo/a *adj.* possessive **1.3**
posible *adj.* possible **3.1**
  es posible it's possible **3.1**
  no es posible it's not possible **3.1**
postal *f.* postcard **1.4**
postre *m.* dessert **2.3**
practicar *v.* to practice **1.2**
  practicar deportes *m., pl.* to play sports **1.4**
precio (fijo) *m.* (fixed; set) price **1.6**
preferir (e:ie) *v.* to prefer **1.4**
pregunta *f.* question
preguntar *v.* to ask (*a question*) **1.2**
premio *m.* prize; award **3.5**
prender *v.* to turn on **2.5**
prensa *f.* press **3.6**
preocupado/a (por) *adj.* worried (about) **1.5**
preocuparse (por) *v.* to worry (about) **2.1**
preparar *v.* to prepare **1.2**
preposición *f.* preposition
presentación *f.* introduction
presentar *v.* to introduce; to present **3.5**; to put on (*a performance*) **3.5**
  Le presento a... I would like to introduce (name) to you... (*form.*) **1.1**
  Te presento a... I would like to introduce (name) to you... (*fam.*) **1.1**
presiones *f., pl.* pressures **3.3**
prestado/a *adj.* borrowed
préstamo *m.* loan **3.2**
prestar *v.* to lend; to loan **1.6**
primavera *f.* spring **1.5**
primer, primero/a *adj.* first **1.5**
primo/a *m., f.* cousin **1.3**
principal *adj. m., f.* main **2.2**
prisa *f.* haste **1.3**
  darse prisa *v.* to hurry; to rush **3.3**
probable *adj. m., f.* probable **3.1**
  es probable it's probable **3.1**
  no es probable it's not probable **3.1**
probar (o:ue) *v.* to taste; to try **2.2**
probarse (o:ue) *v.* to try on **2.1**
problema *m.* problem **1.1**
profesión *f.* profession **1.3, 3.4**
profesor(a) *m., f.* teacher **1.1, 1.2**
programa *m.* **1.1**
  programa de computación *m.* software **2.5**
  programa de entrevistas *m.* talk show **3.5**
programador(a) *m., f.* computer programmer **1.3**
prohibir *v.* to prohibit **2.4**; to forbid

pronombre *m.* pronoun
pronto *adv.* soon **2.4**
propina *f.* tip **2.3**
propio/a *adj.* own **3.4**
proteger *v.* to protect **3.1**
proteína *f.* protein **3.3**
próximo/a *adj.* next **3.4**
prueba *f.* test; quiz **1.2**
psicología *f.* psychology **1.2**
psicólogo/a *m., f.* psychologist **3.4**
publicar *v.* to publish **3.5**
público *m.* audience **3.5**
pueblo *m.* town **1.4**
puerta *f.* door **1.2**
Puerto Rico *m.* Puerto Rico **1.1**
puertorriqueño/a *adj.* Puerto Rican **1.3**
pues *conj.* well **1.2, 3.5**
puesto *m.* position; job **3.4**
puesto/a *p.p.* put **3.2**
puro/a *adj.* pure **3.1**

Q

que *pron.* that; which; who **2.6**
  ¿En qué...? In which...? **1.2**
  ¡Qué...! How...! **1.3**
  ¡Qué dolor! What pain!
  ¡Qué ropa más bonita! What pretty clothes! **1.6**
  ¡Qué sorpresa! What a surprise!
  ¿qué? what? **1.1**
  ¿Qué día es hoy? What day is it? **1.2**
  ¿Qué hay de nuevo? What's new? **1.1**
  ¿Qué hora es? What time is it? **1.1**
  ¿Qué les parece? What do you (*pl.*) think?
  ¿Qué pasa? What's happening? What's going on? **1.1**
  ¿Qué pasó? What happened? **2.5**
  ¿Qué precio tiene? What is the price?
  ¿Qué tal...? How are you?; How is it going? **1.1**; How is/are...? **1.2**
  ¿Qué talla lleva/usa? What size do you wear? **1.6**
  ¿Qué tiempo hace? How's the weather? **1.5**
quedar *v.* to be left over; to fit (*clothing*) **2.1**; to be left behind; to be located **3.2**
quedarse *v.* to stay; to remain **2.1**
quehaceres domésticos *m., pl.* household chores **2.6**
quemado/a *adj.* burned (out) **2.5**
quemar *v.* to burn (a CD) **2.5**
querer (e:ie) *v.* to want; to love **1.4**
queso *m.* cheese **2.2**
quien(es) *pron.* who; whom; that **2.6**
  ¿quién(es)? who?; whom? **1.1**
  ¿Quién es...? Who is...? **1.1**

¿Quién habla? Who is speaking? (*telephone*) **2.5**
química *f.* chemistry **1.2**
quince fifteen **1.1**
  menos quince quarter to (time) **1.1**
  y quince quarter after (time) **1.1**
quinceañera *f.* young woman's fifteenth birthday celebration/ fifteen-year-old girl **2.3**
quinientos/as *adj.* five hundred **1.2**
quinto/a *adj.* fifth **1.5**
quisiera *v.* I would like **3.5**
quitar el polvo *v.* to dust **2.6**
quitar la mesa *v.* to clear the table **2.6**
quitarse *v.* to take off **2.1**
quizás *adv.* maybe **1.5**

R

racismo *m.* racism **3.6**
radio *f.* radio (*medium*) **1.2**; *m.* radio (set) **1.2**
radiografía *f.* X-ray **2.4**
rápido/a *adv.* quickly **2.4**
ratón *m.* mouse **2.5**
ratos libres *m., pl.* spare (free) time **1.4**
raya *f.* stripe **1.6**
razón *f.* reason **1.3**
rebaja *f.* sale **1.6**
recado *m.* (telephone) message **2.5**
receta *f.* prescription **2.4**
recetar *v.* to prescribe **2.4**
recibir *v.* to receive **1.3**
reciclaje *m.* recycling **3.1**
reciclar *v.* to recycle **3.1**
recién casado/a *m., f.* newly- wed **2.3**
recoger *v.* to pick up **3.1**
recomendar (e:ie) *v.* to recommend **2.2, 2.6**
recordar (o:ue) *v.* to remember **1.4**
recorrer *v.* to tour an area
recurso *m.* resource **3.1**
  recurso natural *m.* natural resource **3.1**
red *f.* network; Web **2.5**
reducir *v.* to reduce **3.1**
refresco *m.* soft drink **2.2**
refrigerador *m.* refrigerator **2.6**
regalar *v.* to give (a gift) **2.3**
regalo *m.* gift **1.6**
regatear *v.* to bargain **1.6**
región *f.* region; area **3.1**
regresar *v.* to return **1.2**
regular *adj. m., f.* so-so.; OK **1.1**
reído *p.p.* laughed **3.2**
reírse (e:i) *v.* to laugh **2.3**
relaciones *f., pl.* relationships
relajarse *v.* to relax **2.3**
reloj *m.* clock; watch **1.2**
renunciar (a) *v.* to resign (from) **3.4**
repetir (e:i) *v.* to repeat **1.4**

reportaje *m.* report **3.6**
reportero/a *m., f.* reporter;
   journalist **3.4**
representante *m., f.* representative **3.6**
reproductor de DVD *m.* DVD
   player **2.5**
reproductor de MP3 *m.* MP3
   player **2.5**
resfriado *m.* cold (*illness*) **2.4**
residencia estudiantil *f.*
   dormitory **1.2**
resolver (o:ue) *v.* to resolve; to
   solve **3.1**
respirar *v.* to breathe **3.1**
respuesta *f.* answer
restaurante *m.* restaurant **1.4**
resuelto/a *p.p.* resolved **3.2**
reunión *f.* meeting **3.4**
revisar *v.* to check **2.5**
   revisar el aceite *v.* to check
     the oil **2.5**
revista *f.* magazine **1.4**
rico/a *adj.* rich **1.6**; *adj.* tasty;
   delicious **2.2**
ridículo/a *adj.* ridiculous **3.1**
río *m.* river **3.1**
riquísimo/a *adj.* extremely
   delicious **2.2**
rodilla *f.* knee **2.4**
rogar (o:ue) *v.* to beg; to
   plead **2.6**
rojo/a *adj.* red **1.6**
romántico/a *adj.* romantic **3.5**
romper *v.* to break **2.4**
   romperse la pierna *v.* to break
     one's leg **2.4**
romper (con) *v.* to break up
   (with) **2.3**
ropa *f.* clothing; clothes **1.6**
   ropa interior *f.* underwear **1.6**
rosado/a *adj.* pink **1.6**
roto/a *adj.* broken **2.4, 3.2**
rubio/a *adj.* blond(e) **1.3**
ruso/a *adj.* Russian **1.3**
rutina *f.* routine **2.1**
   rutina diaria *f.* daily routine **2.1**

S

sábado *m.* Saturday **1.2**
saber *v.* to know; to know
   how **1.6**; to taste **2.2**
   saber a to taste like **2.2**
sabrosísimo/a *adj.* extremely
   delicious **2.2**
sabroso/a *adj.* tasty; delicious **2.2**
sacar *v.* to take out
   sacar fotos to take photos **1.5**
   sacar la basura to take out
     the trash **2.6**
   sacar(se) un diente to have a
     tooth removed **2.4**
sacudir *v.* to dust **2.6**
   sacudir los muebles to dust
     the furniture **2.6**

sal *f.* salt **2.2**
sala *f.* living room **2.6**; room
   sala de emergencia(s) emer-
     gency room **2.4**
salario *m.* salary **3.4**
salchicha *f.* sausage **2.2**
salida *f.* departure; exit **1.5**
salir *v.* to leave **1.4**; to go out
   salir (con) to go out (with);
     to date **2.3**
   salir de to leave from
   salir para to leave for (*a place*)
salmón *m.* salmon **2.2**
salón de belleza *m.* beauty
   salon **3.2**
salud *f.* health **2.4**
saludable *adj.* healthy **2.4**
saludar(se) *v.* to greet (each
   other) **2.5**
saludo *m.* greeting **1.1**
   saludos a... greetings to... **1.1**
sandalia *f.* sandal **1.6**
sandía *f.* watermelon
sándwich *m.* sandwich **2.2**
sano/a *adj.* healthy **2.4**
se *ref. pron.* himself, herself,
   itself, *form.* yourself, themselves,
   yourselves **2.1**
se *impersonal* one **2.4**
   Se nos dañó... The... broke
     down. **2.5**
   Se hizo... He/she/it became...
   Se nos pinchó una llanta.
     We had a flat tire. **2.5**
secadora *f.* clothes dryer **2.6**
secarse *v.* to dry oneself **2.1**
sección de (no) fumar *f.* (non)
   smoking section **2.2**
secretario/a *m., f.* secretary **3.4**
secuencia *f.* sequence
sed *f.* thirst **1.3**
seda *f.* silk **1.6**
sedentario/a *adj.* sedentary;
   related to sitting **3.3**
seguir (e:i) *v.* to follow; to
   continue **1.4**
según according to
segundo/a *adj.* second **1.5**
seguro/a *adj.* sure; safe;
   confident **1.5**
seis six **1.1**
seiscientos/as six
   hundred **1.2**
sello *m.* stamp **3.2**
selva *f.* jungle **3.1**
semana *f.* week **1.2**
   fin *m.* **de semana** weekend **1.4**
   semana *f.* **pasada** last
     week **1.6**
semestre *m.* semester **1.2**
sendero *m.* trail; trailhead **3.1**
sentarse (e:ie) *v.* to sit down **2.1**
sentir(se) (e:ie) *v.* to feel **2.1**; to
   be sorry; to regret **3.1**
señor (Sr.); don *m.* Mr.; sir **1.1**
señora (Sra.); doña *f.* Mrs.;
   ma'am **1.1**

señorita (Srta.) *f.* Miss **1.1**
separado/a *adj.* separated **2.3**
separarse (de) *v.* to separate
   (from) **2.3**
septiembre *m.* September **1.5**
séptimo/a *adj.* seventh **1.5**
ser *v.* to be **1.1**
   ser aficionado/a (a) to be a
     fan (of) **1.4**
   ser alérgico/a (a) to be allergic
     (to) **2.4**
   ser gratis to be free of
     charge **3.2**
serio/a *adj.* serious
servilleta *f.* napkin **2.6**
servir (e:i) *v.* to help **1.5**; to
   serve **2.2**
sesenta sixty **1.2**
setecientos/as seven
   hundred **1.2**
setenta seventy **1.2**
sexismo *m.* sexism **3.6**
sexto/a *adj.* sixth **1.5**
sí *adv.* yes **1.1**
si *conj.* if **1.4**
SIDA *m.* AIDS **3.6**
sido *p.p.* been **3.3**
siempre *adv.* always **2.1**
siete seven **1.1**
silla *f.* seat **1.2**
sillón *m.* armchair **2.6**
similar *adj. m., f.* similar
simpático/a *adj.* nice; likeable **1.3**
sin *prep.* without **1.2, 3.1**
   sin duda without a doubt
   sin embargo however
   sin que *conj.* without **3.1**
sino but (rather) **2.1**
síntoma *m.* symptom **2.4**
sitio *m.* **web;** website **2.5**
situado/a *p.p.* located
sobre *m.* envelope **3.2**; *prep.*
   on; over **1.2**
sobrino/a *m., f.* nephew; niece **1.3**
sociología *f.* sociology **1.2**
sofá *m.* couch; sofa **2.6**
sol *m.* sun **1.4; 1.5; 3.1**
solar *adj. m., f.* solar **3.1**
soldado *m., f.* soldier **3.6**
soleado/a *adj.* sunny
solicitar *v.* to apply (*for a job*) **3.4**
solicitud (de trabajo) *f.* (job)
   application **3.4**
sólo *adv.* only **1.3**
solo/a *adj.* alone
soltero/a *adj.* single **2.3**
solución *f.* solution **3.1**
sombrero *m.* hat **1.6**
Son las dos. It's two o'clock. **1.1**
sonar (o:ue) *v.* to ring **2.5**
sonreído *p.p.* smiled **3.2**
sonreír (e:i) *v.* to smile **2.3**
sopa *f.* soup **2.2**
sorprender *v.* to surprise **2.3**
sorpresa *f.* surprise **2.3**
sótano *m.* basement; cellar **2.6**
soy I am **1.1**

Soy de... I'm from... **1.1**
Soy yo. That's me. **1.1**
su(s) *poss. adj.* his; her; its; *form.* your; their **1.3**
subir(se) a *v.* to get on/into (*a vehicle*) **2.5**
sucio/a *adj.* dirty **1.5**
sucre *m.* Former Ecuadorian currency **1.6**
sudar *v.* to sweat **3.3**
suegro/a *m., f.* father-in-law; mother-in-law **1.3**
sueldo *m.* salary **3.4**
suelo *m.* floor **2.6**
sueño *m.* sleep **1.3**
suerte *f.* luck **1.3**
suéter *m.* sweater **1.6**
sufrir *v.* to suffer **2.4**
  sufrir muchas presiones to be under a lot of pressure **3.3**
  sufrir una enfermedad to suffer an illness **2.4**
sugerir (e:ie) *v.* to suggest **2.6**
supermercado *m.* supermarket **3.2**
suponer *v.* to suppose **1.4**
sur *m.* south **3.2**
sustantivo *m.* noun
suyo(s)/a(s) *poss.* (of) his/her; (of) hers; (of) its; (of) *form.* your, (of) yours, (of) their **2.5**

T

tal vez *adv.* maybe **1.5**
talentoso/a *adj.* talented **3.5**
talla *f.* size **1.6**
  talla grande *f.* large **1.6**
taller *m.* **mecánico** garage; mechanic's repairshop **2.5**
también *adv.* also; too **1.2; 2.1**
tampoco *adv.* neither; not either **2.1**
tan *adv.* so **1.5**
  tan... como as... as **2.2**
  tan pronto como *conj.* as soon as **3.1**
tanque *m.* tank **2.5**
tanto *adv.* so much
  tanto... como as much... as **2.2**
  tantos/as... como as many... as **2.2**
tarde *f.* afternoon; evening; P.M. **1.1;** *adv.* late **2.1**
tarea *f.* homework **1.2**
tarjeta *f.* (post) card
tarjeta de crédito *f.* credit card **1.6**
tarjeta postal *f.* postcard **1.4**
taxi *m.* taxi **1.5**
taza *f.* cup **2.6**
te *sing., fam., d.o. pron.* you **1.5;** *sing., fam., i.o. pron.* to/for you **1.6**
  Te presento a... *fam.* I would like to introduce... to you **1.1**
  ¿Te gustaría? Would you like to? **3.5**

¿Te gusta(n)... ? Do you like... ? **1.2**
té *m.* tea **2.2**
  té helado *m.* iced tea **2.2**
teatro *m.* theater **3.5**
teclado *m.* keyboard **2.5**
técnico/a *m., f.* technician **3.4**
tejido *m.* weaving **3.5**
teleadicto/a *m., f.* couch potato **3.3**
teléfono (celular) *m.* (cell) telephone **2.5**
telenovela *f.* soap opera **3.5**
teletrabajo *m.* telecommuting **3.4**
televisión *f.* television **1.2; 2.5**
televisión por cable *f.* cable television **2.5**
televisor *m.* television set **2.5**
temer *v.* to fear **3.1**
temperatura *f.* temperature **2.4**
temprano *adv.* early **2.1**
tenedor *m.* fork **2.6**
tener *v.* to have **1.3**
  tener... años to be... years old **1.3**
  Tengo... años. I'm... years old. **1.3**
  tener (mucho) calor to be (very) hot **1.3**
  tener (mucho) cuidado to be (very) careful **1.3**
  tener dolor to have a pain **2.4**
  tener éxito to be successful **3.4**
  tener fiebre to have a fever **2.4**
  tener (mucho) frío to be (very) cold **1.3**
  tener ganas de (+ *inf.*) to feel like (*doing something*) **1.3**
  tener (mucha) hambre *f.* to be (very) hungry **1.3**
  tener (mucho) miedo (de) to be (very) afraid (of); to be (very) scared (of) **1.3**
  tener miedo (de) que to be afraid that
  tener planes *m., pl.* to have plans **1.4**
  tener (mucha) prisa to be in a (big) hurry **1.3**
  tener que (+ *inf.*) *v.* to have to (*do something*) **1.3**
  tener razón *f.* to be right **1.3**
  tener (mucha) sed *f.* to be (very) thirsty **1.3**
  tener (mucho) sueño to be (very) sleepy **1.3**
  tener (mucha) suerte to be (very) lucky **1.3**
  tener tiempo to have time **1.4**
  tener una cita to have a date; to have an appointment **2.3**
tenis *m.* tennis **1.4**
tensión *f.* tension **3.3**
tercer, tercero/a *adj.* third **1.5**
terminar *v.* to end; to finish **1.2**
  terminar de (+*inf.*) *v.* to finish (*doing something*) **1.4**
terremoto *m.* earthquake **3.6**

terrible *adj. m., f.* terrible **3.1**
ti *prep., obj. of prep., fam.* you
tiempo *m.* time **1.4;** weather **1.5**
  tiempo libre free time
tienda *f.* shop; store **1.6**
  tienda de campaña tent
tierra *f.* land; soil **3.1**
tinto/a *adj.* red (wine) **2.2**
tío/a *m., f.* uncle; aunt **1.3**
tíos *m., pl.* aunts and uncles **1.3**
título *m.* title
tiza *f.* chalk **1.2**
toalla *f.* towel **2.1**
tobillo *m.* ankle **2.4**
tocadiscos compacto *m.* compact disc player **2.5**
tocar *v.* to touch **3.1;** to play (*a musical instrument*) **3.5**
todavía *adv.* yet; still **1.5**
todo *m.* everything **1.5**
  en todo el mundo throughout the world **3.1**
  Todo está bajo control. Everything is under control. **2.1**
  todo derecho straight (ahead) **3.2**
todo(s)/a(s) *adj.* all **1.4;** whole
todos *m., pl.* all of us; *m., pl.* everybody; everyone
  ¡Todos a bordo! All aboard! **1.1**
todos los días *adv.* every day **2.4**
tomar *v.* to take; to drink **1.2**
  tomar clases *f., pl.* to take classes **1.2**
  tomar el sol to sunbathe **1.4**
  tomar en cuenta to take into account
  tomar fotos *f., pl.* to take photos **1.5**
  tomar la temperatura to take someone's temperature **2.4**
tomate *m.* tomato **2.2**
tonto/a *adj.* silly; foolish **1.3**
torcerse (o:ue) (el tobillo) *v.* to sprain (one's ankle) **2.4**
torcido/a *adj.* twisted; sprained **2.4**
tormenta *f.* storm **3.6**
tornado *m.* tornado **3.6**
tortilla *f.* tortilla **2.2**
  tortilla de maíz corn tortilla **2.2**
tos *f., sing.* cough **2.4**
toser *v.* to cough **2.4**
tostado/a *adj.* toasted **2.2**
tostadora *f.* toaster **2.6**
trabajador(a) *adj.* hard-working **1.3**
trabajar *v.* to work **1.2**
trabajo *m.* job; work **3.4**
traducir *v.* to translate **1.6**
traer *v.* to bring **1.4**
tráfico *m.* traffic **2.5**
tragedia *f.* tragedy **3.5**
traído/a *p.p.* brought **3.2**
traje *m.* suit **1.6**
  traje (de baño) *m.* (bathing) suit **1.6**

tranquilo/a *adj.* calm; quiet **3.3**
  Tranquilo. Don't worry.; Be cool. **2.1**
transmitir *v.* to broadcast **3.6**
tratar de (+ *inf.*) *v.* to try (*to do something*) **3.3**
Trato hecho. You've got a deal. **3.5**
trece thirteen **1.1**
treinta thirty **1.1, 1.2**
  y treinta thirty minutes past the hour (time) **1.1**
tren *m.* train **1.5**
tres three **1.1**
trescientos/as three hundred **1.2**
trimestre *m.* trimester; quarter **1.2**
triste *adj.* sad **1.5**
tú *fam. sub. pron.* you **1.1**
  Tú eres... You are... **1.1**
tu(s) *fam. poss. adj.* your **1.3**
turismo *m.* tourism **1.5**
turista *m., f.* tourist **1.1**
turístico/a *adj.* touristic
tuyo(s)/a(s) *fam. poss. pron.* your; (of) yours **2.5**

U

Ud. *form. sing.* you **1.1**
Uds. *form., pl.* you **1.1**
último/a *adj.* last
un, uno/a *indef. art.* a; one **1.1**
  uno/a *m., f., sing. pron.* one **1.1**
    a la una at one o'clock **1.1**
  una vez once; one time **1.6**
  una vez más one more time **2.3**
único/a *adj.* only **1.3**
universidad *f.* university; college **1.2**
unos/as *m., f., pl. indef. art.* some **1.1**
  unos/as *pron.* some **1.1**
urgente *adj.* urgent **2.6**
usar *v.* to wear; to use **1.6**
usted (Ud.) *form. sing.* you **1.1**
  ustedes (Uds.) *form., pl.* you **1.1**
útil *adj.* useful
uva *f.* grape **2.2**

V

vaca *f.* cow **3.1**
vacaciones *f. pl.* vacation **1.5**
valle *m.* valley **3.1**
vamos let's go **1.4**
vaquero *m.* cowboy **3.5**
  de vaqueros *m., pl.* western (genre) **3.5**
varios/as *adj. m. f., pl.* various; several **2.2**
vaso *m.* glass **2.6**
veces *f., pl.* times **1.6**
vecino/a *m., f.* neighbor **2.6**
veinte twenty **1.1**
veinticinco twenty-five **1.1**
veinticuatro twenty-four **1.1**

veintidós twenty-two **1.1**
veintinueve twenty-nine **1.1**
veintiocho twenty-eight **1.1**
veintiséis twenty-six **1.1**
veintisiete twenty-seven **1.1**
veintitrés twenty-three **1.1**
veintiún, veintiuno/a twenty-one **1.1**
vejez *f.* old age **2.3**
velocidad *f.* speed **2.5**
  velocidad máxima *f.* speed limit **2.5**
vendedor(a) *m., f.* salesperson **1.6**
vender *v.* to sell **1.6**
venir *v.* to come **1.3**
ventana *f.* window **1.2**
ver *v.* to see **1.4**
  a ver *v.* let's see **1.2**
  ver películas *f., pl.* to see movies **1.4**
verano *m.* summer **1.5**
verbo *m.* verb
verdad *f.* truth **1.4**
  ¿verdad? right? **1.1**
verde *adj., m. f.* green **1.6**
verduras *pl., f.* vegetables **2.2**
vestido *m.* dress **1.6**
vestirse (e:i) *v.* to get dressed **2.1**
vez *f.* time **1.6**
viajar *v.* to travel **1.2**
viaje *m.* trip **1.5**
viajero/a *m., f.* traveler **1.5**
vida *f.* life **2.3**
video *m.* video **1.1**
video(casete) *m.* video (cassette) **2.5**
videocasetera *f.* VCR **2.5**
videoconferencia *f.* videoconference **3.4**
videojuego *m.* video game **1.4**
vidrio *m.* glass **3.1**
viejo/a *adj.* old **1.3**
viento *m.* wind **1.5**
viernes *m., sing.* Friday **1.2**
vinagre *m.* vinegar **2.2**
vino *m.* wine **2.2**
  vino blanco *m.* white wine **2.2**
  vino tinto *m.* red wine **2.2**
violencia *f.* violence **3.6**
visitar *v.* to visit **1.4**
  visitar monumentos *m., pl.* to visit monuments **1.4**
visto/a *p.p.* seen **3.2**
vitamina *f.* vitamin **3.3**
viudo/a *adj.* widower/widow **2.3**
vivienda *f.* housing **2.6**
vivir *v.* to live **1.3**
vivo/a *adj.* bright; lively; living
volante *m.* steering wheel **2.5**
volcán *m.* volcano **3.1**
vóleibol *m.* volleyball **1.4**
volver (o:ue) *v.* to return **1.4**
volver a ver(te, lo, la) *v.* to see (you, him, her) again **3.6**
vos *pron.* you
vosotros/as *form., pl.* you **1.1**
votar *v.* to vote **3.6**

vuelta *f.* return trip
vuelto/a *p.p.* returned **3.2**
vuestro(s)/a(s) *poss. adj.* your **1.3**; (of) yours *fam.* **2.5**

W

walkman *m.* walkman

Y

y *conj.* and **1.1**
  y cuarto quarter after (time) **1.1**
  y media half-past (time) **1.1**
  y quince quarter after (time) **1.1**
  y treinta thirty (minutes past the hour) **1.1**
  ¿Y tú? *fam.* And you? **1.1**
  ¿Y usted? *form.* And you? **1.1**
ya *adv.* already **1.6**
yerno *m.* son-in-law **1.3**
yo *sub. pron.* I **1.1**
  Yo soy... I'm... **1.1**
yogur *m.* yogurt **2.2**

Z

zanahoria *f.* carrot **2.2**
zapatería *f.* shoe store **3.2**
zapatos de tenis *m., pl.* tennis shoes, sneakers **1.6**

English-Spanish

A

a **un/a** *m., f., sing.; indef. art.* **1.1**
@ (*symbol*) **arroba** *f.* **2.5**
A.M. **mañana** *f.* **1.1**
able: be able to **poder (o:ue)** *v.* **1.4**
aboard **a bordo** **1.1**
accident **accidente** *m.* **2.4**
accompany **acompañar** *v.* **3.2**
account **cuenta** *f.* **3.2**
  on account of **por** *prep.* **2.5**
accountant **contador(a)** *m., f.* **3.4**
accounting **contabilidad** *f.* **1.2**
ache **dolor** *m.* **2.4**
acid **ácido/a** *adj.* **3.1**
  acid rain **lluvia ácida** **3.1**
acquainted: be acquainted with
  conocer *v.* **1.6**
action (genre) **de acción** *f.* **3.5**
active **activo/a** *adj.* **3.3**
actor **actor** *m.,* **actriz** *f.* **3.4**
addict (*drug*) **drogadicto/a** *adj.* **3.3**
additional **adicional** *adj.*
address **dirección** *f.* **3.2**
adjective **adjetivo** *m.*
adolescence **adolescencia** *f.* **2.3**
adventure (genre) **de aventura** *f.* **3.5**
advertise **anunciar** *v.* **3.6**
advertisement **anuncio** *m.* **3.4**
advice **consejo** *m.* **1.6**
  give advice **dar consejos** **1.6**
advise **aconsejar** *v.* **2.6**
advisor **consejero/a** *m., f.* **3.4**
aerobic **aeróbico/a** *adj.* **3.3**
  aerobics class **clase de
    ejercicios aeróbicos** **3.3**
  to do aerobics **hacer ejercicios
    aeróbicos** **3.3**
affected **afectado/a** *adj.* **3.1**
  be affected (by) **estar** *v.*
    afectado/a (por) **3.1**
affirmative **afirmativo/a** *adj.*
afraid: be (very) afraid (of) **tener
  (mucho) miedo (de)** **1.3**
  be afraid that **tener miedo
    (de) que**
after **después de** *prep.* **2.1;**
  después de que *conj.* **3.1**
afternoon **tarde** *f.* **1.1**
afterward **después** *adv.* **2.1**
again **otra vez**
age **edad** *f.* **2.3**
agree **concordar** *v.*
agree **estar** *v.* **de acuerdo** **3.4**
  I agree (completely). **Estoy
    (completamente) de
    acuerdo.** **3.4**
  I don't agree. **No estoy de
    acuerdo.** **3.4**
agreement **acuerdo** *m.* **3.4**
AIDS **SIDA** *m.* **3.6**
air **aire** *m.* **3.1**
  air pollution **contaminación
    del aire** **3.1**

airplane **avión** *m.* **1.5**
airport **aeropuerto** *m.* **1.5**
alarm clock **despertador** *m.* **2.1**
alcohol **alcohol** *m.* **3.3**
  to consume alcohol **consumir
    alcohol** **3.3**
alcoholic **alcohólico/a** *adj.* **3.3**
all **todo(s)/a(s)** *adj.* **1.4**
  All aboard! **¡Todos a bordo!** **1.1**
  all of us **todos** **1.1**
  all over the world **en todo el
    mundo**
allergic **alérgico/a** *adj.* **2.4**
  be allergic (to) **ser alérgico/a
    (a)** **2.4**
alleviate **aliviar** *v.*
almost **casi** *adv.* **2.4**
alone **solo/a** *adj.*
along **por** *prep.* **2.5**
already **ya** *adv.* **1.6**
also **también** *adv.* **1.2; 2.1**
alternator **alternador** *m.* **2.5**
although **aunque** *conj.*
aluminum **aluminio** *m.* **3.1**
  (made) of aluminum **de
    aluminio** **3.1**
always **siempre** *adv.* **2.1**
American (*North*)
  norteamericano/a *adj.* **1.3**
among **entre** *prep.* **1.2**
amusement **diversión** *f.*
and **y** **1.1, e** (*before words
  beginning with i or hi*) **1.4**
  And you? **¿Y tú?** *fam.* **1.1;**
    ¿Y usted? *form.* **1.1**
angry **enojado/a** *adj.* **1.5**
  get angry (with) **enojarse** *v.*
    (con) **2.1**
animal **animal** *m.* **3.1**
ankle **tobillo** *m.* **2.4**
anniversary **aniversario** *m.* **2.3**
  (wedding) anniversary
    aniversario *m.*
    (de bodas) **2.3**
announce **anunciar** *v.* **3.6**
announcer (*TV/radio*) **locutor(a)**
  m., f. **3.6**
annoy **molestar** *v.* **2.1**
another **otro/a** *adj.* **1.6**
answer **contestar** *v.* **1.2;**
  respuesta *f.*
answering machine **contestadora**
  f. **2.5**
antibiotic **antibiótico** *m.* **2.4**
any **algún, alguno/a(s)** *adj.* **2.1**
anyone **alguien** *pron.* **2.1**
anything **algo** *pron.* **2.1**
apartment **apartamento** *m.* **2.6**
apartment building **edificio de
  apartamentos** **2.6**
appear **parecer** *v.*
appetizers **entremeses** *m., pl.* **2.2**
applaud **aplaudir** *v.* **3.5**
apple **manzana** *f.* **2.2**
appliance (electric) **electrodoméstico** *m.* **2.6**
applicant **aspirante** *m., f.* **3.4**

application **solicitud** *f.* **3.4**
  job application **solicitud de
    trabajo** **3.4**
apply (*for a job*) **solicitar** *v.* **3.4**
  apply for a loan **pedir (e:ie)** *v.*
    un préstamo **3.2**
appointment **cita** *f.* **2.3**
  have an appointment **tener** *v.*
    una cita **2.3**
appreciate **apreciar** *v.* **3.5**
April **abril** *m.* **1.5**
aquatic **acuático/a** *adj.*
archaeologist **arqueólogo/a**
  m., f. **3.4**
architect **arquitecto/a** *m., f.* **3.4**
area **región** *f.* **3.1**
arm **brazo** *m.* **2.4**
armchair **sillón** *m.* **2.6**
army **ejército** *m.* **3.6**
around **por** *prep.* **2.5**
  around here **por aquí** **2.5**
arrange **arreglar** *v.* **2.5**
arrival **llegada** *f.* **1.5**
arrive **llegar** *v.* **1.2**
art **arte** *m.* **1.2**
  (fine) arts **bellas artes** *f., pl.* **3.5**
article *m.* **artículo** **3.6**
artist **artista** *m., f.* **1.3**
artistic **artístico/a** *adj.* **3.5**
arts **artes** *f., pl.* **3.5**
as **como** **2.2**
  as a child **de niño/a** **2.4**
  as... as **tan... como** **2.2**
  as many... as **tantos/as...
    como** **2.2**
  as much... as **tanto...
    como** **2.2**
  as soon as **en cuanto** *conj.* **3.1;**
    tan pronto como *conj.* **3.1**
ask (*a question*) **preguntar** *v.* **1.2**
  ask for **pedir (e:i)** *v.* **1.4**
asparagus **espárragos** *m., pl.* **2.2**
aspirin **aspirina** *f.* **2.4**
at **a** *prep.* **1; en** *prep.* **1.2**
  at + *time* **a la(s) +** *time* **1.1**
  at home **en casa** **2.1**
  at least **por lo menos** **2.4**
  at night **por la noche** **2.1**
  at the end (of) **al fondo (de)** **2.6**
  At what time...? **¿A qué
    hora...?** **1.1**
  At your service. **A sus
    órdenes.** **2.5**
ATM **cajero automático** *m.* **3.2**
attend **asistir (a)** *v.* **1.3**
attic **altillo** *m.* **2.6**
attract **atraer** *v.* **1.4**
audience **público** *m.* **3.5**
August **agosto** *m.* **1.5**
aunt **tía** *f.* **1.3**
  aunts and uncles **tíos** *m., pl.* **1.3**
automobile **automóvil** *m.* **1.5;**
  carro *m.;* **coche** *m.* **2.5**
autumn **otoño** *m.* **1.5**
avenue **avenida** *f.*
avoid **evitar** *v.* **3.1**
award **premio** *m.* **3.5**

B

backpack **mochila** *f.* 1.2
bad **mal, malo/a** *adj.* 1.2
  It's bad that... **Es malo que...** 2.6
  It's not at all bad. **No está nada mal.** 1.5
bag **bolsa** *f.* 1.6
bakery **panadería** *f.* 3.2
balanced **equilibrado/a** *adj.* 3.3
  to eat a balanced diet **comer una dieta equilibrada** 3.3
balcony **balcón** *m.* 2.6
ball **pelota** *f.* 1.4
banana **banana** *f.* 2.2
band **banda** *f.* 3.5
bank **banco** *m.* 3.2
bargain **ganga** *f.* 1.6; **regatear** *v.* 1.6
baseball (*game*) **béisbol** *m.* 1.4
basement **sótano** *m.* 2.6
basketball (*game*) **baloncesto** *m.* 1.4
bathe **bañarse** *v.* 2.1
bathing suit **traje** *m.* **de baño** 1.6
bathroom **baño** *m.* 2.1; **cuarto de baño** *m.* 2.1
be **ser** *v.* 1.1; **estar** *v.* 1.2
  be... years old **tener... años** 1.3
beach **playa** *f.* 1.5
beans **frijoles** *m., pl.* 2.2
beautiful **hermoso/a** *adj.* 1.6
beauty **belleza** *f.* 3.2
  beauty salon **peluquería** *f.* 3.2; **salón** *m.* **de belleza** 3.2
because **porque** *conj.* 1.2
  because of **por** *prep.* 2.5
become (+ *adj.*) **ponerse (+ adj.)** 2.1; **convertirse** *v.*
bed **cama** *f.* 1.5
  go to bed **acostarse (o:ue)** *v.* 2.1
bedroom **alcoba** *f.;* **dormitorio** *m.* 2.6; **recámara** *f.*
beef **carne de res** *f.* 2.2
  beef soup **caldo de patas** 2.2
been **sido** *p.p.* 3.3
beer **cerveza** *f.* 2.2
before **antes** *adv.* 2.1; **antes de** *prep.* 2.1; **antes (de) que** *conj.* 3.1
beg **rogar (o:ue)** *v.* 2.6
begin **comenzar (e:ie)** *v.* 1.4; **empezar (e:ie)** *v.* 1.4
behalf: on behalf of **de parte de** 2.5
behind **detrás de** *prep.* 1.2
believe (in) **creer** *v.* **(en)** 1.3; **creer** *v.* 3.1
  not to believe **no creer** 3.1
believed **creído/a** *p.p.* 3.2
bellhop **botones** *m., f. sing.* 1.5
below **debajo de** *prep.* 1.2
belt **cinturón** *m.* 1.6
benefit **beneficio** *m.* 3.4
beside **al lado de** *prep.* 1.2
besides **además (de)** *adv.* 2.4

best **mejor** *adj.*
  the best **el/la mejor** *m., f.* 2.2; **lo mejor** *neuter* 3.6
better **mejor** *adj.* 2.2
  It's better that... **Es mejor que...** 2.6
between **entre** *prep.* 1.2
beverage **bebida** *f.*
  alcoholic beverage **bebida alcohólica** *f.* 3.3
bicycle **bicicleta** *f.* 1.4
big **gran, grande** *adj.* 1.3
bill **cuenta** *f.* 2.3
billion **mil millones**
biology **biología** *f.* 1.2
bird **ave** *f.* 3.1; **pájaro** *m.* 3.1
birth **nacimiento** *m.* 2.3
birthday **cumpleaños** *m., sing.* 2.3
  have a birthday **cumplir** *v.* **años** 2.3
black **negro/a** *adj.* 1.6
blackberry **mora** *f.* 2.2
blackboard **pizarra** *f.* 1.2
blanket **manta** *f.* 2.6
block (city) **cuadra** *f.* 3.2
blond(e) **rubio/a** *adj.* 1.3
blouse **blusa** *f.* 1.6
blue **azul** *adj. m., f.* 1.6
boarding house **pensión** *f.*
boat **barco** *m.* 1.5
body **cuerpo** *m.* 2.4
bone **hueso** *m.* 2.4
book **libro** *m.* 1.2
bookcase **estante** *m.* 2.6
bookshelves **estante** *m.* 2.6
bookstore **librería** *f.* 1.2
boot **bota** *f.* 1.6
bore **aburrir** *v.* 2.1
bored **aburrido/a** *adj.* 1.5
  be bored **estar** *v.* **aburrido/a** 1.5
  get bored **aburrirse** *v.* 3.5
boring **aburrido/a** *adj.* 1.5
born: be born **nacer** *v.* 2.3
borrow **pedir (e:ie)** *v.* **prestado** 3.2
borrowed **prestado/a** *adj.*
boss **jefe** *m.,* **jefa** *f.* 3.4
bother **molestar** *v.* 2.1
bottle **botella** *f.* 2.3
  bottle of wine **botella de vino** 2.3
bottom **fondo** *m.*
boulevard **bulevar** *m.*
boy **chico** *m.* 1; **muchacho** *m.* 1.3
boyfriend **novio** *m.* 1.3
brakes **frenos** *m., pl.*
bread **pan** *m.* 2.2
break **romper** *v.* 2.4
  break (one's leg) **romperse (la pierna)** 2.4
  break down **dañar** *v.* 2.4
  The... broke down. **Se nos dañó el/la...** 2.5
  break up (with) **romper** *v.* **(con)** 2.3
breakfast **desayuno** *m.* 1.2, 2.2
  have breakfast **desayunar** *v.* 1.2

breathe **respirar** *v.* 3.1
bring **traer** *v.* 1.4
broadcast **transmitir** *v.* 3.6; **emitir** *v.* 3.6
brochure **folleto** *m.*
broken **roto/a** *adj.* 2.4, 3.2
  be broken **estar roto/a** 2.4
brother **hermano** *m.* 1.3
  brother-in-law **cuñado** *m., f.* 1.3
  brothers and sisters **hermanos** *m., pl.* 1.3
brought **traído/a** *p.p.* 3.2
brown **café** *adj.* 1.6; **marrón** *adj.* 1.6
brunet(te) **moreno/a** *adj.* 1.3
brush **cepillar** *v.* 2.1
  brush one's hair **cepillarse el pelo** 2.1
  brush one's teeth **cepillarse los dientes** 2.1
build **construir** *v.* 1.4
building **edificio** *m.* 2.6
bump into (*something accidentally*) **darse con** 2.4; (*someone*) **encontrarse** *v.* 2.5
burn (a CD) **quemar** *v.* 2.5
burned (out) **quemado/a** *adj.* 2.5
bus **autobús** *m.* 1.1
  bus station **estación** *f.* **de autobuses** 1.5
business **negocios** *m. pl.* 3.4
  business administration **administración** *f.* **de empresas** 1.2
  business-related **comercial** *adj.* 3.4
businessperson **hombre** *m.* **/ mujer** *f.* **de negocios** 3.4
busy **ocupado/a** *adj.* 1.5
but **pero** *conj.* 1.2; (rather) **sino** *conj.* (*in negative sentences*) 2.1
butcher shop **carnicería** *f.* 3.2
butter **mantequilla** *f.* 2.2
buy **comprar** *v.* 1.2
by **por** *prep.* 2.5; **para** *prep.* 2.5
  by means of **por** *prep.* 2.5
  by phone **por teléfono** 2.5
  by plane **en avión** 1.5
  by way of **por** *prep.* 2.5
bye **chau** *interj. fam.* 1.1

C

cabin **cabaña** *f.* 1.5
cable television **televisión** *f.* **por cable** *m.* 2.5
café **café** *m.* 1.4
cafeteria **cafetería** *f.* 1.2
caffeine **cafeína** *f.* 3.3
cake **pastel** *m.* 2.3
  chocolate cake **pastel de chocolate** *m.* 2.3
calculator **calculadora** *f.* 2.5
call **llamar** *v.* 2.5
  be called **llamarse** *v.* 2.1 call on the phone **llamar por teléfono**

calm **tranquilo/a** *adj.* 3.3
calorie **caloría** *f.* 3.3
camera **cámara** *f.* 2.5
camp **acampar** *v.* 1.5
can *(tin)* **lata** *f.* 3.1
can **poder (o:ue)** *v.* 1.4
Canadian **canadiense** *adj.* 1.3
candidate **aspirante** *m., f.* 3.4;
  candidate **candidato/a** *m., f.* 3.6
candy **dulces** *m., pl.* 2.3
capital city **capital** *f.* 1.1
car **coche** *m.* 2.5; **carro** *m.* 2.5;
  auto(móvil) *m.* 1.5
caramel **caramelo** *m.* 2.3
card **tarjeta** *f.;* *(playing)*
  carta *f.* 1.5
care **cuidado** *m.* 1.3
  Take care! **¡Cuídense!** *v.* 3.3
  take care of **cuidar** *v.* 3.2
career **carrera** *f.* 3.4
careful: be (very) careful **tener** *v.*
  (mucho) cuidado 1.3
caretaker **ama** *m., f.* **de casa** 2.6
carpenter **carpintero/a** *m., f.* 3.4
carpet **alfombra** *f.* 2.6
carrot **zanahoria** *f.* 2.2
carry **llevar** *v.* 1.2
cartoons **dibujos** *m, pl.*
  animados 3.5
case: in case (that) **en caso (de)**
  que 3.1
cash (a check) **cobrar** *v.* 3.2;
  cash **(en) efectivo** 1.6
  cash register **caja** *f.* 1.6
  pay in cash **pagar** *v.* **al contado**
  3.2; **pagar en efectivo** 3.2
cashier **cajero/a** *m., f.*
cat **gato** *m.* 3.1
CD-ROM **cederrón** *m.* 2.5
celebrate **celebrar** *v.* 2.3
celebration **celebración** *f.*
  young woman's fifteenth
  birthday celebration
  quinceañera *f.* 2.3
cellar **sótano** *m.* 2.6
cellular **celular** *adj.* 2.5
  cellular telephone **teléfono**
  celular *m.* 2.5
cereal **cereales** *m., pl.* 2.2
certain **cierto** *m.;* **seguro** *m.* 3.1
  it's (not) certain **(no) es**
  cierto/seguro 3.1
chalk **tiza** *f.* 1.2
champagne **champán** *m.* 2.3
change **cambiar** *v.* **(de)** 2.3
channel *(TV)* **canal** *m.* 2.5; 3.5
character *(fictional)* **personaje**
  m. 2.5, 3.5
  (main) character *m.* **personaje**
  (principal) 3.5
chat **conversar** *v.* 1.2
chauffeur **conductor(a)** *m., f.* 1.1
cheap **barato/a** *adj.* 1.6
check **comprobar (o:ue)** *v.;*
  revisar *v.* 2.5; *(bank)* **cheque**
  m. 3.2
  check the oil **revisar el aceite** 2.5

checking account **cuenta** *f.*
  corriente 3.2
cheese **queso** *m.* 2.2
chef **cocinero/a** *m., f.* 3.4
chemistry **química** *f.* 1.2
chest of drawers **cómoda** *f.* 2.6
chicken **pollo** *m.* 2.2
child **niño/a** *m., f.* 1.3
childhood **niñez** *f.* 2.3
children **hijos** *m., pl.* 1.3
Chinese **chino/a** *adj.* 1.3
chocolate **chocolate** *m.* 2.3
  chocolate cake **pastel** *m.* **de**
  chocolate 2.3
cholesterol **colesterol** *m.* 3.3
choose **escoger** *v.* 2.2
chop *(food)* **chuleta** *f.* 2.2
Christmas **Navidad** *f.* 2.3
church **iglesia** *f.* 1.4
citizen **ciudadano/a** *adj.* 3.6
city **ciudad** *f.* 1.4
class **clase** *f.* 1.2
  take classes **tomar clases** 1.2
classical **clásico/a** *adj.* 3.5
classmate **compañero/a** *m., f.* **de**
  clase 1.2
clean **limpio/a** *adj.* 1.5;
  limpiar *v.* 2.6
  clean the house *v.* **limpiar la**
  casa 2.6
clear *(weather)* **despejado/a** *adj.*
  clear the table **quitar la**
  mesa 2.6
  It's (very) clear. *(weather)*
  Está (muy) despejado.
clerk **dependiente/a** *m., f.* 1.6
climb **escalar** *v.* 1.4
  climb mountains **escalar**
  montañas 1.4
clinic **clínica** *f.* 2.4
clock **reloj** *m.* 1.2
close **cerrar (e:ie)** *v.* 1.4
closed **cerrado/a** *adj.* 1.5
closet **armario** *m.* 2.6
clothes **ropa** *f.* 1.6
  clothes dryer **secadora** *f.* 2.6
clothing **ropa** *f.* 1.6
cloud **nube** *f.* 3.1
cloudy **nublado/a** *adj.* 1.5
  It's (very) cloudy. **Está (muy)**
  nublado. 1.5
coat **abrigo** *m.* 1.6
coffee **café** *m.* 2.2
  coffee maker **cafetera** *f.* 2.6
cold **frío** *m.* 1.5;
  (illness) **resfriado** *m.* 2.4
  be *(feel)* (very) cold **tener**
  (mucho) frío 1.3
  It's (very) cold. *(weather)* **Hace**
  (mucho) frío. 1.5
college **universidad** *f.* 1.2
collision **choque** *m.* 3.6
color **color** *m.* 1.6
comb one's hair **peinarse** *v.* 2.1
come **venir** *v.* 1.3
comedy **comedia** *f.* 3.5
comfortable **cómodo/a** *adj.* 1.5

commerce **negocios** *m., pl.* 3.4
commercial **comercial** *adj.* 3.4
communicate (with) **comunicarse**
  v. **(con)** 3.6
communication **comunicación**
  f. 3.6
  means of communication
  medios *m. pl.* **de**
  comunicación 3.6
community **comunidad** *f.* 1.1
compact disc (CD) **disco** *m.*
  compacto 2.5
  compact disc player **tocadiscos**
  m. sing. **compacto** 2.5
company **compañía** *f.* 3.4;
  empresa *f.* 3.4
comparison **comparación** *f.*
completely **completamente**
  adv. 3.4
composer **compositor(a)** *m., f.* 3.5
computer **computadora** *f.* 1.1
  computer disc **disco** *m.*
  computer monitor **monitor**
  m. 2.5
  computer programmer
  programador(a) *m., f.* 1.3
  computer science **computación**
  f. 1.2
concert **concierto** *m.* 3.5
conductor *(musical)* **director(a)**
  m., f. 3.5
confident **seguro/a** *adj.* 1.5
confirm **confirmar** *v.* 1.5
  confirm a reservation **confirmar**
  una reservación 1.5
confused **confundido/a** *adj.* 1.5
congested **congestionado/a**
  adj. 2.4
Congratulations! *(for an event such*
  as a birthday or anniversary)
  ¡Felicidades! 2.3; *(for an*
  event such as an engagement
  or a good grade on a test)
  f., pl. **¡Felicitaciones!** 2.3
conservation **conservación** *f.* 3.1
conserve **conservar** *v.* 3.1
considering **para** *prep.* 2.3
consume **consumir** *v.* 3.3
container **envase** *m.* 3.1
contamination **contaminación** *f.*
content **contento/a** *adj.* 1.5
contest **concurso** *m.* 3.5
continue **seguir (e:i)** *v.* 1.4
control **control** *m.;* **controlar** *v.* 3.1
  be under control **estar bajo**
  control 2.1
conversation **conversación** *f.* 1.1
converse **conversar** *v.* 1.2
cook **cocinar** *v.* 2.6; **cocinero/a**
  m., f. 3.4
cookie **galleta** *f.* 2.3
cool **fresco/a** *adj.* 1.5
  Be cool. **Tranquilo.** 2.1
  It's cool. *(weather)* **Hace**
  fresco. 1.5
corn **maíz** *m.* 2.2
corner **esquina** *f.* 3.2

cost **costar (o:ue)** *v.* 1.6
cotton **algodón** *f.* 1.6
  (made of) cotton **de algodón** 1.6
couch **sofá** *m.* 2.6
couch potato **teleadicto/a** *m., f.* 3.3
cough **tos** *f.* 2.4; **toser** *v.* 2.4
counselor **consejero/a** *m., f.* 3.4
count (on) **contar (o:ue)** *v.* **(con)** 1.4, 2.6
country (*nation*) **país** *m.* 1.1
countryside **campo** *m.* 1.5
(married) couple **pareja** *f.* 2.3
course **curso** *m.* 1.2; **materia** *f.* 1.2
courtesy **cortesía** *f.*
cousin **primo/a** *m., f.* 1.3
cover **cubrir** *v.*
covered **cubierto/a** *p.p.*
cow **vaca** *f.* 3.1
crafts **artesanía** *f.* 3.5
craftsmanship **artesanía** *f.* 3.5
crater **cráter** *m.* 3.1
crazy **loco/a** *adj.* 1.6
create **crear** *v.*
credit **crédito** *m.* 1.6
  credit card **tarjeta** *f.* **de crédito** 1.6
crime **crimen** *m.* 3.6
cross **cruzar** *v.* 3.2
culture **cultura** *f.* 3.5
cup **taza** *f.* 2.6
currency exchange **cambio** *m.* **de moneda**
current events **actualidades** *f., pl.* 3.6
curtains **cortinas** *f., pl.* 2.6
custard (*baked*) **flan** *m.* 2.3
custom **costumbre** *f.* 1.1
customer **cliente/a** *m., f.* 1.6
customs **aduana** *f.* 1.5
  customs inspector **inspector(a)** *m., f.* **de aduanas** 1.5
cybercafé **cibercafé** *m.* 2.5
cycling **ciclismo** *m.* 1.4

D

dad **papá** *m.* 1.3
daily **diario/a** *adj.* 2.1
  daily routine **rutina** *f.* **diaria** 2.1
damage **dañar** *v.* 2.4
dance **bailar** *v.* 1.2; **danza** *f.* 3.5; **baile** *m.* 3.5
dancer **bailarín/bailarina** *m., f.* 3.5
danger **peligro** *m.* 3.1
dangerous **peligroso/a** *adj.* 3.6
date (*appointment*) **cita** *f.* 2.3; (*calendar*) **fecha** *f.* 1.5; (*someone*) **salir** *v.* **con (alguien)** 2.3
  have a date **tener una cita** 2.3
daughter **hija** *f.* 1.3
daughter-in-law **nuera** *f.* 1.3
day **día** *m.* 1.1

day before yesterday **anteayer** *adv.* 1.6
deal **trato** *m.* 3.5
  It's not a big deal. **No es para tanto.** 2.6
  You've got a deal! **¡Trato hecho!** 3.5
death **muerte** *f.* 2.3
decaffeinated **descafeinado/a** *adj.* 3.3
December **diciembre** *m.* 1.5
decide **decidir** *v.* **(+ inf.)** 1.3
decided **decidido/a** *adj. p.p.* 3.2
declare **declarar** *v.* 3.6
deforestation **deforestación** *f.* 3.1
delicious **delicioso/a** *adj.* 2.2; **rico/a** *adj.* 2.2; **sabroso/a** *adj.* 2.2
delighted **encantado/a** *adj.* 1.1
dentist **dentista** *m., f.* 2.4
deny **negar (e:ie)** *v.* 3.1
  not to deny **no dudar** 3.1
department store **almacén** *m.* 1.6
departure **salida** *f.* 1.5
deposit **depositar** *v.* 3.2
describe **describir** *v.* 1.3
described **descrito/a** *p.p.* 3.2
desert **desierto** *m.* 3.1
design **diseño** *m.*
designer **diseñador(a)** *m., f.* 3.4
desire **desear** *v.* 1.2
desk **escritorio** *m.* 1.2
dessert **postre** *m.* 2.3
destroy **destruir** *v.* 3.1
develop **desarrollar** *v.* 3.1
diary **diario** *m.* 1.1
dictatorship **dictadura** *f.* 3.6
dictionary **diccionario** *m.* 1.1
die **morir (o:ue)** *v.* 2.2
died **muerto/a** *p.p.* 3.2
diet **dieta** *f.* 3.3; **alimentación**
  balanced diet **dieta equilibrada** 3.3
  be on a diet **estar a dieta** 3.3
difficult **difícil** *adj. m., f.* 1.3
digital camera **cámara** *f.* **digital** 2.5
dining room **comedor** *m.* 2.6
dinner **cena** *f.* 1.2, 2.2
  have dinner **cenar** *v.* 1.2
direct **dirigir** *v.* 3.5
directions **direcciones** *f., pl.* 3.2
  give directions **dar direcciones** 3.2
director **director(a)** *m., f.* 3.5
dirty **ensuciar** *v.*; **sucio/a** *adj.* 1.5
  get (something) dirty **ensuciar** *v.* 2.6
disagree **no estar de acuerdo**
disaster **desastre** *m.* 3.6
discover **descubrir** *v.* 3.1
discovered **descubierto/a** *p.p.* 3.2
discrimination **discriminación** *f.* 3.6
dish **plato** *m.* 2.2, 2.6
  main dish *m.* **plato principal** 2.2

dishwasher **lavaplatos** *m., sing.* 2.6
disk **disco** *m.*
disorderly **desordenado/a** *adj.* 1.5
dive **bucear** *v.* 1.4
divorce **divorcio** *m.* 2.3
divorced **divorciado/a** *adj.* 2.3
  get divorced (from) **divorciarse** *v.* **(de)** 2.3
dizzy **mareado/a** *adj.* 2.4
do **hacer** *v.* 1.4
  do aerobics **hacer ejercicios aeróbicos** 3.3
  do household chores **hacer quehaceres domésticos** 2.6
  do stretching exercises **hacer ejercicios de estiramiento** 3.3
  (I) don't want to. **No quiero.** 1.4
doctor **doctor(a)** *m., f.* 1.3; 2.4; **médico/a** *m., f.* 1.3
documentary (*film*) **documental** *m.* 3.5
dog **perro** *m.* 3.1
domestic **doméstico/a** *adj.*
  domestic appliance **electrodoméstico** *m.*
done **hecho/a** *p.p.* 3.2
door **puerta** *f.* 1.2
dormitory **residencia** *f.* **estudiantil** 1.2
double **doble** *adj.* 1.5
  double room **habitación** *f.* **doble** 1.5
doubt **duda** *f.* 3.1; **dudar** *v.* 3.1
  not to doubt 3.1
  There is no doubt that... **No cabe duda de** 3.1; **No hay duda de** 3.1
Down with... ! **¡Abajo el/la...!**
download **descargar** *v.* 2.5
downtown **centro** *m.* 1.4
drama **drama** *m.* 3.5
dramatic **dramático/a** *adj.* 3.5
draw **dibujar** *v.* 1.2
drawing **dibujo** *m.* 3.5
dress **vestido** *m.* 1.6
  get dressed **vestirse (e:i)** *v.* 2.1
drink **beber** *v.* 1.3; **bebida** *f.* 2.2; **tomar** *v.* 1.2
drive **conducir** *v.* 1.6; **manejar** *v.* 2.5
driver **conductor(a)** *m., f.* 1.1
drug **droga** *f.* 3.3
  drug addict **drogadicto/a** *adj.* 3.3
dry oneself **secarse** *v.* 2.1
during **durante** *prep.* 2.1; **por** *prep.* 2.5
dust **sacudir** *v.* 2.6; **quitar** *v.* **el polvo** 2.6
  dust the furniture **sacudir los muebles** 2.6
DVD player **reproductor** *m.* **de DVD** 2.5

E

each **cada** *adj.* 1.6
eagle **águila** *f.*
ear (outer) **oreja** *f.* 2.4
early **temprano** *adv.* 2.1
earn **ganar** *v.* 3.4
earthquake **terremoto** *m.* 3.6
ease **aliviar** *v.*
east **este** *m.* 3.2
   to the east **al este** 3.2
easy **fácil** *adj. m., f.* 1.3
eat **comer** *v.* 1.3
ecology **ecología** *f.* 3.1
economics **economía** *f.* 1.2
ecotourism **ecoturismo** *m.* 3.1
Ecuador **Ecuador** *m.* 1.1
Ecuadorian **ecuatoriano/a** *adj.* 1.3
effective **eficaz** *adj. m., f.*
egg **huevo** *m.* 2.2
eight **ocho** 1.1
eight hundred **ochocientos/as** 1.2
eighteen **dieciocho** 1.1
eighth **octavo/a** 1.5
eighty **ochenta** 1.2
either... or **o... o** *conj.* 2.1
eldest **el/la mayor** 2.2
elect **elegir** *v.* 3.6
election **elecciones** *f. pl.* 3.6
electric appliance
   electrodoméstico *m.* 2.6
electrician **electricista** *m., f.* 3.4
electricity **luz** *f.* 2.6
elegant **elegante** *adj. m., f.* 1.6
elevator **ascensor** *m.* 1.5
eleven **once** 1.1
e-mail **correo** *m.* **electrónico** 1.4
e-mail address **dirrección** *f.*
   electrónica 2.5
   e-mail message **mensaje** *m.*
      electrónico 1.4
   read e-mail **leer** *v.* **el correo**
      electrónico 1.4
embarrassed **avergonzado/a**
   adj. 1.5
embrace (each other) **abrazar(se)**
   v. 2.5
emergency **emergencia** *f.* 2.4
   emergency room **sala** *f.* **de**
      emergencia 2.4
employee **empleado/a** *m., f.* 1.5
employment **empleo** *m.* 3.4
end **fin** *m.* 1.4; **terminar** *v.* 1.2
   end table **mesita** *f.* 2.6
energy **energía** *f.* 3.1
engaged: get engaged (to) **comprometerse** *v.* **(con)** 2.3
engineer **ingeniero/a** *m., f.* 1.3
English (*language*) **inglés** *m.* 1.2;
   inglés, inglesa *adj.* 1.3
enjoy **disfrutar** *v.* **(de)** 3.3
enough **bastante** *adv.* 2.4
entertainment **diversión** *f.* 1.4
entrance **entrada** *f.* 2.6
envelope **sobre** *m.* 3.2
environment **medio ambiente**
   m. 3.1

equality **igualdad** *f.* 3.6
equipped **equipado/a** *adj.* 3.3
erase **borrar** *v.* 2.5
eraser **borrador** *m.* 1.2
errand **diligencia** *f.* 3.2
establish **establecer** *v.*
evening **tarde** *f.* 1.1
event **acontecimiento** *m.* 3.6
every day **todos los días** 2.4
everybody **todos** *m., pl.*
everything **todo** *m.* 1.5
   Everything is under control.
      Todo está bajo control. 2.1
exactly **en punto** 1.1
exam **examen** *m.* 1.2
excellent **excelente** *adj.* 1.5
excess **exceso** *m.* 3.3
   in excess **en exceso** 3.3
exchange **intercambiar** *v.*
   in exchange for **por** 2.5
exciting **emocionante** *adj. m., f.*
excursion **excursión** *f.*
excuse **disculpar** *v.*
Excuse me. (*May I?*) **Con
   permiso.** 1.1; (*I beg your pardon.*) **Perdón.** 1.1
exercise **ejercicio** *m.* 3.3
   hacer *v.* **ejercicio** 3.3
exit **salida** *f.* 1.5
expensive **caro/a** *adj.* 1.6
experience **experiencia** *f.* 3.6
explain **explicar** *v.* 1.2
explore **explorar** *v.*
expression **expresión** *f.*
extinction **extinción** *f.* 3.1
extremely delicious **riquísimo/a**
   adj. 2.2
extremely serious **gravísimo**
   adj. 3.1
eye **ojo** *m.* 2.4

F

fabulous **fabuloso/a** *adj.* 1.5
face **cara** *f.* 2.1
facing **enfrente de** *prep.* 3.2
fact: in fact **de hecho**
fall (down) **caerse** *v.* 2.4
   fall asleep **dormirse (o:ue)**
      v. 2.1
   fall in love (with) **enamorarse**
      v. **(de)** 2.3
fall (season) **otoño** *m.* 1.5
fallen **caído/a** *p.p.* 3.2
family **familia** *f.* 1.3
famous **famoso/a** *adj.* 3.4
fan **aficionado/a** *adj.* 1.4
   be a fan (of) **ser aficionado/a
      (a)** 1.4
far from **lejos de** *prep.* 1.2
farewell **despedida** *f.*
fascinate **fascinar** *v.* 2.1
fashion **moda** *f.* 1.6
   be in fashion **estar de
      moda** 1.6
fast **rápido/a** *adj.*

fat **gordo/a** *adj.* 1.3; **grasa** *f.* 3.3
father **padre** *m.* 1.3
father-in-law **suegro** *m.* 1.3
favorite **favorito/a** *adj.* 1.4
fax (machine) **fax** *m.* 2.5
fear **miedo** *m.* 1.3; **temer** *v.* 3.1
February **febrero** *m.* 1.5
feel **sentir(se) (e:ie)** *v.* 2.1
   feel like (*doing something*) **tener
      ganas de (+ *inf.*)** 1.3
festival **festival** *m.* 3.5
fever **fiebre** *f.* 2.4
   have a fever **tener** *v.* **fiebre** 2.4
few **pocos/as** *adj. pl.*
   fewer than **menos de
      (+ *number*)** 2.2
field: major field of study **especialización** *f.*
fifteen **quince** 1.1
   fifteen-year-old girl **quinceañera** *f.*
   young woman's fifteenth birthday
      celebration **quinceañera** *f.* 2.3
fifth **quinto/a** 1.5
fifty **cincuenta** 1.2
fight (for/against) **luchar** *v.* **(por/
   contra)** 3.6
figure (*number*) **cifra** *f.*
file **archivo** *m.* 2.5
fill **llenar** *v.* 2.5
   fill out (a form) **llenar (un
      formulario)** 3.2
   fill the tank **llenar el
      tanque** 2.5
finally **finalmente** *adv.* 3.3; **por
   último** 2.1; **por fin** 2.5
find **encontrar (o:ue)** *v.* 1.4
   find (each other) **encontrar(se)**
fine **multa** *f.*
   That's fine. **Está bien.** 2.5
(fine) arts **bellas artes** *f., pl.* 3.5
finger **dedo** *m.* 2.4
finish **terminar** *v.* 1.2
   finish (*doing something*)
      terminar *v.* **de (+ *inf.*)** 1.4
fire **incendio** *m.* 3.6; **despedir
   (e:i)** *v.* 3.4
firefighter **bombero/a** *m., f.* 3.4
firm **compañía** *f.* 3.4; **empresa**
   f. 3.4
first **primer, primero/a** 1.5
fish (*food*) **pescado** *m.* 2.2;
   pescar *v.* 1.5; (*live*) **pez** *m.* 3.1
   fish market **pescadería** *f.* 3.2
fisherman **pescador** *m.*
fisherwoman **pescadora** *f.*
fishing **pesca** *f.*
fit (*clothing*) **quedar** *v.* 2.1
five **cinco** 1.1
five hundred **quinientos/as** 1.2
fix (*put in working order*) **arreglar**
   v. 2.5
fixed **fijo/a** *adj.* 1.6
flag **bandera** *f.*
flank steak **lomo** *m.* 2.2
flat tire: We had a flat tire. **Se nos
   pinchó una llanta.** 2.5
flexible **flexible** *adj.* 3.3

flood **inundación** f. 3.6
floor (of a building) **piso** m. 1.5;
 suelo m. 2.6
 ground floor **planta baja** f. 1.5
 top floor **planta** f. **alta**
flower **flor** f. 3.1
flu **gripe** f. 2.4
fog **niebla** f.
folk **folklórico/a** adj. 3.5
follow **seguir (e:i)** v. 1.4
food **comida** f. 2.2; **alimento**
foolish **tonto/a** adj. 1.3
foot **pie** m. 2.4
football **fútbol** m. **americano** 1.4
for **para** prep. 2.5; **por** prep. 2.5
 for example **por ejemplo** 2.5
 for me **para mí** 2.2
forbid **prohibir** v.
foreign **extranjero/a** adj. 3.5
 foreign languages **lenguas**
 f., pl. **extranjeras** 1.2
forest **bosque** m. 3.1
forget **olvidar** v. 2.4
fork **tenedor** m. 2.6
form **formulario** m. 3.2
forty **cuarenta** m. 1.2
four **cuatro** 1.1
four hundred **cuatrocientos/**
 as 1.2
fourteen **catorce** 1.1
fourth **cuarto/a** m., f. 1.5
free **libre** adj. m., f. 1.4
 be free (of charge) **ser**
 gratis 3.2
 free time **tiempo libre**; spare
 (free) time **ratos libres** 1.4
freedom **libertad** f. 3.6
freezer **congelador** m. 2.6
French **francés, francesa** adj. 1.3
 French fries **papas** f., pl.
 fritas 2.2; **patatas** f., pl.
 fritas 2.2
frequently **frecuentemente**
 adv. 2.4; **con frecuencia**
 adv. 2.4
Friday **viernes** m., sing. 1.2
fried **frito/a** adj. 2.2
 fried potatoes **papas** f., pl.
 fritas 2.2; **patatas** f., pl.
 fritas 2.2
friend **amigo/a** m., f. 1.3
friendly **amable** adj. m., f. 1.5
friendship **amistad** f. 2.3
from **de** prep. 1.1; **desde** prep. 1.6
 from the United States
 estadounidense m., f.
 adj. 1.3
 from time to time **de vez en**
 cuando 2.4
 He/She/It is from... **Es de...;**
 I'm from... **Soy de...** 1.1
fruit **fruta** f. 2.2
 fruit juice **jugo** m. **de fruta** 2.2
 fruit store **frutería** f. 3.2
full **lleno/a** adj. 2.5
fun **divertido/a** adj. 2.1
 fun activity **diversión** f. 1.4

have fun **divertirse (e:ie)** v. 2.3
function **funcionar** v.
furniture **muebles** m., pl. 2.6
furthermore **además (de)** adv. 2.4
future **futuro** adj. 3.4; **porvenir**
 m. 3.4
 Here's to the future! **¡Por el**
 porvenir! 3.4
 in the future **en el futuro** 3.4

G

gain weight **aumentar** v. **de**
 peso 3.3; **engordar** v. 3.3
game **juego** m.; (match)
 partido m. 1.4
 game show **concurso** m. 3.5
garage (in a house) **garaje** m. 2.6;
 garaje m. 2.5; **taller**
 (mecánico) 2.5
garden **jardín** m. 2.6
garlic **ajo** m. 2.2
gas station **gasolinera** f. 2.5
gasoline **gasolina** f. 2.5
geography **geografía** f. 1.2
German **alemán, alemana** adj. 1.3
get **conseguir (e:i)** v. 1.4;
 obtener v. 3.4
 get along well/badly (with)
 llevarse bien/mal (con) 2.3
 get bored **aburrirse** v. 3.5
 get off of (a vehicle) **bajar(se)** v.
 de 2.5
 get on/into (a vehicle) **subir(se)**
 v. **a** 2.5
 get out of (a vehicle) **bajar(se)**
 v. **de** 2.5
 get up **levantarse** v. 2.1
gift **regalo** m. 1.6
girl **chica** f. 1.1; **muchacha** f. 1.3
girlfriend **novia** f. 1.3
give **dar** v. 1.6, 2.3;
 (as a gift) **regalar** 2.3
glass (drinking) **vaso** m. 2.6;
 vidrio m. 3.1
 (made) of glass **de vidrio** 3.1
glasses **gafas** f., pl. 1.6
 sunglasses **gafas** f., pl.
 de sol 1.6
gloves **guantes** m., pl. 1.6
go **ir** v. 1.4
 go away **irse** 2.1
 go by boat **ir en barco** 1.5
 go by bus **ir en autobús** 1.5
 go by car **ir en auto(móvil)** 1.5
 go by motorcycle **ir en**
 motocicleta 1.5
 go by taxi **ir en taxi** 1.5
 go by the bank **pasar por el**
 banco 3.2
 go down; **bajar(se)** v.
 go on a hike (in the mountains)
 ir de excursión (a las
 montañas) 1.4
 go out **salir** v. 2.3
 go out (with) **salir** v. **(con)** 2.3

go up **subir** v.
go with **acompañar** v. 3.2
Let's go. **Vamos.** 1.4
goblet **copa** f. 2.6
going to: be going to (do something) **ir a (+ inf.)** 1.4
golf **golf** m. 1.4
good **buen, bueno/a** adj. 1.3, 1.6
 Good afternoon. **Buenas**
 tardes. 1.1
 Good evening. **Buenas**
 noches. 1.1
 Good idea. **Buena idea.** 1.4
 Good morning. **Buenos días.** 1.1
 Good night. **Buenas noches.** 1.1
 It's good that... **Es bueno**
 que... 2.6
goodbye **adiós** m. 1.1
 say goodbye (to) **despedirse** v.
 (de) (e:i) 2.1
good-looking **guapo/a** adj. 1.3
government **gobierno** m. 3.1
graduate (from/in) **graduarse** v.
 (de/en) 2.3
grains **cereales** m., pl. 2.2
granddaughter **nieta** f. 1.3
grandfather **abuelo** m. 1.3
grandmother **abuela** f. 1.3
grandparents **abuelos** m., pl. 1.3
grandson **nieto** m. 1.3
grape **uva** f. 2.2
grass **hierba** f. 3.1
grave **grave** adj. 2.4
gray **gris** adj. m., f. 1.6
great **fenomenal** adj. m., f. 1.5
great-grandfather **bisabuelo** m. 1.3
great-grandmother **bisabuela** f. 1.3
green **verde** adj. m., f. 1.6
greet (each other) **saludar(se)** v. 2.5
greeting **saludo** m. 1.1
 Greetings to... **Saludos a...** 1.1
grilled (food) **a la plancha** 2.2
 grilled flank steak **lomo a la**
 plancha 2.2
ground floor **planta baja** f. 1.5
guest (at a house/hotel) **huésped**
 m., f. 1.5; (invited to a function)
 invitado/a m., f. 2.3
guide **guía** m., f. 3.1
gymnasium **gimnasio** m. 1.4

H

hair **pelo** m. 2.1
hairdresser **peluquero/a** m.,
 f. 3.4
half **medio/a** adj. 1.3
 half-brother **medio herma-**
 no 1.3 half-sister **media her-**
 mana 1.3
 half-past... (time) **...y**
 media 1.1
hallway **pasillo** m. 2.6
ham **jamón** m. 2.2
hamburger **hamburguesa** f. 2.2
hand **mano** f. 1.1

Eng-Span

Hands up! **¡Manos arriba!**
handsome **guapo/a** *adj.* 1.3
happen **ocurrir** *v.* 3.6
happiness **algería** *v.* 2.3
Happy birthday! **¡Feliz cumpleaños!** 2.3
happy **alegre** *adj.* 1.5; **contento/
a** *adj.* 1.5; **feliz** *adj. m., f.* 1.5
    be happy **alegrarse** *v.* **(de)** 3.1
hard **difícil** *adj. m., f.* 1.3
hard-working **trabajador(a)**
    adj. 1.3
hardly **apenas** *adv.* 2.4
haste **prisa** *f.* 1.3
hat **sombrero** *m.* 1.6
hate **odiar** *v.* 2.3
have **tener** *v.* 1.3
    Have a good trip! **¡Buen
    viaje!** 1.1
    have time **tener tiempo** 1.4
    have to (*do something*) **tener
    que (+ *inf.*)** 1.3; **deber (+ *inf.*)**
    have a tooth removed **sacar(se)
    un diente** 2.4
he **él** 1.1
head **cabeza** *f.* 2.4
headache **dolor** *m.* **de cabeza** 2.4
health **salud** *f.* 2.4
healthy **saludable** *adj. m., f.* 2.4;
    sano/a *adj.* 2.4
    lead a healthy lifestyle **llevar** *v.*
    una vida sana 3.3
hear **oír** *v.* 1.4
heard **oído/a** *p.p.* 3.2
hearing: sense of hearing **oído**
    m. 2.4
heart **corazón** *m.* 2.4
heat **calor** *m.* 1.5
Hello. **Hola.** 1.1; (*on the telephone*) **Aló.** 2.5; **¿Bueno?** 2.5;
    Diga. 2.5
help **ayudar** *v.* 2.6; **servir (e:i)**
    v. 1.5
    help each other **ayudarse** *v.* 2.5
her **su(s)** *poss. adj.* 1.3; (of) hers
    suyo(s)/a(s) *poss.* 2.5
    her **la** *f., sing., d.o. pron.* 1.5
    to/for her **le** *f., sing., i.o. pron.* 1.6
here **aquí** *adv.* 1.1
    Here it is. **Aquí está.** 1.5
    Here we are at/in... **Aquí
    estamos en...** 1.2
Hi. **Hola.** 1.1
highway **autopista** *f.* 2.5;
    carretera *f.* 2.5
hike **excursión** *f.* 1.4
    go on a hike **hacer una excur-
    sión** 1.5; **ir de excursión** 1.4
hiker **excursionista** *m., f.*
hiking **de excursión** 1.4
him: to/for him **le** *m., sing., i.o.
    pron.* 1.6
hire **contratar** *v.* 3.4
his **su(s)** *poss. adj.* 1.3; (of) his
    suyo(s)/a(s) *poss. pron.* 2.5
    his **lo** *m., sing., d.o. pron.* 1.5
history **historia** *f.* 1.2; 3.5

hobby **pasatiempo** *m.* 1.4
hockey **hockey** *m.* 1.4
holiday **día** *m.* **de fiesta** 2.3
home **casa** *f.* 1.2
    home page **página** *f.*
    principal 2.5
homework **tarea** *f.* 1.2
hood **capó** *m.* 2.5; **cofre** *m.* 2.5
hope **esperar** *v.* **(+ *inf.*)** 1.2;
    esperar *v.* 3.1
    I hope (that) **ojalá (que)** 3.1
horror (genre) **de horror** *m.* 3.5
hors d'oeuvres **entremeses** *m.,
    pl.* 2.2
horse **caballo** *m.* 1.5
hospital **hospital** *m.* 2.4
hot: be (*feel*) (very) hot **tener
    (mucho) calor** 1.3
    It's (very) hot. **Hace (mucho)
    calor.** 1.5
hotel **hotel** *m.* 1.5
hour **hora** *f.* 1.1
house **casa** *f.* 1.2
household chores **quehaceres** *m.
    pl.* **domésticos** 2.6
housekeeper **ama** *m., f.* **de casa** 2.6
housing **vivienda** *f.* 2.6
How... ! **¡Qué...!** 1.3
    how **¿cómo?** *adv.* 1.1
    How are you? **¿Qué tal?** 1.1
    How are you? **¿Cómo estás?**
    fam. 1.1
    How are you? **¿Cómo está
    usted?** *form.* 1.1
    How can I help you? **¿En qué
    puedo servirles?** 1.5
    How did it go for you...?
    ¿Cómo le/les fue...? 3.3
    How is it going? **¿Qué tal?** 1.1
    How is/are...? **¿Qué tal...?** 1.2
    How is the weather? **¿Qué
    tiempo hace?** 3.3
    How much/many?
    ¿Cuánto(s)/a(s)? 1.1
    How much does... cost?
    ¿Cuánto cuesta...? 1.6
    How old are you? **¿Cuántos
    años tienes?** *fam.* 1.3
however **sin embargo**
hug (each other) **abrazar(se)** *v.* 2.5
humanities **humanidades** *f., pl.* 1.2
hundred **cien, ciento** 1.2
hunger **hambre** *f.* 1.3
hungry: be (very) hungry **tener** *v.*
    (mucha) hambre 1.3
hunt **cazar** *v.* 3.1
hurricane **huracán** *m.* 3.6
hurry **apurarse** *v.* 3.3; **darse prisa**
    v. 3.3
    be in a (big) hurry **tener** *v.*
    (mucha) prisa 1.3
hurt **doler (o:ue)** *v.* 2.4
    It hurts me a lot... **Me duele
    mucho...** 2.4
husband **esposo** *m.* 1.3

I

I **yo** 1.1
    I am... **Yo soy...** 1.1
    I hope (that) **Ojalá (que)**
    interj. 3.1
    I wish (that) **Ojalá (que)**
    interj. 3.1
ice cream **helado** *m.* 2.3
    ice cream shop **heladería** *f.* 3.2
iced **helado/a** *adj.* 2.2
    iced tea **té** *m.* **helado** 2.2
idea **idea** *f.* 1.4
if **si** *conj.* 1.4
illness **enfermedad** *f.* 2.4
important **importante** *adj.* 1.3
    be important to **importar** *v.* 2.1
    It's important that... **Es
    importante que...** 2.6
impossible **imposible** *adj.* 3.1
    it's impossible **es imposible** 3.1
improbable **improbable** *adj.* 3.1
    it's improbable **es
    improbable** 3.1
improve **mejorar** *v.* 3.1
in **en** *prep.* 1.2; **por** *prep.* 2.5
    in the afternoon **de la tarde** 1.1;
    por la tarde 2.1
    in a bad mood **de mal
    humor** 1.5
    in the direction of **para** *prep.* 1.1;
    in the early evening **de la
    tarde** 1.1
    in the evening **de la noche** 1.1;
    por la tarde 2.1
    in a good mood **de buen
    humor** 1.5
    in the morning **de la
    mañana** 1.1; **por la
    mañana** 2.1
    in love (with)
    enamorado/a (de) 1.5
    in search of **por** *prep.* 2.5
    in front of **delante de** *prep.* 1.2
increase **aumento** *m.* 3.4
incredible **increíble** *adj.* 1.5
inequality **desigualdad** *f.* 3.6
infection **infección** *f.* 2.4
inform **informar** *v.* 3.6
injection **inyección** *f.* 2.4
    give an injection *v.* **poner una
    inyección** 2.4
injure (oneself) **lastimarse** 2.4
    injure (one's foot) **lastimarse** *v.*
    (el pie) 2.4
inner ear **oído** *m.* 2.4
inside **dentro** *adv.*
insist (on) **insistir** *v.* **(en)** 2.6
installments: pay in installments
    pagar *v.* **a plazos** 3.2
intelligent **inteligente** *adj.* 1.3
intend to **pensar** *v.* **(+ *inf.*)** 1.4
interest **interesar** *v.* 2.1
interesting **interesante** *adj.* 1.3
    be interesting to **interesar** *v.* 2.1
international **internacional**
    adj. m., f. 3.6

Internet **Internet** 2.5
interview **entrevista** *f.* 3.4; interview **entrevistar** *v.* 3.4
interviewer **entrevistador(a)** *m., f.* 3.4
introduction **presentación** *f.*
I would like to introduce (name) to you… **Le presento a…** *form.* 1.1; **Te presento a…** *fam.* 1.1
invest **invertir (e:ie)** *v.* 3.4
invite **invitar** *v.* 2.3
iron (clothes) **planchar** *v.* **la ropa** 2.6
it **lo/la** *sing., d.o., pron.* 1.5
Italian **italiano/a** *adj.* 1.3
its **su(s)** *poss. adj.* 1.3, **suyo(s)/a(s)** *poss. pron.* 2.5
It's me. **Soy yo.** 1.1

J

jacket **chaqueta** *f.* 1.6
January **enero** *m.* 1.5
Japanese **japonés, japonesa** *adj.* 1.3
jeans **bluejeans** *m., pl.* 1.6
jewelry store **joyería** *f.* 3.2
job **empleo** *m.* 3.4; **puesto** *m.* 3.4; **trabajo** *m.* 3.4
job application **solicitud** *f.* **de trabajo** 3.4
jog **correr** *v.*
journalism **periodismo** *m.* 1.2
journalist **periodista** *m., f.* 1.3; **reportero/a** *m., f.* 3.4
joy **alegría** *f.* 2.3
give joy **dar** *v.* **alegría** 2.3
joyful **alegre** *adj.* 1.5
juice **jugo** *m.* 2.2
July **julio** *m.* 1.5
June **junio** *m.* 1.5
jungle **selva, jungla** *f.* 3.1
just **apenas** *adv.*
have just done something **acabar de (+ inf.)** 1.6

K

key **llave** *f.* 1.5
keyboard **teclado** *m.* 2.5
kilometer **kilómetro** *m.* 2.5
kind: That's very kind of you. **Muy amable.** 1.5
kiss **beso** *m.* 2.3
kiss each other **besarse** *v.* 2.5
kitchen **cocina** *f.* 2.6
knee **rodilla** *f.* 2.4
knife **cuchillo** *m.* 2.6
know **saber** *v.* 1.6; **conocer** *v.* 1.6
know how **saber** *v.* 1.6

L

laboratory **laboratorio** *m.* 1.2

lack **faltar** *v.* 2.1
lake **lago** *m.* 3.1
lamp **lámpara** *f.* 2.6
land **tierra** *f.* 3.1
landlord **dueño/a** *m., f.* 2.2
landscape **paisaje** *m.* 1.5
language **lengua** *f.* 1.2
laptop (computer) **computadora** *f.* **portátil** 2.5
large **grande** *adj.* 1.3
large (clothing size) **talla grande** 1.6
last **durar** *v.* 3.6; **pasado/a** *adj.* 1.6; **último/a** *adj.*
last name **apellido** *m.* 1.3
last night **anoche** *adv.* 1.6
last week **semana** *f.* **pasada** 1.6
last year **año** *m.* **pasado** 1.6
late **tarde** *adv.* 2.1
later (on) **más tarde** 2.1
See you later. **Hasta la vista.** 1.1; **Hasta luego.** 1.1
laugh **reírse (e:i)** *v.* 2.3
laughed **reído** *p.p.* 3.2
laundromat **lavandería** *f.* 3.2
law **ley** *f.* 3.1
lawyer **abogado/a** *m., f.* 3.4
lazy **perezoso/a** *adj.*
learn **aprender** *v.* **(a + inf.)** 1.3
least, at **por lo menos** *adv.* 2.4
leave **salir** *v.* 1.4; **irse** *v.* 2.1
leave a tip **dejar una propina** 2.3
leave behind **dejar** *v.* 3.4
leave for (a place) **salir para**
leave from **salir de**
left **izquierdo/a** *adj.* 1.2
be left over **quedar** *v.* 2.1
to the left of **a la izquierda de** 1.2
leg **pierna** *f.* 2.4
lemon **limón** *m.* 2.2
lend **prestar** *v.* 1.6
less **menos** *adv.* 2.4
less… than **menos… que** 2.2
less than **menos de (+ number)**
lesson **lección** *f.* 1.1
let **dejar** *v.* 2.6
let's see **a ver** 1.2
letter **carta** *f.* 1.4, 3.2
lettuce **lechuga** *f.* 2.2
liberty **libertad** *f.* 3.6
library **biblioteca** *f.* 1.2
license (driver's) **licencia** *f.* **de conducir** 2.5
lie **mentira** *f.* 1.4
life **vida** *f.* 2.3
of my life **de mi vida** 3.3
lifestyle: lead a healthy lifestyle **llevar una vida sana** 3.3
lift **levantar** *v.* 3.3
lift weights **levantar pesas** 3.3
light **luz** *f.* 2.6
like **gustar** *v.* 1.2; **como** *prep.* 2.2
I don't like them at all. **No me gustan nada.** 1.2

I like… **Me gusta(n)…** 1.2
like this **así** *adv.* 2.4
like very much **encantar** *v.;* **fascinar** *v.* 2.1
Do you like…? **¿Te gusta(n)…?** 1.2
likeable **simpático/a** *adj.* 1.3
likewise **igualmente** *adv.* 1.1
line **línea** *f.* 1.4; **cola** (queue) *f.* 3.2
listen (to) **escuchar** *v.* 1.2
Listen! (command) **¡Oye!** *fam., sing.* 1.1; **¡Oiga/Oigan!** *form., sing./pl.* 1.1
listen to music **escuchar música** 1.2
listen (to) the radio **escuchar la radio** 1.2
literature **literatura** *f.* 1.2
little (quantity) **poco/a** *adj.* 1.5; **poco** *adv.* 2.4
live **vivir** *v.* 1.3
living room **sala** *f.* 2.6
loan **préstamo** *m.* 3.2; **prestar** *v.* 1.6, 3.2
lobster **langosta** *f.* 2.2
located **situado/a** *adj.*
be located **quedar** *v.* 3.2
long **largo/a** *adj.* 1.6
look (at) **mirar** *v.* 1.2
look for **buscar** *v.* 1.2
lose **perder (e:ie)** *v.* 1.4
lose weight **adelgazar** *v.* 3.3
lost **perdido/a** *adj.* 3.2
be lost **estar perdido/a** 3.2
lot, a **muchas veces** *adv.* 2.4
lot of, a **mucho/a** *adj.* 1.2, 1.3
love (another person) **querer (e:ie)** *v.* 1.4; (inanimate objects) **encantar** *v.* 2.1 ; **amor** *m.* 2.3
in love **enamorado/a** *adj.* 1.5
I loved it! **¡Me encantó!** 3.3
luck **suerte** *f.* 1.3
lucky: be (very) lucky **tener (mucha) suerte** 1.3
luggage **equipaje** *m.* 1.5
lunch **almuerzo** *m.* 2.2
have lunch **almorzar (o:ue)** *v.* 1.4

M

ma'am **señora (Sra.); doña** *f.* 1.1
mad **enojado/a** *adj.* 1.5
magazine **revista** *f.* 1.4
magnificent **magnífico/a** *adj.* 1.5
mail **correo** *m.* 3.2; **enviar** *v.,* **mandar** *v.* 3.2; **echar (una carta) al buzón** 3.2
mail **correo** *m.* 3.2; **enviar** *v.,* **mandar** *v.* 3.2
mail carrier **cartero** *m.* 3.2
mailbox **buzón** *m.* 3.2
main **principal** *adj. m., f.* 2.2
maintain **mantener** *v.* 3.3
major **especialización** *f.* 1.2
make **hacer** *v.* 1.4

make the bed **hacer la cama** 2.6
makeup **maquillaje** *m.* 2.1
  put on makeup **maquillarse** *v.* 2.1
man **hombre** *m.* 1.1
manager **gerente** *m., f.* 3.4
many **mucho/a** *adj.* 1.3
  many times **muchas veces** 2.4
map **mapa** *m.* 1.2
March **marzo** *m.* 1.5
margarine **margarina** *f.* 2.2
marinated fish **ceviche** *m.* 2.2
  lemon-marinated shrimp **ceviche** *m.* **de camarón** 2.2
marital status **estado** *m.* **civil** 2.3
market **mercado** *m.* 1.6
  open-air market **mercado al aire libre** 1.6
marriage **matrimonio** *m.* 2.3
married **casado/a** *adj.* 2.3
  get married (to) **casarse** *v.* **(con)** 2.3
marvelous **maravilloso/a** *adj.* 1.5
marvelously **maravillosamente** *adv.* 3.6
massage **masaje** *m.* 3.3
masterpiece **obra maestra** *f.* 3.5
match (*sports*) **partido** *m.* 1.4
match (with) **hacer** *v.* **juego (con)** 1.6
mathematics **matemáticas** *f., pl.* 1.2
matter **importar** *v.* 2.1
maturity **madurez** *f.* 2.3
maximum **máximo/a** *adj.* 2.5
May **mayo** *m.* 1.5
maybe **tal vez** 1.5; **quizás** 1.5
mayonnaise **mayonesa** *f.* 2.2
me **me** *sing., d.o. pron.* 1.5
  to/for me **me** *sing., i.o. pron.* 1.6
meal **comida** *f.* 2.2
means of communication **medios** *m., pl.* **de comunicación** 3.6
meat **carne** *f.* 2.2
mechanic **mecánico/a** *m., f.* 2.5
  mechanic's repair shop **taller mecánico** 2.5
media **medios** *m., pl.* **de comunicación** 3.6
medical **médico/a** *adj.* 2.4
medication **medicamento** *m.* 2.4
medicine **medicina** *f.* 2.4
medium **mediano/a** *adj.*
meet (each other) **encontrar(se)** *v.* 2.5; **conocerse(se)** *v.* 2.2
meeting **reunión** *f.* 3.4
menu **menú** *m.* 2.2
message (*telephone*) **recado** *m.* 2.5, **mensaje** *m.*
Mexican **mexicano/a** *adj.* 1.3
Mexico **México** *m.* 1.1
microwave **microonda** *f.* 2.6
  microwave oven **horno** *m.* **de microondas** 2.6
middle age **madurez** *f.* 2.3

midnight **medianoche** *f.* 1.1
mile **milla** *f.* 2.5
milk **leche** *f.* 2.2
million **millón** *m.* 1.2
  million of **millón de** 1.2
mine **mío(s)/a(s)** *poss.* 2.5
mineral **mineral** *m.* 3.3
  mineral water **agua** *f.* **mineral** 2.2
minute **minuto** *m.* 1.1
mirror **espejo** *m.* 2.1
Miss **señorita (Srta.)** *f.* 1.1
miss **perder (e:ie)** *v.* 1.4
mistaken **equivocado/a** *adj.*
modem **módem** *m.*
modern **moderno/a** *adj.* 3.5
mom **mamá** *f.* 1.3
Monday **lunes** *m., sing.* 1.2
money **dinero** *m.* 1.6
monitor **monitor** *m.* 2.5
month **mes** *m.* 1.5
monument **monumento** *m.* 1.4
moon **luna** *f.* 3.1
more **más** 1.2
  more... than **más... que** 2.2
  more than **más de (+ number)** 2.2
morning **mañana** *f.* 1.1
mother **madre** *f.* 1.3
mother-in-law **suegra** *f.* 1.3
motor **motor** *m.*
motorcycle **motocicleta** *f.* 1.5
mountain **montaña** *f.* 1.4
mouse **ratón** *m.* 2.5
mouth **boca** *f.* 2.4
move (*from one house to another*) **mudarse** *v.* 2.6
movie **película** *f.* 1.4
  movie star **estrella** *f.* **de cine** 3.5
  movie theater **cine** *m.* 1.4
MP3 player **reproductor** *m.* **de MP3** 2.5
Mr. **señor (Sr.)**; **don** *m.* 1.1
Mrs. **señora (Sra.)**; **doña** *f.* 1.1
much **mucho/a** *adj.* 1.2, 1.3
  very much **muchísimo/a** *adj.* 1.2
municipal **municipal** *adj. m., f.*
murder **crimen** *m.* 3.6
muscle **músculo** *m.* 3.3
museum **museo** *m.* 1.4
mushroom **champiñón** *m.* 2.2
music **música** *f.* 1.2, 3.5
musical **musical** *adj., m., f.* 3.5
musician **músico/a** *m., f.* 3.5
must **deber** *v.* **(+ inf.)** 3
  It must be... **Debe ser...** 1.6
my **mi(s)** *poss. adj.* 1.3; **mío(s)/a(s)** *poss. pron.* 2.5

N

name **nombre** *m.* 1.1
  be named **llamarse** *v.* 2.1

  in the name of **a nombre de** 1.5
  last name **apellido** *m.*
  My name is... **Me llamo...** 1.1
napkin **servilleta** *f.* 2.6
national **nacional** *adj. m., f.* 3.6
nationality **nacionalidad** *f.* 1.1
natural **natural** *adj. m., f.* 3.1
  natural disaster **desastre** *m.* **natural** 3.6
  natural resource **recurso** *m.* **natural** 3.1
nature **naturaleza** *f.* 3.1
nauseated **mareado/a** *adj.* 2.4
near **cerca de** *prep.* 1.2
neaten **arreglar** *v.* 2.6
necessary **necesario/a** *adj.* 2.6
  It is necessary that... **Hay que...** 2.6, 3.2
neck **cuello** *m.* 2.4
need **faltar** *v.* 2.1; **necesitar** *v.* **(+ inf.)** 1.2
negative **negativo/a** *adj.*
neighbor **vecino/a** *m., f.* 2.6
neighborhood **barrio** *m.* 2.6
neither **tampoco** *adv.* 2.1
neither... nor **ni... ni** *conj.* 2.1
nephew **sobrino** *m.* 1.3
nervous **nervioso/a** *adj.* 1.5
network **red** *f.* 2.5
never **nunca** *adj.* 2.1; **jamás** 2.1
new **nuevo/a** *adj.* 1.6
newlywed **recién casado/a** *m., f.* 2.3
news **noticias** *f., pl.* 3.6; **actualidades** *f., pl.* 3.6
newscast **noticiero** *m.* 3.6
newspaper **periódico** 1.4; **diario** *m.* 3.6
next **próximo/a** *adj.* 3.4
  next to **al lado de** *prep.* 1.2
nice **simpático/a** *adj.* 1.3; **amable** *adj. m., f.* 1.5
niece **sobrina** *f.* 1.3
night **noche** *f.* 1.1
  night stand **mesita** *f.* **de noche** 2.6
nine **nueve** 1.1
nine hundred **novecientos/as** 1.2
nineteen **diecinueve** 1.1
ninety **noventa** 1.2
ninth **noveno/a** 1.5
no **no** 1.1; **ningún, ninguno/a(s)** *adj.* 2.1
  no one **nadie** *pron.* 2.1
  No problem. **No hay problema.** 2.1
  no way **de ninguna manera** 3.4
nobody **nadie** 2.1
none **ningún, ninguno/a(s)** *adj.* 2.1
noon **mediodía** *m.* 1.1
nor **ni** *conj.* 2.1
north **norte** *m.* 3.2
  to the north **al norte** 3.2
nose **nariz** *f.* 2.4
not **no** 1.1

not any **ningún, ninguno/a(s)** *adj.* 2.1
not anyone **nadie** *pron.* 2.1
not anything **nada** *pron.* 2.1
not bad at all **nada mal** 1.5
not either **tampoco** *adv.* 2.1
not ever **nunca** *adv.* 2.1; **jamás** *adv.* 2.1
not very well **no muy bien** 1.1
not working **descompuesto/a** *adj.* 2.5
notebook **cuaderno** *m.* 1.1
nothing **nada** 1.1; 2.1
noun **sustantivo** *m.*
November **noviembre** *m.* 1.5
now **ahora** *adv.* 1.2
nowadays **hoy día** *adv.*
nuclear **nuclear** *adj. m., f.* 3.1
nuclear energy **energía nuclear** 3.1
number **número** *m.* 1.1
nurse **enfermero/a** *m., f.* 2.4
nutrition **nutrición** *f.* 3.3
nutritionist **nutricionista** *m., f.* 3.3

O

o'clock: It's… o'clock **Son las…** 1.1
   It's one o'clock. **Es la una.** 1.1
obey **obedecer** *v.* 3.6
obligation **deber** *m.* 3.6
obtain **conseguir (e:i)** *v.* 1.4; **obtener** *v.* 3.4
obvious **obvio/a** *adj.* 3.1
   it's obvious **es obvio** 3.1
occupation **ocupación** *f.* 3.4
occur **ocurrir** *v.* 3.6
October **octubre** *m.* 1.5
of **de** *prep.* 1.1
   Of course. **Claro que sí.** 3.4; **Por supuesto.** 3.4
offer **oferta** *f.* 2.6; **ofrecer (c:zc)** *v.* 1.6
office **oficina** *f.* 2.6
   doctor's office **consultorio** *m.* 2.4
often **a menudo** *adv.* 2.4
Oh! **¡Ay!**
oil **aceite** *m.* 2.2
OK **regular** *adj.* 1.1
   It's okay. **Está bien.**
old **viejo/a** *adj.* 1.3
old age **vejez** *f.* 2.3
older **mayor** *adj. m., f.* 1.3
   older brother, sister **hermano/a mayor** *m., f.* 1.3
oldest **el/la mayor** 2.2
on **en** *prep.* 1.2: **sobre** *prep.* 1.2
   on behalf of **por** *prep.* 2.5
   on the dot **en punto** 1.1
   on time **a tiempo** 2.4
   on top of **encima de** 1.2
once **una vez** 1.6
one **un, uno/a** *m., f., sing. pron.* 1.1
   one hundred **cien(to)** 1.2

one million **un millón** *m.* 1.2
one more time **una vez más** 2.3
one thousand **mil** 1.2
one time **una vez** 1.6
onion **cebolla** *f.* 2.2
only **sólo** *adv.* 1.3; **único/a** *adj.* 1.3 only child **hijo/a único/a** *m., f.* 1.3
open **abierto/a** *adj.* 1.5, 3.2; **abrir** *v.* 1.3
open-air **al aire libre** 1.6
opera **ópera** *f.* 3.5
operation **operación** *f.* 2.4
opposite **enfrente de** *prep.* 3.2
or **o** *conj.* 2.1
orange **anaranjado/a** *adj.* 1.6; **naranja** *f.* 2.2
orchestra **orquesta** *f.* 3.5
order **mandar** 2.6; (*food*) **pedir (e:i)** *v.* 2.2
   in order to **para** *prep.* 2.5
orderly **ordenado/a** *adj.* 1.5
ordinal (*numbers*) **ordinal** *adj.*
other **otro/a** *adj.* 1.6
ought to **deber** *v.* (**+ inf.**) *adj.* 1.3
our **nuestro(s)/a(s)** *poss. adj.* 1.3; *poss. pron.* 2.5
out of order **descompuesto/a** *adj.* 2.5
outskirts **afueras** *f., pl.* 2.6
oven **horno** *m.* 2.6
over **sobre** *prep.* 1.2
own **propio/a** *adj.* 3.4
owner **dueño/a** *m., f.* 2.2

P

p.m. **tarde** *f.* 1.1
pack (one's suitcases) **hacer** *v.* **las maletas** 1.5
package **paquete** *m.* 3.2
page **página** *f.* 2.5
pain **dolor** *m.* 2.4
   have a pain **tener** *v.* **dolor** 2.4
paint **pintar** *v.* 3.5
painter **pintor(a)** *m., f.* 3.4
painting **pintura** *f.* 2.6, 3.5
pair **par** *m.* 1.6
   pair of shoes **par** *m.* **de zapatos** 1.6
pants **pantalones** *m., pl.* 1.6
pantyhose **medias** *f., pl.* 1.6
paper **papel** *m.* 1.2; (*report*) **informe** *m.* 3.6
Pardon me. (*May I?*) **Con permiso.** 1.1; (*Excuse me.*) Pardon me. **Perdón.** 1.1
parents **padres** *m., pl.* 1.3; **papás** *m., pl.* 1.3
park **estacionar** *v.* 2.5; **parque** *m.* 1.4
parking lot **estacionamiento** *m.* 3.2
partner (*one of a married couple*) **pareja** *f.* 2.3
party **fiesta** *f.* 2.3

passed **pasado/a** *p.p.*
passenger **pasajero/a** *m., f.* 1.1
passport **pasaporte** *m.* 1.5
past **pasado/a** *adj.* 1.6
pastime **pasatiempo** *m.* 1.4
pastry shop **pastelería** *f.* 3.2
patient **paciente** *m., f.* 2.4
patio **patio** *m.* 2.6
pay **pagar** *v.* 1.6, 2.3
pay in cash **pagar** *v.* **al contado; pagar en efectivo** 3.2
pay in installments **pagar** *v.* **a plazos** 3.2
pay the bill **pagar la cuenta** 2.3
pea **arveja** *m.* 2.2
peace **paz** *f.* 3.6
peach **melocotón** *m.* 2.2
pear **pera** *f.* 2.2
pen **pluma** *f.* 1.2
pencil **lápiz** *m.* 1.1
penicillin **penicilina** *f.* 2.4
people **gente** *f.* 1.3
pepper (*black*) **pimienta** *f.* 2.2
per **por** *prep.* 2.5
perfect **perfecto/a** *adj.* 1.5
perhaps **quizás; tal vez**
permission **permiso** *m.*
person **persona** *f.* 1.3
pharmacy **farmacia** *f.* 2.4
phenomenal **fenomenal** *adj.* 1.5
photograph **foto(grafía)** *f.* 1.1
physical (*exam*) **examen** *m.* **médico** 2.4
physician **doctor(a), médico/a** *m., f.* 1.3
physics **física** *f. sing.* 1.2
pick up **recoger** *v.* 3.1
picture **cuadro** *m.* 2.6; **pintura** *f.* 2.6
pie **pastel** *m.* 2.3
pill (*tablet*) **pastilla** *f.* 2.4
pillow **almohada** *f.* 2.6
pineapple **piña** *f.* 2.2
pink **rosado/a** *adj.* 1.6
place **lugar** *m.* 1.4; **poner** *v.* 1.4
plaid **de cuadros** 1.6
plans **planes** *m., pl.* 1.4
   have plans **tener planes** 1.4
plant **planta** *f.* 3.1
plastic **plástico** *m.* 3.1
   (made) of plastic **de plástico** 3.1
plate **plato** *m.* 2.6
   platter of fried food **fuente** *f.* **de fritada**
play **drama** *m.* 3.5; **comedia** *f.* 3.5; **jugar (u:ue)** *v.* 1.4; (*a musical instrument*) **tocar** *v.* 3.5; (*a role*) **hacer el papel de** 3.5; (*cards*) **jugar a (las cartas)** 1.5; (*sports*) **practicar deportes** 1.4
player **jugador(a)** *m., f.* 1.4
playwright **dramaturgo/a** *m., f.* 3.5
plead **rogar (o:ue)** *v.* 2.6
pleasant **agradable** *adj. m., f.*

please **por favor** 1.1
Pleased to meet you. **Mucho gusto.** 1.1; **Encantado/a.** *adj.* 1.1
pleasing: be pleasing to **gustar** *v.* 2.1
pleasure **gusto** *m.* 1.1; **placer** *m.* 3.3
   It's a pleasure to… **Gusto de** *(+ inf.)* 3.6
   It's been a pleasure. **Ha sido un placer.** 3.3
   The pleasure is mine. **El gusto es mío.** 1.1
poem **poema** *m.* 3.5
poet **poeta** *m., f.* 3.5
poetry **poesía** *f.* 3.5
police (force) **policía** *f.* 2.5
political **político/a** *adj.* 3.6
politician **político/a** *m., f.* 3.4
politics **política** *f.* 3.6
polka-dotted **de lunares** 1.6
poll **encuesta** *f.* 3.6
pollute **contaminar** *v.* 3.1
polluted **contaminado/a** *m., f.* 3.1
   be polluted **estar contaminado/a** 3.1
pollution **contaminación** *f.* 3.1
pool **piscina** *f.* 1.4
poor **pobre** *adj., m., f.* 1.6
population **población** *f.* 3.1
pork **cerdo** *m.* 2.2
   pork chop **chuleta** *f.* **de cerdo** 2.2
portable **portátil** *adj.* 2.5
   portable computer **computadora** *f.* **portátil** 2.5
position **puesto** *m.* 3.4
possessive **posesivo/a** *adj.* 1.3
possible **posible** *adj.* 3.1
   it's (not) possible **(no) es posible** 3.1
post office **correo** *m.* 3.2
postcard **postal** *f.* 1.4
poster **cartel** *m.* 2.6
potato **papa** *f.* 2.2; **patata** *f.* 2.2
pottery **cerámica** *f.* 3.5
practice **entrenarse** *v.* 3.3; **practicar** *v.* 1.2
prefer **preferir (e:ie)** *v.* 1.4
pregnant **embarazada** *adj. f.* 2.4
prepare **preparar** *v.* 1.2
preposition **preposición** *f.*
prescribe *(medicine)* **recetar** *v.* 2.4
prescription **receta** *f.* 2.4
present **regalo** *m.*; **presentar** *v.* 3.5
press **prensa** *f.* 3.6
pressure **presión** *f.*
   be under a lot of pressure **sufrir muchas presiones** 3.3
pretty **bonito/a** *adj.* 1.3; **bastante** *adv.* 3.1
price **precio** *m.* 1.6
   (fixed, set) price **precio** *m.* **fijo** 1.6
print **estampado/a** *adj.*; **imprimir** *v.* 2.5
printer **impresora** *f.* 2.5

private *(room)* **individual** *adj.*
prize **premio** *m.* 3.5
probable **probable** *adj.* 3.1
   it's (not) probable **(no) es probable** 3.1
problem **problema** *m.* 1.1
profession **profesión** *f.* 1.3; 3.4
professor **profesor(a)** *m., f.*
program **programa** *m.* 1.1
programmer **programador(a)** *m., f.* 1.3
prohibit **prohibir** *v.* 2.4
promotion *(career)* **ascenso** *m.* 3.4
pronoun **pronombre** *m.*
protect **proteger** *v.* 3.1
protein **proteína** *f.* 3.3
provided (that) **con tal (de) que** *conj.* 3.1
psychologist **psicólogo/a** *m., f.* 3.4
psychology **psicología** *f.* 1.2
publish **publicar** *v.* 3.5
Puerto Rican **puertorriqueño/a** *adj.* 1.3
Puerto Rico **Puerto Rico** *m.* 1.1
pull a tooth **sacar una muela**
purchases **compras** *f., pl.* 1.5
pure **puro/a** *adj.* 3.1
purple **morado/a** *adj.* 1.6
purse **bolsa** *f.* 1.6
put **poner** *v.* 1.4; **puesto/a** *p.p.* 3.2
   put (a letter) in the mailbox **echar (una carta) al buzón** 3.2
   put on *(a performance)* **presentar** *v.* 3.5
   put on *(clothing)* **ponerse** *v.* 2.1
   put on makeup **maquillarse** *v.* 2.1

Q

quality **calidad** *f.* 1.6
quarter *(academic)* **trimestre** *m.* 1.2
   quarter after *(time)* **y cuarto** 1.1; **y quince** 1.1
   quarter to *(time)* **menos cuarto** 1.1; **menos quince** 1.1
question **pregunta** *f.* 1.2
quickly **rápido** *adv.* 2.4
quiet **tranquilo/a** *adj.* 3.3
quit **dejar** *v.* 3.4
quiz **prueba** *f.* 1.2

R

racism **racismo** *m.* 3.6
radio *(medium)* **radio** *f.* 1.2
   radio (set) **radio** *m.* 2.5
rain **llover (o:ue)** *v.* 1.5; **lluvia** *f.* 3.1

It's raining. **Llueve.** 1.5; **Está lloviendo.** 1.5
raincoat **impermeable** *m.* 1.6
rainforest **bosque** *m.* **tropical** 3.1
raise *(salary)* **aumento de sueldo** 3.4
rather **bastante** *adv.* 2.4
read **leer** *v.* 1.3; **leído/a** *p.p.* 3.2
   read e-mail **leer correo electrónico** 1.4
   read a magazine **leer una revista** 1.4
   read a newspaper **leer un periódico** 1.4
ready **listo/a** *adj.* 1.5
   (Are you) ready? **¿(Están) listos?** 3.3
reap the benefits (of) *v.* **disfrutar** *v.* **(de)** 3.3
receive **recibir** *v.* 1.3
recommend **recomendar (e:ie)** *v.* 2.2; 2.6
record **grabar** *v.* 2.5
recreation **diversión** *f.* 1.4
recycle **reciclar** *v.* 3.1
recycling **reciclaje** *m.* 3.1
red **rojo/a** *adj.* 1.6
red-haired **pelirrojo/a** *adj.* 1.3
reduce **reducir** *v.* 3.1
   reduce stress/tension **aliviar el estrés/la tensión** 3.3
refrigerator **refrigerador** *m.* 2.6
region **región** *f.* 3.1
regret **sentir (e:ie)** *v.* 3.1
related to sitting **sedentario/a** *adj.* 3.3
relatives **parientes** *m., pl.* 1.3
relax **relajarse** *v.* 2.3
remain **quedarse** *v.* 2.1
remember **recordar (o:ue)** *v.* 1.4; **acordarse (o:ue)** *v.* **(de)** 2.1
remote control **control remoto** *m.* 2.5
rent **alquilar** *v.* 2.6; *(payment)* **alquiler** *m.* 2.6
repeat **repetir (e:i)** *v.* 1.4
report **informe** *m.* 3.6; **reportaje** *m.* 3.6
reporter **reportero/a** *m., f.* 3.4
representative **representante** *m., f.* 3.6
request **pedir (e:i)** *v.* 1.4
reservation **reservación** *f.* 1.5
resign (from) **renunciar (a)** *v.* 3.4
resolve **resolver (o:ue)** *v.* 3.1
resolved **resuelto/a** *p.p.* 3.2
resource **recurso** *m.* 3.1
responsibility **deber** *m.* 3.6
   responsabilidad *f.*
rest **descansar** *v.* 1.2
restaurant **restaurante** *m.* 1.4
résumé **currículum** *m.* 3.4
retire (from work) **jubilarse** *v.* 2.3
return **regresar** *v.* 1.2; **volver (o:ue)** *v.* 1.4
returned **vuelto/a** *p.p.* 3.2

rice **arroz** *m.* 2.2
rich **rico/a** *adj.* 1.6
ride a bicycle **pasear** *v.* **en bicicleta** 1.4
ride a horse **montar** *v.* **a caballo** 1.5
ridiculous **ridículo/a** *adj.* 3.1
   it's ridiculous **es ridículo** 3.1
right **derecha** *f.* 1.2
   be right **tener razón** 1.3
   right? *(question tag)* **¿no?** 1.1; **¿verdad?** 1.1
   right away **enseguida** *adv.* 2.3
   right here **aquí mismo** 2.5
   right now **ahora mismo** 1.5
   right there **allí mismo** 3.2
   to the right of **a la derecha de** 1.2
rights **derechos** *m.* 3.6
ring *(a doorbell)* **sonar (o:ue)** *v.* 2.5
river **río** *m.* 3.1
road **camino** *m.*
roast **asado/a** *adj.* 2.2
roast chicken **pollo** *m.* **asado** 2.2
rollerblade **patinar en línea** *v.*
romantic **romántico/a** *adj.* 3.5
room **habitación** *f.* 1.5; **cuarto** *m.* 1.2; 3.5
   living room **sala** *f.* 2.6
roommate **compañero/a** *m., f.* **de cuarto** 1.2
roundtrip **de ida y vuelta** 1.5
   roundtrip ticket **pasaje** *m.* **de ida y vuelta** 1.5
routine **rutina** *f.* 2.1
rug **alfombra** *f.* 2.6
run **correr** *v.* 1.3
   run errands **hacer diligencias** 3.2
   run into *(have an accident)* **chocar (con)** *v.; (meet accidentally)* **encontrar(se) (o:ue)** *v.* 2.5; *(run into something)* **darse (con)** 2.4
   run into (each other) **encontrar(se) (o:ue)** *v.* 2.5
rush **apurarse, darse prisa** *v.* 3.3
Russian **ruso/a** *adj.* 1.3

S

sad **triste** *adj.* 1.5; 3.1
   it's sad **es triste** 3.1
safe **seguro/a** *adj.* 1.5
said **dicho/a** *p.p.* 3.2
salad **ensalada** *f.* 2.2
salary **salario** *m.* 3.4; **sueldo** *m.* 3.4
sale **rebaja** *f.* 1.6
salesperson **vendedor(a)** *m., f.* 1.6
salmon **salmón** *m.* 2.2
salt **sal** *f.* 2.2
same **mismo/a** *adj.* 1.3
sandal **sandalia** *f.* 1.6

sandwich **sándwich** *m.* 2.2
Saturday **sábado** *m.* 1.2
sausage **salchicha** *f.* 2.2
save *(on a computer)* **guardar** *v.* 2.5; save *(money)* **ahorrar** *v.* 3.2
savings **ahorros** *m.* 3.2
   savings account **cuenta** *f.* **de ahorros** 3.2
say **decir** *v.* 1.4; **declarar** *v.* 3.6
say *(that)* **decir (que)** *v.* 1.4, 2.3
   say the answer **decir la respuesta** 1.4
scarcely **apenas** *adv.* 2.4
scared: be (very) scared (of) **tener (mucho) miedo (de)** 1.3
schedule **horario** *m.* 1.2
school **escuela** *f.* 1.1
science *f.* **ciencia** 1.2
   science fiction **ciencia ficción** *f.* 3.5
scientist **científico/a** *m., f.* 3.4
screen **pantalla** *f.* 2.5
scuba dive **bucear** *v.* 1.4
sculpt **esculpir** *v.* 3.5
sculptor **escultor(a)** *m., f.* 3.5
sculpture **escultura** *f.* 3.5
sea **mar** *m.* 1.5
season **estación** *f.* 1.5
seat **silla** *f.* 1.2
second **segundo/a** 1.5
secretary **secretario/a** *m., f.* 3.4
sedentary **sedentario/a** *adj.* 3.3
see **ver** *v.* 1.4
   see (you, him, her) again **volver a ver(te, lo, la)** 3.6
   see movies **ver películas** 1.4
   See you. **Nos vemos.** 1.1
   See you later. **Hasta la vista.** 1.1; **Hasta luego.** 1.1
   See you soon. **Hasta pronto.** 1.1
   See you tomorrow. **Hasta mañana.** 1.1
seem **parecer** *v.* 1.6
seen **visto/a** *p.p.* 3.2
sell **vender** *v.* 1.6
semester **semestre** *m.* 1.2
send **enviar; mandar** *v.* 3.2
separate (from) **separarse** *v.* **(de)** 2.3
separated **separado/a** *adj.* 2.3
September **septiembre** *m.* 1.5
sequence **secuencia** *f.*
serious **grave** *adj.* 2.4
serve **servir (e:i)** *v.* 2.2
set *(fixed)* **fijo** *adj.* 1.6
   set the table **poner la mesa** 2.6
seven **siete** 1.1
seven hundred **setecientos/as** 1.2
seventeen **diecisiete** 1.1
seventh **séptimo/a** 1.5
seventy **setenta** 1.2
several **varios/as** *adj. pl.* 2.2
sexism **sexismo** *m.* 3.6
shame **lástima** *f.* 3.1
   it's a shame **es una lástima** 3.1
shampoo **champú** *m.* 2.1

shape **forma** *f.* 3.3
   be in good shape **estar en buena forma** 3.3
   stay in shape **mantenerse en forma** 3.3
share **compartir** *v.* 1.3
sharp *(time)* **en punto** 1.1
shave **afeitarse** *v.* 2.1
shaving cream **crema** *f.* **de afeitar** 2.1
she **ella** 1.1
shellfish **mariscos** *m., pl.* 2.2
ship **barco** *m.*
shirt **camisa** *f.* 1.6
shoe **zapato** *m.* 1.6
   shoe size **número** *m.* 1.6
   shoe store **zapatería** *f.* 3.2
   tennis shoes **zapatos** *m., pl.* **de tenis** 1.6
shop **tienda** *f.* 1.6
shopping, to go **ir de compras** 1.5
   shopping mall **centro comercial** *m.* 1.6
short *(in height)* **bajo/a** *adj.* 1.3; *(in length)* **corto/a** *adj.* 1.6
short story **cuento** *m.* 3.5
shorts **pantalones cortos** *m., pl.* 1.6
should *(do something)* **deber** *v.* **(+ inf.)** 1.3
show **espectáculo** *m.* 3.5; **mostrar (o:ue)** *v.* 1.4
   game show **concurso** *m.* 3.5
shower **ducha** *f.* 2.1; **ducharse** *v.* 2.1
shrimp **camarón** *m.* 2.2
siblings **hermanos/as** *pl.* 1.3
sick **enfermo/a** *adj.* 2.4
   be sick **estar enfermo/a** 2.4
   get sick **enfermarse** *v.* 2.4
sign **firmar** *v.* 3.2; **letrero** *m.* 3.2
silk **seda** *f.* 1.6
   (made of) **de seda** 1.6
silly **tonto/a** *adj.* 1.3
since **desde** *prep.*
sing **cantar** *v.* 1.2
singer **cantante** *m., f.* 3.5
single **soltero/a** *adj.* 2.3
   single room **habitación** *f.* **individual** 1.5
sink **lavabo** *m.* 2.1
sir **señor (Sr.), don** *m.* 1.1
sister **hermana** *f.* 1.3
sister-in-law **cuñada** *f.* 1.3
sit down **sentarse (e:ie)** *v.* 2.1
six **seis** 1.1
six hundred **seiscientos/as** 1.2
sixteen **dieciséis** 1.1
sixth **sexto/a** 1.5
sixty **sesenta** 1.2
size **talla** *f.* 1.6
   shoe size *m.* **número** 1.6
(in-line) skate **patinar (en línea)** 1.4
skateboard **andar en patineta** *v.* 1.4
ski **esquiar** *v.* 1.4

skiing **esquí** *m.* 1.4
   water-skiing **esquí** *m.*
     acuático 1.4
skirt **falda** *f.* 1.6
sky **cielo** *m.* 3.1
sleep **dormir (o:ue)** *v.* 1.4; **sueño**
   m. 1.3
   go to sleep **dormirse**
     (o:ue) *v.* 2.1
sleepy: be (very) sleepy **tener**
   (mucho) sueño 1.3
slender **delgado/a** *adj.* 1.3
slim down **adelgazar** *v.* 3.3
slippers **pantuflas** *f.* 2.1
slow **lento/a** *adj.* 2.5
slowly **despacio** *adv.* 2.4
small **pequeño/a** *adj.* 1.3
smart **listo/a** *adj.* 1.5
smile **sonreír (e:i)** *v.* 2.3
smiled **sonreído** *p.p.* 3.2
smoggy: It's (very) smoggy. **Hay**
   (mucha) contaminación. 1.4
smoke **fumar** *v.* 2.2; 3.3
   (not) to smoke **(no) fumar** 3.3
smoking section **sección** *f.* **de**
   fumar 2.2
   (non) smoking section *f.* **sección**
   de (no) fumar 2.2
snack **merendar** *v.* 2.2; 3.3; afternoon snack **merienda** *f.* 3.3
   have a snack **merendar** *v.*
sneakers **los zapatos de tenis** 1.6
sneeze **estornudar** *v.* 2.4
snow **nevar (e:ie)** *v.* 1.5; **nieve** *f.*
snowing: It's snowing. **Nieva.** 1.5;
   Está nevando. 1.5
so (*in such a way*) **así** *adv.* 2.4;
   tan *adv.* 1.5
   so much **tanto** *adv.*
   so-so **regular** 1.1, **así así**
   so that **para que** *conj.* 3.1
soap **jabón** *m.* 2.1
   soap opera **telenovela** *f.* 3.5
soccer **fútbol** *m.* 1.4
sociology **sociología** *f.* 1.2
sock(s) **calcetín (calcetines)**
   m. 1.6
sofa **sofá** *m.* 2.6
soft drink **refresco** *m.* 2.2
software **programa** *m.* **de**
   computación 2.5
soil **tierra** *f.* 3.1
solar **solar** *adj., m., f.* 3.1
   solar energy **energía solar** 3.1
soldier **soldado** *m., f.* 3.6
solution **solución** *f.* 3.1
solve **resolver (o:ue)** *v.* 3.1
some **algún, alguno/a(s)**
   adj. 2.1; **unos/as** *pron./ m., f.,*
   pl; indef.
   art. 1.1
somebody **alguien** *pron.* 2.1
someone **alguien** *pron.* 2.1
something **algo** *pron.* 2.1
sometimes **a veces** *adv.* 2.4
son **hijo** *m.* 1.3
song **canción** *f.* 3.5

son-in-law **yerno** *m.* 1.3
soon **pronto** *adv.* 2.4
   See you soon. **Hasta pronto.** 1.1
sorry: be sorry **sentir (e:ie)** *v.* 3.1
   I'm sorry. **Lo siento.** 1.4
   I'm so sorry. **Mil perdones.** 1.4;
     Lo siento muchísimo. 1.4
soup **caldo** *m.* 2.2; **sopa** *f.* 2.2
south **sur** *m.* 3.2
   to the south **al sur** 3.2
Spain **España** *f.* 1.1
Spanish (*language*) **español**
   m. 1.2; **español(a)** *adj.* 1.3
spare (free) time **ratos libres** 1.4
speak **hablar** *v.* 1.2
spectacular **espectacular** *adj. m.,*
   f. 3.3
speech **discurso** *m.* 3.6
speed **velocidad** *f.* 2.5
   speed limit **velocidad** *f.*
     máxima 2.5
spelling **ortografía** *f.*, **ortográ-**
   fico/a *adj.*
spend (*money*) **gastar** *v.* 1.6
spoon (*table or large*) **cuchara**
   f. 2.6
sport **deporte** *m.* 1.4
   sports-related **deportivo/a**
     adj. 1.4
spouse **esposo/a** *m., f.* 1.3
sprain (one's ankle) **torcerse**
   (o:ue) *v.* **(el tobillo)** 2.4
sprained **torcido/a** *adj.* 2.4
   be sprained **estar torcido/a** 2.4
spring **primavera** *f.* 1.5
(city or town) square **plaza** *f.* 1.4
stadium **estadio** *m.* 1.2
stage **etapa** *f.* 2.3
stairs **escalera** *f.* 2.6
stairway **escalera** *f.* 2.6
stamp **estampilla** *f.* 3.2; **sello**
   m. 3.2
stand in line **hacer** *v.* **cola** 3.2
star **estrella** *f.* 3.1
start (*a vehicle*) **arrancar** *v.* 2.5;
   (*establish*) **establecer** *v.* 3.4
station **estación** *f.* 1.5
statue **estatua** *f.* 3.5
status: marital status **estado** *m.*
   civil 2.3
stay **quedarse** *v.* 2.1
   stay in shape **mantenerse en**
     forma 3.3
steak **bistec** *m.* 2.2
steering wheel **volante** *m.* 2.5
step **etapa** *f.*
stepbrother **hermanastro** *m.* 1.3
stepdaughter **hijastra** *f.* 1.3
stepfather **padrastro** *m.* 1.3
stepmother **madrastra** *f.* 1.3
stepsister **hermanastra** *f.* 1.3
stepson **hijastro** *m.* 1.3
stereo **estéreo** *m.* 2.5
still **todavía** *adv.* 1.5
stockbroker **corredor(a)** *m., f.* **de**
   bolsa 3.4
stockings **medias** *f., pl.* 1.6

stomach **estómago** *m.* 2.4
stone **piedra** *f.* 3.1
stop **parar** *v.* 2.5
   stop (*doing something*) **dejar de**
   (+ inf.) 3.1
store **tienda** *f.* 1.6
storm **tormenta** *f.* 3.6
story **cuento** *m.* 3.5; **historia**
   f. 3.5
stove **cocina, estufa** *f.* 2.6
straight **derecho** *adj.* 3.2
   straight (ahead) **derecho** 3.2
straighten up **arreglar** *v.* 2.6
strange **extraño/a** *adj.* 3.1
   it's strange **es extraño** 3.1
strawberry **frutilla** *f.* 2.2, **fresa**
street **calle** *f.* 2.5
stress **estrés** *m.* 3.3
stretching **estiramiento** *m.* 3.3
   do stretching exercises **hacer**
     ejercicios; *m. pl.* **de**
     estiramiento 3.3
strike (*labor*) **huelga** *f.* 3.6
stripe **raya** *f.* 1.6
   striped **de rayas** 1.6
stroll **pasear** *v.* 1.4
strong **fuerte** *adj. m. f.* 3.3
struggle (for/against) **luchar** *v.*
   (por/contra) 3.6
student **estudiante** *m., f.* 1.1; 1.2;
   estudiantil *adj.* 1.2
study **estudiar** *v.* 1.2
stuffed-up (*sinuses*)
   congestionado/a *adj.* 2.4
stupendous **estupendo/a** *adj.* 1.5
style **estilo** *m.*
suburbs **afueras** *f., pl.* 2.6
subway **metro** *m.* 1.5
   subway station **estación** *f.*
     del metro 1.5
success **éxito** *m.* 3.4
successful: be successful **tener**
   éxito 3.4
such as **tales como**
suddenly **de repente** *adv.* 1.6
suffer **sufrir** *v.* 2.4
   suffer an illness **sufrir una**
     enfermedad 2.4
sugar **azúcar** *m.* 2.2
suggest **sugerir (e:ie)** *v.* 2.6
suit **traje** *m.* 1.6
suitcase **maleta** *f.* 1.1
summer **verano** *m.* 1.5
sun **sol** *m.* 1.5; 3.1
sunbathe **tomar** *v.* **el sol** 1.4
Sunday **domingo** *m.* 1.2
(sun)glasses **gafas** *f., pl.*
   (oscuras/de sol) 1.6; **lentes** *m.*
   pl. **(de sol)** 1.6
sunny: It's (very) sunny. **Hace**
   (mucho) sol. 1.5
supermarket **supermercado** *m.* 3.2
suppose **suponer** *v.* 1.4
sure **seguro/a** *adj.* 1.5
   be sure **estar seguro/a** 1.5
surf (*the Internet*) **navegar** *v.* **(en**
   Internet) 2.5

surprise **sorprender** *v.* 2.3;
  sorpresa *f.* 2.3
survey **encuesta** *f.* 3.6
sweat **sudar** *v.* 3.3
sweater **suéter** *m.* 1.6
sweep the floor **barrer el**
  suelo 2.6
sweets **dulces** *m., pl.* 2.3
swim **nadar** *v.* 1.4
swimming **natación** *f.* 1.4
  swimming pool **piscina** *f.* 1.4
symptom **síntoma** *m.* 2.4

T

table **mesa** *f.* 1.2
tablespoon **cuchara** *f.* 2.6
tablet (*pill*) **pastilla** *f.* 2.4
take **tomar** *v.* 1.2; **llevar** *v.* 1.6;
  take care of **cuidar** *v.* 3.1
  take someone's temperature
    tomar *v.* **la temperatura** 2.4
  take (*wear*) a shoe size
    calzar *v.* 1.6
  take a bath **bañarse** *v.* 2.1
  take a shower **ducharse** *v.* 2.1
  take off **quitarse** *v.* 2.1
  take out the trash *v.* **sacar la**
    basura 2.6
  take photos **tomar** *v.* **fotos** 1.5;
    sacar *v.* **fotos** 1.5
talented **talentoso/a** *adj.* 3.5
talk **hablar** *v.* 1.2
  talk show **programa** *m.* **de**
    entrevistas 3.5
tall **alto/a** *adj.* 1.3
tank **tanque** *m.* 2.5
tape recorder **grabadora** *f.* 1.1
taste **probar (o:ue)** *v.* 2.2; **saber**
  v. 2.2
  taste like **saber a** 2.2
tasty **rico/a** *adj.* 2.2; **sabroso/a**
  adj. 2.2
tax **impuesto** *m.* 3.6
taxi **taxi** *m.* 1.5
tea **té** *m.* 2.2
teach **enseñar** *v.* 1.2
teacher **profesor(a)** *m., f.* 1.1, 1.2;
  maestro/a *m., f.* 3.4
team **equipo** *m.* 1.4
technician **técnico/a** *m., f.* 3.4
telecommuting **teletrabajo** *m.* 3.4
telephone **teléfono** 2.5
  cellular telephone **teléfono** *m.*
    celular 2.5
television **televisión** *f.* 1.2; 2.5
  television set **televisor** *m.* 2.5
tell **contar** *v.* 1.4; **decir** *v.* 1.4
tell (that) **decir** *v.* **(que)** 1.4, 2.3
  tell lies **decir mentiras** 1.4
  tell the truth **decir la verdad** 1.4
temperature **temperatura** *f.* 2.4
ten **diez** 1.1
tennis **tenis** *m.* 1.4
  tennis shoes **zapatos** *m., pl.* **de**
    tenis 1.6

tension **tensión** *f.* 3.3
tent **tienda** *f.* **de campaña**
tenth **décimo/a** 1.5
terrible **terrible** *adj. m., f.* 3.1
  it's terrible **es terrible** 3.1
terrific **chévere** *adj.*
test **prueba** *f.* 1.2; **examen** *m.* 1.2
text message **mensaje** *m.* **de**
  texto 2.5
Thank you. **Gracias.** *f., pl.* 1.1
  Thank you (very much).
    (Muchas) gracias. 1.1
  Thank you very, very much.
    Muchísimas gracias. 2.3
  Thanks (a lot). **(Muchas)**
    gracias. 1.1
  Thanks again. (lit. Thanks one
    more time.) **Gracias una vez**
    más. 2.3
  Thanks for everything. **Gracias**
    por todo. 2.3; 3.3
that **que, quien(es), lo que**
  pron. 2.6
  that (one) **ése, ésa, eso**
    pron. 1.6; **ese, esa,** *adj.* 1.6
  that (*over there*) **aquél,**
    aquélla, aquello *pron.* 1.6;
    aquel, aquella *adj.* 1.6
  that which **lo que** *conj.* 2.6
  that's me **soy yo** 1.1
  That's not the way it is. **No es**
    así. 3.4
  that's why **por eso** 2.5
the **el** *m.,* **la** *f. sing.,* **los** *m.,*
  las *f., pl.* 1.1
theater **teatro** *m.* 3.5
their **su(s)** *poss. adj.* 1.3;
  suyo(s)/a(s) *poss. pron.* 2.5
them **los/las** *pl., d.o. pron.* 1.5
  to/for them **les** *pl., i.o. pron.* 1.6
then (*afterward*) **después**
  adv. 2.1; (*as a result*) **enton-**
  ces *adv.* 2.1;   (*next*) **luego**
  adv. 2.1; **pues** *adv.* 3.3
there **allí** *adv.* 1.5
  There is/are... **Hay...** 1.1;
  There is/are not... **No hay...** 1.1
therefore **por eso** 2.5
these **éstos, éstas** *pron.* 1.6;
  estos, estas *adj.* 1.6
they **ellos** *m.,* **ellas** *f. pron.*
thin **delgado/a** *adj.* 1.3
thing **cosa** *f.* 1.1
think **pensar (e:ie)** *v.* 1.4; (believe)
  creer *v.*
  think about **pensar en** *v.* 1.4
third **tercero/a** 1.5
thirst **sed** *f.* 1.3
thirsty: be (very) thirsty **tener**
  (mucha) sed 1.3
thirteen **trece** 1.1
thirty **treinta** 1.1; 1.2; thirty (*min-*
  utes past the hour) **y treinta; y**
  media 1.1
this **este, esta** *adj.;* **éste, ésta,**
  esto *pron.* 1.6

This is... (*introduction*)
  Éste/a es... 1.1
  This is he/she. (*on telephone*)
    Con él/ella habla. 2.5
those **ésos, ésas** *pron.* 1.6; **esos,**
  esas *adj.* 1.6
those (over there) **aquéllos,**
  aquéllas *pron.* 1.6; **aquellos,**
  aquellas *adj.* 1.6
thousand **mil** *m.* 1.6
three **tres** 1.1
three hundred **trescientos/as** 1.2
throat **garganta** *f.* 2.4
through **por** *prep.* 2.5
throughout: throughout the world
  en todo el mundo 3.1
Thursday **jueves** *m., sing.* 1.2
thus (*in such a way*) **así** *adj.*
ticket **boleto** *m.* 3.5; **pasaje** *m.* 1.5
tie **corbata** *f.* 1.6
time **tiempo** *m.* 1.4; **vez** *f.* 1.6
  have a good/bad time **pasarlo**
    bien/mal 2.3
  We had a great time. **Lo**
    pasamos de película. 3.6
  What time is it? **¿Qué hora**
    es? 1.1
  (At) What time...? **¿A qué**
    hora...? 1.1
times **veces** *f., pl.* 1.6
  many times **muchas veces** 2.4
  two times **dos veces** 1.6
tip **propina** *f.* 2.3
tire **llanta** *f.* 2.5
tired **cansado/a** *adj.* 1.5
  be tired **estar cansado/a** 1.5
to **a** *prep.* 1.1
toast (*drink*) **brindar** *v.* 2.3
  toast **pan** *m.* **tostado**
toasted **tostado/a** *adj.* 2.2
  toasted bread **pan tostado**
    m. 2.2
toaster **tostadora** *f.* 2.6
today **hoy** *adv.* 1.2
  Today is... **Hoy es...** 1.2
toe **dedo** *m.* **del pie** 2.4
together **juntos/as** *adj.* 2.3
toilet **inodoro** *m.* 2.1
tomato **tomate** *m.* 2.2
tomorrow **mañana** *f.* 1.1
  See you tomorrow. **Hasta**
    mañana. 1.1
tonight **esta noche** *adv.* 1.4
too **también** *adv.* 1.2; 2.1
  too much **demasiado** *adv.* 1.6;
    en exceso 3.3
tooth **diente** *m.* 2.1
toothpaste **pasta** *f.* **de dientes** 2.1
tornado **tornado** *m.* 3.6
tortilla **tortilla** *f.* 2.2
touch **tocar** *v.* 3.1; 3.5
tour an area **recorrer** *v;* **excur-**
  sión *f.* 1.4
tourism **turismo** *m.* 1.5
tourist **turista** *m., f.* 1.1;
  turístico/a *adj.*

toward **hacia** *prep.* 3.2;
   para *prep.* 2.5
towel **toalla** *f.* 2.1
town **pueblo** *m.* 1.4
trade **oficio** *m.* 3.4
traffic **circulación** *f.* 2.5; **tráfico**
   m. 2.5
   traffic signal **semáforo** *m.*
tragedy **tragedia** *f.* 3.5
trail **sendero** *m.* 3.1
   trailhead **sendero** *m.* 3.1
train **entrenarse** *v.* 3.3; **tren**
   m. 1.5
   train station **estación** *f.* **(de)**
    tren *m.* 1.5
trainer **entrenador(a)** *m., f.* 3.3
translate **traducir** *v.* 1.6
trash **basura** *f.* 2.6
travel **viajar** *v.* 1.2
   travel agent **agente** *m., f.*
    de viajes 1.5
traveler **viajero/a** *m., f.* 1.5
   (traveler's) check **cheque (de**
    viajero) 3.2
treadmill **cinta caminadora** *f.* 3.3
tree **árbol** *m.* 3.1
trillion **billón** *m.*
trimester **trimestre** *m.* 1.2
trip **viaje** *m.* 1.5
   take a trip **hacer un viaje** 1.5
tropical forest **bosque** *m.*
   tropical 3.1
true **verdad** *adj.* 3.1
   it's (not) true **(no) es verdad** 3.1
trunk **baúl** *m.* 2.5
truth **verdad** *f.* 1.4
try **intentar** *v.*; **probar (o:ue)** *v.* 2.2
   try (*to do something*) **tratar de**
    (*+ inf.*) 3.3
   try on **probarse (o:ue)** *v.* 2.1
t-shirt **camiseta** *f.* 1.6
Tuesday **martes** *m., sing.* 1.2
tuna **atún** *m.* 2.2
turkey **pavo** *m.* 2.2
turn **doblar** *v.* 3.2
   turn off (*electricity/appliance*)
    apagar *v.* 2.5
   turn on (*electricity/appliance*)
    poner *v.* 2.5; **prender** *v.* 2.5
twelve **doce** 1.1
twenty **veinte** 1.1
twenty-eight **veintiocho** 1.1
twenty-five **veinticinco** 1.1
twenty-four **veinticuatro** 1.1
twenty-nine **veintinueve** 1.1
twenty-one **veintiún,**
   veintiuno/a 1.1
twenty-seven **veintisiete** 1.1
twenty-six **veintiséis** 1.1
twenty-three **veintitrés** 1.1
twenty-two **veintidós** 1.1
twice **dos veces** 1.6
twin **gemelo/a** *m., f.* 1.3
twisted **torcido/a** *adj.* 2.4
   be twisted **estar torcido/a** 2.4
two **dos** 1.1
   two hundred **doscientos/as** 1.2

two times **dos veces** 1.6

U

ugly **feo/a** *adj.* 1.3
uncle **tío** *m.* 1.3
under **bajo** *adv.* 2.1;
   debajo de *prep.* 1.2
understand **comprender** *v.* 1.3;
   entender (e:ie) *v.* 1.4
underwear **ropa interior** 1.6
unemployment **desempleo** *m.* 3.6
United States **Estados Unidos**
   (EE.UU.) *m. pl.* 1.1
university **universidad** *f.* 1.2
unless **a menos que** *adv.* 3.1
unmarried **soltero/a** *adj.*
unpleasant **antipático/a** *adj.* 1.3
until **hasta** *prep.* 1.6; **hasta que**
   conj. 3.1
up **arriba** *adv.* 3.3
urgent **urgente** *adj.* 2.6
   It's urgent that… **Es urgente**
    que… 3.6
us **nos** *pl., d.o. pron.* 1.5
   to/for us **nos** *pl., i.o. pron.* 1.6
use **usar** *v.* 1.6
used for **para** *prep.* 2.5
useful **útil** *adj. m., f.*

V

vacation **vacaciones** *f., pl.* 1.5
   be on vacation **estar de**
    vacaciones 1.5
   go on vacation **ir de**
    vacaciones 1.5
vacuum **pasar** *v.* **la aspiradora** 2.6
   vacuum cleaner **aspiradora** *f.* 2.6
valley **valle** *m.* 3.1
various **varios/as** *adj. m., f.*
   pl. 2.2
VCR **videocasetera** *f.* 2.5
vegetables **verduras** *pl., f.* 2.2
verb **verbo** *m.*
very **muy** *adv.* 1.1
   very much **muchísimo** *adv.* 1.2
   (Very) well, thank you. **(Muy)**
    bien, gracias. 1.1
video **video** *m.* 1.1
   video camera **cámara** *f.* **de**
    video 2.5
   video(cassette) **video(casete)**
    m. 2.5
   videoconference
    videoconferencia *f.* 3.4
   video game **videojuego** *m.* 1.4
vinegar **vinagre** *m.* 2.2
violence **violencia** *f.* 3.6
visit **visitar** *v.* 1.4
   visit monuments **visitar**
    monumentos 1.4
vitamin **vitamina** *f.* 3.3
volcano **volcán** *m.* 3.1
volleyball **vóleibol** *m.* 1.4
vote **votar** *v.* 3.6

W

wait (for) **esperar** *v.* **(+ *inf.*)** 1.2
waiter/waitress **camarero/a**
   m., f. 2.2
wake up **despertarse (e:ie)**
   v. 2.1
walk **caminar** *v.* 1.2
   take a walk **pasear** *v.* 1.4;
   walk around **pasear por** 1.4
walkman ***walkman*** *m.*
wall **pared** *f.* 2.6
wallet **cartera** *f.* 1.6
want **querer (e:ie)** *v.* 1.4
war **guerra** *f.* 3.6
warm (oneself) up **calentarse**
   (e:ie) *v.* 3.3
wash **lavar** *v.* 2.6
   wash one's face/hands **lavarse**
    la cara/las manos 2.1
   wash (the floor, the dishes)
    lavar (el suelo, los
    platos) 2.6
   wash oneself **lavarse** *v.* 2.1
washing machine **lavadora** *f.* 2.6
wastebasket **papelera** *f.* 1.2
watch **mirar** *v.* 1.2; **reloj** *m.* 1.2
   watch television **mirar (la)**
    televisión 1.2
water **agua** *f.* 2.2
   water pollution **contaminación**
    del agua 3.1
   water-skiing **esquí** *m.*
    acuático 1.4
way **manera** *f.* 3.4
we **nosotros(as)** *m., f.* 1.1
weak **débil** *adj. m., f.* 3.3
wear **llevar** *v.* 1.6; **usar** *v.* 1.6
weather **tiempo** *m.*
   The weather is bad. **Hace mal**
    tiempo. 1.5
   The weather is good. **Hace**
    buen tiempo. 1.5
weaving **tejido** *m.* 3.5
Web **red** *f.* 2.5
website **sitio** *m.* **web** 2.5
wedding **boda** *f.* 2.3
Wednesday **miércoles** *m.,*
   sing. 1.2
week **semana** *f.* 1.2
weekend **fin** *m.* **de semana** 1.4
weight **peso** *m.* 3.3
   lift weights **levantar** *v.* **pesas**
    f., pl. 3.3
welcome **bienvenido(s)/a(s)**
   adj. 2.6
well **pues** *adv.* 1.2, 3.5; **bueno**
   adv. 1.2, 3.5; (Very) well,
   thanks. **(Muy) bien, gra-**
   cias. 1.1
well-being **bienestar** *m.* 3.3
well organized **ordenado/a** *adj.*
west **oeste** *m.* 3.2
   to the west **al oeste** 3.2
western (*genre*) **de vaqueros** 3.5
what **lo que** *pron.* 2.6
what? **¿qué?** 1.1

At what time...? **¿A qué hora...?** 1.1

What a pleasure to... ! **¡Qué gusto (+ inf.)...** 3.6

What day is it? **¿Qué día es hoy?** 1.2

What do you guys think? **¿Qué les parece?** 2.3

What happened? **¿Qué pasó?** 2.5

What is today's date? **¿Cuál es la fecha de hoy?** 1.5

What nice clothes! **¡Qué ropa más bonita!** 1.6

What size do you take? **¿Qué talla lleva (usa)?** 1.6

What time is it? **¿Qué hora es?** 1.1

What's going on? **¿Qué pasa?** 1.1

What's happening? **¿Qué pasa?** 1.1

What's. . . like? **¿Cómo es...?** 1.3

What's new? **¿Qué hay de nuevo?** 1.1

What's the weather like? **¿Qué tiempo hace?** 1.5

What's wrong? **¿Qué pasó?** 2.5

What's your name? **¿Cómo se llama usted?** *form.* 1.1

What's your name? **¿Cómo te llamas (tú)?** *fam.* 1.1

when **cuando** *conj.* 2.1; 3.1

When? **¿Cuándo?** 1.2

where **donde**

where (to)? (*destination*) **¿adónde?** 1.2; (*location*) **¿dónde?** 1.1

Where are you from? **¿De dónde eres (tú)?** (*fam.*) 1.1; **¿De dónde es (usted)?** (*form.*) 1.1

Where is...? **¿Dónde está...?** 1.2

(to) where? **¿adónde?** 1.2

which **que** *pron.*, **lo que** *pron.* 2.6

which? **¿cuál?** 1.2; **¿qué?** 1.2

In which...? **¿En qué...?** 1.2

which one(s)? **¿cuál(es)?** 1.2

while **mientras** *adv.* 2.4

white **blanco/a** *adj.* 1.6

white wine **vino blanco** 2.2

who **que** *pron.* 2.6; **quien(es)** *pron.* 2.6

who? **¿quién(es)?** 1.1

Who is...? **¿Quién es...?** 1.1

Who is calling? (*on telephone*) **¿De parte de quién?** 2.5

Who is speaking? (*on telephone*) **¿Quién habla?** 2.5

whole **todo/a** *adj.*

whom **quien(es)** *pron.* 2.6

whose? **¿de quién(es)?** 1.1

why? **¿por qué?** 1.2

widower/widow **viudo/a** *adj.* 2.3

wife **esposa** *f.* 1.3

win **ganar** *v.* 1.4

wind **viento** *m.* 1.5

window **ventana** *f.* 1.2

windshield **parabrisas** *m., sing.* 2.5

windy: It's (very) windy. **Hace (mucho) viento.** 1.5

wine **vino** *m.* 2.2

red wine **vino tinto** 2.2

white wine **vino blanco** 2.2

wineglass **copa** *f.* 2.6

winter **invierno** *m.* 1.5

wish **desear** *v.* 1.2; **esperar** *v.* 3.1

I wish (that) **ojalá (que)** 3.1

with **con** *prep.* 1.2

with me **conmigo** 1.4; 2.3

with you **contigo** *fam.* 2.3

within (ten years) **dentro de (diez años)** *prep.* 3.4

without **sin** *prep.* 1.2; 3.1; 3.3; **sin que** *conj.* 3.1

woman **mujer** *f.* 1.1

wool **lana** *f.* 1.6

(made of) wool **de lana** 1.6

word **palabra** *f.* 1.1

work **trabajar** *v.* 1.2; **funcionar** *v.* 2.5; **trabajo** *m.* 3.4

work (*of art, literature, music, etc.*) **obra** *f.* 3.5

work out **hacer gimnasia** 3.3

world **mundo** *m.* 3.1

worldwide **mundial** *adj. m., f.*

worried (about) **preocupado/a (por)** *adj.* 1.5

worry (about) **preocuparse** *v.* **(por)** 2.1

Don't worry. **No se preocupe.** *form.* 2.1; **Tranquilo.; No te preocupes.** *fam.* 2.1

worse **peor** *adj. m., f.* 2.2

worst **el/la peor, lo peor** 2.2; 3.6

Would you like to...? **¿Te gustaría...?** *fam.* 1.4

write **escribir** *v.* 1.3

write a letter/post card/e-mail message **escribir una carta/postal/mensaje electrónico** 1.4

writer **escritor(a)** *m., f* 3.5

written **escrito/a** *p.p.* 3.2

wrong **equivocado/a** *adj.* 1.5

be wrong **no tener razón** 1.3

X

X-ray **radiografía** *f.* 2.4

Y

yard **jardín** *m.* 2.6; **patio** *m.* 2.6

year **año** *m.* 1.5

be... years old **tener... años** 1.3

yellow **amarillo/a** *adj.* 1.6

yes **sí** *interj.* 1.1

yesterday **ayer** *adv.* 1.6

yet **todavía** *adv.* 1.5

yogurt **yogur** *m.* 2.2

You **tú** *fam.* **usted (Ud.)** *form. sing.* **vosotros/as** *m., f. fam.* **ustedes (Uds.)** *form.* 1.1; (to, for) you *fam. sing.* **te** *pl.* **os** 1.6; *form. sing.* **le** *pl.* **les** 1.6

you **te** *fam., sing.,* **lo/la** *form., sing.,* **os** *fam., pl.,* **los/las** *form., pl, d.o. pron.* 1.5

You don't say! **¡No me digas!** *fam.;* **¡No me diga!** *form.* 2.5

You are. . . **Tú eres...** (*fam.*), **Usted es...** (*form.*) 1.1

You're welcome. **De nada.** 1.1; **No hay de qué.** 1.1

young **joven** *adj.* 1.3

young person **joven** *m., f.* 1.1

young woman **señorita (Srta.)** *f.*

younger **menor** *adj. m., f.* 1.3

younger: younger brother, sister *m., f.* **hermano/a menor** 1.3

youngest **el/la menor** *m., f.* 2.2

your **su(s)** *poss. adj. form.* 1.3

your **tu(s)** *poss. adj. fam. sing.* 1.3

your **vuestro/a(s)** *poss. adj. form. pl.* 1.3

your(s) *form.* **suyo(s)/a(s)** *poss. pron. form.* 2.5

your(s) **tuyo(s)/a(s)** *poss. fam. sing.* 2.5

your(s) **vuestro(s)/a(s)** *poss. fam.* 2.5

youth *f.* **juventud** 2.3

Z

zero **cero** *m.* 1.1

As in the glossary, the level and lesson of **¡ADELANTE!** where each item is found is indicated by the two numbers separated by a decimal:

- 1.6 = *¡ADELANTE!* **UNO** , Lección 6
- 3.4 = *¡ADELANTE!* **TRES** , Lección 4

Índice

Text Credits

(3.2) **94–95** © Carmen Laforet. Fragment of the novel *Nada*, reprinted by permission of Random House Publishing Group.

(3.3) **142–143** © Gabriel García Márquez, *Un día de éstos*, reprinted by permission of Carmen Balcells.

(3.4) **190–191** © Julia de Burgos, "A Julia de Burgos" from *Song of the Simple Truth: The Complete Poems of Julia de Burgos*, 1996. Published by Curbstone Press. Distributed by Consortium.

(3.5) **242–243** © Federico García Lorca, *Danza, Las seis cuerdas, La guitarra*. Reprinted by permission of Herederos de Federico García Lorca.

Fine Art Credits

[Lv 1] 75 (ml) Diego Velázquez. *Las meninas*. 1656. Derechos reservados © Museo Nacional del Prado, Madrid. Photograph © José Blanco/VHL.

[Lv 1] 113 Oswaldo Guayasamín. *Madre y niño en azul*. 1986. Cortesía Fundación Guayasamín. Quito, Ecuador.

[Lv 2] 148 Frida Kahlo. *Autorretrato con mono*. 1938. Oil on masonite, overall 16 X12" (40.64 x 30.48 cms). Albright-Knox Art Gallery, Buffalo, New York. Bequest of A. Conger Goodyear, 1966.

[Lv 3] 190 Frida Kahlo. *Las dos Fridas*. 1939. Oil on Canvas. 5'8.5" x 5'8.5" © Banco de México Trust. Foto © Schavcwijk/Art Resource, NY.

[Lv 3] 228 (r) Joan Miró. *La lección de esquí*. © ARS, NY/Art Resource, NY.

[Lv 3] 229 (r) Fernando Botero. *El alguacil*. 20th Century © Fernando Botero. Foto © Christie's Images/Corbis.

[Lv 3] 247 José Antonio Velásquez. *San Antonio de Oriente*. 1957. Colección: Art Museum of the Americas, Organization of American States. Washington D.C.

Illustration Credits

Hermann Mejía: [Lv 1] 5, 14, 15, 17, 18, 22, 23, 29, 70, 77, (b) 83, 115, (b) 125, 127, 128, 131, 136, 137, 138, 139, 155, 213, (l) 233, 235, 238, 243, 247, 249 (b), 279, 301. **[Lv 2]** 3, 11, 24, 25, 30, 34, 44, 89, 99, 103, 134, 144, 153, 183, 200, 201, 205, 252, 255, 258, 259, 261, 306, 315, 317. **[Lv 3]** 6, 7, 19, 38, 45, 91, 93, 133, 135, 138, 141, 189, 235, 241, 291, 292–293.

Pere Virgili: [Lv 1] 2–3, 56–57, 78, 112–113, 116–117, 118, 222-223, 224, 125 (t), 238, 242, 249 (t), 276-277, 300. **[Lv 2]** 3 (t & m), 19, 22-23, 76–77, 78, 132–133, 180–181, 236–237, 238, 290–291, 292. **[Lv3]** 7, 22-23, 24, 72-73, 74, 120, 121, 122, 168–169, 220–221, 272–273.

Yayo: [Lv 1] 9, 19, 47, 123, 231, 283. **[Lv 2]** 29, 85, 139, 187, 243, 297. **[Lv 3]** 29, 79, 127, 175, 227, 279.

Deborah Dixon: [Lv 2] 2. **[Lv 3]** 2, 3.

Sophie Casson: [Lv 2] 2, 3. **[Lv3]** 2, 3.

Photography Credits

Martín Bernetti: [Lv 1] 1, 3, 4, 16 (c, m), 19, 32, 33, 42, 57, 68, 69, 70, 71, 79, 80 (tl, tm, r, bml, bmr, br), 90, 95, 97 (r), 98, 106, 107 (b), 109, 112, 113 (t, ml, b), 117 (b), 139, 142, 144, 182, 205, 218, 219, 295 (tl, tr, ml, mr), 296, 297. **[Lv 2]** 35, 38, 39, 50 (tl, tr), 51 (tl, br), 81, 135, 154 (t), 193, 237, 293, 349, 381, 386, 293. **[Lv 3]** 87, 232.

Carlos Gaudier: [Lv 1] 180, 181, 252 (tl, tr, ml, mr), 253 (tl, bl).

Corbis: cover (7) © Dave G. Houser (3) © David Muench **[Lv 1] 11** (tr) © Hans Georg Roth. **19** (r) © 1999 Charles Gupton. **32** (tr) © Robert Holmes. **64** (t) © Pablo Corral V. **74** © Charles Gupton. **86** (m) © Elke Stolzenberg, (b) © Reuters. **87** (br) © Owen Franken, (tl) © Patrick Almasy, (tr) © Jean-Pierre Lescourret. **111** © Ronnie Kaufman. **115** © Jon Feingersh. **117** (t) © George Shelley. **119** © Ronnie Kaufman. **120** (tr) © Rafael Pérez/Reuters, (b) © Martial Trezzini/epa. **121** (t) © Reuters. **124** (b) © Reuters. **125** (t) © Reuters. **134** © José Luis Pelaez, Inc. **141** © Images.com. **143** © AFP Photo/Juan Barreto. **145** © Rick Gómez. **147** (b) © Janet Jarman. **148** (tl) © George D. Lepp, (mr) Peter Guttman, (b) Reuters. **149** (tr) © Bettman, (br) Greg Vaughn. **231** (r) © Jeremy Horner. **233** (b) © Mark A. Johnson. **237** © Ronnie Kaufman. **253** (br) © Steve Chenn. **[Lv 2] 50** (bm) © Charles & Josette Lenars, (lm) © Richard Smith. **51** (bl) © Jeremy Horner. **87** (tr) © Carlos Cazalis, (br) © Carlos Cazalis. **90** © José Luis Pelaez, Inc. **106** (t) © Bob Winsett, (ml, mr, b) © Dave G. Houser. **107** (tl) © Reuters Newmedia, Inc./Jorge Silva, (tr) © Michael & Patricia Fogden, (bl) © Jon Butchofsky-Houser, (br) © Paul W. Liebhardt. **140** (r) © PictureNet. **156** (ml) © Dave G. Houser, (tr, mtr) © Mcduff Everton, (tl) © Pablo Corral V., (mbr) © AFP/Macarena Minguell, (bl, br) © Bettman. **157** (tl) © Wolfgang Kaehler, (bl) © Roger Ressmeyer, (br) © Charles O'rear. **208**

(m) © Jan Butchofsky-Houser, (ml) © Bill Gentile, (mr) © Dave G. Houser, (b) © Bob Winsett. **209** (r,b) © Martin Rogers. **235** © PictureNet. **263** © Laurence Kesterson/SYGMA. **264** (m, mr) Galen Rowell. **265** (t) Pablo Corral V. **289** © Rolf Bruderer. **298** (l) © Dusko Despotovic. **320** (tl) © Kevin Schafer, (tr, b) Danny Lehman. **321** (tl) © Danny Lehman (ml) Ralf A. Clavenger, (b) José & Fuste Raga. **353** © Lawrence Kesterson. **[Lv 3] 21** © Michael de Young. **23** (tr) Stephanie Maze. **34** © Karl & Anne Purcell. **48** (tr) Karl & Anne Purcell. **49** (tl) Gianni Dagli Ortí, (tr) Stringer/Mexico/Reuters, (br) © Jeremy Horner. **95** © Bureau L.A. Collection. **96** (t) John Madere, (mt) Kevin Schafer, (mb) Buddy Mays, (b) Peter Guttmann. **97** (tl) Reuters/NewMedia Inc./ Kimberly White, (bl, br) Pablo Corral V. **136** © Michael Keller. **144** (tl) © Anders Ryman, (m) © Reuters NewMedia Inc./Sergio Moraes, (b) © Pablo Corral V. **145** (tl) © Hubert Stadler, (r) AFP Photo/Gonzalo Espinoza, (bl) © Wolfgang Kaehler. **167** © Peter Beck. **177** (b) © Galen Rowell. **187** © Bill Gentile. **192** (tl) © Jeremy Horner, (tr, m) © Bill Gentile, (b) © Stephen Frink. **193** (tl) © Brian A. Vikander, (r) © Reuters NewMedia Inc./Claudia Daut, (bl) © Gary Braasch. **194** (tr) © Reinhard Eisele, (m) © Richard Bickel. **195** (tl) © Jeremy Horner, (r) © Reuters NewMedia Inc./Marc Serota, (bl) © Lawrence Manning. **229** (l) Raúl Benegas. **244** (tl) © José F. Poblete, (tr) © Peter Guttman, (ml) © Leif Skoogfors, (mr) © Lake County Museum. **245** (tl) © Guy Motil. **246** (tl) © Stuart Westmorland, (tr, ml) © Macduff Everton, (mr) © Tony Arruza. **247** (tl) © Macduff Everton. **271** © Douglas Kirkland. **275** (t) © Owen Franken. **280** (l) © Gustavo Gilabert/Corbis SABA. **289** (l) © Dave G. Houser. **294** (t) © Peter Guttman, (ml) © Paul Almasy, (b) © Carlos Carrión. **295** (r) © Joel Creed; Ecoscene. **296** (tl) © Bettmann, (tr) © Reuters/Andrés Stapff, (m) © Diego Lezama Orezzoli, (b) © Tim Graham. **297** (tl) © Stephanie Maze, (r) © SI/Simon Bruty, (ml) © Reuters/Andrés Stapff, (bl) © Wolfgang Kaehler.

AP Wide World Photos: **[Lv 1] 86** (tl) © David Cantor. **121** (b) © Juanjo Martin. **[Lv 2] 140** (l) © José Luis Magaña. **141** (t) © Simon Cruz, (b) © Karel Navarro. **188** (b) Ricardo Figueroa. **[Lv 3] 231** © Mark Lennihan, File. **281** © Álex Ibañez, HO.

Alamy: **[Lv 1] 65** (b) © Michele Molinari. **149** © Greg Vaughn. **233** (t) © Christopher Pillitz. **[Lv3] 9** JTB Photo Communications, Inc. **30** (t) Clive Tully. **31** (br) David South. **129** (l) VStock. **280** (r) © Homer Sykes.

Getty Images: **[Lv 1] 11** (l) © Mark Mainz. **33** (tl) PhotoDisk. **124** (t) © Javier Soriano/AFP. **125** (b) © Daniel García/ AFP. **147** (t) © AFP/AFP. **157** (tr) © PhotoDisk. **189** (b) Kiko Castro/AFP. **221** © Robert Harding World Imagery. **253** (tr) PhotoDisk. **285** (l) © Guiseppe Carace, (br) © Mark Mainz, (tr) © Carlos Álvarez. **304** (t,b) © PhotoDisk. **305** (tl) © Don Emmert/AFP. **[Lv 2] 1** Denis Doyle **8** Joel Nito/AFP **308** © Tim Graham. **[Lv 3] 128** (l) © Krysztof Dydynski. **247** (r) © Elmer Martínez/AFP.

Lonely Planet Images: **[Lv 1] 86** (b) © Greg Elms. **[Lv 3] 31** (tr) Krzysztof Dydynski, (l) Eric L Wheater.

Masterfile: **[Lv 1] 147** © WireImageStock. **[Lv 2] 75** © Mark Leibowitz.

The Picture-desk: **[Lv 1] 305** (br) © Road Movie Prods/The Kobal Collection. **[Lv 2] 189** (t) The Art Archive/Templo Mayor Library Mexico/Dagli Orti. **[Lv 3] 233** Walt Disney/The Kobal Collection.

Misc.: cover (BK) Jupiter Images, (6) © Robert Frerck/Odyssey **[Lv 1] 10** (r) Oscar Artavia Solano/VHL. **11** (br) Paola Ríos Schaff/VHL. **33** (br) © DominiCanada. **55** © Jimmy Dorantes/Latin Focus. **65** (r) Antonio Contreras Martínez/VHL. **83** (tr) © Hola Images/Workbook.com. **86** (tr, tl) José Blanco/VHL. **87** (ml) José Blanco/VHL. **95** Janet Dracksdorf/VHL. **113** (l) Alí Burafi/VHL. **118** (b) Reprinted by permission of Juana Macíos Alba. **141** (r) Oscar Artavia Solano/VHL, (m) José Blanco/VHL. **143** (bl) Janet Dracksdorf/VHL. **185** (t) © Rodrigo Varela/WireImage.com. **284** (t) © Robert Frerck/Odyssey Productions. **304** (tl, bmr) © Robert Frerck/Odyssey Productions. **[Lv 2] 7** Janet Dracksdorf/VHL. **9** © Emiliano Gatica. **31** José Blanco/VHL. **50** (tm) Paola Ríos Schaff/VHL. **86** (r) José Blanco/VHL. **87** (l) © Studio Bonisolli/StockFood Munich. **131** Index Stock/Network Productions. **155** Armando Brito/VHL. **179** © Jimmy Dorantes/Latin Focus. **188** (t) José Blanco/VHL. **208** (tl) Janet Dracksdorf/ VHL, (tr) Oscar Artavia Solano/VHL. **209** (t, m) Oscar Artavia Solano/VHL. **230** (b) © Yann-Arthus Bertrund. **245** (b) © Gabrielle Wallace, (t) © Esteban Corbo /VHL. **264** (t, ml, b) Alí Burafi/VHL. **265** (r, m, b) Alí Burafi//VHL. **269** © Network Productions/IndexStock Imagery. **299** (bl) Maribel García. **[Lv 3] 23** (bl) Alí Burafi//VHL, (br) Paola Ríos Schaff/VHL. **71** © David R. Frazier/Danita Delimont. **80** (r) José Blanco/VHL, (L) www.metro.df.gob.mx. **81** (t, b) ©2006 Barragán Foundation, Birsfelden, Switzerland/ProLitteris, Zürich, Switzerland, for the work of Luis Barragán. **94** www.joanducros.net Permission Requested. Best efforts made. **119** © ThinkStock, LLC. **128** (r) Janet Dracksdorf/VHL. **129** (r) Janet Dracksdorf/VHL. **154** (b) Esteban Corbo/VHL. **177** (t) © 2002 USPS. **186** Paola Ríos Schaff/VHL. **219** © Leslie Harris/Index Stock Imagery Inc. **275** (b) José Blanco/VHL. **228** (l) Exposición Cuerpo Plural, Museo de Arte Contemporáneo, Caracas, Venezuela, octubre 2005 (Sala 1). Fotografía Morella Muñoz-Tébar. Archivo MAC. **245** (bl) © Romeo A. Escobar, La Sala de La Miniatura, San Salvador. www.ilobasco.net. **295** (tl) © Chris R. Sharp/DDB Stock, (bl) © Francis E. Caldwell/DDB Stock.

About the Author

José A. Blanco founded Vista Higher Learning in 1998. A native of Barranquilla, Colombia, Mr. Blanco holds degrees in Literature and Hispanic Studies from Brown University and the University of California, Santa Cruz. He has worked as a writer, editor, and translator for Houghton Mifflin and D.C. Heath and Company and has taught Spanish at the secondary and university levels. Mr. Blanco is also the co-author of several other Vista Higher Learning programs: **Panorama, Aventuras,** and **¡Viva!** at the introductory level, **Ventanas, Facetas, Enfoques, Imagina,** and **Sueña** at the intermediate level, and **Revista** at the advanced conversation level.

About the Illustrators

Yayo, an internationally acclaimed illustrator, was born in Colombia. He has illustrated children's books, newspapers, and magazines, and has been exhibited around the world. He currently lives in Montreal, Canada.

Pere Virgili lives and works in Barcelona, Spain. His illustrations have appeared in textbooks, newspapers, and magazines throughout Spain and Europe.

Born in Caracas, Venezuela, **Hermann Mejía** studied illustration at the *Instituto de Diseño de Caracas*. Hermann currently lives and works in the United States.